THE BEDFORD READER

SIXTH EDITION

X. J. Kennedy • Dorothy M. Kennedy
Jane E. Aaron

BEDFORD BOOKS ⧏ BOSTON

For Bedford Books

President and Publisher: Charles H. Christensen
General Manager and Associate Publisher: Joan E. Feinberg
Managing Editor: Elizabeth M. Schaaf
Developmental Editor: Alanya Harter
Editorial Assistant: Aron Keesbury
Production Editor: Karen S. Baart
Production Assistant: Deborah Baker
Copyeditor: Nancy Bell Scott
Text Design: Anna George
Cover Design: Night & Day Design
Cover Photograph: Ron Thomas (1991) / FPG International Corp

Library of Congress Catalog Card Number: 96–86772

For information, write: Bedford Books, 75 Arlington Street, Boston, MA 02116
(617–426–7440)

ISBN: 0–312–13634–X

ACKNOWLEDGMENTS

Maya Angelou. "Champion of the World." From *I Know Why the Caged Bird Sings* by Maya Angelou. Copyright © 1969 by Maya Angelou. Reprinted by permission of Random House Inc. In "Maya Angelou on Writing," excerpts from Sheila Weller, "Work in Progress/Maya Angelou," in *Intellectual Digest*, June 1973. Reprinted by permission.

Barbara Lazear Ascher. "On Compassion." From *The Habit of Loving* by Barbara Lazear Ascher. Copyright © 1986, 1987, 1989 by Barbara Lazear Ascher. Reprinted by permission of Random House Inc.

Margaret Atwood. "Bored." © Margaret Atwood. Reprinted by permission of the author. First published in *The Atlantic Monthly*. In "Margaret Atwood on Writing," excerpt from "Great Unexpectations" © Margaret Atwood, 1987. First published in *Ms.* (July/Aug. 1987). Reprinted by permission of the author.

PREFACE
FOR INSTRUCTORS

"A writer," says Saul Bellow, "is a reader moved to emulation." In a nutshell, the aim of *The Bedford Reader* is to move students to be writers, through reading and emulating the best essays available.

Like its predecessor, this sixth edition of *The Bedford Reader* works toward its aim with both a rhetorical and a thematic approach. In Part One we present the rhetorical methods realistically, as we ourselves use them — as natural forms that assist invention and fruition *and* as flexible forms that mix easily for any purpose a writer might have. Then throughout Part One and in the thematic Part Two, we give students plenty to write about with thematic connections in and among chapters.

We polled scores of teachers and students, asking how we could improve this framework and the myriad elements that contribute to it. Some features have proved so popular that we did not tamper with them. But our users' excellent suggestions also prompted many changes, highlighted below with bullets.

REALISTIC RHETORICAL EMPHASIS. At the center of *The Bedford Reader*, ten chapters treat ten methods of development, each presented not as a box to be stuffed full of verbiage but as a tool for inventing and shaping ideas. We take this realistic approach even further, showing how the authors freely combine the methods to achieve their purposes: an "Other Methods" question after every selection helps students analyze how the methods work together, and five chapters in Part Two contain mixed-method essays centered on interesting topics.

In this edition we have bolstered the treatment of mixed methods to make the concept easier to teach:

- New annotations on George Orwell's "Politics and the English Language" show how every one of the methods contributes to that classic essay.
- In the instructor's manual, a list for every rhetorical method indicates the selections elsewhere in the book developed significantly by that method.

We have also improved the introductions to the individual methods, making each one's focus on concepts and process both clearer and more practical:

- A new section discusses and illustrates appropriate thesis sentences.
- A boxed revision checklist highlights essential elements for easy reference.
- New headings provide more signposts throughout the text.
- Marginal annotations on the two sample paragraphs clarify their uses of the method.

VARIED, LIVELY SELECTIONS BY WELL-KNOWN AUTHORS.   The selections in *The Bedford Reader* vary in authorship, topics, even length. Half are by women, and a quarter touch on cultural diversity. Ranging from one to twelve pages, the selections deal with sports, business, history, science, gender, computers, psychology, drug legalization, and many other subjects.

As always, we've added many new selections intended to engage students and inspire them to write:

- Of seventy-one selections, thirty-three are new. Joining proven favorites such as Jessica Mitford and E. B. White are Louise Erdrich, Amy Tan, Dave Barry, and many other fresh voices.
- Three new student essays, bringing the total to six, reassure students that good writing is not exclusive to professionals.
- Three new literary works, bringing the total to four, include a poem by Margaret Atwood and stories by Edgar Allan Poe and Jamaica Kincaid.

EXTENSIVE THEMATIC CONNECTIONS.   To provide substantial topics for class discussion and student writing, *The Bedford Reader* connects essays in many ways. As before, each rhetorical chapter includes two selections that address the same topic, from the ordinary (housekeeping) to the controversial (drug legalization and capital punishment). Every selection ends with a "Connections" writing topic linking the selection to another in the book. An alternate thematic table of contents organizes all the selections into more than two dozen topics. And Part Two organizes the mixed-method essays into thematic chapters that can be used separately or integrated into the rhetorical Part One.

In this edition we've made it easier to use the essays in Part Two:

- The thematic chapters now number five, and they are more focused, with only two or three essays in each. The topics are language, family, gender differences, community life, and community in cyberspace.
- The essays in Part Two each have two "Connections" writing topics, one relating the essay to others in its chapter and one relating it to an essay in the rhetorical Part One.
- In the instructor's manual, a list for each thematic chapter highlights the selections elsewhere in the book that also deal with that theme.

THOROUGH COVERAGE OF CRITICAL READING AND WRITING.   As before, *The Bedford Reader's* general introduction provides detailed advice on developing a critical response to reading. A case study shows the development of a student's response to an essay by M. F. K. Fisher, from annotations on the essay through journal entries and drafts to a final paper. And a "Critical Writing" topic after every selection helps students formulate their own critiques.

In this edition we've expanded the introductory discussion of the writing process:

- Under invention we cover freewriting, journal writing, and other techniques that can help students write fluently, creatively, and confidently.
- We give more advice on thesis sentences and more examples, laying the groundwork for the parallel coverage in each rhetorical introduction.
- We explain the advantages of collaboration in writing and revising, and we offer advice on giving and receiving criticism.

ADVICE ON USING AND DOCUMENTING SOURCES.   Once again, a student paper in *The Bedford Reader* is a researched argument that is fully documented in MLA style. In addition, we've provided new guidance on using sources:

- A new appendix introduces the basics of using sources, including the selections in this book: paraphrasing, summarizing, and quoting; integrating quotations into one's own text; and documenting sources (including electronic sources) in MLA style.

UNIQUE COMMENTS BY WRITERS ON WRITING.   After their essays, forty-eight of the book's writers offer comments on everything from grammar to revision to how they developed the reprinted piece. Besides providing rock-solid advice, these comments also prove that for the pros, too, writing is usually a challenge.

ABUNDANT EDITORIAL APPARATUS.   As always, we've surrounded the selections with a wealth of material designed to get students reading, thinking, and writing. To help structure students' critical approach to the selections, each one comes with two headnotes (on the author and the selection itself), three sets of questions (on meaning, writing strategy, and language), and at least four writing topics. One writing topic emphasizes critical writing, a second stresses connections with other selections, and a third is new:

- To complement the general introduction's increased emphasis on journal writing, a two-part writing topic for every selection encourages students to explore their responses in their journals and then develop their ideas into essays.

Besides the aids with every selection, the book also includes additional writing topics for every rhetorical chapter, a glossary ("Useful Terms") that defines all the terms used in the book (including all those printed in SMALL CAPITAL LETTERS), and an index that alphabetizes authors and titles and important topics (including those in the Writers on Writing sections).

INSTRUCTOR'S MANUAL.   Available as a separate manual or bound with the book, *Notes and Resources for Teaching The Bedford Reader* features a discussion of every method, every selection (with possible answers to the questions), and every Writer on Writing. Some features are new to this edition:

- An introduction suggests ways to integrate journal writing and collaboration into writing classes.
- As noted earlier, each chapter includes a list of the selections in other chapters that illustrate the chapter's method or address its theme.

TWO VERSIONS.   *The Bedford Reader* has a sibling. A shorter edition, *The Brief Bedford Reader*, features forty-five selections instead of seventy-one and omits the five thematic, mixed-method chapters of Part Two.

ACKNOWLEDGMENTS

With each edition we accumulate an enormous debt to teachers and students who help us shape *The Bedford Reader*. The following teachers, patiently answering detailed questionnaires, pointed us toward worthy changes. We heartily thank Joan V. Anderson, Linda Anthon, Syd Bartman, Ted Billy, Carole Brown, Sabrina Caine, Thomas William Cobb, Patricia Coleman, Thomas F. Connolly, Charles Cowdrick, Marcia B. Dinneen, Janet Eber, Peggy Ellington, O. Joseph Fleming II, Louis Graham, John Hackett, Carol Withington Hake, Sally Harvey, Edward M. Jackson, Doni Jeffrey, Carla I. LaGreca, Arthur J. Leo, Mandy McDougal, Jeff McMahon, George J. Mecherly, Thomas D. Patterson, Bryan Polk, Kathryn Presley, Noel Robinson, Alice Royer, Pat Schutjer, Janet Seim, M. S. Shufeser, John D. Simpson, Joan Livingston Smiley, Thomas A. Smith, Paige Dayton Smitten, Lindon Stall, Stephanie J. Stiles, Christina C. Stough, Michael C. Tighe, Susan Trudell, Jill Lynn Tucker, Helen Wilson, and Sander Zulauf.

Bedford Books continues its tradition of spoiling its authors with generosity, warmth, and intelligence. Its bedrock, Charles H. Christensen, provided his usual insight into the needs of composition teachers and students. The developmental editor, Alanya Harter, was so bright, thoughtful, encouraging, and witty that the work of the revision was actually fun. She was supported by Aron Keesbury, who enthusiastically fielded any request. Andrea Kaston, David Gibbs, and Mitch Evich helped shape the apparatus and instructor's manual. And Karen Baart, assisted by Deborah Baker, calmly and deftly shepherded a complex and sometimes unwieldy manuscript through production. We are deeply and happily grateful to all.

CONTENTS

A student questions M. F. K. Fisher's acceptance of physical punishment as a justifiable form of violence.

PART ONE
THE METHODS
37

1   NARRATION: Telling a Story   39

She didn't dare ring up a sale while that epic battle was on. A noted black writer remembers from her early childhood the night when a people's fate hung on a pair of boxing gloves.

Maya Angelou on Writing   53

The writer remembers her teenaged angst when the minister and his cute blond son attended her family's Christmas Eve dinner, an elaborate Chinese feast.

Amy Tan on Writing   57

◄► Indicates thematic pair.

◆▶ Indicates thematic pair.

◀▶ Indicates thematic pair.

◀▶ Indicates thematic pair.

▲ Indicates thematic trio.
◀▶ Indicates thematic pair.

THEMATIC
TABLE OF CONTENTS

AUTOBIOGRAPHY

BIOGRAPHY

CAPITAL PUNISHMENT

CHILDREN, FAMILY, AND GROWING UP

CLASS

COMMUNITY

OTHER PEOPLES, OTHER COUNTRIES

PLACES

PSYCHOLOGY AND BEHAVIOR

READING, WRITING, AND LANGUAGE

SCHOOL AND COLLEGE

SCIENCE AND TECHNOLOGY

SELF-DISCOVERY

WOMEN AND MEN

WORK

INTRODUCTION

WHY READ? WHY WRITE?
WHY NOT PHONE?

Many prophets have forecast the doom of the word on paper. Soon, they have argued, books and magazines will be read on pocket computers. Newspapers will be found only in attics, supplanted by interactive television. The mails will be replaced by electronic message boards.

The prophets have been making such forecasts for many decades, but book sales remain high, magazines and newspapers keep publishing, and the Postal Service has trouble keeping up with volume. In the electronic office, the computer workstation is often an island in a sea of paper. Evidently, the permanent, word-on-paper record still has its advantages.

Even if the day comes when we throw away pens and paper, it is doubtful that the basic aims and methods of writing will completely change. Whether on paper or on screens, we will need to arrange our thoughts in a clear order. We will still have to explain them to others plainly and forcefully.

That is why, in almost any career or profession you may enter, you will be expected to read continually and also to write. This book assumes that reading and writing are a unity. Deepen your mastery of one, and you deepen your mastery of the other. The experience of carefully reading an excellent writer, noticing not only what the writer has to say but also the quality of its saying, rubs off (if you are patient and perceptive) on your own writing. "We go to college," said the poet Robert Frost, "to be given one more chance to learn to read in case we haven't learned in high school. Once we have learned to read, the rest can be trusted to add itself *unto us*."

For any writer, reading is indispensable. It turns up fresh ideas; it stocks the mind with information, understanding, examples, and illustrations; it instills critical awareness of one's surroundings. When you have a well-stocked and girded mental storehouse, you tell truths, even small and ordinary truths, and so write what most readers will find worth reading, instead of building shimmering spires of words in an attempt to make a reader think, "Wow, what a grade A writer." Thornton Wilder, playwright and novelist, put this advice memorably: "If you write to *impress* it will always be bad, but if you write to *express* it will be good."

USING *THE BEDFORD READER*

The Essays

In this book, we trust, you'll find at least a few selections you will enjoy and care to remember. *The Bedford Reader* features work by many of the finest nonfiction writers and even a few sterling fiction writers.

The essays deal with more than just writing and literature and such usual concerns of English courses; they cut broadly across a college curriculum. You'll find writings on science, history, business, law, religion, popular culture, women's studies, sociology, education, communication, the environment, technology, sports, dreams, politics, the media, and minority experience. Some writers recall their childhoods, their families, their own college days, their problems and challenges. Some explore matters likely to spark controversy: drug use, funerals, sex roles, race relations, class distinctions, bilingual schooling, pornography, conservation, the death penalty, multiculturalism. Some writers are intently serious; others, funny. In all, these seventy-one selections—including three stories and one poem—reveal kinds of reading you will meet in other college courses. Such reading is the usual diet of well-informed people with lively minds—who, to be sure, aren't found only on campuses.

The essays have been chosen with one main purpose in mind: to show you how good writers write. Don't feel glum if at first you find an immense gap in quality between E. B. White's writing and yours. Of course there's a gap: White is an immortal with a unique style that he perfected over half a century. You don't have to judge your efforts by comparison. The idea is to gain whatever writing techniques you can. If you're going to learn from other writers, why not go to the best of them? Do you want to know how to define an idea so that the definition is vivid and clear? Read Tom Wolfe on "pornoviolence." Do you want to know how to tell a story about your childhood and make it stick in someone's memory? Read Maya Angelou. Incidentally, not all the selections in this book are the work of professional writers: Students, too, write essays worth studying, as Christine D'Angelo, Brad Manning, Linnea Saukko, Christine Leong, Curtis Chang, and Marco Wilkinson prove.

This book has another aim: to encourage you in critical reading, meaning thoughtful, open-minded, questioning reading. Like everyone else, you face a daily barrage of words—from the information and advertisements on television, from course texts and lectures, even from relatives and friends. Mulling over the views of the writers in this book, figuring out their motives and strategies, agreeing or disagreeing with their ideas, will help you learn to manage, digest, and use, in your own writing, what you read and hear.

The Organization

As a glance over the table of contents will show, the essays in *The Bedford Reader* fall into fifteen chapters: Each of the first ten explains a familiar method of developing ideas, such as DESCRIPTION or CLASSIFICATION or DEFINITION, and the essays illustrate the method; each of the last five chapters focuses on a subject, such as family or gender, and the essays illustrate how, most often, the methods work together.

These methods of development aren't empty jugs to pour full of any old, dull words. Neither are they straitjackets woven by fiendish English teachers to pin your writing arm to your side and keep you from expressing yourself naturally. Amazingly, these methods can be ways to discover what you know, what you need to know, how to think critically about your subject, and how to shape your writing.

Suppose, for example, that you set out to write about two popular singers—their sounds, their styles, their looks, what they are like off-stage—by the method of COMPARISON AND CONTRAST. With luck, you may find the method prompting you to notice similarities and differences between the two singers that you hadn't dreamed of noticing. Using the methods, such little miracles of creating and finding take place with heartening regularity. Give the methods a try. See if they don't help you find more to say, more that you feel is worth saying.

Reading the illustrations in *The Bedford Reader*, you'll discover two important facts about the methods of development. First, they are flexible: Just about any method can point a way into just about any subject, and two writers using the same method will probably approach the same subject very differently. To demonstrate this flexibility, in each method chapter we offer a sample paragraph on television, a sample paragraph drawn from a college textbook, and a pair of essays by different authors on the same general subject (such as sex roles or American customs or capital punishment).

The second thing you'll discover about the methods of development is that a writer never sticks to just one method all the way through an essay. Even when one method predominates, as in all the essays in the methods chapters (1–10), you'll see the writer pick up another method, let it shape a passage, and then move on to yet another method—all to achieve some overriding aim. In "The Black and White Truth About Basketball," Jeff Greenfield mainly compares and contrasts the styles of black and white players, but he begins with a paragraph that follows another method: giving EXAMPLES. Later, he gives still more examples; he briefly describes famous players in action; he defines the terms *rhythm*, *"black" basketball*, and *"white" basketball*; he examines the CAUSES AND EFFECTS of each style of play. The point is that Greenfield employs whatever methods suit his purpose: to explain the differences between two playing styles.

So the methods are like oxygen, iron, and other elements that make up substances in nature: all around us, indispensable to us, but seldom found alone and isolated, in laboratory-pure states. When you read an essay in a chapter called "Description" or "Classification," don't expect it to describe or classify in every line, but do notice how the method is central to the writer's purpose. Then, when you read the essays in the last five, thematic chapters, notice how the "elements" of description, example, comparison, definition, and so on rise to prominence and recede as the writer's need dictates.

The Questions, Writing Topics, and Glossary

Following every essay, you'll find questions on meaning, writing strategy, and language that can help you analyze the selection and learn from it. (You can see a sample of how these questions work when we analyze M. F. K. Fisher's "The Broken Chain," starting on p. 17.) These questions are followed by at least four suggestions for writing, including one that proposes a journal exercise, one that links the essay with one or two others in the book, and one that asks you to read the essay and write about it with your critical faculties alert (more on this in a moment). More writing topics conclude each chapter.

In the material surrounding the essays, certain terms appear in CAPITAL LETTERS. These are words helpful in discussing both the essays in this book and the essays you write. If you'd like to see such a term de-fined and illustrated, you can find it in the glossary at the back of the book: Useful Terms. This section offers more than just brief definitions. It is there to provide you with further information and support.

Writers on Writing

We have tried to give this book another dimension. We want to show that the writers represented here do not produce their readable and informative prose on the first try, as if by magic, leaving the rest of us to cope with writer's block, awkward sentences, and all the other dif-ficulties of writing. Take comfort and cheer: These writers, too, strug-gled to make themselves interesting and clear. In proof, we visit their workshops littered with crumpled paper and forgotten coffee cups. Later in this introduction, when we discuss the writing process briefly and include an essay by a student, Christine D'Angelo, we also include her drafts and her thoughts about them. Then after most of the other essays are statements by the writers, revealing how they write (or wrote), offering their tricks, setting forth things they admire about good writing.

No doubt you'll soon notice some contradictions in these state-ments: The writers disagree about when and how to think about their readers, about whether outlines have any value, about whether style follows subject or vice versa. The reason for the difference of opinion is, simply, that no two writers follow the same path to finished work. Even the same writer may take the left instead of the customary right fork if the writing situation demands a change. A key aim of providing D'Angelo's drafts and the other writers' statements on writing, then, is to suggest the sheer variety of routes open to you, the many approaches to writing and strategies for succeeding at it. At the very end of the book, an index points you toward the writers' comments on such prac-tical matters as writing introductions, finding your point, and revising sentences.

READING AN ESSAY

Whatever career you enter, much of the reading you will do—for business, not for pleasure—will probably be hasty. You'll skim: glance at words here and there, find essential facts, catch the drift of an argu-ment. To cross oceans of print, you won't have time to paddle: You'll need to hop a jet. By skimming, you'll be able to tear through screens full of electronic mail or quickly locate the useful parts of a long report.

But other reading that you do for work, most that you do in college, and all that you do in this book call for reading word for word. You may

be trying to understand how a new company policy affects you, or researching a complicated historical treaty, or (in using this book) looking for pointers to sharpen your reading and writing skills. To learn
from the essays here how to write better yourself, expect to spend an
hour or two in the company of each one. Does the essay assigned for today remain unread, and does class start in five minutes? "I'll just breeze
through this little item," you might tell yourself. But no, give up. You're
a goner.

Good writing, as every writer knows, demands toil, and so does
CRITICAL READING—reading that looks beneath the surface of the writing, that seeks to understand how the piece works and whether it suc-
ceeds. Never try to gulp down a rich and potent essay without chewing;
all it will give you is indigestion. When you're going to read an essay in
depth, seek out some quiet place—a library, a study cubicle, your room
(provided it doesn't also hold a cranky baby or two roommates playing
poker). Flick off the radio, stereo, or television. What writer can out-
sing Aretha Franklin or Luciano Pavarotti, or outshout a kung fu
movie? The fewer the distractions, the easier your task will be and the
more you'll enjoy it.

How do you read an essay? Exactly how, that is, do you read it critically, master its complexities, learn how a good writer writes, and so
write better yourself? To find out, we'll be taking a close look at an
actual essay, M. F. K. Fisher's "The Broken Chain." You'll find it rewards the time you spend on it.

The Preliminaries

Critical reading starts before you read the first word of the essay.
Like a pilot circling an airfield, you take stock of what's before you, lo-
cating clues to the essay's content and the writer's biases.

The Title

Often the title will tell you the writer's subject, as in Thomas Sowell's "Student Loans" or H. L. Mencken's "The Penalty of Death."
Sometimes the title immediately states the THESIS, the main point the
writer will make: "I Want a Wife." The title may set forth the subject as
a question: "Why Don't We Complain?" Some titles spell out the
method a writer proposes to follow: "Grant and Lee: A Study in Contrasts." The TONE of the title may also reveal the writer's attitude toward
the material. If a work is named "Why the Rich Are Getting Richer
and the Poor Poorer," the title gives you an idea of the writer's
approach, all right; and so does that of an informal essay such as "The
Day I Turned Sarcastic." You, in turn, approach each work in a differ-

ent way—with serious intent, or set to chuckle. Some titles reveal more than others. M. F. K. Fisher's title, "The Broken Chain," is a bit mysterious. We may suspect that the author does not mean "chain" literally (a bicycle chain) but figuratively (like a chain of events or a chain reaction). The title hints at change (a chain breaks), so we may guess that this broken chain lies at the heart of a story. The rest is for us to find out.

Whatever it does, a title sits atop its essay like a neon sign. It tells you what's inside or makes you want to venture in. To pick an alluring title for an essay of your own is a skill worth cultivating.

The Author

Whatever you know about a writer—background, special training, previous works, outlook, or ideology—often will help you guess something about the essay before you read a word of it. Is the writer on new taxes a political conservative? Expect an argument against added "revenue enhancement." Is the writer a liberal? Expect an argument that new social programs are worth the price. Is the writer a feminist? an athlete? an internationally renowned philosopher? a popular television comedian? By knowing something about a writer's background or beliefs, you may know beforehand a little of what he or she will say.

To help provide such knowledge, this book supplies biographical notes. The one on M. F. K. Fisher before "The Broken Chain" (p. 9) tells us that Fisher often wrote about food but that she told other stories as well. You won't know until you read it whether "The Broken Chain" is about food. But if you guess from the note that the essay will be thought provoking, enjoyable, and readily understandable, you will be right.

Where the Essay Was First Published

Clearly, it matters to a writer's credibility whether an article called "Living Mermaids: An Amazing Discovery" first saw print in *Scientific American*, a magazine for scientists and interested nonscientists, or in a popular tabloid weekly, sold at supermarket checkout counters, that is full of eye-popping sensations. But no less important, finding out where an essay first appeared can tell you for whom the writer was writing. In this book we'll strongly urge you as a writer to think of your AUDIENCE, your readers, and to try looking at what you write as if through their eyes. To help you develop this ability, we tell you something about the sources and thus the original readers of each essay you study, in a note just before the essay. (Such a note precedes "The Broken Chain" on

p. 9.) After you have read the sample essay, we'll further consider how having a sense of your readers helps you write.

When the Essay Was First Published

Knowing in what year an essay was first printed may give you another key to understanding it. A 1988 essay on mermaids will contain statements of fact more recent and more reliable than an essay printed in 1700—although the older essay might contain valuable information, too, and perhaps some delectable language, folklore, and poetry. In *The Bedford Reader*, the brief introductory note on every essay tells you not only where but also when the essay was originally printed. If you're reading an essay elsewhere—say, in one of the writer's books—you can usually find this information on the copyright page.

The First Reading

On first reading an essay, you don't want to bog down over every troublesome particular. "The Broken Chain" is written for an educated audience, and that means the author may use a few large words when they seem necessary. If you meet any words that look intimidating, take them in your stride. When, in reading a rich essay, you run into an unfamiliar word or name, see if you can figure it out from its surroundings. If a word stops you cold and you feel lost, circle it in pencil; you can always look it up later. (In a little while we'll come back to the helpful habit of reading with a pencil. Indeed, some readers feel more confident with pencil in hand from the start.)

The first time you read an essay, size up the forest; later, you can squint at the acorns all you like. Glimpse the essay in its entirety. When you start to read "The Broken Chain," don't even think about dissecting it. Just see what Fisher has to say.

M. F. K. FISHER

MARY FRANCES KENNEDY FISHER was born in 1908 and began telling stories at age four. Raised in California and educated there and in Illinois and France, Fisher became renowned for her writing about food. Her first book, *Serve It Forth* (1937), was followed by more than sixteen others before her death at eighty-three in 1992. Not all of them concerned eating, and even those on food, such as *How to Cook a Wolf* (1942), expanded the subject to encompass needs and pleasures of all sorts. Besides writing her books, Fisher produced essays, poetry, and a screenplay, kept house, tended a vineyard in Switzerland, and translated a French gastronomical classic, Brillat-Savarin's *The Physiology of Taste*. Her works reveal a keen sense of story, a sharply observant, independent mind, and a search for the truths in her own and others' lives.

The Broken Chain

"The Broken Chain" was written in 1983 and first published in Fisher's last book, *To Begin Again* (1992). Taking her lead from news headlines, Fisher flashes back to an incident in 1920 that transformed her and her father, Rex, and could perhaps help others as well.

1   There has been more talk than usual lately about the abuse and angry beating of helpless people, mostly children and many women. I think about it. I have never been beaten, so empathy is my only weapon against the ugliness I know vicariously. On the radio someone talks about a chain of violence. When is it broken? he asks. How?

2   When I was growing up, I was occasionally spanked and always by my father. I often had to go upstairs with him when he came home from the *News* for lunch, and pull down my panties and lay myself obediently across his long bony knees, and then steel my emotions against the ritualistic whack of five or eight or even ten sharp taps from a wooden hairbrush. They were counted by my age, and by nine or ten he began to use his hand, in an expert upward slap that stung more than the hairbrush. I often cried a little, to prove that I had learned my lesson.

3   I knew that Rex disliked this duty very much, but that it was part of being Father. Mother could not or would not punish us. Instead, she always said, by agreement with him and only when she felt that things were serious enough to drag him into it, that she would have to speak with him about the ugly matter when he came home at noon.

4   This always left me a cooling-off period of thought and regret and conditioned dread, even though I knew that I had been the cause, through my own stupidity, of involving both my parents in the plot.

9

Maybe it was a good idea. I always felt terrible that it was dragged ⁵
out. I wished that Mother would whack me or something and get it
over with. And as I grew older I resented having to take several unde-
served blows because I was the older child and was solemnly expected
to be a model to my younger sister, Anne. She was a comparatively
sickly child, and spoiled and much cleverer than I, and often made it
bitterly clear to me that I was an utter fool to take punishment for her
own small jaunty misdoings. I continued to do this, far past the fatherly
spankings and other parental punishments, because I loved her and
agreed that I was not as clever as she.

Once Rex hit me. I deserved it, because I had vented stupid petu- ⁶
lance on my helpless little brother David. He was perhaps a year old,
and I was twelve. We'd all left the lunch table for the living room and
had left him sitting alone in his high chair, and Father spotted him
through the big doors and asked me to get him down. I felt sulky about
something, and angered, and I stamped back to the table and pulled up
the wooden tray that held the baby in his chair, and dumped him out
insolently on the floor. David did not even cry out, but Rex saw it and
in a flash leapt across the living room toward the dining table and the
empty high chair and gave me a slap across the side of my head that
sent me halfway across the room against the big old sideboard. He
picked up David and stood staring at me. Mother ran in. A couple of
cousins came, looking flustered and embarrassed at the sudden ugliness.

I picked myself up from the floor by the sideboard, really raging ⁷
with insulted anger, and looked disdainfully around me and then went
silently up the stairs that rose from the dining room to all our sleeping
quarters. Behind me I could hear Mother crying, and then a lot of talk.

I sat waiting for my father to come up to the bedroom that Anne ⁸
and I always shared, from her birth until I was twenty, in our two family homes in Whittier, and in Laguna in the summers, and then when
we went away to three different schools. I knew I was going to be punished.

Finally Father came upstairs, looking very tired. "Daughter," he ⁹
said, "your mother wants you to be spanked. You have been bad. Pull
down your panties and lie across my knees."

I was growing very fast and was almost as tall as I am now, with ¹⁰
small growing breasts. I looked straight at him, not crying, and got into
the old position, all long skinny arms and legs, with my bottom bared
to him. I felt insulted and full of fury. He gave me twelve expert upward
stinging whacks. I did not even breathe fast, on purpose. Then I stood
up insolently, pulled up my sensible Munsingwear panties, and stared
down at him as he sat on the edge of my bed.

"That's the last time," he said. ¹¹

"Yes," I said. "And you hit me." ¹²

"I apologize for that," he said, and stood up slowly, so that once   13
again I had to look up into his face as I had always done. He went out
of the room and downstairs, and I stayed alone in the little room under
the eaves of the Ranch house, feeling my insult and anger drain slowly
out and away forever. I knew that a great deal had happened, and I felt
ashamed of behaving so carelessly toward my helpless little brother and
amazed at the way I had simply blown across the room and into the
sideboard under my own father's wild stinging blow across my cheek. I
wished that I would be maimed, so that he would feel shame every time
he looked at my poor face. I tried to forget how silly I'd felt, baring my
pubescent bottom to his heavy dutiful slaps across it. I was full of scowling puzzlements.

My mother came into the room, perhaps half an hour later, and   14
wrapped her arms around me with a tenderness I had never felt from
her before, although she had always been quietly free with her love and
her embraces. She had been crying but was very calm with me, as she
told me that Father had gone back to the *News* and that the cousins
were playing with the younger children. I wanted to stay haughty and
abused with her, but sat there on the bed quietly, while she told me
about Father.

She said that he had been beaten when he was a child and then as   15
a growing boy, my age, younger, older. His father beat him, almost every
Saturday, with a long leather belt. He beat all four of his boys until they
were big enough to tell him that it was the last time. They were all of
them tall strong people, and Mother said without any quivering in her
voice that they were all about sixteen before they could make it clear
that if it ever happened again, they would beat their father worse than
he had ever done it to them.

He did it, she said, because he believed that he was ridding them of   16
the devil, of sin. Grandfather, she said quietly, was not a brute or a
beast, not sinful, not a devil. But he lived in the wild prairies and raised
strong sons to survive, as he had, the untold dangers of frontier life.
When he was starting his family, as a wandering newspaperman and
printer of political broadsides, he got religion. He was born again. He
repented of all his early wildness and tried to keep his four sons from
"sinning," as he came to call what he had done before he accepted God
as his master.

I sat close to Mother as she explained to me how horrible it had   17
been only a few minutes or hours before in my own short life, when Rex
had broken a long vow and struck his own child in unthinking anger.
She told me that before they married, he had told her that he had
vowed when he was sixteen to break the chain of violence and that
never would he strike anyone in anger. She must help him. They
promised each other that they would break the chain. And then today

he had, for the first time in his whole life, struck out, and he had struck his oldest child.

I could feel my mother trembling. I was almost overwhelmed by   18
pity for the two people whom I had betrayed into this by my stupidity. "Then why did he hit me?" I almost yelled suddenly. She said that he hardly remembered doing it, because he was so shocked by my dumping the helpless baby out onto the floor. "Your father does not remember," she repeated. "He simply had to stop you, stop the unthinking way you acted toward a helpless baby. He was . . . He suddenly acted violently. And it is dreadful for him now to see that, after so long, he can be a raging animal. He thought it would never happen. That is why he has never struck any living thing in anger. Until today."

We talked for a long time. It was a day of spiritual purging,   19
obviously. I have never been the same—still stupid but never unthinking, because of the invisible chains that can be forged in all of us, without our knowing it. Rex knew of the chain of violence that was forged in him by his father's whippings, brutal no matter how mistakenly committed in the name of God. I learned of what violence could mean as I sat beside my mother, that day when I was twelve, and felt her tremble as she put her arm over my skinny shoulders and pulled me toward her in an embrace that she was actually giving to her husband.

It is almost certain that I stayed aloof and surly, often, in the   20
next years with my parents. But I was never spanked again. And I know as surely as I do my given name that Rex no longer feared the chain of violence that had bound him when he was a boy. Perhaps it is as well that he hit me, the one time he found that it had not been broken for him.

Rereadings

When first looking into an essay, you are like a person who arrives at the doorway of a large and lively room, surveying a party going on inside. Glancing around the room, you catch the overall picture: the locations of the food and the drinks, of people you know, of people you don't know but would certainly like to. You have just taken such an overview of Fisher's essay. Now, stepping through the doorway of the essay and going on in, you can head for whatever beckons most strongly.

Well, what will it be? If it is writing skills you want, then go for those elements that took skill or flair or thoughtful decision on the writer's part. Most likely, you'll need to reread the essay more than once, go over the difficult parts several times, with all the care of someone combing a snag from the mane of an admirable horse.

Writing While Reading

In giving an essay this going-over, many students—some of the best—find a pencil in hand as good as a currycomb for a horse's mane. The pencil (or pen or computer keyboard) concentrates the attention wonderfully, and, as often happens with writing, it can lead you to unexpected questions and connections. (Some readers favor markers that roll pink or yellow ink over a word or line, making the eye jump to that spot, but you can't use a highlighter to note *why* a word or idea is important.) You can annotate your own books, underlining essential ideas, scoring key passages with vertical lines, writing questions in the margins about difficult words or concepts, venting feelings ("Bull!" "Yes!" "Says who?"). Here, as an example, are the jottings of one student, Christine D'Angelo, on a paragraph of Fisher's essay:

"I apologize for that," he said, and stood up slowly, so that once again I had to look up into his face as I had always done. *What was his expression?*

He went out of the room and downstairs, and I stayed alone in the little room under the eaves of the Ranch house, feeling my insult and anger drain slowly out and away forever. I knew that *already forgives father?*

a great deal had happened, and I felt ashamed of behaving so carelessly toward my helpless little brother and amazed at the way I had simply blown across the room and into the sideboard under my own father's wild stinging blow across my cheek. I *difference in blow and spanking (to author and father)*

wished that I would be maimed, so that he would feel shame every time he looked at my poor face. I tried to forget how silly I'd felt, baring my pubescent bottom to his heavy dutiful slaps across it. I was full of scowling puzzlements.

— Good phrase for child's mixed emotions

If a book is borrowed, you can accomplish the same thing by making notes on a separate sheet of paper.

Whether you own the book or not, you'll need separate paper for responses that are lengthier and more substantial than the margins can contain, such as the informal responses, summaries, detailed analyses, and evaluations discussed below. For such notes, you may find a JOURNAL handy. It can be a repository of your ideas, a comfortable place to record meandering or direct thoughts about what you read. You may be surprised to find that the more you write in an unstructured way, the more you'll have to say when it's time to write a structured essay. (For more on journals, see p. 24.)

Writing and reading help you behold the very spine of an essay, as if in an X-ray view, so that you, as much as any expert, can judge its curves and connections. You'll develop an opinion about what you read, and you'll want to express it. While reading this way, you're being a writer. Your pencil tracks or keystrokes will jog your memory, too, when you review for a test, when you take part in class discussion, or when you want to write about what you've read.

Summarizing

It's usually good practice, especially with more difficult essays, to SUMMARIZE the content in writing to be sure you understand it or, as often happens, to come to understand it. We use summary all the time to fill friends in on the gist of a story—shrinking a two-hour movie to a single sentence, "This woman is recruited to be a spy, and she stops a ring of double agents." In summarizing a work of writing, you digest, *in your own words*, what the author says: You take the essence of the author's meaning, without the supporting evidence and other details that make that gist convincing or interesting. When you are practicing reading and the work is short (the case with the reading you do in this book), you may want to make this a two-step procedure: First write a summary sentence for every paragraph or related group of paragraphs; then summarize those sentences in two or three others that capture the heart of the author's meaning.

Here is a two-step summary of "The Broken Chain." (The numbers in parentheses refer to paragraph numbers in the essay.) First, the longer version:

> (1) Fisher wonders about the "chain of violence" against children and women. (2–3) As a child, she was sometimes spanked on her bare bottom by her father, who carried out the job reluctantly as a father's responsibility. (4–5) The spanking did not occur immediately after the bad behavior, and the delay left Fisher feeling sorry and afraid and often resentful of her younger sister, who escaped such punishment. (6) Then once Fisher peevishly dropped her baby brother on the floor, and her father struck her suddenly and violently in anger. (7–13) She was simply furious at first, but she became remorseful, vindictive, and embarrassed as well when her father later spanked her for her deed and apologized for striking her. (14–16) Her mother then comforted her and explained that her father had been regularly beaten by his own father. (17–18) Her father had sworn that he would "break the chain of violence" by never hitting another person out of anger, and now he was horrified to discover that he, too, could be violent. (19) The incident helped Fisher understand her father and violence. (20) It also broke the chain by releasing her father from his fear that any violence in him must control him as it had his own father.

Now the short summary:

Fisher's father sometimes reluctantly spanked her as punishment, but once when she deliberately dropped her baby brother he struck her suddenly and violently. Her father had not escaped the "chain of violence" begun by his own father's regular beatings, but the incident released him from his fear that the chain must control him.

(We're suggesting that you write summaries for yourself, but the technique is also useful when you discuss other people's works in your writing. Then you must use your own words or use quotation marks for the author's words, and either way you must acknowledge the source in a citation. See pp. 658–67.)

Reading Critically

Summarizing will start you toward understanding the author's meaning, but it won't take you as far as you're capable of going, or as far as you'll need to go in school or work or just to live well in our demanding Information Age. Passive, rote learning (such as memorizing the times tables in arithmetic) won't do. You require techniques for comprehending what you encounter. But more: You need tools for discovering what's beneath the surface of an essay or case study or business letter or political message. You need ways to discriminate between the trustworthy and the not so and to apply what's valid in your own work and life.

We're talking here about critical thinking, reading, and writing—not "negative," the common conception of *critical*, but "thorough, thoughtful, question-asking, judgment-forming." When you approach something critically, you harness your faculties, your fund of knowledge, and your experiences to understand, appreciate, and evaluate the object. Using this book—guided by questions on meaning, writing strategy, and language—you'll read an essay and ask what the author's purpose and main idea are, how clear they are, and how well supported. You'll isolate which writing techniques the author has used to special advantage, what hits you as particularly fresh, clever, or wise—and what *doesn't* work, too. You'll discover exactly what the writer is saying, how he or she says it, and whether, in the end, it was worth saying. In class discussions and in writing, you'll tell others what you think and why.

Critical reading is a process involving several overlapping operations: analysis, inference, synthesis, and evaluation.

Analysis.   Say you're listening to a new album by a band called the Alley Cats. Without thinking much about it, you isolate melodies, song lyrics, and instrumentals—in other words, you ANALYZE the album by separating it into its parts. Analysis is a way of thinking so basic to us that it has its own chapter (6) in this book. For reading in this book, you'll consciously analyze essays by looking at the author's main idea, support for the idea, special writing strategies, and other elements.

Analysis underlies many of the other methods of development discussed in this book, so that while you are analyzing a subject you might also (even unconsciously) begin classifying it, or comparing it with something else, or figuring out what caused it. For instance, you might compare the Alley Cats' new instrumentals with those on their earlier albums, or you might notice that the lyrics seem to be influenced by another band's. Similarly, in analyzing a poem you might compare several images of water, or in analyzing a journal article in psychology you might consider how the author's theories affect her interpretations of behavior.

Inference.   Say that after listening to the Alley Cats' new album, you conclude that it reveals a preoccupation with traditional blues music and themes. Now you are using INFERENCE, drawing conclusions about a work based on your store of information and experience, your knowledge of the creator's background and biases, and your analysis. When you infer, you add to the work, making explicit what was only implicit. In critical reading, inference is especially important in discovering a writer's ASSUMPTIONS: opinions or beliefs, often unstated, that direct the writer's choices of ideas, support, writing strategies, and language. A writer who favors gun control may assume without saying so that some individual rights (such as the right to bear arms) may be infringed for the good of the community. A writer who opposes gun control may assume the opposite—that in this case the individual's right is superior to the community's.

Synthesis.   What are the Alley Cats trying to accomplish with their new album? Is it different from their previous album in its understanding of the blues? Answering such questions leads you into SYNTHESIS, linking elements into a whole, or linking two or more wholes. During synthesis, you use your special aptitudes, interests, and training to reconstitute the work so that it now contains not just the original elements but also your sense of their underpinnings and relationships. About an essay you might ask why the author elicits contradictory feelings from readers, or what this essay has to do with that other essay, or what this essay has to do with your life.

Analysis, inference, and synthesis overlap—so much so that it's often impossible to distinguish one from the other during critical reading. To stave off confusion, in this book we use the word *analysis* to cover all of these operations: identifying elements, drawing conclusions about them, *and* reconstituting them.

understanding what be you have read.

Evaluation. Not all critical reading involves EVALUATION, or judging
the quality of the work. You'll probably form a judgment of the Alley
Cats' new album (is the band getting better or just standing still?), but
often you (and your teachers) will be satisfied with a nonjudgmental
reading of a work. ("Nonjudgmental" does not mean "uncritical": You
will still be expected to analyze, infer, and synthesize.) When you *do*
evaluate, you determine adequacy, significance, value. You answer a
question such as whether an essay moves you as it was intended to, or
whether the author has proved a case, or whether the argument is even
worthwhile.

The following comments on M. F. K. Fisher's "The Broken
Chain" show how a critical reading can work. The headings "Meaning," "Writing Strategy" (p. 19), and "Language" (p. 21) correspond to
those organizing the questions at the end of each essay.

Meaning

"No man but a blockhead," declared Samuel Johnson, "ever wrote
except for money." Perhaps the industrious critic, journalist, and dictionary maker was remembering his own days as a literary drudge in
London's Grub Street; but surely most people who write often do so for
other reasons.

When you read an essay, you'll find it rewarding to ask, "What is this
writer's PURPOSE?" By purpose, we mean the writer's apparent reason for
writing: what he or she was trying to achieve with readers. A purpose is
as essential to a good, pointed essay as a destination is to a trip. It affects
every choice or decision the writer makes. (On vacation, of course, care-
free people sometimes climb into a car without a thought and go happily
rambling around; but if a writer rambles like that in an essay, the reader
may plead, "Let me out!") In making a simple statement of a writer's purpose, we might say that the writer writes *to entertain* readers, or *to explain*
something to them, or *to persuade* them. To state a purpose more fully, we
might say that a writer writes not just to persuade but "to tell readers a
story to illustrate the point that when you are being cheated it's a good
idea to complain," or not just to entertain but "to tell a horror story to
make chills shoot down readers' spines." If the essay is an argument
meant to convince, a fuller statement of its writer's purpose might be "to
win readers over to the writer's opinion that San Antonio is the most liv-
able city in the United States," or "to persuade readers to take action by
writing their representatives and urging more federal spending for the
rehabilitation of criminals."

"But," the skeptic might object, "how can I know a writer's purpose? I'm no mind reader, and even if I were, how could I tell what E. B.
White was trying to do? He's dead and buried." And yet writers living

and dead have revealed their purposes in their writing, just as visibly as a hiker leaves footprints.

What is M. F. K. Fisher's purpose in writing? If you want to be more exact, you can speak of her *main purpose* or *central purpose*, for "The Broken Chain" fulfills more than one. Fisher clearly wants to tell her readers something about her parents and herself as a child. She is not averse to entertaining readers with details capturing the fierce moodiness of a twelve-year-old. But Fisher's main purpose is larger than these and encompasses them. She has heard much lately of child abuse, and a recollection from her own childhood might throw some light on the problem. She wants to help.

How can you tell a writer's purpose? This is where analysis, inference, and synthesis come in. Fisher hints at her purpose in the first paragraph, asking "When is [the chain of violence] broken? . . . How?" The rest of her essay answers these questions: At least for her father, the chain broke when he no longer feared it (para. 20). The opening questions and last paragraph form the THESIS of the essay—the point made for a purpose, the overwhelming idea that the writer communicates. Some writers will come right out, early on, and sum up this central idea in a sentence or two (the THESIS SENTENCE). George Orwell, in his essay "Politics and the English Language," states the gist of his argument in his second paragraph:

> Modern English, especially written English, is full of bad habits which spread by imitation and which can be avoided if one is willing to take the necessary trouble. If one gets rid of these habits one can think more clearly, and to think clearly is a necessary first step towards political regeneration.

Orwell's thesis is obvious early on. Sometimes, however, like Fisher, a writer will introduce and conclude the thesis at the beginning and end. Other writers won't come out and state their theses in any neat Orwellian capsule at all. Even so, the main point of a well-written essay will make itself clear to you—so clear that you can sum it up in a sentence or two of your own. What might that sentence be for Fisher's essay? Perhaps this: The chain of violence against children may be broken when a former victim understands that violence need not take control even when it is expressed.

It's part of your job as an active reader to answer questions like these: What is the writer's purpose? How does it govern the writer's choices? Is it actually achieved? Does the thesis come through? How is it supported? Is the support adequate to convince you of the author's sincerity and truthfulness? (Such conviction is a basic transaction between writer and reader, even when the writer isn't seeking the reader's outright agreement or action.) Sometimes you'll be confused by a writer's point—"What *is* this about?"—and sometimes your confusion won't yield to repeated careful readings. That's when you'll want to toss the book or magazine aside in exasperation, but you won't always have the choice: A school or work assignment or just an urge to figure out the writer's problem may keep you at it. Then it'll be up to you to figure out why the writer fails—in essence, to clarify what's unclear—by, say, digging for buried assumptions that you may not agree with or by spotting where facts and examples fall short.

With some reservations, we think M. F. K. Fisher achieves her purpose. Her essay is engaging. She gives plenty of details to place us in her shoes, to experience what she experienced. Her story about her father rings true, as does the lesson to be learned from it. The story and the lesson do lean on certain assumptions, though, and these are bound to influence a reader's response. One is that the father's spankings are justified and, because they are reluctant and unemotional, do not constitute violence—at least not the abusive violence that concerns Fisher. Even if the spankings are justified, a second, more ticklish assumption is that their manner is appropriate. Fisher describes herself merely as feeling "silly . . . baring my pubescent bottom" for the spanking (para. 13), but these days many readers might condemn her father for expecting her to undress. If you are one of these readers, the essay may be hard to accept. For us, such objections are understandable but ultimately irrelevant because Fisher was writing of a time (1920) when spankings and whippings (even on bare bottoms) were common methods of disciplining children.

Analyzing writers' purposes and their successes and failures makes you an alert and critical reader. Applied to your own writing, this analysis also gives you a decided advantage, for when you write with a clear-cut purpose in mind, aware of your assumptions, you head toward a goal. Of course, sometimes you just can't know what you are going to say until you say it, to echo the English novelist E. M. Forster. In such a situation, your purpose emerges as you write. But the earlier and more exactly you define your purpose, the easier you'll find it to fulfill.

Writing Strategy

author want to put you in his or her class .

To the extent that M. F. K. Fisher holds our interest and engages our sympathies, it pays to ask, "How does she succeed?" (When a writer bores or angers us, we ask why he or she fails.) As we've already hinted, success and failure lie in the eye of the beholder: The reader knows. Almost all writing is a *transaction* between a writer and an audience, maybe one reader, maybe millions. Conscious writers make choices intended to get their audience on their side so that they can achieve their purpose. These choices are what we mean by STRATEGY in writing.

Fisher's audience was the readers of her memoir, *To Begin Again*. She might have assumed that many of these readers would be familiar with her earlier writing and predisposed to like her work. But even for such an appreciative audience, and certainly for newcomers, Fisher would have to be interesting and focused, making readers (us) care about *this* piece. She grabs our attention right at the start by connecting with the disturbing and controversial issue of physical abuse. She doesn't oversell, though—she hasn't been abused herself—so she whets our appetites without setting us up for disappointment. When she begins her story, she keeps involving us by referring to common feelings and experiences in memorably specific terms. Even if we've never been spanked, we can feel her father's "long bony knees" and the "sharp taps" of the brush (para. 2). We share Fisher's resentment of her sister, who "made it bitterly clear to me that I was an utter fool to take punishment for her own small jaunty misdoings" (5). We know that adolescent feeling of "stupid petulance" that caused Fisher to drop her brother (6) and her "raging with insulted anger" at being struck by her father (7). We see that "little room under the eaves" where Fisher found herself "full of scowling puzzlements" (13). We submit as her mother "wrapped her arms around me with a tenderness I had never felt from her before" (14), "an embrace that she was actually giving to her husband" (19). We believe Fisher because of how vivid and precise she is all along.

Part of a writer's strategy—Fisher's, too—is in the methods used to elicit and arrange details such as these. Fisher draws mainly on two methods: narration (telling a story) and description (conveying the evidence of the senses). But she also gives examples of spankings and her feelings about them (2–5), contrasts the "heavy dutiful slaps" of a spanking with the "wild stinging blow" of being struck (13), analyzes her own reactions (13), defines the "chain of violence" (17, 19), and examines the causes and effects of child abuse (15–20). In short, Fisher uses nearly every method discussed in this book, asking each one to perform the work it's best suited for. As we noted earlier, one method or another may predominate in an essay (as narration and description do in Fisher's), but other methods will help the writer explore the subject in paragraphs or shorter passages.

Aside from the details and the methods used to develop them, probably no writing strategy is as crucial to success as finding an appropriate structure. Writing that we find interesting and clear and convincing almost always has UNITY (everything relates to the main idea) and COHERENCE (the relations between parts are clear). When we find an essay wanting, it may be because the writer got lost in digressions or couldn't make the parts fit together.

Sometimes structure almost takes care of itself. When she chose the method of narration, for instance, Fisher also chose a chronological sequence (reporting events as they occurred in time). But she still had to emphasize certain events and de-emphasize others. She lingers over the important moments: dropping her brother and being struck by her father (6–7), the following encounters with her father (8–13) and her mother (14–18). She compresses all the events that contribute background but are not the heart of the story, notably the previous spankings (2–4) and taking the blame for her sister (5).

This kind of handiwork will be even more evident in essays where the method of development doesn't dictate an overall structure. Then the writer must mold and shape ideas and details to pique, hold, and direct our interest. One writer may hit us with the big idea right at the start and then fill us in on the details. Another writer may gradually unfold the idea, leading to a surprise. One writer may arrange information in order of increasing importance; another may do the opposite. Like all other choices in writing, these come out of the writer's purpose: What is the aim? What do I want readers to think or feel? What's the best way to achieve that? As you'll see in this book, there are as many options as there are writers.

Language

To examine the element of language is often to go even more deeply into an essay and how it was made. Fisher, you'll notice, is a writer whose language is rich and varied. It isn't bookish. Many expressions from common speech lend her prose vigor and naturalness. "I always felt terrible that it was dragged out," she writes (5). Her father "gave me a slap across the side of my head that sent me halfway across the room against the big old sideboard" (6). When spanked, she says, "I did not even breathe fast, on purpose" (10). "I have never been the same—" she concludes, "still stupid but never unthinking" (19). These relaxed sentences suit the material: Fisher's recollections of herself as a fresh, moody adolescent. At the same time, Fisher is an adult addressing adults, and her vocabulary reflects as much. Consult a dictionary if you need help defining *vicariously* (1), *ritualistic* (2), *conditioned* (4), *petulance, insolently* (6), *disdainfully* (7), *pubescent* (13), or *haughty* (14).

Fisher's words and sentence structures not only sharpen and animate her meaning but also convey her attitudes and elicit them from readers. They create a TONE, the equivalent of tone of voice in speaking. Whether it's angry, sarcastic, or sad, joking or serious, tone carries almost as much information about a writer's purpose as the words themselves do. Fisher's tone is sincere, matter-of-fact. In true adolescent fashion, she occasionally veers into indignation or embarrassment or

compassion; but she never indulges in histrionics, which would overwhelm the sensations and make her account untrustworthy.

With everything you read, as with "The Broken Chain," it's in-
structive to study the writer's tone so that you are aware of whether
and how it affects you. Pay particular attention to the CONNOTATIONS
of words—their implied meanings, their associations. We sympathize when Fisher takes those "twelve expert upward stinging whacks"
(10)—stinging whacks *hurt*. We identify with her "scowling puzzlements" (13)—the anger and hurt are there and also the confusion.
When one writer calls the homeless "society's downtrodden" and another calls them "human refuse," we know something of their attitudes
and can use that knowledge to analyze and evaluate what they say
about homelessness.

One other use of language is worth noting in Fisher's essay and in
many others in this book: FIGURES OF SPEECH, bits of colorful language not
meant to be taken literally. In one instance, Fisher makes her adolescent gangliness vivid with HYPERBOLE, or exaggeration, describing herself
as "all skinny arms and legs" (10). Most memorable is the extended
METAPHOR of the "chain of violence" (17, 19–20)—not an actual, physical chain, of course, but a pattern of behavior passed from generation
to generation. This chain is "invisible"; it had "bound" Fisher's father
since childhood; and finally, as the title tells us, it was "broken." Such
a colorful comparison—a chain and a destructive behavior—gives
Fisher's essay flavor and force. (More examples of figures of speech can
be found under Useful Terms, p. 676.)

Many questions in this book point to such figures, to oddities of
tone, or to troublesome or unfamiliar words. We don't wish to swamp
you in details or make you a slave to your dictionary, only to get you
thinking about how meaning and effect begin at the most basic level,
with the word. As a writer, you can have no traits more valuable to you
than a fondness and respect for words and a yen to experiment with
them.

WRITING

Suggestions for Writing

Throughout this book every essay is followed by several "Suggestions for Writing." The first of these encourages you to respond to the
essay in two ways: by approaching it in your journal (especially useful if
you feel shy or blocked about responding) and by transforming that
journal entry into an essay for an audience. One of the other writing
suggestions, labeled "Critical Writing," asks you to take a deliberate,
critical look at the essay. And a final suggestion, labeled "Connec-

tions," helps you relate the essay to one or two other essays in the book. You may not wish to take these suggestions exactly as worded; they may merely urge your own thoughts toward what you want to say. Here are four possibilities for M. F. K. Fisher's "The Broken Chain."

1. **JOURNAL WRITING.** Write about a moment in your childhood or adolescence that changed you or someone you know or both. Try to capture the details of the incident: where, why, and how it happened; how the participants looked and behaved; actual dialogue.

   FROM JOURNAL TO ESSAY. Following Fisher's example, shape your journal writing into an essay full of concrete, specific details so that your readers understand the incident and its effects. Use a chronological organization, and take advantage of your distance from the incident to evaluate how it changed you or someone else.

2. If you have had some experience with physical abuse (as a counselor, bystander, victim, abuser) and you care to write about it, compose an essay that develops a thesis about the problem. You do not have to write in the first person (*I*) unless you want to. Draw on personal experience, observation, or reading as needed to support your thesis. (If you draw on reading, be sure to acknowledge your sources.)

3. **CRITICAL WRITING.** Write an essay in which you analyze and evaluate Fisher's attitudes toward physical punishment. Consider what Fisher actually says about spanking and what her words convey about her feelings. (You will have to infer some of her assumptions.) When you are sure you understand Fisher's point of view, explain it and then evaluate it, using specific evidence from the essay and from your own sources (experience, observation, reading). Do you agree with Fisher? Does she omit any important considerations? In your view, do her attitudes toward physical punishment weaken or strengthen the essay? Why?

4. **CONNECTIONS.** Both Fisher's "The Broken Chain" and Brad Manning's "Arm Wrestling with My Father" (p. 113) address the ways love and standards of behavior are passed from one generation to another. Compare and contrast these two essays, looking closely at how Fisher's and Manning's parents love and educate their children. Be specific in your analysis, using evidence from the essays and, if you wish, your own experience. (If you need help with the method of comparison and contrast, see Chap. 4.)

The Writing Process

To complete an assignment like those above, you need in a way to duplicate the reading process, moving from sketchy impressions to rich understandings as you gain mastery over your material. Like critical reading, writing is no snap: As this book's Writers on Writing attest, even professionals do not produce thoughtful, detailed, attention-getting essays in a single draft. Writing well demands, and rewards, a willingness to work recursively — to begin tentatively, perhaps, and then to double back, to welcome change and endure frustration, to recognize and exploit progress. Something of this recursive process is captured in the case study beginning on page 29. A student, Christine D'Angelo, wrote this piece for *The Bedford Reader* in response to M. F. K. Fisher's essay. D'Angelo provided us with her notes and drafts, along with her comments on her progress at each stage.

For you, as for D'Angelo and most writers, the recursive writing process may proceed through three rough stages: discovery, drafting, and revision.

Discovery

During the first phase of the writing process, DISCOVERY, you'll feel your way into an assignment. This is the time when you critically read any text that is part of the assignment and begin to generate ideas for writing. When writing about essays in this book, you'll be reading and rereading and writing, coming to understand the work, figuring out what you think of it, figuring out what you have to *say* about it. From notes during reading to jotted phrases, lists, or half-finished paragraphs after reading, this stage should always be a writing stage. You may even produce a rough draft. The important thing is to let yourself go: Do not, above all, concern yourself with making beautiful sentences or correcting errors. Such self-consciousness at this stage will only jam the flow of thoughts. If your idea of "audience" is "teacher with sharp pencil" (not, by the way, a fair picture), then temporarily blank out your audience, too.

A few techniques can help you let go and open up during the discovery stage. One is keeping a JOURNAL, a notebook or tablet or computer file where you record your thoughts *for yourself.* (Teachers sometimes assign journals and periodically collect them to see how students are doing, but even in these situations the journal is for yourself.) In keeping a journal, you don't have to worry about being understood by a reader or making mistakes: You are free to write however you want, using whatever words, sentence structures, and arrangements work best to get your thoughts down. If you keep a journal regularly— say, for ten or fifteen minutes a day —it can provide a place to work out personal difficulties, explore half-formed ideas, make connections between courses, or respond to reading. Here, for instance, is Christine D'Angelo's initial journal entry on M. F. K. Fisher's "The Broken Chain":

> *I liked this — the writer makes me remember what it's like to be really mad at my parents for being mean, even when part of me knows they might be right (like the time I stole the car and got grounded!). But I don't get why Fisher makes such a big deal about the difference between a slap from her father when she dropped the baby and the regular spankings she got*

from him. She's getting hit either way, right? Got to get at the difference Fisher sees.

Kept faithfully, a journal can limber up your writing muscles, giving you more confidence and flexibility as a writer. Another technique for limbering up, but more in response to specific writing assignments than as a regular habit, is *freewriting*. When freewriting, you write without stopping for ten or fifteen minues, not halting to reread, criticize, edit, or admire. You can use partial sentences, abbreviations, question marks for uncertain words. If you can't think of anything to write about, jot "can't think" over and over until new words come (they will). You can use this technique to find a subject for writing or to explore ideas on a subject you already have. Of course, when you've finished, you'll need to separate the promising passages from the dead ends, using those promising bits as the starting place for more freewriting or perhaps a freely written first draft.

Another discovery technique provides a bit more structure when you already have your subject: Apply each method of development systematically to throw light on your subject, as a headlight illuminates a midnight road. You'll see in the following chapters of this book that these methods can provide approaches as well as light, showing you a direction for your writing. For now, we've given some examples of how the methods can reveal responses, either direct or indirect, to Fisher's "The Broken Chain."

- *Narration:* Tell a story about the subject. Ask the journalist's questions: who, what, when, where, why, how? For instance, consider an incident in your own life that changed you, as Fisher's experience changed her and her father.
- *Description:* Ask about the subject's look, sound, feel, smell, taste — the evidence of the senses. For instance, examine Fisher's use of language to evoke sensation.
- *Example:* Point to instances, or illustrations, of the subject. For instance, give examples that illustrate Fisher's use of language to portray herself as an adolescent.
- *Comparison and contrast:* Set the subject beside something else, noting similarities or differences or both. For instance, compare and contrast Fisher's views of spanking and hitting.
- *Process analysis:* Explain the subject as it happens, step by step. For instance, explain a process for disciplining children that does not involve physical punishment.
- *Division or analysis:* Slice the subject into its parts or elements. For instance, analyze Fisher's tone and its relation to her purpose.
- *Classification:* Sort the subject into kinds of groups. For instance, classify different kinds of family discipline, physical and otherwise.

- *Cause and effect:* Ask why or what if, seeking reasons for or consequences of the subject. For instance, try to understand why parents strike their children.
- *Definition:* Trace a boundary around the subject to discover its meaning. For instance, define *violence* or *child abuse*.
- *Argument and persuasion:* Formulate an opinion or make a proposal about the subject. For instance, argue that Fisher's father did (or did not) abuse her by spanking her.

Drafting

Sooner or later, the discovery stage yields to DRAFTING: arranging ideas in sequence, filling in their details, spelling out their relationships. For most, this is the occasion for further exploration, but with a sharper focus. Here you may be concerned with clarifying your purpose. You may experiment with tone. You may try out different structures. It's best to stay fairly loose during drafting so that you're free to wander down intriguing avenues or consider changing direction altogether. As during discovery, you'll want to keep your eyes on what's ahead, not obsess over the pebbles underfoot—the possible mistakes, "wrong" words, and bumpy sentences that you can attend to later. This is an important message that many inexperienced writers miss: It's okay to make mistakes. You can fix them later.

One important element that should receive some attention during drafting, or shortly after, is the THESIS, often stated in a THESIS SENTENCE or two. The thesis, to recap page 18, is the main idea of a piece of writing, its focus. Without a focus, either expressed or implied, an essay wanders and irritates and falls flat. With a focus, an essay is much more likely to click.

We've already given one example of a thesis sentence (actually two sentences) from George Orwell's "Politics and the English Language" (see p. 18). Here are some other examples from the essays in this book:

> The answer [to the distinction Fisher makes between spanking and hitting] lies in her distinction between justified and unjustified violence. (Christine D'Angelo, "Has the Chain Been Broken?")

> These were two strong men, these oddly different generals [Ulysses S. Grant and Robert E. Lee], and they represented the strengths of two conflicting currents that, through them, had come into final collision. (Bruce Catton, "Grant and Lee: A Study in Contrasts")

> Inanimate objects are classified into three major categories—those that don't work, those that break down and those that get lost. (Russell Baker, "The Plot Against People")

It is possible to stop most drug addiction in the United States within a very short time. Simply make all drugs available and sell them at cost. (Gore Vidal, "Drugs")

These four diverse examples share a few important qualities:

- First, in these thesis sentences the authors assert opinions, taking positions on their subjects. They do not merely state facts, as in "Grant and Lee both signed the document ending the Civil War" or "Grant and Lee were different men."
- Second, each thesis sentence projects a single idea. The thesis may have parts (such as D'Angelo's two kinds of violence or Baker's three categories of objects), but the parts fit under a single umbrella idea.
- Third (as you will see when you read the essays themselves), each thesis sentence accurately forecasts the scope of its essay, neither taking on too much nor leaving out essential parts.
- Finally, these thesis statements hint about each writer's purpose— we can tell that D'Angelo, Catton, and Baker want to explain, whereas Vidal wants mainly to persuade. (Explaining and persuading overlap a great deal; we're talking here about the writer's *primary* purpose.)

Every single essay in this book has a *thesis* because a central, controlling idea is a requirement of good writing. But we can give no rock-hard rules about the *thesis sentence*—how long it must be or where it must appear in an essay or even whether it must appear. Indeed, the essays in this book demonstrate that writers have great flexibility in these areas. For your own writing, we advise stating your thesis explicitly and putting it near the beginning of your essay—at least until you've gained experience as a writer. The stated thesis will help you check that you have that necessary focus, and the early placement will tell your readers what to expect from your writing.

Revision

If it helps you produce writing, you may view your draft as a kind of dialogue with readers, fulfilling their expectations, answering the questions you imagine they would ask. But some writers save this kind of thinking for the next stage, REVISION. Literally "re-seeing," revision is the price you pay for the freedom to experiment and explore. Initially the work centers on you and your material, but gradually it shifts into that transaction we spoke of earlier between you and your reader. And that means stepping outside the intense circle of you-and-the-material to see the work as a reader, with whatever qualities you imagine that reader to have. Questions after most essays in this book ask you to analyze how the writers' ideas of their readers have influenced their writing strategies, and how you as a reader react to the writers' choices. These analyses will teach you much about responding to your own readers.

Like many writers, you will be able to concentrate better if you approach revision as at least a two-step process. First you question fundamental matters, using a checklist like this one:

> Will my purpose be clear to readers? Have I achieved it?
> What is my thesis? Have I proved it?
> Is the essay unified (all parts relate to the thesis)?
> Is the essay coherent (the parts relate clearly)?
> Will readers be able to follow the organization?
> Have I given enough details, examples, and other specifics for readers to understand me and stay with me?
> Is the tone appropriate for my purpose?
> Have I used the methods of development to full advantage?

When these deeper issues are resolved, then you look at the surface of the writing:

> Do PARAGRAPH breaks help readers grasp related information?
> Do TRANSITIONS tell readers where I am making connections, additions, and other changes?
> Are sentences smooth and concise? Do they use PARALLELISM, EMPHASIS, and other techniques to clarify meaning?
> Do words say what I mean, and are they as vivid as I can make them?
> Are my grammar and punctuation correct?
> Are any words misspelled?

Two-step revision is like inspecting a ship before it sails. First check underwater for holes to make sure the boat will stay afloat. Then look above water at what will move the boat and please the passengers: intact sails, sparkling hardware, gleaming decks.

A Note on Collaboration

Your writing teacher may ask you to spend some time talking with your classmates, as a whole class or in small groups or pairs. You may analyze the essays in this book (perhaps answering the end-of-essay questions), read each other's journals or drafts, or plot revision strategies. Such conversation and collaboration—voicing, listening to, and arguing about ideas—can help you develop more confidence in your writing and give you a clearer sense of audience. One classmate may show you that your introduction, which you thought was lame, really worked to get her involved in your essay. Another classmate may question you in a way that helps you see how the introduction sets up expectations in the reader, expectations you're obliged to fulfill.

You may at first be anxious about collaboration: How can I judge others' writing? How can I stand others' criticism of my own writing? These are natural worries, and your teacher will try to help you with both of them—for instance, by providing a checklist to guide your critique of your classmates' writing. (The first checklist on the opposite page works for reading others' drafts as well as your own.) With practice and plentiful feedback, you'll soon appreciate how much you're learning about writing and what a good effect that knowledge has on your work. You're writing for an audience, after all, and you can't beat the immediate feedback of a live one.

An Essay-in-Progress

In the following pages, you have a chance to watch Christine D'Angelo as she develops an essay through journal notes and several drafts. Her topic is the third one on page 23, about M. F. K. Fisher's attitudes toward physical punishment—a topic she had already started exploring in her journal (pp. 24–25). D'Angelo's journal notes during each stage (in handwriting) enlighten us about her thinking as she proceeds through the writing process.

Journal Notes on Reading

"I have never been beaten" — *she doesn't consider her father's punishment as beating. (¶ 1)*

Very conscious of how to play role of victim (excellent description of kids that age).

— "I often cried a little, to prove that I had learned my lesson" (¶ 2)
— wishes she were maimed (¶ 13)
— "I wanted to stay haughty and abused with her" (¶ 14)

"Your mother wants you to be spanked": typical of fathers' tendency not to take responsibility for feelings. More common when trying to express tenderness: "Your mother was worried sick about you," "Your mother and I are going to miss you," "You know we love you," etc. The potentially embarrassing feelings are diluted.

She doesn't seem to consider spankings as violent:

"Once Rex hit me" (¶ 6)
"And you hit me" (¶ 12)

Calling father first name: distancing?
("Father" vs. "Rex")

Justifies father's actions

> *— he "disliked this duty very much" (¶ 3)*
> *— "fatherly spankings" (¶ 5)*
> *— "two people whom I had betrayed into this" (¶ 18)*

Is father's reaction justified by narrator's act? Both are acts of violence. It's easy to understand his anger.

"Once Rex hit me" and "and you hit me" literally confusing until you become aware that she doesn't count spanking as "hitting."

Mother shares same refusal to see spanking as violent.

Fisher's ideas about physical punishment outdated. These days many people would consider spanking abusive.

I think I have a lot of evidence here to answer question 3, about Fisher's attitudes toward physical punishment and whether they weaken or strengthen the essay.

It's clear that she doesn't think of the spankings as violent. I like the idea of talking about how Fisher's assumptions confuse the reader who doesn't share them. I was confused that she opened with "I have never been beaten" and then recounted many spankings. (This could be a good introduction.)

Even though they're interesting ideas, I don't think I'll be able to use anything about the narrator knowing how to play the victim or fathers' inability to express their emotions. (Not in this paper at least.)

First Draft

How is the reader of "The Broken Chain" to reconcile the narrator's ac-   1
count of the physical punishment she suffered from her father up to the
age of twelve with her assumption in the very first paragraph that "I have
never been beaten"?

Knowing that the father has a history of spanking the narrator, the   2
reader has a hard time interpreting her statement "Once Rex hit me." Why
does she say "once" if he actually hit her quite often? In the key scene in
which the narrator is spanked for having dropped her baby brother on the
floor, her father says "That's the last time," after he has finished spanking
her. To which she responds, "Yes. And you hit me." "Once" and "and" make
no sense. Until we realize that spanking seems to fall under the realm of

just punishment but on the other hand violence outside the clear realm of punishment is unjustifiable.

The narrator's mother shares this distinction. Describing her husband's 3 history of violence in the family, she maintains that up until now he had succeeded in breaking the chain. "He has never struck any living thing in anger," she says, "Until today." In other words, the spankings have never counted as part of the chain of violence.

It is interesting to note that the narrator never questions why it should 4 be the father who struggles constantly to keep his violence in check, who has this "duty" rather than the mother. After all, isn't such a choice rather like putting a dieter in charge of guarding the refrigerator?

When we understand that the narrator does not consider her father's 5 spankings to be violent, we can only call this assumption into question, in fact it is easier to justify the father's response to the dumping of the baby on the floor, itself a violent act that could have been deadly, than his more calculated, repeated capital punishment. If the father is so concerned with breaking the "chain of violence" in his family, why can he not look to alternative methods of punishment? And again, why is it him and not the mother who must carry out this punishment?

I can only speculate on Fisher's reasons for not classifying her father's 6 spankings as violent. But capital punishment is no longer considered an acceptable form of punishment--it is recognized as violence in its own right. In writing this essay, Fisher's purpose was to expose in a family the "chain of violence" against children passed down from generation to generation. But she herself is too blind to see that spanking is a form of violence too.

This gets at what I want to say pretty well, but there are some big holes. I need an explicit thesis — an answer to the question I pose in the first paragraph — to tie the whole thing together. The last sentence of paragraph 2 is really my thesis: that the narrator makes a distinction between two kinds of violence — one kind (the spankings) being OK, the other (the slap) unjustified. The rest of the paper goes on to explain this distinction and call it into question. I just need to make this thesis clearer and bring it up into the first paragraph.

Paragraph 2 needs to be developed more, probably expanded into two paragraphs. I think the first paragraph can pretty much stay the way it is, talking about readers' confusion. But the idea of the last sentence — now the thesis — needs to be fleshed out, expanded into an entire paragraph. Need to define the narrator's distinction between justified and unjustified violence.

Paragraph 4 goes nowhere. It's an interesting point, but doesn't fit in with the rest of the paper. Think it's going to have to be cut. (Same for last sentence of paragraph 5.)

The last sentence of the conclusion is too angry and judgmental. Instead, I could say something about how the very fact that Fisher doesn't see the spankings as violent just goes to show how subtle the "chain" is.

Title??? It should work in the thesis somehow.

Big mistake: spanking is <u>corporal</u>, not <u>capital</u>, punishment.

Revised Draft

Has the Chain Been Broken?
Two Ideas of Violence in "The Broken Chain"

How is the reader of "The Broken Chain" to reconcile the narrator's account of the physical punishment she suffered from her father up to the age of twelve with her assumption in the very first paragraph that "I have never been beaten"? *The answer lies in the difference she makes between what is in her view justified and unjustified violence.* 1

¶ *This distinction is never made explicit in the essay and is apt to lead to confusion on the readers' part.* 2

∧ Knowing that the father has a history of spanking the narrator, the reader has a hard time interpreting her statement "Once Rex hit me."
Likewise,   i
~~Why does she say "once"if he actually hit her quite often?~~ In the key scene in which the narrator is spanked for having dropped her baby brother on the floor, her father says "That's the last time," after he has finished spanking her. To which she responds, "Yes. And you hit me."
What does she mean by "and"?
~~"Once" and "and" make no sense. Until we realize that spanking seems to fall under the realm of just punishment but on the other hand violence outside the clear realm of punishment is unjustifiable.~~

The "once" and "and" make no sense until we realize that they do not refer to the fathers spankings. They refer to his violent, immediate reaction to the narrator's dropping the baby. It becomes clear that "spanking" and "hitting" have different values for the narrator depending on the intention behind it. Spanking, in her eyes, falls under the realm of just punishment, unpleasant though it may be, she sees it as an appropriate response to her own crime. On the other hand, violence outside the clear realm of punishment, in this case the blow, is unjustifiable, despite the fact that both are responses to the same wrongdoing (and each probably hurts about as much as the other!). 3
                                    between "just" and "unjust" violence.
The narrator's mother shares this distinction∧ Describing her husband's history of violence in the family, she maintains that up until now 4

he had succeeded in breaking the chain. "He has never struck any living thing in anger," she says, "Until today." In other words, the spankings have never counted as part of the chain of violence.

~~It is interesting to note that the narrator never questions why it should be the father who struggles constantly to keep his violence in check, who has this "duty" rather than the mother. After all, isn't such a choice rather like putting a dieter in charge of guarding the refrigerator?~~

When we understand that the narrator does not consider her father's   5
spankings to be violent, we can only call this assumption into question, in fact it is easier to justify the father's response to the dumping of the baby on the floor, itself a violent act that could have been deadly, than his more calculated, repeated ~~capital~~ *corporal* punishment. If the father is so concerned with breaking the "chain of violence" in his family, why can he not look to alternative methods of punishment? And ~~again, why is it him and not the mother who must carry out this punishment?~~ *In law, a premeditated crime is more serious than one committed on the spur of the moment.*

I can only speculate on Fisher's reasons for not classifying her father's   6
spankings as violent. *Perhaps she loved and respected her parents too much to judge them objectively, even sixty years after the essay.* But ~~capital~~ *corporal* punishment is no longer considered an acceptable form of punishment--it is recognized as violence in its own right. In writing this essay, Fisher's purpose was to expose in a family the "chain of violence" against children passed down from generation to generation. But ~~she herself is too blind to see that spanking is a form of violence too.~~ *her refusal to recognize corporal punishment as a form of violence is a good example of how subtle the chain is, and why it is so hard to break.*

This hangs together much better now; more coherent. Every paragraph has something to do with the distinction between "good" and "bad" violence. The new title incorporates both the thesis (the two standards of violence) and the hint in the conclusion about the chain not necessarily being broken.

The first sentence is abrupt. Need a "cushion" to ease the reader into the paper.

I think saying "the narrator" is too impersonal for an autobiographical essay. Since this is a personal essay, not fiction, I could just say "Fisher." And since the events in the essay really happened, I should change them to the past tense, keeping present tense when referring to Fisher as writer, in 1983. This will help make it clear that there are really two "Fishers" in question.

Conclusion: Last sentence is still too angry. I could change "refusal" to "inability," taking some of the blame off Fisher.

Need to edit for rough or awkward sentences, spelling and grammar mistakes, and poor word choice.

Edited Paragraph

The "once" and "and" make no sense until we realize that they ~~do not~~ ^{not} refer _, to the fathers spankings _{but} ~~They refer~~ to his violent, immediate reaction to ~~the narrator's~~ ^{Fisher's} dropping the baby. It becomes clear that "spanking" and "hitting" have different values for ~~the narrator~~ ^{Fisher} depending on the intention behind ~~it.~~ ^{them.} Spanking, in her eyes, falls under the realm of just punishment^{. U}/ Unpleasant though it may ~~be,~~ ^{have been,} she sees it as an appropriate response to her own ~~crime. On the other hand,~~ ^{misconduct. But} violence outside the ~~clear~~ ^{well-defined} realm of punishment/ in this case the blow/ is unjustifiable, despite the fact that both are responses to the same wrongdoing/(and ~~each~~ probably hurts ~~about as much as the other!).~~ ^{the same!).}

Final Draft

Has the Chain Been Broken?

Two Ideas of Violence in "The Broken Chain"

There is a problem of definition in "The Broken Chain." How is the reader to reconcile M. F. K. Fisher's account of the physical punishment she suffered from her father up to the age of twelve with her assertion in the very first paragraph that "I have never been beaten"? The answer lies in her distinction between justified and unjustified violence.

This distinction is never made explicit in the essay. Knowing that the father had a history of spanking Fisher, the reader has a hard time interpreting her statement "Once Rex hit me." Then after Fisher was spanked for dropping her baby brother on the floor and her father said, "That's the last time," she responded, "Yes. And you hit me." What did she mean by "and"?

The "once" and "and" make no sense until we realize that they refer not to the father's spankings but to his violent, immediate reaction to Fisher's dropping the baby. It becomes clear that "spanking" and "hitting" have different values for Fisher depending on the intention behind them. Spanking, in her eyes, falls under the realm of just punishment. Unpleasant though it may have been, she sees it as an appropriate response to her own misconduct. But violence outside the well-defined realm of punishment--in this case the blow--is unjustifiable, despite the fact that both are responses to the same wrongdoing (and probably hurt the same!).

The mother shared Fisher's distinction between "just" and "unjust" vio-   4
lence. Describing the "chain of violence" passed down from generation to generation in her husband's family, she maintained that up until then he had succeeded in breaking the chain. "He has never struck any living thing in anger," she said. "Until today." In other words, the spankings never counted.

Once we understand that Fisher does not consider her father's spank-   5
ings to be violent, we can only call this assumption into question. In fact, it is easier to justify the father's heated response to the dumping of the baby on the floor, a violent act that could have been deadly, than his more calculated, repeated corporal punishment. In law, a premeditated crime is more serious than one committed on the spur of the moment.

One can only speculate on Fisher's reasons for not classifying her fa-   6
ther's spankings as violent. Perhaps she loves and respects her parents too much to judge them objectively, even sixty years after the events of the essay. But physical punishment is no longer universally considered acceptable; it is recognized as violence in its own right. In writing this essay, Fisher intends to expose the "chain of violence" against children passed from generation to generation in a family. But her inability to recognize corporal punishment as a form of violence is a good example of how subtle the chain is, and why it is so hard to break.

PART ONE

THE METHODS

1

NARRATION

Telling a Story

THE METHOD

"What happened?" you ask a friend who sports a luminous black eye. Unless he merely grunts, "A golf ball," he may answer you with a narrative—a story, true or fictional.

"OK," he sighs, "you know The Tenth Round? That nightclub down by the docks that smells of formaldehyde? Last night I heard they were giving away $500 to anybody who could stand up for three minutes against this karate expert, the Masked Samurai. And so..."

You lean forward. At least, you lean forward *if* you love a story. Most of us do, particularly if the story tells us of people in action or in conflict, and if it is told briskly, vividly, and with insight into the human heart. NARRATION, or storytelling, is therefore a powerful method by which to engage and hold the attention of listeners—readers as well. A little of its tremendous power flows to the public speaker who starts off with a joke, even a stale joke ("A funny thing happened to me on my way over here..."), and to the preacher who at the beginning of a sermon tells of some funny or touching incident. In its opening paragraph, an article in a popular magazine ("Vampires Live Today!") will give us a brief, arresting narrative: perhaps the case history of a car dealer who noticed, one moonlit night, his incisors strangely lengthening.

The term *narrative* takes in abundant territory. A narrative may be short or long, factual or imagined, as artless as a tale told in a locker room or as artful as a novel by Henry James. A narrative may instruct and inform, or simply divert and regale. It may set forth some point or message, or it may be no more significant than a horror tale that aims to curdle your blood.

At least a hundred times a year, you probably resort to narration, not always for the purpose of telling an entertaining story, but often to explain, to illustrate a point, to report information, to argue, or to persuade. That is, although a narrative can run from the beginning of an essay to the end, more often in your writing (as in your speaking) a narrative is only a part of what you have to say. It is there because it serves a larger purpose. In truth, because narration is such an effective way to put across your ideas, the ability to tell a compelling story—on paper, as well as in conversation—may be one of the most useful skills you can acquire.

A novel is a narrative, but a narrative doesn't have to be long. Sometimes an essay will include several brief stories. See, for instance, "Why Don't We Complain?" by William F. Buckley, Jr. (p. 494). A type of story often used to illustrate a point is the ANECDOTE, a short, entertaining account of a single incident. Anecdotes add color and specifics to history and to every issue of *People* magazine, and they often help support an ARGUMENT by giving it the flesh and blood of real life. Besides being vivid, an anecdote can be deeply revealing. In a biography of Samuel Johnson, the great eighteenth-century critic and scholar, W. Jackson Bate uses an anecdote to show that his subject was human and lovable. As Bate tells us, Dr. Johnson, a portly and imposing gentleman of fifty-five, had walked with some friends to the crest of a hill, where the great man,

> delighted by its steepness, said he wanted to "take a roll down." They tried to stop him. But he said he "had not had a roll for a long time," and taking out of his pockets his keys, a pencil, a purse, and other objects, lay down parallel at the edge of the hill, and rolled down its full length, "turning himself over and over till he came to the bottom."

However small the event it relates, this anecdote is memorable—partly because of its attention to detail, such as the exact list of the contents of Johnson's pockets. In such a brief story, a superhuman figure comes down to human size. In one stroke, Bate reveals an essential part of Johnson: his boisterous, hearty, and boyish sense of fun.

An anecdote may be used to explain a point. Asked why he had appointed to a cabinet post Josephus Daniels, the harshest critic of his policies, President Woodrow Wilson replied with an anecdote of a woman he knew. On spying a strange man urinating through her picket fence into her flower garden, she invited the offender into her yard because, as she explained to him, "I'd a whole lot rather have you inside pissing out than have you outside pissing in." By telling this story, Wilson made clear his situation in regard to his political enemy more succinctly and pointedly than if he had given a more abstract explanation.

THE PROCESS

So far, we have considered a few uses of narration. Now let us see how you tell an effective story.

Every good story has a purpose. Perhaps the storyteller seeks to explain what it was like to be an African American in a certain time and place (as Maya Angelou does in "Champion of the World" in this chapter); perhaps the teller seeks merely to entertain us. Whatever the reason for its telling, an effective story holds the attention of readers or listeners; and to do so, the storyteller shapes that story to appeal to its audience. If, for instance, you plan to tell a few friends of an embarrassing moment you had on your way to campus—you tripped and spilled a load of books into the arms of a passing dean—you know how to proceed. Simply to provide a laugh is your purpose, and your listeners, who need no introduction to you or the dean, need to be told only the bare events of the story. Perhaps you'll use some vivid words to convey the surprise on the dean's face when sixty pounds of literary lumber hit her. Perhaps you'll throw in a little surprise of your own. At first, you didn't take in the identity of this passerby on whom you'd dumped a load of literary lumber. Then you realized: It was the dean!

The Narrator in the Story

Such simple, direct storytelling is so common and habitual that we do it without planning in advance. The NARRATOR (or teller) of such a personal experience is the speaker, the one who was there. (All the selections in this chapter tell of such experiences. All except Ralph Ellison use the first PERSON *I*.) The telling is usually SUBJECTIVE, with details and language chosen to express the writer's feelings. Of course, a personal experience told in the first person can use some artful telling and some structuring. (In the course of this discussion, we'll offer advice on telling stories of different kinds.)

When a story isn't your own experience but a recital of someone else's, or of events that are public knowledge, then you proceed differently. Without expressing opinions, you step back and report, content to stay invisible. Instead of saying, "I did this; I did that," you use the third person, *he*, *she*, *it*, or *they*: "The runner did this; he did that." You may have been on the scene; if so, you will probably write as a spectator, from your own POINT OF VIEW (or angle of seeing). If you put together what happened from the testimony of others, you tell the story from the point of view of a nonparticipant (a witness who didn't take part). Generally, a nonparticipant is OBJECTIVE in setting forth events: unbiased, as accurate and dispassionate as possible.

When you narrate a story in the third person, you aren't a character central in the eyes of your audience. Unlike the first-person writer of a personal experience, you aren't the main actor; you are the camera operator, whose job is to focus on what transpires. Most history books and news stories are third-person narratives, and so is much fiction. In narrating actual events, writers stick to the facts and do not invent the thoughts of participants (historical novels, though, do mingle fact and fancy in this way). And even writers of fiction and anecdote imagine the thoughts of their characters only if they want to explore psychology. Note how much Woodrow Wilson's anecdote would lose if the teller had gone into the thoughts of his characters: "The woman was angry and embarrassed at seeing the stranger...."

A final element of the narrator's place in the story is verb tense, whether present (*I stare, he stares*) or past (*I stared, he stared*). Telling a story in the present tense (instead of the past, traditionally favored) gives events a sense of immediacy. Presented as though everything were happening right now, Wilson's story might have begun, "Peering out her window, a woman spies a strange man...." You can try the present tense, if you like, and see how immediate it seems to you. Be warned, however, that it can seem artificial (because we're used to reading stories in the past tense), and it can be difficult to sustain throughout an entire narrative. The past tense may be more removed, but it is still powerful: Just look at Edgar Allan Poe's toe-curling story "The Tell-Tale Heart," at the end of this chapter.

What to Emphasize

Whether you tell of your own experience or of someone else's, even if it is brief, you need a whole story to tell. If the story is complex, do some searching and discovering in writing. One trusty method to test your memory (or to make sure you have all the necessary elements of a story) is that of a news reporter. Ask yourself:

1. *What* happened?
2. *Who* took part?
3. *When?*
4. *Where?*
5. *Why* did this event (or these events) take place?
6. *How* did it (or they) happen?

That last *how* isn't merely another way of asking what happened. It means: In exactly what way or under what circumstances? If the event was a murder, how was it done—with an ax or with a bulldozer? Journalists call this handy list of questions "the five *W*'s and the *H*."

Well-prepared storytellers, those who first search their memories (or do some research and legwork), have far more information on hand than they can use. The writing of a good story calls for careful choice. In choosing, remember your purpose and your audience. If you're writing that story of the dean and the books to give pleasure to readers who are your friends, delighted to hear about the discomfort of a pompous administrator, you will probably dwell lovingly on each detail of her consternation. You would tell the story differently if your audience were strangers who didn't know the dean from Eve. They would need more information on her background, reputation for stiffness, and appearance. If, suspected of having deliberately contrived the dean's humiliation, you were writing a report of the incident for the campus police, you'd want to give the plainest possible account of the story—without drama, without adornment, without background, and certainly without any humor whatsoever.

Your purpose and your audience, then, clearly determine which of the two main strategies of narration you're going to choose: to tell a story by SCENE or to tell it by SUMMARY. When you tell a story in a scene, or in scenes, you visualize each event as vividly and precisely as if you were there—as though it were a scene in a film, and your reader sat before the screen. This is the strategy of most fine novels and short stories—and of much excellent nonfiction as well. Instead of just mentioning people, you portray them. You recall dialogue as best you can, or you invent some that could have been spoken. You include DESCRIPTION (a mode of writing to be dealt with fully in our next chapter).

For a lively example of a well-drawn scene, see Maya Angelou's account of a tense crowd's behavior as, jammed into a small-town store, they listen to a fight broadcast (in "Champion of the World," beginning on p. 49). Angelou prolongs one scene for almost her entire essay. Sometimes, though, a writer will draw a scene in only two or three sentences. This is the brevity we find in W. Jackson Bate's glimpse of the hill-rolling Johnson. Unlike Angelou, Bate evidently seeks not to weave a tapestry of detail but to show, in telling of one brief event, a trait of his hero's character.

When, on the other hand, you tell a story by the method of summary, you relate events concisely. Instead of depicting people and their surroundings in great detail, you set down just the essentials of what happened. Most of us employ this method in most stories we tell, for it takes less time and fewer words. A summary is to a scene, then, as a simple stick figure is to a portrait in oils. This is not to dismiss stick figures as inferior. The economy of a story told in summary as effective as the lavish detail of a story told in scene

Again, your choice of a method depends on your answer to the questions you ask yourself: What is my purpose? Who is my audience? How fully to flesh out a scene, how much detail to include—these choices depend on what you seek to do, and on how much your audience needs to know to follow you. Read the life of some famous person in an encyclopedia, and you will find the article telling its story in summary form. Its writer's purpose, evidently, is to recount the main events of a whole life in a short space. But glance through a book-length biography of the same celebrity, and you will probably find scenes in it. A biographer writes with a different purpose: to present a detailed portrait roundly and thoroughly, bringing the subject vividly to life.

To be sure, you can use both methods in telling a single story. Often, summary will serve a writer who passes briskly from one scene to the next, or hurries over events of lesser importance. Were you to write, let's say, the story of a man's fiendish passion for horse racing, you might decide to give short shrift to most other facts of his life. To emphasize what you consider essential, you might begin a scene with a terse summary: "Seven years went by, and after three marriages and two divorces, Lars found himself again back at Hialeah." (A detailed scene might follow.)

Good storytellers know what to emphasize. They do not fall into a boring drone: "And then I went down to the club and I had a few beers and I noticed this sign, Go 3 Minutes with the Masked Samurai and Win $500, so I went and got knocked out and then I had pizza and went home." In this lazily strung-out summary, the narrator reduces all events to equal unimportance. A more adept storyteller might leave out the pizza and dwell in detail on the big fight.

In *The Bedford Reader*, we are concerned with the kind of writing you do every day in college: nonfiction writing in which you generally explain ideas, organize information you have learned, analyze other people's ideas, or argue a case. In fiction, though, we find an enormously popular and appealing use of narration and certain devices of storytelling from which all storytellers can learn. For these reasons, this chapter includes one celebrated short story by a master storyteller, Edgar Allan Poe. But fiction and fact barely separate Poe's story and the equally compelling true memoirs in this chapter. All the authors strive to make people and events come alive for us. All of them also use a tool that academic writers generally do not: dialogue. Reported speech, in quotation marks, is invaluable for revealing characters' feelings.

Organization

In any kind of narration, the simplest approach is to set down ᵉnts in CHRONOLOGICAL ORDER, the way they happened. To do so is to your story already organized for you. A chronological order is therefore an excellent sequence to follow unless you can see some special advantage in violating it. Ask: What am I trying to do? If you are trying to capture your readers' attention right away, you might begin *in medias res* (Latin, "in the middle of things") and open with a colorful, dramatic event, even though it took place late in the chronology. If trying for dramatic effect, you might save the most exciting or impressive event for last, even though it actually happened early. By this means, you can keep your readers in suspense for as long as possible. (You can return to earlier events by a FLASHBACK, an earlier scene recalled.) Let your purpose be your guide.

The writer Calvin Trillin has recalled why, in a narrative titled "The Tunica Treasure," he deliberately chose not to follow a chronology:

> I wrote a story on the discovery of the Tunica treasure which I couldn't begin by saying, "Here is a man who works as a prison guard in Angola State Prison, and on his weekends he sometimes looks for buried treasure that is rumored to be around the Indian village." Because the real point of the story centered around the problems caused when an amateur wanders onto professional territory, I thought it would be much better to open with how momentous the discovery was, that it was the most important archeological discovery about Indian contact with the European settlers to date, and *then* to say that it was discovered by a prison guard. So I made a conscious choice *not* to start with Leonard Charrier working as a prison guard, not to go back to his boyhood in Bunkie, Louisiana, not to talk about how he'd always been interested in treasure hunting—hoping that the reader would assume I was about to say that the treasure was found by an archeologist from the Peabody Museum at Harvard.

Trillin, by saving the fact that a prison guard made the earthshaking discovery, effectively took his reader by surprise.

No matter what order you choose, either following chronology or departing from it, make sure your audience can follow it. The sequence of events has to be clear. This calls for TRANSITIONS of time, whether they are brief phrases that point out exactly when each event happened ("Seven years later," "A moment earlier"), or whole sentences that announce an event and clearly locate it in time ("If you had known Leonard Charrier ten years earlier, you would have found him voraciously poring over every archeology text he could lay his hands on in the public library").

The Point

In writing a news story, a reporter often begins with the conclusion, placing the main event in the opening paragraph (called the lead) so that readers get the essentials up front. Similarly, in using an anecdote to explain something or to argue a point, you'll want to tell readers directly what you think the story demonstrates. But in most other kinds of narration, whether fiction or nonfiction, whether to entertain or to make an idea clear, the storyteller refrains from revealing the gist of the story, its point, right at the beginning. In fact, many narratives do not contain a THESIS SENTENCE, a statement of the idea behind the story, because such a statement can rob the reader of the very pleasure of narration, the excitement of seeing a story build. That doesn't mean the story lacks a focal point—far from it. The writer has every obligation to construct the narrative as if a thesis sentence directed the way, even when it doesn't.

By the end of the story, that focal point should become obvious, as the writer builds toward a memorable CONCLUSION. In a story Mark Twain liked to tell aloud, a woman's ghost returns to claim her artificial arm made of gold, which she wore in life and which her greedy husband had unscrewed from her corpse. Carefully, Twain would build up suspense as the ghost pursued the husband upstairs to his bedroom, stood by his bed, breathed her cold breath on him, and intoned, *"Who's got my golden arm?"* Twain used to end his story by suddenly yelling at a member of the audience, *"You've* got it!"—and enjoying the victim's shriek of surprise. That final punctuating shriek may be a technique that will work only in oral storytelling; yet, like Twain, most storytellers like to end with a bang if they can. For another example, take specific notice of Edgar Allan Poe's ending for "The Tell-Tale Heart" (*after* you've read the whole story, that is). The final impact need not be as dramatic as Twain's and Poe's, either. As Maya Angelou and Barbara Huttmann demonstrate in their narratives in this chapter, you can achieve a lot just by leading to your point, stating your thesis sentence at the very end. And as James Thurber shows, you can sometimes make your point just by saving the best incident for last—the most dramatic or, in Thurber's case, the funniest and most baffling.

CHECKLIST FOR REVISING A NARRATIVE

✔ **POINT OF VIEW.** Is your narrator's position in the story appropriate for your purpose and consistent throughout the story? Check for awkward or confusing shifts in point of view (participant or nonparticipant; first, second, or third person) and in the tenses of verbs (present to past or vice versa).

✔ **SELECTION OF EVENTS.** Have you selected and emphasized events to suit your audience and fulfill your purpose? Tell the important parts of the story in the greatest detail. Summarize the less important, connective events.

✔ **ORGANIZATION.** If your organization is not strictly chronological (first event to last), do you have a compelling reason for altering it? If you start somewhere other than the beginning of the story or use flashbacks at any point, will your readers benefit from your creativity?

✔ **TRANSITIONS.** Have you used transitions to help clarify the order of events and their duration?

✔ **DIALOGUE.** If you have used dialogue, quoting participants in the story, is it appropriate for your purpose? Is it concise, telling only the important, revealing lines? Does the language sound like spoken English?

✔ **THE POINT.** What is the point of your narrative? Will it be clear to readers by the end? Even if you haven't stated it in a thesis sentence, your story should focus on a central idea. If you can't risk readers' misunderstanding — if, for instance, you're using narration to support an argument or explain a concept — then have you stated your thesis outright?

NARRATION IN A PARAGRAPH: TWO ILLUSTRATIONS

Using Narration to Write About Television

Oozing menace from beyond the stars or from the deeps, televised horror powerfully stimulates a child's already frisky imagination. As parents know, a "Creature Double Feature" has an impact that lasts long after the click of the *off* button. Recently a neighbor reported the strange case of her eight-year-old. Discovered late at night in the game room watching *The Exorcist*, the girl was promptly sent to bed. An hour later, her parents could hear her chanting something in the darkness of her bedroom. On tiptoe, they stole to her door to listen. The creak of springs told them that their daughter was swaying rhythmically to and fro, and the smell of acrid smoke warned them that something was burning. At once, they shoved open the door to find the room flickering with shadows cast by a lighted candle. Their daughter was sitting in bed, rocking back and forth as she intoned over and over, "Fiend in human form …Fiend in human form…" This case may be unique; still, it seems likely that similar events take place each night all over the screen-watching world.

> Claim to be supported by narrative

> Anecdote builds suspense:
>
> Mystery
>
> Warnings
>
> Crisis
>
> Transitions (underlined) clarify sequence and pace of events
>
> Conclusion broadens claim

Using Narration in an Academic Discipline

The news media periodically relate the terrifying and often grim details of landslides. On May 31, 1970, one such event occurred when a gigantic rock avalanche buried more than 20,000 people in Yungay and Ranrahirca, Peru. There was little warning of the impending disaster; it began and ended in

> Generalization illustrated by narrative

> Anecdote helps explain landslides:

just a matter of a few minutes. The avalanche started 14 kilo-
meters from Yungay, near the summit of 6,700-meter-high
Nevados Huascaran, the loftiest peak in the Peruvian Andes.
Triggered by the ground motion from a strong offshore earthquake, a huge mass of rock and ice broke free from the precipi-
tous north face of the mountain. After plunging nearly one
kilometer, the material pulverized on impact and immediately
began rushing down the mountainside, made fluid by trapped
air and melted ice. The initial mass ripped loose additional millions of tons of debris as it roared downhill. The shock waves
produced by the event created thunderlike noise and stripped
nearby hillsides of vegetation. Although the material followed
a previously eroded gorge, a portion of the debris jumped a
200–300-meter-high bedrock ridge that had protected Yungay
from past rock avalanches and buried the entire city. After
inundating another town in its path, Ranrahirca, the mass of
debris finally reached the bottom of the valley where its mo-
mentum carried it across the Rio Santa and tens of meters up
the opposite bank.

—Edward J. Tarbuck and Frederick K. Lutgens,
The Earth: An Introduction to Physical Geology

Sudden beginning

Fast movement

Irresistible force

*Transitions (underlined)
clarify sequence and pace
of events*

MAYA ANGELOU

MAYA ANGELOU was born Marguerite Johnson in Saint Louis in 1928. After an unpleasantly eventful youth by her account ("from a broken family, raped at eight, unwed mother at sixteen"), she went on to join a dance company, star in an off-Broadway play (*The Blacks*), write six books of poetry, produce a series on Africa for PBS-TV, act in the television-special series *Roots*, serve as a coordinator for the Southern Christian Leadership Conference, and accept several honorary doctorates. She is best known, however, for the five books of her searching, frank, and joyful autobiography—beginning with *I Know Why the Caged Bird Sings* (1970), which she adapted for television, through *All God's Children Need Traveling Shoes* (1986). Her latest book is a collection of essays, *Wouldn't Take Nothing for My Journey Now* (1993). In 1993 Angelou read a specially commissioned poem, "On the Pulse of Morning," at the inauguration of President Bill Clinton. She is Reynolds Professor of American Studies at Wake Forest University.

Champion of the World

"Champion of the World" is the nineteenth chapter in *I Know Why the Caged Bird Sings;* the title is a phrase taken from the chapter. Remembering her childhood, the writer tells how she and her older brother, Bailey, grew up in a town in Arkansas. The center of their lives was Grandmother and Uncle Willie's store, a gathering place for the black community. On the night when this story takes place, Joe Louis, the "Brown Bomber" and the hero of his people, defends his heavyweight boxing title against a white contender.

The last inch of space was filled, yet people continued to wedge 1 themselves along the walls of the Store. Uncle Willie had turned the radio up to its last notch so that youngsters on the porch wouldn't miss a word. Women sat on kitchen chairs, dining-room chairs, stools, and upturned wooden boxes. Small children and babies perched on every lap available and men leaned on the shelves or on each other.

The apprehensive mood was shot through with shafts of gaiety, as 2 a black sky is streaked with lightning.

"I ain't worried 'bout this fight. Joe's gonna whip that cracker like 3 it's open season."

"He gone whip him till that white boy call him Momma." 4

At last the talking finished and the string-along songs about razor 5 blades were over and the fight began.

49

"A quick jab to the head." In the Store the crowd grunted. "A left   6
to the head and a right and another left." One of the listeners cackled
like a hen and was quieted.

"They're in a clinch, Louis is trying to fight his way out."   7

Some bitter comedian on the porch said, "That white man don't   8
mind hugging that niggah now, I betcha."

"The referee is moving in to break them up, but Louis finally   9
pushed the contender away and it's an uppercut to the chin. The contender is hanging on, now he's backing away. Louis catches him with a
short left to the jaw."

A tide of murmuring assent poured out the door and into the yard.   10

"Another left and another left. Louis is saving that mighty right ..."   11
The mutter in the Store had grown into a baby roar and it was pierced
by the clang of a bell and the announcer's "That's the bell for round
three, ladies and gentlemen."

As I pushed my way into the Store I wondered if the announcer   12
gave any thought to the fact that he was addressing as "ladies and gentlemen" all the Negroes around the world who sat sweating and pray-
ing, glued to their "Master's voice."[1]

There were only a few calls for RC Colas, Dr Peppers, and Hires   13
root beer. The real festivities would begin after the fight. Then even
the old Christian ladies who taught their children and tried themselves
to practice turning the other cheek would buy soft drinks, and if the
Brown Bomber's victory was a particularly bloody one they would order
peanut patties and Baby Ruths also.

Bailey and I laid the coins on top of the cash register. Uncle Willie   14
didn't allow us to ring up sales during a fight. It was too noisy and might
shake up the atmosphere. When the gong rang for the next round
we pushed through the near-sacred quiet to the herd of children
outside.

"He's got Louis against the ropes and now it's a left to the body and   15
a right to the ribs. Another right to the body, it looks like it was
low ... Yes, ladies and gentlemen, the referee is signaling but the contender keeps raining the blows on Louis. It's another to the body, and it
looks like Louis is going down."

My race groaned. It was our people falling. It was another lynching,   16
yet another Black man hanging on a tree. One more woman ambushed
and raped. A Black boy whipped and maimed. It was hounds on the
trail of a man running through slimy swamps. It was a white woman
slapping her maid for being forgetful.

---

[1] "His master's voice," accompanied by a picture of a little dog listening to a
phonograph, was a familiar advertising slogan. (The picture still appears on some RCA
recordings.) — EDS.

The men in the Store stood away from the walls and at attention.   17
Women greedily clutched the babes on their laps while on the porch
the shufflings and smiles, flirtings and pinching of a few minutes before
were gone. This might be the end of the world. If Joe lost we were back
in slavery and beyond help. It would all be true, the accusations that we
were lower types of human beings. Only a little higher than apes. True
that we were stupid and ugly and lazy and dirty and, unlucky and worst
of all, that God Himself hated us and ordained us to be hewers of wood
and drawers of water, forever and ever, world without end.

We didn't breathe. We didn't hope. We waited.   18

"He's off the ropes, ladies and gentlemen. He's moving towards the   19
center of the ring." There was no time to be relieved. The worst might
still happen.

"And now it looks like Joe is mad. He's caught Carnera with a left   20
hook to the head and a right to the head. It's a left jab to the body and
another left to the head. There's a left cross and a right to the head.
The contender's right eye is bleeding and he can't seem to keep his
block up. Louis is penetrating every block. The referee is moving in,
but Louis sends a left to the body and it's an uppercut to the chin and
the contender is dropping. He's on the canvas, ladies and gentlemen."

Babies slid to the floor as women stood up and men leaned toward   21
the radio.

"Here's the referee. He's counting. One, two, three, four, five, six, 22
seven...Is the contender trying to get up again?"

All the men in the store shouted, "NO."   23

"—eight, nine, ten." There were a few sounds from the audience, but   24
they seemed to be holding themselves in against tremendous pressure.

"The fight is all over, ladies and gentlemen. Let's get the micro-   25
phone over to the referee...Here he is. He's got the Brown Bomber's
hand, he's holding it up...Here he is..."

Then the voice, husky and familiar, came to wash over us—"The   26
winnah, and still heavyweight champeen of the world...Joe Louis."

Champion of the world. A Black boy. Some Black mother's son.   27
He was the strongest man in the world. People drank Coca-Colas like
ambrosia and ate candy bars like Christmas. Some of the men went behind the Store and poured white lightning in their soft-drink bottles,
and a few of the bigger boys followed them. Those who were not chased
away came back blowing their breath in front of themselves like proud
smokers.

It would take an hour or more before the people would leave the   28
Store and head for home. Those who lived too far had made arrangements to stay in town. It wouldn't do for a Black man and his family to
be caught on a lonely country road on a night when Joe Louis had
proved that we were the strongest people in the world.

QUESTIONS ON MEANING

1. What do you take to be the author's PURPOSE in telling this story?
2. What connection does Angelou make between the outcome of the fight and the pride of African Americans? To what degree do you think the author's view is shared by the others in the store listening to the broadcast?
3. To what extent are the statements in paragraphs 16 and 17 to be taken literally? What function do they serve in Angelou's narrative?
4. Primo Carnera was probably *not* the Brown Bomber's opponent on the night Maya Angelou recalls. Louis fought Carnera only once, on June 25, 1935, and it was not a title match; Angelou would have been no more than seven years old at the time. Does the author's apparent error detract from her story?

QUESTIONS ON WRITING STRATEGY

1. What details in the opening paragraphs indicate that an event of crucial importance is about to take place?
2. How does Angelou build up SUSPENSE in her account of the fight? At what point were you able to predict the winner?
3. Comment on the IRONY in Angelou's final paragraph.
4. What EFFECT does the author's use of direct quotation have on her narrative?
5. **OTHER METHODS.** Besides narration, Angelou also relies heavily on the method of DESCRIPTION. Analyze how narration depends on description in paragraph 27 alone.

QUESTIONS ON LANGUAGE

1. Explain what the author means by "string-along songs about razor blades" (para. 5).
2. How does Angelou's use of NONSTANDARD ENGLISH contribute to her narrative?
3. Be sure you know the meanings of these words: apprehensive (para. 2); assent (10); ambushed, maimed (16); ordained (17); ambrosia, white lightning (27).

SUGGESTIONS FOR WRITING

1. **JOURNAL WRITING.** What groups do you belong to, and how do you know you're a member? Consider groups based on race, ethnic background, religion, sports, hobbies, politics, friendship, kinship, or any other ties. **FROM JOURNAL TO ESSAY.** Choose one of the groups from your journal entry, and explore your sense of membership through a narrative that tells of an incident when that sense was strong. Try to make the incident come alive for your readers with vivid details, dialogue, and tight sequencing of events.
2. Write an essay based on some childhood experience of your own, still vivid in your memory.

3. **CRITICAL WRITING.** Angelou does not directly describe relations between African Americans and whites, yet her essay implies quite a lot. Write a brief essay about what you can INFER from the exaggeration of paragraphs 16–17 and the obliqueness of paragraph 28. Focus on Angelou's details and the language she uses to present them.
4. **CONNECTIONS.** Angelou's "Champion of the World" and the next essay, Amy Tan's "Fish Cheeks," both tell stories of children who felt like outsiders in predominantly white America. COMPARE AND CONTRAST the two writers' perceptions of what sets them apart from the dominant culture. How does the event each reports affect that sense of difference? Use specific examples from both essays as your EVIDENCE.

MAYA ANGELOU ON WRITING

Maya Angelou's writings have shown great variety: She has done notable work as an autobiographer, poet, short-story writer, screenwriter, journalist, and song lyricist. Asked by interviewer Sheila Weller, "Do you start each project with a specific idea?" Angelou replied:

"It starts with a definite subject, but it might end with something entirely different. When I start a project, the first thing I do is write down, in longhand, everything I know about the subject, every thought I've ever had on it. This may be twelve or fourteen pages. Then I read it back through, for quite a few days, and find—given that subject—what its rhythm is. 'Cause everything in the universe has a rhythm. So if it's free form, it still has a rhythm. And once I hear the rhythm of the piece, then I try to find out what are the salient points that I must make. And then it begins to take shape.

"I try to set myself up in each chapter by saying: 'This is what I want to go from—from B to, say, G-sharp. Or from D to L.' And then I find the hook. It's like the knitting, where, after you knit a certain amount, there's one thread that begins to pull. You know, you can see it right along the cloth. Well, in writing, I think: 'Now where is that one hook, that one little thread?' It may be a sentence. If I can catch that, then I'm home free. It's the one that tells me where I'm going. It may not even turn out to be in the final chapter. I may throw it out later or change it. But if I follow it through, it leads me right out."

FOR DISCUSSION

1. How would you define the word *rhythm* as Maya Angelou uses it?
2. What response would you give a student who said, "Doesn't Angelou's approach to writing waste more time and thought than it's worth?"

AMY TAN

AMY TAN is a gifted storyteller whose first novel, *The Joy Luck Club* (1989), met with critical acclaim and huge success. The relationships it details between immigrant Chinese mothers and their Chinese American daughters came from Tan's firsthand experience. She was born in 1952 in Oakland, California, the daughter of immigrants who had fled China's Cultural Revolution in the late 1940s. She majored in English and linguistics at San Jose State University, where she received a B.A. in 1973 and an M.A. in 1974. After two more years of graduate work, Tan became a consultant in language development for disabled children and then started her own company writing reports and speeches for business corporations. Tan began writing fiction to explore her ethnic ambivalence and to find a voice for herself. After *The Joy Luck Club*, she published *The Kitchen God's Wife* (1991), a fictional account of her mother's harrowing life in China, and *The Hundred Secret Senses* (1995), a novel. Tan has also written children's books and contributed essays to *McCall's*, *Life*, *Glamour*, *The Atlantic Monthly*, and other magazines.

Fish Cheeks

In this very brief narrative, Tan deftly portrays the ambivalence — the contradictory feelings — of a child with feet in different cultures. "Fish Cheeks" first appeared in *Seventeen*, a magazine for teenage girls and young women, in 1987.

I fell in love with the minister's son the winter I turned fourteen. He was not Chinese, but as white as Mary in the manger. For Christmas I prayed for this blond-haired boy, Robert, and a slim new American nose. 1

When I found out that my parents had invited the minister's family over for Christmas Eve dinner, I cried. What would Robert think of our shabby Chinese Christmas? What would he think of our noisy Chinese relatives who lacked proper American manners? What terrible disappointment would he feel upon seeing not a roasted turkey and sweet potatoes but Chinese food? 2

On Christmas Eve I saw that my mother had outdone herself in creating a strange menu. She was pulling black veins out of the backs of fleshy prawns. The kitchen was littered with appalling mounds of raw food: A slimy rock cod with bulging eyes that pleaded not to be thrown into a pan of hot oil. Tofu, which looked like stacked wedges of rubbery white sponges. A bowl soaking dried fungus back to life. A plate of squid, their backs crisscrossed with knife markings so they resembled bicycle tires. 3

And then they arrived—the minister's family and all my relatives 4
in a clamor of doorbells and rumpled Christmas packages. Robert
grunted hello, and I pretended he was not worthy of existence.

Dinner threw me deeper into despair. My relatives licked the ends 5
of their chopsticks and reached across the table, dipping them into the
dozen or so plates of food. Robert and his family waited patiently for
platters to be passed to them. My relatives murmured with pleasure
when my mother brought out the whole steamed fish. Robert grimaced.
Then my father poked his chopsticks just below the fish eye and
plucked out the soft meat. "Amy, your favorite," he said, offering me
the tender fish cheek. I wanted to disappear.

At the end of the meal my father leaned back and belched loudly, 6
thanking my mother for her fine cooking. "It's a polite Chinese custom
to show you are satisfied," explained my father to our astonished guests.
Robert was looking down at his plate with a reddened face. The minister managed to muster up a quiet burp. I was stunned into silence for
the rest of the night.

After everyone had gone, my mother said to me, "You want to be 7
the same as American girls on the outside." She handed me an early
gift. It was a miniskirt in beige tweed. "But inside you must always be
Chinese. You must be proud you are different. Your only shame is to
have shame."

And even though I didn't agree with her then, I knew that she 8
understood how much I had suffered during the evening's dinner. It
wasn't until many years later—long after I had gotten over my crush
on Robert—that I was able to fully appreciate her lesson and the true
purpose behind our particular menu. For Christmas Eve that year, she
had chosen all my favorite foods.

QUESTIONS ON MEANING

1. Why does Tan cry when she finds out that the boy she is in love with is
coming to dinner?
2. Why does Tan's mother go out of her way to prepare a disturbingly
traditional Chinese dinner for her daughter and guests? What one sentence best sums up the lesson Tan was not able to understand until years
later?
3. How does the fourteen-year-old Tan feel about her Chinese background?
About her mother?
4. What is Tan's PURPOSE in writing this essay? Does she just want to entertain
readers, or might she have a weightier goal?

QUESTIONS ON WRITING STRATEGY

1. How does Tan draw the reader into her story right from the beginning?
2. How does Tan use TRANSITIONS both to drive and to clarify her narrative?
3. What is the IRONY of the last sentence of the essay?
4. **OTHER METHODS.** Paragraph 3 is a passage of pure DESCRIPTION. Why does Tan linger over the food? What is the EFFECT of this paragraph?

QUESTIONS ON LANGUAGE

1. The SIMILE about Mary in the second sentence of the essay is surprising. Why? Why is it amusing?
2. How does the narrator's age affect the TONE of this essay? Give EXAMPLES of language particularly appropriate to a fourteen-year-old.
3. Make sure you know the meanings of the following words: prawns, tofu (para. 3); clamor (4); grimaced (5); muster (6).

SUGGESTIONS FOR WRITING

1. **JOURNAL WRITING.** Think of an occasion when, for whatever reason, you were ashamed of being different. How did you react? Did you try to hide your difference in order to fit in, or did you reveal or celebrate your uniqueness?
   FROM JOURNAL TO ESSAY. Using Tan's essay as a model, write a brief narrative based on the sketch from your journal. Try to imitate the way Tan integrates the external events of the dinner with her own feelings about what is going on. Your story may be humorous, like Tan's, or more serious.
2. Take a perspective like that of the minister's son, Robert: Write a narrative essay about a time when you had to adjust to participating in a culture different from your own. It could be a meal, a wedding or other rite of passage, a religious ceremony, a trip to another country. What did you learn from your experience, about yourself and others?
3. **CRITICAL WRITING.** From this essay one can INFER two very different sets of ASSUMPTIONS about the extent to which immigrants should seek to integrate themselves into the culture of their adopted country. Take either of these positions, in favor of or against assimilation (cultural integration), and make an ARGUMENT for your case.
4. **CONNECTIONS.** Both Tan and Maya Angelou, in "Champion of the World" (p. 49), write about difference from white Americans, but their POINTS OF VIEW are not the same: Tan's is a teenager's lament about not fitting in; Angelou's is an oppressed child's excitement about proving the injustice of oppression. In an essay, ANALYZE the two authors' uses of narration to convey their perspectives. What details do they focus on? What internal thoughts do they report? Is one essay more effective than the other? Why, or why not?

AMY TAN ON WRITING

In 1989 Amy Tan delivered a lecture titled "Mother Tongue" at the State of the Language Symposium in San Francisco. The lecture, later published in *The Threepenny Review* in 1990, addresses Tan's own experience as a bilingual child speaking both Chinese and English. "I do think that the language spoken in the family, especially in immigrant families, which are more insular, plays a large role in shaping the language of the child. And I believe that it affected my results on achievement tests, IQ tests, and the SAT. While my English skills were never judged as poor, compared to math English could not be considered my strong suit.... This was understandable. Math is precise; there is only one correct answer. Whereas, for me at least, the answers on English tests were always a judgment call, a matter of opinion and personal experience."

Tan goes on to say that the necessity of adapting to different styles of expression may affect other children from bilingual households. "I've been asked, as a writer, why there are not more Asian-Americans represented in American literature. Why are there few Asian-Americans enrolled in creative-writing programs? Why do so many Chinese students go into engineering? Well, these are broad sociological questions I can't begin to answer. But I have noticed in surveys...that Asian students, as a whole, always do significantly better on math achievement tests than in English. And this makes me think that there are other Asian-American students whose English spoken in the home might also be described as 'broken' or 'limited.' And perhaps they also have teachers who are steering them away from writing and into math and science, which is what happened to me."

Tan admits that when she first began writing fiction, she wrote "what I thought to be wittily crafted sentences, sentences that would finally prove I had mastery over the English language." But they were awkward and self-conscious, so she changed her tactic. "I later decided I should envision a reader for the stories I would write. And the reader I decided upon was my mother, because these were stories about mothers. So with this reader in mind—and in fact, she did read my early drafts—I began to write stories using all the Englishes I grew up with: the English I spoke to my mother,...the English she used with me,...my translation of her Chinese,...and what I imagined to be her translation of her Chinese if she could speak in perfect English, her internal language, and for that I sought to preserve the essence, but not either an English or a Chinese structure. I wanted to capture what language ability tests can never reveal: her intent, her passion, her imagery, the rhythms of her speech and the nature of her thoughts.

"Apart from what any critic had to say about my writing, I knew I had succeeded where it counted when my mother finished reading my book and gave me her verdict: 'So easy to read.'"

FOR DISCUSSION

1. How could growing up in a household of "broken" English be a handicap for a student taking an achievement test?
2. What does the author suggest is the reason why more Asian Americans enter engineering than English?
3. Why did Amy Tan's mother make a good reader?

ANNIE DILLARD

ANNIE DILLARD is accomplished as a prose writer, poet, and literary critic. Born in 1945, she earned a B.A. (1967) and an M.A. (1968) from Hollins College in Virginia. She now teaches writing at Wesleyan University in Connecticut. Dillard's first published prose, *Pilgrim at Tinker Creek* (1974), is a work alive with close, intense, and poetic descriptions of the natural world. It won her a Pulitzer Prize and comparison with Thoreau. Since then, Dillard's entranced and entrancing writing has appeared regularly in *Harper's, American Scholar, The Atlantic Monthly*, and other magazines and in her books: *Tickets for a Prayer Wheel* (1975), poems; *Holy the Firm* (1978), a prose poem; *Living by Fiction* (1982), literary criticism; *Teaching a Stone to Talk* (1982), nonfiction; *Encounters with Chinese Writers* (1984), an account of a trip to China; *An American Childhood* (1987), an autobiography; *The Writing Life* (1989), anecdotes and metaphors about writing; and *The Living* (1992), a historical novel set in the Pacific Northwest. Dillard's latest publication is *Modern American Memoirs* (1995), an anthology she edited.

The Chase

In this chapter from her autobiography, *An American Childhood*, Dillard leads us running desperately through snow-filled backyards. Like all of Dillard's writing, this romp shows an unparalleled enthusiasm for life and skill at expressing it.

Some boys taught me to play football. This was fine sport. You 1 thought up a new strategy for every play and whispered it to the others. You went out for a pass, fooling everyone. Best, you got to throw yourself mightily at someone's running legs. Either you brought him down or you hit the ground flat out on your chin, with your arms empty before you. It was all or nothing. If you hesitated in fear, you would miss and get hurt: you would take a hard fall while the kid got away, or you would get kicked in the face while the kid got away. But if you flung yourself wholeheartedly at the back of his knees—if you gathered and joined body and soul and pointed them diving fearlessly—then you likely wouldn't get hurt, and you'd stop the ball. Your fate, and your team's score, depended on your concentration and courage. Nothing girls did could compare with it.

Boys welcomed me at baseball, too, for I had, through enthusiastic 2 practice, what was weirdly known as a boy's arm. In winter, in the snow, there was neither baseball nor football, so the boys and I threw snow-

balls at passing cars. I got in trouble throwing snowballs, and have seldom been happier since.

On one weekday morning after Christmas, six inches of new snow   3
had just fallen. We were standing up to our boot tops in snow on a front
yard on trafficked Reynolds Street, waiting for cars. The cars traveled
Reynolds Street slowly and evenly; they were targets all but wrapped in
red ribbons, cream puffs. We couldn't miss.

I was seven; the boys were eight, nine, and ten. The oldest two Fa-   4
hey boys were there—Mikey and Peter—polite blond boys who lived
near me on Lloyd Street, and who already had four brothers and sisters.
My parents approved Mikey and Peter Fahey. Chickie McBride was
there, a tough kid, and Billy Paul and Mackie Kean too, from across
Reynolds, where the boys grew up dark and furious, grew up skinny,
knowing, and skilled. We had all drifted from our houses that morning
looking for action, and had found it here on Reynolds Street.

It was cloudy but cold. The cars' tires laid behind them on the   5
snowy street a complex trail of beige chunks like crenellated castle
walls. I had stepped on some earlier; they squeaked. We could have
wished for more traffic. When a car came, we all popped it one. In the
intervals between cars we reverted to the natural solitude of children.

I started making an iceball—a perfect iceball, from perfectly white   6
snow, perfectly spherical, and squeezed perfectly translucent so no
snow remained all the way through. (The Fahey boys and I considered
it unfair actually to throw an iceball at somebody, but it had been
known to happen.)

I had just embarked on the iceball project when we heard tire   7
chains come clanking from afar. A black Buick was moving toward us
down the street. We all spread out, banged together some regular snowballs, took aim, and, when the Buick drew nigh, fired.

A soft snowball hit the driver's windshield right before the driver's   8
face. It made a smashed star with a hump in the middle.

Often, of course, we hit our target, but this time, the only time in   9
all of life, the car pulled over and stopped. Its wide black door opened;
a man got out of it, running. He didn't even close the car door.

He ran after us, and we ran away from him, up the snowy Reynolds   10
sidewalk. At the corner, I looked back; incredibly, he was still after us.
He was in city clothes: a suit and tie, street shoes. Any normal adult
would have quit, having sprung us into flight and made his point. This
man was gaining on us. He was a thin man, all action. All of a sudden,
we were running for our lives.

Wordless, we split up. We were on our turf; we could lose ourselves   11
in the neighborhood backyards, everyone for himself. I paused and

considered. Everyone had vanished except Mikey Fahey, who was just rounding the corner of a yellow brick house. Poor Mikey, I trailed him. The driver of the Buick sensibly picked the two of us to follow. The man apparently had all day.

He chased Mikey and me around the yellow house and up a back- 12 yard path we knew by heart: under a low tree, up a bank, through a hedge, down some snowy steps, and across the grocery store's delivery driveway. We smashed through a gap in another hedge, entered a scruffy backyard and ran around its back porch and tight between houses to Edgerton Avenue; we ran across Edgerton to an alley and up our own sliding woodpile to the Halls' front yard; he kept coming. We ran up Lloyd Street and wound through mazy backyards toward the steep hilltop at Willard and Lang.

He chased us silently, block after block. He chased us silently over 13 picket fences, through thorny hedges, between houses, around garbage cans, and across streets. Every time I glanced back, choking for breath, I expected he would have quit. He must have been as breathless as we were. His jacket strained over his body. It was an immense discovery, pounding into my hot head with every sliding, joyous step, that this or- dinary adult evidently knew what I thought only children who trained at football knew: that you have to fling yourself at what you're doing, you have to point yourself, forget yourself, aim, dive.

Mikey and I had nowhere to go, in our own neighborhood or out of 14 it, but away from this man who was chasing us. He impelled us forward; we compelled him to follow our route. The air was cold; every breath tore my throat. We kept running, block after block; we kept improvis- ing, backyard after backyard, running a frantic course and choosing it simultaneously, failing always to find small places or hard places to slow him down, and discovering always, exhilarated, dismayed, that only bare speed could save us—for he would never give up, this man—and we were losing speed.

He chased us through the backyard labyrinths of ten blocks before 15 he caught us by our jackets. He caught us and we all stopped.

We three stood staggering, half blinded, coughing, in an obscure 16 hilltop backyard: a man in his twenties, a boy, a girl. He had released our jackets, our pursuer, our captor, our hero: he knew we weren't going anywhere. We all played by the rules. Mikey and I unzipped our jackets. I pulled off my sopping mittens. Our tracks multiplied in the backyard's new snow. We had been breaking new snow all morning. We didn't look at each other. I was cherishing my excite- ment. The man's lower pants legs were wet; his cuffs were full of snow, and there was a prow of snow beneath them on his shoes and socks. Some trees bordered the little flat backyard, some messy winter trees. There was no one around: a clearing in a grove, and we the only players.

It was a long time before he could speak. I had some difficulty at 17 first recalling why we were there. My lips felt swollen; I couldn't see out of the sides of my eyes; I kept coughing.

"You stupid kids," he began perfunctorily. 18

We listened perfunctorily indeed, if we listened at all, for the chew- 19 ing out was redundant, a mere formality, and beside the point. The point was that he had chased us passionately without giving up, and so he had caught us. Now he came down to earth. I wanted the glory to last forever.

But how could the glory have lasted forever? We could have run 20 through every backyard in North America until we got to Panama. But when he trapped us at the lip of the Panama Canal, what precisely could he have done to prolong the drama of the chase and cap its glory? I brooded about this for the next few years. He could only have fried Mikey Fahey and me in boiling oil, say, or dismembered us piecemeal, or staked us to anthills. None of which I really wanted, and none of which any adult was likely to do, even in the spirit of fun. He could only chew us out there in the Panamanian jungle, after months or years of exalting pursuit. He could only begin, "You stupid kids," and con- tinue in his ordinary Pittsburgh accent with his normal righteous anger and the usual common sense.

If in that snowy backyard the driver of the black Buick had cut off 21 our heads, Mikey's and mine, I would have died happy, for nothing has required so much of me since as being chased all over Pittsburgh in the middle of winter—running terrified, exhausted—by this sainted, skinny, furious red-headed man who wished to have a word with us. I don't know how he found his way back to his car.

QUESTIONS ON MEANING

1. What is Dillard's PURPOSE in this essay? Obviously, she wants to entertain readers, but does she have another purpose as well?
2. Does the persistence of the pursuer seem reasonable to you, given the chil- dren's prank?
3. What does the pursuer represent for the narrator? How do her feelings about him change after the chase is over, and why?
4. Why does Dillard describe the "chewing out," seemingly the object of the chase, as "redundant, a mere formality, and beside the point" (para. 19)?

QUESTIONS ON WRITING STRATEGY

1. Why does Dillard open her story with a discussion of football? In what way does the game of football serve as a METAPHOR in the story? (Hint: Look at para. 13, as well as the sentence "It was all or nothing" in para. 1.)
2. Identify the two rapid TRANSITIONS in paragraph 2. Do they contribute to or detract from the COHERENCE of the essay?
3. Why does Dillard interrupt the story of the chase with an "immense discovery" (para. 13)? Does this interruption weaken the narrative?
4. Discuss Dillard's POINT OF VIEW. Is her perspective that of a seven-year-old girl, or that of an adult writer reflecting on her childhood experience?
5. **OTHER METHODS.** Dillard's story implicitly COMPARES AND CONTRASTS a child's and an adult's way of looking at life. What are some of the differences that Dillard implies?

QUESTIONS ON LANGUAGE

1. Look up the meaning of any of the following words you don't already know: crenellated (para. 5); translucent (6); nigh (7); impelled, compelled (14); prow (16); perfunctorily (18); redundant (19); dismembered, piecemeal, exalting, righteous (20).
2. Explain the contradiction in this statement: "I got in trouble throwing snowballs, and have seldom been happier since" (para. 2). Can you find other examples of PARADOX in what the narrator says? How is this paradox related to the narrator's apparent view of children?
3. What is the EFFECT of the last sentence of the essay?

SUGGESTIONS FOR WRITING

1. **JOURNAL WRITING.** What incidents in your childhood seem to you momentous even now? List these significant incidents, along with some notes about their importance.

   FROM JOURNAL TO ESSAY. Choose one significant incident from your journal list, and narrate it as vividly as you can. Include the details: Where did the event take place? What did people say? How were they dressed? What was the weather like? Follow Dillard's model in putting CONCRETE IMAGES to work for an idea, in this case an idea about the significance of the incident to you then and now.
2. From what you have seen of children and adults, do you agree with Dillard's characterization of the two groups (see "Writing Strategy" question 5)? Write an essay comparing and contrasting children's and adults' attitudes toward play. (You will have to GENERALIZE, of course, but try to keep your broad statements grounded in a reality your readers will share.)
3. **CRITICAL WRITING.** Dillard's narration of the chase is only six paragraphs long (paras. 10–15), but it seems longer, as if almost in real time. What techniques does Dillard use in these paragraphs to hold our attention and re-create the breathlessness of the chase? Look at concrete details, repetition, PARALLELISM, and the near absence of time-marking transitions. In ANALYZING Dillard's techniques, use plenty of quotations from the essay.

4. **CONNECTIONS.** Dillard's essay and Merrill Markoe's "The Day I Turned Sarcastic" (p. 154) both deal with childhood values and how they are transformed in adulthood. In a brief essay, compare and contrast the two writers' treatment of this subject. How does the humor differ between the two essays? The TONE?

ANNIE DILLARD ON WRITING

Writing for *The Bedford Reader*, Dillard has testified to her work habits. Rarely satisfied with an essay until it has gone through many drafts, she sometimes goes on correcting and improving it even after it has been published. "I always have to condense or toss openings," she affirms; "I suspect most writers do. When you begin something, you're so grateful to have begun you'll write down anything, just to prolong the sensation. Later, when you've learned what the writing is really about, you go back and throw away the beginning and start over."

Often she replaces a phrase or sentence with a shorter one. In one essay, to tell how a drop of pond water began to evaporate on a microscope slide, she first wrote, "Its contours pulled together." But that sentence seemed to suffer from "tortured abstraction." She made the sentence read instead, "Its edges shrank." Dillard observes, "I like short sentences. They're forceful, and they can get you out of big trouble."

FOR DISCUSSION

1. Why, according to Dillard, is it usually necessary for writers to revise the opening paragraphs of what they write?
2. Dillard says that short sentences "can get you out of big trouble." What kinds of "big trouble" do you suppose she means?

RALPH ELLISON

RALPH WALDO ELLISON is best known for his award-winning novel *Invisible Man* (1952), about a black man who seeks his identity somewhere beyond white and black stereotypes. Born in 1919, Ellison studied music and read literature at Tuskegee Institute in Alabama but left before graduating for lack of money. He began publishing stories in the late 1930s and has written essays of autobiography, criticism, and cultural history that have been collected in *Shadow and Act* (1964) and *Going to the Territory* (1986). At New York University, Ellison was Albert Schweitzer Professor in Humanities for almost a decade, and he lectured at Rutgers, Yale, and many other universities. Ellison died in 1994, but his words continue to be published: *Collected Essays* and *Conversations with Ralph Ellison* both appeared in 1995, and his long-awaited second novel is being compiled from his drafts by his literary executor, John Callahan.

On Being the Target of Discrimination

Ellison grew up in Oklahoma, where he felt that "relationships between the races were more fluid and thus more human than in the old slave states." Still, as a boy he knew discrimination in "brief impersonal encounters, stares, vocal inflections, hostile laughter, or public reversals of private expectations." Some of these slights are recounted in this essay, which first appeared in 1989 in *A World of Difference*, a special *New York Times* supplement devoted to reducing racial and ethnic prejudice.

It got to you first at the age of six, and through your own curiosity. 1
With kindergarten completed and the first grade ahead, you were eagerly anticipating your first day of public school. For months you had been imagining your new experience and the children, known and unknown, with whom you would study and play. But the physical framework of your imagining, an elementary school in the process of construction, lay close at hand on the block-square site across the street from your home. For over a year you had watched it rise and spread in the air to become a handsome structure of brick and stone, then seen its broad encircling grounds arrayed with seesaws, swings, and baseball diamonds. You had imagined this picture-book setting as the scene of your new experience, and when enrollment day arrived, with its grounds astir with bright colors and voices of kids like yourself, it did, indeed, become the site of your very first lesson in public schooling — though not within its classrooms, as you had imagined, but well

outside its walls. For while located within a fairly mixed neighborhood this new public school was exclusively for whites.

It was then you learned that you would attend a school located far 2 to the south of your neighborhood, and that reaching it involved a journey which took you over, either directly or by way of a viaduct which arched head-spinning high above, a broad expanse of railroad tracks along which a constant traffic of freightcars, switch engines, and passenger trains made it dangerous for a child to cross. And that once the tracks were safely negotiated you continued past warehouses, factories, and loading docks, and then through a notorious red-light district where black prostitutes in brightly colored housecoats and Mary Jane shoes supplied the fantasies and needs of a white clientele. Considering the fact that you couldn't attend school with white kids this made for a confusion that was further confounded by the giggling jokes which older boys whispered about the district's peculiar form of integration. For you it was a grown-up's mystery, but streets being no less schools than routes to schools, the district would soon add a few forbidden words to your vocabulary.

It took a bit of time to forget the sense of incongruity aroused by 3 your having to walk *past* a school to get *to* a school, but soon you came to like your school, your teachers, and most of your schoolmates. Indeed, you soon enjoyed the long walks and anticipated the sights you might see, the adventures you might encounter, and the many things not taught in school that could be learned along the way. Your school was not nearly so fine as that which faced your home but it had its attractions. Among them its nearness to a park, now abandoned by whites, in which you picnicked and played. And there were the two tall cylindrical fire-escapes on either wing of its main building down which it was a joy to lie full-length and slide, spiraling down and around three stories to the ground—providing no outraged teacher was waiting to strap your legs once you sailed out of its chute like a shot off a fireman's shovel. Besides, in your childish way you were learning that it was better to take self-selected risks and pay the price than be denied the joy or pain of risk-taking by those who begrudged your existence.

Beginning when you were four or five you had known the joy of 4 trips to the city's zoo, but one day you would ask your mother to take you there and have her sigh and explain that it was now against the law for Negro kids to view the animals. Had someone done something bad to the animals? No. Had someone tried to steal them or feed them poison? No. Could white kids still go? Yes! So why? Quit asking questions, it's the law and only because some white folks are out to turn this state into a part of the South.

This sudden and puzzling denial of a Saturday's pleasure was disap- 5 pointing and so angered your mother that later, after the zoo was moved north of the city, she decided to do something about it. Thus one warm Saturday afternoon with you and your baby brother dressed in your best she took you on a long streetcar ride which ended at a strange lakeside park, in which you found a crowd of noisy white people. Having assumed that you were on your way to the integrated cemetery where at the age of three you had been horrified beyond all tears or forgetting when you saw your father's coffin placed in the ground, you were bewildered. But now as your mother herded you and your brother in to the park you discovered that you'd come to the zoo and were so delighted that soon you were laughing and babbling as excitedly as the kids around you.

Your mother was pleased and as you moved through the crowd of white parents and children she held your brother's hand and allowed as much time for staring at the cages of rare animals as either of you desired. But once your brother began to tire she herded you out of the park and toward the streetcar line. And then it happened.   6

Just as you reached the gate through which crowds of whites were coming and going you had a memorable lesson in the strange ways of segregated-democracy as instructed by a guard in civilian clothes. He was a white man dressed in a black suit and a white straw hat, and when he looked at the fashion in which your mother was dressed, then down to you and your brother, he stiffened, turned red in the face, and stared as though at something dangerous.   7

"Girl," he shouted, "where are your *white* folks!"   8

"*White* folks," your mother said. "What white folks? I don't *have* any white folks, I'm a Negro!"   9

"Now don't you get smart with me, colored gal," the white man said. "I mean where are the white folks you come *out* here with!"   10

"But I just told you that I didn't come here with any white people," your mother said. "I came here with my boys..."   11

"Then what are you doing in this park," the white man said.   12

And now when your mother answered you could hear the familiar sound of anger in her voice.   13

"I'm here," she said, "because I'm a *taxpayer*, and I thought it was about time that my boys have a look at those animals. And for that I didn't *need* any *white* folks to show me the way!"   14

"Well," the white man said, "*I'm* here to tell you that you're breaking the law! So now you'll have to leave. Both you and your chillun too. The rule says no niggers is allowed in the zoo. That's the law and I'm enforcing it!"   15

"Very well," your mother said, "we've seen the animals anyway and were on our way to the streetcar line when you stopped us."   16

"That's fine," the white man said, "and when that car comes you be sure that you get on it, you hear? You and your chillun too!"   17

So it was quite a day. You had enjoyed the animals with your baby   18
brother and had another lesson in the sudden ways good times could be
turned into bad when white people looked at your color instead of *you*.
But better still, you had learned something of your mother's courage
and were proud that she had broken an unfair law and stood up for her
right to do so. For while the white man kept staring until the streetcar
arrived she ignored him and answered your brother's questions about
the various animals. Then the car came with its crowd of white parents
and children, and when you were entrained and rumbling home past
the fine lawns and houses your mother gave way to a gale of laughter;
in which, hesitantly at first, and then with assurance and pride, you
joined. And from that day the incident became the source of a family
joke that was sparked by accidents, faux pas, or obvious lies. Then one
of you was sure to frown and say, "Well, I think you'll have to go now,
both you and your chillun too!" And the family would laugh hilari-
ously. Discrimination teaches one to discriminate between discrimina-
tors while countering absurdity with black (Negro? Afro-American?
African-American?) comedy.

When you were eight you would move to one of the white sections   19
through which you often passed on the way to your father's grave and
your truly last trip to the zoo. For now your mother was the custodian
of several apartments located in a building which housed on its street
floor a drug store, a tailor shop, a Piggly Wiggly market, and a branch
post office. Built on a downward slope, the building had at its rear a
long driveway which led from the side street past an empty lot to a
group of garages in which the apartments' tenants stored their cars.
Built at an angle with wings facing north and east, the structure supported a servant's quarters which sat above its angle like a mock watch-
tower atop a battlement, and it was there that you now lived.

Reached by a flight of outside stairs, it consisted of four small   20
rooms, a bath, and a kitchen. Windows on three of its sides provided a
view across the empty frontage to the street, of the back yards behind
it, and of the back wall and windows of the building in which your
mother worked. It was quite comfortable but you secretly disliked the
idea of your mother living in service and missed your friends who now
lived far away. Nevertheless, the neighborhood was pleasant, served by
a sub-station of the streetcar line, and marked by a variety of activities
which challenged your curiosity. Even its affluent alleys were more exciting to explore than those of your old neighborhood, and the one
white friend you were to acquire in the area lived nearby.

This friend was a brilliant but sickly boy who was tutored at home,   21
and with him you shared your new interest in building radios, a hobby
at which he was quite skilled. Your friendship eased your loneliness and
helped dispel some of the mystery and resentment imposed by segrega-

tion. Through access to his family, headed by an important Episco-
palian minister, you learned more about whites and thus about yourself.
With him you could make comparisons that were not so distorted by
the racial myths which obstructed your thrust toward self-perception;
compare their differences in taste, discipline, and manners with those
of Negro families of comparable status and income; observe variations
between your friend's boyish lore and your own, and measure his intelligence, knowledge, and ambitions against your own. For you this was a
most important experience and a rare privilege, because up to now the
prevailing separation of the races had made it impossible to learn how
you and your Negro friends compared with boys who lived on the white
side of the color line. It was said by word of mouth, proclaimed in
newsprint, and dramatized by acts of discriminatory law that you were
inferior. You were barred from vying with them in sports and games,
competing in the classroom or the world of art. Yet what you saw,
heard, and smelled of them left irrepressible doubts. So you ached for
objective proof, for a fair field of testing.

Even your school's proud marching band was denied participation   22
in the statewide music contests so popular at the time, as though so airy
and earth-transcending an art as music would be contaminated if performed by musicians of different races.

Which was especially disturbing because after the father of a friend   23
who lived next door in your old neighborhood had taught you the be-
ginner's techniques required to play valved instruments you had decided to become a musician. Then shortly before moving among whites
your mother had given you a brass cornet, which in the isolation of the
servant's quarters you practiced hours on end. But you yearned to play
with other musicians and found none available. Now you lived less
than a block from a white school with a famous band, but there was no
one in the neighborhood with whom to explore the mysteries of the
horn. You could hear the school band's music and watch their marching, but joining in making the thrilling sounds was impossible. Nor did
it help that you owned the scores to a few of their marches and could
play with a certain facility and fairly good tone. So there, surrounded
by sounds but unable to share a sound, you went it alone. You turned
yourself into a one-man band.

You played along as best you could with the phonograph, read the   24
score to *The Carnival of Venice* while listening to Del Steigers executing
triple-tongue variations on its themes; played the trumpet parts of your
bandbook's marches while humming in your head the supporting
voices of horns and reeds. And since your city was a seedbed of South-
western jazz you played Kansas City riffs, bugle calls, and wha-wha-
muted imitations of blues singers' pleas. But none of this made up for
your lack of fellow musicians. And then, late one Saturday afternoon

when your mother and brother were away, and when you had dozed off while reading, you awoke to the nearby sound of live music. At first you thought you were dreaming, and then that you were listening to the high school band, but that couldn't be the source because, instead of floating over building tops and bouncing off wall and windowpane, the sounds you heard rose up, somewhat muffled, from below.

With that you ran to a window which faced the driveway, and 25 looking down through the high windowpane of the lighted post office you could see the metal glint of instruments. Then you were on your feet and down the stairs, keeping to the shadows as you drew close and peeped below. And there you looked down upon a room full of men and women postal workers who were playing away at a familiar march. It was like the answer to a silent prayer because you could tell by the sound that they were beginners like yourself and the covers of the thicket of bandbooks revealed that they were of the same set as yours. For a while you listened and hummed along, unseen but shaking with excitement in the dimming twilight. And then, hardly before the idea formed in your head, you were skipping up the stairs to grab your cornet, lyre, and bandbook and hurtling down again to the drive.

For a while you listened, hearing the music come to a pause and the 26 sound of the conductor's voice. Then came a rap on a music stand and once again the music. And now turning to the march by the light from the window, you snapped score to lyre, raised horn to lip, and began to play; at first silently tonguing the notes through the mouthpiece and then, carried away with the thrill of stealing a part of the music, you tensed your diaphragm and blew. And as you played, keeping time with your foot on the concrete drive, you realized that you were a better cornetist than some in the band and grew bold in the pride of your sound. Now in your mind you were marching along a downtown street to the flying of flags, the tramping of feet, and the cheering of excited crowds. For at last by an isolated act of brassy cunning you had become a member of the band.

Yes, but unfortunately you then let yourself become so carried away 27 that you forgot to listen for the conductor's instructions which you were too high and hidden to see. Suddenly the music faded and you opened your ears to the fact that you were now rendering a lonely solo in the startled quietness. And before you could fully return to reality there came the sound of table legs across a floor and a rustle of movement ending in the appearance of a white startled face in the opened window. Then you heard a man's voice exclaim, "I'll be damn, it's a little nigger!" whereupon you took off like quail at the sound of sudden shotgun fire.

Next thing you knew, you were up the stairs and on your bed, cry- 28 ing away in the dark your guilt and embarrassment. You cried and cried, asking yourself how could you have been so lacking in pride as to shame yourself and your entire race by butting in where you weren't wanted. And this just to make some amateur music. To this you had no answers but then and there you made a vow that it would never happen again. And then, slowly, slowly, as you lay in the dark, your earlier lessons in the absurd nature of racial relations came to your aid. And suddenly you found yourself laughing, both at the way you'd run away and the shock you'd caused by joining unasked in the music.

Then you could hear yourself intoning in your eight-year-old's im- 29 itation of a white Southern accent. "Well boy, you broke the law, so you have to go, and that means you and your chillun too!"

QUESTIONS ON MEANING

1. What do you see as Ellison's PURPOSE in writing this essay?
2. What does the phrase "You and your chillun too" mean in paragraph 17? What does it come to mean in the writer's family? What does it mean at the end of the essay?
3. How does the writer's self-image change from the beginning of the narrative to the end?

♍ QUESTIONS ON WRITING STRATEGY

1. What is the narrator's POINT OF VIEW? What PERSON does the narrator use? What EFFECT does this choice of person have on you as reader?
2. Why do you think this essay was published in a newspaper supplement designed to reduce discrimination (see the note on the essay, p. 65)? How did the essay affect your understanding of or attitude toward discrimination?
3. Why does Ellison narrate several events instead of just one? What is the point of each incident?
4. How do we learn that the narrator's father is dead? Is this fact important to the narrative? Is the narrator's handling of it effective?
5. **OTHER METHODS.** Comment on Ellison's use of EXAMPLES in paragraphs 3 and 24. What do they add?

♌ QUESTIONS ON LANGUAGE

1. What do the DESCRIPTION and dialogue in paragraphs 7–17 tell you about Ellison's attitude toward the white zoo guard?
2. What is generally meant by "black comedy" or "black humor"? What joke is Ellison making at the end of paragraph 18?
3. Define: astir (para. 1); viaduct, clientele (2); incongruity, begrudged (3); faux pas (18); battlement (19); lore, vying (21); intoning (29).

SUGGESTIONS FOR WRITING

1. **JOURNAL WRITING.** Have you ever broken a code (whether an unwritten rule or a recorded law) to do something? How did the experience make you feel? Did you get caught?

   FROM JOURNAL TO ESSAY. Write an essay that EVALUATES the worth of break-ing the code you described in your journal. What did you risk and gain (or lose)? Make sure to use concrete details to narrate both the incident and the outcome.

2. Write a narrative about a childhood event in which you discovered some-thing about your place in the world. Give careful consideration to point of view and the use of dialogue.

3. Relate an incident from your childhood that illustrates how you felt about a particular environment—a house, rooftop, school, neighborhood, clear-ing in the woods. Use description to create a clear picture of the place.

4. **CRITICAL WRITING.** Ellison's use of *you* for the participant in his story is un-usual; we might expect *I* or, less commonly, *he*. To ANALYZE this strategy, first rewrite paragraph 28, substituting *I/my* and then *he/his* for *you/your*. (You'll need to change verbs to match the new pronouns.) Read the paragraphs aloud, analyzing the effect of each pronoun: Does it create distance or im-mediacy? Does it elicit more or less sympathy for the narrator? Is it clear or confusing? What can you INFER about Ellison's reasons for choosing *you*? In an essay, evaluate Ellison's choice on the basis of your analysis, supporting your ideas with examples from the essay or your rewrites.

5. **CONNECTIONS.** If you haven't already, read Maya Angelou's "Champion of the World" (p. 49). COMPARE AND CONTRAST the ways the African Americans in Ellison's and Angelou's essays find their value as human beings.

❧ RALPH ELLISON ON WRITING

In his introduction to his essay collection *Shadow and Act* (1964), Ralph Ellison talks about how he came to be a writer. "When the first of these essays [reprinted in *Shadow and Act*] was published I regarded myself—in my most secret heart at least—a musician.... Writing was far from a serious matter.... Nor had I invested in writing any long hours of practice and study. Rather it was a reflex of reading, an exten-sion of a source of pleasure, escape, and instruction.... It was not, then, the *process* of writing which initially claimed my attention, but the fin-ished creations, the artifacts—poems, plays, novels.... The pleasure I derived from reading had long been a necessity, and in the *act* of read-ing, that marvelous collaboration between the writer's artful vision and the reader's sense of life, I had become acquainted with other possible selves—freer, more courageous and ingenuous and, during the course of the narrative at least, even wise."

The process of writing did not attract Ellison as strongly until he actually started writing. "Once involved," he says, "I soon became consciously concerned with craft, with technique....I was gradually led, often reluctantly, to become consciously concerned with the nature of the culture and the society out of which American fiction is fabricated."

For Ellison, "the act of writing requires a constant plunging back into the shadow of the past where time hovers ghostlike.... [It is] the agency of my efforts to answer the question: Who am I, what am I, how did I come to be? What shall I make of the life around me, what celebrate, what reject, how confront the snare of good and evil which is inevitable? What does American society *mean* when regarded out of my *own* eyes, when informed by my *own* sense of the past and viewed by my *own* complex sense of the present? How, in other words, should I think of myself and my pluralistic sense of the world, how express my vision of the human predicament?"

FOR DISCUSSION

1. How did reading prepare Ellison for writing?
2. What connection does Ellison see between writing and personal identity?

Significant Events: is an event that caused you directly or indirectly to be impacted.

JAMES THURBER

JAMES THURBER (1894–1961), a native of Columbus, Ohio, made himself immortal with his humorous stories of shy, bumbling men (such as "The Secret Life of Walter Mitty") and his cartoons of men, women, and dogs that look as though he had drawn them with his foot. (In fact, Thurber suffered from weak eyesight and had to draw his cartoons in crayon on sheets of paper two or three feet wide.) As Thurber aged and approached blindness, he drew less and less and wrote more and more. His first book, written with his friend E. B. White, is a takeoff on self-help manuals, *Is Sex Necessary?* (1929). His later prose includes *My Life and Hard Times* (1933), from which "University Days" is taken; *The Thirteen Clocks*, a fable for children (1950); and *The Years with Ross* (1959), a memoir of his years on the staff of *The New Yorker*.

University Days

Ohio State University during World War I may seem remote from your own present situation, but see if you don't agree that this story of campus frustration is as fresh as the day it was first composed. Notice how, with beautiful brevity, Thurber draws a scene, introduces bits of revealing dialogue, and shifts briskly from one scene to another.

I passed all the other courses that I took at my university, but I 1 could never pass botany. This was because all botany students had to spend several hours a week in a laboratory looking through a microscope at plant cells, and I could never see through a microscope. I never once saw a cell through a microscope. This used to enrage my instructor. He would wander around the laboratory pleased with the progress all the students were making in drawing the involved and, so I am told, interesting structure of flower cells, until he came to me. I would just be standing there. "I can't see anything," I would say. He would begin patiently enough, explaining how anybody can see through a microscope, but he would always end up in a fury, claiming that I could *too* see through the microscope but just pretended that I couldn't. "It takes away from the beauty of flowers anyway," I used to tell him. "We are not concerned with beauty in this course," he would say. "We are concerned solely with what I may call the *mechanics* of flars." "Well," I'd say, "I can't see anything." "Try it just once again," he'd say, and I would put my eye to the microscope and see nothing at all, except now and again a nebulous milky substance—a phenomenon of maladjustment. You were supposed to see a vivid, restless clockwork of sharply defined plant cells. "I see what looks like a lot of milk," I would tell him. This, he claimed, was the result of my not having adjusted the microscope properly, so he would readjust it for me, or rather, for himself. And I would look again and see milk.

I finally took a deferred pass, as they called it, and waited a year and tried again. (You had to pass one of the biological sciences or you couldn't graduate.) The professor had come back from vacation brown as a berry, bright-eyed, and eager to explain cell-structure again to his classes. "Well," he said to me, cheerily, when we met in the first laboratory hour of the semester, "we're going to see cells this time, aren't we?" "Yes, sir," I said. Students to right of me and to left of me and in front of me were seeing cells; what's more, they were quietly drawing pictures of them in their notebooks. Of course, I didn't see anything.

"We'll try it," the professor said to me, grimly, "with every adjustment of the microscope known to man. As God is my witness, I'll arrange this glass so that you see cells through it or I'll give up teaching. In twenty-two years of botany, I—" He cut off abruptly for he was beginning to quiver all over, like Lionel Barrymore,[1] and he genuinely wished to hold onto his temper; his scenes with me had taken a great deal out of him.

So we tried it with every adjustment of the microscope known to man. With only one of them did I see anything but blackness or the familiar lacteal opacity, and that time I saw, to my pleasure and amazement, a variegated constellation of flecks, specks, and dots. These I hastily drew. The instructor, noting my activity, came back from an adjoining desk, a smile on his lips and his eyebrows high in hope. He looked at my cell drawing. "What's that?" he demanded, with a hint of a squeal in his voice. "That's what I saw," I said. "You didn't, you didn't, you *didn't!*" he screamed, losing control of his temper instantly, and he bent over and squinted into the microscope. His head snapped up. "That's your eye!" he shouted. "You've fixed the lens so that it reflects! You've drawn your eye!"

Another course that I didn't like, but somehow managed to pass, was economics. I went to that class straight from the botany class, which didn't help me any in understanding either subject. I used to get them mixed up. But not as mixed up as another student in my economics class who came there direct from a physics laboratory. He was a tackle on the football team, named Bolenciecwcz. At that time Ohio State University had one of the best football teams in the country, and Bolenciecwcz was one of its outstanding stars. In order to be eligible to play it was necessary for him to keep up in his studies, a very difficult matter, for while he was not dumber than an ox he was

---

[1] A noted American stage, radio, and screen actor (1878–1954). —Eds.

not any smarter. Most of his professors were lenient and helped him along. None gave him more hints in answering questions or asked him simpler ones than the economics professor, a thin, timid man named Bassum. One day when we were on the subject of transportation and distribution, it came Bolenciecwcz's turn to answer a question. "Name one means of transportation," the professor said to him. No light came into the big tackle's eyes. "Just any means of transportation," said the professor. Bolenciecwcz sat staring at him. "That is," pursued the professor, "any medium, agency, or method of going from one place to another." Bolenciecwcz had the look of a man who is being led into a trap. "You may choose among steam, horse-drawn, or electrically propelled vehicles," said the instructor. "I might suggest the one which we commonly take in making long journeys across land." There was a profound silence in which everybody stirred uneasily, including Bolenciecwcz and Mr. Bassum. Mr. Bassum abruptly broke this silence in an amazing manner. "Choo-choo-choo," he said, in a low voice, and turned instantly scarlet. He glanced appealingly around the room. All of us, of course, shared Mr. Bassum's desire that Bolenciecwcz should stay abreast of the class in economics, for the Illinois game, one of the hardest and most important of the season, was only a week off. "Toot, too, too-toooooot!" some student with a deep voice moaned, and we all looked encouragingly at Bolenciecwcz. Somebody else gave a fine imitation of a locomotive letting off steam. Mr. Bassum himself rounded off the little show. "Ding, dong, ding, dong," he said, hopefully. Bolenciecwcz was staring at the floor now, trying to think, his great brow furrowed, his huge hands rubbing together, his face red.

"How did you come to college this year, Mr. Bolenciecwcz?" asked 6 the professor. "*Chuffa* chuffa, *chuffa* chuffa."

"M'father sent me," said the football player.   7

"What on?" asked Bassum.   8

"I git an 'lowance," said the tackle, in a low, husky voice, obviously 9 embarrassed.

"No, no," said Bassum. "Name a means of transportation. What did 10 you *ride* here on?"

"Train," said Bolenciecwcz.   11

"Quite right," said the professor. "Now, Mr. Nugent, will you tell 12 us—"

If I went through anguish in botany and economics—for different 13 reasons—gymnasium work was even worse. I don't even like to think about it. They wouldn't let you play games or join the exercises with your glasses on and I couldn't see with mine off. I bumped into professors, horizontal bars, agricultural students, and swinging iron rings. Not being able to see, I could take it but I couldn't dish it out. Also, in order to pass gymnasium (and you had to pass it to graduate) you had to learn to swim if you didn't know how. I didn't like the swimming pool, I didn't like swimming, and I didn't like the swimming instructor, and after all these years I still don't. I never swam but I passed my gym work anyway, by having another student give my gymnasium number (978) and swim across the pool in my place. He was a quiet, amiable blond youth, number 473, and he would have seen through a microscope for me if we could have got away with it, but we couldn't get away with it. Another thing I didn't like about gymnasium work was that they made you strip the day you registered. It is impossible for me to be happy when I am stripped and being asked a lot of questions. Still, I did better than a lanky agricultural student who was cross-examined just before I was. They asked each student what college he was in — that is, whether Arts, Engineering, Commerce, or Agriculture. "What college are you in?" the instructor snapped at the youth in front of me. "Ohio State University," he said promptly.

It wasn't that agricultural student but it was another a whole lot 14 like him who decided to take up journalism, possibly on the ground that when farming went to hell he could fall back on newspaper work. He didn't realize, of course, that that would be very much like falling back full-length on a kit of carpenter's tools. Haskins didn't seem cut out for journalism, being too embarrassed to talk to anybody and unable to use a typewriter, but the editor of the college paper assigned him to the cow barns, the sheep house, the horse pavilion, and the animal husbandry department generally. This was a genuinely big "beat," for it took up five times as much ground and got ten times as great a legislative appropriation as the College of Liberal Arts. The agricultural student knew animals, but nevertheless his stories were dull and colorlessly written. He took all afternoon on each of them, on account of having to hunt for each letter on the typewriter. Once in a while he had to ask somebody to help him hunt. C and L, in particular, were hard letters for him to find. His editor finally got pretty much annoyed at the farmer-journalist because his pieces were so uninteresting. "See here, Haskins," he snapped at him one day, "why is it we never have anything hot from you on the horse pavilion? Here we have two hundred head of horses on this campus — more than any other university in the Western Conference except Purdue — and yet you never get any real lowdown on them. Now shoot over to the horse barns and dig up something lively." Haskins shambled out and came back in about an hour; he said he had something. "Well, start if off snappily," said the editor. "Something people will read." Haskins set to work and in a couple of hours brought a sheet of typewritten paper to the desk; it was a two-hundred-word story about some disease that had broken out among the horses. Its opening sentence was simple but arresting. It read: "Who has noticed the sores on the tops of the horses in the animal husbandry building?"

Ohio State was a land grant university and therefore two years of 15 military drill was compulsory. We drilled with old Springfield rifles and studied the tactics of the Civil War even though the World War was going on at the time. At 11 o'clock each morning thousands of freshmen and sophomores used to deploy over the campus, moodily creeping up on the old chemistry building. It was good training for the kind of warfare that was waged at Shiloh but it had no connection with what was going on in Europe. Some people used to think there was German money behind it, but they didn't say so or they would have been thrown in jail as German spies. It was a period of muddy thought and marked, I believe, the decline of higher education in the Middle West.

As a soldier I was never any good at all. Most of the cadets were 16 glumly indifferent soldiers, but I was no good at all. Once General Littlefield, who was commandant of the cadet corps, popped up in front of me during regimental drill and snapped, "You are the main trouble with this university!" I think he meant that my type was the main trouble with the university but he may have meant me individually. I was mediocre at drill, certainly — that is, until my senior year. By that time I had drilled longer than anybody else in the Western Conference, having failed at military at the end of each preceding year so that I had to do it all over again. I was the only senior still in uniform. The uniform which, when new, had made me look like an interurban railway conductor, now that it had become faded and too tight made me look like Bert Williams in his bellboy act.[2] This had a definitely bad effect on my morale. Even so, I had become by sheer practice little short of wonderful at squad maneuvers.

One day General Littlefield picked our company out of the whole 17 regiment and tried to get it mixed up by putting it through one movement after another as fast as we could execute them: squads right, squads left, squads on right into line, squads right about, squads left front into line, etc. In about three minutes one hundred and nine men were marching in one direction and I was marching away from them at an angle of forty degrees all alone. "Company, halt!" shouted General Littlefield. "That man is the only man who has it right!" I was made a corporal for my achievement.

The next day General Littlefield summoned me to his office. He 18 was swatting flies when I went in. I was silent and he was silent too, for

---

[2] A popular vaudeville and silent-screen comedian of the time, Williams in one routine played a hotel porter in a shrunken suit. — Eds.

a long time. I don't think he remembered me or why he had sent for me, but he didn't want to admit it. He swatted some more flies, keeping his eyes on them narrowly before he let go with the swatter. "Button up your coat!" he snapped. Looking back on it now I can see that he meant me although he was looking at a fly, but I just stood there. Another fly came to rest on a paper in front of the general and began rubbing its hind legs together. The General lifted the swatter cautiously. I moved restlessly and the fly flew away. "You startled him!" barked General Littlefield, looking at me severely. I said I was sorry. "That won't help the situation!" snapped the General, with cold military logic. I didn't see what I could do except offer to chase some more flies toward his desk, but I didn't say anything. He stared out the window at the far-away figures of co-eds crossing the campus toward the library. Finally, he told me I could go. So I went. He either didn't know which cadet I was or else he forgot what he wanted to see me about. It may have been that he wished to apologize for having called me the main trouble with the university; or maybe he had decided to compliment me on my brilliant drilling of the day before and then at the last minute decided not to. I don't know. I don't think about it much any more.

QUESTIONS ON MEANING

1. In what light does Thurber portray himself in "University Days"? Is his self-portrait sympathetic?
2. Are Bolenciecwcz and Haskins stereotypes? Discuss.
3. To what extent does Thurber sacrifice believability for humorous EFFECT? What is his main PURPOSE?

QUESTIONS ON WRITING STRATEGY

1. How do Thurber's INTRODUCTION, his TRANSITIONS, and his CONCLUSION heighten the humor of his essay?
2. Criticize the opening sentence of the story Haskins writes about horse disease (quoted in para. 14).
3. Thurber does not explain in "University Days" how he ever did fulfill his biological science requirement for graduation. Is this an important omission? Explain.
4. **OTHER METHODS.** Each of Thurber's anecdotes is also an EXAMPLE, but the GENERALIZATION illustrated by these examples is not stated. How would you phrase this generalization? What idea do the examples add up to? (Avoid a vague assertion like "College can be frustrating.") Does the absence of a stated generalization weaken or strengthen the essay?

QUESTIONS ON LANGUAGE

1. Be sure to know what the following words mean: nebulous (para. 1); lacteal opacity, variegated (4).
2. Explain how Thurber's word choices heighten the IRONY in the following phrases: "like falling back full-length on a kit of carpenter's tools" (para. 14); "a genuinely big 'beat'" (14); "the decline of higher education in the Middle West" (15).
3. What is a land grant university (para. 15)?
4. Where in his essay does Thurber use colloquial DICTION? What is its effect?

SUGGESTIONS FOR WRITING

1. **JOURNAL WRITING.** The humor of Thurber's essay stems partly from his ability to laugh at himself. What experiences in your past—no doubt serious at the time—can you now look back on and laugh at?
   FROM JOURNAL TO ESSAY. Take a series of related incidents suggested by your journal entry, or one significant enough to stand alone, and write a narrative essay that reveals how your perspective on the incident(s) has changed over time.
2. Write an essay called "High-School Days" in which, with a light touch, you recount two or three related ANECDOTES from your own experience, educational or otherwise.
3. How does Thurber's picture of campus life during the days of World War I compare with campus life today? What has changed? What has stayed the same? Develop your own ideas in a brief essay.
4. **CRITICAL WRITING.** ANALYZE the details and language Thurber uses to exploit a stereotype in the football player Bolenciecwcz (paras. 5–12). (If you need help defining *stereotype*, see p. 450.) In an essay, explain your analysis and EVALUATE the characterization: Do you, for instance, find it funny or offensive? Why?
5. **CONNECTIONS.** James Thurber and E. B. White were friends and colleagues at *The New Yorker*, and both are here represented by reminiscences. But Thurber's "University Days" and White's "Once More to the Lake" (p. 104) are very different in substance and TONE. After reading White's essay, write an essay of your own comparing these two works. What attitudes does each author convey, and how does he do it? (Use quotations and PARAPHRASES from both essays to support your points.)

JAMES THURBER ON WRITING

In an interview with writers George Plimpton and Max Steele, James Thurber revealingly fielded some questions.

"Is the act of writing easy for you?" the interviewers wanted to know.

"For me," Thurber replied, "it's mostly a question of rewriting. It's part of a constant attempt on my part to make the finished version smooth, to make it seem effortless. A story I've been working on — 'The Train on Track Six,' it's called — was rewritten fifteen complete times. There must have been close to 240,000 words in all the manuscripts put together, and I must have spent two thousand hours working at it. Yet the finished version can't be more than twenty thousand words."

"Then it's rare that your work comes out right the first time?"

"Well," said Thurber, "my wife took a look at the first version of something I was doing not long ago and said, 'Goddamn it, Thurber, that's high-school stuff.' I have to tell her to wait until the seventh draft, it'll work out all right. I don't know why that should be so, that the first or second draft of everything I write reads as if it was turned out by a charwoman. I've only written one piece quickly. I wrote a thing called 'File and Forget' in one afternoon — but only because it was a series of letters just as one would ordinarily dictate. And I'll have to admit that the last letter of the series, after doing all the others that one afternoon, took me a week. It was the end of the piece and I had to fuss over it."

"Does the fact that you're dealing with humor slow down the production?"

"It's possible. With humor you have to look out for traps. You're likely to be very gleeful with what you've first put down, and you think it's fine, very funny. One reason you go over and over it is to make the piece sound less as if you were having a lot of fun with it yourself."

In his own book *Thurber Country*, Thurber set forth, with tongue in cheek, some general principles for comic writing. "I have established a few standing rules of my own about humor," he wrote, "after receiving dozens of humorous essays and stories from strangers over a period of twenty years. (1) The reader should be able to find out what the story is about. (2) Some inkling of the general idea should be apparent in the first five hundred words. (3) If the writer has decided to change the name of his protagonist from Ketcham to McTavish, Ketcham should not keep bobbing up in the last five pages. A good way to eliminate this confusion is to read the piece over before sending it out, and remove Ketcham completely. He is a nuisance. (4) The word *I'll* should not be divided so that the *I* is on one line and *'ll* on the next. The

reader's attention, after the breaking up of *I'll*, can never be successfully recaptured. (5) It also never recovers from such names as Ann S.
Thetic, Maud Lynn, Sally Forth, Bertha Twins, and the like. (6) Avoid
comic stories about plumbers who are mistaken for surgeons, sheriffs
who are terrified by gunfire, psychiatrists who are driven crazy by
women patients, doctors who faint at the sight of blood, adolescent
girls who know more about sex than their fathers do, and midgets who
turn out to be the parents of a two-hundred-pound wrestler."

FOR DISCUSSION

1. By what means does Thurber make his writing look "effortless"?
2. Is there any serious advice to be extracted from Thurber's "standing rules
   about humor"? If so, what is it?

BARBARA HUTTMANN

BARBARA HUTTMANN is a registered nurse, a health-care administrator, and a writer on health-care issues. She was born in 1935 and received a B.S. in nursing and an M.S. in nursing administration. Since 1980 she has directed a consulting firm for hospitals, nursing organizations, and health-care consumers. Huttmann has written two books, *The Patient's Advocate* (1981) and *Code Blue: A Nurse's True-Life Story* (1982). She lives in California.

A Crime of Compassion

As a nurse, Huttmann has had to care for many people who are dying. This essay tells of one such patient, Mac, whose rapid decline Huttmann witnessed and whose death she finally did nothing to prevent. The essay was first published in *Newsweek* in 1983.

"Murderer," a man shouted. "God help patients who get *you* for a 1 nurse."

"What gives you the right to play God?" another one asked. 2

It was the Phil Donahue show where the guest is a fatted calf and 3 the audience a 200-strong flock of vultures hungering to pick at the bones. I had told them about Mac, one of my favorite cancer patients. "We resuscitated him 52 times in just one month. I refused to resuscitate him again. I simply sat there and held his hand while he died."

There wasn't time to explain that Mac was a young, witty, macho cop 4 who walked into the hospital with 32 pounds of attack equipment, looking as if he could single-handedly protect the whole city, if not the entire state. "Can't get rid of this cough," he said. Otherwise, he felt great.

Before the day was over, tests confirmed that he had lung cancer. 5 And before the year was over, I loved him, his wife, Maura, and their three kids as if they were my own. All the nurses loved him. And we all battled his disease for six months without ever giving death a thought. Six months isn't such a long time in the whole scheme of things, but it was long enough to see him lose his youth, his wit, his macho, his hair, his bowel and bladder control, his sense of taste and smell, and his ability to do the slightest thing for himself. It was also long enough to watch Maura's transformation from a young woman into a haggard, beaten old lady.

When Mac had wasted away to a 60-pound skeleton kept alive 6 by liquid food we poured down a tube, i.v. solutions we dripped into

83

his veins, and oxygen we piped to a mask on his face, he begged us: "Mercy...for God's sake, please just let me go."

The first time he stopped breathing, the nurse pushed the button ⁷ that calls a "code blue" throughout the hospital and sends a team rushing to resuscitate the patient. Each time he stopped breathing, sometimes two or three times in one day, the code team came again. The doctors and technicians worked their miracles and walked away. The nurses stayed to wipe the saliva that drooled from his mouth, irrigate the big craters of bedsores that covered his hips, suction the lung fluids that threatened to drown him, clean the feces that burned his skin like lye, pour the liquid food down the tube attached to his stomach, put pillows between his knees to ease the bone-on-bone pain, turn him every hour to keep the bedsores from getting worse, and change his gown and linen every two hours to keep him from being soaked in perspiration.

At night I went home and tried to scrub away the smell of decay-   8 ing flesh that seemed woven into the fabric of my uniform. It was in my hair, the upholstery of my car—there was no washing it away. And every night I prayed that Mac would die, that his agonized eyes would never again plead with me to let him die.

Every morning I asked his doctor for a "no-code" order. Without   9 that order, we had to resuscitate every patient who stopped breathing. His doctor was one of several who believe we must extend life as long as we have the means and knowledge to do it. To not do it is to be liable for negligence, at least in the eyes of many people, including some nurses. I thought about what it would be like to stand before a judge, accused of murder, if Mac stopped breathing and I didn't call a code.

And after the fifty-second code, when Mac was still lucid enough   10 to beg for death again, and Maura was crumbled in my arms again, and when no amount of pain medication stilled his moaning and agony, I wondered about a spiritual judge. Was all this misery and suffering supposed to be building character or infusing us all with the sense of humility that comes from impotence?

Had we, the whole medical community, become so arrogant that   11 we believed in the illusion of salvation through science? Had we become so self-righteous that we thought meddling in God's work was our duty, our moral imperative and our legal obligation? Did we really believe that we had the right to force "life" on a suffering man who had begged for the right to die?

Such questions haunted me more than ever early one morning   12 when Maura went home to change her clothes and I was bathing Mac. He had been still for so long, I thought he at last had the blessed relief of coma. Then he opened his eyes and moaned, "Pain...no more...Barbara...do something...God, let me go."

The desperation in his eyes and voice riddled me with guilt. "I'll 13
stop," I told him as I injected the pain medication.

I sat on the bed and held Mac's hands in mine. He pressed his bony 14
fingers against my hand and muttered, "Thanks." Then there was one
soft sigh and I felt his hands go cold in mine. "Mac?" I whispered, as I
waited for his chest to rise and fall again.

A clutch of panic banded my chest, drew my finger to the code but- 15
ton, urged me to do something, anything...but sit there alone with
death. I kept one finger on the button, without pressing it, as a waxen
pallor slowly transformed his face from person to empty shell. Nothing
I've ever done in my 47 years has taken so much effort as it took *not* to
press that code button.

Eventually, when I was as sure as I could be that the code team 16
would fail to bring him back, I entered the legal twilight zone and
pushed the button. The team tried. And while they were trying, Maura
walked into the room and shrieked, "No... don't let them do this to
him...for God's sake...please, no more."

Cradling her in my arms was like cradling myself, Mac, and all 17
those patients and nurses who had been in this place before, who do
the best they can in a death-denying society.

So a TV audience accused me of murder. Perhaps I am guilty. If a 18
doctor had written a no-code order, which is the only *legal* alternative,
would he have felt any less guilty? Until there is legislation making it a
criminal act to code a patient who has requested the right to die, we
will all of us risk the same fate as Mac. For whatever reason, we developed the means to prolong life, and now we are forced to use it. We do
not have the right to die.

QUESTIONS ON MEANING

1. Is Huttmann's PURPOSE in this essay personal (wanting to justify her act) or
   social (wanting to establish the right to die) or both? Explain.
2. What is the contradiction in the title of the essay?
3. What personal risk does Huttmann assume when she decides not to press
   the button? What does she mean by "legal twilight zone" (para. 16)?
4. Is Huttmann confident that she made the right decision?
5. Where does Huttmann state her THESIS?

QUESTIONS ON WRITING STRATEGY

1. Why does Huttmann begin the essay the way she does? What do we ASSUME
   about the nurse referred to in the first sentence, and at what point do we
   begin to question that assumption?

2. What is the TONE of this piece? How does Huttmann manage to avoid the SENTIMENTALITY one might expect of an essay on this subject? (Cite specific EXAMPLES from the text.)
3. How does the detail about resuscitating Mac fifty-two times in one month (para. 3) contribute to the effectiveness of Huttmann's ARGUMENT?
4. **OTHER METHODS.** This essay illustrates how narrative can help promote an argument. Summarize Huttmann's argument. What does she gain by supporting it with a story?

QUESTIONS ON LANGUAGE

1. Consult a dictionary for any of the following words whose meanings you are unsure of: resuscitate (para. 3); haggard (5); irrigate, suction, feces, lye, bedsores (7); lucid, infusing, impotence (10); imperative (11); riddled (13); banded, pallor (15).
2. Some of the words in the vocabulary list above are medical terminology, but perhaps fewer than one would expect, given the subject. What about her AUDIENCE (originally readers of *Newsweek* magazine) would influence Huttmann's use of terms?
3. Find words in the essay that illustrate Huttmann's particular fondness for Mac. What difference does the closeness of their relationship make to her argument?
4. Explain the METAPHOR in paragraph 3.

SUGGESTIONS FOR WRITING

1. **JOURNAL WRITING.** What do you think of Huttmann's essay? Does a terminally ill patient have a right to choose when to die? Should a doctor or anyone else be legally empowered to overrule a patient's wish for death? **FROM JOURNAL TO ESSAY.** After exploring your opinions and beliefs in your journal, write an essay arguing for or against the right of a terminally ill patient to choose when to die. You may, like Huttmann, support your argument with a narrative of personal experience. Or you may argue on other grounds—religious, moral, humanitarian, medical, and so on. In your argument, be sure to acknowledge the views of those who might oppose you, as you understand those views. This acknowledgment will help show your fairness and reach out to more readers.
2. Think back to a moment in your life when you had to make a difficult choice, one with important consequences. (The stakes need not have been as high as in Huttmann's essay.) What were the circumstances? What was the result of the decision you made? In a narrative essay, start by stating the choice you had to make and its implications; then go back and relate the circumstances; and, finally, conclude by explaining the results of your choice and its effectiveness.
3. Huttmann presents two opposed ideas of God's role in human life and death. For the member of Phil Donahue's audience, only God can decide to stop someone's life; anyone who tries to make that decision in "playing God" (para. 2). For Huttmann, in contrast, sustaining life artificially is "meddling in God's work" (para. 11). Which view do you agree with, and why? (If you'd rather not debate the role of God, try "nature" instead.)

4. **CRITICAL WRITING.** When they take the Hippocratic oath, physicians promise to "do no harm." It could be argued that neither choice available to Huttmann avoids harm to her patient. Given the circumstances of the patient she describes, did she choose the less harmful alternative? Why, or why not? Can your argument be generalized: Is it applicable in every case?

5. **CONNECTIONS.** Huttmann writes, "For whatever reason, we developed the means to prolong life, and now we are forced to use it" (para. 18). Although the purpose and tone of his essay are very different from Huttmann's, Edward Tenner makes a similar claim, in his "Voice Mail and Fire Ants" (p. 323), about technology's unintended consequences. In your opinion, does better technology usually result in a better quality of life, or does it usually end up creating more problems than it solves? Support your claim with EVIDENCE from your own experience, observations, and reading.

EDGAR ALLAN POE

EDGAR ALLAN POE (1809–49) was the first American writer to gain a reputation outside the United States. His short stories and poems, famously mysterious or frightening, were popular both at home and in Europe, and his literary criticism helped shape the course of French poetry. Poe was born in Boston, grew up in England and Virginia, and died in Baltimore at only forty years of age. His short life was often clouded by family troubles, disciplinary problems (he was expelled from West Point), and heavy drinking; yet he held jobs on magazines, wrote volumes of criticism, published collections of poetry, and crafted immortal stories. Poe is perhaps best known for such stories as "The Tell-Tale Heart" (printed here), "The Pit and the Pendulum" (1843), and "The Cask of Amontillado" (1846), as well as for his poems "Annabel Lee" (1849, addressed to his recently deceased wife) and "The Raven" (1845). In honor of the famous poet who died there, the city of Baltimore in 1996 named its football team the Baltimore Ravens, thus making Poe, as the humorist Russell Baker observed, "the first literary man to break into professional sports."

The Tell-Tale Heart

This masterpiece of paranoid terror was first published in 1843. If you've never read the story before, bear with the occasionally old-fashioned style until you swing into the narrator's groove (as you certainly will). If you have read the story, read it again just for the pleasure, noticing how Poe's narrative technique pulls you in and along.

True!—nervous—very, very dreadfully nervous I had been and 1 am; but why *will* you say that I am mad? The disease had sharpened my senses—not destroyed—not dulled them. Above all was the sense of hearing acute. I heard all things in the heaven and in the earth. I heard many things in hell. How, then, am I mad? Hearken! and observe how healthily—how calmly I can tell you the whole story.

It is impossible to say how first the idea entered my brain; but once 2 conceived, it haunted me day and night. Object there was none. Passion there was none. I loved the old man. He had never wronged me. He had never given me insult. For his gold I had no desire. I think it was his eye! yes, it was this! One of his eyes resembled that of a vulture—a pale blue eye, with a film over it. Whenever it fell upon me, my blood ran cold; and so by degrees—very gradually—I made up my mind to take the life of the old man, and thus rid myself of the eye for ever.

Now this is the point. You fancy me mad. Madmen know nothing. 3 But you should have seen *me*. You should have seen how wisely I proceeded—with what caution—with what foresight—with what dissimulation I went to work! I was never kinder to the old man than during the whole week before I killed him. And every night, about midnight, I turned the latch of his door and opened it—oh, so gently! And then, when I had made an opening sufficient for my head, I put in a dark lantern, all closed, closed, so that no light shone out, and then I thrust in my head. Oh, you would have laughed to see how cunningly I thrust it in! I moved it slowly—very, very slowly, so that I might not disturb the old man's sleep. It took me an hour to place my whole head within the opening so far that I could see him as he lay upon his bed. Ha—would a madman have been so wise as this? And then, when my head was well in the room, I undid the lantern cautiously—oh, so cautiously—cautiously (for the hinges creaked)—I undid it just so much that a single thin ray fell upon the vulture eye. And this I did for seven long nights—every night just after midnight—but I found the eye always closed; and so it was impossible to do the work; for it was not the old man who vexed me, but his Evil Eye. And every morning, when the day broke, I went boldly into the chamber, and spoke courageously to him, calling him by name in a hearty tone, and inquiring how he had passed the night. So you see he would have been a very profound old man, indeed, to suspect that every night, just at twelve, I looked in upon him while he slept.

Upon the eighth night I was more than usually cautious in opening 4 the door. A watch's minute hand moves more quickly than did mine. Never before that night had I *felt* the extent of my own powers—of my sagacity. I could scarcely contain my feelings of triumph. To think that there I was, opening the door, little by little, and he not even to dream of my secret deeds or thoughts. I fairly chuckled at the idea; and perhaps he heard me; for he moved on the bed suddenly, as if startled. Now you may think that I drew back—but no. His room was as black as pitch with the thick darkness (for the shutters were close fastened, through fear of robbers), and so I knew that he could not see the opening of the door, and I kept pushing it on steadily, steadily.

I had my head in, and was about to open the lantern, when my 5 thumb slipped upon the tin fastening, and the old man sprang up in the bed, crying out—"Who's there?"

I kept quite still and said nothing. For a whole hour I did not move 6 a muscle, and in the meantime I did not hear him lie down. He was still sitting up in the bed listening;—just as I have done, night after night, hearkening to the death watches in the wall.

Presently I heard a slight groan, and I knew it was the groan of mor-   7
tal terror. It was not a groan of pain or of grief—oh, no!—it was the
low stifled sound that arises from the bottom of the soul when over-
charged with awe. I knew the sound well. Many a night, just at midnight, when all the world slept, it has welled up from my own bosom,
deepening with its dreadful echo, the terrors that distracted me. I say I
knew it well. I knew what the old man felt, and pitied him, although I
chuckled at heart. I knew that he had been lying awake ever since the
first slight noise, when he had turned in the bed. His fears had been
ever since growing upon him. He had been trying to fancy them cause-
less, but could not. He had been saying to himself—"It is nothing but
the wind in the chimney—it is only a mouse crossing the floor," or "it
is merely a cricket which has made a single chirp." Yes, he has been trying to comfort himself with these suppositions; but he had found all in
vain. *All in vain*; because Death, in approaching him, had stalked with
his black shadow before him, and enveloped the victim. And it was
the mournful influence of the unperceived shadow that caused him to
feel—although he neither saw nor heard—to *feel* the presence of my
head within the room.

When I had waited a long time, very patiently, without hearing   8
him lie down, I resolved to open a little—a very, very little crevice in
the lantern. So I opened it—you cannot imagine how stealthily,
stealthily—until, at length, a single dim ray, like the thread of the spider, shot from out the crevice and full upon the vulture eye.

It was open—wide, wide open—and I grew furious as I gazed upon   9
it. I saw it with perfect distinctness—all a dull blue, with a hideous veil
over it that chilled the very marrow in my bones, but I could see nothing else of the old man's face or person: for I had directed the ray as if
by instinct, precisely upon the damned spot.

And now have I not told you that what you mistake for madness is   10
but over-acuteness of the senses?—now, I say, there came to my ears a
low, dull, quick sound, such as a watch makes when enveloped in cotton. I knew *that* sound well too. It was the beating of the old man's
heart. It increased my fury, as the beating of a drum stimulates the soldier into courage.

But even yet I refrained and kept still. I scarcely breathed. I held   11
the lantern motionless. I tried how steadily I could maintain the ray
upon the eye. Meantime the hellish tattoo of the heart increased. It
grew quicker and quicker, and louder and louder every instant. The old
man's terror *must* have been extreme! It grew louder, I say, louder every
moment!—do you mark me well? I have told you that I am nervous: so
I am. And now at the dead hour of the night, amid the dreadful silence
of that old house, so strange a noise as this excited me to uncontrol-
lable terror. Yet, for some minutes longer I refrained and stood still. But

the beating grew louder, louder! I thought the heart must burst. And now a new anxiety seized me — the sound would be heard by a neighbor! The old man's hour had come! With a loud yell, I threw open the lantern and leaped into the room. He shrieked once — once only. In an instant I dragged him to the floor, and pulled the heavy bed over him. I then smiled gaily, to find the deed so far done. But, for many minutes, the heart beat on with a muffled sound. This, however, did not vex me; it would not be heard through the wall. At length it ceased. The old man was dead. I removed the bed and examined the corpse. Yes, he was stone, stone dead. I placed my hand upon the heart and held it there many minutes. There was no pulsation. He was stone dead. His eye would trouble me no more.

If still you think me mad, you will think so no longer when I describe the wise precautions I took for the concealment of the body. The night waned, and I worked hastily, but in silence. First of all I dismembered the corpse. I cut off the head and the arms and the legs.   12

I then took up three planks from the flooring of the chamber, and deposited all between the scantlings. I then replaced the boards so cleverly, so cunningly, that no human eye — not even *his* — could have detected anything wrong. There was nothing to wash out — no stain of any kind — no blood-spot whatever. I had been too wary for that. A tub had caught all — ha! ha!   13

When I had made an end of these labors, it was four o'clock — still dark as midnight. As the bell sounded the hour, there came a knocking at the street door. I went down to open it with a light heart — for what had I *now* to fear? There entered three men, who introduced themselves, with perfect suavity, as officers of the police. A shriek had been heard by a neighbor during the night; suspicion of foul play had been aroused; information had been lodged at the police office, and they (the officers) had been deputed to search the premises.   14

I smiled — for *what* had I to fear? I bade the gentlemen welcome. The shriek, I said, was my own in a dream. The old man, I mentioned, was absent in the country. I took my visitors all over the house. I bade them search — search *well*. I led them, at length, to *his* chamber. I showed them his treasures, secure, undisturbed. In the enthusiasm of my confidence, I brought chairs into the room, and desired them *here* to rest from their fatigues, while I myself, in the wild audacity of my perfect triumph, placed my own seat upon the very spot beneath which reposed the corpse of the victim.   15

The officers were satisfied. My *manner* had convinced them. I was singularly at ease. They sat, and while I answered cheerily, they chatted familiar things. But, ere long, I felt myself getting pale and wished them gone. My head ached, and I fancied a ringing in my ears: but still they sat and still chatted. The ringing became more distinct: — it continued   16

and became more distinct: I talked more freely to get rid of the feeling:
but it continued and gained definitiveness—until, at length, I found
that the noise was *not* within my ears.

No doubt I now grew *very* pale;—but I talked more fluently, and   17
with a heightened voice. Yet the sound increased—and what could I
do? It was *a low, dull, quick sound—much such a sound as a watch makes
when enveloped in cotton.* I gasped for breath—and yet the officers
heard it not. I talked more quickly—more vehemently; but the noise
steadily increased. I arose and argued about trifles, in a high key and
with violent gesticulations, but the noise steadily increased. Why
would they not be gone? I paced the floor to and fro with heavy strides,
as if excited to fury by the observation of the men—but the noise
steadily increased. Oh God! what *could* I do? I foamed—I raved—I
swore! I swung the chair upon which I had been sitting, and grated it
upon the boards, but the noise arose over all and continually increased.
It grew louder—louder—*louder!* And still the men chatted pleasantly,
and smiled. Was it possible they heard not? Almighty God—no, no!
They heard!—they suspected!—they *knew!*—they were making a
mockery of my horror—this I thought, and this I think. But any thing
was better than this agony! Any thing was more tolerable than this
derision! I could bear those hypocritical smiles no longer! I felt that
I must scream or die—and now—again!—hark! louder! louder!
louder! *louder!* —

"Villains!" I shrieked, "dissemble no more! I admit the deed!—tear   18
up the planks—here, here!—it is the beating of his hideous heart!"

QUESTIONS ON MEANING

1. On what basis does the narrator claim to be sane? Is he convincing?
2. In paragraph 7 the narrator empathizes with his victim's fears. How does he
   know so much of what the old man feels?
3. Why does the narrator choose to sit directly above the buried heart during
   his interview with the police?
4. Why does the narrator unnecessarily give himself away in the end?
5. What, in your opinion, was Poe's PURPOSE in writing this story?

QUESTIONS ON WRITING STRATEGY

1. What is the purpose of the opening paragraph? Why does Poe delay the
   opening of the story?
2. What is the EFFECT of the narrator's addressing the reader directly as *you* (for
   example, para. 3)?

3. What is the IRONY in the fact that the old man's shutters were always closed (para. 4)?
4. Note the conciseness of the narration in the second half of paragraph 14. From whose POINT OF VIEW is the story being told here? How do you know?
5. **OTHER METHODS.** The narrator complains that he suffers from "over-acuteness of the senses" (para. 10), an affliction that gives Poe an opportunity for rich DESCRIPTION. ANALYZE Poe's treatment of the sense of sound in paragraph 11. How does Poe play on the contrast between sound and silence, stillness and movement, in this paragraph?

QUESTIONS ON LANGUAGE

1. What effect is created by Poe's frequent use of repetition—for instance, "Slowly—very, very slowly" (para. 3); "stealthily, stealthily" (8); "The old man was dead.... Yes, he was stone, stone dead.... He was stone dead" (11)? Is this bad prose? Why, or why not?
2. Poe is a master of forceful FIGURES OF SPEECH. In paragraph 4 he writes, "A watch's minute hand moves more quickly than did mine" (para. 4). Substitute the word *hour* for *minute*. Which is more effective, and why? What other powerful figures of speech can you find in the story?
3. What is the effect of Poe's use of italics throughout the story, especially in paragraph 17? Do any of the choices of italicized words seem strange or arbitrary?
4. This story contains a number of words that may be unfamiliar, including a couple of familiar words used in unfamiliar ways (these are asterisked). Look up any words you're unsure of: hearken (para. 1); foresight, dissimulation, cunningly, vexed (3); sagacity (4); stifled, suppositions, mournful (7); crevice, stealthily (8); refrained, tattoo,* mark* (11); dismembered (12); scantlings (13); suavity, deputed (14); bade, fatigues, audacity (15); ere (16); vehemently, gesticulations, derision, hypocritical, hark (17); dissemble (18).

SUGGESTIONS FOR WRITING

1. **JOURNAL WRITING.** Write about an actual crime you know of, setting down the facts as completely and OBJECTIVELY as you can. (If you need ideas for crimes, try looking in a tabloid newspaper or watching a true-crime program on television.)
   FROM JOURNAL TO ESSAY. Retell the events of the crime you have written about from the point of view of the criminal. Choose any psychology you like for the criminal: articulate but mad (like the narrator of Poe's story), guilt-ridden, unjustly accused—use your imagination. Like Poe, you will need to add IMAGES and details to spice up the objective account in your journal.
2. Look up the clinical DEFINITIONS of *obsessive-compulsive disorder* and *paranoia* in an encyclopedia or a psychology textbook. How well does Poe's narrator fit either of these definitions? Make a case for a clinical basis to the narrator's madness, drawing on both the narrator's own descriptions of his mental states and faculties and the textbook definitions of the two mental disorders.

3. **CRITICAL WRITING.** Notice how much effort Poe devotes to recounting an event as simple as the opening of a door or lantern. How does Poe manage to keep readers on the edge of their seats while working on such a microscopic level? How does he indicate the passing of time? How does he create SUSPENSE? In a brief essay, ANALYZE the rhythm of Poe's narrative, paying close attention to TRANSITIONS.
4. **CONNECTIONS.** In "Safe-Sex Lies" (p. 380) Meghan Daum writes about a very different kind of paranoia from that of Poe's narrator—what she sees as the unreasonable fear of AIDS among low-risk groups. Although it will be easier to CONTRAST than to COMPARE the two essays, try to find as many common points as you can between the narrator's paranoia and the one Daum describes.

EDGAR ALLAN POE ON WRITING

Writing in *Graham's Magazine* in 1842, Edgar Allan Poe commented on the stories of his contemporary Nathaniel Hawthorne and in the process revealed much about his own views of narration. What he says could apply equally to fiction and to nonfiction. (It could also apply equally to female and to male writers. Poe uses the generalized *he*, once universally understood to mean "he or she.")

Poe emphasizes that "in almost all classes of composition, the unity of effect or impression is a point of the greatest importance," something achievable in "the short prose narrative, requiring from a half-hour to one or two hours in its perusal.... In the brief tale,...the author is enabled to carry out the fullness of his intention, be it what it may. During the hour of perusal the soul of the reader is at the writer's control....

"A skillful literary artist has constructed a tale. If wise, he has not fashioned his thoughts to accommodate his incidents; but having conceived, with deliberate care, a certain unique or single *effect* to be wrought out,...he then combines such events as may best aid him in establishing this preconceived effect. If his very initial sentence tend not to the outbringing of this effect, then he has failed in his first step. In the whole composition there should be no word written, of which the tendency, direct or indirect, is not to the one pre-established design. And by such means, with such care and skill, a picture is at length painted which leaves in the mind of him who contemplates it with a kindred art, a sense of the fullest satisfaction."

FOR DISCUSSION

1. Why, according to Poe, is the "unity of effect" so important to a narrative?
2. What role do you see for revision in Poe's narrative process? Do you think he means that the first sentence must be perfect the first time it's written? Why, or why not?

ADDITIONAL WRITING TOPICS

Narration

1. Write a narrative with one of the following as your subject. It may be (as your instructor may advise) either a first-PERSON memoir or a story written in the third person, observing the experience of someone else. Decide before you begin what your PURPOSE is and whether you are writing (1) an anecdote; (2) an essay consisting mainly of a single narrative; or (3) an essay that includes more than one story.

   A memorable experience from your early life
   A lesson you learned the hard way
   A trip into unfamiliar territory
   An embarrassing moment that taught you something
   A monumental misunderstanding
   An accident
   An unexpected encounter
   A story about a famous person, or someone close to you
   A conflict or contest
   A destructive storm
   An assassination attempt
   A historical event of significance

2. Tell a true story of your early or recent school days, either humorous or serious, showing what a struggle school or college has been for you. (For comparable stories, see Ellison's "On Being the Target of Discrimination" and Thurber's "University Days.")

Note: Writing topics combining narration and description appear on page 137.

2

DESCRIPTION
Writing with Your Senses

THE METHOD

Like narration, DESCRIPTION is a familiar method of expression, already a working part of you. In any talk-fest with friends, you probably do your share of describing. You depict in words someone you've met by describing her clothes, the look on her face, the way she walks. You describe somewhere you've been, something you admire, something you just can't abide. In a diary or in a letter to a friend, you describe your college (cast concrete buildings, crowded walks, pigeons rattling their wings); or perhaps you describe your brand-new secondhand car, from the snakelike glitter of its hubcaps to the odd antiques in its trunk, bequeathed by its previous owner. You hardly can live a day without describing (or hearing described) some person, place, or thing. Small wonder that, in written discourse, description is almost as indispensable as paper.

Description reports the testimony of your senses. It invites your readers to imagine that they, too, not only see but perhaps also hear, taste, smell, and touch the subject you describe. Usually, you write a description for either of two PURPOSES: (1) to convey information without bias or emotion; or (2) to convey it with feeling.

In writing with the first purpose in mind, you write an OBJECTIVE (or *impartial, public,* or *functional*) description. You describe your subject so clearly and exactly that your reader will understand it or recognize it, and you leave your emotions out. Technical or scientific descriptive writing is usually objective: a manual detailing the parts of an internal combustion engine, a biology report on a previously unknown species of frog. You write this kind of description in sending a friend directions for finding your house: "Look for the green shutters on the windows and a new garbage can at the front door." Although in a personal letter describing your house you might very well become emotionally involved with it (and call it, perhaps, a "fleabag"), in writing an objective description your purpose is not to convey your feelings. You are trying to make the house easily recognized.

The other type of descriptive writing is SUBJECTIVE (or *emotional, personal,* or *impressionistic*) description. This is the kind included in a magazine advertisement for a new car. It's what you write in your letter to a friend setting forth what your college is like—whether you are pleased or displeased with it. In this kind of description, you may use biases and personal feelings—in fact, they are essential. Let us consider a splendid example: a subjective description of a storm at sea. Charles Dickens, in his memoir *American Notes,* conveys his passenger's-eye view of an Atlantic steamship on a morning when the ocean is wild:

> Imagine the ship herself, with every pulse and artery of her huge body swollen and bursting ... sworn to go on or die. Imagine the wind howling, the sea roaring, the rain beating; all in furious array against her. Picture the sky both dark and wild, and the clouds in fearful sympathy with the waves, making another ocean in the air. Add to all this the clattering on deck and down below; the tread of hurried feet; the loud hoarse shouts of seamen; the gurgling in and out of water through the scuppers; with every now and then the striking of a heavy sea upon the planks above, with the deep, dead, heavy sound of thunder heard within a vault; and there is the head wind of that January morning.
>
> I say nothing of what may be called the domestic noises of the ship; such as the breaking of glass and crockery, the tumbling down of stewards, the gambols, overhead, of loose casks and truant dozens of bottled porter, and the very remarkable and far from exhilarating sounds raised in their various staterooms by the seventy passengers who were too ill to get up to breakfast.

Notice how many *sounds* are included in this primarily ear-minded description. We can infer how Dickens feels about the storm. It is a terrifying event that reduces the interior of the vessel to chaos; and yet the writer (in hearing the loose barrels and beer bottles merrily gambol, in finding humor in the seasick passengers' plight) apparently delights in it. Writing subjectively, he intrudes his feelings. Think of what a starkly different description of the very same storm the captain might set down—objectively—in the ship's log: "At 0600 hours, watch reported a wind from due north of 70 knots. Whitecaps were noticed, in height two ells above the bow. Below deck, much gear was reported adrift, and ten casks of ale were broken and their staves strewn about. Mr. Liam Jones, chief steward, suffered a compound fracture of the left leg...." But Dickens, not content simply to record information, strives to ensure that the mind's eye is dazzled and the mind's ear regaled.

Description is usually found in the company of other methods of writing. Often, for instance, it will enliven NARRATION and make the people in the story and the setting unmistakably clear. Writing an ARGUMENT in his essay "Why Don't We Complain?" (p. 494), William F. Buckley, Jr., begins with a description of eighty suffering commuters perspiring in an overheated train; the description makes the argument more powerful. Description will help a writer in examining the EFFECTS of a flood, or in COMPARING AND CONTRASTING two towns. Keep the method of description in mind when you come to try expository and argumentative writing.

THE PROCESS

Purpose, Audience, and Dominant Impression

Understand, first of all, your purpose in writing a description. Are you going to write a subjective description, expressing your personal feelings? Or, instead, do you want to write an objective description, trying only to see and report, leaving out your emotions and biases?

Give a little thought to your AUDIENCE. What do your readers need to be told, if they are to share the feelings you would have them share, if they are clearly to behold what you want them to? If, let's say, you are describing a downtown street on a Saturday night for an audience of fellow students who live in the same city and know it well, then you need not dwell on the street's familiar geography. What must you tell? Only those details that make the place different on a Saturday night. But if you are remembering your home city, and writing for readers who don't know it, you'll need to establish a few central landmarks to sketch (in their minds) an unfamiliar street on a Saturday night.

Before you begin to write a description, go look at your subject. If that is not possible, your next best course is to spend a few minutes imagining the subject until, in your mind's eye, you can see every flyspeck on it.

Then, having fixed your subject in mind, ask yourself which of its features you'll need to report to your particular audience, for your particular purpose. Ask, "What am I out to accomplish? What main impression of my subject am I trying to give?" Let your description, as a

whole, convey this one DOMINANT IMPRESSION. If you plan to write a subjective description of an old house, laying weight on its spooky atmosphere for readers you wish to make shiver, then you might mention its
squeaking bats and its shadowy halls, leaving out any reference to its
busy swimming pool and the stomping dance music that billows from
its interior. If, however, you are describing the house in a classified ad,
for an audience of possible buyers, you might focus instead on its eat-
in kitchen, working fireplace, and proximity to public transportation.
Details have to be carefully selected. Feel no grim duty to include
every perceptible detail. To do so would only invite chaos—or perhaps, for the reader, mere tedium. Pick out the features that matter
most.

Your dominant impression is like the THESIS of your description—
the main idea about your subject that you want readers to take away
with them. When you use description to explain or to argue, it's usually
a good strategy to state that dominant impression outright, tying it to
your essay's thesis or a part of it. In a biology report on a previously unknown species of frog, for instance, you might preface your description
with a statement like this one:

> A number of unique features distinguish this frog from those already
> known and classified.

Or in an argument in favor of cleaning a local toxic waste site, you
might begin with a description of the site and then state your point
about it:

> This landscape is as poisonous as it looks, for underneath its barren
> crust are enough toxic chemicals to sicken a small village.

When you use subjective description more for its own sake—to
show the reader a place or a person, to evoke feelings—you needn't always state your dominant impression as a THESIS SENTENCE, as long as the
impression is there dictating the details. Sometimes, though, stating
your dominant impression can bring your writing to a climax. That's
what E. B. White does halfway through his essay "Once More to the
Lake" in this chapter (para. 8):

> Summertime, oh, summertime, pattern of life indelible, the fade-
> proof lake, the woods unshatterable, the pasture with the sweetfern
> and the juniper forever and ever, summer without end; this was the
> background....

Organization

You can organize a description in several ways. In depicting the
storm at sea—a subjective description—Charles Dickens sorts out

the pandemonium for us. He groups the various sounds into two classes: those of sea and sailors, and the "domestic noises" of the ship's passengers—their smashing dishes, their rolling bottles, the crashing of stewards who wait on them. Others writers of description rely on their POINT OF VIEW to help them arrange details—the physical angle from which they're perceiving and describing. In the previous chapter, on narration, we spoke of point of view: how essential it is for a story to have a narrator—one who, from a certain position, reports what takes place. A description, too, needs a consistent point of view: that of an observer who stays put and observes steadily. From this point of view, you can make a carefully planned inspection tour of your subject, moving spatially (from left to right, from near to far, from top to bottom, from center to periphery), or perhaps moving from prominent objects to tiny ones, from dull to bright, from commonplace to extraordinary—or vice versa. The plan you choose is the one that best fulfills your purpose. If you were to describe, for instance, a chapel in the middle of a desert, you might begin with the details of the lonely terrain. Then, as if approaching the chapel with the aid of a zoom lens, you might detail its exterior and then go on inside. That might be a workable method to write a description *if* you wanted to create the dominant impression of the chapel as an island of beauty and feeling in the midst of desolation. Say, however, that you had a different impression in mind: to emphasize the spirituality of the chapel's interior. You might then begin your description inside the structure, perhaps with its most prominent feature, the stained glass windows. You might mention the surrounding desert later in your description, but only incidentally. An effective description makes a definite impression. The writer arranges details so that the reader is firmly left with the feeling the writer intends to convey.

Whatever method you follow in arranging details, stick with it all the way through. Don't start out describing a group of cats by going from old cats to kittens, then switch in the middle of your description and line up the cats according to color. If your arrangement would cause any difficulty for the reader, you need to rearrange your details. If a writer, in describing a pet shop, should skip about wildly from clerks to cats to customers to cat food to customers to cat food to clerks, the reader may quickly be lost. Instead, the writer might group clerks together with customers, and cats together with cat food (or in some other clear order). But suppose (the writer might protest) it's a wildly confused pet shop I'm trying to describe? No matter—the writer nevertheless has to write in an orderly manner, if the reader is to understand. Dickens describes a scene of shipboard chaos, yet his prose is orderly.

Details

Luckily, to write a memorable description, you don't need a storm at sea or any other awe-inspiring subject. As E. B. White demonstrates in "Once More to the Lake," you can write about a summer cabin on a lake as effectively as you can write about a tornado. The secret is in the vividness, the evocativeness, of the details. Like most masters of description, White relies heavily on IMAGES (language calling up concrete sensory experiences), including FIGURES OF SPEECH (expressions that do not mean literally what they say, often describing one thing in terms of another). White writes of motorboats that "whined about one's ears like mosquitoes" (a SIMILE) and of "small waves...chucking the rowboat under the chin" (a *metaphor*). Another writer, the humorist S. J. Perelman, uses metaphor to convey the garish brightness of a certain low-rent house. Notice how he makes clear the spirit of the place: "After a few days, I could have sworn that our faces began to take on the hue of Kodachromes, and even the dog, an animal used to bizarre surroundings, developed a strange, off-register look, as if he were badly printed in overlapping colors."

When you, too, write an effective description, you'll convey your sensory experience as exactly as possible. Find vigorous, specific words, and you will enable your reader to behold with the mind's eye — and to feel with the mind's fingertips.

CHECKLIST FOR REVISING A DESCRIPTION

✔ **SUBJECTIVE OR OBJECTIVE.** Given your purpose and audience, is your description appropriately subjective (emphasizing feelings) or objective (unemotional)?

✔ **DOMINANT IMPRESSION.** What is the dominant impression of your subject? If you haven't stated it, will your readers be able to express it accurately to themselves?

✔ **POINT OF VIEW AND ORGANIZATION.** Do your point of view and organization work together to make your subject clear in readers' minds? Are they consistent?

✔ **DETAILS.** Have you provided all the details — and just those — needed to convey your dominant impression? What needs expanding? What needs condensing or cutting?

✔ **CONCRETE LANGUAGE.** Have you used words that appeal to the senses of sight, hearing, touch, taste, and smell? A vague word such as *loud* does little for readers; a concrete word such as *screeching* works harder, and a fresh figure of speech such as *a screech like a 747 directly overhead* does even more.

DESCRIPTION IN A PARAGRAPH:
TWO ILLUSTRATIONS

Using Description to Write About Television

At 2:59 this Monday afternoon, a thick hush settles like cigarette smoke inside the sweat-scented TV room of Harris Hall. First to arrive, freshman Lee Ann squashes down into the catbird seat in front of the screen. Soon she is flanked by roommates Lisa and Kate, silent, their mouths straight lines, their upturned faces lit by the nervous flicker of a detergent ad. To the left and right of the couch, Pete and Anse crouch on the floor, leaning forward like runners awaiting a starting gun. Behind them, stiff standees line up at attention. Farther back still, English majors and jocks compete for an unobstructed view. Fresh from class, shirttail flapping, arm crooking a bundle of books, Dave barges into the room demanding, "Has it started? Has it started yet?" He is shushed. Somebody shushes a popped-open can of Dr Pepper whose fizz is distractingly loud. What do these students so intently look forward to—the announcement of World War III? A chord of music climbs and the screen dissolves to a title: *General Hospital.*

Dominant impression (not stated): tense expectation of something vital

Details (underlined) contribute to dominant impression

Organization proceeds from front of room (at TV) to back

Using Description in an Academic Discipline

While working on *The Battle of Anghiari*, Leonardo painted his most famous portrait, the *Mona Lisa*. The delicate *sfumato* already noted in the *Madonna of the Rocks* is here so perfected that it seemed miraculous to the artist's contemporaries. The forms are built from layers of glazes so gossamer-thin that the entire panel seems to glow with a gentle light from within. But the fame of the *Mona Lisa* comes not from this pictorial subtlety alone; even more intriguing is the psychological fascination of the sitter's personality. Why, among all the smiling faces ever painted, has this particular one been singled out as "mysterious"? Perhaps the reason is that, as a portrait, the picture does not fit our expectations. The features are too individual for Leonardo to have simply depicted an ideal type, yet the element of idealization is so strong that it blurs the sitter's character. Once again the artist has brought two opposites into harmonious balance. The smile, too, may be read in two ways: as the echo of a momentary mood, and as a timeless, symbolic expression (somewhat like the "Archaic smile" of the Greeks...). Clearly, the *Mona Lisa* embodies a quality of maternal tenderness which was to Leonardo the essence of womanhood. Even the landscape in the background, composed mainly of rocks and water, suggests elemental generative forces.

—H. W. Janson, *History of Art*

(Sfumato: soft gradations of light and dark)

Main idea (topic sentence) of the paragraph, supported by description of "pictorial subtlety" (above) and "psychological fascination" (below)

Details (underlined) contribute to dominant impression

E. B. WHITE

ELWYN BROOKS WHITE (1899–1985) for half a century was a regular contributor to *The New Yorker*, and his essays, editorials, anonymous features for "The Talk of the Town," and fillers helped build the magazine a reputation for wit and good writing. If as a child you read *Charlotte's Web* (1952), you have met E. B. White before. The book reflects some of his own life on a farm in North Brooklin, Maine. His *Letters* were collected in 1976, his *Essays* in 1977, and his *Poems and Sketches* in 1981. On July 4, 1963, President Kennedy named White in the first group of Americans to receive the Presidential Medal of Freedom, with a citation that called him "an essayist whose concise comment...has revealed to yet another age the vigor of the English sentence."

Once More to the Lake

"Once More to the Lake" first appeared in *Harper's* magazine in 1941. Perhaps if a duller writer had written the essay, or an essay with the same title, we wouldn't much care about it, for at first its subject seems as personal and ordinary as a letter home. White's loving and exact description, however, brings this lakeside camp to life for us. In the end, the writer arrives at an awareness that shocks him—shocks us, too, with a familiar sensory detail.

August 1941

One summer, along about 1904, my father rented a camp on a lake 1 in Maine and took us all there for the month of August. We all got ringworm from some kittens and had to rub Pond's Extract on our arms and legs night and morning, and my father rolled over in a canoe with all his clothes on; but outside of that the vacation was a success and from then on none of us ever thought there was any place in the world like that lake in Maine. We returned summer after summer—always on August 1 for one month. I have since become a salt-water man, but sometimes in summer there are days when the restlessness of the tides and the fearful cold of the sea water and the incessant wind that blows across the afternoon and into the evening make me wish for the placidity of a lake in the woods. A few weeks ago this feeling got so strong I bought myself a couple of bass hooks and a spinner and returned to the lake where we used to go, for a week's fishing and to revisit old haunts.

I took along my son, who had never had any fresh water up his nose 2 and who had seen lily pads only from train windows. On the journey over to the lake I began to wonder what it would be like. I wondered

how time would have marred this unique, this holy spot—the coves
and streams, the hills that the sun set behind, the camps and the paths
behind the camps. I was sure that the tarred road would have found it
out, and I wondered in what other ways it would be desolated. It is
strange how much you can remember about places like that once you
allow your mind to return into the grooves that lead back. You remember one thing, and that suddenly reminds you of another thing. I guess
I remembered clearest of all the early mornings, when the lake was cool
and motionless, remembered how the bedroom smelled of the lumber it
was made of and of the wet woods whose scent entered through the
screen. The partitions in the camp were thin and did not extend clear
to the top of the rooms, and as I was always the first up I would dress
softly so as not to wake the others, and sneak out into the sweet outdoors and start out in the canoe, keeping close along the shore in the
long shadows of the pines. I remembered being very careful never to
rub my paddle against the gunwale for fear of disturbing the stillness of
the cathedral.

The lake had never been what you would call a wild lake. There 3
were cottages sprinkled around the shores, and it was in farming country although the shores of the lake were quite heavily wooded. Some of
the cottages were owned by nearby farmers, and you would live at the
shore and eat your meals at the farmhouse. That's what our family did.
But although it wasn't wild, it was a fairly large and undisturbed lake
and there were places in it that, to a child at least, seemed infinitely remote and primeval.

I was right about the tar: It led to within half a mile of the shore. 4
But when I got back there, with my boy, and we settled into a camp
near a farmhouse and into the kind of summertime I had known, I
could tell that it was going to be pretty much the same as it had been
before—I knew it, lying in bed the first morning smelling the bedroom
and hearing the boy sneak quietly out and go off along the shore in a
boat. I began to sustain the illusion that he was I, and therefore, by simple transposition, that I was my father. This sensation persisted, kept
cropping up all the time we were there. It was not an entirely new feeling, but in this setting it grew much stronger. I seemed to be living a
dual existence. I would be in the middle of some simple act, I would be
picking up a bait box or laying down a table fork, or I would be saying
something and suddenly it would be not I but my father who was saying the words or making the gesture. It gave me a creepy sensation.

We went fishing the first morning. I felt the same damp moss cov- 5
ering the worms in the bait can, and saw the dragonfly alight on the tip
of my rod as it hovered a few inches from the surface of the water. It was
the arrival of this fly that convinced me beyond any doubt that everything was as it always had been, that the years were a mirage and that

there had been no years. The small waves were the same, chucking the rowboat under the chin as we fished at anchor, and the boat was the same boat, the same color green and the ribs broken in the same places, and under the floorboards the same fresh water leavings and debris— the dead hellgrammite, the wisps of moss, the rusty discarded fishhook, the dried blood from yesterday's catch. We stared silently at the tips of our rods, at the dragonflies that came and went. I lowered the tip of mine into the water, tentatively, pensively dislodging the fly, which darted two feet away, poised, darted two feet back, and came to rest again a little farther up the rod. There had been no years between the ducking of this dragonfly and the other one—the one that was part of memory. I looked at the boy, who was silently watching his fly, and it was my hands that held his rod, my eyes watching. I felt dizzy and didn't know which rod I was at the end of.

We caught two bass, hauling them in briskly as though they were   6 mackerel, pulling them over the side of the boat in a businesslike manner without any landing net, and stunning them with a blow on the back of the head. When we got back for a swim before lunch, the lake was exactly where we had left it, the same number of inches from the dock, and there was only the merest suggestion of a breeze. This seemed an utterly enchanted sea, this lake you could leave to its own devices for a few hours and come back to, and find that it had not stirred, this constant and trustworthy body of water. In the shallows, the dark, water-soaked sticks and twigs, smooth and old, were undulating in clusters on the bottom against the clean ribbed sand, and the track of the mussel was plain. A school of minnows swam by, each minnow with its small individual shadow, doubling the attendance, so clear and sharp in the sunlight. Some of the other campers were in swimming, along the shore, one of them with a cake of soap, and the water felt thin and clear and unsubstantial. Over the years there had been this person with the cake of soap, this cultist, and here he was. There had been no years.

Up to the farmhouse to dinner through the teeming dusty field, the   7 road under our sneakers was only a two-track road. The middle track was missing, the one with the marks of the hooves and the splotches of dried, flaky manure. There had always been three tracks to choose from in choosing which track to walk in; now the choice was narrowed down to two. For a moment I missed terribly the middle alternative. But the way led past the tennis court, and something about the way it lay there in the sun reassured me; the tape had loosened along the backline, the alleys were green with plantains and other weeds, and the net (installed in June and removed in September) sagged in the dry noon, and the whole place steamed with midday heat and hunger and emptiness. There was a choice of pie for dessert, and one was blueberry and one was apple, and the waitresses were the same country girls, there having been no passage of time, only the illusion of it as in a dropped curtain—the waitresses were still fifteen; their hair had been washed, that was the only difference—they had been to the movies and seen the pretty girls with the clean hair.

Summertime, oh, summertime, pattern of life indelible, the fade- 8 proof lake, the woods unshatterable, the pasture with the sweetfern and the juniper forever and ever, summer without end; this was the background, and the life along the shore was the design, the cottages with their innocent and tranquil design, their tiny docks with the flagpole and the American flag floating against the white clouds in the blue sky, the little paths over the roots of the trees leading from camp to camp and the paths leading back to the outhouses and the can of lime for sprinkling, and at the souvenir counters at the store the miniature birchbark canoes and the postcards that showed things looking a little better than they looked. This was the American family at play, escaping the city heat, wondering whether the newcomers in the camp at the head of the cove were "common" or "nice," wondering whether it was true that the people who drove up for Sunday dinner at the farmhouse were turned away because there wasn't enough chicken.

It seemed to me, as I kept remembering all this, that those times 9 and those summers had been infinitely precious and worth saving. There had been jollity and peace and goodness. The arriving (at the beginning of August) had been so big a business in itself, at the railway station the farm wagon drawn up, the first smell of the pine-laden air, the first glimpse of the smiling farmer, and the great importance of the trunks and your father's enormous authority in such matters, and the feel of the wagon under you for the long ten-mile haul, and at the top of the last long hill catching the first view of the lake after eleven months of not seeing this cherished body of water. The shouts and cries of the other campers when they saw you, and the trunks to be unpacked, to give up their rich burden. (Arriving was less exciting nowadays, when you sneaked up in your car and parked it under a tree near the camp and took out the bags and in five minutes it was all over, no fuss, no loud wonderful fuss about trunks.)

Peace and goodness and jollity. The only thing that was wrong 10 now, really, was the sound of the place, an unfamiliar nervous sound of the outboard motors. This was the note that jarred, the one thing that would sometimes break the illusion and set the years moving. In those other summertimes all motors were inboard; and when they were at a little distance, the noise they made was a sedative, an ingredient of summer sleep. They were one-cylinder and two-cylinder engines, and some were make-and-break and some were jump-spark, but they all made a sleepy sound across the lake. The one-lungers throbbed and fluttered, and the twin-cylinder ones purred and purred, and that was a quiet sound, too. But now the campers all had outboards. In the daytime, in the hot mornings, these motors made a petulant irritable sound; at night in the still evening when the afterglow lit the water, they whined about one's ears like mosquitoes. My boy loved our rented outboard, and his great desire was to achieve single-handed mastery over it, and authority, and he soon learned the trick of choking it a little (but not too much), and the adjustment of the needle valve. Watching him I would remember the things you could do with the old one-cylinder engine with the heavy flywheel, how you could have it eating out of your hand if you got really close to it spiritually. Motorboats in those days didn't have clutches, and you would make a landing by shutting off the motor at the proper time and coasting in with a dead rudder. But there was a way of reversing them, if you learned the trick, by cutting the switch and putting it on again exactly on the final dying revolution of the flywheel, so that it would kick back against compression and begin reversing. Approaching a dock in a strong following breeze, it was difficult to slow up sufficiently by the ordinary coasting method, and if a boy felt he had complete mastery over his motor, he was tempted to keep it running beyond its time and then reverse it a few feet from the dock. It took a cool nerve, because if you threw the switch a twentieth of a second too soon you would catch the flywheel when it still had speed enough to go up past center, and the boat would leap ahead, charging bull-fashion at the dock.

We had a good week at the camp. The bass were biting well and the sun shone endlessly, day after day. We would be tired at night and lie down in the accumulated heat of the little bedrooms after the long hot day and the breeze would stir almost imperceptibly outside and the smell of the swamp drift in through the rusty screens. Sleep would come easily and in the morning the red squirrel would be on the roof, tapping out his gay routine. I kept remembering everything, lying in bed in the mornings—the small steamboat that had a long rounded stern like the lip of a Ubangi, and how quietly she ran on the moonlight sails, when the older boys played their mandolins and the girls sang and we ate doughnuts dipped in sugar, and how sweet the music was on the water in the shining night, and what it had felt like to think about girls then. After breakfast we would go up to the store and the things were in the same place—the minnows in a bottle, the plugs and spinners disarranged and pawed over by the youngsters from the boys' camp, the Fig Newtons and the Beeman's gum. Outside, the road was tarred and cars stood in front of the store. Inside, all was just as it had always been, except there was more Coca-Cola and not so much Moxie and root beer and birch beer and sarsaparilla. We would walk out with the bottle of pop apiece and sometimes the pop would backfire up our noses and hurt. We explored the streams, quietly, where the turtles slid off the sunny logs and dug their way into the soft bottom; and we lay on the town wharf and fed worms to the tame bass. Everywhere we went I had trouble making out which was I, the one walking at my side, the one walking in my pants.

One afternoon while we were at the lake a thunderstorm came up. 12 It was like the revival of an old melodrama that I had seen long ago with childish awe. The second-act climax of the drama of the electrical disturbance over a lake in America had not changed in any important respect. This was the big scene, still the big scene. The whole thing was so familiar, the first feeling of oppression and heat and a general air around camp of not wanting to go very far away. In midafternoon (it was all the same) a curious darkening of the sky, and a lull in everything that had made life tick; and then the way the boats suddenly swung the other way at their moorings with the coming of a breeze out of the new quarter, and the premonitory rumble. Then the kettle drum, then the snare, then the bass drum and cymbals, then crackling light against the dark, and the gods grinning and licking their chops in the hills. Afterward the calm, the rain steadily rustling in the calm lake, the return of light and hope and spirits, and the campers running out in joy and relief to go swimming in the rain, their bright cries perpetuating the deathless joke about how they were getting simply drenched, and the children screaming with delight at the new sensation of bathing in the rain, and the joke about getting drenched linking the generations in a strong indestructible chain. And the comedian who waded in carrying an umbrella.

When the others went swimming my son said he was going in, too. 13 He pulled his dripping trunks from the line where they had hung all through the shower and wrung them out. Languidly, and with no thought of going in, I watched him, his hard little body, skinny and bare, saw him wince slightly as he pulled up around his vitals the small, soggy, icy garment. As he buckled the swollen belt, suddenly my groin felt the chill of death.

————————

QUESTIONS ON MEANING

1. How do you account for the distortions that creep into the author's sense of time?
2. What does the discussion of inboard and outboard motors (para. 10) have to do with the author's divided sense of time?
3. To what degree does White make us aware of his son's impression of this trip to the lake?

4. What do you take to be White's main PURPOSE in the essay? At what point do you become aware of it?

QUESTIONS ON WRITING STRATEGY

1. In paragraph 4 the author first introduces his confused feeling that he has gone back in time to his own childhood, an idea that he repeats and expands throughout his account. What is the function of these repetitions?
2. Try to describe the impact of the essay's final paragraph. By what means is it achieved?
3. To what extent is this essay written to appeal to any but middle-aged readers? Is it comprehensible to anyone whose vacations were never spent at a Maine summer cottage?
4. What is the TONE of White's essay?
5. **OTHER METHODS.** White's essay is both a description and a COMPARISON of the lake when he was a boy and when he revisits it with his son. What changes does he find at the lake? What things have stayed the same?

QUESTIONS ON LANGUAGE

1. Be sure you know the meanings of the following words: incessant, placidity (para. 1); gunwale (2); primeval (3); transposition (4); hellgrammite (5); undulating, cultist (6); indelible, tranquil (8); petulant (10); imperceptibly (11); premonitory (12); languidly (13).
2. Comment on White's DICTION in his reference to the lake as "this unique, this holy spot" (para. 2).
3. Explain what White is describing in the sentence that begins, "Then the kettle drum..." (para. 12). Where else does the author use FIGURES OF SPEECH?
4. Find effective IMAGES that are not figures of speech — that are, in other words, literal descriptions of sensory impressions.

SUGGESTIONS FOR WRITING

1. **JOURNAL WRITING.** What place or places were most important to you as a child? What was important about them?
   FROM JOURNAL TO ESSAY. Choose one of the places suggested by your journal entry, and write an essay describing the place now, revisiting it as an adult. (If you haven't visited the place since childhood, you can imagine what seeing it now would be like.) Your description should draw on your childhood memories, making them as vivid as possible for the reader, but you should also consider how your POINT OF VIEW toward the place differs now.
2. In a descriptive paragraph about a real or imagined place, try to appeal to each of your reader's five senses.
3. **CRITICAL WRITING.** While on the vacation he describes, White wrote to his wife, Katharine, "This place is as American as a drink of Coca Cola. The white collar family having its annual liberty." Obviously, not everyone has a chance at the lakeside summers White enjoyed. To what extent, if at

all, does White's privileged point of view deprive his essay of universal meaning and significance? Write an essay answering this question. Back up your ideas with EVIDENCE from White's essay.
4. **CONNECTIONS.** In White's "Once More to the Lake" and the next essay, Brad Manning's "Arm Wrestling with My Father," both writers reveal a changing sense of what it means to be a father. Write an essay that examines the similarities and differences in their definitions of fatherhood. How does a changing idea of what it means to be a son connect with this redefinition of fatherhood?

E. B. WHITE ON WRITING

"You asked me about writing—how I did it," E. B. White replied to a seventeen-year-old who had written to him, wanting to become a professional writer but feeling discouraged. "There is no trick to it. If you like to write and want to write, you write, no matter where you are or what else you are doing or whether anyone pays any heed. I must have written half a million words (mostly in my journal) before I had anything published, save for a couple of short items in *St. Nicholas*.[1] If you want to write about feelings, about the end of the summer, about growing, write about it. A great deal of writing is not 'plotted'—most of my essays have no plot structure, they are a ramble in the woods, or a ramble in the basement of my mind. You ask, 'Who cares?' Everybody cares. You say, 'It's been written before.' Everything has been written before....Henry Thoreau, who wrote *Walden*, said, 'I learned this at least by my experiment: that if one advances confidently in the direction of his dreams and endeavors to live the life which he has imagined, he will meet with a success unexpected in common hours.' The sentence, after more than a hundred years, is still alive. So, advance confidently."

In trying to characterize his own writing, White was modest in his claims. To his brother Stanley Hart White, he once remarked, "I discovered a long time ago that writing of the small things of the day, the trivial matters of the heart, the inconsequential but near things of this living, was the only kind of creative work which I could accomplish with any sincerity or grace. As a reporter, I was a flop, because I always came back laden not with facts about the case, but with a mind full of the little difficulties and amusements I had encountered in my travels. Not till *The New Yorker* came along did I ever find any means of expressing those impertinences and irrelevancies. Thus yesterday, setting out to get a story on how police horses are trained, I ended by writing a

[1] A magazine for children, popular early in the century.—EDS.

story entitled "How Police Horses Are Trained" which never even mentions a police horse, but has to do entirely with my own absurd adventures at police headquarters. The rewards of such endeavor are not that I have acquired an audience or a following, as you suggest (fame of any kind being a Pyrrhic victory), but that sometimes in writing of myself—which is the only subject anyone knows intimately—I have occasionally had the exquisite thrill of putting my finger on a little capsule of truth, and heard it give the faint squeak of mortality under my pressure, an antic sound."

FOR DISCUSSION

1. Sometimes young writers are counseled to study the market and then try to write something that will sell. How would you expect E. B. White to have reacted to such advice?
2. What, exactly, does White mean when he says, "Everything has been written before"? How might an aspiring writer take this remark as encouragement?
3. What interesting distinction does White make between reporting and essay writing?

BRAD MANNING

BRAD MANNING was born in Little Rock, Arkansas, in 1967 and grew up near Charlottesville, Virginia. He attended Harvard University, graduating in 1990 with a B.A. in history and religion. At Harvard he played intramural sports and wrote articles and reviews for the *Harvard Independent*. After graduation Manning wrote features and news stories for the *Charlotte Observer* and then attended law school at the University of Virginia, graduating in 1995. Now living in Richmond, Virginia, with his wife and son, Manning practices law and takes courses in preparation for medical school.

Arm Wrestling with My Father

In this essay written for his freshman composition course, Manning describes his physical contact with his father over the years, perceiving gradual changes that are, he realizes, inevitable. This essay has been published in a Harvard collection of students' writing; in *Student Writers at Work: The Bedford Prizes*, an anthology of prize-winning essays edited by Nancy Sommers and Donald McQuade; and in *Montage*, a collection of Russian and American stories published in Russian.

"Now you say when" is what he always said before an arm-wrestling 1 match. He liked to put the responsibility on me, knowing that he would always control the outcome. "When!" I'd shout, and it would start. And I would tense up, concentrating and straining and trying to push his wrist down to the carpet with all my weight and strength. But Dad would always win; I always had to lose. "Want to try it again?" he would ask, grinning. He would see my downcast eyes, my reddened, sweating face, and sense my intensity. And with squinting eyes he would laugh at me, a high laugh, through his perfect white teeth. Too bitter to smile, I would not answer or look at him, but I would just roll over on my back and frown at the ceiling. I never thought it was funny at all.

That was the way I felt for a number of years during my teens, after 2 I had lost my enjoyment of arm wrestling and before I had given up that same intense desire to beat my father. Ours had always been a physical relationship, I suppose, one determined by athleticism and strength. We never communicated as well in speech or in writing as in a strong hug, battling to make the other gasp for breath. I could never find him at one of my orchestra concerts. But at my lacrosse games, he would be there in the stands, with an angry look, ready to coach me after the game on how I could do better. He never helped me write a paper or a poem. Instead, he would take me outside and show me a new move for my game, in the hope that I would score a couple of goals and gain confidence in my ability. Dad knew almost nothing about lacrosse and his movements were all wrong and sad to watch. But at those times I could just feel how hard he was trying to communicate, to help me, to show the love he had for me, the love I could only assume was there.

His words were physical. The truth is, I have never read a card or a 3 letter written in his hand because he never wrote to me. Never. Mom wrote me all the cards and letters when I was away from home. The closest my father ever came, that I recall, was in a newspaper clipping Mom had sent with a letter. He had gone through and underlined all the important words about the dangers of not wearing a bicycle helmet. Our communication was physical, and that is why we did things like arm wrestle. To get down on the floor and grapple, arm against arm, was like having a conversation.

This ritual of father-son competition in fact had started early in my 4 life, back when Dad started the matches with his arm almost horizontal, his wrist an inch from defeat, and still won. I remember in those battles how my tiny shoulders would press over our locked hands, my whole upper body pushing down in hope of winning that single inch from his calm, unmoving forearm. "Say when," he'd repeat, killing my concentration and causing me to squeal, "I did, I did!" And so he'd grin with his eyes fixed on me, not seeming to notice his own arm, which would begin to rise slowly from its starting position. My greatest efforts could not slow it down. As soon as my hopes had disappeared I'd start to cheat and use both hands. But the arm would continue to move steadily along its arc toward the carpet. My brother, if he was watching, would sometimes join in against the arm. He once even wrapped his little legs around our embattled wrists and pulled back with everything he had. But he did not have much and, regardless of the opposition, the man would win. My arm would lie at rest, pressed into the carpet beneath a solid, immovable arm. In that pinned position, I could only giggle, happy to have such a strong father.

My feelings have changed, though. I don't giggle anymore, at least 5 not around my father. And I don't feel pressured to compete with him the way I thought necessary for years. Now my father is not really so strong as he used to be and I am getting stronger. This change in strength comes at a time when I am growing faster mentally than at any time before. I am becoming less my father and more myself. And as a result, there is less of a need to be set apart from him and his command. I am no longer a rebel in the household, wanting to stand up against the master with clenched fists and tensing jaws, trying to impress him with my education or my views on religion. I am no longer a challenger, quick to correct his verbal mistakes, determined to beat him whenever possible in physical competition.

I am not sure when it was that I began to feel less competitive with my father, but it all became clearer to me one day this past January. I was home in Virginia for a week between exams, and Dad had stayed home from work because the house was snowed in deep. It was then that I learned something I never could have guessed. 6

I don't recall who suggested arm wrestling that day. We hadn't done it for a long time, for months. But there we were, lying flat on the carpet, face to face, extending our right arms. Our arms were different. His still resembled a fat tree branch, one which had leveled my wrist to the ground countless times before. It was hairy and white with some pink moles scattered about. It looked strong, to be sure, though not so strong as it had in past years. I expect that back in his youth it had looked even stronger. In high school he had played halfback and had been voted "best-built body" of the senior class. Between college semesters he had worked on road crews and on Louisiana dredges. I admired him for that. I had begun to row crew in college and that accounted for some small buildup along the muscle lines, but it did not seem to be enough. The arm I extended was lanky and featureless. Even so, he insisted that he would lose the match, that he was certain I'd win. I had to ignore this, however, because it was something he always said, whether or not he believed it himself. 7

Our warm palms came together, much the same way we had shaken hands the day before at the airport. Fingers twisted and wrapped about once again, testing for a better grip. Elbows slid up and back making their little indentations on the itchy carpet. My eyes pinched closed in concentration as I tried to center as much of my thought as possible on the match. Arm wrestling, I knew, was a competition that depended less on talent and experience than on one's mental control and confidence. I looked up into his eyes and was ready. He looked back, smiled at me, and said softly (did he sound nervous?), "You say when." 8

It was not a long match. I had expected him to be stronger, faster. I was conditioned to lose and would have accepted defeat easily. However, after some struggle, his arm yielded to my efforts and began to move unsteadily toward the carpet. I worked against his arm with all the strength I could find. He was working hard as well, straining, breathing heavily. It seemed that this time was different, that I was going to win. Then something occurred to me, something unexpected. I discovered that I was feeling sorry for my father. I wanted to win but I did not want to see him lose. 9

It was like the thrill I had once experienced as a young boy at my grandfather's lake house in Louisiana when I hooked my first big fish. There was that sudden tug that made me leap. The red bobber was 10 sucked down beneath the surface and I pulled back against it, reeling it in excitedly. But when my cousin caught sight of the fish and shouted out, "It's a keeper," I realized that I would be happier for the fish if it were let go rather than grilled for dinner. Arm wrestling my father was now like this, like hooking "Big Joe," the old fish that Lake Quachita holds but you can never catch, and when you finally think you've got him, you want to let him go, cut the line, keep the legend alive.

Perhaps at that point I could have given up, letting my father win. But it was so fast and absorbing. How could I have learned so quickly how it would feel to have overpowered the arm that had protected and provided for me all of my life? His arms have always protected me and the family. Whenever I am near him I am unafraid, knowing his arms are ready to catch me and keep me safe, the way they caught my mother one time when she fainted halfway across the room, the way he carried me, full grown, up and down the stairs when I had mononucleosis, the way he once held my feet as I stood on his shoulders to put up a new basketball net. My mother may have had the words or the touch that sustained our family, but his were the arms that protected us. And his were the arms now that I had pushed to the carpet, first the right arm, then the left. 11

I might have preferred him to be always the stronger, the one who carries me. But this wish is impossible now; our roles have begun to switch. I do not know if I will ever physically carry my father as he has carried me, though I fear that someday I may have that responsibility. More than once this year I have hesitated before answering the phone late at night, fearing my mother's voice calling me back to help carry his wood coffin. When I am home with him and he mentions a sharp pain in his chest, I imagine him collapsing onto the floor. And in that second vision I see me rushing to him, lifting him onto my shoulders, and running. 12

A week after our match, we parted at the airport. The arm-wrestling match was by that time mostly forgotten. My thoughts were on school. I had been awake most of the night studying for my last exam, and by that morning I was already back into my college-student manner of reserve and detachment. To say goodbye, I kissed and hugged my mother and I prepared to shake my father's hand. A handshake had always seemed easier to handle than a hug. His hugs had always been powerful ones, intended I suppose to give me strength. They made me suck in my breath and struggle for control, and the way he would pound his hand on my back made rumbles in my ears. So I offered a handshake; but he offered a hug. I accepted it, bracing myself for the impact. Once our arms were wrapped around each other, however, I sensed a different message. His embrace was softer, longer than before. 13

I remember how it surprised me and how I gave an embarrassed laugh as if to apologize to anyone watching.

I got on the airplane and my father and mother were gone. But as the plane lifted my throat was hurting with sadness. I realized then that Dad must have learned something as well, and what he had said to me in that last hug was that he loved me. Love was a rare expression between us, so I had denied it at first. As the plane turned north, I had a sudden wish to go back to Dad and embrace his arms with all the love I felt for him. I wanted to hold him for a long time and to speak with him silently, telling him how happy I was, telling him all my feelings, in that language we shared.

In his hug, Dad had tried to tell me something he himself had discovered. I hope he tries again. Maybe this spring, when he sees his first crew match, he'll advise me on how to improve my stroke. Maybe he has started doing pushups to rebuild his strength and challenge me to another match—if this were true, I know I would feel less challenged than loved. Or maybe, rather than any of this, he'll just send me a card.

QUESTIONS ON MEANING

1. In paragraph 3 Manning says that his father's "words were physical." What does this mean?
2. After his most recent trip home, Manning says, "I realized then that Dad must have learned something as well" (para. 14). What is it that father and son have each learned?
3. Manning says in the last paragraph that he "would feel less challenged than loved" if his father challenged him to a rematch. Does this statement suggest that he did not feel loved earlier? Why, or why not?
4. What do you think is Manning's PURPOSE in this essay? Does he want to express love for his father, or is there something more as well?

QUESTIONS ON WRITING STRATEGY

1. Why does Manning start his essay with a match that leaves him "too bitter to smile" and then move backward to earlier bouts of arm wrestling?
2. In the last paragraph Manning suggests that his father might work harder at competing with him and pushing him to be competitive, or he might just send his son a card. Why does Manning present both of these options? Are we supposed to know which will happen?
3. Explain the fishing ANALOGY Manning uses in paragraph 10.
4. **OTHER METHODS.** Manning's essay is as much a NARRATIVE as a description: The author gives brief stories, like video clips, to show the dynamic of his relationship with his father. Look at the story in paragraph 4. How does Manning mix elements of both methods to convey his powerlessness?

QUESTIONS ON LANGUAGE

1. Manning uses the word *competition* throughout this essay. Why is this a more accurate word than *conflict* to describe Manning's relationship with his father?
2. What is the EFFECT of "the arm" in this line from paragraph 4: "But the arm would continue to move steadily along its arc toward the carpet"?
3. In paragraph 9 Manning writes, "I wanted to win but I did not want to see him lose." What does this apparent contradiction mean?
4. If any of these words is unfamiliar, look it up in a dictionary: embattled (para. 4); dredges, crew (7); conditioned (9); mononucleosis (11).

SUGGESTIONS FOR WRITING

1. JOURNAL WRITING. When have you felt strongly conflicting emotions over a person or an event: a relative, friend, breakup, ceremony, move?
   FROM JOURNAL TO ESSAY. Expand your journal entry into a descriptive essay that brings your feelings to life for your reader. Focus less on the circumstances and events than on emotions, both positive and negative.
2. Write an essay that describes your relationship with a parent or another close adult. You may want to focus on just one aspect of your relationship, or one especially vivid moment, in order to give yourself the space and time to build many sensory details into your description.
3. CRITICAL WRITING. In paragraph 12 Manning writes, "our roles have begun to switch." Does this seem like an inevitable switch, or one that this father and son have been working to achieve? Use EVIDENCE from Manning's essay to support your answer. Also consider whether Manning and his father would respond the same way to this question.
4. CONNECTIONS. Manning writes about the "ritual of father-son competition," while E. B. White, in "Once More to the Lake" (p. 104), writes about a vacation ritual that binds father and son. Both authors imply that fathers and sons don't communicate through words. COMPARE AND CONTRAST the kind of communication that occurs between each father-son pair. What seems to be the relationship between rituals and communication for each?

BRAD MANNING ON WRITING

For *The Bedford Reader*, Brad Manning offered some valuable concrete advice on writing as a student.

"You hear this a lot, but writing takes a long time. For me, this is especially true. The only difference between the 'Arm Wrestling' essay and all the other essays I wrote in college (and the only reason it's in this book and not thrown away) is that I rewrote it six or seven times over a period of weeks.

"If I have something to write, I need to start early. In college, I had a bad habit of putting off papers until 10 P.M. the night before they were due and spending a desperate night typing whatever ideas the coffee inspired. But putting off papers didn't just lower my writing quality; it robbed me of a good time.

"I like starting early because I can jot down notes over a stretch of days; then I type them up fast, ignoring typos; I print the notes with narrow margins, cut them up, and divide them into piles that seem to fit together; then it helps to get away for a day and come back all fresh so I can throw away the corny ideas. Finally, I sit on the floor and make an outline with all the cutouts of paper, trying at the same time to work out some clear purpose for the essay.

"When the writing starts, I often get hung up most on trying to 'sound' like a good writer. If you're like me and came to college from a shy family that never discussed much over dinner, you might think your best shot is to sound like a famous writer like T. S. Eliot and you might try to sneak in words that aren't really your own like *ephemeral* or *the lilacs smelled like springtime*. But the last thing you really want a reader thinking is how good or bad a writer you are.

"Also, in the essay on arm wrestling, I got hung up thinking I had to make my conflict with my father somehow 'universal.' So in an early draft I wrote in a classical allusion—Aeneas lifting his old father up onto his shoulders and carrying him out of the burning city of Troy.[1] I'd read that story in high school and guessed one classical allusion might make the reader think I knew a lot more. But Aeneas didn't help the essay much, and I'm glad my teacher warned me off trying to universalize. He told me to write just what was true for me.

"But that was hard, too, and still is—especially in the first draft. I don't know anyone who enjoys the first draft. If you do, I envy you. But in my early drafts, I always get this sensation like I have to impress somebody and I end up overanalyzing the effects of every word I am about to write. This self-consciousness may be unavoidable (I get self-conscious calling L. L. Bean to order a shirt), but, in this respect, writing is great for shy people because you can edit all you want, all day long, until it finally sounds right. I never feel that I am being myself until the third or fourth draft, and it's only then that it gets personal and starts to be fun.

"When I said that putting off papers robbed me of a good time, I really meant it. Writing the essay about my father turned out to be a high point in my life. And on top of having a good time with it, I now have a record of what happened. And my ten-month-old son, when he

---

[1] In the *Aeneid*, by the Roman poet Vergil (70–19 B.C.), the mythic hero Aeneas escaped from the city of Troy when it was sacked by the Greeks and went on to found Rome.—EDS.

grows up, can read things about his grandfather and father that he'd probably not have learned any other way."

FOR DISCUSSION

1. What did Manning miss by writing his college papers at the last minute?
2. Why does Manning say that "writing is great for shy people"? Have you ever felt that you could express yourself in writing better than in speech?

JOAN DIDION

A writer whose fame is fourfold—as novelist, essayist, journalist, and screenwriter—JOAN DIDION was born in 1934 in California, where her family has lived for five generations. After graduation from the University of California, Berkeley, she spent a few years in New York, working as a feature editor for *Vogue*, a fashion magazine. In 1964 she returned to California, where she worked as a freelance journalist and wrote four much-discussed novels: *River Run* (1963), *Play It As It Lays* (1971), *A Book of Common Prayer* (1977), and *Democracy* (1984). *Salvador* (1983), her book-length essay based on a visit to war-torn El Salvador, and *Miami* (1987), a study of Cuban exiles in Florida, also received wide attention. With her husband, John Gregory Dunne, Didion has coauthored screenplays, notably for *A Star Is Born* (1976), *True Confessions* (1981), and, most recently, *Up Close and Personal* (1996). Didion's latest books are *After Henry* (1992), a collection of essays, and *The Last Thing He Wanted* (1996), a novel.

Marrying Absurd

"Marrying Absurd" appeared originally in 1967 in *The Saturday Evening Post*, a general-interest magazine, and was reprinted in a book of Didion's essays, *Slouching Towards Bethlehem* (1968). As you will see, the essay is no aged relic of the 1960s. Didion's descriptions of Las Vegas and the people who marry there are enduringly fresh and funny.

To be married in Las Vegas, Clark County, Nevada, a bride must   1 swear that she is eighteen or has parental permission and a bridegroom that he is twenty-one or has parental permission. Someone must put up five dollars for the license. (On Sundays and holidays, fifteen dollars. The Clark County Courthouse issues marriage licenses at any time of the day or night except between noon and one in the afternoon, between eight and nine in the evening, and between four and five in the morning.) Nothing else is required. The State of Nevada, alone among these United States, demands neither a premarital blood test nor a waiting period before or after the issuance of a marriage license. Driving in across the Mojave from Los Angeles, one sees the signs way out on the desert, looming up from the moonscape of rattlesnakes and mesquite, even before the Las Vegas lights appear like a mirage on the horizon: "GETTING MARRIED? Free License Information First Strip Exit." Perhaps the Las Vegas wedding industry achieved its peak operational efficiency between 9:00 P.M. and midnight of August 26, 1965, an otherwise unremarkable Thursday which happened to be, by Presidential order, the last day on which anyone could improve his draft status merely by getting married. One hundred and seventy-one couples were pronounced man and wife in the name of Clark County and the State of Nevada that night, sixty-seven of them by a single justice of the peace, Mr. James A. Brennan. Mr. Brennan did one wedding at the Dunes and the other sixty-six in his office, and charged each couple eight dollars. One bride lent her veil to six others. "I got it down from five to three minutes," Mr. Brennan said later of his feat. "I could've married them *en masse*, but they're people, not cattle. People expect more when they get married."

What people who get married in Las Vegas actually do expect— what, in the largest sense, their "expectations" are—strikes one as a curious and self-contradictory business. Las Vegas is the most extreme and allegorical of American settlements, bizarre and beautiful in its venality and in its devotion to immediate gratification, a place the tone of which is set by mobsters and call girls and ladies' room attendants with amyl nitrate poppers in their uniform pockets. Almost everyone notes that there is no "time" in Las Vegas, no night and no day and no past and no future (no Las Vegas casino, however, has taken the obliteration of the ordinary time sense quite so far as Harold's Club in Reno, which for a while issued, at odd intervals in the day and night, mimeographed "bulletins" carrying news from the world outside); neither is there any logical sense of where one is. One is standing on a highway in the middle of a vast hostile desert looking at an eighty-foot sign which blinks "STARDUST" or "CAESAR'S PALACE." Yes, but what does that explain? This geographical implausibility reinforces the sense that what happens there has no connection with "real" life; Nevada cities like Reno and Carson are ranch towns, Western towns, places behind which there is some historical imperative. But Las Vegas seems to exist only in the eye of the beholder. All of which makes it an extraordinarily stimulating and interesting place, but an odd one in which to want to wear a candlelight satin Priscilla of Boston wedding dress with Chantilly lace insets, tapered sleeves and a detachable modified train.

And yet the Las Vegas wedding business seems to appeal to precisely that impulse. "Sincere and Dignified Since 1954," one wedding chapel advertises. There are nineteen such wedding chapels in Las Vegas, intensely competitive, each offering better, faster, and, by implication, more sincere services than the next: Our Photos Best Anywhere, Your Wedding on a Phonograph Record, Candlelight with Your Ceremony, Honeymoon Accommodations, Free Transportation from Your Motel to Courthouse to Chapel and Return to Motel, Religious or Civil Ceremonies, Dressing Rooms, Flowers, Rings, Announcements, Witnesses Available, and Ample Parking. All of these services, like most others in Las Vegas (sauna baths, payroll-check cashing, chinchilla coats for sale or rent), are offered twenty-four hours a day, seven days a week, presumably on the premise that marriage, like craps, is a game to be played when the table seems hot.

But what strikes one most about the Strip chapels, with their wishing wells and stained-glass paper windows and their artificial bouvardia, is that so much of their business is by no means a matter of simple convenience, of late-night liaisons between show girls and baby Crosbys. Of course there is some of that. (One night about eleven o'clock in Las Vegas I watched a bride in an orange minidress and masses of flame-colored hair stumble from a Strip chapel on the arm of her bridegroom, who looked the part of the expendable nephew in movies like *Miami Syndicate*. "I gotta get the kids," the bride whimpered. "I gotta pick up the sitter, I gotta get to the midnight show." "What you gotta get," the bridegroom said, opening the door of a Cadillac Coupe de Ville and watching her crumple on the seat, "is sober.") But Las Vegas seems to offer something other than "convenience"; it is merchandising "niceness," the facsimile of proper ritual, to children who do not know how else to find it, how to make the arrangements, how to do it "right." All day and evening long on the Strip, one sees actual wedding parties, waiting under the harsh lights at a crosswalk, standing uneasily in the parking lot of the Frontier while the photographer hired by The Little Church of the West ("Wedding Place of the Stars") certifies the occasion, takes the picture: the bride in a veil and white satin pumps, the bridegroom usually in a white dinner jacket, and even an attendant or two, a sister or a best friend in hot-pink *peau de soie*, a flirtation veil, a carnation nosegay. "When I Fall in Love It Will Be Forever," the organist plays, and then a few bars of Lohengrin. The mother cries; the stepfather, awkward in his role, invites the chapel hostess to join them for a drink at the Sands. The hostess declines with a professional smile; she has already transferred her interest to the group waiting outside. One bride out, another in, and again the sign goes up on the chapel door: "One moment please—Wedding."

I sat next to one such wedding party in a Strip restaurant the last time I was in Las Vegas. The marriage had just taken place; the bride still wore her dress, the mother her corsage. A bored waiter poured out a few swallows of pink champagne ("on the house") for everyone but the bride, who was too young to be served. "You'll need something with more kick than that," the bride's father said with heavy jocularity to his new son-in-law; the ritual jokes about the wedding night had a certain Panglossian character, since the bride was clearly several months pregnant. Another round of pink champagne, this time not on the house, and the bride began to cry. "It was just as nice," she sobbed, "as I hoped and dreamed it would be."

QUESTIONS ON MEANING

1. Why do people from other states choose to get married in Nevada?
2. Why does Didion feel that in Las Vegas there is "no night and no day" (para. 2)?
3. What is Didion's THESIS in this essay? Where is it stated?
4. Does Didion seem sympathetic to her subjects?

QUESTIONS ON WRITING STRATEGY

1. To which of our senses does Didion's description primarily appeal? Why might that be?
2. What kinds of EVIDENCE does Didion use to support her impressions?
3. How would you characterize Didion's POINT OF VIEW in this essay? Note her use of pronouns—she is "one" until the middle of paragraph 4, when she appears as "I."
4. What is the essay's DOMINANT IMPRESSION?
5. **OTHER METHODS.** Over the course of her essay, Didion offers a PROCESS ANALYSIS of the Las Vegas wedding. Outline this process.

QUESTIONS ON LANGUAGE

1. Is Didion's DICTION well matched to her subject matter? How would you describe it?
2. What is the TONE of this essay? Give EXAMPLES to support your opinion.
3. What is the EFFECT of Didion's use of brand names, place names, and business slogans? Look closely at paragraphs 3 and 4. How do strings of commercial phrases help reinforce Didion's thesis?
4. What does Didion ALLUDE to with the expression "Panglossian character" (para. 5)?
5. Check a dictionary for the meanings of the following words: allegorical, venality, implausibility, imperative (para. 2); chinchilla (3); bouvardia, *peau de soie* (4); jocularity (5).

SUGGESTIONS FOR WRITING

1. **JOURNAL WRITING.** Do you find the Las Vegas wedding industry and its clients, as described by Didion, to be depressing or contemptible or funny (or all or none)? Why?
   FROM JOURNAL TO ESSAY. Write an essay, drawn from your journal entry, in which you spell out and explain your response to Didion's essay. If you find it depressing, for instance, what depresses you—the marrying couples? the people who marry them? both? Why do you think these people do what they do? Why do they depress you? What do you think these people say about American culture?
2. Didion's description of Las Vegas weddings illustrates some contemporary attitudes toward marriage. Along the same lines, write an essay describing

another ritual or social custom (for example, a graduation, military induction, presidential inauguration, religious service). What does the conduct
of this custom tell us about our attitudes toward it? Try to convey a strong
DOMINANT IMPRESSION.

3. Like Los Angeles, New York, and some other American cities, Las Vegas is
a place with a reputation. What does Las Vegas mean to you? Base your answer on firsthand experience if you can, but also on information in the media (TV, movies, books, magazines). In an essay giving specific examples,
describe the city as you understand it.

4. **CRITICAL WRITING.** Didion is well known for her detached, wryly IRONIC
tone. Reread the essay, making note of how its tone is set. Write a brief essay analyzing Didion's use of words and sentence structures to create this
tone.

5. **CONNECTIONS.** After reading Didion's essay, turn to Jessica Mitford's "Behind the Formaldehyde Curtain" (p. 228). How are the wedding and funeral industries similar or different? Use quotations from both essays to
support your comparison. (If you need help with COMPARISON AND CONTRAST,
see Chap. 4.)

JOAN DIDION ON WRITING

In "Why I Write," an essay published by the *New York Times Book
Review,* adapted from her Regents' Lecture at the University of California at Berkeley, Joan Didion writes, "Of course I stole the title for
this talk, from George Orwell [excerpts of his essay appear on pages
541–43]. One reason I stole it was that I like the sound of the words:
Why I Write. There you have three short unambiguous words that
share a sound, and the sound they share is this:

I

I

I

In many ways writing is the act of saying *I,* of imposing oneself upon
other people, of saying *listen to me, see it my way, change your mind....*"

Didion's "way," though, comes not from notions of how the world
works or should work but from its observable details. She writes, "I am
not in the least an intellectual, which is not to say that when I hear the
word 'intellectual' I reach for my gun, but only to say that I do not
think in abstracts. During the years when I was an undergraduate at
Berkeley I tried, with a kind of hopeless late-adolescent energy, to buy
some temporary visa into the world of ideas, to forge for myself a mind
that could deal with the abstract.... In short, I tried to think. I failed.
My attention veered inexorably back to the specific, to the tangible, to
what was generally considered, by everyone I knew then and for that
matter have known since, the peripheral. I would try to contemplate

the Hegelian dialectic and would find myself concentrating instead on the flowering pear tree outside my window and the particular way the petals fell on my floor."

Later in the essay, Didion writes, "During those years I was traveling on what I knew to be a very shaky passport, forged papers: I knew that I was no legitimate resident in any world of ideas. I knew I couldn't think. All I knew then was what I wasn't, and it took me some years to discover what I was.

"Which was a writer.

"By which I mean not a 'good' writer or a 'bad' writer but simply a writer, a person whose most absorbed and passionate hours are spent arranging words on pieces of paper. Had my credentials been in order I would never have become a writer. Had I been blessed with even limited access to my own mind there would have been no reason to write. I write entirely to find out what I'm thinking, what I'm looking at, what I see, and what it means. What I want and what I fear. . . . *What is going on in these pictures in my mind?*"

In the essay, Didion emphasizes that these mental pictures have a grammar. "Grammar is a piano I play by ear, since I seem to have been out of school the year the rules were mentioned. All I know about grammar is its infinite power. To shift the structure of a sentence alters the meaning of that sentence, as definitely and inflexibly as the position of a camera alters the meaning of the object photographed. Many people know about camera angles now, but not so many know about sentences. The arrangement of the words matters, and the arrangement you want can be found in the picture in your mind. The picture dictates the arrangement. The picture dictates whether this will be a sentence with or without clauses, a sentence that ends hard or a dying-fall sentence, long or short, active or passive. The picture tells you how to arrange the words and the arrangement of the words tells you, or tells me, what's going on in the picture."

FOR DISCUSSION

1. What is Didion's definition of thinking? Do you agree with it?
2. To what extent does Didion's writing support her remarks about how and why she writes?
3. What does Didion mean when she says that grammar has "infinite power"? Power to do what?

LOUISE ERDRICH

Known mainly for her fiction, LOUISE ERDRICH has been called "a sorceress with language" for her unusual, lyrical prose. Part Chippewa Indian, she was born in 1954 and raised in North Dakota. Her parents worked at the Bureau of Indian Affairs boarding school that she attended. Erdrich graduated from Dartmouth College (B.A., 1976), where she met her future husband and frequent collaborator, Michael Dorris, a writer who is also part Native American. In 1979 Erdrich received an M.A. degree in creative writing from Johns Hopkins University. Beginning in 1984 with the hugely successful *Love Medicine*, she wrote a series of four novels that follow generations of Chippewa families in North Dakota; the other volumes are *The Beet Queen* (1986), *Tracks* (1988), and *The Bingo Palace* (1994). Her publications also include two volumes of poetry, two other novels (one, *The Crown of Columbus*, cowritten with Dorris), and a children's book. Erdrich, Dorris, and their six children live in New Hampshire.

Beneath My House

This nonfiction piece first appeared in *The Georgia Review* in 1992, then in *Harper's* magazine in 1993; a slightly different version was later included in *The Bluejay's Dance* (1995), Erdrich's meditation on motherhood. With great economy and power, Erdrich uses description to transform an incident that might happen to anyone with a kitten.

It was as if the house itself had given birth. One day the floor cried 1 where I stepped on it, and I jumped back. I was near a heating vent, and when I bent and pried the cover off and thrust my hand in, I briefly grabbed a ball of fur that hissed and spat. I heard the kitten scrambling away, the tin resounding like small thunder along the length of its flight.

I went down to the basement, looking for it with a flashlight, but, 2 of course, at my step the untamed creature fled from the concrete-floored area and off into the earthen crawl space — draped with spiderwebs as thick as cotton, a place of unpeeled log beams, the underside of the house. I put out milk in a saucer. I crouched on the other side of the furnace, and I waited until I fell half-asleep. But the kitten was too young to drink from a dish and never came. Instead, she set up, from just beyond where I could catch her, a piteous crying that I could hardly stand to hear.

I went after her. The earth was moldy, a dense clay. No sun had 3 fallen here for over two centuries. I climbed over the brick retaining

127

wall and crawled toward the sound of the kitten. As I neared, as it
sensed my presence was too large to be its mother, it went silent and
scrabbled away from the reach of my hand. I brushed fur, though, and
that slight warmth filled me with what must have been a mad calm because when the creature squeezed into a bearing wall of piled stones, I
inched forward on my stomach. My back was now scraping along the
beams that bore the weight of the whole house above me. Tons and
tons of plaster, boards, appliances, and furniture. This was no crawl
space anymore. I could hardly raise my shoulders to creep forward,
could move only by shifting my hips up and down. On the edge of
panic—I had never before been in a space so tight—one thought
pressed in: if I heard the house creak, if it settled very suddenly upon
my back, my last crushed words would be, "Shit! I don't even *like* cats."
Because I *don't* like cats, just find their silken ways irresistible.

Its face popped out right in front of me, and vanished. How far   4
back did the piled rock go? If I moved a rock, would the whole house
fall on me? I reached for the kitten, missed, reached again, missed. I
tried to breathe, to be patient. Then, after a time, the kitten backed toward me, away from a clump of dirt I managed to throw at the far wall.
Its tail flicked through a space in the rocks, and I snatched it. Held it,
drew it toward me. Out it came with a squeak of terror, a series of pant-
ing comic hisses, and a whirl of claws and teeth, tiny needles it didn't
yet know how to use.

She is a pretty cat, a calico marbled evenly with orange and black.   5
Rocky. She sits near as I write, leaps into the warmth of my chair when
I leave, and is jealous of the baby.

The night after I pulled her from the house, the darkness pressed   6
down on me until I woke. I'd swum weightlessly into a smaller and
smaller space. What the body remembers of birth it anticipates as
death. In the house of my dreams the basement is the most fearful: the
awful place filled with water, the place of both comfort and death. I fear
in particular the small space, the earth closing in on me, the house like
a mother settling its cracked bones and plumbing.

That afternoon, from underneath, I had heard the house all around   7
me like an old familiar body. I hadn't told anybody else that I was going
after the kitten, so nobody knew I was below. The normal sounds of my
family's daily life were magnified. Their steps trailed and traveled
around me, boomed in my ears. Their voices jolted me, their words
loud but meaningless, warped by their travel through the walls and
beams. Water flowed through invisible pipes around me, hitched and
gurgled. It was like being dead, or unborn. I hadn't thought about it
then, but now I could clearly see part of me, the husk of myself, still

buried against the east wall: a person sacrificed to ensure the good luck of a temple, a kind of house god, a woman lying down there, still, an empty double.

QUESTIONS ON MEANING

1. The first line of this essay is "It was as if the house itself had given birth." What does this METAPHOR refer to? Where does it reappear in the essay? How does it change?
2. Why does Erdrich decide to follow the kitten?
3. What does Erdrich mean when she says her "empty double" is still lying underneath her house (para. 7)?

QUESTIONS ON WRITING STRATEGY

1. What is the DOMINANT IMPRESSION of Erdrich's description?
2. Why is Erdrich so careful to build the image of the house as weighty (para. 3)?
3. Why doesn't Erdrich speculate about where the kitten came from?
4. **OTHER METHODS.** In describing the basement as "the place of comfort and death" (para. 6), Erdrich sets up a COMPARISON AND CONTRAST between the reassuring and the scary. List qualities of the basement that contribute to both feelings.

QUESTIONS ON LANGUAGE

1. Make sure you know the meanings of the following words: resounding (para. 1); piteous (2); scrabbled (3); husk (7).
2. In paragraph 3 Erdrich describes herself as filled with a "mad calm." What does this contradictory IMAGE mean in this context?
3. How does Erdrich use language to build the metaphor equating the basement with the womb?
4. If you don't know what a "retaining wall" is (para. 3), look it up. What is significant about Erdrich's going over the retaining wall to follow the kitten?

SUGGESTIONS FOR WRITING

1. **JOURNAL WRITING.** Indulge in your own fears. What place frightens you? Why? (If you need inspiration, look back at Erdrich's para. 6, where she explains how in the house of her dreams she fears the "small space, the earth closing in on me.")
   FROM JOURNAL TO ESSAY. When have you come closest to entering the place you fear? Using lots of concrete details and images, describe facing, or not facing, your fears. Did you learn anything from the experience?

2. Explore the connections between a family and its home. Using a real EX-
   AMPLE (your own or another family's), consider how the home protects the
   family (and from what) and how the home reflects the family (for instance,
   chaotic or neat, spacious or tight, rooms matching individuals' personalities).
3. **CRITICAL WRITING.** Erdrich writes in paragraph 6, "What the body remembers of birth it anticipates as death." This statement suggests the presence
   of a human unconscious that understands and anticipates things of which
   we may not be consciously aware. How convincingly does Erdrich's essay
   support this suggestion? Write an essay using EVIDENCE from the essay to support your answer.
4. **CONNECTIONS.** In "Homeless" (p. 149) Anna Quindlen says (para. 4): "I
   love my home. . . . I love dumb things about it: the hot-water heater, the
   plastic rack you drain the dishes in, the roof over my head, which occasionally leaks. And yet it is precisely these dumb things that make it what
   it is—a place of certainty, stability, predictability, privacy, for me and for
   my family." Erdrich seems to share Quindlen's feelings, but her experience
   in the basement causes contrasting feelings as well. In a brief essay, examine the cracks that appear in Erdrich's sense of her house's protectiveness.
   How is the house threatening as well?

LOUISE ERDRICH ON WRITING

Louise Erdrich and her husband, the writer Michael Dorris, collaborate thoroughly on each other's writing and speak freely of their collaboration. Thus it seems appropriate to hear from them both on this
remarkable process. In a joint interview with Michael Schumacher for
Writer's Digest, the two writers explained their way of working together.

ERDRICH: "One person—the one whose name is to be on the book
—will write the draft, will actually be confronted with those blank
pages. But we have this continual process of talking about the work:
We get ideas and discuss them, often before we write anything down."

DORRIS: "It's like that all the way through. 'Don't use this line.' Or,
'How about if such and such happens?' Or, 'How about if this word
comes in?'. . . As we've worked on more and more books together, it's
become harder to separate one or another's contribution. . . . The point
to make is that ours isn't just an editing relationship."

ERDRICH: "It's terribly important to have someone who cares about
the work as much as I do, who is involved in the same way. We're probably a lot harder on each other than other editors are with writers because we really have more at stake in each other's work. We each tend
to be quite ruthless about our ideas for the direction of the other's
books. That can be very difficult sometimes because it's very hard to tell
someone, 'This doesn't work.'. . . Marriage is a process of coming to trust

the other person over the years, and it's the same thing with our writing. I started out being very wary of collaboration and working together, but I trusted it and trusted it, and when I would have trouble with it, I would really look at the work and I'd realize that it was better for the efforts. In a lot of ways, I'd have to sacrifice the ego for the work."

Erdrich discussed her collaboration with Dorris elsewhere as well. With Miriam Berkley of *Publishers Weekly*, she addressed the skeptics. "Some people don't believe it's possible to collaborate that closely, although we both have solitude and private anguish as well. You develop this very personal relationship with your work, and it seems fragile; you're afraid to destroy it. But I trust Michael enough so that we can talk about it. And every time I've been afraid to open it up, it has always been better for the work."

FOR DISCUSSION

1. What, according to Erdrich, is the advantage of her collaboration with her husband?
2. What good experiences have you had with collaboration, in writing class or elsewhere, either giving or taking suggestions? When collaboration hasn't worked, why do you think it failed?

MARGARET ATWOOD

Born in 1939 in Ottawa, Canada, MARGARET ATWOOD is a poet, fiction writer, and literary critic well known for her refined imagery and exploration of conflicts between individuals and cultures. She graduated from the University of Toronto (B.A., 1961) and Radcliffe College (M.A., 1962) and at Harvard University did much of the work for a Ph.D. in Victorian literature and Gothic romances. Her poems were first published in the early 1960s, and to date she has produced eleven collections of poetry. Volumes of selected poems appeared in 1976 and 1987; the most recent collection is *Morning in the Buried House* (1995). Well respected as a poet, Atwood is probably more widely known as a novelist: Her eight novels include *The Edible Woman* (1967), *The Handmaid's Tale* (1985), *Cat's Eye* (1988), and *The Robber Bride* (1993). As a Canadian and a critic, Atwood has focused on Canadian literature, publishing *Survival: A Thematic Guide to Canadian Literature* (1972) and anthologies of Canadian poems and stories. She lives in Toronto.

Bored

Atwood's father studied forest insects for the Canadian government and was, as Atwood has put it, "a very woodsy man." This poem about time spent with her father when she was young reveals the contradictory responses of the girl and the woman she became.

All those times I was bored
out of my mind. Holding the log
while he sawed it. Holding
the string while he measured, boards,
distances between things, or pounded   5
stakes into the ground forrows and rows
of lettuces and beets, which I then (bored)
weeded. Or sat in the back
of the car, or sat still in boats,
sat, sat, while at the prow, stern, wheel   10
he drove, steered, paddled. It
wasn't even boredom, it was looking,
looking hard and up close at the small
details. Myopia. The worn gunwales,
the intricate twill of the seat   15
cover. The acid crumbs of loam, the granular
pink rock, its igneous veins, the sea-fans

of dry moss, the blackish and then the greying
bristles on the back of his neck.
Sometimes he would whistle, sometimes   20
I would. The boring rhythm of doing
things over and over, carrying
the wood, drying
the dishes. Such minutiae. It's what
the animals spend most of their time at,   25
ferrying the sand, grain by grain, from their tunnels,
shuffling the leaves in their burrows. He pointed
such things out, and I would look
at the whorled texture of his square finger, earth under
the nail. Why do I remember it as sunnier   30
all the time then, although it more often
rained, and more birdsong?
I could hardly wait to get
the hell out of there to
anywhere else. Perhaps though   35
boredom is happier. It is for dogs or
groundhogs. Now I wouldn't be bored.
Now I would know too much.
Now I would know.

QUESTIONS ON MEANING

1. Atwood's "Bored" centers on the emotion of its title. What does the speaker "know" about boredom at the end that she didn't know at the beginning? What does your answer tell you about Atwood's PURPOSE in writing this poem?
2. Lines 11 and 12 mark a shift in the poem from doing to looking: "It / wasn't even boredom, it was looking." PARAPHRASE these lines. What is "it" in these lines?
3. Why is the question the speaker asks herself in lines 30–32 important? What is the TONE of the poem before and after this question?

QUESTIONS ON WRITING STRATEGY

1. Atwood uses repetition and restatement to build her poem—most obviously, variations of the word *bored*. Find examples of repetition and restatement, whether a word, verb form, image, or idea. What function do these examples serve in the poem?
2. The first mention of a male figure is in line 3—the speaker is holding a log

"while he sawed it." What EVIDENCE from the poem suggests that this "he" is the speaker's father? Why has he been included in the poem?

3. In lines 24–26 the speaker suggests that carrying wood and drying dishes resemble ants carrying grains of sand or groundhogs arranging their nests. What do you make of this COMPARISON?

4. **OTHER METHODS.** Atwood uses many concrete EXAMPLES to explain an abstract concept. Pick out the images, and explain why they are important to the concept.

QUESTIONS ON LANGUAGE

1. Make sure you know the meanings of the following words: prow, stern (line 10): gunwales (14); twill (15); loam, granular (16); igneous (17); minutiae (24); whorled (29).

2. Look up the word *myopia* (line 14). Why do you think Atwood uses this word?

3. Consider the level of the DICTION in this poem. How does word choice help us see the speaker simultaneously as both a child and an adult?

SUGGESTIONS FOR WRITING

1. **JOURNAL WRITING.** The central idea in "Bored" could be rephrased as a CLICHÉ: "If only I had it to do over again." Like many clichés, this one is often repeated because it captures the way many people feel about their past life. Do you feel sympathy for the speaker in this poem, or do you think she should have been able to appreciate what she had when she had it? **FROM JOURNAL TO ESSAY.** Pretend that you are a judge and the speaker in "Bored" is on trial. Write an essay in which you maintain either that she deserves a second chance to relive her childhood or that she doesn't. Use your response in your journal entry and evidence from the poem (treating the poem as testimony from the speaker). Keep your focus on the poem, not on your own personal memories.

2. Have you ever tried to write a poem? Try it now, choosing, like Atwood, an emotion. Don't worry too much about meter and rhyme, but do think carefully about your choice of words and images, building the poem through description.

3. **CRITICAL WRITING.** The last two lines of "Bored" are "Now I would know too much./Now I would know." Why does the speaker repeat herself, and why is her new knowledge important? Write an essay in which you answer these questions in the context of the poem. This will require a careful line-by-line reading of the poem so that you can explain what's happening, why certain words and ideas are important, how the poem moves. Write a paper that moves through your reading (which may take more than one draft to work out fully) and concludes with your explanation of the last two lines.

4. **CONNECTIONS.** Read Richard Rodriguez's essay "Aria: A Memoir of a Bilingual Childhood" (p. 570). Rodriguez writes about the private loss and public gain involved in assimilation and concludes by saying, "If I rehearse here the changes in my private life after my Americanization, it is finally to

emphasize a public gain. The loss implies the gain" (para. 40). The speaker in "Bored" is dealing with loss and gain, too. Write an essay in which you compare and contrast the nature of the loss and gain that Atwood's speaker and Rodriguez experience. Who loses more? Who gains more? Do they think about loss and gain in the same way?

MARGARET ATWOOD ON WRITING

Margaret Atwood decided to be a writer in her teens, but her way was not clear to her until much later. In "Great Unexpectations," an essay she wrote for *Ms.* magazine in 1987, Atwood confesses that she "was scared to death" by her decision. She thought she would end up "writing masterpieces in a freezing-cold garret at night, and getting TB, like [the English poet] Keats." The alternative, it seemed, was the traditional view of Canadian women's writing, equivalent to "flower painting and making roses out of wool. As one friend of my mother's put it, trying to take a cheerful view of my eccentricity, 'Well, that's nice, dear, because you can do it at home, can't you?' She was right, as it turned out, but at that moment she aroused nothing but loathing in my adolescent soul. Home, hell. It was garret or nothing. What did she think I was, inauthentic?"

Atwood considered her fate. "My choices were between excellence and doom on the one hand, and mediocrity and coziness on the other. I gritted my teeth, set my face to the wind, gave up double-dating, and wore horn-rims and a scowl so I would not be mistaken for a puffball." She resolved, she says, to "live by myself in a suitably painted attic (black) and have lovers whom I would dispose of in appropriate ways, though I drew the line at bloodshed....I would never, never own an automatic washer-dryer."

As it happened, Atwood's attic life was of short duration, and she eventually settled into domestic life—house, family, garden, washer-dryer. "This state of affairs was not achieved without struggle," she says, but the stereotypes about writers, and especially woman writers, reside now outside herself, in the minds of some reviewers.

FOR DISCUSSION

1. What was the choice Atwood believed she faced as a young writer? Why? How did she resolve the conflict?
2. Search your mind for any stereotypes of writers that may be lurking there. Do they, or should they, live a certain way? Do they fit a certain personality type? What causes these images? Does Atwood strengthen or dispel any of them?

ADDITIONAL WRITING TOPICS

Description

1. This is an in-class writing experiment. Describe another person in the room so clearly and unmistakably that when you read your description aloud, your subject will be recognized. (Be OBJECTIVE. No insulting descriptions, please!)

2. Write a paragraph describing one subject from *each* of the following categories. It will be up to you to make the general subject refer to a particular person, place, or thing. Write at least one paragraph as an OBJECTIVE description and at least one as a SUBJECTIVE description.

   PERSON
   A friend or roommate
   A typical rap, heavy metal, or country musician
   One of your parents
   An elderly person you know
   A prominent politician
   A historical figure

   PLACE
   An office
   A classroom
   A college campus
   A vacation spot
   A hospital emergency room
   A forest

   THING
   A dentist's drill
   A painting or photograph
   A foggy day
   A season of the year
   A musical instrument
   A train

3. In a brief essay, describe your ideal place: an apartment, a bookstore, a dorm room, a vacation spot, a classroom, a restaurant, a gym, a supermarket or convenience store, a garden, a golf course. With concrete details, try to make the ideal seem actual.

Narration and Description

4. Use a combination of narration and description to develop any one of the following topics:

Your first day on the job
Your first day at college
Returning to an old neighborhood
Getting lost
A brush with a celebrity
Delivering bad (or good) news

3

EXAMPLE

Pointing to Instances

THE METHOD

"There have been many women runners of distinction," a writer begins, and quickly goes on, "among them Joan Benoit, Grete Waitz, Florence Griffith Joyner...."

You have just seen examples at work. An EXAMPLE (from the Latin *exemplum:* "one thing selected from among many") is an instance that reveals a whole type. By selecting an example, a writer shows the nature or character of the group from which it is taken. In a written essay, examples will often serve to illustrate a general statement, or GENERAL-IZATION. Here, for instance, the writer Linda Wolfe makes a point about the food fetishes of Roman emperors (Domitian and Claudius ruled in the first century A.D.).

> The emperors used their gastronomical concerns to indicate their contempt of the country and the whole task of governing it. Domitian humiliated his cabinet by forcing them to attend him at his villa to help solve a serious problem. When they arrived he kept them waiting for hours. The problem, it finally appeared, was that the emperor had just purchased a giant fish, too large for any dish he owned, and he needed the learned brains of his ministers to decide

whether the fish should be minced or whether a larger pot should be sought. The emperor Claudius one day rode hurriedly to the Senate and demanded they deliberate the importance of a life without pork. Another time he sat in his tribunal ostensibly administering justice but actually allowing the litigants to argue and orate while he grew dreamy, interrupting the discussions only to announce, "Meat pies are wonderful. We shall have them for dinner."

Wolfe might have allowed the opening sentence of her paragraph —the TOPIC SENTENCE—to remain a vague generalization. Instead, she supports it with three examples, each a brief story of an emperor's contemptuous behavior. With these examples, Wolfe not only explains and supports her generalization but also animates it.

The method of giving examples—of illustrating what you're saying with a "for instance"—is not merely helpful to practically all kinds of writing, it is indispensable. Bad writers—those who bore us, or lose us completely—often have an ample supply of ideas; their trouble is that they never pull their ideas down out of the clouds. A dull writer, for instance, might declare, "The emperors used food to humiliate their governments," and then, instead of giving examples, go on, "They also manipulated their families," or something—adding still another large, unillustrated idea. Specific examples are *needed* elements in good prose. Not only do they make ideas understandable, but they also keep readers awake. (The previous paragraphs have tried—by giving examples from Linda Wolfe and from "a dull writer"—to illustrate this point.)

THE PROCESS

The Generalization

Examples illustrate a generalization, such as Linda Wolfe's opening statement about the Roman emperors, and any example essay is bound to have a generalization as its THESIS STATEMENT. Here are a few examples from the essays in this chapter:

> Sometimes I think we would be better off [in dealing with social problems] if we forgot about the broad strokes and concentrated on the details. (Anna Quindlen, "Homeless")

> It is a strangely pleasurable thing to read your own words from widely varying periods and phases of your life. (Merrill Markoe, "The Day I Turned Sarcastic")

> That first encounter, and those that followed, signified that a vast, unnerving gulf lay between nighttime pedestrians—particularly women—and me. (Brent Staples, "Black Men and Public Space")

Such a generalization forms the backbone, the central idea, of an essay developed by example. With specifics, the idea comes to earth for readers.

Example   **141**

The Examples

Where do you find examples? In anything you know—or care to learn. Start close to home. Seek examples in your own immediate knowledge and experience. When assigned an elephant-sized subject that you think you know nothing about—ethical dilemmas, for instance—rummage your memory and you may discover that you know more than you thought. In what ethical dilemmas have you ever found yourself? Deciding whether or not to date your friend's fiancé (or fiancée) when your friend is out of town? Being tempted to pilfer from the jelly jar of a small boy's Kool-Aid stand when you need a quarter for a bus? No doubt you can supply your own examples. It is the method—exemplifying—that matters. To bring some huge and ethereal concept down to earth may just set your expository faculties galloping over the plains of your own life to the sound of "hi-ho, Silver!" For different examples, you can explore your conversations with others, your studies, and the storehouse of information you have gathered from books, newspapers, magazines, radio, and TV, and from popular hearsay: proverbs and sayings, bits of wisdom you've heard voiced in your family, folklore, popular song.

Now and again, you may feel an irresistible temptation to make up an example out of thin air. This procedure is risky, but can work wonderfully—if, that is, you have a wonder-working imagination. When Henry David Thoreau, in *Walden*, attacks Americans' smug pride in the achievements of nineteenth-century science and industry, he wants to illustrate that kind of invention or discovery "which distracts our attention from serious things." And so he makes up the examples—farfetched at the time, but pointed—of a transatlantic speaking tube and what it might convey: "We are eager to tunnel under the Atlantic and bring the Old World some weeks nearer to the New; but perchance the first news that will leak through into the broad, flapping American ear will be that the Princess Adelaide has the whooping cough." (Thoreau would be appalled at our immersion in the British Royal Family via just the sort of communication he imagined.)

Thoreau's examples (and the sarcastic phrase about the American ear) bespeak genius; but, of course, not every writer can be a Thoreau—or needs to be. A hypothetical example may well be better than no example at all; yet, as a rule, an example from fact or experience is likely to carry more weight. Suppose you have to write about the benefits—any benefits—that recent science has conferred upon the nation. You might imagine one such benefit: the prospect of one day being able to vacation in outer space and drift about in free-fall like a soap bubble. That imagined benefit would be all right, but it is obviously a conjecture that you dreamed up without going to the library. Do a little digging in recent books and magazines (for the latter, with the aid of the *Readers' Guide to Periodical Literature*). Your reader will feel better informed to be told that science—specifically, the NASA space program—has produced useful inventions. You add:

> Among these are the smoke detector, originally developed as Skylab equipment; the inflatable air bag to protect drivers and pilots, designed to cushion astronauts in splashdowns; a walking chair that enables paraplegics to mount stairs and travel over uneven ground, derived from the moonwalkers' surface buggy; the technique of cryosurgery, the removal of cancerous tissue by fast freezing.

By using specific examples like these, you render the idea of "benefits to society" more concrete and more definite. Such examples are not prettifications of your essay; they are necessary if you are to hold your readers' attention and convince them that you are worth listening to.

When giving examples, you'll find other methods useful. Sometimes, as in the paragraph by Linda Wolfe, an example takes the form of a NARRATIVE (Chap. 1): a brief story, an ANECDOTE, or a case history. Sometimes an example embodies a vivid DESCRIPTION of a person, place, or thing (Chap. 2).

Lazy writers think, "Oh well, I can't come up with any example here—I'll just leave it to the reader to find one." The flaw in this ASSUMPTION is that the reader may be as lazy as the writer. As a result, a perfectly good idea may be left suspended in the stratosphere. The linguist and writer S. I. Hayakawa tells the story of a professor who, in teaching a philosophy course, spent a whole semester on the theory of beauty. When students asked him for a few examples of beautiful paintings, symphonies, or works of nature, he refused, saying, "We are interested in principles, not in particulars." The professor himself may well have been interested in principles, but it is a safe bet that his classroom resounded with snores. In written EXPOSITION, it is undoubtedly the particulars—the pertinent examples—that keep a reader awake and having a good time, and taking in the principles besides.

CHECKLIST FOR REVISING AN EXAMPLE ESSAY

✔ **GENERALIZATION.** What general statement do your examples illustrate? Will it be clear to readers what ties the examples together?

✔ **SUPPORT.** Do you have enough examples to establish your generalization, or will readers be left needing more?

Example   **143**

✔ **SPECIFICS.** Are your examples detailed? Does each capture some aspects of the generalization?

✔ **RELEVANCE.** Do all your examples relate to your generalization? Should any be cut because they go off-track?

EXAMPLE IN A PARAGRAPH:
TWO ILLUSTRATIONS

Using Example to Write About Television

To simulate reality must be among television's main concerns, for the airwaves glow with programs that create a smooth and enjoyable imitation of life. Take, for example, | *Generalization to be illustrated*

wrestling. Stripped to their essentials (and to their gaudy tights), the heroes and villains of TV wrestling matches parade before us like walking abstractions: the Sly Braggart, the Well-Barbered Athlete, the Evil Russian. Larger than life, wrestlers are also louder. They seldom speak; they bellow instead. Part of our enjoyment comes from recognizing the phoniness of it all: When blows fail to land, the intended recipients groan anyway. | *First example, with its own examples of wrestlers*

Some TV simulations are less obvious than wrestling: for instance, the long-running *People's Court.* "What you're about to see is real," a voice-over tells us. In fact, the litigants are not professional actors but people who have filed to appear in a small claims court. Enticed to drop their complaints and instead appear on *People's Court* before the admirably fair Judge Wapner, they play themselves and are rewarded with instant fame and a paycheck. We enjoy the illusion that a genuine legal dispute can be as dramatic as a soap opera. And happily, it can always be settled in exactly ten minutes, between commercials. | *Second example*

— Michael Sorkin, "Faking It,"
in *Watching Television*, ed. Todd Gitlin

Using Example in an Academic Discipline

The primary function of the market is to bring together suppliers and demanders so that they can trade with one another. Buyers and sellers do not necessarily have to be in face-to-face contact; they can signal their desires and intentions through various intermediaries. For example, the | *Generalization to be illustrated*

demand for green beans in California is not expressed directly by the green bean consumers to the green bean growers. People who want green beans buy them at a grocery store; the store orders them from a vegetable wholesaler; the wholesaler buys them from a bean cooperative, whose | *Single extended example*

manager tells local farmers of the size of the current demand
for green beans. The demanders of green beans are able to
signal their demand schedule to the original suppliers, the
farmers who raise the beans, without any personal communication between the two parties.

—Lewis C. Solmon, *Microeconomics*

BARBARA LAZEAR ASCHER

BARBARA LAZEAR ASCHER was born in 1946 and educated at Bennington College and Cardozo School of Law. She practiced law for two years in a private firm, where she found herself part of a power structure in which those on top resembled "the two-year-old with the biggest plastic pail and shovel on the beach. It's a life of nervous guardianship." Ascher quit the law to devote herself to writing, to explore, as she says, "what really matters." Her essays have appeared in the *New York Times*, the *Yale Review*, *Vogue*, and other periodicals and have been collected in *Playing After Dark* (1986) and *The Habit of Loving* (1989). She is a contributing editor of *Self* magazine. Her most recent book, *Landscape Without Gravity: A Memoir of Grief* (1993), is about her brother's death from AIDS. Ascher lives with her family in New York City.

On Compassion

Ascher often writes about life in New York City, where human problems sometimes seem larger and more stubborn than in other places. But this essay concerns an experience most of us have had, wherever we live: responding to those who need help. First published in *Elle* magazine in 1988, the essay was later reprinted in *The Habit of Loving*. (The essay following this one, Anna Quindlen's "Homeless," addresses the same issue.)

The man's grin is less the result of circumstance than dreams or 1 madness. His buttonless shirt, with one sleeve missing, hangs outside the waist of his baggy trousers. Carefully plaited dreadlocks bespeak a better time, long ago. As he crosses Manhattan's Seventy-ninth Street, his gait is the shuffle of the forgotten ones held in place by gravity rather than plans. On the corner of Madison Avenue, he stops before a blond baby in an Aprica stroller. The baby's mother waits for the light to change and her hands close tighter on the stroller's handle as she sees the man approach.

The others on the corner, five men and women waiting for the 2 crosstown bus, look away. They daydream a bit and gaze into the weak rays of November light. A man with a briefcase lifts and lowers the shiny toe of his right shoe, watching the light reflect, trying to catch and balance it, as if he could hold and make it his, to ease the heavy gray of coming January, February, and March. The winter months that will send snow around the feet, calves, and knees of the grinning man as he heads for the shelter of Grand Central or Pennsylvania Station.

But for now, in this last gasp of autumn warmth, he is still. His eyes   3
fix on the baby. The mother removes her purse from her shoulder and
rummages through its contents: lipstick, a lace handkerchief, an address book. She finds what she's looking for and passes a folded dollar
over her child's head to the man who stands and stares even though the
light has changed and traffic navigates about his hips.

His hands continue to dangle at his sides. He does not know his   4
part. He does not know that acceptance of the gift and gratitude are
what make this transaction complete. The baby, weary of the unwavering stare, pulls its blanket over its head. The man does not look away.
Like a bridegroom waiting at the altar, his eyes pierce the white veil.

The mother grows impatient and pushes the stroller before her,   5
bearing the dollar like a cross. Finally, a black hand rises and closes
around green.

Was it fear or compassion that motivated the gift?   6

Up the avenue, at Ninety-first Street, there is a small French bread   7
shop where you can sit and eat a buttery, overpriced croissant and wash
it down with rich cappuccino. Twice when I have stopped here to stave
hunger or stay the cold, twice as I have sat and read and felt the warm
rush of hot coffee and milk, an old man has wandered in and stood inside the entrance. He wears a stained blanket pulled up to his chin, and
a woolen hood pulled down to his gray, bushy eyebrows. As he stands,
the scent of stale cigarettes and urine fills the small, overheated room.

The owner of the shop, a moody French woman, emerges from the   8
kitchen with steaming coffee in a Styrofoam cup, and a small paper bag
of...of what? Yesterday's bread? Today's croissant? He accepts the offering as silently as he came, and is gone.

Twice I have witnessed this, and twice I have wondered, what com-   9
pels this woman to feed this man? Pity? Care? Compassion? Or does she
simply want to rid her shop of his troublesome presence? If expulsion
were her motivation she would not reward his arrival with gifts of food.
Most proprietors do not. They chase the homeless from their midst
with expletives and threats.

As winter approaches, the mayor of New York City is moving the   10
homeless off the streets and into Bellevue Hospital. The New York
Civil Liberties Union is watchful. They question whether the rights of
these people who live in our parks and doorways are being violated by
involuntary hospitalization.

I think the mayor's notion is humane, but I fear it is something else   11
as well. Raw humanity offends our sensibilities. We want to protect
ourselves from an awareness of rags with voices that make no sense and
scream forth in inarticulate rage. We do not wish to be reminded of the
tentative state of our own well-being and sanity. And so, the troublesome presence is removed from the awareness of the electorate.

Like other cities, there is much about Manhattan now that resem- 12
bles Dickensian London. Ladies in high-heeled shoes pick their way
through poverty and madness. You hear more cocktail party complaints
than usual, "I just can't take New York anymore." Our citizens dream of
the open spaces of Wyoming, the manicured exclusivity of Hobe
Sound.

And yet, it may be that these are the conditions that finally give 13
birth to empathy, the mother of compassion. We cannot deny the existence of the helpless as their presence grows. It is impossible to insulate
ourselves against what is at our very doorstep. I don't believe that one
is born compassionate. Compassion is not a character trait like a sunny
disposition. It must be learned, and it is learned by having adversity at
our windows, coming through the gates of our yards, the walls of our
towns, adversity that becomes so familiar that we begin to identify and
empathize with it.

For the ancient Greeks, drama taught and reinforced compassion 14
within a society. The object of Greek tragedy was to inspire empathy in
the audience so that the common response to the hero's fall was:
"There, but for the grace of God, go I." Could it be that this was the response of the mother who offered the dollar, the French woman who
gave the food? Could it be that the homeless, like those ancients, are
reminding us of our common humanity? Of course, there is a difference.
This play doesn't end — and the players can't go home.

QUESTIONS ON MEANING

1. What do the two men in Ascher's essay exemplify?
2. What is Ascher's THESIS? What is her PURPOSE?
3. What solution to homelessness is introduced in paragraph 10? What does
   Ascher think of this possibility?
4. How do you interpret Ascher's last sentence? Is she optimistic or pessimistic about whether people will learn compassion?

QUESTIONS ON WRITING STRATEGY

1. Which comes first, the GENERALIZATIONS or the supporting examples? Why
   has Ascher chosen this order?
2. What assumptions does the author make about her AUDIENCE?
3. Why do the other people at the bus stop look away (para. 2)? What does
   Ascher's description of their activities say about them?
4. **OTHER METHODS.** Ascher explores CAUSES AND EFFECTS. Do you agree with
   her that exposure to others' helplessness increases our compassion? Why, or
   why not?

QUESTIONS ON LANGUAGE

1. What is the difference between empathy and compassion? Why does Ascher say that "empathy [is] the mother of compassion" (para. 13)?
2. Find definitions for the following words: plaited, dreadlocks, bespeaks (para. 1); stave, stay (7); expletives (9); inarticulate, electorate (11).
3. What are the implications of Ascher's ALLUSION to "Dickensian London" (para. 12)?
4. Examine the language Ascher uses to describe the two homeless men. Is it OBJECTIVE? sympathetic? negative?

SUGGESTIONS FOR WRITING

1. **JOURNAL WRITING.** Write about a personal experience with misfortune. Have you needed to beg on the street, been evicted from an apartment, had to scrounge for food? Have you worked in a soup kitchen, been asked for money by beggars, helped out in a city hospital?
   FROM JOURNAL TO ESSAY. Write an essay on the experience you explored in your journal, using examples to convey the effect the experience had on you.
2. Write an essay on the problem of homelessness in your town or city. Use examples to support your view of the problem and a possible solution.
3. Ascher refers to the efforts of New York City to move the homeless off the streets (para. 10). In October 1987, one of New York's homeless, Joyce Brown, was taken off the sidewalk where she lived to Bellevue Hospital. The American Civil Liberties Union sued on her behalf, claiming that she was not a danger to herself or to others—the grounds for involuntary hospitalization. Although Brown was eventually released in January 1988, the issue of the city's right to hospitalize her was never resolved. Consult the *New York Times Index* and the *Times* itself for news articles and editorials on this situation. Write an essay arguing for or against Joyce Brown's freedom to live on the street, supporting your argument with evidence from the newspaper and from your own experience.
4. **CRITICAL WRITING.** In her last paragraph, Ascher mentions but does not address another key difference between the characters in Greek tragedy and the homeless on today's streets: The former were "heroes"—gods and goddesses, kings and queens—whereas the latter are placeless, poor, anonymous, even reviled. Does this difference negate Ascher's comparison between Greek theatergoers and ourselves or her larger point about how compassion is learned? Answer in a brief essay, saying why or why not.
5. **CONNECTIONS.** The next essay, Anna Quindlen's "Homeless," also uses examples to make a point about homelessness. What are some of the differences in the examples each writer uses? In a brief essay, explore whether and how these differences create different TONES in the two works.

ANNA QUINDLEN

ANNA QUINDLEN was born in 1952 and graduated from Barnard College in 1974. She worked as a reporter for the *New York Post* and the *New York Times* before taking over the *Times*'s "About New York" column, serving as the paper's deputy metropolitan editor, and in 1986 creating her own weekly column, "Life in the Thirties." Many of the essays from this popular column were collected in *Living Out Loud* (1988). Between 1989 and 1994 Quindlen wrote a twice-weekly op-ed column for the *Times*, on social and political issues. The columns earned her the Pulitzer Prize in 1992, and many of them were collected in *Thinking Out Loud: On the Personal, the Political, the Public, and the Private* (1993). Quindlen has also published two successful novels, *Object Lessons* (1991) and *One True Thing* (1994).

Homeless

In this essay from *Living Out Loud*, Quindlen explores the same topic as Barbara Lazear Ascher (p. 145), but with a different slant. Typically for Quindlen, she mingles a reporter's respect for details with a passionate regard for life.

Her name was Ann, and we met in the Port Authority Bus Termi- 1 nal several Januarys ago. I was doing a story on homeless people. She said I was wasting my time talking to her; she was just passing through, although she'd been passing through for more than two weeks. To prove to me that this was true, she rummaged through a tote bag and a manila envelope and finally unfolded a sheet of typing paper and brought out her photographs.

They were not pictures of family, or friends, or even a dog or cat, its 2 eyes brown-red in the flashbulb's light. They were pictures of a house. It was like a thousand houses in a hundred towns, not suburb, not city, but somewhere in between, with aluminum siding and a chain-link fence, a narrow driveway running up to a one-car garage and a patch of backyard. The house was yellow. I looked on the back for a date or a name, but neither was there. There was no need for discussion. I knew what she was trying to tell me, for it was something I had often felt. She was not adrift, alone, anonymous, although her bags and her raincoat with the grime shadowing its creases had made me believe she was. She had a house, or at least once upon a time had had one. Inside were curtains, a couch, a stove, potholders. You are where you live. She was somebody.

I've never been very good at looking at the big picture, taking the 3 global view, and I've always been a person with an overactive sense of place, the legacy of an Irish grandfather. So it is natural that the thing that seems most wrong with the world to me right now is that there are so many people with no homes. I'm not simply talking about shelter from the elements, or three square meals a day or a mailing address to which the welfare people can send the check—although I know that all these are important for survival. I'm talking about a home, about precisely those kinds of feelings that have wound up in cross-stitch and French knots on samplers over the years.

Home is where the heart is. There's no place like it. I love my home 4 with a ferocity totally out of proportion to its appearance or location. I love dumb things about it: the hot-water heater, the plastic rack you drain dishes in, the roof over my head, which occasionally leaks. And yet it is precisely those dumb things that make it what it is—a place of certainty, stability, predictability, privacy, for me and for my family. It is where I live. What more can you say about a place than that? That is everything.

Yet it is something that we have been edging away from gradually 5 during my lifetime and the lifetimes of my parents and grandparents. There was a time when where you lived often was where you worked and where you grew the food you ate and even where you were buried. When that era passed, where you lived at least was where your parents had lived and where you would live with your children when you became enfeebled. Then, suddenly where you lived was where you lived for three years, until you could move on to something else and something else again.

And so we have come to something else again, to children who do 6 not understand what it means to go to their rooms because they have never had a room, to men and women whose fantasy is a wall they can paint a color of their own choosing, to old people reduced to sitting on molded plastic chairs, their skin blue-white in the lights of a bus station, who pull pictures of houses out of their bags. Homes have stopped being homes. Now they are real estate.

People find it curious that those without homes would rather sleep 7 sitting up on benches or huddled in doorways than go to shelters. Certainly some prefer to do so because they are emotionally ill, because they have been locked in before and they are damned if they will be locked in again. Others are afraid of the violence and trouble they may find there. But some seem to want something that is not available in shelters, and they will not compromise, not for a cot, or oatmeal, or a shower with special soap that kills the bugs. "One room," a woman with a baby who was sleeping on her sister's floor, once told me, "painted blue." That was the crux of it; not size or location, but pride of ownership. Painted blue.

This is a difficult problem, and some wise and compassionate 8
people are working hard at it. But in the main I think we work around it,
just as we walk around it when it is lying on the sidewalk or sitting in the
bus terminal—the problem, that is. It has been customary to take
people's pain and lessen our own participation in it by turning it into an
issue, not a collection of human beings. We turn an adjective into a
noun: the poor, not poor people; the homeless, not Ann or the man who
lives in the box or the woman who sleeps on the subway grate.

Sometimes I think we would be better off if we forgot about the 9
broad strokes and concentrated on the details. Here is a woman without a bureau. There is a man with no mirror, no wall to hang it on.
They are not the homeless. They are people who have no homes. No
drawer that holds the spoons. No window to look out upon the world.
My God. That is everything.

QUESTIONS ON MEANING

1. What is Quindlen's THESIS?
2. What distinction is Quindlen making in her CONCLUSION with the sentences
   "They are not the homeless. They are people who have no homes"?
3. Why does Quindlen feel a home is so important?

QUESTIONS ON WRITING STRATEGY

1. Why do you think Quindlen begins with the story of Ann? How else might
   Quindlen have begun her essay?
2. What is the EFFECT of Quindlen's examples of her own home?
3. What key ASSUMPTIONS does the author make about her AUDIENCE? Are the
   assumptions reasonable? Where does she specifically address an assumption
   that might undermine her view?
4. **OTHER METHODS.** Quindlen uses examples to support an ARGUMENT. What
   position does she want readers to recognize and accept?

QUESTIONS ON LANGUAGE

1. What is the effect of "My God" in the last paragraph?
2. How might Quindlen be said to give new meaning to the old CLICHÉ "Home
   is where the heart is" (para. 4)?
3. What is meant by "crux" (para. 7)? Where does the word come from?

SUGGESTIONS FOR WRITING

1. **JOURNAL WRITING.** What does the word *home* mean to you? Does it involve material things or a sense of permanence?

FROM JOURNAL TO ESSAY. Write an essay that gives a detailed DEFINITION of *home* by using your own home(s), hometown(s), or experiences with home(s) as supporting examples.

2. Have you ever moved from one place to another? What sort of experience was it? Write an essay about leaving an old home and moving to a new one. Was there an activity or a piece of furniture that helped ease the transition?

3. Address Quindlen's contention that turning homelessness into an issue avoids the problem, that we might "be better off if we forgot about the broad strokes and concentrated on the details."

4. **CRITICAL WRITING.** Write a brief essay in which you agree or disagree with Quindlen's assertion that a home is "everything." Can one, for instance, be a fulfilled person without a home? In your answer, take account of the values that might underlie an attachment to home; Quindlen mentions "certainty, stability, predictability, privacy" (para. 4), but there are others, including some (such as fear) that are less positive.

5. **CONNECTIONS.** COMPARE AND CONTRAST the views of homelessness and its solution in Quindlen's "Homeless" and Barbara Lazear Ascher's "On Compassion" (p. 145). Use specific passages from each essay to support your comparison.

ANNA QUINDLEN ON WRITING

Anna Quindlen started her writing career as a newspaper reporter. "I had wanted to be a writer for most of my life," she recalls in the introduction to her book *Living Out Loud*, "and in the service of the writing I became a reporter. For many years I was able to observe, even to feel, life vividly, but at second hand. I was able to stand over the chalk outline of a body on a sidewalk dappled with black blood; to stand behind the glass and look down into an operating theater where one man was placing a heart in the yawning chest of another; to sit in the park on the first day of summer and find myself professionally obligated to record all the glories of it. Every day I found answers: who, what, when, where, and why."

Quindlen was a good reporter, but the business of finding answers did not satisfy her personally. "In my own life," she continues, "I had only questions." Then she switched from reporter to columnist at the *New York Times*. It was "exhilarating," she says, that "my work became a reflection of my life. After years of being a professional observer of other people's lives, I was given the opportunity to be a professional observer of my own. I was permitted—and permitted myself—to write a column, not about my answers, but about my questions. Never did I make so much sense of my life as I did then, for it was inevitable that as a writer I would find out most clearly what I thought, and what I only thought I thought, when I saw it written down.... After years of feeling secondhand, of feeling the pain of the widow, the joy of the winner, I was able to allow myself to feel those emotions for myself."

FOR DISCUSSION

1. What were the advantages and disadvantages of news reporting, according to Quindlen?
2. What did Quindlen feel she could accomplish in a column that she could not accomplish in a news report? What evidence of this difference do you see in her essay "Homeless"?

MERRILL MARKOE

A comedian and comedy writer, MERRILL MARKOE was born in New York City in 1950 and received an M.F.A. from the University of California at Berkeley, in 1974. She worked for one year as a drawing teacher and then tried stand-up comedy. While performing in Los Angeles in 1977, she met David Letterman and went on to win four Emmy Awards as a writer for *Late Night with David Letterman*. She wrote and starred in several cable TV specials, including *This Week Indoors* and *Merrill Markoe's Guide to Glamorous Living*. She won Writers' Guild and Ace awards for *Not Necessarily the News*. Markoe's essays for *New York Woman* are collected in *What the Dogs Have Taught Me* (1992). Her latest book is *Bad Dog, Bo: A Story and Pictures* (1994). The creator of Stupid Pet Tricks lives in Malibu, California, with her four dogs.

The Day I Turned Sarcastic

People magazine once called Markoe "the funniest woman in America." In this essay from *What the Dogs Have Taught Me*, Markoe uses her humor to tell how she got her start—and, incidentally, how worthwhile a journal can be, even one written in childhood.

On January 1, 1959, these immortal words were recorded: "Dear 1 Diary. Today the weather was not too nice. Little Bruce came over and got bitten by a slug. We ate hamburgers on the grill. Now it is 1959. Sincerely, Merrill." I was nine years old, and it was the beginning of an era. Well, maybe not an *era*, but it *was* the beginning of my close relationship with my diary.

It is a strangely pleasurable thing to read your own words from 2 widely varying periods and phases of your life. You can hear not just how you thought but how you sounded at the moment you were thinking it. It's so much clearer and more specific than when your memory plays it back.

For instance, these days my brother and I are good friends, but this 3 was not the case on January 22, 1959, when my rage moved me to scrawl in black India ink, "Today is Glenn's party, and he does not want me to come. He is a very greedy boy. When it was my birthday party he ate with the girls and played all the games and everything. And now it is his party and he says that I have to eat at a separate table from them and that I can't even talk to the boys, let alone play the games. I won't stand for it. I'll go to Jill's house where I'm welcome. Who needs his stinky party anyway." I can still vaguely remember the anger, but I would never have imagined it in those terms. It's been a while since I used the word *stinky* as effectively.

Part of the fun of reading about your own past is to chart your growth. On March 26, 1959, after viewing *The Story of Menstruation* with the rest of Girl Scout Troop 511, I had the following comments to make: "It was interesting. I decided that I would not wear lipstick or makeup until I was at least in my twenties. In fact, I might never wear it." On January 8, 1960, I amended that resolution slightly: "I decided that I wasn't going to wait until eighteen to wear lipstick but that I would wear it when fourteen." Then on June 1, 1960, "I decided that I am not going to wait until I am fourteen to wear lipstick but would wear it when I'm thirteen." And *then,* undated, but just a couple of pages later, "I decided that I wouldn't wait until thirteen to wear lipstick but would wear it when I go out to dinner or something at twelve."

It's a good thing I didn't have access to any sort of time-travel mechanism or I might have kept this lipstick rumination up indefinitely. It was hardly prophetic, anyway, since I didn't really get around to the whole lipstick thing until somewhere in my thirties.

Recently I found myself leafing through these early volumes in an attempt to discover the primitive roots of my need for self-expression. Self-expression was not the original motive. What fascinated me initially about diaries was the fact that these small, plastic-coated volumes decorated with drawings of teenage girls came equipped with a *lock* and a *key.* These temporarily kept safe from the prying eyes of family and strangers the sanctity of such top secret passages as "January 24, 1959. Went to school. At night I watched *77 Sunset Strip.* It was real good. 'Kookie' (Ed [*sic*] Byrnes) went skin diving."[1] Or "February 28, 1959. After piano lessons we went to the Grand Union where Jim Dooley [a local TV personality] was. He came in a helicopter. Mr. Moke [a monkey] and his trainer came also. Mr. Moke did some tricks and we all got free Jim Dooley potato chips (ugg). I got Jim Dooley's autograph. He looks much much older in person."

Some of the entries were a little more controversial. On March 7: "I had a piano recital and did terrible. Miss Clemson gave me one day notice and told me to play 'Wheatlands.' Then the next day, which was the recital, she told me I had to play 'Waltz of the Flowers' AND 'Wheatlands.' I did awful on 'Waltz of the Flowers.' I hate her so much I feel like puking just at the sight of her."

The idea of the diary as a locked document only lasted until I discovered that every diary known to mankind was operated by the same

4

5

6

7

8

---

[1] The star of the popular television show *77 Sunset Strip* spells his first name "Edd." *Sic,* in brackets, means "in this manner" in Latin. With it, Markoe indicates that the mistake was in the original text (in this case, the diary).—Eds.

key. And, what was worse, any bobby pin or scissor point could do the trick as well. That's how the idea of locking things up tight became secondary to a new motive—gaining a readership. Suddenly I was dropping asides to "whoever is reading this" or an invisible "you" (as in, "In case you want to know").

Seldom has the birth of a writer been so specifically documented. 9 For instance, I now know that January 21, 1960, can be hailed as "The Day I Turned Sarcastic." The occasion was a Girl Scout Troop 511 rehearsal of the song selected by the troop leader as the one that would be performed at a countrywide jamboree. "Linda Andrew found it in one of her baby piano books and we go around in a circle stamping our feet while we sing it. It's called 'Dance with Us, Sing with Us, Gretchen and Hans,' and we had to practice it over and over and over because *it's so hard to learn*, HA HA!"

It's probably significant that this kind of writerly awareness began 10 to occur during the year when I first became sensitive about being treated like a child (read: chump), as seen in the entry for April 21, 1960, when "Mrs. Edwards was our teacher because Mr. Wilson had to go to a convention. She must have thought we were two-year-olds because she made us play 'Did you ever see a Lassie, a Lassie, a Lassie.' We were *DISGUSTED*."

This was also the time that I began my first misguided attempts at 11 trying to interact in an appealing way with members of the opposite sex (an area in which to date I have made only the most marginal progress). On May 26, 1960, "I drew a picture on a piece of paper and wrote 'To Wayne; Roses are red, violets are blue. I killed my dog cause he looked like you' and then I left the note on his bicycle." At the bottom of the page, I added wistfully, "I wonder if he found it," as clueless then as to why verbal abuse may not be an effective come-on with guys as I was the other day when it fell through for me again for the hundred-thousandth time.

My biographers will want to make special note of July 15, 1960, 12 which seems to mark the beginning of what can loosely be construed as some kind of a general world view. That was the day when I wrote, "Stayed home again. Still have a stuffed nose. In the evening the Democratic Convention nominated some guys for president."

The following year's events must remain shrouded in mystery, until 13 the "lost writings of 1961" surface. But by 1962, I had ripened considerably, as a person as well as a journalist. And now I was pretty consistently addressing the proceedings to some kind of theoretical "you" as seen on January 1, when "my mother caught me reading Daddy's sexy desk calendar and took it away. It's unfit reading for a twelve-year-old, or so she says. I'll get it again though. Don't *you* worry."

The desire to get my message out to some kind of an audience was 14 becoming more urgent—even if the message itself was still pretty dopey. On January 4, I phoned in a comment to the WFUN Radio newscast *and* diligently made a diary entry to record it for the ages. "In the news they talked about how a woman was complaining about the Coppertone billboard where they have the little girl with her butt exposed," I explained. "They wanted public opinions, so I called in and they played my comment at 7, 8 and again at 10. They called it a comment from a teenager. I said, 'With so many important things to criticize in the world I think this lady should use her voice to criticize more important things instead of picking on what I think is a cute ad. I wonder what she would have done if the little girl had been a grown woman.'" Now, I actually have no idea what I meant by that comment. Perhaps I was trying to say that we should all be grateful the ad was not much worse. Whatever it meant, this was the first documented moment of my ability to understand "the sound bite." Also to say nothing much succinctly.

Which brings us to the crux of the matter. Not long afterward I began to come under the influence of *The Diary of Anne Frank*.[2] It was, to my teen eyes, less an account of the horror and tragedy of the Holocaust than an example of a girl my own age who had really done well in the diary game.   15

Suddenly I knew that I was going to have to roll out some big guns if I wanted to attract a readership throughout the ages, the way Anne Frank had, because I had not been given the gift of of a tragic personal life to work with. Which is why, suddenly, my Month at a Glance highlight summaries began to read as follows: 16

September 13—Had my braces removed   17

September 17—Got a retainer   18

End of September sometime—A lot of trouble at U. of Miss. when Negro James Meredith tried to enter. Rioting. He got in though.   19

October 1—Lois's party   20

October 2—Candy's party   21

October 3—Walter Schirra made a sixth orbital flight. It was very successful and he returned nine hours later in good health and spirits.   22

But all this was just a prelude to the glorious day of October 22, when, through the grace of God, I was handed the first significant world event I could really milk diary-wise. October 22 was the beginning of the Cuban missile crisis, and we were living in Miami. At last, something nearby of greater theatricality than my brother's bad behavior! Oh sure, I was able to generate a little thirteen-year-old angst here and there with a few "I'm a social outcast. Everyone is going to the   23

[2] Anne Frank (1929–45) was a young German Jew who kept a journal while hiding with her family from the German Gestapo. She died in the Bergen-Belsen concentration camp. Her journal was published in 1947.—Eds.

dance except me"–type musings, but they were nothing compared to this first visitation of a national nightmare right in my own backyard (sort of). The entries for October 22 and 23 read: "Turned in our home ec. notebooks. In the afternoon President Kennedy made a public address. He spoke of the fastly being erected USSR missile bases in Cuba and how this could not be tolerated. He said that a quarantine would begin around Cuba and all ships would be checked for offensive weapons. Four Russian ships are on their way. There's a possibility that this may be the last Tuesday I'll ever live through. The next forty-eight hours will decide whether there will be peace or war. I feel like crying but I can't I don't want to die. There's so much out of life I've never experienced. I'll never complete my education or fall in love or be married and have children. I'll never see the rest of the world. God. I'm only thirteen and there's still so much ahead. I don't want to die." Never mind that the entry the next night was business as usual. "Went to Andi's party," I wrote. "The highlight of the whole thing was a scavenger hunt."

Never mind that twenty-seven years later I have made good on 24 only *one* of my top five reasons for living through the Cuban missile crisis. For at least one fabulous day, global politics and international strife had done a little something on my behalf. And so I was able to find a small measure of diary fulfillment, however short-lived.

By 1963 I had entirely given up on the idea of incorporating world 25 events into my diaries. I was hard at work on my first and only novel. My influence had changed from Anne Frank to Holden Caulfield,[3] and so was born 125 pages in which I detailed, amid plenty of casual swearing, my acute ability to distinguish the phonies from the real people. Entitled *The Cheese Stands Alone*, this remains such an intensely embarrassing piece of work that I think I'll just go ahead and end right here.

QUESTIONS ON MEANING

1. What is the THESIS of Markoe's essay? What is its PURPOSE?
2. Markoe reveals that as a teenager she viewed *The Diary of Anne Frank* as "an example of a girl my own age who had done really well in the diary game" (para. 15). What does this statement mean? Does it belittle the Holocaust? Why, or why not?
3. Markoe mentions several times her wish when writing her diary to have

---

[3] Holden Caulfield is the narrator of J. D. Salinger's novel of adolescence, *The Catcher in the Rye* (1951). — EDS.

readers for it (for example, paras. 8, 12). Does she really think someone is reading the diary or will do so?

QUESTIONS ON WRITING STRATEGY

1. Why do you think Markoe chose one of her examples (para. 9) as the basis for her essay's title? Where else in this essay do you find Markoe using SAR-CASM? What is its EFFECT?
2. Many of the examples from Markoe's diary reveal a concern with her AUDI-ENCE. How do we know from the TONE of this essay that the author still has this concern?
3. How do this essay's TRANSITIONS help to connect Markoe the child and Markoe the adult? Look, for example, at the first sentences of paragraphs 3, 9, and 10. Try to locate more transitions yourself.
4. **OTHER METHODS.** Markoe uses DIVISION or ANALYSIS to examine her diary entries, considering elements such as the freshness of emotion (para. 3) and the steps in growth (4–5). What other elements does Markoe identify?

QUESTIONS ON LANGUAGE

1. Look up any of the following words if they are unfamiliar to you: amended, resolution (para. 4); rumination, prophetic (5); sanctity (6); jamboree (9); wistfully (11); construed (12); shrouded, theoretical (13); diligently, succinctly (14); crux (15); angst, quarantine (23).
2. What does the word *primitive* mean in the context of paragraph 6? Why do you think Markoe chose it?
3. One of Markoe's examples documents her first conscious use of a "sound bite" (para. 14). What is a "sound bite"? How might it be said to apply to Markoe's essay as a whole?

SUGGESTIONS FOR WRITING

1. **JOURNAL WRITING.** Markoe's essay proves that the entries in a journal or diary can be amusing when reread. What might be the risks of writing in a journal?
   FROM JOURNAL TO ESSAY. Have you ever written something personal that created difficulties, either for you or for someone else? Write an essay that explores the risks of personal writing, using one or more examples from your own experience of how writing can come back to haunt you.
2. Markoe's most vivid, detailed example quotes her diary entry on October 22, 1962, when the Cuban missile crisis was brewing. (It ended October 28.) Write an essay in which you report on an event that affected you deeply—a world event or one closer to home, such as a storm or a crime. Try to recapture the way you felt at the time, but also view the event from the present: What do you think of your reactions? What have been the long-term effects of the event on you?
3. **CRITICAL WRITING.** Markoe states that "by 1962, I had ripened considerably, as a person as well as a journalist" (para. 13). Write an essay analyzing her "ripening." What do you know of Markoe the person from this essay? Use specific examples and quotations as your EVIDENCE.

4. **CONNECTIONS.** Like Markoe's essay, Maya Angelou's "Champion of the
   World" (p. 49) looks back on the past. Angelou relies on recollection,
   while Markoe draws from accounts actually written in the past moments.
   Write an essay COMPARING AND CONTRASTING these two writers' different
   methods of remembering and presenting the past. Do you find one method
   more convincing or legitimate than the other? Why?

STEPHEN KING

A prolific and hugely popular master of horror and dread, STEPHEN KING has written more than thirty books in the twenty-plus years he has been publishing. He was born in Portland, Maine, in 1947 and grew up in Indiana, Connecticut, and Maine, where he has lived for most of his adult life. He graduated in 1970 from the University of Maine at Orono, worked in an industrial laundry, and taught high-school English before the sales of his books allowed him to write full-time. Among King's best-known novels are *Carrie* (1974), *The Shining* (1977), *The Dead Zone* (1979), *Misery* (1987), and *Dolores Claiborne* (1992)—all of them also made into movies. His own screenplays include *Creepshow* (1982) and *Pet Sematary* (1987, from the 1985 novel). King has also published several books under the pen name Richard Bachman, most recently *The Regulators* (1996). His latest projects under his own name are two novels also published in 1996: *The Green Mile*, which appeared in six monthly installments, and *Desperation*.

"Ever Et Raw Meat?"

King's books have sold nearly 100 million copies, and his readers are naturally curious about him. In this essay published in the *New York Times Book Review* in 1987, King reveals that he finds the public's interest sometimes gratifying, sometimes annoying, and sometimes very funny.

It seems to me that, in the minds of readers, writers actually exist to 1 serve two purposes, and the more important may not be the writing of books and stories. The primary function of writers, it seems, is to answer readers' questions. These fall into three categories. The third is the one that fascinates me most, but I'll identify the other two first.

The One-of-a-Kind Questions

Each day's mail brings a few of these. Often they reflect the writer's 2 field of interest—history, horror, romance, the American West, outer space, big business. The only thing they have in common is their uniqueness. Novelists are frequently asked where they get their ideas (see category No. 2), but writers must wonder where this relentless curiosity, these really strange questions, come from.

There was, for instance, the young woman who wrote to me from a 3 penal institution in Minnesota. She informed me she was a kleptomaniac. She further informed me that I was her favorite writer, and she had stolen every one of my books she could get her hands on. "But after I stole *Different Seasons* from the library and read it, I felt moved to send it back," she wrote. "Do you think this means you wrote this one the best?" After due consideration, I decided that reform on the part of the reader has nothing to do with artistic merit. I came close to writing back to find out if she had stolen *Misery* yet but decided I ought to just keep my mouth shut.

From Bill V. in North Carolina: "I see you have a beard. Are you   4
morbid of razors?"

From Carol K. in Hawaii: "Will you soon write of pimples or some   5
other facial blemish?"

From Don G., no address (and a blurry postmark): "Why do you   6
keep up this disgusting mother worship when anyone with any sense knows a MAN has no use to his mother once he is weaned?"

From Raymond R. in Mississippi: "Ever et raw meat?" (It's the la-   7
conic ones like this that really get me.)

I have been asked if I beat my children and/or my wife. I have been   8
asked to parties in places I have never been and hope never to go. I was once asked to give away the bride at a wedding, and one young woman sent me an ounce of pot, with the attached question: "This is where I get my inspiration—where do you get yours?" Actually, mine usually comes in envelopes—the kind through which you can view your name and address printed by a computer—that arrive at the end of every month.

My favorite question of this type, from Anchorage, asked simply: 9
"How could you write such a why?" Unsigned. If E. E. Cummings[1] were still alive, I'd try to find out if he'd moved to the Big North.

The Old Standards

These are the questions writers dream of answering when they are   10
collecting rejection slips, and the ones they tire of quickest once they start to publish. In other words, they are the questions that come up without fail in every dull interview the writer has ever given or will ever give. I'll enumerate a few of them:

Where do you get your ideas? (I get mine in Utica.)   11

How do you get an agent? (Sell your soul to the Devil.)   12

Do you have to know somebody to get published? (Yes; in fact, it   13
helps to grovel, toady, and be willing to perform twisted acts of sexual depravity at a moment's notice, and in public if necessary.)

How do you start a novel? (I usually start by writing the number 1   14
in the upper right-hand corner of a clean sheet of paper.)

[1] E. E. Cummings (1894–1962) was an American poet noted for wordplay like that in the question King quotes. —Eds.

How do you write best sellers? (Same way you get an agent.)   15

How do you sell your book to the movies? (Tell them they don't   16
want it.)

What time of day do you write? (It doesn't matter; if I don't keep   17
busy enough, the time inevitably comes.)

Do you ever run out of ideas? (Does a bear defecate in the woods?)   18

Who is your favorite writer? (Anyone who writes stories I would   19
have written had I thought of them first.)

There are others, but they're pretty boring, so let us march on.   20

The Real Weirdies

Here I am, bopping down the street, on my morning walk, when   21
some guy pulls over in his pickup truck or just happens to walk by and
says, "Hi, Steve! Writing any good books lately?" I have an answer for
this; I've developed it over the years out of pure necessity. I say, "I'm
taking some time off." I say that even if I'm working like mad, thun-
dering down homestretch on a book. The reason *why* I say this is because no other answer seems to fit. Believe me, I know. In the course of
the trial and error that has finally resulted in "I'm taking some time
off," I have discarded about 500 other answers.

Having an answer for "You writing any good books lately?" is a   22
good thing, but I'd be lying if I said it solves the problem of *what the
question means*. It is this inability on my part to make sense of this odd
query, which reminds me of that Zen riddle — "Why is a mouse when it
runs?" — that leaves me feeling mentally shaken and impotent. You
see, it isn't just *one* question; it is a *bundle* of questions, cunningly
wrapped up in one package. It's like that old favorite, "Are you still
beating your wife?"

If I answer in the affirmative, it means I may have written — how   23
many books? two? four? — (all of them good) in the last — how long?
Well, how long is "lately"? It could mean I wrote maybe three good
books just last week, or maybe two *on this very walk up to Bangor International Airport and back!* On the other hand, if I say no, what does *that*
mean? I wrote three or four *bad* books in the last "lately" (surely "lately"
can be no longer than a month, six weeks at the outside)?

Or here I am, signing books at the Betts' Bookstore or B. Dalton's   24
in the local consumer factory (nicknamed "the mall"). This is something I do twice a year, and it serves much the same purpose as those
little bundles of twigs religious people in the Middle Ages used to braid
into whips and flagellate themselves with. During the course of this exercise in madness and self-abnegation, at least a dozen people will approach the little coffee table where I sit behind a barrier of books and
ask brightly, "Don't you wish you had a rubber stamp?"

I have an answer to this one, too, an answer that has been devel- 25
oped over the years in a trial-and-error method similar to "I'm taking
some time off." The answer to the rubber-stamp question is: "No, I
don't mind."

Never mind if I really do or don't (this time it's my own motiva- 26
tions I want to skip over, you'll notice); the question is, Why does such
an illogical query occur to so many people? My signature is actually
stamped on the covers of several of my books, but people seem just as
eager to get these signed as those that aren't so stamped. Would these
questioners stand in line for the privilege of watching me slam a rubber
stamp down on the title page of *The Shining* or *Pet Sematary*? I don't
think they would.

If you still don't sense something peculiar in these questions, this 27
one might help convince you. I'm sitting in the cafe around the corner
from my house, grabbing a little lunch by myself and reading a book
(reading at the table is one of the few bad habits acquired in my youth
that I have nobly resisted giving up) until a customer or maybe even a
waitress sidles up and asks, "How come you're not reading one of your
own books?"

This hasn't happened just once, or even occasionally; it happens *a* 28
lot. The computer-generated answer to this question usually gains a
chuckle, although it is nothing but the pure, logical and apparent
truth. "I know how they all come out," I say. End of exchange. Back to
lunch, with only a pause to wonder why people assume you want to
read what you wrote, rewrote, read again following the obligatory editorial conference and yet again during the process of correcting the
mistakes that a good copy editor always prods, screaming, from their
hiding places (I once heard a crime writer suggest that God could have
used a copy editor, and while I find the notion slightly blasphemous, I
tend to agree).

And then people sometimes ask in that chatty, let's-strike-up-a- 29
conversation way people have, "How long does it take you to write a
book?" Perfectly reasonable question — at least until you try to answer
it and discover there *is* no answer. This time the computer-generated
answer is a total falsehood, but it at least serves the purpose of advancing the conversation to some more discussable topic. "Usually about
nine months," I say, "the same length of time it takes to make a baby."
This satisfies everyone but me. I know that nine months is just an average, and probably a completely fictional one at that. It ignores *The
Running Man* (published under the name Richard Bachman), which
was written in four days during a snowy February vacation when I was
teaching high school. It also ignores *It* and my latest, *The Tommyknockers*. *It* is over 1,000 pages long and took four years to write. *The
Tommyknockers* is 400 pages shorter but took five years to write.

Do I mind these questions? Yes . . . and no. Anyone minds questions 30 that have no real answers and thus expose the fellow being questioned to be not a real doctor but a sort of witch doctor. But no one—at least no one with a modicum of simple human kindness—resents questions from people who honestly want answers. And now and then someone will ask a really interesting question, like, Do you write in the nude? The answer—not generated by computer—is: I don't think I ever have, but if it works, I'm willing to try it.

QUESTIONS ON MEANING

1. What is the THESIS of this essay? Why do you think King wrote it: to entertain readers? to gain sympathy for himself? to discourage readers from writing to him? some other reason? Explain your answer.
2. What is so "peculiar" about the questions King calls the "real weirdies" (paras. 21–29)?
3. In paragraph 24 King draws a comparison between his signing of books and the self-flagellation (self-whipping) by people in the Middle Ages. What does he mean by this ANALOGY?

QUESTIONS ON WRITING STRATEGY

1. How do King's many examples illustrate his GENERALIZATION that the "primary function of writers, it seems, is to answer readers' questions" (para. 1)? What do all the examples have in common?
2. What is King's relationship with his AUDIENCE in this essay? How do you know? Recall that he wrote the essay for the *New York Times Book Review* and so could expect a well-educated and well-read audience.
3. How does King's concluding paragraph modify his response to readers' questions?
4. **OTHER METHODS.** This essay is a CLASSIFICATION of examples. What distinguishes King's three categories of questions: What makes each one different from the others?

QUESTIONS ON LANGUAGE

1. Make sure you know the meanings of the following words: kleptomaniac (para. 3); morbid (4); weaned (6); laconic (7); enumerate (10); grovel, depravity (13); defecate (18); impotent (22); affirmative (23); self-abnegation (24); sidles (27); obligatory, blasphemous (28); modicum (30).
2. King directly addresses his readers at certain points—for instance, "Believe me" (para. 21), "You see" (22), "you'll notice" (26), and "If you still don't sense something peculiar . . ." (27). Why do you think he addresses readers? What is the EFFECT?

3. In paragraphs 28–30 King mentions the "computer-generated answer" to some of the questions he has been asked. What does he mean by this METAPHOR?

SUGGESTIONS FOR WRITING

1. **JOURNAL WRITING.** At some point you have probably faced questions that were either unanswerable or unbearably tedious—maybe in school or on a job or from a younger or older relative. Write about these questions and how they made you feel.
   FROM JOURNAL TO ESSAY. Develop your journal entry into an essay that uses specific examples to reveal the problem of being you when you are asked such questions. How have you coped with the problem?
2. Teachers often tell us that the only stupid question is the one we don't ask. But King seems to think there are lots of stupid questions that unfortunately *do* get asked. Is there such a thing as a stupid question? How do you identify one?
3. **CRITICAL WRITING.** One might reasonably claim that those who are famous owe something to the fans who made them popular. Write an essay on this claim, using King as an extended example. Does King have an obligation to his fans? If so, does he live up to it? Use his work as EVIDENCE for your answers, including his fiction as well as "'Ever Et Raw Meat?'"
4. **CONNECTIONS.** Stephanie Ericsson, in "The Ways We Lie" (p. 337), suggests that lies can help us maintain a sense of being connected to others in good ways. King implies that questions to famous writers may do the same. After reading Ericsson's essay, write an essay of your own that examines how lies and questions may work as social glue. Consider all possible positions—lying versus being lied to, asking questions versus answering them. Is the sense of connection one-sided? Why, or why not?

STEPHEN KING ON WRITING

The impressive publishing record of Stephen King depends on his regular writing habits. In 1992 he told W. C. Stoby of *Writer's Digest* that he works "four, four-and-a-half hours a day, seven days a week." It may be surprising, then, that King faces the same demons of procrastination that most of us do. "For me," King says, "a lot of times the real barrier to getting to work—to getting to the typewriter or the word processsor—comes before I get there. I had one of those days today when I thought to myself, 'I'm not sure if I can do this.' I have lot of days like that. I think it's kind of funny, really, that people think, 'Well, you're Stephen King; that doesn't happen to you,' as if I wasn't really the same as everybody else."

On the day in question King avoided getting to work by reading the sports page twice and working out at the Y. Eventually, though, he sat down to work. "And then," he says, "there's always those first few things where you feel awkward and there's a feeling of being in a medium where you don't precisely belong. But then you acclimate. There's nothing really very magical about it. If you've done it day in and day out, the cylinders all sort of fire over. I think the best trick is experience. After you've done that a certain amount of time, you know that it's going to get better."

In a 1991 interview, this time with Bill Goldstein of *Publishers Weekly*, King talked of his audience in a way that helps explain some of the attitudes toward readers expressed in "'Ever Et Raw Meat?'" "If the stuff you're writing is not for yourself, it won't work. I feel a certain pressure about my writing, and I have an idea of who reads my books; I am concerned with my readership. But it's kind of a combination love letter/poison-pen relationship, a sweet-and-sour thing. . . . I feel I ought to write something because people want to read something. But I think, 'Don't give them what they want—give them what *you* want.'"

FOR DISCUSSION

1. King writes fiction mostly. Do you think his ideas on overcoming procrastination and thinking about readers have any relevance to writing nonfiction such as college papers? Why, or why not?
2. If King writes for himself more than for his readers, how do you think he manages to appeal to so many readers?

BRENT STAPLES

BRENT STAPLES is a member of the editorial board of the *New York Times*. Born in 1951 in Chester, Pennsylvania, Staples has a B.A. in behavioral science from Widener University in Chester and a Ph.D. in psychology from the University of Chicago. Before joining the *New York Times* in 1985, he worked for the *Chicago Sun-Times*, the *Chicago Reader*, *Chicago* magazine, and *Down Beat* magazine. At the *Times*, Staples writes on culture and politics. He has also contributed to the *New York Times Magazine*, *New York Woman*, *Ms.*, *Harper's*, and other magazines. His memoir, *Parallel Time: Growing Up in Black and White*, appeared in 1994.

Black Men and Public Space

"Black Men and Public Space" appeared in the December 1986 issue of *Harper's* magazine and has recently been published, in a slightly different version, in Staples's memoir, *Parallel Time*. The essay relates incidents Staples has experienced "as a night walker in the urban landscape."

My first victim was a woman—white, well dressed, probably in her late twenties. I came upon her late one evening on a deserted street in Hyde Park, a relatively affluent neighborhood in an otherwise mean, impoverished section of Chicago. As I swung onto the avenue behind her, there seemed to be a discreet, uninflammatory distance between us. Not so. She cast back a worried glance. To her, the youngish black man—a broad six feet two inches with a beard and billowing hair, both hands shoved into the pockets of a bulky military jacket—seemed menacingly close. After a few more quick glimpses, she picked up her pace and was soon running in earnest. Within seconds she disappeared into a cross street.

That was more than a decade ago. I was twenty-two years old, a graduate student newly arrived at the University of Chicago. It was in the echo of that terrified woman's footfalls that I first began to know the unwieldy inheritance I'd come into—the ability to alter public space in ugly ways. It was clear that she thought herself the quarry of a mugger, a rapist, or worse. Suffering a bout of insomnia, however, I was stalking sleep, not defenseless wayfarers. As a softy who is scarcely able to take a knife to a raw chicken—let alone hold one to a person's throat—I was surprised, embarrassed, and dismayed all at once. Her flight made me feel like an accomplice in tyranny. It also made it clear that I was indistinguishable from the muggers who occasionally seeped into the area from the surrounding ghetto. That first encounter, and those that followed, signified that a vast, unnerving gulf lay between nighttime pedestrians—particularly women—and me. And I soon gathered that being perceived as dangerous is a hazard in itself. I only needed to turn a corner into a dicey situation, or crowd some frightened, armed person in a foyer somewhere, or make an errant move after being pulled over by a policeman. Where fear and weapons meet— and they often do in urban America—there is always the possibility of death.

In that first year, my first away from my hometown, I was to become 3 thoroughly familiar with the language of fear. At dark, shadowy intersections, I could cross in front of a car stopped at a traffic light and elicit the *thunk, thunk, thunk, thunk* of the driver—black, white, male, or female—hammering down the door locks. On less traveled streets after dark, I grew accustomed to but never comfortable with people crossing to the other side of the street rather than pass me. Then there were the standard unpleasantries with policemen, doormen, bouncers, cabdrivers, and others whose business it is to screen out troublesome individuals *before* there is any nastiness.

I moved to New York nearly two years ago and I have remained an 4 avid night walker. In central Manhattan, the near-constant crowd cover minimizes tense one-on-one street encounters. Elsewhere—in SoHo, for example, where sidewalks are narrow and tightly spaced buildings shut out the sky—things can get very taut indeed.

After dark, on the warrenlike streets of Brooklyn where I live, I 5 often see women who fear the worst from me. They seem to have set their faces on neutral, and with their purse straps strung across their chests bandolier-style, they forge ahead as though bracing themselves against being tackled. I understand, of course, that the danger they perceive is not a hallucination. Women are particularly vulnerable to street violence, and young black males are drastically overrepresented among the perpetrators of that violence. Yet these truths are no solace against the kind of alienation that comes of being ever the suspect, a fearsome entity with whom pedestrians avoid making eye contact.

It is not altogether clear to me how I reached the ripe old age of 6 twenty-two without being conscious of the lethality nighttime pedestrians attributed to me. Perhaps it was because in Chester, Pennsylvania, the small, angry industrial town where I came of age in the 1960s, I was scarcely noticeable against a backdrop of gang warfare, street knifings, and murders. I grew up one of the good boys, had perhaps a half-dozen fistfights. In retrospect, my shyness of combat has clear sources.

As a boy, I saw countless tough guys locked away; I have since 7 buried several, too. They were babies, really—a teenage cousin, a brother of twenty-two, a childhood friend in his mid-twenties—all gone down in episodes of bravado played out in the streets. I came to doubt the virtues of intimidation early on. I chose, perhaps unconsciously, to remain a shadow—timid, but a survivor.

The fearsomeness mistakenly attributed to me in public places often has a perilous flavor. The most frightening of these confusions occurred in the late 1970s and early 1980s, when I worked as a journalist in Chicago. One day, rushing into the office of a magazine I was writing for with a deadline story in hand, I was mistaken for a burglar. The office manager called security and, with an ad hoc posse, pursued me through the labyrinthine halls, nearly to my editor's door. I had no way of proving who I was. I could only move briskly toward the company of someone who knew me.   8

Another time I was on assignment for a local paper and killing time before an interview. I entered a jewelry store on the city's affluent Near North Side. The proprietor excused herself and returned with an enormous red Doberman pinscher straining at the end of a leash. She stood, the dog extended toward me, silent to my questions, her eyes bulging nearly out of her head. I took a cursory look around, nodded, and bade her good night.   9

Relatively speaking, however, I never fared as badly as another black male journalist. He went to nearby Waukegan, Illinois, a couple of summers ago to work on a story about a murderer who was born there. Mistaking the reporter for the killer, police officers hauled him from his car at gunpoint and but for his press credentials would probably have tried to book him. Such episodes are not uncommon. Black men trade tales like this all the time.   10

Over the years, I learned to smother the rage I felt at so often being taken for a criminal. Not to do so would surely have led to madness. I now take precautions to make myself less threatening. I move about with care, particularly late in the evening. I give a wide berth to nervous people on subway platforms during the wee hours, particularly when I have exchanged business clothes for jeans. If I happen to be entering a building behind some people who appear skittish, I may walk by, letting them clear the lobby before I return, so as not to seem to be following them. I have been calm and extremely congenial on those rare occasions when I've been pulled over by the police.   11

And on late-evening constitutionals I employ what has proved to be an excellent tension-reducing measure: I whistle melodies from Beethoven and Vivaldi and the more popular classical composers. Even steely New Yorkers hunching toward nighttime destinations seem to relax, and occasionally they even join in the tune.   12

Virtually everybody seems to sense that a mugger wouldn't be warbling bright, sunny selections from Vivaldi's *Four Seasons*. It is my equivalent of the cowbell that hikers wear when they know they are in bear country.

QUESTIONS ON MEANING

1. What is the PURPOSE of this essay? Do you think Staples believes that he (or other African American men) will cease "to alter public space in ugly ways" in the near future? Does he suggest any long-term solution for "the kind of alienation that comes of being ever the suspect" (para. 5)?
2. In paragraph 5 Staples says he understands that the danger women fear when they see him "is not a hallucination." Do you take this to mean that Staples perceives himself to be dangerous? Explain.
3. Staples says, "I chose, perhaps unconsciously, to remain a shadow—timid, but a survivor" (para. 7). What are the usual CONNOTATIONS of the word *survivor*? Is "timid" one of them? How can you explain this apparent discrepancy?

QUESTIONS ON WRITING STRATEGY

1. The concept of altering public space is relatively abstract. How does Staples convince you that this phenomenon really takes place?
2. The author employs a large number of examples in a fairly small space. He cites three specific instances that involved him, several general situations, and one incident involving another African American man. How does Staples avoid having the piece sound like a list? How does he establish COHERENCE among all these examples? (Look, for example, at details and TRANSITIONS.)
3. **OTHER METHODS.** Many of Staples's examples are actually ANECDOTES—brief NARRATIVES. The opening paragraph is especially notable. Why is it so effective?

QUESTIONS ON LANGUAGE

1. What does the author accomplish by using the word *victim* in the essay's first paragraph? Is the word used literally? What TONE does it set for the essay?
2. Be sure you know how to define the following words, as used in this essay: affluent, uninflammatory (para. 1); unwieldy, tyranny, pedestrians (2); intimidation (7); congenial (11); constitutionals (12).
3. The word *dicey* (para. 2) comes from British slang. Without looking it up in your dictionary, can you figure out its meaning from the context in which it appears?

SUGGESTIONS FOR WRITING

1. **JOURNAL WRITING.** Have you ever felt as if *you* altered public space — in other words, as if you changed people's attitudes or behavior just by being in a place or entering a situation?
   FROM JOURNAL TO ESSAY. Write an essay narrating the experience you explored in your journal or, alternatively, the experience of being a witness as someone else altered public space. What changes did you observe in the behavior of the people around you? Was your behavior similarly affected? In retrospect, do you think your reactions were justified?
2. Write an essay using examples to show how a trait of your own or of someone you know well always seems to affect people, whether positively or negatively.
3. **CRITICAL WRITING.** Consider, more broadly than Staples does, what it means to alter public space. Staples would rather not have the power to do so, but it *is* a power, and it could perhaps be positive in some circumstances (wielded by a street performer, for instance, or the architect of a beautiful new building on campus). Write an essay expanding on Staples's essay in which you examine the pros and cons of altering public space. Use specific examples as your EVIDENCE.
4. **CONNECTIONS.** Like Staples, Barbara Lazear Ascher, in "On Compassion" (p. 145), considers how people regard and respond to "the Other," the one who is viewed as different. In an essay, COMPARE AND CONTRAST the POINTS OF VIEW of these two authors. How does point of view affect each author's selection of details and tone?

BRENT STAPLES ON WRITING

In comments written especially for *The Bedford Reader*, Brent Staples talks about the writing of "Black Men and Public Space." "I was only partly aware of how I felt when I began this essay. I knew only that I had this collection of experiences (facts) and that I felt uneasy with them. I sketched out the experiences one by one and strung them together. The bridge to the essay — what I wanted to say, but did not know when I started — sprang into life quite unexpectedly as I sat looking over these experiences. The crucial sentence comes right after the opening anecdote, in which my first 'victim' runs away from me: 'It was in the echo of that woman's footfalls that I first began to know the unwieldy inheritance I'd come into — the ability to alter public space in ugly ways.' 'Aha!' I said, 'This is why I feel bothered and hurt and frustrated when this happens. I don't want people to think I'm stalking them. I want some fresh air. I want to stretch my legs. I want to be as anonymous as any other person out for a walk in the night.'"

A news reporter and editor by training and trade, Staples sees much similarity between the writing of a personal essay like "Black Men and Public Space" and the writing of, say, a murder story for a daily newspaper. "The newspaper murder," he says, "begins with standard newspaper information: the fact that the man was found dead in an alley in such-and-such a section of the city; his name, occupation, and where he lived; that he died of gunshot wounds to such-and-such a part of his body; that arrests were or were not made; that such-and-such a weapon was found at the scene; that the police have established no motive; etc.

"Personal essays take a different tack, but they, too, begin as assemblies of facts. In 'Black Men and Public Space,' I start out with an anecdote that crystalizes the issue I want to discuss—what it is like to be viewed as a criminal all the time. I devise a sentence that serves this purpose and also catches the reader's attention: 'My first victim was a woman—white, well dressed, probably in her late twenties.' The piece gives examples that are meant to illustrate the same point and discusses what those examples mean.

"The newspaper story stacks its details in a specified way, with each piece taking a prescribed place in a prescribed order. The personal essay begins often with a flourish, an anecdote, or the recounting of a crucial experience, then goes off to consider related experiences and their meanings. But both pieces rely on reporting. Both are built of facts. Reporting is the act of finding and analyzing facts.

"A fact can be a state of the world—a date, the color of someone's eyes, the arc of a body that flies through the air after having been struck by a car. A fact can also be a feeling—sorrow, grief, confusion, the sense of being pleased, offended, or frustrated. 'Black Men and Public Space' explores the relationship between two sets of facts: (1) the way people cast worried glances at me and sometimes run away from me on the streets after dark, and (2) the frustration and anger I feel at being made an object of fear as I try to go about my business in the city."

Personal essays and news stories share one other quality as well, Staples thinks: They affect the writer even when the writing is finished. "The discoveries I made in 'Black Men and Public Space' continued long after the essay was published. Writing about the experiences gave me access to a whole range of internal concerns and ideas, much the way a well-reported news story opens the door onto a given neighborhood, situation, or set of issues."

FOR DISCUSSION

1. In recounting how his essay developed, what does Staples reveal about his writing process?
2. How, according to Staples, are essay writing and news writing similar? How are they different?
3. What does Staples mean when he says that "writing about the experiences gave me access to a whole range of internal concerns and ideas"?

ADDITIONAL WRITING TOPICS

Example

1. Select one of the following general statements, or set forth a general statement of your own that one of these inspires. Making it your central idea (or THESIS), support it in an essay full of examples. Draw your examples from your reading, your studies, your conversation, or your own experience.

   People one comes to admire don't always at first seem likable.
   Fashions this year are loonier than ever before.
   Good (or bad) habits are necessary to the nation's economy.
   Each family has its distinctive lifestyle.
   Certain song lyrics, closely inspected, promote violence.
   Comic books are going to the dogs.
   At some point in life, most people triumph over crushing difficulties.
   Churchgoers aren't perfect.
   TV commercials suggest: Buy this product and your love life will improve like crazy.
   Home cooking can't win over fast food.
   Ordinary lives sometimes give rise to legends.
   Some people I know are born winners (or losers).
   Books can change our lives.
   Certain machines *do* have personalities.
   Some road signs lead drivers astray.

2. In a brief essay, make a GENERALIZATION about either the terrors or the joys that members of minority groups seem to share. To illustrate your generalization, draw examples from personal experience, from outside reading, or from two or three of the following essays in this book: Maya Angelou's "Champion of the World" (p. 49), Amy Tan's "Fish Cheeks" (p. 54), Ralph Ellison's "On Being the Target of Discrimination" (p. 65), Brent Staples's "Black Men and Public Space" (p. 168), Judith Ortiz Cofer's "Advanced Biology" (p. 209), Gloria Naylor's "The Meanings of a Word" (p. 407), Christine Leong's "Being a Chink" (p. 413), Curtis Chang's "Streets of Gold" (p. 482), Martin Luther King, Jr.'s "I Have a Dream" (p. 502), Marco Wilkinson's "Exposing Truth for the Lie That It Is" (p. 550), and Richard Rodriguez's "Aria" (p. 570).

4

COMPARISON
AND CONTRAST
Setting Things Side by Side

THE METHOD

Should we pass laws to regulate pornography, or just let pornography run wild? Which team do you place your money on, the Cowboys or the Forty-Niners? To go to school full-time or part-time: What are the rewards and drawbacks of each way of life? How do the Republican and the Democratic platforms stack up against each other? How is the work of Picasso like or unlike that of Matisse? These are questions that may be addressed by the dual method of COMPARISON AND CONTRAST. In comparing, you point to similar features of the subjects; in contrasting, to different features. (The features themselves you identify by the method of DIVISION or ANALYSIS; see Chap. 6.)

With the aid of comparison and contrast, you can show why you prefer one thing to another, one course of action to another, one idea to another. In an argument in which you support one of two possible choices, a careful and detailed comparison and contrast of the choices may be extremely convincing. In an expository essay, it can demonstrate that you understand your subjects thoroughly. That is why, on exams that call for essay answers, often you will be asked to compare and contrast. Sometimes the examiner will come right out and say,

"Compare and contrast nineteenth-century methods of treating drug addiction with those of the present day." Sometimes, however, comparison and contrast won't even be mentioned by name; instead, the examiner will ask, "What resemblances and differences do you find between John Updike's short story 'A & P' and the Grimm fairy tale 'Godfather Death'?" Or, "Explain the relative desirability of holding a franchise as against going into business as an independent proprietor." But those — as you realize when you begin to plan your reply — are just other ways of asking you to compare and contrast.

In practice, the two methods are usually inseparable. A little reflection will show you why you need both. Say you intend to write a portrait-in-words of two people. No two people are in every respect exactly the same or entirely dissimilar. Simply to compare them or to contrast them would not be true to life. To set them side by side and portray them accurately, you must consider both similarities and differences.

A good essay in comparing and contrasting serves a purpose. Most of the time, the writer of such an essay has one of two purposes in mind:

1. *The purpose of showing each of two subjects distinctly by considering both, side by side.* Writing with such a purpose, the writer doesn't necessarily find one of the subjects better than the other. In "The Black and White Truth About Basketball" in this chapter, Jeff Greenfield details two styles of playing the game; and his conclusion is not that either "black" or "white" basketball is the more beautiful, but that the two styles can complement each other on the same court.

2. *The purpose of choosing between two things.* In daily life, we often EVALUATE two possibilities to choose between them: which college course to elect, which movie to see, which luncheon special to take — chipped beef over green noodles or fried smelt on a bun? Our thinking on a matter such as the last is quick and informal: "Hmmmm, the smelt *looks* better. Red beef, green noodles — ugh, what a sight! Smelt has bones, but the beef is rubbery. Still, I don't like the smell of that smelt. I'll go for the beef (or maybe just grab a hamburger after class)." In essays, too, a writer, by comparing and evaluating points, decides which of two things is more admirable: "Organic Gardening, Yes; Gardening with Chemical Fertilizers, No!" — or "Skydiving Versus the Safe, Sane Life." In writing, as in thinking, you need to consider the main features of both subjects, the positive features and the negative, and to choose the subject whose positive features more clearly predominate.

THE PROCESS

Subjects for Comparison

The first step in comparing and contrasting is to select subjects that will display a clear basis for comparison. In other words, you have to pick two subjects that have enough in common to be worth placing side by side. You'll have the best luck if you choose two of a kind: two California wines, two mystery writers, two schools of political thought.

It can sometimes be effective to find similarities between evidently unlike subjects—a city and a country town, say—and a special form of comparison, ANALOGY, always equates two very unlike things, explaining one in terms of the other. (In an analogy you might explain how the human eye works by comparing it to a simple camera, or you might explain the forces in a thunderstorm by comparing them to armies in battle.) In any comparison of unlike things, you must have a valid reason for bringing the two together. In his essay "Grant and Lee," Bruce Catton compares the characters of the two Civil War generals. But in an essay called "General Grant and Mick Jagger" you would be hard-pressed to find any real basis for comparison. Although you might wax ingenious and claim, "Like Grant, Jagger posed a definite threat to Nashville," the ingenuity would wear thin and soon the yoking together of general and rock star would fall apart.

Basis for Comparison

Just identifying shared features may give you two subjects for a comparison, but the comparison won't be manageable for you or interesting to your readers unless you also limit it. You would be overly ambitious to try to compare and contrast the Russian way of life with the American way of life in five hundred words; you couldn't include all the important similarities and differences. In a brief paper, you would be wise to select a single basis for comparison: to show, for instance, how day-care centers in Russia and the United States are both alike and dissimilar.

This basis for comparison will eventually underpin the THESIS of your essay—the claim you have to make about the similarities and dissimilarities of two things or about one thing's superiority over another. Here, from essays in this chapter, are THESIS SENTENCES that clearly lay out what's being compared and why:

Neat people are lazier and meaner than sloppy people. (Suzanne Britt, "Neat People vs. Sloppy People")

These were two strong men, these oddly different generals, and they represented the strengths of two conflicting currents that, through them, had come into collision. (Bruce Catton, "Grant and Lee: A Study in Contrasts")

Most simply (remembering that we are talking about culture, not chromosomes), "black" basketball is the use of superb athletic skill to adapt to the limits of space imposed by the game. "White" ball is the pulverization of that space by sheer intensity. (Jeff Greenfield, "The Black and White Truth About Basketball")

Notice that each of these authors not only identifies his or her subjects (neat and sloppy people, Grant and Lee, "black" and "white" basketball styles) but also previews the purpose of the comparison, whether to evaluate (Britt) or to explain (Catton, Greenfield).

Organization

Even with a limited basis for comparison, the method of comparison and contrast can be tricky without some planning. We suggest that you make an outline (preferably in writing), using one of two organizations described below. Say you're writing an essay on two banjo-pickers, Jed and Jake. Your purpose is to explain the distinctive identities of the two players, and your thesis sentence might be the following:

Jed and Jake are both excellent banjo-pickers whose differences reflect their training.

Here are the two ways you might arrange your comparison:

1. *Subject by subject.* Set forth all your facts about Jed, then do the same for Jake. Next, sum up their similarities and differences. In your conclusion, state what you think you have shown.

1. *Jed*
   Training
   Choice of material
   Technical dexterity
   Playing style

2. *Jake*
   Training
   Choice of material
   Technical dexterity
   Playing style

   SUMMARY
   CONCLUSION

This procedure works for a paper of a few paragraphs, but for a longer one, it has a built-in disadvantage. Readers need to remember all the facts about subject 1 while they read about subject 2. If the essay is long and lists many facts, this procedure may be burdensome.

2. *Point by point.* Usually more workable in writing a long paper than the first method, the second scheme is to compare and contrast as you go. You consider one point at a time, taking up your two subjects alternately. In this way, you continually bring the subjects together, perhaps in every paragraph. Notice the differences in the outline:

1. *Training*
   Jed: studied under Scruggs
   Jake: studied under Segovia

2. *Choice of material*
   Jed: traditional
   Jake: innovative

3. *Technical dexterity*
   Jed: highly skilled
   Jake: highly skilled

4. *Playing style*
   Jed: likes to show off
   Jake: keeps work simple

For either the subject-by-subject or the point-by-point scheme, your conclusion might be: Although similar in skill, the two differ greatly in aims and in personalities. Jed is better suited to the Grand Ol' Opry; Jake, to a concert hall.

No matter how you group your points, they have to balance; you can't discuss Jed's on-stage manner without discussing Jake's too. If you have nothing to say about Jake's on-stage manner, then you might as well omit the point. A surefire loser is the paper that proposes to compare and contrast two subjects but then proceeds to discuss quite different elements in each: Jed's playing style and Jake's choice of material, Jed's fondness for smelt on a bun and Jake's hobby of antique-car collecting. The writer of such a paper doesn't compare and contrast the two musicians at all, but provides two quite separate discussions.

By the way, a subject-by-subject organization works most efficiently for a *pair* of subjects. If you want to write about *three* banjo-pickers, you might first consider Jed and Jake, then Jake and Josh, then Josh and Jed —but it would probably be easiest to compare and contrast all three point by point.

Flexibility

As you write, an outline will help you see the shape of your paper and keep your procedure in mind. But don't be the simple tool of your outline. Few essays are more boring to read than the long comparison and contrast written mechanically. The reader comes to feel like a weary tennis spectator whose head has to swivel from side to side: now Jed, now Jake; now Jed again, now back to Jake. You need to mention the same features of both subjects, it is true, but no law decrees *how* you must mention them. You need not follow your outline in lockstep order, or cover similarities and differences at precisely the same length, or spend a hundred words on Jed's banjo-picking skill just because you spend a hundred words on Jake's. Your essay, remember, doesn't need to be as symmetrical as a pair of salt and pepper shakers. What is your outline but a simple means to organize your account of a complicated reality? As you write, keep casting your thoughts upon a living, particular world—not twisting and squeezing that world into a rigid scheme, but moving through it with open senses, being patient and faithful and exact in your telling of it.

CHECKLIST FOR REVISING A COMPARISON AND CONTRAST

✔ **PURPOSE.** What is the aim of your comparison: to explain two subjects or evaluate them? Will the purpose be clear to readers from the start?

✔ **SUBJECTS.** Are the subjects enough alike, sharing enough features, to make comparison worthwhile?

✔ **THESIS.** Does your thesis establish a limited basis for comparison so that you have room and time to cover all the relevant similarities and differences?

✔ **ORGANIZATION.** Does your arrangement of material, whether subject by subject or point by point, do justice to your subjects and help readers follow the comparison?

✔ **BALANCE AND FLEXIBILITY.** Have you covered the same features of both subjects? At the same time, have you avoided a rigid back-and-forth movement that could bore or exhaust a reader?

COMPARISON AND CONTRAST
IN A PARAGRAPH: TWO ILLUSTRATIONS

Using Comparison and Contrast
to Write About Television

Seen on aged 16-millimeter film, the original production of Paddy Chayevsky's *Marty* makes clear the differences between television drama of 1953 and that of today. Today there's no weekly Goodyear Playhouse to showcase original one-hour plays; most scriptwriters write serials about familiar characters. *Marty* features no car chases, no bodice ripping, no mansions. Instead, it simply shows the awakening of love between a heavyset butcher and a mousy high-school teacher: both single, lonely, and shy, never twice dating the same person. Unlike the writer of today, Chayevsky couldn't set scenes outdoors or on location. In one small studio, in slow lingering takes (some five minutes long—not eight to twelve seconds, as we now expect), the camera probes the faces of two seated characters as Marty and his pal Angie plan Saturday night ("What do you want to do?" —"I dunno, what do *you*?"). Oddly, the effect is spellbinding. To bring such scenes to life, the actors must project with vigor; and like the finer actors of today, Rod Steiger as Marty exploits each moment. In 1953, plays were telecast live. Today, well-edited videotape may eliminate blown lines, but a chill slickness prevails. Technically, *Marty* is primitive, yet it probes souls. Most televised drama today displays a physically larger world—only to nail a box around it.

Point-by-point comparison supporting this topic sentence

1. *Original plays vs. serials*

2. *Simple love story vs. violence and sex*

3. *Studio sets with long takes vs. locations with short takes*

4. *Good acting vs. good acting*

5. *Live vs. videotaped*

6. *Primitive and probing vs. big and limited*

Transitions (underlined) clarify the comparison

Using Comparison and Contrast
in an Academic Discipline

In Russia, too, modernists fell into two camps. They squared off against each other in public debate and in Vkhutemas, a school of architecture organized in 1920 along lines parallel to the Bauhaus. "The measure of architecture is architecture," went the motto of one camp. They believed in an unfettered experimentalism of form. The rival camp had a problem-solving orientation. The architect's main mission, in their view, was to share in the common task of achieving the transformation of society promised by the October Revolution [of 1917]. They were keen on standardization, user interviews, and ideological prompting. They worked on new building programs that would consolidate the social order of communism. These they referred to as "social condensers."

— Spiro Kostof, *A History of Architecture*

Subject-by-subject comparison supporting this topic sentence

1. *First camp: experimental*

2. *Second camp: problem-solving (receives more attention because it eventually prevailed)*

SUZANNE BRITT

Suzanne Britt was born in Winston-Salem, North Carolina, and studied at Salem College and Washington University, where she earned an M.A. in English. She writes a regular column for *North Carolina Gardens & Homes* and for the *Dickens Dispatch,* a national newsletter for Charles Dickens disciples, and she occasionally contributes to *Books and Religion,* a newspaper of social and theological comment, published by Duke University. Britt has written for the *New York Times, Newsweek,* the *Boston Globe,* and many other publications. She teaches English part-time at Meredith College in North Carolina and has published a history of the college and two English textbooks. Her other books are collections of her essays: *Skinny People Are Dull and Crunchy like Carrots* (1982) and *Show and Tell* (1983).

Neat People
vs.
Sloppy People

"Neat People vs. Sloppy People" appears in Britt's collection *Show and Tell*. Mingling humor with seriousness (as she often does), Britt has called the book a report on her journey into "the awful cave of self: You shout your name and voices come back in exultant response, telling you their names." In this essay about certain inescapable personality traits, you may recognize some aspects of your *own* self, awful or otherwise. For a different approach to a similar subject, see the next essay, by Dave Barry.

I've finally figured out the difference between neat people and 1
sloppy people. The distinction is, as always, moral. Neat people are lazier and meaner than sloppy people.

Sloppy people, you see, are not really sloppy. Their sloppiness is 2 merely the unfortunate consequence of their extreme moral rectitude. Sloppy people carry in their mind's eye a heavenly vision, a precise plan, that is so stupendous, so perfect, it can't be achieved in this world or the next.

Sloppy people live in Never-Never Land. Someday is their métier. 3 Someday they are planning to alphabetize all their books and set up home catalogs. Someday they will go through their wardrobes and mark certain items for tentative mending and certain items for passing on to relatives of similar shape and size. Someday sloppy people will make family scrapbooks into which they will put newspaper clippings, postcards, locks of hair, and the dried corsage from their senior prom.

Someday they will file everything on the surface of their desks, including the cash receipts from coffee purchases at the snack shop. Someday they will sit down and read all the back issues of *The New Yorker*.

For all these noble reasons and more, sloppy people never get neat. 4
They aim too high and wide. They save everything, planning someday to file, order, and straighten out the world. But while these ambitious plans take clearer and clearer shape in their heads, the books spill from the shelves onto the floor, the clothes pile up in the hamper and closet, the family mementos accumulate in every drawer, the surface of the desk is buried under mounds of paper and the unread magazines threaten to reach the ceiling.

Sloppy people can't bear to part with anything. They give loving 5
attention to every detail. When sloppy people say they're going to tackle the surface of a desk, they really mean it. Not a paper will go unturned; not a rubber band will go unboxed. Four hours or two weeks into the excavation, the desk looks exactly the same, primarily because the sloppy person is meticulously creating new piles of papers with new headings and scrupulously stopping to read all the old book catalogs before he throws them away. A neat person would just bulldoze the desk.

Neat people are bums and clods at heart. They have cavalier atti- 6
tudes toward possessions, including family heirlooms. Everything is just another dust-catcher to them. If anything collects dust, it's got to go and that's that. Neat people will toy with the idea of throwing the children out of the house just to cut down on the clutter.

Neat people don't care about process. They like results. What they 7
want to do is get the whole thing over with so they can sit down and watch the rasslin' on TV. Neat people operate on two unvarying principles: Never handle any item twice, and throw everything away.

The only thing messy in a neat person's house is the trash can. The 8
minute something comes to a neat person's hand, he will look at it, try to decide if it has immediate use and, finding none, throw it in the trash.

Neat people are especially vicious with mail. They never go 9
through their mail unless they are standing directly over a trash can. If the trash can is beside the mailbox, even better. All ads, catalogs, pleas for charitable contributions, church bulletins and money-saving coupons go straight into the trash can without being opened. All letters from home, postcards from Europe, bills and paychecks are opened, immediately responded to, then dropped in the trash can. Neat people keep their receipts only for tax purposes. That's it. No sentimental salvaging of birthday cards or the last letter a dying relative ever wrote. Into the trash it goes.

Neat people place neatness above everything, even economics. 10
They are incredibly wasteful. Neat people throw away several toys

every time they walk through the den. I knew a neat person once who threw away a perfectly good dish drainer because it had mold on it. The drainer was too much trouble to wash. And neat people sell their furniture when they move. They will sell a La-Z-Boy recliner while you are reclining in it.

Neat people are no good to borrow from. Neat people buy every-   11
thing in expensive little single portions. They get their flour and sugar in two-pound bags. They wouldn't consider clipping a coupon, saving a leftover, reusing plastic nondairy whipped cream containers or rinsing off tin foil and draping it over the unmoldy dish drainer. You can never borrow a neat person's newspaper to see what's playing at the movies. Neat people have the paper all wadded up and in the trash by 7:05 A.M.

Neat people cut a clean swath through the organic as well as the   12
inorganic world. People, animals, and things are all one to them. They are so insensitive. After they've finished with the pantry, the medicine cabinet, and the attic, they will throw out the red geranium (too many leaves), sell the dog (too many fleas), and send the children off to boarding school (too many scuff-marks on the hardwood floors).

QUESTIONS ON MEANING

1. "Suzanne Britt believes that neat people are lazy, mean, petty, callous, wasteful, and insensitive." How would you respond to this statement?
2. Is the author's main PURPOSE to make fun of neat people, to assess the habits of neat and sloppy people, to help neat and sloppy people get along better, to defend sloppy people, to amuse and entertain, or to prove that neat people are morally inferior to sloppy people? Discuss.
3. What is meant by "as always" in the sentence "The distinction is, as always, moral" (para. 1)? Does the author seem to be suggesting that any and all distinctions between people are moral?

QUESTIONS ON WRITING STRATEGY

1. What is the general TONE of this essay? What words and phrases help you determine that tone?
2. Britt mentions no similarities between neat and sloppy people. Does that mean this is not a good comparison and contrast essay? Why might a writer deliberately focus on differences and give very little or no time to similarities?
3. Consider the following GENERALIZATIONS: "For all these noble reasons and more, sloppy people never get neat" (para. 4) and "The only thing messy in a neat person's house is the trash can" (para. 8). How can you tell that these

statements are generalizations? Look for other generalizations in the essay. What is the EFFECT of using so many?

4. **OTHER METHODS.** Although filled with generalizations, Britt's essay does not lack for EXAMPLES. Study the examples in paragraph 11 and explain how they do and don't work the way examples are supposed to, to bring the generalizations about people down to earth.

QUESTIONS ON LANGUAGE

1. Consult your dictionary for definitions of these words: rectitude (para. 2); métier, tentative (3); accumulate (4); excavation, meticulously, scrupulously (5); salvaging (9).
2. How do you understand the use of the word *noble* in the first sentence of paragraph 4? Is it meant literally? Are there other words in the essay that appear to be written in a similar tone?

SUGGESTIONS FOR WRITING

1. **JOURNAL WRITING.** Although Britt is writing tongue-in-cheek when she says, "Neat people are lazier and meaner than sloppy people," her essay suggests that grouping people according to oppositions like neat/sloppy reveals other things about them. What oppositions do you use to evaluate people? Smart/dumb? Fit/out of shape? Rich/poor? Outgoing/shy?

   FROM JOURNAL TO ESSAY. Choose your favorite opposition for evaluating people, and write an essay in which you compare and contrast those who pass your "test" with those who fail it. You may choose to write your essay tongue-in-cheek, as Britt does, or seriously.
2. Write an essay in which you compare and contrast two apparently dissimilar groups of people: for example, blue-collar workers and white-collar workers, people who write letters and people who don't write letters, runners and football players, readers and TV watchers, or any other variation you choose. Your approach may be either lighthearted or serious, but make sure you come to some conclusion about your subjects. Which group do you favor? Why?
3. ANALYZE the similarities and differences between two characters in your favorite novel, story, film, or television show. Which aspects of their personalities make them work well together, within the context in which they appear? Which characteristics work against each other, and therefore provide the necessary conflict to hold the readers' or viewers' attention?
4. **CRITICAL WRITING.** Britt's essay is remarkable for its exaggeration of the two types. Write a brief essay analyzing and contrasting the ways Britt characterizes sloppy people and neat people. Be sure to consider the CONNOTATIONS of the words, such as "moral rectitude" for sloppy people (para. 2) and "cavalier" for neat people (6).
5. **CONNECTIONS.** Write an essay about the humor gained from exaggeration, relying on Britt's essay and the next one, Dave Barry's "Batting Clean-Up and Striking Out." Consider why exaggeration is often funny and what qualities humorous exaggeration has. Use quotations and PARAPHRASES from Britt's and Barry's essays as your support.

SUZANNE BRITT ON WRITING

Asked to tell how she writes, Suzanne Britt contributed the following comment to *The Bedford Reader*.

"The question 'How do you write?' gets a snappy, snappish response from me. The first commandment is 'Live!' And the second is like unto it: 'Pay attention!' I don't mean that you have to live high or fast or deep or wise or broad. And I certainly don't mean you have to live true and upright. I just mean that you have to suck out all the marrow of whatever you do, whether it's picking the lint off the navy-blue suit you'll be wearing to Cousin Ione's funeral or popping an Aunt Jemimah frozen waffle into the toaster oven or lying between sand dunes, watching the way the sea oats slice the azure sky. The ominous question put to me by students on all occasions of possible accountability is 'Will this count?' My answer is rock bottom and hard: 'Everything counts,' I say, and silence falls like prayers across the room.

"The same is true of writing. Everything counts. Despair is good. Numbness can be excellent. Misery is fine. Ecstasy will work — or pain or sorrow or passion. The only thing that won't work is indifference. A writer refuses to be shocked and appalled by anything going or coming, rising or falling, singing or soundless. The only thing that shocks me, truth to tell, is indifference. How dare you not fight for the right to the crispy end piece on the standing-rib roast? How dare you let the fragrance of Joy go by without taking a whiff of it? How dare you not see the old woman in the snap-front housedress and the rolled-down socks, carrying her Polident and Charmin in a canvas tote that says, simply, elegantly, Le Bag?

"After you have lived, paid attention, seen connections, felt the harmony, writhed under the dissonance, fixed a Diet Coke, popped a big stick of Juicy Fruit in your mouth, gathered your life around you as a mother hen gathers her brood, as a queen settles the folds in her purple robes, you are ready to write. And what you will write about, even if you have one of those teachers who makes you write about, say, Guatemala, will be something very exclusive and intimate — something just between you and Guatemala. All you have to find out is what that small intimacy might be. It is there. And having found it, you have to make it count.

"There is no rest for a writer. But there is no boredom either. A Sunday morning with a bottle of extra-strength aspirin within easy reach and an ice bag on your head can serve you very well in writing. So can a fly buzzing at your ear or a heart-stopping siren in the night or an interminable afternoon in a biology lab in front of a frog's innards.

"All you need, really, is the audacity to believe, with your whole being, that if you tell it right, tell it truly, tell it so we can all see it, the 'it' will play in Peoria, Poughkeepsie, Pompeii, or Podunk. In the South we call that conviction, that audacity, an act of faith. But you can call it writing."

FOR DISCUSSION

1. What advice does Britt offer a student assigned to write a paper about, say, Guatemala? If you were that student, how would you go about taking her advice?
2. Where in her comment does the author use colorful and effective FIGURES OF SPEECH?
3. What is the TONE of Britt's remarks? Sum up her attitude toward her subject, writing.

DAVE BARRY

DAVE BARRY is a humorist whom the *New York Times* has called "the funniest man in America." Barry was born in 1947 in Armonk, New York, and graduated from Haverford College in 1969. He worked as a journalist for five years and lectured businesspeople on writing for eight years while he began to establish himself as a columnist. His humor writing now appears in several hundred newspapers and has been collected in twenty or so books, including *Bad Habits: A 100% Fact Free Book* (1985) and *The World According to Dave Barry* (1994). In 1988 Barry received the Pulitzer Prize for "distinguished commentary," although, he says, "nothing I've ever written fits the definition." (He thinks he won because his columns stood out from the "earthshakingly important" competition.) Most recently, Barry has inspired a television sitcom, *Dave's World*. He lives in Miami with his family.

Batting Clean-Up and Striking Out

This essay from *Dave Barry's Greatest Hits* (1988) illustrates Barry's gift, in the words of critic Alison Teal, "for taking things at face value and rendering them funny on those grounds alone, for rendering every ounce of humor out of a perfectly ordinary experience." Like Suzanne Britt in the previous essay, Barry sees two styles of dealing with a mess.

The primary difference between men and women is that women can see extremely small quantities of dirt. Not when they're babies, of course. Babies of both sexes have a very low awareness of dirt, other than to think it tastes better than food.

But somewhere during the growth process, a hormonal secretion takes place in women that enables them to see dirt that men cannot see, dirt at the level of *molecules*, whereas men don't generally notice it until it forms clumps large enough to support agriculture. This can lead to tragedy, as it did in the ill-fated ancient city of Pompeii, where the residents all got killed when the local volcano erupted and covered them with a layer of ash twenty feet deep.[1] Modern people often ask, "How come, when the ashes started falling, the Pompeii people didn't just *leave?*" The answer is that in Pompeii, it was the custom for the men to do the housework. They never even *noticed* the ash until it had for the most part covered the children. "Hey!" the men said (in Latin).

[1] Pompeii, in what is now southern Italy, was buried in the eruption of Mount Vesuvius in A.D. 79. — EDS.

"It's mighty quiet around here!" This is one major historical reason why, to this very day, men tend to do extremely little in the way of useful housework.

What often happens in my specific family unit is that my wife will say to me: "Could you clean Robert's bathroom? It's filthy." So I'll gather up the Standard Male Cleaning Implements, namely a spray bottle of Windex and a wad of paper towels, and I'll go into Robert's bathroom, and it *always looks perfectly fine*. I mean, when I hear the word "filthy" used to describe a bathroom, I think about this bar where I used to hang out called Joe's Sportsman's Lounge, where the men's room had bacteria you could enter in a rodeo.

Nevertheless, because I am a sensitive and caring kind of guy, I "clean" the bathroom, spraying Windex all over everything including the six hundred action figures each sold separately that God forbid Robert should ever take a bath without, and then I wipe it back off with the paper towels, and I go back to whatever activity I had been engaged in, such as doing an important project on the Etch-a-Sketch, and a little while later my wife will say: "I hate to rush you, but could you do Robert's bathroom? It's really *filthy*." She is in there looking at the very walls I *just Windexed*, and she is seeing *dirt! Everywhere!* And if I tell her I already *cleaned* the bathroom, she gives me this look that she has perfected, the same look she used on me the time I selected Robert's outfit for school and part of it turned out to be pajamas.

The opposite side of the dirt coin, of course, is sports. This is an area where men tend to feel very sensitive and women tend to be extremely callous. I have written about this before and I always get irate letters from women who say they are the heavyweight racquetball champion of some place like Iowa and are sensitive to sports to the point where they could crush my skull like a ripe grape, but I feel these women are the exception.

A more representative woman is my friend Maddy, who once invited some people, including my wife and me, over to her house for an evening of stimulating conversation and jovial companionship, which sounds fine except that this particular evening occurred *during a World Series game*. If you can imagine such a social gaffe.

We sat around the living room and Maddy tried to stimulate a conversation, but we males could not focus our attention on the various suggested topics because we could actually *feel* the World Series television and radio broadcast rays zinging through the air, penetrating right into our bodies, causing our dental fillings to vibrate, and all the while the women were behaving *as though nothing were wrong*. It was exactly like that story by Edgar Allan Poe where the murderer can hear the victim's heart beating louder and louder even though he (the murder victim) is dead, until finally he (the murderer) can't stand it anymore, and he just *has* to watch the World Series on television.[2] That was how we felt.

Maddy's husband made the first move, coming up with an ab-   8
solutely brilliant means of escape: *He used their baby.* He picked up Jus-
tine, their seven-months-old daughter, who was fussing a little, and
announced: "What this child needs is to have her bottle and watch the
World Series." And just like that he was off to the family room, moving very quickly for a big man holding a baby. A second male escaped
by pretending to clear the dessert plates. Soon all four of us were in
there, watching the Annual Fall Classic, while the women prattled
away about human relationships or something. It turned out to be an
extremely pivotal game.

QUESTIONS ON MEANING

1. What is the PURPOSE of Barry's essay? How do you know?
2. How OBJECTIVE is Barry's portrayal of men and women? Does he seem to understand one sex better than the other? Does he seek to justify and excuse
   male sloppiness and antisocial behavior?
3. What can you INFER about Barry's attitude toward the differences between
   the sexes? Does he see a way out?

QUESTIONS ON WRITING STRATEGY

1. Barry's comparison is organized point by point—differences in sensitivity
   to dirt, then differences in sensitivity to sports. What is the EFFECT of this organization? Or, from another angle, what would have been the effect of a
   subject-by-subject organization—just men, then women (or vice versa)?
2. How does Barry set the TONE of this piece from the very first paragraph?
3. The first sentence looks like a THESIS SENTENCE (if a tongue-in-cheek one).
   At what point in the essay does it become clear that it is not? Does it hurt
   or help the essay that it actually has no thesis sentence?
4. How does Barry's ALLUSION to Poe's "The Tell-Tale Heart" enhance Barry's
   own story?
5. **OTHER METHODS.** How persuasive is the historical EXAMPLE cited in paragraph 2 as EVIDENCE for Barry's claims about men's and women's differing
   abilities to perceive dirt? Must examples always be persuasive?

QUESTIONS ON LANGUAGE

1. Define these words: hormonal (para. 2); implements (3); callous, irate (5);
   jovial, gaffe (6); prattled, pivotal (8).

---

[2] Barry refers to Poe's story "The Tell-Tale Heart" (1843). The story (minus Barry's
World Series ending) appears on pages 88–92 of this book. —EDS.

2. Paragraph 4 begins with a textbook example of a run-on sentence. Does Barry need a better copy editor, or is he deliberately going for an effect here? If so, what is it?
3. What effect does Barry achieve through his frequent use of italics (for example, "*just Windexed*," para. 4) and capital letters ("Standard Male Cleaning Implements," 3)?
4. Why does Barry use the word *males* instead of *men* in paragraphs 7 and 8?

SUGGESTIONS FOR WRITING

1. **JOURNAL WRITING.** Make a list of traits of the opposite sex you find foreign or bewildering. (They would rather talk to you on the phone than in person. They would rather watch sports on TV than play them....)
   FROM JOURNAL TO ESSAY. Choose the trait on your list about the opposite sex that seems to have the most potential for humor. Write an essay similar to Barry's, exaggerating the difference to the point where it becomes the defining distinction between men and women.
2. How well do you conform to Barry's GENERALIZATIONS about your gender? In what ways are you stereotypically male or female? Do such generalizations amuse or merely annoy you? Why?
3. **CRITICAL WRITING.** Barry is obviously not afraid of offending women: He claims to have already done so (para. 5), and yet he persists. Do you take offense at any of this essay's stereotypes of women and men? If so, explain the nature of the offense as coolly as you can. Whether you take offense or not, can you see any virtue in using such stereotypes for humor? For instance, does the humor help undermine the stereotypes or merely strengthen them? Write an essay in which you address these questions, using quotations from Barry as examples and evidence.
4. **CONNECTIONS.** Like Barry, Suzanne Britt (p. 182) relies heavily on exaggeration and generalization in her characterizations of "neat" and "sloppy" people. Write an essay about the humor gained from these two techniques, using quotations and PARAPHRASES from both essays. You might want to address the potential risks of using these methods to get a laugh, and the degree to which Barry and Britt have succeeded in avoiding them.

DAVE BARRY ON WRITING

For Dave Barry, coming up with ideas for humorous writing is no problem. "Just about anything's a topic for a humor column," he told an interviewer for *Contemporary Authors* in 1990, "any event that occurs in the news, anything that happens in daily life—driving, shopping, reading, eating. You can look at just about anything and see humor in it somewhere."

Writing challenges, for Barry, occur after he has his idea. "Writing has always been hard for me," he says. "The hard part is getting the jokes to come, and it never happens all at once for me. I very rarely have any idea where a column is going to go when it starts. It's a matter of piling a little piece here and a little piece there, fitting them together, going on to the next part, then going back and gradually shaping the whole piece into something. I know what I want in terms of reaction, and I want it to have a certain feel. I know when it does and when it doesn't. But I'm never sure when it's going to get there. That's what writing is. That's why it's so painful and slow. But that's more technique than anything else. You don't rely on inspiration—I don't, anyway, and I don't think most writers do. The creative process is just not an inspirational one for most people. There's a little bit of that and a whole lot of polishing."

A humor writer must be sensitive to readers, trying to make them smile, but Barry warns against catering to an audience. "I think it's a big mistake to write humor for anybody but yourself, to try to adopt any persona other than your own. If I don't at some point think something is funny, then I'm not going to write it." Not that his own sense of humor will always make a piece fly. "Thinking of it in rough form is one thing," Barry confesses, "and shaping and polishing it so that you like the way it reads is so agonizingly slow that by the time you're done, you don't think anything is funny. You think this is something you might use to console a widow."

More often, though, the shaping and polishing—the constant revision—do work. "Since I know how to do that," Barry says, "since I do it every day of the week and have for years and years, I'm confident that if I keep at it I'll get something."

FOR DISCUSSION

1. Do you agree with Barry that "you can look at just about anything and see humor in it somewhere"? What topics do you think would be off-limits for humor?
2. What does successful writing depend on, according to Barry? What role does inspiration play?
3. How might Barry's views on writing be relevant to your own experiences as a writer? What can a humor writer teach a college writer?

BRUCE CATTON

BRUCE CATTON (1899–1978) became America's best-known historian of the Civil War. As a boy in Benzonia, Michigan, Catton acted out historical battles on local playing fields. In his memoir *Waiting for the Morning Train* (1972), he recalls how he would listen by the hour to the memories of Union Army veterans. His studies at Oberlin College interrupted by service in World War I, Catton never finished his bachelor's degree. Instead, he worked as a reporter, columnist, and editorial writer for the *Cleveland Plain Dealer* and other newspapers, then became a speechwriter and information director for government agencies. Of Catton's eighteen books, seventeen were written after his fiftieth year. *A Stillness at Appomattox* (1953) won him both a Pulitzer Prize for history and a National Book Award; other notable works include *This Hallowed Ground* (1956) and *Gettysburg: The Final Fury* (1974). From 1954 until his death, Catton edited *American Heritage*, a magazine of history. President Gerald Ford awarded him a Medal of Freedom for his life's accomplishment.

Grant and Lee: A Study in Contrasts

"Grant and Lee: A Study in Contrasts" first appeared in *The American Story*, a book of essays written by eminent historians for interested general readers. In his discussion of the two great Civil War generals, Catton contrasts not only two very different men but also the conflicting traditions they represented. Catton's essay builds toward the conclusion that, in one outstanding way, the two leaders were more than a little alike.

When Ulysses S. Grant and Robert E. Lee met in the parlor of a 1 modest house at Appomattox Court House, Virginia, on April 9, 1865, to work out the terms for the surrender of Lee's Army of Northern Virginia, a great chapter in American life came to a close, and a great new chapter began.

These men were bringing the Civil War to its virtual finish. To be 2 sure, other armies had yet to surrender, and for a few days the fugitive confederate government would struggle desperately and vainly, trying to find some way to go on living now that its chief support was gone. But in effect it was all over when Grant and Lee signed the papers. And the little room where they wrote out the terms was the scene of one of the poignant, dramatic contrasts in American history.

They were two strong men, these oddly different generals, and they 3

193

represented the strengths of two conflicting currents that, through them, had come into final collision.

Back of Robert E. Lee was the notion that the old aristocratic con-   4
cept might somehow survive and be dominant in American life.

Lee was tidewater Virginia, and in his background were family,   5
culture, and tradition...the age of chivalry transplanted to a New World which was making its own legends and its own myths. He embodied a way of life that had come down through the age of knighthood and the English country squire. America was a land that was beginning all over again, dedicated to nothing much more complicated than the rather hazy belief that all men had equal rights, and should have an equal chance in the world. In such a land Lee stood for the feeling that it was somehow of advantage to human society to have a pronounced inequality in the social structure. There should be a leisure class, backed by ownership of land; in turn, society itself should be keyed to the land as the chief source of wealth and influence. It would bring forth (according to this ideal) a class of men with a strong sense of obligation to the community; men who lived not to gain advantage for themselves, but to meet the solemn obligations which had been laid on them by the very fact that they were privileged. From them the country would get its leadership; to them it could look for the higher values—of thought, of conduct, of personal deportment—to give it strength and virtue.

Lee embodied the noblest elements of this aristocratic ideal.   6
Through him, the landed nobility justified itself. For four years, the Southern states had fought a desperate war to uphold the ideals for which Lee stood. In the end, it almost seemed as if the Confederacy fought for Lee; as if he himself was the Confederacy...the best thing that the way of life for which the Confederacy stood could ever have to offer. He had passed into legend before Appomattox. Thousands of tired, underfed, poorly clothed Confederate soldiers, long-since past the simple enthusiasm of the early days of the struggle, somehow considered Lee the symbol of everything for which they had been willing to die. But they could not quite put this feeling into words. If the Lost Cause, sanctified by so much heroism and so many deaths, had a living justification, its justification was General Lee.

Grant, the son of a tanner on the Western frontier, was everything   7
Lee was not. He had come up the hard way, and embodied nothing in particular except the eternal toughness and sinewy fiber of the men who grew up beyond the mountains. He was one of a body of men who owed reverence and obeisance to no one, who were self-reliant to a fault, who cared hardly anything for the past but who had a sharp eye for the future.

These frontier men were the precise opposites of the tidewater aris-   8 tocrats. Back of them, in the great surge that had taken people over the Alleghenies and into the opening Western country, there was a deep, implicit dissatisfaction with a past that had settled into grooves. They stood for democracy, not from any reasoned conclusion about the proper ordering of human society, but simply because they had grown up in the middle of democracy and knew how it worked. Their society might have privileges, but they would be privileges each man had won for himself. Forms and patterns meant nothing. No man was born to anything, except perhaps to a chance to show how far he could rise. Life was competition.

Yet along with this feeling had come a deep sense of belonging to a   9
national community. The Westerner who developed a farm, opened a shop, or set up in business as a trader could hope to prosper only as his own community prospered—and his community ran from the Atlantic to the Pacific and from Canada down to Mexico. If the land was settled, with towns and highways and accessible markets, he could better himself. He saw his fate in terms of the nation's own destiny. As its horizons expanded, so did his. He had, in other words, an acute dollars-and-cents stake in the continued growth and development of his country.

And that, perhaps, is where the contrast between Grant and Lee   10
becomes most striking. The Virginia aristocrat, inevitably, saw himself in relation to his own region. He lived in a static society which could endure almost anything except change. Instinctively, his first loyalty would go to the locality in which that society existed. He would fight to the limit of endurance to defend it, because in defending it he was defending everything that gave his own life its deepest meaning.

The Westerner, on the other hand, would fight with an equal   11
tenacity for the broader concept of society. He fought so because everything he lived by was tied to growth, expansion, and a constantly widening horizon. What he lived by would survive or fall with the nation itself. He could not possibly stand by unmoved in the face of an attempt to destroy the Union. He would combat it with everything he had, because he could only see it as an effort to cut the ground out from under his feet.

So Grant and Lee were in complete contrast, representing two di-   12
ametrically opposed elements in American life. Grant was the modern man emerging; beyond him, ready to come on the stage, was the great age of steel and machinery, of crowded cities and a restless, burgeoning vitality. Lee might have ridden down from the old age of chivalry, lance in hand, silken banner fluttering over his head. Each man was the perfect champion of his cause, drawing both his strengths and his weaknesses from the people he led.

Yet it was not all contrast, after all. Different as they were—in   13 background, in personality, in underlying aspiration—these two great soldiers had much in common. Under everything else, they were marvelous fighters. Furthermore, their fighting qualities were really very much alike.

Each man had, to begin with, the great virtue of utter tenacity and 14 fidelity. Grant fought his way down the Mississippi Valley in spite of acute personal discouragement and profound military handicaps. Lee hung on in the trenches at Petersburg after hope itself had died. In each man there was an indomitable quality...the born fighter's refusal to give up as long as he can still remain on his feet and lift his two fists.

Daring and resourcefulness they had, too; the ability to think faster 15 and move faster than the enemy. These were the qualities which gave Lee the dazzling campaigns of Second Manassas and Chancellorsville and won Vicksburg for Grant.

Lastly, and perhaps greatest of all, there was the ability, at the end, 16 to turn quickly from war to peace once the fighting was over. Out of the way these two men behaved at Appomattox came the possibility of a peace of reconciliation. It was a possibility not wholly realized, in the years to come, but which did, in the end, help the two sections to become one nation again...after a war whose bitterness might have seemed to make such a reunion wholly impossible. No part of either man's life became him more than the part he played in their brief meeting in the McLean house at Appomattox. Their behavior there put all succeeding generations of Americans in their debt. Two great Americans, Grant and Lee—very different, yet under everything very much alike. Their encounter at Appomattox was one of the great moments of American history.

QUESTIONS ON MEANING

1. What is Bruce Catton's PURPOSE in writing: to describe the meeting of two generals at a famous moment in history; to explain how the two men stood for opposing social forces in America; or to show how the two differed in personality?
2. SUMMARIZE the background and the way of life that produced Robert E. Lee; then do the same for Ulysses S. Grant. According to Catton, what ideals did each man represent?
3. In the historian's view, what essential traits did the two men have in common? Which trait does Catton think most important of all? For what reason?
4. How does this essay help you understand why Grant and Lee were such determined fighters?

QUESTIONS ON WRITING STRATEGY

1. From the content of this essay, and from knowing where it first appeared, what can you infer about Catton's original AUDIENCE? At what places in his essay does the writer expect of his readers a familiarity with United States history?
2. What effect does the writer achieve by setting both his INTRODUCTION and his CONCLUSION in Appomattox?
3. For what reasons does Catton contrast the two generals *before* he compares them? Suppose he had reversed his outline, and had dealt first with Grant's and Lee's mutual resemblances. Why would his essay have been less effective?
4. Pencil in hand, draw a single line down the margin of every paragraph in which you find the method of contrast. Then draw a *double* line next to every paragraph in which you find the method of comparison. How much space does Catton devote to each method? Why didn't he give comparison and contrast equal time?
5. Closely read the first sentence of every paragraph and underline each word or phrase in it that serves as a TRANSITION. Then review your underlinings. How much COHERENCE has Catton given his essay?
6. What is the TONE of this essay — that is, what is the writer's attitude toward his two subjects? Is Catton poking fun at Lee by imagining the Confederate general as a knight of the Middle Ages, "lance in hand, silken banner fluttering over his head" (para. 12)?
7. **OTHER METHODS.** In identifying "two conflicting currents," Catton uses CLASSIFICATION to sort Civil War–era Americans into two groups represented by Lee and Grant. Catton then uses ANALYSIS to tease out the characteristics of each current, each type. How do classification and analysis serve Catton's comparison and contrast?

QUESTIONS ON LANGUAGE

1. In his opening paragraph, Catton uses a METAPHOR: American life is a book containing chapters. Find other FIGURES OF SPEECH in his essay. What do they contribute?
2. Look up *poignant* in the dictionary. Why is it such a fitting word in paragraph 2? Why wouldn't *touching, sad,* or *teary* have been as good?
3. What information do you glean from the sentence "Lee was tidewater Virginia" (para. 5)?
4. Define *aristocratic* as Catton uses it in paragraphs 4 and 6.
5. Define *obeisance* (para. 7); *indomitable* (14).

SUGGESTIONS FOR WRITING

1. **JOURNAL WRITING.** During the American Civil War, nearly every citizen had an opinion and chose sides. Do you think Americans today are generally as interested in political issues? Why, or why not?
   FROM JOURNAL TO ESSAY. Write an essay that offers an explanation for public participation in or commitment to political and social causes. What fires people up or turns them off? To help focus your essay, zero in on a specific issue, such as wartime patriotism, voting, education, or government spending.

2. In a brief essay full of specific examples, discuss: Do the "two diametrically opposed elements in American life" (as Catton calls them) still exist in the country today? Are there still any "landed nobility"?
3. In your thinking and your attitudes, whom do you more closely resemble — Grant or Lee? Compare and contrast your outlook with that of one famous American or the other. (A serious tone for this topic isn't required.)
4. **CRITICAL WRITING.** Although slavery, along with other issues, helped precipitate the Civil War, Catton in this particular essay does not deal with it. Perhaps he assumes that his readers will supply the missing context themselves. Is this a fair ASSUMPTION? If Catton had recalled the facts of slavery, would he have undermined any of his assertions about Lee? (Though the general of the pro-slavery Confederacy, Lee was personally opposed to slavery.) In a brief essay, judge whether or not the omission of slavery weakens the essay, and explain why.
5. **CONNECTIONS.** Ishmael Reed, in "America: The Multinational Society" (p. 476), argues that this country's cultural diversity has always been its greatest strength. In an essay, position this view of America alongside that attributed by Catton to Ulysses S. Grant: "No man was born to anything, except perhaps a chance to show how far he could rise. Life was competition." Questions to consider: In a culturally diverse society, who benefits from such competition? What does competition do for the United States? How does diversity help or hinder competition?

BRUCE CATTON ON WRITING

Most of Bruce Catton's comments on writing, those that have been preserved, refer to the work of others. As editor of *American Heritage*, he was known for his blunt, succinct comments on unsuccessful manuscripts: "This article can't be repaired and wouldn't be much good if it were." Or: "The high-water mark of this piece comes at the bottom of page one, where the naked Indian nymph offers the hero strawberries. Unfortunately, this level is not maintained."

In a memoir published in *Bruce Catton's America* (1979), Catton's associate Oliver Jensen has marveled that, besides editing *American Heritage* for twenty-four years (and contributing to nearly every issue), Catton managed to produce so many substantial books. "Concentration was no doubt the secret, that and getting an early start. For many years Catton was always the first person in the office, so early that most of the staff never knew when he did arrive. On his desk the little piles of yellow sheets grew slowly, with much larger piles in the wastebasket. A neat and orderly man, he preferred to type a new page than correct very much in pencil."

His whole purpose as a writer, Catton once said, was "to reexamine [our] debt to the past."

FOR DISCUSSION

1. To which of Catton's traits does Oliver Jensen attribute the historian's impressive output?
2. Which characteristics of Catton the editor would you expect to have served him well as a writer?

JEFF GREENFIELD

JEFF GREENFIELD, born in 1943, graduated from the University of Wisconsin and Yale University School of Law. He became a sportswriter, humorist, and media commentator for CBS-TV, and now he is a political and media analyst for ABC News, a regular guest anchor on the news show *Nightline*, and a syndicated columnist. Earlier in his career, he served as a staff aide and writer of speeches for both John V. Lindsay, former mayor of New York City, and the late attorney general Robert F. Kennedy. His books include *A Populist Manifesto* (1972), *Where Have You Gone, Joe DiMaggio?* (1973), *The World's Greatest Team* (history of the Boston Celtics, 1976), *Television: The First 50 Years* (1977), *Playing to Win: An Insider's Guide to Politics* (1980), *The Real Campaign* (1982), and *The People's Choice* (1995).

The Black and White Truth
About Basketball

When Jeff Greenfield's survey of "black" and "white" basketball, subtitled "A Skin-Deep Theory of Style," was first published in *Esquire* in 1975, it provoked immediate interest and controversy. Greenfield has updated the essay for Bedford Books, most recently in 1993. (His thesis is unchanged.)

The dominance of black athletes over professional basketball is beyond dispute. Two-thirds of the players are black, and the number would be greater were it not for the continuing practice of picking white bench warmers for the sake of balance. Over the last two decades, no more than three white players have been among the ten starting players on the National Basketball Association's All-Star team, and in the last quarter century, only two white players—Dave Cowens and Larry Bird of the Boston Celtics—have ever been chosen as the NBA's Most Valuable Player.

And at a time when a baseball executive can lose his job for asserting that blacks lack "the necessities" to become pro sports executives and when the National Football League only in 1989 had its first black head coach, the NBA stands as a pro sports league that hired its first black head coach in 1968 (Bill Russell) and its first black general manager in the early 1970s (Wayne Embry of the Milwaukee Bucks). What discrimination remains—lack of equal opportunity for speaking engagements and product endorsements—has more to do with society than with basketball.

This dominance reflects a natural inheritance: Basketball is a pastime of the urban poor. The current generation of black athletes are heirs to a tradition more than half a century old. In a neighborhood without the money for bats, gloves, hockey sticks and ice skates, or shoulder pads, basketball is an eminently accessible sport. "Once it was the game of the Irish and Italian Catholics in Rockaway and the Jews on Fordham Road in the Bronx," writes David Wolf in his brilliant book, *Foul!* "It was recreation, status, and a way out." But now the ethnic names have been changed: Instead of the Red Holzmans, Red Auerbachs, and the McGuire brothers, there are the Michael Jordans and Charles Barkleys, the Shaquille O'Neals and Patrick Ewings. And professional basketball is a sport with national television exposure and million-dollar salaries.

But the mark on basketball of today's players can be measured by   4
more than money or visibility. It is a question of style. For there is a clear difference between "black" and "white" styles of play that is as clear as the difference between 155th Street at Eighth Avenue and Crystal City, Missouri. Most simply (remembering we are talking about culture, not chromosomes), "black" basketball is the use of superb athletic skill to adapt to the limits of space imposed by the game. "White" ball is the pulverization of that space by sheer intensity.[1]

It takes a conscious effort to realize how constricted the space is on   5
a basketball court. Place a regulation court (ninety-four by fifty feet) in a football field, and it will reach from the back of the end zone to the twenty-one-yard line; its width will cover less than a third of the field. On a baseball diamond, a basketball court will reach from home plate to first base. Compared to its principal indoor rival, ice hockey, basketball covers about one-fourth the playing area. Moreover, during the normal flow of the game, most of the action takes place on the third of the court nearest the basket. It is in this dollhouse space that ten men, each of them half a foot taller than the average man, come together to battle each other.

There is, thus, no room; basketball is a struggle for the edge: the   6
half step with which to cut around the defender for a lay-up, the half second of freedom with which to release a jump shot, the instant a head turns allowing a pass to a teammate breaking for the basket. It is an arena for the subtlest of skills: the head fake, the shoulder fake, the shift of body weight to the right and the sudden cut to the left. Deception is crucial to success; and to young men who have learned early and

---

[1] This distinction has nothing to do with the question of whether whites can play as "well" as blacks. In 1987, the Detroit Pistons' Isiah Thomas quipped that the Celtics' Larry Bird was "a pretty good player," but would be much less celebrated and wealthy if he were black. As Thomas later said, Bird was one of the greatest pro players in history. Nor is this distinction about "smart," although the ex–Los Angeles Laker great Magic Johnson was right when he said that too many journalists attribute brilliant strategic moves by black players to "innate" ability.

painfully that life is a battle for survival, basketball is one of the few pursuits in which the weapon of deception is a legitimate tactic rather than a source of trouble.

If there is, then, the need to compete in a crowd, to battle for the edge, then the surest strategy is to develop the *unexpected:* to develop a shot that is simply and fundamentally different from the usual methods of putting the ball in the basket. Drive to the hoop, but go under it and come up the other side; hold the ball at waist level and shoot from there instead of bringing the ball up to eye level; leap into the air, but fall away from the basket instead of toward it. All these tactics, which a fan can see embodied in the astonishing play of the Chicago Bulls' Michael Jordan, take maximum advantage of the crowding on the court. They also stamp uniqueness on young men who may feel it nowhere else.

"For many young men in the slums," David Wolf writes, "the school yard is the only place they can feel true pride in what they do, where they can move free of inhibitions and where they can, by being spectacular, rise for the moment against the drabness and anonymity of their lives. Thus, when a player develops extraordinary 'school yard' moves and shots...[they] become his measure as a man."

So the moves that begin as tactics for scoring soon become calling cards. You don't just lay the ball in for an uncontested basket; you take the ball in both hands, leap as high as you can, and slam the ball through the hoop. When you jump in the air, fake a shot, bring the ball back to your body, and throw up a shot, all without coming back down, you have proven your worth in uncontestable fashion.

This liquid grace is an integral part of "black" ball, almost exclusively the province of the playground player. Some white stars like Bob Cousy, Billy Cunningham, Doug Collins, and Kevin McHale had it; John Stockton of the Utah Jazz has it now: the body control, the moves to the basket, the free-ranging mobility. Most of them also possessed the surface ease that is integral to the "black" style; an incorporation of the ethic of mean streets—to "make it" is not just to have wealth but to have it without strain. Whatever the muscles and organs are doing, the face of the "black" star almost never shows it. Magic Johnson of the Lakers could bring the ball downcourt with two men on him, whip a pass through an invisible opening, cut to the basket, take a return pass, and hit the shot all with no more emotion than a quick smile. So stoic was San Antonio Spurs great George Gervin that he earned the nickname "Ice Man." (Interestingly, a black coach like San Antonio's John Lucan exhibits far less emotion on the bench than a white counterpart like Portland's Rick Adelman.)

If there is a single trait that characterizes "black" ball it is leaping ability. Bob Cousy, ex-Celtic great and former pro coach, says that "when coaches get together, one is sure to say, 'I've got the one black kid in the country who can't jump.' When coaches see a white boy who can jump or who moves with extraordinary quickness, they say, 'He should have been born black, he's that good.'" This pervasive belief was immortalized by the title of the hit film *White Men Can't Jump*.

Don Nelson, now a top executive with the Golden State Warriors, recalls that back in 1970, Dave Cowens, then a relatively unknown graduate of Florida State, prepared for his rookie pro season by playing in the Rucker League, an outdoor competition in Harlem playgrounds that pits pros against college kids and playground stars. So ferocious was Cowens's leaping ability, Nelson says, that "when the summer was over, everyone wanted to know who the white son of a bitch was who could jump so high." That's another way to overcome a crowd around the basket—just go over it. 12

Speed, mobility, quickness, acceleration, "the moves"—all of these are catch-phrases that surround the "black" playground athlete, the style of play. So does the most racially tinged of attributes, "rhythm." Yet rhythm is what the black stars themselves talk about: feeling the flow of the game, finding the tempo of the dribble, the step, the shot. It is an instinctive quality (although it stems from hundreds of hours of practice), and it is one that has led to difficulty between system-oriented coaches and free-form players. "Cats from the street have their own rhythm when they play," said college dropout Bill Spivey, onetime New York high school star. "It's not a matter of somebody setting you up and you shooting. You *feel* the shot. When a coach holds you back, you lose the feel and it isn't fun anymore." 13

When legendary Brooklyn playground star Connie Hawkins was winding up his NBA career under Laker coach Bill Sharman, he chafed under the methodical style of play. "He's systematic to the point where it begins to be a little too much. It's such an action-reaction type of game that when you have to do everything the same way, I think you lose something." 14

There is another kind of basketball that has grown up in America. It is not played on asphalt playgrounds with a crowd of kids competing for the court; it is played on macadam driveways by one boy with a ball and a backboard nailed over the garage; it is played in gyms in the frigid winter of the rural Midwest and on Southern dirt courts. It is a mechanical, precise development of skills (when Don Nelson was an Iowa farm boy, his incentive to make his shots was that an errant rebound would land in the middle of chicken droppings). It is a game without frills, without flow, but with effectiveness. It is "white" basketball: jagged, sweaty, stumbling, intense. Where a "black" player overcomes an obstacle with finesse and body control, a "white" player reacts by outrunning or overpowering the obstacle. 15

By this definition, the Boston Celtics have been classically "white" 16
regardless of the pigmentation of the players. They have rarely suited
up a player with dazzling moves; indeed, such a player would probably
have made Red Auerbach swallow his cigar. Instead, the Celtic philosophy has been to wear you down with execution, with constant running, with the same play run again and again. The rebound by Bill
Russell (or Dave Cowens or Robert Parrish) triggers the fast break, as
everyone races downcourt; the ball goes to Bob Cousy (or John
Havlicek or Larry Bird), who pulls up and takes the shot, or who drives
and then finds Sam Jones (or Kevin McHale or M. L. Carr) free for an
easy basket.

Perhaps the most definitively "white" position is that of the quick 17
forward, one without great moves to the basket, without highly developed shots, without the height and mobility for rebounding effectiveness. So what does he do?

He runs. He runs from the opening jump to the final buzzer. He 18
runs up and down the court, from base line to base line, back and forth
under the basket, looking for the opening, the pass, the chance to take
a quick step, the high-percentage shot. To watch Detroit's Bill Laimbeer or the Suns' Dan Majerle, players without speed or obvious
moves, is to wonder what they are doing in the NBA—until you see
them swing free and throw up a shot that, without demanding any apparent skill, somehow goes in the basket more frequently than the
shots of many of their more skilled teammates. And to have watched
the New York Knicks' (now U.S. Senator) Bill Bradley, or the Celtics'
John Havlicek, is to have watched "white" ball at its best.

Havlicek or Laimbeer or the Phoenix Suns' Danny Ainge stands in 19
dramatic contrast to Michael Jordan or to the Philadelphia 76ers legend Julius Erving. Erving had the capacity to make legends come true,
leaping from the foul line and slam-dunking the ball on his way down;
going up for a lay-up, pulling the ball to his body, and driving under and
up the other side of the rim, defying gravity and probability with impossible moves and jumps. Michael Jordan of the Chicago Bulls has
been seen by thousands spinning a full 360 degrees in midair before
slamming the ball through the hoop.

When John Havlicek played, by contrast, he was the living em- 20
bodiment of his small-town Ohio background. He would bring the ball
downcourt, weaving left, then right, looking for a path. He would
swing the ball to a teammate, cut behind the pick, take the pass, and
release the shot in a flicker of time. It looked plain, unvarnished. But it
was a blend of skills that not more than half a dozen other players in
the league possessed.

To former pro Jim McMillian, a black who played quick forward 21
with "white" attributes, "it's a matter of environment. Julius Erving

grew up in a different environment from Havlicek. John came from a very small town in Ohio. There everything was done the easy way, the shortest distance between two points. It's nothing fancy; very few times will he go one-on-one. He hits the lay-up, hits the jump shot, makes the free throw, and after the game you look up and say, 'How did he hurt us that much?'"

"White" ball, then, is the basketball of patience, method, and   22
sometimes brute strength. "Black" ball is the basketball of electric self-expression. One player has all the time in the world to perfect his skills, the other a need to prove himself. These are slippery categories, because a poor boy who is black can play "white" and a white boy of middle-class parents can play "black." Charles Oakley of the New York Knicks and John Paxson of the Chicago Bulls are athletes who seem to defy these categories.

And what makes basketball the most intriguing of sports is how   23
these styles do not necessarily clash; how the punishing intensity of "white" players and the dazzling moves of the "blacks" can fit together, a fusion of cultures that seems more and more difficult in the world beyond the out-of-bounds line.

QUESTIONS ON MEANING

1. According to Greenfield, how did black athletes come to dominate professional basketball?
2. What differences does the author discern between "black" and "white" styles of play? How do exponents of the two styles differ in showing emotion?
3. Explain the author's reference to the word *rhythm* as "the most racially tinged of attributes" (para. 13).
4. Does Greenfield stereotype black and white players? Where in his essay does he admit there are players who don't fit neatly into his two categories?

QUESTIONS ON WRITING STRATEGY

1. How much do we have to know about professional basketball to appreciate Greenfield's essay? Is it written only for basketball fans, or for a general AUDIENCE?
2. In what passage in his essay does Greenfield begin comparing and contrasting? What is the function of the paragraphs that come before this passage?
3. In paragraph 5, the author compares a basketball court to a football field, a baseball diamond, and an ice hockey arena. What is the basis for his comparison?
4. **OTHER METHODS.** In addition to comparison and contrast and a good deal of DESCRIPTION, Greenfield uses CAUSE AND EFFECT when he accounts for the

differences in playing style. In your own words, SUMMARIZE the author's point about school yards (para. 8) and his point about macadam driveways, gyms, and dirt courts (15). Explain "the ethic of mean streets" (10).

QUESTIONS ON LANGUAGE

1. Consult the dictionary if you need help in defining the following words: ethnic (para. 3); constricted (5); inhibitions, anonymity (8); uncontestable (9); finesse (15); execution (16); embodiment (20).
2. Talk to someone who knows basketball if you need help in understanding the head fake, the shoulder fake (para. 6); the fast break (16); the high-percentage shot (18); the jump shot (21). What kind of DICTION do you find in these instances?
3. When Greenfield says, "We are talking about culture, not chromosomes" (para. 4), how would you expect him to define these terms?

SUGGESTIONS FOR WRITING

1. **JOURNAL WRITING.** Is it a problem that Greenfield's argument relies on GENERALIZATIONS about groups of people? Why, or why not?
   FROM JOURNAL TO ESSAY. Write an essay that discusses how well (or not) Greenfield has surmounted the difficulties facing any writer who makes generalizations about people. Consider as background what makes a generalization reasonable or responsible.
2. Compare and contrast a college basketball and professional basketball team, or the styles of two athletes in any sport.
3. Compare and contrast the styles of two people in the same line of work, showing how their work is affected by their different personalities. You might take, for instance, two singers, two taxi drivers, two bank tellers, two evangelists, two teachers, or two symphony orchestra conductors.
4. **CRITICAL WRITING.** Do you agree with Greenfield's observations about basketball styles? Consider the exceptions Greenfield cites (paras. 10, 21, 22), and muster any of your own. In an essay, EVALUATE whether Greenfield's essay can withstand these exceptions: In your opinion, are Greenfield's ideas valid?
5. **CONNECTIONS.** Like Greenfield, Annie Dillard, in "The Chase" (p. 59), uses sports as a point of departure for exploring larger, more universal themes. Write a brief essay comparing and contrasting the two authors' treatments of sports as a METAPHOR. What does each writer seem to see as the function of sports in our society?

JEFF GREENFIELD ON WRITING

For *The Bedford Reader*, Jeff Greenfield told how he gathered his information for "The Black and White Truth About Basketball" from basketball professionals, and how he tried to contrast the two styles of play with humor and goodwill. "In the early 1970s," he commented, "I was spending a good deal of time playing hooky from my work as a political consultant writing books and magazine articles; and no writing was more enjoyable than sports reporting.... Coming from the world of politics where everything was debatable—who would win, whose position was right, who was engaging in 'desperation smear tactics'—I relished the world of sports, where winners and losers were clearly identifiable....

"It was while writing about various star basketball players of the time —men like the New York Knicks' Willis Reed, the Boston Celtics' Dave Cowens—that I first began noticing how often offhand, utterly unmalicious racial references were being thrown about. A white player in practice would miss a rebound, and a black teammate would joke, 'Come on, man, jump like a brother.' A black player would lose a footrace for a ball, and someone would quip, 'Looks black, plays white.' It slowly became clear to me that many of those in the basketball world freely acknowledged that there were different styles of play that broke down, roughly speaking, into black and white characteristics.

"At first, it did not even occur to me that this would make a publishable magazine piece. For one thing, I came from a typical postwar liberal family, repulsed by the racial stereotypes which still dominated 'respectable' conversation. In a time when black Americans were heavily portrayed as happy-go-lucky, shiftless, childlike adults, consigned to success as athletes and tap-dancers, the idea that there was anything like a 'black' or 'white' way to play basketball would have seemed something out of a segregationist manifesto.

"For another, I have always been an enthusiastic follower of the sports pages and had never seen any such analysis in the many newspapers I read. Apparently, most sportswriters felt equally uncomfortable with a foray into race; it had, after all, taken baseball more than a half a century to admit blacks into its ranks. Indeed, one of the more common assertions of bigots in the 1930s and 1940s was that blacks could not be great athletes because 'they couldn't take the pressure.' It is easy to understand why race was not a comfortable basis on which to analyze athletic grace.

"In the end, I decided to write about 'black' and 'white' basketball because it made the game more enjoyable to me. Clearly, there *were* different ways to play the game; clearly the kind of self-assertion represented by the spectacular moves of black schoolyard ball was a reflection of how important the game was to an inner-city kid, for whom the asphalt court was the cheapest—maybe the only—release from a nasty, sometimes brutish, existence. And books such as Pete Axthelm's *The City Game* and David Wolf's *Foul!* had brilliantly explored the significance of basketball in the urban black world of modern America.

"I talked with players and sportswriters alike when I wrote the article; without exception, they approached the subject as I did: with humor, un-self-consciously. Perhaps it is a measure of the progress we have made in racial matters that no one—black or white—thought it insulting or offensive to remark on the different styles of play, to note that the gravity-defying slam-dunks of a Michael Jordan and the carefully calibrated shots of a Dan Majerle are two facets of the same game."

FOR DISCUSSION

1. What gave Greenfield the idea for his essay?
2. What aspects of his topic made Greenfield hesitant to write about it? What persuaded him to go ahead?

JUDITH ORTIZ COFER

A native of Puerto Rico who has lived most of her life in the United States, JUDITH ORTIZ COFER writes poetry, fiction, and essays about her heritage and the balancing of two cultures. Born in Hormigueros, Puerto Rico, in 1952, she earned a B.A. from Augusta College in 1974 and an M.A. from Florida Atlantic University in 1977, the same year she attended Oxford University as scholar of the English Speaking Union. Cofer started out as a bilingual teacher in the schools of Palm Beach County, Florida, and she has taught English at several colleges and universities. Her publications include collections of poetry, among them *Peregrina* (1986) and *Terms of Survival* (1987); a novel, *The Line of the Sun* (1989); a book of essays, *Silent Dancing* (1990); and a book of stories for young people, *An Island like You: Stories from the Barrio* (1995). As a native Spanish speaker who challenged herself to learn English, she is always experimenting, she says, with "the 'infinite variety' and power of language."

Advanced Biology

Her Puerto Rican heritage and American upbringing often pulled Cofer in opposite directions. In this essay from her collection *The Latin Deli: Prose and Poetry* (1993), she seeks "cultural compromise" in remembering high-school biology class.

As I lay out clothes for the trip to Miami to do a reading from my 1 recently published novel, then on to Puerto Rico to see my mother, I take a close look at my travel wardrobe—the tailored skirts in basic colors easily coordinated with my silk blouses—I have to smile to myself remembering what my mother had said about my conservative outfits when I visited her the last time—that I looked like the Jehovah's Witnesses who went from door to door in her pueblo trying to sell tickets to heaven to the die-hard Catholics. I would scare people she said. They would bolt their doors if they saw me approaching with my briefcase. As for her, she dresses in tropical colors—a red skirt and parakeet-yellow blouse look good on her tan skin, and she still has a good enough figure that she can wear a tight, black cocktail dress to go dancing at her favorite club, *El Palacio*, on Saturday nights. And, she emphasizes, still make it to the 10 o'clock mass on Sunday. Catholics can have fun and still be saved, she has often pointed out to me, but only if you pay your respects to God and all His Court with the necessary rituals. She has never accepted my gradual slipping out of the faith in which I was so strictly brought up.

As I pack my clothes into the suitcase, I recall our early days in 2

Paterson, New Jersey, where we lived for most of my adolescence while
my father was alive and stationed in Brooklyn Yard in New York. At
that time, my mother's views on everything from clothing to (the forbidden subject) sex were ruled by the religious fervor that she had developed as a shield against the cold foreign city. These days we have
traded places in a couple of areas since she has "gone home" after my father's death, and "gone native." I chose to attend college in the United
States and make a living as an English teacher and, lately, on the lecture circuit as a novelist and poet. But, though our lives are on the surface radically different, my mother and I have affected each other
reciprocally over the past twenty years; she has managed to liberate
herself from the rituals, mores, and traditions that "cramp" her style,
while retaining her femininity and "Puertoricanness," while I struggle
daily to consolidate my opposing cultural identities. In my adolescence,
divided into my New Jersey years and my Georgia years, I received an
education in the art of cultural compromise.

In Paterson in the 1960s I attended a public school in our neigh-   3
borhood. Still predominantly white and Jewish, it was rated very well
academically in a city where the educational system was in chaos, de-
teriorating rapidly as the best teachers moved on to suburban schools
following the black and Puerto Rican migration into, and the white ex-
odus from, the city proper.

The Jewish community had too much at stake to make a fast re-   4
treat; many of the small businesses and apartment buildings in the city's
core were owned by Jewish families of the World War II generation.
They had seen worse things happen than the influx of black and brown
people that was scaring away the Italians and the Irish. But they too
would gradually move their families out of the best apartments in their
buildings and into houses in East Paterson, Fairlawn, and other places
with *lawns*. It was how I saw the world then; either you lived without
your square of grass or you bought a house to go with it. But for most of
my adolescence, I lived among the Jewish people of Paterson. We
rented an apartment owned by the Milsteins, proprietors also of the
deli on the bottom floor. I went to school with their children. My father took his business to the Jewish establishments, perhaps because
these men symbolized "dignified survival" to him. He was obsessed with
privacy, and could not stand the personal turns conversations almost
always took when two or more Puerto Ricans met casually over a store
counter. The Jewish men talked too, but they concentrated on externals. They asked my father about his job, politics, his opinion on Vietnam, Lyndon Johnson. And my father, in his quiet voice, answered
their questions knowledgeably. Sometimes before we entered a store,
the cleaners, or a shoe-repair shop, he would tell me to look for the

blue-inked numbers on the owner's left forearm.[1] I would stare at these numbers, now usually faded enough to look like veins in the wrong place. I would try to make them out. They were a telegram from the past, I later decided, informing the future of the deaths of millions. My father discussed the Holocaust with me in the same hushed tones my mother used to talk about God's Mysterious Ways. I could not reconcile both in my mind. This conflict eventually led to my first serious clash with my mother over irreconcilable differences between the "real world" and religious doctrine.

It had to do with the Virgin Birth.   5

And it had to do with my best friend and study partner, Ira Nathan,   6
the acknowledged scientific genius at school. In junior high school it was almost a requirement to be "in love" with an older boy. I was an eighth grader and Ira was in the ninth grade that year and preparing to be sent away to some prep school in New England. I chose him as my boyfriend (in the eyes of my classmates, if a girl spent time with a boy that meant they were "going together") because I needed tutoring in biology — one of his best subjects. I ended up having a crush on him af-ter our first Saturday morning meeting at the library. Ira was my first ex-posure to the wonders of an analytical mind.

The problem was the subject. Biology is a dangerous topic for   7
young teenagers who are themselves walking laboratories, experiment-ing with interesting combinations of chemicals every time they make a choice. In my basic biology class, we were looking at single-cell organ-isms under the microscope, and watching them reproduce in slow-motion films in a darkened classroom. Though the process was as unexciting as watching a little kid blow bubbles, we were aroused by the concept itself. Ira's advanced class was dissecting fetal pigs. He brought me a photograph of his project, inner organs labeled neatly on the paper the picture had been glued to. My eyes refused to budge from the line drawn from "genitals" to a part of the pig it pertained to. I felt a wave of heat rising from my chest to my scalp. Ira must have seen my discomfort, though I tried to keep my face behind the black curtain of my hair, but as the boy-scientist, he was relentless. He actually traced the line from label to pig with his pencil.

"All mammals reproduce sexually," he said in a teacherly mono-   8
tone.

The librarian, far off on the other side of the room, looked up at us   9
and frowned. Logically, it was not possible that she could have heard Ira's pronouncement, but I was convinced that the mention of sex en-hanced the hearing capabilities of parents, teachers and librarians by

---

[1] Jews held in German concentration camps during World War II were tattooed on their forearms with identity numbers. — EDS.

one hundred percent. I blushed more intensely, and peeked through my hair at Ira.

He was holding the eraser of his pencil on the pig's blurry sexual   10
parts and smiling at me. His features were distinctly Eastern European. I had recently seen the young singer Barbra Streisand on the Red Skelton show and had been amazed at how much similarity there was in their appearances. She could have been his sister. I was particularly attracted to the wide mouth and strong nose. No one that I knew in school thought that Ira was attractive, but his brains had long ago overshadowed his looks as his most impressive attribute. Like Ira, I was also a straight A student and also considered odd because I was one of the few Puerto Ricans on the honor roll. So it didn't surprise anyone that Ira and I had drifted toward each other. Though I could not have articulated it then, Ira was seducing me with his No. 2 pencil and the laboratory photograph of his fetal pig. The following Saturday, Ira brought in his advanced biology book and showed me the transparencies of the human anatomy in full color that I was not meant to see for a couple more years. I was shocked. The cosmic jump between paramecium and the human body was almost too much for me to take in. These were the first grown people I had ever seen naked and they revealed too much.

"Human sexual reproduction can only take place when the male's   11
sperm is introduced into the female womb and fertilization of the egg takes place," Ira stated flatly.

The book was open to the page labeled "The Human Reproductive   12
System." Feeling that my maturity was being tested, as well as my intelligence, I found my voice long enough to contradict Ira.

"There has been one exception to this, Ira." I was feeling a little   13
smug about knowing something that Ira obviously did not.

"Judith, there are no exceptions in biology, only mutations, and   14
adaptations through evolution." He was smiling in a superior way.

"The Virgin Mary had a baby without..." I couldn't say *having sex*   15
in the same breath as the name of the Mother of God. I was totally unprepared for the explosion of laughter that followed my timid statement. Ira had crumped in his chair and was laughing so hard that his thin shoulders shook. I could hear the librarian approaching. Feeling humiliated, I started to put my books together. Ira grabbed my arm.

"Wait, don't go," he was still giggling uncontrollably, "I'm sorry.   16
Let's talk a little more. Wait, give me a chance to explain."

Reluctantly, I sat down again mainly because the librarian was al-   17
ready at our table, hands on hips, whispering angrily: "If you *children* cannot behave in this *study area*, I will have to ask you to leave." Ira and I both apologized, though she gave him a nasty look because his mouth was still stretched from ear to ear in a hysterical grin.

"Listen, listen. I'm sorry that I laughed like that. I know you're   18

Catholic and you believe in the Virgin Birth (he bit his lower lip trying to regain his composure), but it's just not biologically possible to have a baby without…(he struggled for control)…losing your virginity."

I sank down on my hard chair. "Virginity." He had said another of   19
the forbidden words. I glanced back at the librarian who was keeping her eye on us. I was both offended and excited by Ira's blasphemy. How could he deny a doctrine that people had believed in for 2,000 years? It was part of my prayers every night. My mother talked about *La Virgen* as if she were our most important relative.

Recovering from his fit of laughter, Ira kept his hand discreetly on   20
my elbow as he explained in the seductive language of the scientific laboratory how babies were made, and how it was impossible to violate certain natural laws.

"Unless God will it," I argued feebly.   21

"There is no God," said Ira, and the last shred of my innocence fell   22
away as I listened to his arguments backed up by irrefutable scientific evidence.

Our meetings continued all that year, becoming more exciting   23
with every chapter in his biology book. My grades improved dramatically since one-celled organisms were no mystery to a student of advanced biology. Ira's warm, moist hand often brushed against mine under the table at the library, and walking home one bitter cold day, he asked me if I would wear his Beta Club pin. I nodded and when we stepped inside the hallway of my building where he removed his thick mittens which his mother had knitted, he pinned the blue enamel B to my collar. And to the hissing of the steam heaters, I received a serious kiss from Ira. We separated abruptly when we heard Mrs. Milstein's door open.

"Hello, Ira."   24

"Hello, Mrs. Milstein."   25

"And how is your mother? I haven't seen Fritzie all week. She's not   26
sick, is she?"

"She's had a mild cold, Mrs. Milstein. But she is steadily improv-   27
ing." Ira's diction became extremely precise and formal when he was in the presence of adults. As an only child and a prodigy, he had to live up to very high standards.

"I'll call her today," Mrs. Milstein said, finally looking over at me.   28
Her eyes fixed on the collar of my blouse which was, I later saw in our hall mirror, sticking straight up with Ira's pin attached crookedly to the edge.

"Good-bye, Mrs. Milstein."   29

"Nice to see you, Ira."   30

Ira waved awkwardly to me as he left. Mrs. Milstein stood in the   31
humid hallway of her building watching me run up the stairs.

Our "romance" lasted only a week; long enough for Mrs. Milstein   32
to call Ira's mother, and for Mrs. Nathan to call my mother. I was subjected to a lecture on moral behavior by my mother, who, carried away
by her anger and embarrassed that I had been seen kissing a boy (understood: a boy who was not even Catholic), had begun a chain
of metaphors for the loss of virtue that was on the verge of the tragi/
comical:

"A *perdida,* a cheap item," she said trembling before me as I sat on   33
the edge of my bed, facing her accusations, "a girl begins to look like
one when she allows herself to be *handled* by men."

"Mother..." I wanted her to lower her voice so that my father, sit-   34
ting at the kitchen table reading, would not hear. I had already
promised her that I would confess my sin that Saturday and take communion with a sparkling clean soul. I had not been successful at keeping the sarcasm out of my voice. Her fury was fueled by her own bitter
litany.

"A dirty joke, a burden to her family..." She was rolling with her   35
Spanish now; soon the Holy Mother would enter into the picture for
good measure. "It's not as if I had not taught you better. Don't you
know that those people do not have the example of the Holy Virgin
Mary and her Son to follow and that is why they do things for the
wrong reasons. Mrs. Nathan said she did not want her son messing
around with you—not because of the wrongness of it—but because it
would interfere with his studies!" She was yelling now. "She's afraid
that he will (she crossed herself at the horror of the thought) make you
pregnant!"

"We could say an angel came down and put a baby in my stomach,   36
Mother." She had succeeded in dragging me into her field of hysteria.
She grabbed my arm and pulled me to my feet.

"I do not want you associating any more than necessary with   37
people who do not have God, do you hear me?"

"They have a god!" I was screaming now too, trying to get away   38
from her suffocating grasp: "They have an intelligent god who doesn't
ask you to believe that a woman can get pregnant without having sex!"
That's when she slapped me. She looked horrified at what she had in-
stinctively done.

"Nazi," I hissed, out of control by then too, "I bet you'd like to send   39
Ira and his family to a concentration camp!" At that time I thought
that was the harshest thing I could have said to anyone. I was certain
that I had sentenced my soul to eternal damnation the minute the
words came out of my mouth; but my cheek was burning from the slap
and I wanted to hurt her. Father walked into my room at that moment looking shocked at the sight of the two of us entangled in mortal
combat.

"Please, please," his voice sounded agonized. I ran to him and he   40
held me in his arms while I cried my heart out on his starched white
shirt. My mother, also weeping quietly, tried to walk past us, but he
pulled her into the circle. After a few moments, she put her trembling
hand on my head.

"We are a family," my father said, "there is only the three of us   41
against the world. Please, please..." But he did not follow the "please"
with any suggestions as to what we could do to make things right in a
world that was as confusing to my mother as it was to me.

I finished the eighth grade in Paterson, but Ira and I never got to-   42
gether to study again. I sent his Beta club pin back to him via a mutual
friend. Once in a while I saw him in the hall or the playground. But he
seemed to be in the clouds, where he belonged. In the fall, I was enrolled at St. Joseph's Catholic High School where everyone believed in
the Virgin Birth, and I never had to take a test on the human reproductive system. It was a chapter that was not emphasized.

In 1968, the year Paterson, like many U.S. cities, exploded in racial   43
violence, my father moved us to Augusta, Georgia, where two of his
brothers had retired from the army at Fort Gordon. They had convinced him that it was a healthier place to rear teenagers. For me it was
a shock to the senses, like moving from one planet to another: where
Paterson had concrete to walk on and gray skies, bitter winters, and a
smorgasbord of an ethnic population, Georgia was red like Mars, and
Augusta was green—exploding in colors in more gardens of azaleas
and dogwood and magnolia trees—more vegetation than I imagined
was possible anywhere not tropical like Puerto Rico. People seemed to
come in two basic colors: black and blond. And I could barely understand my teachers when they talked in a slowed-down version of English like one of those old 78-speed recordings played at 33. But I was
placed in all advanced classes and one of them was biology. This is
where I got to see my first real fetal pig which my assigned lab partner
had chosen. She picked it up gingerly by the ends of the plastic bag in
which it was stored: "Ain't he cute?" she asked. I nodded, nearly faint-
ing from the overwhelming combination of the smell of formaldehyde
and my sudden flashback to my brief but intense romance with Ira
Nathan.

"What you want to call him?" My partner unwrapped our specimen   44
on the table, and I surprised myself by my instant recall of Ira's chart. I
knew all the parts. In my mind's eye I saw the pencil lines, the labeled
photograph. I had had an excellent teacher.

"Let's call him Ira."   45

"That's a funny name, but OK." My lab partner, a smart girl des-   46
tined to become my mentor in things Southern, then gave me a conspiratorial wink and pulled out a little perfume atomizer from her purse.

She sprayed Ira from snout to tail with it. I noticed this operation was taking place at other tables too. The teacher had conveniently left the room a few minutes before. I was once again stunned—almost literally knocked out by a fist of smell: "What is it?"

"*Intimate*," my advanced biology partner replied smiling.   47

And by the time our instructor came back to the room, we were   48 ready to delve into this mystery of muscle and bone; eager to discover the secrets that lie just beyond fear a little past loathing; of acknowledging the corruptibility of the flesh, and our own fascination with the subject.

As I finish packing, the telephone rings and it's my mother. She is   49 reminding me to be ready to visit relatives, to go to a dance with her, and, of course, to attend a couple of the services at the church. It is the feast of the Black Virgin, revered patron saint of our home town in Puerto Rico. I agree to everything, and find myself anticipating the eclectic itinerary. Why not allow Evolution and Eve, Biology and the Virgin Birth? Why not take a vacation from logic? I will not be away for too long, I will not let myself be tempted to remain in the sealed garden of blind faith; I'll stay just long enough to rest myself from the exhausting enterprise of leading the examined life.

QUESTIONS ON MEANING

1. Locate Cofer's statement of THESIS.
2. What are the "irreconcilable differences between the 'real world' and religious doctrine" to which Cofer refers in paragraph 4?
3. What is the EFFECT of Ira's pronouncement: "There is no God" (para. 22)? How "irrefutable" do you think his scientific evidence for this claim could be?
4. What is the major difference between Ira's family and Cofer's? What do they have in common?
5. Has Cofer entirely renounced her religious upbringing? At what point does she suggest that she finds comfort in the religion of her youth?

QUESTIONS ON WRITING STRATEGY

1. Why does Cofer begin her story with a contrast between her own and her mother's clothing styles? Is this difference a trivial one? What is the IRONY in the mother's flamboyant style of dressing? What does it tell us about the mother?
2. Why does Cofer recount the ANECDOTE of the Jewish shopkeepers (para. 4) before her main story? What is the relationship between the two stories?

3. What is the TONE of the scenes in the library (paras. 6–22)? How does Cofer convey her feelings at the time?
4. How does Cofer establish COHERENCE between the beginning and end of this essay?
5. **OTHER METHODS.** In paragraphs 3 and 4, Cofer uses CAUSE AND EFFECT to explain why her high school was predominantly white and Jewish in a city mostly inhabited by African Americans and Puerto Ricans. SUMMARIZE her explanation.

QUESTIONS ON LANGUAGE

1. Why does Cofer put "in love" and "going together" (para. 6) and "romance" (32) in quotation marks?
2. What is the effect of "No. 2 pencil" in paragraph 10?
3. Look up any unfamiliar words in a dictionary: pueblo (para. 1); reciprocally (2); influx, reconcile, irreconcilable, doctrine (4); fetal (7); monotone (8); articulated, paramecium (10); fertilization (11); mutations (14); blasphemy (19); discreetly (20); irrefutable (22); prodigy (27); litany (34); smorgasbord, gingerly, formaldehyde (43); conspiratorial, atomizer (46); loathing, corruptibility (48); eclectic (49).

SUGGESTIONS FOR WRITING

1. **JOURNAL WRITING.** Is this essay dismissive of religion? Respond to Cofer's attitudes toward religion as expressed throughout the essay, but especially in paragraph 49. Is she fair?
   FROM JOURNAL TO ESSAY. Explain how Cofer arrived at the view, expressed in paragraph 49, that religion is somehow not a part of "the exhausting enterprise of leading the examined life." Then agree or disagree with her, drawing on your own reading and experiences.
2. In paragraph 43 Cofer contrasts Paterson, New Jersey, and Augusta, Georgia. Write an essay of your own comparing and contrasting two places you have lived—people, land, buildings, weather. (If you have lived in only one place, compare and contrast it with another place you know in reality or imagination—a vacation spot, a relative's home, a movie setting.) If your essay is short enough, you can use the subject-by-subject organization described in the introduction to this chapter. Otherwise, you will probably want to follow the point-by-point organization.
3. **CRITICAL WRITING.** Cofer is a first-generation American who, with the help of a good education and the support of her family, could be said to have achieved the "American Dream." As this story makes clear, however, Cofer's success has come at the expense of a certain alienation from her family and the values of the culture from which she came. Using Cofer's essay as your starting point, write a brief essay about the "downside" of the American Dream. You may also want to draw on your own experience, if you believe it is relevant to the topic.
4. **CONNECTIONS.** Cofer's experience of being between two cultures resembles Amy Tan's as reported in "Fish Cheeks" (p. 54). Focusing on the two mother-daughter relationships, compare and contrast the two women's recollections. Use EXAMPLES from both essays for your EVIDENCE.

JUDITH ORTIZ COFER ON WRITING

In the 1980s Cofer told *Contemporary Authors* why she so often chooses her family as her writing subject. She was speaking of her poetry, but the same could be said of her stories and essays as well. "My family is one of the main topics of my poetry," Cofer explained, "the ones left behind on the island of Puerto Rico, and the ones who came to the United States. In tracing their lives, I discover more about mine. The place of birth itself becomes a metaphor for the things we all must leave behind; the assimilation of a new culture is the coming into maturity by accepting the terms necessary for survival. My poetry is the study of this process of change, assimilation, and transformation."

FOR DISCUSSION

1. What does Cofer mean when she says that "the assimilation of a new culture is the coming into maturity by accepting the terms necessary for survival"? Does this statement apply only to immigrants or to nonimmigrants as well? Why?
2. If you have ever written about your family or a relative, what did the experience tell you about your kin? What did it tell you about yourself?

ADDITIONAL WRITING TOPICS

Comparison and Contrast

1. In an essay replete with examples, compare and contrast the two subjects in any one of the following pairs:

   The main characters of two films, stories, or novels
   Women and men as consumers
   The styles of two runners
   Alexander Hamilton and Thomas Jefferson: their opposing views of central government
   How city dwellers and country dwellers spend their leisure time
   The presentation styles of two television news commentators

2. Approach a comparison and contrast essay on one of the following general subjects by explaining why you prefer one thing to the other:

   Two buildings on campus or in town
   Two football teams
   German-made cars and Detroit-made cars
   Two horror movies
   Television when you were a child and television today
   City life and small-town or rural life
   Malls and main streets
   Two neighborhoods
   Two sports

3. Write an essay in which you compare a reality (what actually exists) with an ideal (what should exist). Some possible topics:

   The affordable car
   Available living quarters
   A job
   The college curriculum
   Public transportation
   Financial aid to college students

5

PROCESS ANALYSIS
Explaining Step by Step

THE METHOD

A chemist working for a soft-drink firm is asked to improve on a competitor's product, Orange Quench. First, she chemically tests a sample to figure out what's in the drink. This is the method of DIVISION or ANALYSIS, the separation of something into its parts in order to understand it (see the following chapter). Then the chemist writes a report telling her boss how to make a drink like Orange Quench, but better. This recipe is a special kind of analysis, called PROCESS ANALYSIS: explaining step by step how to do something or how something is done.

Like any type of analysis, process analysis divides a subject into its components: It divides a continuous action into stages. Processes much larger and more involved than the making of an orange drink also may be analyzed. When geologists explain how a formation such as the Grand Canyon occurred—a process taking several hundred million years—they describe the successive layers of sediment deposited by oceans, floods, and wind; then the great uplift of the entire region by underground forces; and then the erosion, visible to us today, by the Colorado River and its tributaries, by little streams and flash floods, by crumbling and falling rock, and by wind. Exactly what are the geologists doing in this explanation? They are taking a complicated event (or process) and dividing it into parts. They are telling us what happened first, second, and third, and what is still happening today.

Because it is useful in explaining what is complicated, process analysis is a favorite method of scientists such as geologists. The method, however, may be useful to anybody. Two kinds of process analysis are very familiar to you:

- A DIRECTIVE process analysis tells how to do something or make something. You meet it when you read a set of instructions for assembling newly purchased stereo components, or follow the directions to a stereo store ("Turn right at the blinker and follow Patriot Boulevard for 2.4 miles...").
- An INFORMATIVE process analysis tells how something is done or how it takes place. This is the kind we often read out of curiosity. Such an essay may tell of events beyond our control: how atoms behave when split, how lions hunt, how a fertilized egg develops into a child.

In this chapter, you will find examples of both kinds of process analysis —both the "how to" and the "how." For instance, Benjamin Franklin offers a charming directive on how to have pleasant dreams, while Jessica Mitford spellbindingly informs us of how corpses are embalmed (but, clearly, she doesn't expect us to rush down to our basements and give her instructions a try).

Sometimes process analysis is used very imaginatively. Foreseeing that the sun eventually will cool, the earth shrink, the oceans freeze, and all life perish, an astronomer who cannot possibly behold the end of the world nevertheless can write a process analysis of it. An exercise in learned guesswork, such an essay divides a vast and almost inconceivable event into stages that, taken one at a time, become clearer and more readily imaginable.

Whether it is useful or useless (but fun to imagine), an effective process analysis can grip readers and even hold them fascinated. Say you were proposing a change in the procedures for course registration at your school. You could argue your point until you were out of words, but you would get nowhere if you failed to tell your readers exactly how the new process would work: That's what makes your proposal sing. Leaf through a current issue of a newsstand magazine, and you will find that process analysis abounds. You may meet, for instance, articles telling you how to tenderize cuts of meat, sew homemade designer jeans, lose fat, cut hair, play the money markets, arouse a bored mate, and program a computer. Less practical, but not necessarily less interesting, are the informative articles: how brain surgeons work, how diamonds are formed, how cities fight crime. Readers, it seems, have an unslakable thirst for process analysis. In every issue of the *New York Times Book Review*, we find an entire best-seller list devoted to "Advice, How-to and Miscellaneous," including books on how to make money in real estate, how to lose weight, how to find a good mate, and how to lose a bad one. Evidently, if anything will still make an American crack open a book, it is a step-by-step explanation of how he or she, too, can be a success at living.

THE PROCESS

Here are suggestions for writing an effective process analysis of your own. (In fact, what you are about to read is itself a process analysis.)

1. *Understand clearly the process you are about to analyze.* Think it through. This preliminary survey will make the task of writing far easier for you.
2. *Think about preparatory steps.* If the reader should do something before beginning the process, list these steps. For instance, you might begin, "Remove the packing from the components," or, "First, lay out three eggs, one pound of Sheboygan bratwurst...."
3. *List the steps or stages in the process.* Try setting them down in chronological order, one at a time—if this is possible. Some processes, however, do not happen in an orderly sequence, but occur all at once. If, for instance, you are writing an account of a typical earthquake, what do you mention first? The shifting of underground rock strata? Cracks in the earth? Falling houses? Bursting water mains? Toppling trees? Mangled cars? Casualties? Here is a subject for which the method of CLASSIFICATION (Chap. 7) may come to your aid. You might sort out apparently simultaneous events into categories: injury to people; damage to homes, to land, to public property.
4. *Check the completeness and order of the steps.* Make sure your list includes *all* the steps in the right order. Sometimes a stage of a process may contain a number of smaller stages. Make sure none has been left out. If any seems particularly tricky or complicated, underline it on your list to remind yourself when you write your essay to slow down and detail it with extra care.
5. *Consider your thesis.* What is the point of your process analysis: Why are you bothering to tell readers about it? The THESIS SENTENCE for a process analysis need do no more than say what the subject is and maybe outline its essential stages. For instance:

   The main stages in writing a process analysis are listing the steps in the process, drafting to explain the steps, and revising to clarify the steps.

But your readers will surely appreciate something livelier and more pointed, something that says "You can use this" or "This may surprise you" or "Listen up." Here are three examples from essays in this chapter:

[In a mortuary the body] is in short order sprayed, sliced, pierced, pickled, trussed, trimmed, creamed, waxed, painted, rouged, and neatly dressed—transformed from a common corpse into a Beautiful Memory Picture. (Jessica Mitford, "Behind the Formaldehyde Curtain")

Poisoning the earth can be difficult because the earth is always trying to cleanse and renew itself. (Linnea Saukko, "How to Poison the Earth")

As a great part of our life is spent in sleep during which we have sometimes pleasant and sometimes painful dreams, it becomes of some consequence to obtain the one kind and avoid the other. (Benjamin Franklin, "The Art of Procuring Pleasant Dreams")

6. *Define your terms.* Ask yourself, "Do I need any specialized or technical terms?" If so, be sure to define them. You'll sympathize with your reader if you have ever tried to work a Malaysia-made VCR that comes with an instruction booklet written in translatorese, full of unexplained technical JARGON; or if you have ever tried to assemble a plastic tricycle according to a directive that reads, "Position sleeve casing on wheel center in fork with shaft in tong groove, and gently but forcibly tap in medium pal nut head...."

7. *Use time-markers or* TRANSITIONS. These words or phrases indicate *when* one stage of a process stops and the next begins, and they greatly aid your reader in following you. Here, for example, is a paragraph of plain medical prose that makes good use of the helpful time-markers printed in *italics.* (The paragraph is adapted from Alan F. Guttmacher's *Pregnancy and Birth.*)

In the human, *thirty-six hours after* the egg is fertilized, a two-cell egg appears. A twelve-cell development takes place *in seventy-two hours.* The egg is *still* round and has increased little in diameter. In this respect it is like a real estate development. *At first* a road bisects the whole area; *then* a cross road divides it into quarters, and *later* other roads divide it into eighths and twelfths. This happens without the taking of any more land, simply by subdivision of the original tract. *On the third or fourth day,* the egg passes from the Fallopian tube into the uterus. *By the fifth day* the original single large cell has subdivided into sixty small cells and floats about the slitlike uterine cavity *a day or two longer, then* adheres to the cavity's inner lining. *By the twelfth day* the human egg is already firmly implanted. Impregnation is *now* completed, *as yet* unbeknown to the woman. *At present,* she has not even had time to miss her first menstrual period, and other symptoms of pregnancy are *still several days distant.*

Brief as these time-markers are, they define each stage of the human egg's journey. Note how the writer, after declaring in the second sentence that the egg forms twelve cells, backtracks for a moment and retraces the process by which the egg has subdivided, comparing it (by a brief ANALOGY) to a piece of real estate. When using time-markers, vary them so that they won't seem mechanical. If you can, avoid the monotonous repetition of a fixed phrase (*In the fourteenth stage...*, *In the fifteenth stage...*). Even boring time-markers, though, are better than none at all. As in any chronological narrative, words and phrases such as *in the beginning, first, second, next, after that, three seconds later, at the same time,* and *finally* can help a process to move smoothly in the telling and lodge firmly in the reader's mind.

8. *Be specific.* When you write a first draft, state your analysis in generous detail, even at the risk of being wordy. When you revise, it will be easier to delete than to amplify.

9. *Revise.* When your essay is finished, reread it carefully against the checklist below. You might also enlist a friend's help. If your process analysis is a directive ("How to Eat an Ice Cream Cone Without Dribbling"), see if the friend can follow your instructions without difficulty. If your process analysis is informative ("How a New Word Enters the Dictionary"), ask the friend whether the process unfolds as clearly in his or her mind as it does in yours.

CHECKLIST FOR REVISING A PROCESS ANALYSIS

✔ **ORGANIZATION.** Have you arranged the steps of your process in a clear chronological order? If steps occur simultaneously, have you grouped them so that readers perceive some order?

✔ **COMPLETENESS.** Have you included all the necessary steps and explained each one fully? Is it clear how each one contributes to the result?

✔ **THESIS.** Does your process analysis have a point? Have you made sure readers know what it is?

✔ **DEFINITIONS.** Have you explained the meanings of any terms your readers may not know?

✔ **TRANSITIONS.** Do time-markers distinguish the steps and clarify their sequence?

PROCESS ANALYSIS IN A PARAGRAPH: TWO ILLUSTRATIONS

Using Process Analysis to Write About Television

The timer on your videocassette recorder permits you to record up to eight programs over a two-week period even when you are not at home. For each program you wish to record in your absence, locate an empty program number by pushing the *P* button until a flashing number appears on the TV screen. The next four steps set the information for the program. First, push the *Day* button until the day and date show on the screen. The screen will flash *On*. Next set the starting time (be sure the time is set correctly for A.M. or P.M.). Then push the *Off* button and set the ending time (again, watching A.M. or P.M.). When the times have been set, push the *Chan* button and set the channel using the unit's channel selector. You may review the program information by pushing the *Check* button. When you are satisfied that the settings are correct, push *Timer* to set the timer to operate. (The unit cannot be operated manually while the timer is on.)

Process to be explained with directive analysis

Step 1

Preview of steps 2–5
Step 2
Step 3

Step 4

Step 5
Step 6
Step 7

Transitions (underlined) clarify steps

Using Process Analysis in an Academic Discipline

When you first climb into bed, close your eyes, and relax, your brain emits bursts of *alpha waves* in a regular, high-amplitude, low-frequency rhythm of 8–12 cycles per second. Alpha is associated with relaxing or not concentrating on anything in particular. Gradually these waves slow down even further and you drift into the Land of Nod, passing through four stages, each deeper than the previous one.

Steps preceding process

Process to be explained with informative analysis

1. *Stage 1.* Your brain waves become small and irregular, indicating activity with low voltage and mixed frequencies. You feel yourself drifting on the edge of consciousness, in a state of light sleep. If awakened, you may recall fantasies or a few visual images.
2. *Stage 2.* Your brain emits occasional short bursts of rapid, high-peaking waves called *sleep spindles*. Light sounds or minor noises probably won't disturb you.
3. *Stage 3.* In addition to the waves characteristic of stage 2, your brain occasionally emits very slow waves of about 1–3 cycles per second, with very high peaks. These *delta waves* are a sure sign that you will be hard to arouse. Your breathing and pulse have slowed down, your temperature has dropped, and your muscles are relaxed.
4. *Stage 4.* Delta waves have now largely taken over, and

Step 1

Step 2

Step 3

Step 4

you are in deep sleep. It will take vigorous shaking or a loud noise to awaken you, and you won't be very happy about it. Oddly enough, though, if you talk or walk in your sleep, this is when you are likely to do so.

—Carole Wade and Carol Tavris, *Psychology*

JESSICA MITFORD

Born in Batsford Mansion, England, in 1917, the daughter of Lord and Lady Redesdale, JESSICA MITFORD devoted much of her early life to defying her aristocratic upbringing. In her autobiography *Daughters and Rebels* (1960), she tells how she received a genteel schooling at home, then as a young woman moved to Loyalist Spain during the violent Spanish Civil War. Later, she emigrated to America, where for a time she worked in Miami as a bartender. She became one of her adopted country's most noted reporters: *Time* called her "Queen of the Muckrakers." Exposing with her typewriter what she regarded as corruption, abuse, and absurdity, Mitford wrote *The American Way of Death* (1963, revised 1996), *Kind and Unusual Punishment: The Prison Business* (1973), and *The American Way of Birth* (1992). *Poison Penmanship* (1979) collects articles from *The Atlantic*, *Harper's*, and other magazines. *A Fine Old Conflict* (1976) is the second volume of Mitford's autobiography. And a novel, *Grace Had an English Heart* (1989), examines how the media transform ordinary people into celebrities. Jessica Mitford died in 1996.

Behind the Formaldehyde Curtain

The most famous (or notorious) thing Jessica Mitford wrote is *The American Way of Death*. The following essay is a self-contained selection from it. In the book, Mitford criticizes the mortuary profession; and when her work landed on best-seller lists, the author was the subject of bitter attacks from funeral directors all over North America. To finish reading the essay, you will need a stable stomach as well as an awareness of Mitford's outrageous sense of humor. "Behind the Formaldehyde Curtain" is a clear, painstaking process analysis, written with masterly style.

The drama begins to unfold with the arrival of the corpse at the mortuary. 1

Alas, poor Yorick! How surprised he would be to see how his counterpart of today is whisked off to a funeral parlor and is in short order sprayed, sliced, pierced, pickled, trussed, trimmed, creamed, waxed, painted, rouged, and neatly dressed—transformed from a common corpse into a Beautiful Memory Picture. This process is known in the trade as embalming and restorative art, and is so universally employed in the United States and Canada that the funeral director does it routinely, without consulting corpse or kin. He regards as eccentric those few who are hardy enough to suggest that it might be dispensed with. 2

Yet no law requires embalming, no religious doctrine commends it, nor is it dictated by considerations of health, sanitation, or even of personal daintiness. In no part of the world but in Northern America is it widely used. The purpose of embalming is to make the corpse presentable for viewing in a suitably costly container; and here too the funeral director routinely, without first consulting the family, prepares the body for public display.

Is all this legal? The processes to which a dead body may be subjected are after all to some extent circumscribed by law. In most states, for instance, the signature of next of kin must be obtained before an autopsy may be performed, before the deceased may be cremated, before the body may be turned over to a medical school for research purposes; or such provision must be made in the decedent's will. In the case of embalming, no such permission is required nor is it ever sought.[1] A textbook, *The Principles and Practices of Embalming*, comments on this: "There is some question regarding the legality of much that is done within the preparation room." The author points out that it would be most unusual for a responsible member of a bereaved family to instruct the mortician, in so many words, to "embalm" the body of a deceased relative. The very term *embalming* is so seldom used that the mortician must rely upon custom in the matter. The author concludes that unless the family specifies otherwise, the act of entrusting the body to the care of a funeral establishment carries with it an implied permission to go ahead and embalm.

Embalming is indeed a most extraordinary procedure, and one must wonder at the docility of Americans who each year pay hundreds of millions of dollars for its perpetuation, blissfully ignorant of what it is all about, what is done, how it is done. Not one in ten thousand has any idea of what actually takes place. Books on the subject are extremely hard to come by. They are not to be found in most libraries or bookshops.

In an era when huge television audiences watch surgical operations in the comfort of their living rooms, when, thanks to the animated cartoon, the geography of the digestive system has become familiar territory even to the nursery school set, in a land where the satisfaction of curiosity about almost all matters is a national pastime, the secrecy surrounding embalming can, surely, hardly be attributed to the inherent gruesomeness of the subject. Custom in this regard has within this century suffered a complete reversal. In the early days of American embalming, when it was performed in the home of the deceased, it was almost mandatory for some relative to stay by the embalmer's side and

---

[1] Partly because of Mitford's attack, the Federal Trade Commission now requires the funeral industry to provide families with itemized price lists, including the price of embalming, to state that embalming is not required, and to obtain the family's consent to embalming before charging for it. — EDS.

witness the procedure. Today, family members who might wish to be in attendance would certainly be dissuaded by the funeral director. All others, except apprentices, are excluded by law from the preparation room.

A close look at what does actually take place may explain in large   6 measure the undertaker's intractable reticence concerning a procedure that has become his major *raison d'être*. Is it possible he fears that public information about embalming might lead patrons to wonder if they really want this service? If the funeral men are loath to discuss the subject outside the trade, the reader may, understandably, be equally loath to go on reading at this point. For those who have the stomach for it, let us part the formaldehyde curtain....

The body is first laid out in the undertaker's morgue—or rather,   7 Mr. Jones is reposing in the preparation room—to be readied to bid the world farewell.

The preparation room in any of the better funeral establish-   8 ments has the tiled and sterile look of a surgery, and indeed the embalmer–restorative artist who does his chores there is beginning to adopt the term *dermasurgeon* (appropriately corrupted by some mortician-writers as "demi-surgeon") to describe his calling. His equipment, consisting of scalpels, scissors, augers, forceps, clamps, needles, pumps, tubes, bowls, and basins, is crudely imitative of the surgeon's, as is his technique, acquired in a nine- or twelve-month post-high-school course in an embalming school. He is supplied by an advanced chemical industry with a bewildering array of fluids, sprays, pastes, oils, powders, creams, to fix or soften tissue, shrink or distend it as needed, dry it here, restore the moisture there. There are cosmetics, waxes, and paints to fill and cover features, even plaster of Paris to replace entire limbs. There are ingenious aids to prop and stabilize the cadaver: a Vari-Pose Head Rest, the Edwards Arm and Hand Positioner, the Repose Block (to support the shoulders during the embalming), and the Throop Foot Positioner, which resembles an old-fashioned stocks.

Mr. John H. Eckels, president of the Eckels College of Mortuary   9 Science, thus describes the first part of the embalming procedure: "In the hands of a skilled practitioner, this work may be done in a comparatively short time and without mutilating the body other than by slight incision—so slight that it scarcely would cause serious inconvenience if made upon a living person. It is necessary to remove the blood, and doing this not only helps in the disinfecting, but removes the principal cause of disfigurements due to discoloration."

Another textbook discusses the all-important time element: "The   10 earlier this is done, the better, for every hour that elapses between death and embalming will add to the problems and complications encountered...." Just how soon should one get going on the embalming? The author tells us, "On the basis of such scanty information made available to this profession through its rudimentary and haphazard system of technical research, we must conclude that the best results are to be obtained if the subject is embalmed before life is completely extinct —that is, before cellular death has occurred. In the average case, this would mean within an hour after somatic death." For those who feel that there is something a little rudimentary, not to say haphazard, about this advice, a comforting thought is offered by another writer. Speaking of fears entertained in early days of premature burial, he points out, "One of the effects of embalming by chemical injection, however, has been to dispel fears of live burial." How true; once the blood is removed, chances of live burial are indeed remote.

To return to Mr. Jones, the blood is drained out through the veins and replaced by embalming fluid pumped in through the arteries. As noted in *The Principles and Practices of Embalming,* "every operator has a favorite injection and drainage point—a fact which becomes a handicap only if he fails or refuses to forsake his favorites when conditions demand it." Typical favorites are the carotid artery, femoral artery, jugular vein, subclavian vein. There are various choices of embalming fluid. If Flextone is used, it will produce a "mild, flexible rigidity. The skin retains a velvety softness, the tissues are rubbery and pliable. Ideal for women and children." It may be blended with B. and G. Products Company's Lyf-Lyk tint, which is guaranteed to reproduce "nature's own skin texture...the velvety appearance of living tissue." Suntone comes in three separate tints: Suntan; Special Cosmetic Tint, a pink shade "especially indicated for female subjects"; and Regular Cosmetic Tint, moderately pink. 11

About three to six gallons of a dyed and perfumed solution of formaldehyde, glycerin, borax, phenol, alcohol, and water is soon circulating through Mr. Jones, whose mouth has been sewn together with a "needle directed upward between the upper lip and gum and brought out through the left nostril," with the corners raised slightly "for a more pleasant expression." If he should be bucktoothed, his teeth are cleaned with Bon Ami and coated with colorless nail polish. His eyes, meanwhile, are closed with flesh-tinted eye caps and eye cement. 12

The next step is to have at Mr. Jones with a thing called a trocar. This is a long, hollow needle attached to a tube. It is jabbed into the abdomen, poked around the entrails and chest cavity, the contents of which are pumped out and replaced with "cavity fluid." This done, and the hole in the abdomen sewn up, Mr. Jones's face is heavily creamed (to protect the skin from burns which may be caused by leakage of the chemicals), and he is covered with a sheet and left unmolested for a while. But not for long—there is more, much more, in store for him. He has been embalmed, but not yet restored, and the best time to start the restorative work is eight to ten hours after embalming, when the tissues have become firm and dry. 13

The object of all this attention to the corpse, it must be remem- 14
bered, is to make it presentable for viewing in an attitude of healthy repose. "Our customs require the presentation of our dead in the
semblance of normality...unmarred by the ravages of illness, disease,
or mutilation," says Mr. J. Sheridan Mayer in his *Restorative Art*. This is
rather a large order since few people die in the full bloom of health, un-
ravaged by illness and unmarked by some disfigurement. The funeral
industry is equal to the challenge: "In some cases the gruesome appearance of a mutilated or disease-ridden subject may be quite discouraging.
The task of restoration may seem impossible and shake the confidence
of the embalmer. This is the time for intestinal fortitude and determination. Once the formative work is begun and affected tissues are
cleaned or removed, all doubts of success vanish. It is surprising and
gratifying to discover the results which may be obtained."

The embalmer, having allowed an appropriate interval to elapse, re- 15
turns to the attack, but now he brings into play the skill and equipment
of sculptor and cosmetician. Is a hand missing? Casting one in plaster of
Paris is a simple matter. "For replacement purposes, only a cast of the
back of the hand is necessary; this is within the ability of the average operator and is quite adequate." If a lip or two, a nose, or an ear should be
missing, the embalmer has at hand a variety of restorative waxes with
which to model replacements. Pores and skin texture are simulated by
stippling with a little brush, and over this cosmetics are laid on. Head
off? Decapitation cases are rather routinely handled. Ragged edges are
trimmed, and head joined to torso with a series of splints, wires, and sutures. It is a good idea to have a little something at the neck—a scarf or
a high collar—when time for viewing comes. Swollen mouth? Cut out
tissue as needed from inside the lips. If too much is removed, the surface
contour can easily be restored by padding with cotton. Swollen necks
and cheeks are reduced by removing tissue through vertical incisions
made down each side of the neck. "When the deceased is casketed, the
pillow will hide the suture incisions...as an extra precaution against
leakage, the suture may be painted with liquid sealer."

The opposite condition is more likely to present itself—that of 16
emaciation. His hypodermic syringe now loaded with massage cream,
the embalmer seeks out and fills the hollowed and sunken areas by injection. In this procedure the backs of the hands and fingers and the
under-chin area should not be neglected.

Positioning the lips is a problem that recurrently challenges the in- 17
genuity of the embalmer. Closed too tightly, they tend to give a stern,
even disapproving expression. Ideally, embalmers feel, the lips should
give the impression of being ever so slightly parted, the upper lip protruding slightly for a more youthful appearance. This takes some engineering, however, as the lips tend to drift apart. Lip drift can sometimes

be remedied by pushing one or two straight pins through the inner margin of the lower lip and then inserting them between the two front upper teeth. If Mr. Jones happens to have no teeth, the pins can just as easily be anchored in his Armstrong Face Former and Denture Replacer. Another method to maintain lip closure is to dislocate the lower jaw, which is then held in its new position by a wire run through holes which have been drilled through the upper and lower jaws at the midline. As the French are fond of saying, *il faut souffrir pour être belle*.[2]

If Mr. Jones has died of jaundice, the embalming fluid will very   18
likely turn him green. Does this deter the embalmer? Not if he has intestinal fortitude. Masking pastes and cosmetics are heavily laid on, burial garments and casket interiors are color-correlated with particular care, and Jones is displayed beneath rose-colored lights. Friends will say "How *well* he looks." Death by carbon monoxide, on the other hand, can be rather a good thing from the embalmer's viewpoint: "One advantage is the fact that this type of discoloration is an exaggerated form of a natural pink coloration." This is nice because the healthy glow is already present and needs but little attention.

The patching and filling completed, Mr. Jones is now shaved,   19
washed, and dressed. Cream-based cosmetic, available in pink, flesh, suntan, brunette, and blond, is applied to his hands and face, his hair is shampooed and combed (and, in the case of Mrs. Jones, set), his hands manicured. For the horny-handed son of toil special care must be taken; cream should be applied to remove ingrained grime, and the nails cleaned. "If he were not in the habit of having them manicured in life, trimming and shaping is advised for better appearance—never questioned by kin."

Jones is now ready for casketing (this is the present participle of the   20
verb "to casket"). In this operation his right shoulder should be depressed slightly "to turn the body a bit to the right and soften the appearance of lying flat on the back." Positioning the hands is a matter of importance, and special rubber positioning blocks may be used. The hands should be cupped slightly for a more lifelike, relaxed appearance. Proper placement of the body requires a delicate sense of balance. It should lie as high as possible in the casket, yet not so high that the lid, when lowered, will hit the nose. On the other hand, we are cautioned, placing the body too low "creates the impression that the body is in a box."

Jones is next wheeled into the appointed slumber room where a   21
few last touches may be added—his favorite pipe placed in his hand or, if he was a great reader, a book propped into position. (In the case of little Master Jones a Teddy bear may be clutched.) Here he will hold open house for a few days, visiting hours 10 A.M. to 9 P.M.

---

[2] You have to suffer to be beautiful. —EDS.

All now being in readiness, the funeral director calls a staff confer- 22
ence to make sure that each assistant knows his precise duties. Mr.
Wilber Kriege writes: "This makes your staff feel that they are a part of
the team, with a definite assignment that must be properly carried out
if the whole plan is to succeed. You never heard of a football coach who
failed to talk to his entire team before they go on the field. They have
drilled on the plays they are to execute for hours and days, and yet the
successful coach knows the importance of making even the bench-
warming third-string substitute feel that he is important if the game is
to be won." The winning of *this* game is predicated upon glass-smooth
handling of the logistics. The funeral director has notified the pallbearers whose names were furnished by the family, has arranged for the
presence of clergyman, organist, and soloist, has provided transportation for everybody, has organized and listed the flowers sent by friends.
In *Psychology of Funeral Service* Mr. Edward A. Martin points out, "He
may not always do as much as the family thinks he is doing, but it is his
helpful guidance that they appreciate in knowing they are proceeding
as they should.... The important thing is how well his services can be
used to make the family believe they are giving unlimited expression to
their own sentiment."

The religious service may be held in a church or in the chapel of 23
the funeral home; the funeral director vastly prefers the latter arrangement, for not only is it more convenient for him but it affords him the
opportunity to show off his beautiful facilities to the gathered mourners. After the clergyman has had his say, the mourners queue up to file
past the casket for a last look at the deceased. The family is *never* asked
whether they want an open-casket ceremony; in the absence of their
instruction to the contrary, this is taken for granted. Consequently well
over 90 per cent of all American funerals feature the open casket — a
custom unknown in other parts of the world. Foreigners are astonished
by it. An English woman living in San Francisco described her reaction
in a letter to the writer:

> I myself have attended only one funeral here — that of an elderly
> fellow worker of mine. After the service I could not understand why
> everyone was walking towards the coffin (sorry, I mean casket), but
> thought I had better follow the crowd. It shook me rigid to get there
> and find the casket open and poor old Oscar lying there in his brown
> tweed suit, wearing a suntan makeup and just the wrong shade of lip-
> stick. If I had not been extremely fond of the old boy, I have a hor-
> rible feeling that I might have giggled. Then and there I decided that
> I could never face another American funeral — even dead.

The casket (which has been resting throughout the service on a 24
Classic Beauty Ultra Metal Casket Bier) is now transferred by a hy-

draulically operated device called Porto-Lift to a balloon-tired, Glide Easy casket carriage which will wheel it to yet another conveyance, the Cadillac Funeral Coach. This may be lavender, cream, light green— anything but black. Interiors, of course, are color-correlated, "for the man who cannot stop short of perfection."

At graveside, the casket is lowered into the earth. This office, once 25 the prerogative of friends of the deceased, is now performed by a patented mechanical lowering device. A "Lifetime Green" artificial grass mat is at the ready to conceal the sere earth, and overhead, to conceal the sky, is a portable Steril Chapel Tent ("resists the intense heat and humidity of summer and the terrific storms of winter...available in Silver Gray, Rose, or Evergreen"). Now is the time for the ritual scattering of earth over the coffin, as the solemn words "earth to earth, ashes to ashes, dust to dust" are pronounced by the officiating cleric. This can today be accomplished "with a mere flick of the wrist with the Gordon Leak-Proof Earth Dispenser. No grasping of a handful of dirt, no soiled fingers. Simple, dignified, beautiful, reverent! The modern way!" The Gordon Earth Dispenser (at $5) is of nickel-plated brass construction. It is not only "attractive to the eye and long wearing"; it is also "one of the 'tools' for building better public relations" if presented as "an appropriate non-commercial gift" to the clergyman. It is shaped something like a saltshaker.

Untouched by human hand, the coffin and the earth are now 26 united.

It is in the function of directing the participants through this maze 27 of gadgetry that the funeral director has assigned to himself his relatively new role of "grief therapist." He has relieved the family of every detail, he has revamped the corpse to look like a living doll, he has arranged for it to nap for a few days in a slumber room, he has put on a well-oiled performance in which the concept of *death* has played no part whatsoever—unless it was inconsiderately mentioned by the clergyman who conducted the religious service. He has done everything in his power to make the funeral a real pleasure for everybody concerned. He and his team have given their all to score an upset victory over death.

QUESTIONS ON MEANING

1. What was your emotional response to this essay? Can you analyze your feelings?
2. To what does the author attribute the secrecy that surrounds the process of embalming?

3. What, according to Mitford, is the mortician's intent? What common ob-stacles to fulfilling it must be surmounted?
4. What do you understand from Mitford's remark in paragraph 10, on dis-pelling fears of live burial: "How true; once the blood is removed, chances of live burial are indeed remote"?
5. Do you find any implied PURPOSE in this essay? Does Mitford seem primarily out to rake muck, or does she offer any positive suggestions to Americans?

QUESTIONS ON WRITING STRATEGY

1. What is Mitford's TONE? In her opening two paragraphs, exactly what shows her attitude toward her subject?
2. Why do you think Mitford goes into so much grisly detail? How does it serve her purpose?
3. What is the EFFECT of calling the body Mr. Jones (or Master Jones)?
4. Paragraph by paragraph, what TRANSITIONS does the author employ? (If you need a refresher on this point, see the discussion of transitions on pp. 224–25.)
5. Into what stages has the author divided the embalming process?
6. To whom does Mitford address her process analysis? How do you know she isn't writing for an AUDIENCE of professional morticians?
7. Consider one of the quotations from the journals and textbooks of profes-sionals and explain how it serves the author's general purpose.
8. **OTHER METHODS.** In paragraph 8, Mitford uses CLASSIFICATION in listing the embalmer's equipment and supplies. What groups does she identify, and why does she bother sorting the items at all?

QUESTIONS ON LANGUAGE

1. Explain the ALLUSION to Yorick in paragraph 2.
2. What IRONY do you find in Mitford's statement in paragraph 7, "The body is first laid out in the undertaker's morgue—or rather, Mr. Jones is reposing in the preparation room"? Pick out any other words or phrases in the essay that seem ironic. Comment especially on those you find in the essay's last two sentences.
3. Why is it useful to Mitford's purpose that she cites the brand names of mor-ticians' equipment and supplies (the Edwards Arm and Hand Positioner, Lyf-Lyk tint)? List all the brand names in the essay that are memorable.
4. Define the following words or terms: counterpart (para. 2); circumscribed, autopsy, cremated, decedent, bereaved (3); docility, perpetuation (4); in-herent, mandatory (5); intractable, reticence, *raison d'être*, formaldehyde (6); "dermasurgeon," augers, forceps, distend, stocks (8); somatic (10); carotid artery, femoral artery, jugular vein, subclavian vein, pliable (11); glycerin, borax, phenol, bucktoothed (12); trocar, entrails (13); stippling, sutures (15); emaciation (16); jaundice (18); predicated (22); queue (23); hydraulically (24); cleric (25); therapist (27).

SUGGESTIONS FOR WRITING

1. **JOURNAL WRITING.** Presumably, morticians embalm and restore corpses, and survivors support the work, because the practices are thought to ease the shock of death. Now that you know what goes on behind the scenes, how do you feel about a loved one's undergoing these procedures?

   FROM JOURNAL TO ESSAY. Drawing on your personal response to Mitford's process analysis, write a brief essay that ARGUES either for or against embalming and restoration. Consider the purposes served by these practices, both for the mortician and for the dead person's relatives and friends, as well as their costs and effects.

2. With the aid of the *Readers' Guide to Periodical Literature*, find information about the recent phenomenon of quick-freezing the dead. Set forth this process, including its hoped-for result of reviving the corpses in the far future.

3. ANALYZE some other process whose operations may not be familiar to everyone. (Have you ever held a job, or helped out in a family business, that has taken you behind the scenes? How is fast food prepared? How are cars serviced? How is a baby sat? How is a house constructed?) Detail it step by step in an essay that includes time-markers.

4. **CRITICAL WRITING.** In attacking the funeral industry, Mitford also, implicitly, attacks the people who pay for and comply with the industry's attitudes and practices. What ASSUMPTIONS does Mitford seem to make about how we ought to deal with death and the dead? (Consider, for instance, her statements about the "docility of Americans, . . . blissfully ignorant" [para. 4] and the funeral director's making "the funeral a real pleasure for everybody concerned" [27].) Write an essay in which you interpret Mitford's assumptions and agree or disagree with them, based on your own reading and experience. If you like, defend the ritual of the funeral, or the mortician's profession, against Mitford's attack.

5. **CONNECTIONS.** Both Jessica Mitford and the author of the following essay, Horace Miner, use process analysis to reveal something about human behavior. How are the two authors' intentions the same or different? What does each want to accomplish with her or his analysis? Use EXAMPLES from both essays to support your claims.

JESSICA MITFORD ON WRITING

"Choice of subject is of cardinal importance," declared Jessica Mitford in *Poison Penmanship*. "One does by far one's best work when besotted by and absorbed in the matter at hand." After *The American Way of Death* was published, Mitford received hundreds of letters suggesting alleged rackets that ought to be exposed, and to her surprise, an overwhelming majority of these letters complained about defective and overpriced hearing aids. But Mitford never wrote a book blasting the hearing aid industry. "Somehow, although there may well be need for such an exposé, I could not warm up to hearing aids as a subject for the kind of thorough, intensive, long-range research that would be needed to do an effective job." She once taught a course at Yale in muckraking, with each student choosing a subject to investigate. "Those who tackled hot issues on campus, such as violations of academic freedom or failure to implement affirmative-action hiring policies, turned in some excellent work; but the lad who decided to investigate 'waste in the Yale dining halls' was predictably unable to make much of this trivial topic." (The editors interject: We aren't sure that the topic is necessarily trivial, but obviously not everyone would burn to write about it!)

The hardest problem Mitford faced in writing *The American Way of Death*, she recalled, was doing her factual, step-by-step account of the embalming process. She felt "determined to describe it in all its revolting details, but how to make this subject palatable to the reader?" Her solution was to cast the whole process analysis in the official JARGON of the mortuary industry, drawing on lists of taboo words and their EUPHEMISMS (or acceptable synonyms), as published in the trade journal *Casket & Sunnyside*: "Mr., Mrs., Miss Blank, not corpse or body; preparation room, not morgue; reposing room, not laying-out room...." The story of Mr. Jones thus took shape, and Mitford's use of jargon, she found, added macabre humor to the proceedings.

FOR DISCUSSION

1. What seem to be Mitford's criteria for an effective essay or book?
2. What is muckraking? Why do you suppose anyone would want to do it?

HORACE MINER

An anthropologist and teacher, HORACE MINER specialized in the cultures of Africa. He was born in 1912 in Saint Paul, Minnesota, and received degrees from the University of Kentucky (B.A., 1933) and the University of Chicago (M.A., 1935; Ph.D., 1937). Miner taught anthropology and sociology at Wayne State University and for many years at the University of Michigan, where he was also a researcher in the Museum of Anthropology. He retired from Michigan in 1980. Based on his field research, Miner wrote numerous journal articles and books, including *St. Denis: A French-Canadian Parish* (1939), *Culture and Agriculture* (1953), *Oasis and Casbah: Algerian Culture and Personality in Change* (1960), and *The City in Modern Africa* (1967). Miner died in 1993.

Body Ritual Among the Nacirema

As an anthropologist, Miner was adept at *ethnography*, studying and reporting on specific cultures. Miner's specialty was African cultures, but here he turned his ethnographer's eye on a North American culture that may seem familiar to you. The essay first appeared in the journal *American Anthropologist* in June 1956 and has often been reprinted.

The anthropologist has become so familiar with the diversity of 1 ways in which different peoples behave in similar situations that he is not apt to be surprised by even the most exotic customs. In fact, if all of the logically possible combinations of behavior have not been found somewhere in the world, he is apt to suspect that they must be present in some yet undescribed tribe. This point has, in fact, been expressed with respect to clan organization by Murdock.[1] In this light, the magical beliefs and practices of the Nacirema present such unusual aspects that it seems desirable to describe them as an example of the extremes to which human behavior can go.

Professor Linton first brought the ritual of the Nacirema to the 2 attention of anthropologists twenty years ago, but the culture of this people is still very poorly understood. They are a North American group living in the territory between the Canadian Cree, the Yaqui and Tarahumare of Mexico, and the Carib and Arawak of the Antilles. Little is known of their origin, although tradition states that they came from the east....

---

[1] George Peter Murdock (1897–1985) was an American anthropologist who attempted to identify and classify the cultures of the world. —EDS.

Nacirema culture is characterized by a highly developed market 3
economy which has evolved in a rich natural habitat. While much of
the people's time is devoted to economic pursuits, a large part of the
fruits of these labors and a considerable portion of the day are spent in
ritual activity. The focus of this activity is the human body, the appearance and health of which loom as a dominant concern in the ethos of
the people. While such a concern is certainly not unusual, its ceremonial aspects and associated philosophy are unique.

The fundamental belief underlying the whole system appears to be 4
that the human body is ugly and that its natural tendency is to debility
and disease. Incarcerated in such a body, man's only hope is to avert
these characteristics through the use of the powerful influences of ritual and ceremony. Every household has one or more shrines devoted to
this purpose. The more powerful individuals in the society have several
shrines in their houses and, in fact, the opulence of a house is often referred to in terms of the number of such ritual centers it possesses. Most
houses are of wattle and daub construction, but the shrine rooms of the
more wealthy are walled with stone. Poorer families imitate the rich by
applying pottery plaques to their shrine walls.

While each family has at least one such shrine, the rituals associ- 5
ated with it are not family ceremonies but are private and secret. The
rites are normally only discussed with children, and then only during
the period when they are being initiated into these mysteries. I was
able, however, to establish sufficient rapport with the natives to examine these shrines and to have the rituals described to me.

The focal point of the shrine is a box or chest which is built into 6
the wall. In this chest are kept the many charms and magical potions
without which no native believes he could live. These preparations are
secured from a variety of specialized practitioners. The most powerful
of these are the medicine men, whose assistance must be rewarded with
substantial gifts. However, the medicine men do not provide the curative potions for their clients, but decide what the ingredients should be
and then write them down in an ancient and secret language. This
writing is understood only by the medicine men and by the herbalists
who, for another gift, provide the required charm.

The charm is not disposed of after it has served its purpose, but is 7
placed in the charm-box of the household shrine. As these magical materials are specific for certain ills, and the real or imagined maladies of
the people are many, the charm-box is usually full to overflowing. The
magical packets are so numerous that people forget what their purposes
were and fear to use them again. While the natives are very vague on this
point, we can only assume that the idea in retaining all the old magical
materials is that their presence in the charm-box, before which the body
rituals are conducted, will in some way protect the worshipper.

Beneath the charm-box is a small font. Each day every member of   8
the family, in succession, enters the shrine room, bows his head before
the charm-box, mingles different sorts of holy water in the font, and
proceeds with a brief rite of ablution. The holy waters are secured from
the Water Temple of the community, where the priests conduct elaborate ceremonies to make the liquid ritually pure.

In the hierarchy of magical practitioners, and below the medicine   9
men in prestige, are specialists whose designation is best translated
"holy-mouth-men." The Nacirema have an almost pathological horror
of and fascination with the mouth, the condition of which is believed
to have a supernatural influence on all social relationships. Were it not
for the rituals of the mouth, they believe that their teeth would fall out,
their gums bleed, their jaws shrink, their friends desert them, and their
lovers reject them. They also believe that a strong relationship exists
between oral and moral characteristics. For example, there is a ritual
ablution of the mouth for children which is supposed to improve their
moral fiber.

The daily body ritual performed by everyone includes a mouth-rite.   10
Despite the fact that these people are so punctilious about care of the
mouth, this rite involves a practice which strikes the uninitiated
stranger as revolting. It was reported to me that the ritual consists of inserting a small bundle of hog hairs into the mouth, along with certain
magical powders, and then moving the bundle in a highly formalized
series of gestures.

In addition to the private mouth-rite, the people seek out a holy-   11
mouth-man once or twice a year. These practitioners have an impressive set of paraphernalia, consisting of a variety of augers, awls, probes,
and prods. The use of these objects in the exorcism of the evils of the
mouth involves almost unbelievable ritual torture of the client. The
holy-mouth-man opens the client's mouth and, using the above mentioned tools, enlarges any holes which decay may have created in the
teeth. Magical materials are put into these holes. If there are not naturally occurring holes in the teeth, large sections of one or more teeth
are gouged out so that the supernatural substance can be applied. In the
client's view, the purpose of these ministrations is to arrest decay and to
draw friends. The extremely sacred and traditional character of the rite
is evident in the fact that the natives return to the holy-mouth-men
year after year, despite the fact that their teeth continue to decay.

It is to be hoped that, when a thorough study of the Nacirema is   12
made, there will be careful inquiry into the personality structure of
these people. One has but to watch the gleam in the eye of a holy-
mouth-man, as he jabs an awl into an exposed nerve, to suspect that a
certain amount of sadism is involved. If this can be established, a very
interesting pattern emerges, for most of the population shows definite

masochistic tendencies. It was to these that Professor Linton referred in discussing a distinctive part of the daily body ritual which is performed only by men. This part of the rite involves scraping and lacerating the surface of the face with a sharp instrument. Special women's rites are performed only four times during each lunar month, but what they lack in frequency is made up in barbarity. As part of this ceremony, women bake their heads in small ovens for about an hour. The theoretically interesting point is that what seems to be a preponderantly masochistic people have developed sadistic specialists.

The medicine men have an imposing temple, or *latipso*, in every   13
community of any size. The more elaborate ceremonies required to treat very sick patients can only be performed at this temple. These ceremonies involve not only the thaumaturge but a permanent group of vestal maidens who move sedately about the temple chambers in distinctive costume and headdress.

The *latipso* ceremonies are so harsh that it is phenomenal that a fair   14
proportion of the really sick natives who enter the temple ever recover. Small children whose indoctrination is still incomplete have been known to resist attempts to take them to the temple because "that is where you go to die." Despite this fact, sick adults are not only willing but eager to undergo the protracted ritual purification, if they can afford to do so. No matter how ill the supplicant or how grave the emergency, the guardians of many temples will not admit a client if he cannot give a rich gift to the custodian. Even after one has gained admission and survived the ceremonies, the guardians will not permit the neophyte to leave until he makes still another gift.

The supplicant entering the temple is first stripped of all his or her   15
clothes. In everyday life the Nacirema avoids exposure of his body and its natural functions. Bathing and excretory acts are performed only in the secrecy of the household shrine, where they are ritualized as part of the body-rites. Psychological shock results from the fact that body secrecy is suddenly lost upon entry into the *latipso*. A man, whose own wife has never seen him in an excretory act, suddenly finds himself naked and assisted by a vestal maiden while he performs his natural functions into a sacred vessel. This sort of ceremonial treatment is necessitated by the fact that the excreta are used by a diviner to ascertain the course and nature of the client's sickness. Female clients, on the other hand, find their naked bodies are subjected to the scrutiny, manipulation and prodding of the medicine men.

Few supplicants in the temple are well enough to do anything but   16
lie on their hard beds. The daily ceremonies, like the rites of the holy-mouth-men, involve discomfort and torture. With ritual precision, the vestals awaken their miserable charges each dawn and roll them about on their beds of pain while performing ablutions, in the formal move-

ments of which the maidens are highly trained. At other times they insert magic wands in the supplicant's mouth or force him to eat substances which are supposed to be healing. From time to time the medicine men come to their clients and jab magically treated needles into their flesh. The fact that these temple ceremonies may not cure, and may even kill the neophyte, in no way decreases the people's faith in the medicine men.

There remains one other kind of practitioner, known as a "listener." This witchdoctor has the power to exorcise the devils that lodge in the heads of people who have been bewitched. The Nacirema believe that parents bewitch their own children. Mothers are particularly suspected of putting a curse on children while teaching them the secret body rituals. The counter-magic of the witchdoctor is unusual in its lack of ritual. The patient simply tells the "listener" all his troubles and fears, beginning with the earliest difficulties he can remember. The memory displayed by the Nacirema in these exorcism sessions is truly remarkable. It is not uncommon for the patient to bemoan the rejection he felt upon being weaned as a babe, and a few individuals even see their troubles going back to the traumatic effects of their own birth.   17

In conclusion, mention must be made of certain practices which have their base in native esthetics but which depend upon the pervasive aversion to the natural body and its functions. There are ritual fasts to make fat people thin and ceremonial feasts to make thin people fat. Still other rites are used to make women's breasts larger if they are small, and smaller if they are large. General dissatisfaction with breast shape is symbolized in the fact that the ideal form is virtually outside the range of human variation. A few women afflicted with almost inhuman hyper-mammary development are so idolized that they make a handsome living by simply going from village to village and permitting the natives to stare at them for a fee.   18

Reference has already been made to the fact that excretory functions are ritualized, routinized, and relegated to secrecy. Natural reproductive functions are similarly distorted. Intercourse is taboo as a topic and scheduled as an act. Efforts are made to avoid pregnancy by the use of magical materials or by limiting intercourse to certain phases of the moon. Conception is actually very infrequent. When pregnant, women dress so as to hide their condition. Parturition takes place in secret, without friends or relatives to assist, and the majority of women do not nurse their infants.   19

Our review of the ritual life of the Nacirema has certainly shown them to be a magic-ridden people. It is hard to understand how they have managed to exist so long under the burdens which they have imposed upon themselves. But even such exotic customs as these take on   20 real meaning when they are viewed with the insight provided by Malinowski[2] when he wrote:

> Looking from far and above, from our high places of safety in the developed civilization, it is easy to see all the crudity and irrelevance of magic. But without its power and guidance early man could not have mastered his practical difficulties as he has done, nor could man have advanced to the higher stages of civilization.

QUESTIONS ON MEANING

1. At what point did you realize what Miner's true subject is? What tipped you off? Did you see the big hint in the spelling of *Nacirema*?
2. One of Miner's purposes is clearly to amuse readers through social SATIRE. But what other purposes does he seem to have?
3. What stereotype does Miner exploit for its humor at the end of paragraph 6?
4. At the beginning and end of the essay, Miner refers to the Nacirema as having "magical beliefs and practices" (para. 1) and as being "magic-ridden" (20). What kinds of cultures are usually described in this way? Why does Miner use such terms to describe the Nacerima?

QUESTIONS ON WRITING STRATEGY

1. Miner explains several processes under the umbrella of "body rituals." What are these processes in Americanese — that is, in the words we commonly use for them?
2. What is the EFFECT of Miner's opening paragraph? What do the academic TONE and mention of the anthropologist Murdock's work accomplish?
3. This essay originally appeared in *American Anthropologist*, a serious academic journal. In what ways are anthropologists the perfect AUDIENCE for Miner's humor? How do you respond differently to this essay than you think an anthropologist would?
4. This essay was first published more than four decades ago. In what ways does it seem dated? What parts of it still seem fresh?
5. **OTHER METHODS.** Miner's humor involves DEFINITIONS of things that ordinarily need no defining: For instance, he refers to a toothbrush as a "small bundle of hog hairs" (para. 10). Find other examples of bizarre definitions of ordinary things. Other than humor, what is the effect of such definitions?

QUESTIONS ON LANGUAGE

1. Why do you think Miner chose the name "Nacirema" for his subjects? What associations does this name call up for you?
2. Explain the IRONY of the last paragraph.

---

[2]Bronislaw Malinowski (1884–1942) was a Polish-born British anthropologist who saw customs in terms of their functions in a culture. —EDS.

3. This essay includes many words specific to the discipline of anthropology. Make sure you know the definitions of the following words: ethos (para. 3); debility, incarcerated, opulence, wattle and daub (4); curative (6); font, ablution (8); hierarchy (9); punctilious (10); augers, awls, gouged, ministrations (11); sadism, masochistic, lacerating, preponderantly (12); thaumaturge (13); indoctrination, supplicant, neophyte (14); excretory, vestal, vessel, excreta, diviner (15); esthetics (18); parturition (19).

SUGGESTIONS FOR WRITING

1. **JOURNAL WRITING.** Think about all the little "rituals" you perform regularly: doing the dishes, walking the dog, going to the movies. Write out all the steps of three or four of these routines, in chronological order, in as much detail as you can.

   FROM JOURNAL TO ESSAY. Imagine that you are an observer from another planet reporting back to your authorities on Earth customs. Write them a letter describing the processes you have detailed in your journal. Remember, you don't understand the language of these earthlings and have no names for the processes you are writing about.

2. Miner satirizes our society's obsession with physical appearance, our hypochondria, our shame over our bodies, our overdependence on psychoanalysis — all in 1956. Evaluate the relevance of this essay at the end of the twentieth century, considering where the concerns with our bodies have brought us. Do you think we are better or worse off, physically and mentally, than we were a hundred or even forty years ago? What's better? What's worse? Be specific.

3. **CRITICAL WRITING.** Anthropologists have sometimes been criticized for turning the people they study into weird and mysterious "others." How does Miner manage to criticize anthropology while working within it, on its own terms, and using its own langauge and methodology? Focus in particular on the implications of the last paragraph.

4. **CONNECTIONS.** Read or reread Jessica Mitford's "Behind the Formaldehyde Curtain" (p. 228). Taken together, what do Miner's and Mitford's essays say about the importance of the body in our culture? Write an essay either defending or criticizing Americans' obsession with the way they look.

LINNEA SAUKKO

LINNEA SAUKKO was born in Warren, Ohio, in 1956. After receiving a degree in environmental quality control from Muskingum Area Technical College, she spent three years as an environmental technician, developing hazardous waste programs and acting as adviser on chemical safety at a large corporation. Concerned about the lack of safe methods for disposing of hazardous waste, Saukko went back to school to earn a B.A. in geology (Ohio State University, 1985) so that she could help address this issue. She currently lives in Hilliard, Ohio, and works as a groundwater supervisor at the Ohio Environmental Protection Agency, evaluating various sites for possible contamination of the groundwater. She is also researching routine spraying in workplaces and its link with workers' chemical sensitivities.

How to Poison the Earth

"How to Poison the Earth" was written in response to an assignment given in a freshman composition class and was awarded a Bedford Prize in Student Writing. It was subsequently published in *Student Writers at Work: The Bedford Prizes*, edited by Nancy Sommers and Donald McQuade (1984). In this SATIRE, Saukko shares with readers some of what she has learned on the job and suggests one way we can guarantee the fate of the earth.

Poisoning the earth can be difficult because the earth is always trying to cleanse and renew itself. Keeping this in mind, we should generate as much waste as possible from substances such as uranium-238, which has a half-life (the time it takes for half of the substance to decay) of one million years, or plutonium, which has a half-life of only 0.5 million years but is so toxic that if distributed evenly, ten pounds of it could kill every person on the earth. Because the United States generates about eighteen tons of plutonium per year, it is about the best substance for long-term poisoning of the earth. It would help if we would build more nuclear power plants because each one generates only 500 pounds of plutonium each year. Of course, we must include persistent toxic chemicals such as polychlorinated biphenyl (PCB) and dichlorodiphenyl trichloroethane (DDT) to make sure we have enough toxins to poison the earth from the core to the outer atmosphere. First, we must develop many different ways of putting the waste from these nuclear and chemical substances in, on, and around the earth.

Putting these substances in the earth is a most important step in the poisoning process. With deep-well injection we can ensure that the earth is poisoned all the way to the core. Deep-well injection involves drilling a hole that is a few thousand feet deep and injecting toxic substances at extremely high pressures so they will penetrate deep into the earth. According to the Environmental Protection Agency (EPA), there are about 360 such deep injection wells in the United States. We cannot forget the groundwater aquifers that are closer to the surface. These must also be contaminated. This is easily done by shallow-well injection, which operates on the same principle as deep-well injection, only closer to the surface. The groundwater that has been injected with toxins will spread contamination beneath the earth. The EPA estimates that there are approximately 500,000 shallow injection wells in the United States.

Burying the toxins in the earth is the next best method. The toxins from landfills, dumps, and lagoons slowly seep into the earth, guaranteeing that contamination will last a long time. Because the EPA estimates there are only about 50,000 of these dumps in the United States, they should be located in areas where they will leak to the surrounding ground and surface water.   3

Applying pesticides and other poisons on the earth is another part of the poisoning process. This is good for coating the earth's surface so that the poisons will be absorbed by plants, will seep into the ground, and will run off into surface water.   4

Surface water is very important to contaminate because it will transport the poisons to places that cannot be contaminated directly. Lakes are good for long-term storage of pollutants while they release some of their contamination to rivers. The only trouble with rivers is that they act as a natural cleansing system for the earth. No matter how much poison is dumped into them, they will try to transport it away to reach the ocean eventually.   5

The ocean is very hard to contaminate because it has such a large volume and a natural buffering capacity that tends to neutralize some of the contamination. So in addition to the pollution from rivers, we must use the ocean as a dumping place for as many toxins as possible. The ocean currents will help transport the pollution to places that cannot otherwise be reached.   6

Now make sure that the air around the earth is very polluted. Combustion and evaporation are major mechanisms for doing this. We must continuously pollute because the wind will disperse the toxins while rain washes them from the air. But this is good because a few lakes are stripped of all living animals each year from acid rain. Because the lower atmosphere can cleanse itself fairly easily, we must explode nuclear tests bombs that shoot radioactive particles high into the upper atmosphere where they will circle the earth for years. Gravity must pull   7 some of the particles to earth, so we must continue exploding these bombs.

So it is that easy. Just be sure to generate as many poisonous sub-   8
stances as possible and be sure they are distributed in, on, and around the entire earth at a greater rate than it can cleanse itself. By following these easy steps we can guarantee the poisoning of the earth.

QUESTIONS ON MEANING

1. Is the author's main PURPOSE to amuse and entertain, to inform readers of ways they can make better use of natural resources, to warn readers about threats to the future of our planet, or to make fun of scientists? Support your answer with EVIDENCE from the essay.
2. Describe at least three of the earth's mechanisms for cleansing its land, water, and atmosphere, as presented in this essay.
3. According to Saukko, many of our actions are detrimental, if not outright destructive, to our environment. Identify these practices and discuss them. If these activities are harmful to the earth, why are they permitted? Do they serve some other important goal or purpose? If so, what? Are there other ways that these goals might be reached?

QUESTIONS ON WRITING STRATEGY

1. How detailed and specific are Saukko's instructions for poisoning the earth? Which steps in this process would you be able to carry out, once you finished reading the essay? In what instances might an author choose not to provide concrete, comprehensive instructions for a procedure? Relate your answer to the TONE and purpose of this essay.
2. How is Saukko's essay organized? Follow the process carefully to determine whether it happens chronologically, with each step depending on the one before it, or whether it follows another order. How effective is this method of organization and presentation?
3. For what AUDIENCE is this essay intended? How can you tell?
4. What is the tone of this essay? Consider especially the title and the last paragraph as well as examples from the body of the essay. How does the tone contribute to Saukko's SATIRE?
5. **OTHER METHODS.** Saukko doesn't mention every possible pollutant but instead focuses on certain EXAMPLES. Why do you think she chooses these particular examples? What serious pollutants can you think of that Saukko doesn't mention specifically?

QUESTIONS ON LANGUAGE

1. How do the phrases "next best method" (para. 3), "another part of the poisoning process" (4), and "lakes are good for long-term storage of pollutants"

(5) signal the tone of this essay? Should they be read literally, IRONICALLY, metaphorically, or some other way?

2. Be sure you know how to define the following words: generate, nuclear, toxins (para. 1); lagoons, contamination (3); buffering, neutralize (6); combustion (7).

SUGGESTIONS FOR WRITING

1. **JOURNAL WRITING.** In everyday conversations, we often use satire or SAR-CASM to suggest solutions to problems that seem ridiculous or overwhelming. For example, we suggest breaking all the dishes so that we don't have to wash them again or barring pedestrians from city streets so that they don't interfere with cars. What kinds of situations drive you to make suggestions like these? Are the suggestions ever serious?

   FROM JOURNAL TO ESSAY. Choose one of the solutions you wrote about in your journal, or propose a solution to a problem that your journal entry has suggested. Write an essay detailing this satirical solution, paying careful attention to explaining each step of the process and to maintaining your satiric tone throughout.

2. Write an essay defending and justifying the use of nuclear power plants, pesticides, or another pollutant Saukko mentions. This essay will require some research because you will need to argue that the benefits of these methods outweigh their hazardous and destructive effects. Be sure to support your claims with factual information and statistics. Or approach the issue from the same point of view that Saukko did, and argue against the use of nuclear power plants or pesticides. Substantiate your argument with data and facts, and be sure to propose alternative sources of power or alternative methods of insect control.

3. **CRITICAL WRITING.** What does Saukko gain or lose by using satire and irony to make her point? What would be the comparative strengths and weaknesses of an essay that approached the same pollution problems straightforwardly and sincerely, perhaps urging or pleading with readers to stop polluting?

4. **CONNECTIONS.** Saukko is not the only writer of irony in this book: James Thurber (p. 74), Joan Didion (p. 121), Merrill Markoe (p. 154), Suzanne Britt (p. 182), Dave Barry (p. 188), Jessica Mitford (p. 228), Horace Miner (p. 239), Judy Brady (p. 274), H. L. Mencken (p. 455), and Jonathan Swift (p. 508) also employ it. Based on Saukko's essay and essays by at least two of these others, define *irony*. If you need a boost, supplement the definition in this book's glossary with one in a dictionary of literary or rhetorical terms. But go beyond others' definitions to construct one of your own, using quotations from the essays as your support.

LINNEA SAUKKO ON WRITING

"After I have chosen a topic," says Linnea Saukko, "the easiest thing for me to do is to write about how I really feel about it. The goal of 'How to Poison the Earth' was to inform people, or more specifically, to open their eyes.

"As soon as I decided on my topic, I made a list of all the types of pollution and I sat down and basically wrote the paper in less than two hours. The information seemed to pour from me onto the page. Of course I did a lot of editing afterward, but I never changed the idea and the tone that I started with."

FOR DISCUSSION

When have you had the experience of writing on a subject that compelled your words to pour forth with little effort? What was the subject? What did you learn from this experience?

BENJAMIN FRANKLIN

Printer, postmaster, author, inventor, scientist, diplomat, and Founding Father, BENJAMIN FRANKLIN is one of America's most revered historical figures. He was born in 1706 in Boston, left school at age ten, and at age seventeen ran away from a printing apprenticeship to find his own life in Philadelphia. Just a bare list of Franklin's accomplishments could fill pages. Some highlights: He invented bifocals and the lightning rod, wrote and published *Poor Richard's Almanac* and many political tracts, wrote a durable *Autobiography*, served as a delegate to the Second Continental Congress, helped to write and then signed the Declaration of Independence, helped to negotiate the end of the Revolutionary War, contributed to the Constitutional Convention, and served as ambassador to France. Franklin died in 1790 at age eighty-four. Writing in the *Encyclopaedia Britannica,* the critic Theodore Hornberger said of Franklin, "Of all the Founding Fathers of the United States, Franklin, were there such a thing as reincarnation, would adapt himself most readily to the complexities of the later half of the twentieth century. His modernity is nothing less than astonishing."

The Art of Procuring Pleasant Dreams

Even during his lifetime, Franklin was renowned for his practicality. Many of his writings, including the essay here, combined common sense and a scientific spirit in advice for living healthfully and prosperously. "The Art of Procuring Pleasant Dreams" first appeared in 1786. Its great age may make reading a bit difficult at first, because Franklin uses a style no longer common, but the advice remains lively and serviceable.

As a great part of our life is spent in sleep during which we have 1
sometimes pleasant and sometimes painful dreams, it becomes of some consequence to obtain the one kind and avoid the other; for whether real or imaginary, pain is pain and pleasure is pleasure. If we can sleep without dreaming, it is well that painful dreams are avoided. If while we sleep we can have any pleasing dream, it is, as the French say, *autant de gagné,* so much added to the pleasure of life.

To this end it is, in the first place, necessary to be careful in pre- 2
serving health, by due exercise and great temperance; for, in sickness, the imagination is disturbed, and disagreeable, sometimes terrible, ideas are apt to present themselves. Exercise should precede meals, not immediately follow them; the first promotes, the latter, unless moderate, obstructs digestion. If, after exercise, we feed sparingly, the diges-

tion will be easy and good, the body lightsome, the temper cheerful, and all the animal functions performed agreeably. Sleep, when it follows, will be natural and undisturbed; while indolence, with full feeding, occasions nightmares and horrors inexpressive; we fall from precipices, are assaulted by wild beasts, murderers and demons, and experience every variety of distress. Observe, however, that the quantities of food and exercise are relative things; those who move much may, and indeed ought to eat more; those who use little exercise should eat little. In general, mankind, since the improvement of cookery, eat about twice as much as nature requires. Suppers are not bad, if we have not dined; but restless nights naturally follow hearty suppers after full dinners. Indeed, as there is a difference in constitutions, some rest well after these meals; it costs them only a frightful dream and an apoplexy, after which they sleep till doomsday. Nothing is more common in the newspapers, than instances of people who, after eating a hearty supper, are found dead abed in the morning.

Another means of preserving health, to be attended to, is the having a constant supply of fresh air in your bed-chamber. It has been a great mistake, the sleeping in rooms exactly closed, and in beds surrounded by curtains. No outward air that may come in to you is so unwholesome as the unchanged air, often breathed, of a close chamber. As boiling water does not grow hotter by longer boiling, if the particles that receive greater heat can escape; so living bodies do not putrefy, if the particles, so fast as they become putrid, can be thrown off. Nature expels them by the pores of the skin and the lungs, and in a free, open air they are carried off; but in a close room we receive them again and again, though they become more and more corrupt. A number of persons crowded into a small room thus spoil the air in a few minutes, and even render it mortal as in the Black Hole at Calcutta. A single person is said to spoil only a gallon of air per minute, and therefore requires a longer time to spoil a chamber-full; but it is done, however, in proportion, and many putrid disorders hence have their origin. It is recorded of Methusalem,[1] who, being the longest liver, may be supposed to have best preserved his health, that he slept always in the open air; for, when he had lived five hundred years, an angel said to him; "Arise, Methusalem, and build thee an house, for thou shalt live yet five hundred years longer." But Methusalem answered, and said, "If I am to live but five hundred years longer, it is not worth while to build me an house; I will sleep in the air, as I have been used to do." Physicians, after having for ages contended that the sick should not be indulged with fresh air, have at length discovered that it may do them good. It is

---

[1] As told in the Bible's Book of Genesis, Chapter 5, Methusalem, or more commonly Methuselah, was a near descendant of Adam who lived to age 969. —Eds.

therefore to be hoped, that they may in time discover likewise, that it is not hurtful to those who are in health, and that we may be then cured of the *aërophobia*,[2] that at present distresses weak minds, and makes them choose to be stifled and poisoned, rather than leave open the window of a bed-chamber, or put down the glass of a coach.

Confined air, when saturated with perspirable matter, will not re- 4 ceive more; and that matter must remain in our bodies, and occasion diseases; but it gives some previous notice of its being about to be hurt-ful, by producing certain uneasiness, slight indeed at first, which as with regard to the lungs is a trifling sensation, and to the pores of the skin a kind of restlessness, which is difficult to describe, and few that feel it know the cause of it. But we may recollect, that sometimes on waking in the night, we have, if warmly covered, found it difficult to get asleep again. We turn often without finding repose in any position. This fidgettiness (to use a vulgar expression for want of a better) is oc-casioned wholly by an uneasiness in the skin, owing to the retention of the perspirable matter—the bed-clothes having received their quan-tity, and, being saturated, refusing to take any more. To become sen-sible of this by an experiment, let a person keep his position in the bed, but throw off the bed-clothes, and suffer fresh air to approach the part uncovered of his body; he will then feel that part suddenly refreshed; for the air will immediately relieve the skin, by receiving, licking up, and carrying off, the load of perspirable matter that incommoded it. For every portion of cool air that approaches the warm skin, in receiving its part of that vapour, receives therewith a degree of heat that rarefies and renders it lighter, when it will be pushed away with its burthen, by cooler and therefore heavier fresh air, which for a moment supplies its place, and then, being likewise changed and warmed, gives way to a succeeding quantity. This is the order of nature, to prevent animals be-ing infected by their own perspiration. He will now be sensible of the difference between the part exposed to the air and that which, remain-ing sunk in the bed, denies the air access: for this part now manifests its uneasiness more distinctly by the comparison, and the seat of the un-easiness is more plainly perceived than when the whole surface of the body was affected by it.

Here, then, is one great and general cause of unpleasing dreams. 5 For when the body is uneasy, the mind will be disturbed by it, and dis-agreeable ideas of various kinds will in sleep be the natural conse-quences. The remedies, preventive and curative, follow:

1. By eating moderately (as before advised for health's sake) less 6 perspirable matter is produced in a given time; hence the bed-clothes

---

[2] Fear of air. — EDS.

receive it longer before they are saturated, and we may therefore sleep longer before we are made uneasy by their refusing to receive any more.

2. By using thinner and more porous bed-clothes, which will suffer the perspirable matter more easily to pass through them, we are less incommoded, such being longer tolerable.

3. When you are awakened by this uneasiness, and find you cannot easily sleep again, get out of bed, beat up and turn your pillow, shake the bed-clothes well, with at least twenty shakes, then throw the bed open and leave it to cool; in the meanwhile, continuing undrest, walk about your chamber till your skin has had time to discharge its load, which it will do sooner as the air may be dried and colder. When you begin to feel the cold air unpleasant, then return to your bed, and you will soon fall asleep, and your sleep will be sweet and pleasant. All the scenes presented to your fancy will be too of the pleasing kind. I am often as agreeably entertained with them, as by the scenery of an opera. If you happen to be too indolent to get out of bed, you may, instead of it, lift up your bed-clothes with one arm and leg, so as to draw in a good deal of fresh air, and by letting them fall force it out again. This, repeated twenty times, will so clear them of the perspirable matter they have imbibed, as to permit your sleeping well for some time afterwards. But this latter method is not equal to the former.

Those who do not love trouble, and can afford to have two beds, will find great luxury in rising, when they wake in a hot bed, and going into the cool one. Such shifting of beds would also be of great service to persons ill of a fever, as it refreshes and frequently procures sleep. A very large bed, that will admit a removal so distant from the first situation as to be cool and sweet, may in a degree answer the same end.

One or two observations more will conclude this little piece. Care must be taken, when you lie down, to dispose your pillow so as to suit your manner of placing your head, and to be perfectly easy; then place your limbs so as not to bear inconveniently hard upon one another, as for instance, the joints of your ankles; for, though a bad position may at first give but little pain and be hardly noticed, yet a continuance will render it less tolerable, and the uneasiness may come on while you are asleep, and disturb your imagination. These are the rules of the art. But, though they will generally prove effectual in producing the end intended, there is a case in which the most punctual observance of them will be totally fruitless. I need not mention the case to you, my dear friend, but my account of the art would be imperfect without it. The case is, when the person who desires to have pleasant dreams has not taken care to preserve, what is necessary above all things,

A GOOD CONSCIENCE.

QUESTIONS ON MEANING

1. How appropriate is the title of this essay? Does it accurately reflect Franklin's PURPOSE as you understand it?
2. What does Franklin mean by "pain is pain and pleasure is pleasure" (para. 1)?
3. What are the two basic requirements for good sleep governing all the advice in the essay?
4. What, according to Franklin, is the one case in which his advice will have no effect?

QUESTIONS ON WRITING STRATEGY

1. What purpose does the first sentence of the essay serve?
2. Why does Franklin propose a do-it-yourself experiment in paragraph 4? Does he actually intend for readers to try this procedure?
3. What is the EFFECT of Franklin's instructions (twice in para. 8) to repeat things twenty times?
4. Locate two instances in which Franklin draws parallels between humans and animals. How do these parallels contribute to the effectiveness of his instructions?
5. **OTHER METHODS.** Paragraph 3, which may at first seem loosely constructed, is actually organized around a single ARGUMENT. SUMMARIZE this argument in a sentence.

QUESTIONS ON LANGUAGE

1. Explain why "those who do not love trouble" (para. 9) is a EUPHEMISM. How else could Franklin have referred, less politely, to the same people?
2. Explain the humor in the quotation from Methusalem (para. 3).
3. What is the effect of Franklin's calling his essay "this little piece" (para. 10)?
4. What is the effect of Franklin's addressing his reader directly in paragraph 10: "I need not mention the case to you, my dear friend"?
5. Look up any of the following words you are unsure of (the asterisked words are familiar ones used by Franklin in perhaps unfamiliar ways): temperance, lightsome, indolence, precipices, constitutions,* apoplexy, abed (para. 2); putrefy, putrid, chamber* (3); saturated, occasion,* trifling, repose, vulgar,* retention, sensible,* therewith, rarefies, burthen, succeeding* (4); curative (5); porous, suffer,* incommoded (7); imbibed (8); procures (9); dispose,* effectual, punctual* (10).

SUGGESTIONS FOR WRITING

1. **JOURNAL WRITING.** All of us, whether through conscious reflection or simple trial and error, develop ways of doing things efficiently; we're all experts at something, however modest our expertise may seem. Make a list of processes you have managed to perfect. These may be as simple as making the perfect cup of coffee or as complex as getting a plant go grow successfully or hanging wallpaper.

FROM JOURNAL TO ESSAY. Choose one of the processes from your list and write a directive, "how-to" process analysis. Your directions should be detailed enough for a general reader with no special knowledge or skills to carry them out.

2. Eighteenth-century prose such as Franklin's often comes across today as unnecessarily wordy or overexplained. Rewrite paragraph 4 or 8 of Franklin's essay for a contemporary AUDIENCE, transforming it into something that might appear in, say, a health and fitness magazine. You will want to use a plain, straightforward vocabulary and a no-nonsense TONE.

3. **CRITICAL WRITING.** How useful is this essay? How much of what Franklin says is merely common sense or unneeded detail? Can you think of any function the essay might serve for today's reader other than its original intended one? In other words, what—other than how to sleep and dream well—do we learn from the essay?

4. **CONNECTIONS.** While Franklin is concerned with maintaining a healthy body, Linnea Saukko, in "How to Poison the Earth" (p. 246), is worried about the health of the planet. ANALYZE both writers' use of process analysis as a way of persuading readers to make the changes, whether individual or social, that they advocate. What role does tone play in this persuasion?

BENJAMIN FRANKLIN ON WRITING

In his *Autobiography*, written between 1771 and 1788 and published after his death, Benjamin Franklin explained how as a teenager he came to acquire "what little Ability" he had as a writer. (The punctuation, spelling, and grammar of this passage have not been updated to match our contemporary preferences.)

"There was another Bookish Lad in the Town [Boston], John Collins by Name, with whom I was intimately acquainted. We sometimes disputed, and very fond we were of Argument, & very desirous of confuting one another....A Question was once some how or other started between Collins & me, of the Propriety of educating the Female Sex in Learning, & their Abilities for Study. He was of Opinion that it was improper; & that they were naturally unequal to it. I took the contrary Side, perhaps a little for Dispute sake. He was naturally more eloquent, had a ready Plenty of Words, and sometimes as I thought bore me down more by his Fluency than by the Strength of his Reasons. As we parted without settling the Point, & were not to see one another again for some time, I sat down to put my Arguments in Writing, which I copied fair & sent to him. He answer'd & I reply'd. Three or four Letters of a Side had pass'd, when my Father happen'd to find my Papers, and read them. Without entring into the Discussion, he took occasion to talk to me about the Manner of my Writing, observ'd that tho' I had the Advantage of my Antagonist in correct Spelling & pointing (which I ow'd to the Printing House) I fell far short in elegance of Expression, in Method and in Perspicuity, of which he convinc'd me by several Instances. I saw the Justice of his Remarks, & thence grew more attentive to the *Manner* in Writing, and determin'd to endeavour at Improvement. —

"About this time I met with an odd Volume of the Spectator.[1] I had never before seen any of them. I bought it, read it over and over, and was much delighted with it. I thought the Writing excellent, & wish'd if possible to imitate it. With that View, I took some of the Papers, & making short Hints of the Sentiment in each Sentence, laid them by a few Days, and then without looking at the Book, try'd to compleat the Papers again, by expressing each hinted Sentiment at length & as fully as it had been express'd before, in any suitable Words that should come to hand.

"Then I compar'd my Spectator with the Original, discover'd some of my Faults & corrected them. But I found I wanted—a Stock of Words or a Readiness in recollecting & using them, which I thought I should have acquir'd before that time, if I had gone on making Verses, since the continual Occasion for Words of the same Import but of different Length, to suit the Measure, or of different Sound for the Rhyme, would have laid me under a constant Necessity of searching for Variety, and also have tended to fix that Variety in my Mind, & make me a Master of it. Therefore I took some of the Tales & turn'd them into Verse: And after a time, when I had pretty well forgotten the Prose, turn'd them back again. I also sometimes jumbled my Collections of Hints into Confusion, and after some Weeks, endeavour'd to reduce them into the best Order, before I began to form the full Sentences, & compleat the Paper. This was to teach me Method in the Arrangement of Thoughts. By comparing my Work afterwards with the original, I discover'd many faults and amended them; but I sometimes had the Pleasure of Fancying that in certain Particulars of small Import, I had been lucky enough to improve the Method or the Language and this encourag'd me to think I might possibly in time come to be a tolerable English Writer, of which I was extreamly ambitious."

FOR DISCUSSION

1. What did Franklin learn by imitating the writing of *The Spectator* and rewriting some of its essays as "Verse" (or poetry)?
2. Have you ever imitated the work of someone you admired—writing, perhaps, or acting, playing an instrument or a sport, doing a job? Did the imitation help you improve? Why, or why not?

---

[1] *The Spectator* (1711–12) was a collection of witty, sharply observant essays on society. — EDS.

PETER ELBOW

PETER ELBOW is well known as a director of writing programs for community groups and for college students. Born in 1935, he received his education at Williams College and at Brandeis, Harvard, and Oxford. He has taught at Wesleyan University, MIT, Franconia College, the Harvard Graduate School of Education, the University of Hawaii, and Evergreen State College. He started the highly acclaimed Institute for Writing and Thinking at Bard College and served as director of the Writing Program at the State University of New York, Stony Brook. He is the author of many articles and of several influential books, including *Writing Without Teachers* (1973), *Writing with Power* (1981), *Embracing Contraries: Explorations in Learning and Teaching* (1986), and *What Is English?* (1990). Currently, he teaches at the University of Massachusetts, Amherst.

Desperation Writing

What do you do when a paper's deadline looms but you can't think of a word to say about the assigned subject? Take heart: Peter Elbow has a solution. What's more, following his advice, you may find writing much less painful than you expected. "Desperation Writing" has offered solace and help to thousands since it first appeared in *Writing Without Teachers*.

I know I am not alone in my recurring twinges of panic that I won't 1 be able to write something when I need to, I won't be able to produce coherent speech or thought. And that lingering doubt is a great hindrance to writing. It's a constant fog or static that clouds the mind. I never got out of its clutches till I discovered that it was possible to write something—not something great or pleasing but at least something usable, workable—when my mind is out of commission. The trick is that you have to do all your cooking out on the table: Your mind is incapable of doing any inside. It means using symbols and pieces of paper not as a crutch but as a wheelchair.

The first thing is to admit your condition: Because of some mood or 2 event or whatever, your mind is incapable of anything that could be called thought. It can put out a babbling kind of speech utterance, it can put a simple feeling, perception or sort-of-thought into understandable (though terrible) words. But it is incapable of considering anything in relation to anything else. The moment you try to hold that thought or feeling up against some other to see the relationship, you simply lose the picture—you get nothing but buzzing lines or waving colors.

So admit this. Avoid anything more than one feeling, perception, or thought. Simply write as much as possible. Try simply to steer your mind in the direction or general vicinity of the thing you are trying to write about and start writing and keep writing.

Just write and keep writing. (Probably best to write on only one side of the paper in case you should want to cut parts out with scissors—but you probably won't.) Just write and keep writing. It will probably come in waves. After a flurry, stop and take a brief rest. But don't stop too long. Don't think about what you are writing or what you have written or else you will overload the circuit again. Keep writing as though you are drugged or drunk. Keep doing this till you feel you have a lot of material that might be useful; or, if necessary, till you can't stand it any more—even if you doubt that there's anything useful there.

Then take a pad of little pieces of paper—or perhaps 3 × 5 cards—and simply start at the beginning of what you were writing, and as you read over what you wrote, every time you come to any thought, feeling, perception, or image that could be gathered up into one sentence or one assertion, do so and write it by itself on a little sheet of paper. In short, you are trying to turn, say, ten or twenty pages of wandering mush into twenty or thirty hard little crab apples. Sometimes there won't be many on a page. But if it seems to you that there are none on a page, you are making a serious error—the same serious error that put you in this comatose state to start with. You are mistaking lousy, stupid, second-rate, wrong, childish, foolish, worthless ideas for no ideas at all. Your job is not to pick out *good* ideas but to pick out ideas. As long as you were conscious, your words will be full of things that could be called feelings, utterances, ideas—things that can be squeezed into one simple sentence. This is your job. Don't ask for too much.

After you have done this, take those little slips or cards, read through them a number of times—not struggling with them, simply wandering and mulling through them; perhaps shifting them around and looking through in various sequences. In a sense these are cards you are playing solitaire with, and the rules of this particular game permit shuffling the unused pile.

The goal of this procedure with the cards is to get them to distribute themselves in two or three or ten or fifteen different piles on your desk. You can get them to do this almost by themselves if you simply keep reading through them in different orders; certain cards will begin to feel like they go with other cards. I emphasize this passive, thoughtless mode because I want to talk about desperation writing in its pure state. In practice, almost invariably at some point in the procedure, your sanity begins to return. It is often at this point. You actually are moved to have thoughts or—and the difference between active and passive is crucial here—to *exert* thought; to hold two cards together and *build* or *assert* a relationship. It is a matter of bringing energy to bear.

So you may start to be able to do something active with these cards,   8
and begin actually to think. But if not, just allow the cards to find their own piles with each other by feel, by drift, by intuition, by mindlessness.

You have now engaged in the two main activities that will permit   9
you to get something cooked out on the table rather than in your brain: writing out into messy words, summing up into single assertions, and even sensing relationships between assertions. You can simply continue to deploy these two activities.

If, for example, after the first round of writing, assertion-making,   10
and pile-making, your piles feel as though they are useful and satisfactory for what you are writing—paragraphs or sections or trains of thought—then you can carry on from there. See if you can gather each pile up into a single assertion. When you can, then put the subsidiary assertions of that pile into their best order to fit with that single unifying one. If you *can't* get the pile into one assertion, then take the pile as the basis for doing some more writing out into words. In the course of this writing, you may produce for yourself the single unifying assertion you were looking for; or you may have to go through the cycle of turning the writing into assertions and piles and so forth. Perhaps more than once. The pile may turn out to want to be two or more piles itself; or it may want to become part of a pile you already have. This is natural. This kind of meshing into one configuration, then coming apart, then coming together and meshing into a different configuration— this is growing and cooking. It makes a terrible mess, but if you can't do it in your head, you have to put up with a cluttered desk and a lot of confusion.

If, on the other hand, all that writing *didn't* have useful material in   11
it, it means that your writing wasn't loose, drifting, quirky, jerky, associative enough. This time try especially to let things simply remind you of things that are seemingly crazy or unrelated. Follow these odd associations. Make as many metaphors as you can—be as nutty as possible —and explore the metaphors themselves—open them out. You may have all your energy tied up in some area of your experience that you are leaving out. Don't refrain from writing about whatever else is on your mind: how you feel at the moment, what you are losing your mind over, randomness that intrudes itself on your consciousness, the pattern on the wallpaper, what those people you see out the window have on their minds—though keep coming back to the whateveritis you are

supposed to be writing about. Treat it, in short, like ten-minute writing exercises. Your best perceptions and thoughts are always going to be tied up in whatever is really occupying you, and that is also where your energy is. You may end up writing a love poem — or a hate poem — in one of those little piles while the other piles will finally turn into a lab report on data processing or whatever you have to write about. But you couldn't, in your present state of having your head shot off, have written that report without also writing the poem. And the report will have some of the juice of the poem in it and vice versa.

QUESTIONS ON MEANING

1. On what ASSUMPTIONS does Elbow base his advice?
2. Where in his essay does the author reveal his PURPOSE?
3. What value does Elbow discern in "lousy, stupid, second-rate, wrong, childish, foolish, worthless ideas" (para. 5)?
4. In your own words, describe the role of the unconscious in the process Elbow analyzes. Where in the process does the conscious mind have to do its part?
5. How does the author justify writing a poem when the assignment is to write a lab report?

QUESTIONS ON WRITING STRATEGY

1. What EFFECT does the author achieve by opening his essay in the first PERSON (I)?
2. At what AUDIENCE does Elbow direct his advice?
3. Into how many steps does the author break down the process he analyzes? What are they?
4. Point to effective samples of TRANSITIONS in this essay. (Transitions are discussed on pp. 224–25.)
5. Point to phrases or sentences in the essay that seem to you designed to offer encouragement and comfort.
6. **OTHER METHODS.** When Elbow says that he wants "to talk about desperation writing in its pure state," he calls attention to a developing DEFINITION. In your own words, what is "pure" desperation writing?

QUESTIONS ON LANGUAGE

1. Where in his essay does the author make good use of FIGURES OF SPEECH?
2. Using a dictionary if necessary, define the following words: coherent, hindrance (para. 1); assertion, comatose (5); configuration (10).

SUGGESTIONS FOR WRITING

1. **JOURNAL WRITING.** See if Peter Elbow's method works for you. Without spending time thinking about the subject beforehand, write steadily in your journal about some recent event, book, idea, or experience that made an impression on you. Spend about twenty minutes writing. If you can't write without stopping for this long, write in flurries with pauses, as Elbow recommends (para. 4). Remember that the key is to *keep writing*: Even if you can't always keep your words focused on the topic you have chosen, just keep your fingers moving.

   FROM JOURNAL TO ESSAY. Go through the prose you generated in your journal to see what ideas emerge. Can you find main points and supporting details (the unifying and subsidiary assertions Elbow describes in para. 10) in what you wrote? Can you organize these into a coherent essay? Now, either write the essay that this free-association journal entry has yielded, or write an essay that explains why you do not think this process works for you.

2. In a brief essay, explain how to tackle any job you're not in the mood for: researching a paper, preparing a speech, performing a lab experiment, studying for a test, cleaning your house, washing your car, getting up in the morning. The process should involve at least three steps.

3. **CRITICAL WRITING.** Write an EVALUATION of Elbow's essay as a work of directive process analysis. First try out Elbow's process, as suggested in the first writing topic. Then test Elbow's advice against your experience. Which suggestions are especially helpful? Which aren't? Why?

4. **CONNECTIONS.** Read or reread Suzanne Britt's "Neat People vs. Sloppy People" (p. 182). Do you think a sloppy person like Britt would be more or less likely than a neat person to take to Elbow's method of writing? Based on Britt's characterization of the two types and your own experience as one of the other, how do you see neat and sloppy people as proceeding differently in writing? How are the final products of the two types likely to compare?

PETER ELBOW ON WRITING

Peter Elbow's best-known work is devoted, like "Desperation Writing," to encouraging people to write. Much of his advice comes from his writing experience. His own life is the source for a recent article, "Closing My Eyes as I Speak: An Argument for Ignoring Audience."

That it often helps writers to be aware of their readers is an article of faith for many college writing instructors; it is an assumption we make in *The Bedford Reader*. Without denying that a sense of audience is sometimes valuable, Elbow makes a persuasive case for sometimes trying to forget that an audience is there. "When I am talking to a person or a group," he begins, "and struggling to find words or thoughts, I often find myself involuntarily closing my eyes as I speak. I realize now that this behavior is an instinctive attempt to blot out awareness of audience when I need all my concentration for just trying to figure out or express what I want to say. Because the audience is so imperiously *present* in a speaking situation, my instinct reacts with this active attempt to avoid audience awareness. This behavior—in a sense impolite or antisocial—is not so uncommon. Even when we write, alone in a room to an absent audience, there are occasions when we are struggling to figure something out and need to push aside awareness of those absent readers."

Some audiences—like a readership of close friends—are helpful to keep in mind. "When we think about them from the start, we think of more and better things to say." But other audiences are powerfully inhibiting, and keeping them in mind as we write may put up writer's blocks. "For example, when we have to write to someone we find intimidating (and of course students often perceive teachers as intimidating), we often start thinking wholly defensively. As we write down each thought or sentence, our mind fills with thoughts of how the intended reader will criticize or object to it. So we try to qualify or soften what we've just written—or write out some answer to a possible objection. Our writing becomes tangled. Sometimes we get so tied in knots that we cannot even figure out what we think."

The solution? "We can ignore that audience altogether during the *early* stages of writing and direct our words only to ourselves or to no one in particular—or even to the 'wrong' audience, that is, to an *inviting* audience of trusted friends or allies.... Putting audience out of mind is of course a traditional practice: Serious writers have long used private journals for early explorations of feeling, thinking, or language." In contrast, inferior newspaper or business writing often reminds us of "the ineffective actor whose consciousness of self distracts us: He makes us too aware of his own awareness of us. When we read such prose, we wish the writer would stop thinking about us—would stop trying to adjust or fit what he is saying to our frame of reference. 'Damn it, put all your attention on what you are saying,' we want to say, 'and forget about us and how we are reacting.'

"When we examine really good student or professional writing, we can often see that its goodness comes from the writer's having gotten sufficiently wrapped up in her meaning and her language as to forget all about audience needs: The writer manages to 'break through.'"

To overcome the problem of being painfully conscious of readers, if it is a problem you've met, Elbow advises writing more than one draft of everything. "*After* we have figured out our thinking in copious exploratory or draft writing—perhaps finding the right voice or stance as well—*then* we can follow the traditional rhetorical advice: Think about readers and revise carefully to adjust our words and thoughts to our intended audience."

FOR DISCUSSION

1. How closely do Peter Elbow's observations reflect your own writing experience? Do you ever worry so hard about what your reader will think that you
   become pen-tied? Or do you usually close your eyes to your audience, and
   just write?
2. What is wrong with the following attempt to state Elbow's thesis: "A writer
   should simply forget about audience"?
3. If you feel uncomfortable when you write, too keenly aware of the reader
   "looking over your shoulder," what advice of Elbow's might you follow?
   Can you suggest any other advice to relieve a writer's self-consciousness?

ADDITIONAL WRITING TOPICS

Process Analysis

1. Write a *directive* process analysis (a "how-to" essay) in which, drawing on your own knowledge, you instruct someone in doing or making something. Divide the process into steps and be sure to detail each step thoroughly. Some possible subjects (any of which may be modified or narrowed):

   How to find games (or other software) on the Internet
   How to enlist people's confidence
   How to bake bread
   How to meditate
   How to teach a child to swim
   How to select a science fiction novel
   How to drive a car in snow or rain
   How to prepare yourself to take an intelligence test
   How to compose a photograph
   How to judge cattle
   How to buy a used motorcycle
   How to enjoy an opera
   How to organize your own rock group
   How to eat an artichoke
   How to groom a horse
   How to bellydance
   How to make a movie or videotape
   How to build (or fly) a kite
   How to start weight training
   How to aid a person who is choking
   How to behave on a first date
   How to get your own way
   How to kick a habit
   How to lose weight
   How to win at poker
   How to make an effective protest or complaint

   Or, if you don't like any of those topics, what else do you know that others might care to learn from you?

2. Step by step, working in chronological order, write a careful *informative* analysis of any one of the following processes. (This is not to be a "how-to" essay, but an essay that explains how something works or happens.) Make use of DESCRIPTION wherever necessary, and be sure to include frequent TRANSITIONS. If one of these topics gives you a better idea for a paper, go with your own subject.

   How a student is processed during orientation or registration
   How the student newspaper gets published
   How an Internet browser works

How a professional umpire (or an insurance underwriter, or some other professional) does his or her job

How an amplifier (or other stereo component) works

How an air conditioner (or other household appliance) works

How a political candidate runs for office

How birds teach their young (or some other process in the natural world: how sharks feed, how a snake swallows an egg, how the human liver works)

How police control crowds

How people usually make up their minds when shopping for new cars (or new clothes)

3. Write a directive process analysis in which you use a light TONE. Although you need not take your subject in deadly earnest, your humor will probably be effective only if you take the method of process analysis seriously. Make clear each stage of the process and explain it in sufficient detail. Possible topics:

How to get through the month of November (or March)

How to flunk out of college swiftly and efficiently

How to outwit a pinball machine

How to choose a mate

How to go broke

How to sell something that nobody wants

6

DIVISION OR ANALYSIS
Slicing into Parts

THE METHOD

A chemist working for a soft-drink company is asked to improve on a competitor's product, Orange Quench. (In Chap. 5, the same chemist was working on a different part of the same problem.) To do the job, the chemist first has to figure out what's in the drink. She smells the stuff and tastes it. Then she tests a sample chemically to discover the actual ingredients: water, corn syrup, citric acid, sodium benzoate, coloring. Methodically, the chemist has performed DIVISION or ANALYSIS: She has separated the beverage into its components. Orange Quench stands revealed, understood, ready to be bettered.

Division or analysis (the terms are interchangeable) is a key skill in learning and in life. It is an instrument allowing you to slice a large and complicated subject into smaller parts that you can grasp and relate to one another. With analysis you comprehend—and communicate— the structure of things. And when it works, you find in the parts an idea or conclusion about the subject that makes it clearer, truer, more comprehensive, or more vivid than before you started.

If you have worked with the previous two chapters, you have already used division or analysis in explaining a process (Chap. 5) and in comparing and contrasting (Chap. 4). To make a better Orange Quench (a process), the chemist might prepare a recipe that divides the process into separate steps or actions ("First, boil a gallon of water..."). When the batch was done, she might taste-test the two drinks, analyzing and then comparing their orange flavor, sweetness, and acidity. As you'll see in following chapters, too, division or analysis figures in all the other methods of developing ideas, for it is basic to any concerted thought, explanation, or evaluation.

Kinds of Division or Analysis

Although division or analysis always works the same way—separating a whole, singular subject into its elements, slicing it into parts—the method can be more or less difficult depending on how unfamiliar, complex, and abstract the subject is. Obviously, it's going to be much easier to analyze a chicken (wings, legs, thighs...) than a poem by T. S. Eliot (this image, that allusion...), easier to analyze why you won a swimming race than why the French and then the Americans got involved in Vietnam. Just about any subject *can* be analyzed and will be the clearer for it. In "I Want a Wife," an essay in this chapter, Judy Brady divides the role of a wife into its various functions or services. In an essay called "Teacher" from his book *Pot Shots at Poetry* (1980), Robert Francis divides the knowledge of poetry he imparted to his class into six pie sections. The first slice is what he told his students that they knew already.

> The second slice is what I told them that they could have found out just as well or better from books. What, for instance, is a sestina?
> The third slice is what I told them that they refused to accept. I could see it on their faces, and later I saw the evidence in their writing.
> The fourth slice is what I told them that they were willing to accept and may have thought they accepted but couldn't accept since they couldn't fully understand. This also I saw in their faces and in their work. Here, no doubt, I was mostly to blame.
> The fifth slice is what I told them that they discounted as whimsy or something simply to fill up time. After all, I was being paid to talk.
> The sixth slice is what I didn't tell them, for I didn't try to tell them all I knew. Deliberately I kept back something—a few professional secrets, a magic formula or two.

There are always multiple ways to divide or analyze a subject, just as there are many ways to slice a pie. Francis could have divided his knowledge of poetry into knowledge of rhyme, knowledge of meter, knowledge of imagery, and so forth—basically following the components of a poem. In other words, the outcome of an analysis depends on the rule or principle used to do the slicing. This fact accounts for some of the differences among academic disciplines: A psychologist, say, may look at the individual person primarily as a bundle of drives and needs, whereas a sociologist may emphasize the individual's roles in society. Even within disciplines, different factions analyze differently, using different principles of division or analysis. Some psychologists are interested mainly in thought, others mainly in behavior; some psychologists focus mainly on emotional development, others mainly on moral development.

Analysis and Critical Thinking

Analysis plays a fundamental role in CRITICAL THINKING, READING, AND WRITING, topics discussed in this book's introduction (pp. 15–17). In fact, *analysis* and *criticism* are deeply related: The first comes from a Greek word meaning "to undo," the second from a Greek word meaning "to separate."

Critical thinking, reading, and writing go beneath the surface of the object, word, image, or whatever the subject is. When you work critically, you divide the subject into its elements, INFER the buried meanings and ASSUMPTIONS that define its essence, and SYNTHESIZE the parts into a new whole. Say a campaign brochure quotes a candidate as favoring "reasonable government expenditures on reasonable highway projects." The candidate will support new roads, right? Wrong. As a critical reader of the brochure, you quickly sense something fishy in the use (twice) of "reasonable." As an informed reader, you know (or find out) that the candidate has consistently opposed new roads, so the chances of her finding a highway project "reasonable" are slim. At the same time, her stand has been unpopular, so of course she wants to seem "reasonable" on the issue. Read critically, then, a campaign statement that seems to offer mild support for highways is actually a slippery evasion of any such commitment.

Analysis (a convenient term for the overlapping operations of analysis, inference, and synthesis) is very useful for exposing such evasiveness, but that isn't its only function. It may also help you understand a short story, perceive the importance of a sociological case study, or form a response to an environmental impact report.

If you've read this far in this book, you've already done quite a bit of analytical/critical thinking as you've read and analyzed the essays. In this chapter, two of the essays themselves—by Barbara Ehrenreich and Michiko Kakutani—show concerted critical thinking.

THE PROCESS

Subjects and Theses

Keep an eye out for writing assignments requiring division or analysis—in college and work, they won't be few or hard to find. They will probably include the word *analyze* or a word implying analysis such as *evaluate*, *interpret*, *discuss*, or *criticize*. Any time you spot such a term, you know your job is to separate the subject into its elements, to infer their meanings, to explore the relations among them, and to draw a conclusion about the subject.

Almost any coherent entity—object, person, place, concept—is a fit subject for analysis *if* the analysis will add to the subject's meaning or significance. Little is deadlier than the rote analytical exercise that leaves the parts neatly dissected and the subject comatose on the page. As a writer, you have to animate the subject, and that means finding your interest. What about your subject seems curious? What's appealing? or mysterious? or awful?

Such questions can help you find the rule or principle you will use to divide the subject into parts. (As we mentioned before, there's more than one way to slice most subjects.) Say you're contemplating a hunk of bronze in the park. What elements of its creation and physical form make this sculpture art? Or what is the point of such public art? Or what does this sculpture do for this park? Or vice versa? Any of these questions would give you an angle of vision, a slant on your subject, a framework, and get your analysis moving.

Finding your principle of analysis will lead you to your essay's THESIS as well—the main point you want to make about your subject. Expressed in a THESIS SENTENCE, this idea will help keep you focused and help your readers see your subject as a whole rather than a bundle of parts. Your essay on the bronze in the park, for instance, might have one of these thesis sentences:

> Though it may not be obvious at first, this bronze sculpture represents the city dweller's relationship with nature.
>
> Like much public art today, this bronze sculpture seems chiefly intended to make people ignore it.
>
> The huge bronze sculpture in the middle of McBean Park demonstrates that so-called public art does little for the public interest.

After any of these thesis sentences, you would go on to identify and explain the relevant elements of the sculpture: in the first case, maybe the sculpture's hints of plants and water and connection; in the second case, maybe the sculpture's blandness, lack of a clear message, and lack of artistic rigor; in the third case, maybe the sculpture's cost, uselessness, and ugliness. (Notice that each approach reveals something different in the sculpture, with very different results.)

In developing an essay by analysis, having an outline at your elbow can be a help. You don't want to overlook any parts or elements that should be included in your framework. (You needn't mention every feature in your final essay or give them all equal treatment, but any omissions or variations should be conscious.) And you want to use your framework consistently, not switching carelessly (and confusingly) from, say, the form of the sculpture to the cost of public art. In writing her brief essay "I Want a Wife," Judy Brady must have needed an outline to work out carefully the different activities of a wife, so that she covered them all and clearly distinguished them.

Evidence

Making a valid analysis is chiefly a matter of giving your subject thought, but for the result to seem useful and convincing to your readers, it will have to refer to the concrete world. The method requires not only cogitation, but open eyes and a willingness to provide EVIDENCE. The nature of the evidence will depend entirely on what you are analyzing—physical details for a sculpture, quotations for a poem, financial data for a business case study, statistics for a psychology case study, and so forth. The idea is to supply enough evidence to justify and support your particular slant on the subject.

A final caution: It's possible to get carried away with one's own analysis, to become so enamored of the details that the subject itself becomes dim or distorted. You can avoid this danger by keeping the subject literally in front of you as you work (or at least imagining it vividly) and by maintaining an outline. It often helps to reassemble your subject at the end of the essay: That gives you a chance to place your subject in a larger context, speculate on its influence, or affirm its significance. By the end of the essay, your subject must be a coherent whole truly represented by your analysis, not twisted, diminished, inflated, or obliterated. The reader should be intrigued by your subject, yes, but also able to recognize it on the street.

CHECKLIST FOR REVISING A DIVISION OR ANALYSIS

✔ **PRINCIPLE OF ANALYSIS.** What is your particular slant on your subject, the rule or principle you have used to divide your subject into its elements? Where do you tell readers what it is?

✔ **COMPLETENESS.** Have you considered all the subject's elements required by your principle of analysis?

✔ **CONSISTENCY.** Have you applied your principle of analysis consistently, viewing your subject from a definite slant?

✔ **EVIDENCE.** Is your division or analysis well supported with concrete details, quotations, data, or statistics, as appropriate?

✔ **SIGNIFICANCE.** Why should readers care about your analysis? Have you told them something about your subject that wasn't obvious on its surface?

✔ **TRUTH TO SUBJECT.** Is your analysis faithful to the subject, not distorted, exaggerated, deflated?

DIVISION OR ANALYSIS IN A PARAGRAPH: TWO ILLUSTRATIONS

Using Division or Analysis to Write About Television

Most television comedies, even some that boast live audiences, rely on the laugh machine to fill too-quiet moments on the soundtrack. The effect of a canned laugh comes from its four overlapping elements. The first is style, from titter to belly laugh. The second is intensity, the volume, ranging from mild to medium to ear splitting. The third ingredient is duration, the length of the laugh, whether quick, medium, or extended. And finally, there's the number of laughers, from a lone giggler to a roaring throng. According to rumor (for its exact workings are a secret), the machine contains a bank of thirty-two tapes. Furiously working keys and tromping pedals, the operator plays the tapes singly or in combination to blend the four ingredients, as a maestro weaves a symphony out of brass, woodwinds, percussion, and strings.

Principle of analysis: elements creating the effect of a canned laugh

1. Style
2. Intensity
3. Duration

4. Number

Details and examples clarify elements

Using Division or Analysis in an Academic Discipline

The model of social relationship which fits these conditions [of realistic equality between patient and doctor] is that of the contract or covenant. The notion of contract should not be loaded with legalistic implications, but taken in its more symbolic form as in the traditional religious or marriage "contract" or "covenant." Here two individuals or groups are interacting in a way where there are obligations and expected benefits for both parties. The obligations and benefits are limited in scope, though, even if they are expressed in somewhat vague terms. The basic norms of freedom, dignity, truth-telling, promise-keeping, and justice are essential to a contractual relationship. The premise is trust and con-

Principle of analysis: elements of a contract between doctor and patient

1. Obligations and benefits for both parties

2. Obligations and benefits limited

3. Freedom, dignity, and other norms

4. Trust and confidence

fidence even though it is recognized that there is not a full mutuality of interests. Social sanctions institutionalize and stand behind the relationship, in case there is a violation of the contract, but for the most part the assumption is that there will be a faithful fulfillment of the obligations.

—Robert M. Veatch,
"Models for Medicine in a Revolutionary Age"

5. *Support of social sanctions (meaning that society upholds the relationship)*

JUDY BRADY

JUDY BRADY, born in 1937 in San Francisco, where she now lives, earned a B.F.A. in painting from the University of Iowa in 1962. Drawn into political action by her work in the feminist movement, she went to Cuba in 1973, where she studied class relationships as a way of understanding change in a society. "I am not a 'writer,'" Brady declares, "but really am a disenfranchised (and fired) housewife, now secretary." Despite her disclaimer, Brady has published articles occasionally—on union organizing and education in Cuba, among other topics—and she writes a regular column for the Women's Cancer Research Center. In 1991 she published *1 in 3: Women with Cancer Confront an Epidemic*, an anthology of writings by women. Asked by an interviewer if she had won any awards lately, Brady responded, "People who do what I do don't get awards."

I Want a Wife

"I Want a Wife" first appeared in the Spring 1972 issue of Ms. magazine and has been reprinted there often. The essay is one of the best-known manifestos in popular feminist writing. In it, Brady trenchantly divides the work of a wife into its multiple duties and functions, leading to an inescapable conclusion.

I belong to that classification of people known as wives. I am A 1 Wife. And, not altogether incidentally, I am a mother.

Not too long ago a male friend of mine appeared on the scene fresh 2 from a recent divorce. He had one child, who is, of course, with his ex-wife. He is looking for another wife. As I thought about him while I was ironing one evening, it suddenly occurred to me that I, too, would like to have a wife. Why do I want a wife?

I would like to go back to school so that I can become economi- 3 cally independent, support myself, and, if need be, support those dependent upon me. I want a wife who will work and send me to school. And while I am going to school I want a wife to take care of my children. I want a wife to keep track of the children's doctor and dentist appointments. And to keep track of mine, too. I want a wife to make sure my children eat properly and are kept clean. I want a wife who will wash the children's clothes and keep them mended. I want a wife who is a good nurturant attendant to my children, who arranges for their schooling, makes sure that they have an adequate social life with their peers, takes them to the park, the zoo, etc. I want a wife who takes care of the children when they are sick, a wife who arranges to be around when the children need special care, because, of course, I cannot miss classes at school. My wife must arrange to lose time at work and not lose the job. It may mean a small cut in my wife's income from time to time, but I guess I can tolerate that. Needless to say, my wife will arrange and pay for the care of the children while my wife is working.

I want a wife who will take care of *my* physical needs. I want a wife 4
who will keep my house clean. A wife who will pick up after my children, a wife who will pick up after me. I want a wife who will keep my clothes clean, ironed, mended, replaced when need be, and who will see to it that my personal things are kept in their proper place so that I can find what I need the minute I need it. I want a wife who cooks the meals, a wife who is a *good* cook. I want a wife who will plan the menus, do the necessary grocery shopping, prepare the meals, serve them pleasantly, and then do the cleaning up while I do my studying. I want a wife who will care for me when I am sick and sympathize with my pain and loss of time from school. I want a wife to go along when our family takes vacation so that someone can continue to care for me and my children when I need a rest and change of scene.

I want a wife who will not bother me with rambling complaints 5
about a wife's duties. But I want a wife who will listen to me when I feel the need to explain a rather difficult point I have come across in my course of studies. And I want a wife who will type my papers for me when I have written them.

I want a wife who will take care of the details of my social life. 6
When my wife and I are invited out by my friends, I want a wife who will take care of the babysitting arrangements. When I meet people at school that I like and want to entertain, I want a wife who will have the house clean, will prepare a special meal, serve it to me and my friends, and not interrupt when I talk about things that interest me and my friends. I want a wife who will have arranged that the children are fed and ready for bed before my guests arrive so that the children do not bother us. I want a wife who takes care of the needs of my guests so that they feel comfortable, who makes sure that they have an ashtray, that they are passed the hors d'oeuvres, that they are offered a second helping of the food, that their wine glasses are replenished when necessary, that their coffee is served to them as they like it. And I want a wife who knows that sometimes I need a night out by myself.

I want a wife who is sensitive to my sexual needs, a wife who makes 7
love passionately and eagerly when I feel like it, a wife who makes sure that I am satisfied. And, of course, I want a wife who will not demand sexual attention when I am not in the mood for it. I want a wife who assumes the complete responsibility for birth control, because I do not want more children. I want a wife who will remain sexually faithful to me so that I do not have to clutter up my intellectual life with jeal-

ousies. And I want a wife who understands that *my* sexual needs may entail more than strict adherence to monogamy. I must, after all, be able to relate to people as fully as possible.

If, by chance, I find another person more suitable as a wife than the   8
wife I already have, I want the liberty to replace my present wife with another one. Naturally, I will expect a fresh, new life; my wife will take the children and be solely responsible for them so that I am left free.

When I am through with school and have a job, I want my wife to   9
quit working and remain at home so that my wife can more fully and completely take care of a wife's duties.

My God, who *wouldn't* want a wife?   10

QUESTIONS ON MEANING

1. Sum up the duties of a wife as Brady sees them.
2. To what inequities in the roles traditionally assigned to men and to women does "I Want a Wife" call attention?
3. What is the THESIS of this essay? Is it stated or implied?
4. Is Brady unfair to men?

QUESTIONS ON WRITING STRATEGY

1. What EFFECT does Brady obtain with the title "I Want a Wife"?
2. What do the first two paragraphs accomplish?
3. What is the TONE of this essay?
4. How do you explain the fact that Brady never uses the pronoun *she* to refer to a wife? Does this make her prose unnecessarily awkward?
5. What principle does Brady use to analyze the role of wife? Can you think of some other principle for analyzing the job?
6. Knowing that this essay was first published in Ms. magazine in 1972, what can you guess about its intended readers? Does "I Want a Wife" strike a college AUDIENCE today as revolutionary?
7. **OTHER METHODS.** Although she mainly divides or analyzes the role of wife, Brady also uses CLASSIFICATION to sort the many duties and responsibilities into manageable groups. What are the groups?

QUESTIONS ON LANGUAGE

1. What is achieved by the author's frequent repetition of the phrase "I want a wife"?
2. Be sure you know how to define the following words as Brady uses them: nurturant (para. 3); replenished (6); adherence, monogamy (7).
3. In general, how would you describe the DICTION of this essay? How well does it suit the essay's intended audience?

SUGGESTIONS FOR WRITING

1. **JOURNAL WRITING.** Brady addresses the traditional obligations of a wife and mother. What are the parallel obligations of a husband and father? **FROM JOURNAL TO ESSAY.** Write an essay titled "I Want a Husband" in which, using examples as Brady does, you enumerate the roles traditionally assigned to men in our society.

2. Imagining that you want to employ someone to do a specific job, divide the task into its duties and functions. Then, guided by your analysis, write an accurate job description in essay form.

3. **CRITICAL WRITING.** In an essay, SUMMARIZE Brady's view as you understand it and then EVALUATE her essay. Consider: Is Brady fair? (If not, is unfairness justified?) Is the essay relevant today? (If not, what has changed?) Provide specific EVIDENCE from your experience, observation, and reading.

4. **CONNECTIONS.** Both "I Want a Wife" and Armin A. Brott's "Not All Men Are Sly Foxes" (next page) challenge traditional ideas about how men and women are supposed to divide the labor in a marriage. However, Brady's STYLE is fast-paced and her tone is sarcastic, while Brott is more methodical and earnest. Which method of addressing these issues do you find more effective? Why? Write an essay that COMPARES AND CONTRASTS the essays' tones, styles, POINTS OF VIEW, and OBJECTIVE versus SUBJECTIVE language. What conclusions can you draw about the connection between the writers' strategies and their messages?

ARMIN A. BROTT

Armin A. Brott is a freelance writer living in San Francisco. Born in 1958, he received a B.A. in Russian from San Francisco State University and an M.B.A. that he calls "less useful than the degree in Russian" before embarking on a career in marketing. He turned to writing when his first child was born because he "wanted to be an active, involved father." Since that time he has contributed to the *New York Times Magazine*, the *Washington Post*, *Reader's Digest*, *Family Circle*, the *Saturday Evening Post*, *Playboy*, and other magazines. He treats issues that affect men: education, health, fatherhood. His first book, *The Expectant Father: Facts, Tips, and Advice for Dads to Be*, was written with Jennifer Ash and published in 1995. Brott is currently working on a book that will take fathers through a baby's first three years.

Not All Men Are Sly Foxes

In this essay from a 1992 *Newsweek* magazine, Brott offers a different view of men from that taken by Judy Brady in the previous essay. While acknowledging that women and men are not yet equal in child care, Brott holds that children's books are hardly helping. In them, the Sly Fox remains much more common than the Caring Dad.

If you thought your child's bookshelves were finally free of openly (and not so openly) discriminatory materials, you'd better check again. In recent years groups of concerned parents have persuaded textbook publishers to portray more accurately the roles that women and minorities play in shaping our country's history and culture. *Little Black Sambo* has all but disappeared from library and bookstore shelves; feminist fairy tales by such authors as Jack Zipes have, in many homes, replaced the more traditional (and obviously sexist) fairy tales. Richard Scarry, one of the most popular children's writers, has reissued new versions of some of his classics; now female animals are pictured doing the same jobs as male animals. Even the terminology has changed: Males and females are referred to as mail "carriers" or "firefighters."

There is, however, one very large group whose portrayal continues to follow the same stereotypical lines as always: fathers. The evolution of children's literature didn't end with *Goodnight Moon* and *Charlotte's Web*. My local public library, for example, previews 203 new children's picture books (for the under-five set) each *month*. Many of these books make a very conscious effort to take women characters out of the

278

kitchen and the nursery and give them professional jobs and responsibilities.

Despite this shift, mothers are by and large still shown as the primary caregivers and, more important, as the primary nurturers of their children. Men in these books—if they're shown at all—still come home late after work and participate in the child rearing by bouncing baby around for five minutes before putting the child to bed. 3

In one of my two-year-old daughter's favorite books, *Mother Goose and the Sly Fox*, "retold" by Chris Conover, a single mother (Mother Goose) of seven tiny goslings is pitted against (and naturally outwits) the sly Fox. Fox, a neglectful and presumably unemployed single father, lives with his filthy, hungry pups in a grimy hovel littered with the bones of their previous meals. Mother Goose, a successful entrepreneur with a thriving lace business, still finds time to serve her goslings homemade soup in pretty porcelain cups. The story is funny and the illustrations marvelous, but the unwritten message is that women take better care of their kids and men have nothing else to do but hunt down and kill innocent, law-abiding geese. 4

The majority of other children's classics perpetuate the same negative stereotypes of fathers. Once in a great while, people complain about *Babar*'s colonialist slant (little jungle-dweller finds happiness in the big city and brings civilization—and fine clothes—to his backward village). But I've never heard anyone ask why, after his mother is killed by the evil hunter, Babar is automatically an "orphan." Why can he find comfort only in the arms of another female? Why do Arthur's and Celeste's mothers come alone to the city to fetch their children? Don't the fathers care? Do they even have fathers? I need my answers ready for when my daughter asks. 5

I recently spent an entire day on the children's floor of the local library trying to find out whether these same negative stereotypes are found in the more recent classics-to-be. The librarian gave me a list of the twenty most popular contemporary picture books and I read every one of them. Of the twenty, seven don't mention a parent at all. Of the remaining thirteen, four portray fathers as much less loving and caring than mothers. In *Little Gorilla*, we are told that the little gorilla's "mother loves him" and we see Mama gorilla giving her little one a warm hug. On the next page we're also told that his "father loves him," but in the illustration, father and son aren't even touching. Six of the remaining nine books mention or portray mothers as the only parent, and only three of the twenty have what could be considered "equal" treatment of mothers and fathers. 6

The same negative stereotypes also show up in literature aimed at the *parents* of small children. In *What to Expect the First Year*, the authors answer almost every question the parents of a newborn or toddler 7 could have in the first year of their child's life. They are meticulous in alternating between references to boys and girls. At the same time, they refer almost exclusively to "mother" or "mommy." Men, and their feelings about parenting, are relegated to a nine-page chapter just before the recipe section.

Unfortunately, it's still true that, in our society, women do the bulk of the child care, and that thanks to men abandoning their families, there are too many single mothers out there. Nevertheless, to say that portraying fathers as unnurturing or completely absent is simply "a reflection of reality" is unacceptable. If children's literature only reflected reality, it would be like prime-time TV and we'd have books filled with child abusers, wife beaters and criminals. 8

Young children believe what they hear — especially from a parent figure. And since, for the first few years of a child's life, adults select the reading material, children's literature should be held to a high standard. Ignoring men who share equally in raising their children, and continuing to show nothing but part-time or no-time fathers is only going to create yet another generation of men who have been told since boyhood — albeit subtly — that mothers are the truer parents and that fathers play, at best, a secondary role in the home. We've taken major steps to root out discrimination in what our children read. Let's finish the job. 9

QUESTIONS ON MEANING

1. What is the THESIS of Brott's essay? Where is it stated succinctly?
2. What does Brott ASSUME about his AUDIENCE in this essay? To what extent do you fit his assumptions?
3. Brott points out a difference between the illustration of the little gorilla with his mother and the one of him with his father (para. 6). Why is this difference significant?
4. What is the EFFECT of Brott's concluding sentences: "We've taken major steps to root out discrimination in what our children read. Let's finish the job"?

QUESTIONS ON WRITING STRATEGY

1. What principle of analysis does Brott use in examining the children's books? What elements does he perceive in these books?
2. What purpose does paragraph 7, with its reference to books for parents, serve in this essay about children's books?
3. **OTHER METHODS.** In paragraph 4, Brott provides vivid DESCRIPTION of Mother Goose's and Sly Fox's homes to show the differences between the two parents. What concrete details help explain these differences?

QUESTIONS ON LANGUAGE

1. What is the difference between "caregivers" and "nurturers" as Brott uses the words in paragraph 3?
2. How would you analyze Brott's TONE? Give specific words and sentences that you think contribute to the tone.
3. If some of the following words are unfamiliar, look them up in a dictionary: discriminatory (para. 1); stereotypical, evolution (2); goslings, neglectful, hovel, entrepreneur, porcelain (4); perpetuate, colonialist (5); meticulous, exclusively, relegated (7); albeit, subtly (9).

QUESTIONS FOR WRITING

1. **JOURNAL WRITING.** Do you remember being read to as a child—either at home or at school? Does a particular book stand out in your memory? What made this book come alive so that you still remember it today—the words, the illustrations, the story?

   FROM JOURNAL TO ESSAY. Write a brief essay that explores the messages sent by one of your childhood books. Did the book contain positive role models? negative ones? moral messages? values that you now embrace or reject? Did you learn anything in particular from this book? Based on your recollections, come to your own conclusions about what's appropriate or not in children's books.
2. Write an essay that analyzes another type of writing by examining its elements. You may choose any kind of writing that's familiar to you: news article, sports article, mystery, romance, science fiction, biography, and so on. Be sure to make your principle of analysis clear to your readers.
3. **CRITICAL WRITING.** "If children's literature only reflected reality," Brott claims, "it would be like prime-time TV and we'd have books filled with child abusers, wife beaters and criminals" (para. 8). However, Brott also suggests that "reality" contains a significant number of responsible, loving fathers. Does the claim about "reality" being "like prime-time TV" detract from Brott's argument on behalf of good fathers? Write an essay in which you explain how (or whether) Brott resolves this contradiction in his essay. It will probably be helpful to DEFINE clearly what *reality* means in this context.
4. **CONNECTIONS.** Look over Judy Brady's "I Want a Wife" (p. 274) and make a list of her implied complaints about the traditional roles of a wife. Now make a list of the responsibilities that Brott implies a good father is happy to take on. How could Brott's essay be viewed as a sort of response or solution to some of the problems Brady raises? Write an essay explaining the changes in traditional gender roles suggested by "I Want a Wife" and "Not All Men Are Sly Foxes" together.

BARBARA EHRENREICH

BARBARA EHRENREICH was born in 1941 in Butte, Montana. After she graduated from Reed College, she took her Ph.D. at Rockefeller University, then taught at the State University of New York in Old Westbury in the early 1970s. She has contributed to many periodicals, among them *The New Republic*, *Mother Jones*, *Ms.*, and, most recently, *Time*, for which she writes a column. Ehrenreich's range encompasses investigative journalism, popular history, and astute social and political commentary. Her books include *Complaints and Disorders: The Sexual Politics of Sickness* (1973); *For Her Own Good: 150 Years of the Experts' Advice to Women* (with Deirdre English; 1978); *The Hearts of Men: American Dreams and the Flight from Commitment* (1983); *Fear of Falling: The Inner Life of the Middle Class* (1989); *The Worst Years of Our Lives* (1990) and *The Snarling Citizen* (1995), both collections of essays; and *Kipper's Game* (1993), a novel.

In Defense of Talk Shows

They may have peaked, but talk shows still prevail on daytime television and still raise people's dander. In this typically lively work of cultural criticism, Ehrenreich maintains that talk shows have their merits. This essay first appeared in *Time* magazine in December 1995.

Up until now, the targets of Bill (*The Book of Virtues*) Bennett's[1] 1 crusades have at least been plausible sources of evil. But the latest victim of his wrath—TV talk shows of the *Sally Jessy Raphael* variety—are in a whole different category from drugs and gangsta rap. As anyone who actually watches them knows, the talk shows are one of the most excruciatingly moralistic forums the culture has to offer. Disturbing and sometimes disgusting, yes, but their very business is to preach the middle-class virtues of responsibility, reason and self-control.

Take the case of Susan, recently featured on *Montel Williams* as an 2 example of a woman being stalked by her ex-boyfriend. Turns out Susan is also stalking the boyfriend and—here's the sexual frisson—has slept with him only days ago. In fact Susan is neck deep in trouble without any help from the boyfriend: She's serving a yearlong stretch of home incarceration for assaulting another woman, and home is the tiny trailer she shares with her nine-year-old daughter.

---

[1] William Bennett (born 1943) has held posts in Republican administrations and urged moral and cultural reform. In *The Book of Virtues* (1993), Bennett collects the fables, folklore, and stories that he sees as the root of American values. —EDS.

But no one is applauding this life spun out of control. Montel 3
scolds Susan roundly for neglecting her daughter and failing to confront her role in the mutual stalking. A therapist lectures her about this
unhealthy "obsessive kind of love." The studio audience jeers at her
every evasion. By the end Susan has lost her cocky charm and dissolved
into tears of shame.

The plot is always the same. People with problems — "husband says 4
she looks like a cow," "pressured to lose her virginity or else," "mate
wants more sex than I do" — are introduced to rational methods of
problem solving. People with moral failings — "boy crazy," "dresses like
a tramp," "a hundred sex partners" — are introduced to external standards of morality. The preaching — delivered alternately by the studio
audience, the host and the ever present guest therapist — is relentless.
"This is wrong to do this," Sally Jessy tells a cheating husband. "Feel
bad?" Geraldo asks the girl who stole her best friend's boyfriend. "Any
sense of remorse?" The expectation is that the sinner, so hectored, will
see her way to reform. And indeed, a Sally Jessy update found "boy
crazy," who'd been a guest only weeks ago, now dressed in schoolgirlish
plaid and claiming her "attitude [had] changed" — thanks to the rough-
and-ready therapy dispensed on the show.

All right, the subjects are often lurid and even bizarre. But there's 5
no part of the entertainment spectacle, from *Hard Copy* to *Jade*, that
doesn't trade in the lurid and bizarre. At least in the talk shows, the
moral is always loud and clear: Respect yourself, listen to others, stop
beating on your wife. In fact it's hard to see how *The Bill Bennett Show*,
if there were to be such a thing, could deliver a more pointed sermon.
Or would he prefer to see the feckless Susan, for example, tarred and
feathered by the studio audience instead of being merely booed and
shamed?

There *is* something morally repulsive about the talks, but it's not 6
anything Bennett or his co-crusader Senator Joseph Lieberman has
seen fit to mention. Watch for a few hours, and you get the claustrophobic sense of lives that have never seen the light of some external
judgment, of people who have never before been listened to, and certainly never been taken seriously if they were. "What kind of people
would let themselves be humiliated like this?" is often asked, sniffily, by
the shows' detractors. And the answer, for the most part, is people who
are so needy — of social support, of education, of material resources and
self-esteem — that they mistake being the center of attention for being
actually loved and respected.

What the talks are about, in large part, is poverty and the distor- 7
tions it visits on the human spirit. You'll never find investment bankers
bickering on *Rolonda*, or the host of *Gabrielle* recommending therapy to
sobbing professors. With few exceptions the guests are drawn from

trailer parks and tenements, from bleak streets and narrow, crowded rooms. Listen long enough, and you hear references to unpaid bills, to welfare, to twelve-hour workdays and double shifts. And this is the real shame of the talks: that they take lives bent out of shape by poverty and hold them up as entertaining exhibits. An announcement appearing between segments of *Montel* says it all: The show is looking for "pregnant women who sell their bodies to make ends meet."

This is class exploitation, pure and simple. What next—"homeless   8 people so hungry they eat their own scabs"? Or would the next step be to pay people outright to submit to public humiliation? For $50 would you confess to adultery in your wife's presence? For $500 would you reveal your thirteen-year-old's girlish secrets on *Ricki Lake*? If you were poor enough, you might.

It is easy enough for those who can afford spacious homes and pri-   9 vate therapy to sneer at their financial inferiors and label their pathetic moments of stardom vulgar. But if I had a talk show, it would feature a whole different cast of characters and category of crimes than you'll ever find on the talks: "CEOs[2] who rake in millions while their employees get downsized" would be an obvious theme, along with "Senators who voted for welfare and Medicaid cuts"—and, if he'll agree to appear, "well-fed Republicans who dithered about talk shows while trailer-park residents slipped into madness and despair."

QUESTIONS ON MEANING

1. Ehrenreich's essay takes exception to Bill Bennett's criticism of talk shows. In your own words, what is Ehrenreich's THESIS?
2. What does Ehrenreich say is the role of a talk show's studio audience?
3. According to this essay, what are a talk show's main methods of "helping" the people who participate as panelists?
4. Why does Ehrenreich think talk shows are "morally repulsive" (paras. 6–8)?

QUESTIONS ON WRITING STRATEGY

1. What are the four parts of talks shows that Ehrenreich identifies in her analysis?
2. Does Ehrenreich seem to assume that her readers are also watchers of talk shows? What EVIDENCE supports your answer?
3. What TONE does Ehrenreich use in paragraph 8? How does this reflect the criticisms she is making?

[2] Chief Executive Officers, the heads of corporations. —EDS.

4. **OTHER METHODS.** In her CONCLUSION, Ehrenreich offers alternative talk show topics. What is the point of this COMPARISON AND CONTRAST with real shows? Do you find this conclusion effective?

QUESTIONS ON LANGUAGE

1. How does Ehrenreich's description of the talk show as "lurid and even bizarre," "a spectacle" (para. 5), contribute to her analysis of these shows?
2. Ehrenreich calls the "therapy" on talk shows "rough-and-ready" (para. 4). What are the CONNOTATIONS of this expression?
3. Why does Ehrenreich pose this RHETORICAL QUESTION in paragraph 5: "Or would [Bennett] prefer to see the feckless Susan, for example, tarred and feathered by the studio audience instead of being merely booed and shamed?"
4. Look up the definitions if any of the following words are unfamiliar to you: plausible, wrath, excruciatingly, moralistic, forums (para. 1); frisson, incarceration (2); roundly, jeers, evasion (3); hectored (4); feckless (5); claustrophobic, detractors (6); tenements (7); exploitation (8); vulgar, dithered (9).

SUGGESTIONS FOR WRITING

1. **JOURNAL WRITING.** If you have never watched a talk show, you may want to sample a few programs. Once you are familiar with the shows' format and content, write your reactions to them in your journal.

   FROM JOURNAL TO ESSAY. Using one episode of a talk show as an EXAMPLE, write an essay analyzing the role of the show's "stars." Do you agree with Ehrenreich that the show exploits its participants? Why, or why not?
2. Write an essay that analyzes another kind of television show. How do the elements of the show come together to send a specific message or achieve certain goals?
3. **CRITICAL WRITING.** Throughout this essay, Ehrenreich uses a number of religious METAPHORS to help explain what goes on during talk shows. Locate some of these metaphors. In light of the arguments against talk shows made by William Bennett and others, why do you think Ehrenreich uses such metaphors? Write an essay explaining how they reinforce her argument about the morality of talk shows.
4. **CONNECTIONS.** At the end of "The Case for Slavery" (p. 370), A. M. Rosenthal asserts that "callousness of class" enables people to argue for the legalization of drugs. How is this concept of class callousness related to the problem Ehrenreich labels "class exploitation" (para. 8)? Write an essay comparing these two explanations of how class differences cause misunderstandings.

BARBARA EHRENREICH ON WRITING

The printed word, in the view of Barbara Ehrenreich, should be a powerful instrument for reform. In an article in *Mother Jones*, though, she complains about a tacit censorship in American magazines that has sometimes prevented her from fulfilling her purpose as a writer. Ehrenreich recalls the difficulties she had in trying to persuade the editor of a national magazine to assign her a story on the plight of Third World women refugees. "Sorry," said the editor, "Third World women have never done anything for me."

Ehrenreich infers that writers who write for such magazines must follow a rule: "You must learn not to stray from your assigned sociodemographic stereotype." She observes, "As a woman, I am generally asked to write on 'women's topics,' such as cooking, divorce, how to succeed in business, diet fads, and the return of the bustle. These are all fine topics and give great scope to my talents, but when I ask, in faltering tones, for an assignment...on the trade deficit, I am likely to be told that *anyone* (Bill, Gerry, Bob) could cover that, whereas my 'voice' is *essential* for the aerobic toothbrushing story. This is not, strictly speaking, 'censorship'—just a division of labor in which white men cover politics, foreign policy, and the economy, and the rest of us cover what's left over, such as the bustle."

Over the years Ehrenreich has had many manuscripts rejected by editors who comment, "too angry," "too depressing," and "Where's the bright side?" She agrees with writer Herbert Gold, who once deduced that the American media want only "happy stories about happy people with happy problems." She concludes, "You can write about anything —death squads, AIDS...—so long as you make it 'upbeat.'" Despite such discouragements, Ehrenreich continues her battle to "disturb the stupor induced by six straight pages of Calvin Klein ads."

FOR DISCUSSION

1. Is Ehrenreich right about what she calls "a tacit censorship in American magazines"? Check a recent issue of a magazine that prints signed articles. How many of the articles *not* on "women's topics" are written by women? How many are written by men?
2. How many women can you name who write serious newspaper and magazine articles reporting on or arguing matters of general interest, as opposed to those meant to appeal chiefly to women?
3. To what extent do you agree with Ehrenreich—and with Herbert Gold— that the American media are interested only in "upbeat" stories?

MICHIKO KAKUTANI

MICHIKO KAKUTANI is principal book reviewer for the *New York Times*, a position she has held since 1983, and she also writes criticism and feature stories on literary and cultural issues. She has published one book, a collection of interviews she conducted at the *Times* titled *The Poet at the Piano: Portraits of Writers, Filmmakers, Playwrights, and Other Artists at Work* (1988). Kakutani was born in 1955 in New Haven, Connecticut, and earned a B.A. from Yale University in 1976. After graduation she worked at the *Washington Post*, served as a staff writer for *Time* magazine, and joined the *New York Times* as a cultural reporter in 1979. She lives in Manhattan.

The Word Police

"The Word Police" is a kind of book review in which Kakutani goes beyond particular books to comment on the entire cultural trend they represent — in this case, efforts by some to rid the language of its biases. The essay first appeared in the *New York Times* in January 1993.

This month's inaugural festivities,[1] with their celebration, in Maya   1
Angelou's words, of "humankind" — "the Asian, the Hispanic, the Jew /
The African, the Native American, the Sioux, / The Catholic, the Muslim, the French, the Greek / The Irish, the Rabbi, the Priest, the Sheik, /
The Gay, the Straight, the Preacher, / The privileged, the homeless,
the Teacher" — constituted a kind of official embrace of multiculturalism and a new politics of inclusion.

The mood of political correctness, however, has already made firm   2
inroads into popular culture. Washington boasts a store called Politically Correct that sells pro-whale, anti-meat, ban-the-bomb T-shirts,
bumper stickers and buttons, as well as a local cable television show
called *Politically Correct Cooking* that features interviews in the kitchen
with representatives from groups like People for the Ethical Treatment
of Animals. The Coppertone suntan lotion people are planning to give
their longtime cover girl, Little Miss (Ms?) Coppertone, a male equivalent, Little Mr. Coppertone. And even Superman (Superperson?) is
rumored to be returning this spring, reincarnated as four ethnically diverse clones: an African-American, an Asian, a Caucasian and a
Latino.

[1] The inauguration of President Bill Clinton in 1993, at which Angelou read the
poem quoted. — EDS.

287

Nowhere is the P.C. mood more striking than in the increasingly 3
noisy debate over language that has moved from university campuses to
the country at large—a development that both underscores Americans' puritanical zeal for reform and their unwavering faith in the talismanic power of words.

Certainly no decent person can quarrel with the underlying im- 4
pulse behind political correctness: a vision of a more just, inclusive society in which racism, sexism and prejudice of all sorts have been
erased. But the methods and fervor of the self-appointed language police can lead to a rigid orthodoxy—and unintentional self-parody—
opening the movement to the scorn of conservative opponents and the
mockery of cartoonists and late-night television hosts.

It's hard to imagine women earning points for political correctness 5
by saying *ovarimony* instead of *testimony*—as one participant at the recent Modern Language Association convention was overheard to suggest. It's equally hard to imagine people wanting to flaunt their lack of
prejudice by giving up such words and phrases as *bull market, kaiser roll,
Lazy Susan,* and *charley horse.*

Several books on bias-free language have already appeared, and the 6
1991 edition of the Random House *Webster's College Dictionary* boasts
an appendix titled "Avoiding Sexist Language." The dictionary also includes such linguistic mutations as *womyn* (women, "used as an alternative spelling to avoid the suggestion of sexism perceived in the
sequence m-e-n") and *waitron* (a gender-blind term for waiter or waitress).

Many of these dictionaries and guides not only warn the reader 7
against offensive racial and sexual slurs, but also try to establish and enforce a whole new set of usage rules. Take, for instance, *The Bias-Free
Word Finder, a Dictionary of Nondiscriminatory Language* by Rosalie
Maggio (Beacon Press)—a volume often indistinguishable, in its
meticulous solemnity, from the tongue-in-cheek *Official Politically Correct Dictionary and Handbook* put out last year by Henry Beard and
Christopher Cerf (Villard Books). Ms. Maggio's book supplies the
reader intent on using kinder, gentler language with writing guidelines
as well as a detailed listing of more than 5,000 "biased words and
phrases."

Whom are these guidelines for? Somehow one has a tough time 8
picturing them replacing *Fowler's Modern English Usage* in the classroom, or being adopted by the average man (sorry, individual) in the
street.

The "pseudogeneric *he,*" we learn from Ms. Maggio, is to be 9
avoided like the plague, as is the use of the word *man* to refer to humanity. *Fellow, king, lord* and *master* are bad because they're "male-
oriented words," and *king, lord* and *master* are especially bad because

they're also "hierarchical, dominator society terms." The politically correct lion becomes the "monarch of the jungle," new-age children play "someone on the top of the heap," and the *Mona Lisa* goes down in history as Leonardo's "acme of perfection."

As for the word *black*, Ms. Maggio says it should be excised from   10 terms with a negative spin: She recommends substituting words like *mouse* for *black eye*, *ostracize* for *blackball*, *payola* for *blackmail*, and *outcast* for *black sheep*. Clearly, some of these substitutions work better than others: Somehow the "sinister humor" of Kurt Vonnegut or *Saturday Night Live* doesn't quite make it; nor does the "denouncing" of the Hollywood 10.

For the dedicated user of politically correct language, all these rules   11 can make for some messy moral dilemmas. Whereas *battered wife* is a gender-biased term, the gender-free term *battered spouse*, Ms. Maggio notes, incorrectly implies "that men and women are equally battered."

On one hand, say Francine Wattman Frank and Paula A. Treichler   12 in their book *Language, Gender, and Professional Writing* (Modern Language Association), *he or she* is an appropriate construction for talking about an individual (like a jockey, say) who belongs to a profession that's predominantly male — it's a way of emphasizing "that such occupations are not barred to women or that women's concerns need to be kept in mind." On the other hand, they add, using masculine pronouns rhetorically can underscore ongoing male dominance in those fields, implying the need for change.

And what about the speech codes adopted by some universities in   13 recent years? Although they were designed to prohibit students from uttering sexist and racist slurs, they would extend, by logic, to blacks who want to use the word *nigger* to strip the term of its racist connotations, or homosexuals who want to use the word *queer* to reclaim it from bigots.

In her book, Ms. Maggio recommends applying bias-free usage   14 retroactively: She suggests paraphrasing politically incorrect quotations, or replacing "the sexist words or phrases with ellipsis dots and/or bracketed substitutes," or using *sic* "to show that the sexist words come from the original quotation and to call attention to the fact that they are incorrect."

Which leads the skeptical reader of *The Bias-Free Word Finder*   15 to wonder whether *All the King's Men* should be retitled *All the Ruler's People; Pet Sematary, Animal Companion Graves; Birdman of Alcatraz, Birdperson of Alcatraz;* and *The Iceman Cometh, The Ice Route Driver Cometh?*

Will making such changes remove the prejudice in people's mind?   16 Should we really spend time trying to come up with non-male-based alternatives to *Midas touch*, *Achilles' heel*, and *Montezuma's revenge?* Will tossing out Santa Claus—whom Ms. Maggio accuses of reinforcing "the cultural male-as-norm system"—in favor of Belfana, his Italian female alter ego, truly help banish sexism? Can the avoidance of "violent expressions and metaphors" like *kill two birds with one stone, sock it to 'em* or *kick an idea around* actually promote a more harmonious world?

The point isn't that the excesses of the word police are comical. 17
The point is that their intolerance (in the name of tolerance) has disturbing implications. In the first place, getting upset by phrases like *bullish on America* or *the City of Brotherly Love* tends to distract attention from the real problems of prejudice and injustice that exist in society at large, turning them into mere questions of semantics. Indeed, the emphasis currently put on politically correct usage has uncanny parallels with the academic movement of deconstruction—a method of textual analysis that focuses on language and linguistic pyrotechnics —which has become firmly established on university campuses.

In both cases, attention is focused on surfaces, on words and 18
metaphors; in both cases, signs and symbols are accorded more importance than content. Hence, the attempt by some radical advocates to remove *The Adventures of Huckleberry Finn* from curriculums on the grounds that Twain's use of the word *nigger* makes the book a racist text —never mind the fact that this American classic (written in 1884) depicts the spiritual kinship achieved between a white boy and a runaway slave, never mind the fact that the "nigger" Jim emerges as the novel's most honorable, decent character.

Ironically enough, the P.C. movement's obsession with language is 19
accompanied by a strange Orwellian willingness to warp the meaning of words by placing them under a high-powered ideological lens. For instance, the *Dictionary of Cautionary Words and Phrases*—a pamphlet issued by the University of Missouri's Multicultural Management Program to help turn "today's journalists into tomorrow's multicultural newsroom managers"—warns that using the word *articulate* to describe members of a minority group can suggest the opposite, "that 'those people' are not considered well educated, articulate and the like."

The pamphlet patronizes minority groups, by cautioning the reader 20
against using the words *lazy* and *burly* to describe any member of such groups; and it issues a similar warning against using words like *gorgeous* and *petite* to describe women.

As euphemism proliferates with the rise of political correctness, 21
there is a spread of the sort of sloppy, abstract language that Orwell said is "designed to make lies sound truthful and murder respectable, and to give an appearance of solidity to pure wind." *Fat* becomes *big boned* and *differently sized; stupid* becomes *exceptional; stoned* becomes *chemically inconvenienced.*

Wait a minute here? Aren't such phrases eerily reminiscent of the 22 euphemisms coined by the government during Vietnam and Watergate? Remember how the military used to speak of "pacification," or how President Richard M. Nixon's press secretary, Ronald L. Ziegler, tried to get away with calling a lie an "inoperative statement"?

Calling the homeless "the underhoused" doesn't give them a place   23
to live; calling the poor "the economically marginalized" doesn't help them pay the bills. Rather, by playing down their plight, such language might even make it easier to shrug off the seriousness of their situation.

Instead of allowing free discussion and debate to occur, many gung-   24
ho advocates of politically correct language seem to think that simple suppression of a word or concept will magically make the problem disappear. In *The Bias-Free Word Finder*, Ms. Maggio entreats the reader not to perpetuate the negative stereotype of Eve. "Be extremely cautious in referring to the biblical Eve," she writes; "this story has profoundly contributed to negative attitudes toward women throughout history, largely because of misogynistic and patriarchal interpretations that labeled her evil, inferior, and seductive."

The story of Bluebeard, the rake (whoops!—the libertine) who   25
killed his seven wives, she says, is also to be avoided, as is the biblical story of Jezebel. Of Jesus Christ, Ms. Maggio writes: "There have been few individuals in history as completely androgynous as Christ, and it does his message a disservice to overinsist on his maleness." She doesn't give the reader any hints on how this might be accomplished; presumably, one is supposed to avoid describing him as the Son of God.

Of course the P.C. police aren't the only ones who want to pro-   26
scribe what people should say or give them guidelines for how they may use an idea; Jesse Helms and his supporters are up to exactly the same thing when they propose to patrol the boundaries of the permissible in art. In each case, the would-be censor aspires to suppress what he or she finds distasteful—all, of course, in the name of the public good.

In the case of the politically correct, the prohibition of certain   27
words, phrases and ideas is advanced in the cause of building a brave new world free of racism and hate, but this vision of harmony clashes with the very ideals of diversity and inclusion that the multicultural movement holds dear, and it's purchased at the cost of freedom of speech.

In fact, the utopian world envisioned by the language police would   28
be bought at the expense of the ideals of individualism and democracy articulated in the "Gettysburg Address": "Four score and seven years ago our fathers brought forth on this continent a new nation, conceived in liberty and dedicated to the proposition that all mean are created equal."

Of course, the P.C. police have already found Lincoln's words   29
hopelessly "phallocentric." No doubt they would rewrite the passage:

"Four score and seven years ago our foremothers and forefathers brought forth on this continent a new nation, formulated with liberty, and dedicated to the proposition that all humankind is created equal."

QUESTIONS ON MEANING

1. Why is *The Bias-Free Word Finder* "indistinguishable" from the satiric *Official Politically Correct Dictionary and Handbook* (para. 7)?
2. In your own words, restate Kakutani's THESIS. What is her PURPOSE?
3. Why, in Kakutani's opinion, do the "word police" hurt the cause they are trying to help?
4. How are advocates of "political correctness" like advocates of right-wing censorship?

QUESTIONS ON WRITING STRATEGY

1. The *New York Times*, where this essay was first published, is one of the nation's most widely read newspapers. Who in the paper's vast AUDIENCE does Kakutani seem to ASSUME will read the essay?
2. What is Kakutani's TONE? (Look, for instance, at paras. 7–8, 14–15, and 24–25.) How might it affect her audience? How does it affect *you*?
3. Which of Kakutani's EXAMPLES do you think are the most effective? Which are the least effective? Why?
4. **OTHER METHODS.** Kakutani's analysis of books on bias-free language develops from her understanding of CAUSES AND EFFECTS. What does she think causes "political correctness"? What are its consequences?

QUESTIONS ON LANGUAGE

1. Give meanings for any of these words that are unfamiliar: puritanical, talismanic (para. 3); fervor, orthodoxy (4); meticulous (7); pseudogeneric, hierarchical (9); excised (10); semantics, pyrotechnics (17); ideological (19); misogynistic, patriarchal (24); androgynous (25); proscribe (26); phallocentric (29).
2. Locate some words and phrases of Kakutani's that might be seen as unacceptable by the "word police." Do they offend or disturb you?
3. What are some of the CONNOTATIONS of the phrase "politically correct"?
4. What does Kakutani mean by the phrase "Orwellian willingness to warp the meaning of words" (para. 19)?

QUESTIONS FOR WRITING

1. **JOURNAL WRITING.** Kakutani argues that "[politically correct] language might even make it easier to shrug off the seriousness" of many people's sit-

uations (para. 23). Have you ever seen individuals or groups hurt by too-careful language? Or have you ever witnessed problems caused by careless use of language? Which seems to be more common?

FROM JOURNAL TO ESSAY. Write an essay exploring what you see as the effects of the movement toward bias-free language. Does this trend seem to be creating more problems than it solves? Use examples (from your journal entry or other sources) to support your ideas.

2. Kakutani writes, "The mood of political correctness…has already made firm inroads into popular culture" (para. 2), and gives examples from television, suntan-lotion ads, and comic books to support her claim. Do you agree or disagree? Write a short essay arguing that popular culture has, or has not, become more "politically correct." Support your claims with EVIDENCE. You may want to COMPARE AND CONTRAST past movies, comics, pop songs, or television shows with their present-day counterparts as a way of making your case.

3. **CRITICAL WRITING.** In an essay, ANALYZE Kakutani's assumptions about the connections between language and action. How do they compare with the assumptions Kakutani attributes to the advocates of "political correctness"? With whose assumptions are you more comfortable, and why?

4. **CONNECTIONS.** Kakutani is concerned that "many gung-ho advocates of politically correct language seem to think the simple suppression of a word or concept will magically make the problem disappear" (para. 24). In "The Meanings of a Word" (p. 407), Gloria Naylor advocates *not* suppressing language that might be called "politically incorrect." She writes, "Meeting the word [*nigger*] head-on, [my relatives] proved it had absolutely nothing to do with the way they were determined to live their lives" (para. 14). How similar are these two writers' positions? In an essay, first SUMMARIZE each ARGUMENT, and then compare the two, considering each author's ideas about why language is or should be suppressed or not.

GAIL SHEEHY

GAIL SHEEHY was born in 1937. She earned her B.S. degree from the University of Vermont in 1958 and was a fellow in Columbia University's Journalism School in 1970. A contributor to the *New York Times Magazine*, *Esquire*, *McCall's*, *Ms.*, *Cosmopolitan*, *Rolling Stone*, and other magazines, she has also written a novel, *Lovesounds* (1970), and many popular studies of contemporary life: *Speed Is of the Essence* (1971), *Panthermania* (1971), *Hustling* (1973), *Passages* (1976), *Pathfinders* (1981), *Character: America's Search for Leadership* (1988), *The Man Who Changed the World: The Lives of Mikhail S. Gorbachev* (1991), *Silent Passage* (1992), and *New Passages* (1995). In *The Spirit of Survival* (1986), Sheehy has written a history of strife and deprivation in Cambodia. The book includes a narrative told from the point of view of Mohm, a twelve-year-old Cambodian child adopted by Sheehy and her husband, Clay Felker, a New York editor.

Predictable Crises of Adulthood

"Predictable Crises of Adulthood" is adapted from the second chapter of *Passages*. In the essay, Sheehy identifies six stages that most people experience between the ages of eighteen and fifty. The author, as she herself makes clear, is not a theorist or a scholar; she is an artful reporter, in this case of findings in adult development. Not everyone goes through the stages Sheehy traces at exactly the same time, but see whether any of the following crises sound familiar to you.

We are not unlike a particularly hardy crustacean. The lobster 1 grows by developing and shedding a series of hard, protective shells. Each time it expands from within, the confining shell must be sloughed off. It is left exposed and vulnerable until, in time, a new covering grows to replace the old.

With each passage from one stage of human growth to the next we, 2 too, must shed a protective structure. We are left exposed and vulnerable—but also yeasty and embryonic again, capable of stretching in ways we hadn't known before. These sheddings may take several years or more. Coming out of each passage, though, we enter a longer and more stable period in which we can expect relative tranquility and a sense of equilibrium regained....

As we shall see, each person engages the steps of development in 3 his or her own characteristic *step-style*. Some people never complete the whole sequence. And none of us "solves" with one step—by jumping out of the parental home into a job or marriage, for example—the problems in separating from the caregivers of childhood. Nor do we

294

"achieve" autonomy once and for all by converting our dreams into concrete goals, even when we attain those goals. The central issues or tasks of one period are never fully completed, tied up, and cast aside. But when they lose their primacy and the current life structure has served its purpose, we are ready to move on to the next period.

Can one catch up? What might look to others like listlessness, con- 4 trariness, a maddening refusal to face up to an obvious task may be a person's own unique detour that will bring him out later on the other side. Developmental gains won can later be lost—and rewon. It's plausible, though it can't be proven, that the mastery of one set of tasks fortifies us for the next period and the next set of challenges. But it's important not to think too mechanistically. Machines work by units. The bureaucracy (supposedly) works step by step. Human beings, thank God, have an individual inner dynamic that can never be precisely coded.

Although I have indicated the ages when Americans are likely to 5 go through each stage, and the differences between men and women where they are striking, do not take the ages too seriously. The stages are the thing, and most particularly the sequence.

Here is the briefest outline of the developmental ladder. 6

Pulling Up Roots

Before 18, the motto is loud and clear: "I have to get away from my 7 parents." But the words are seldom connected to action. Generally still safely part of our families, even if away at school, we feel our autonomy to be subject to erosion from moment to moment.

After 18, we begin Pulling Up Roots in earnest. College, military 8 service, and short-term travels are all customary vehicles our society provides for the first round trips between family and a base of one's own. In the attempt to separate our view of the world from our family's view, despite vigorous protestations to the contrary—"I know exactly what I want!"—we cast about for any beliefs we can call our own. And in the process of testing those beliefs we are often drawn to fads, preferably those most mysterious and inaccessible to our parents.

Whatever tentative memberships we try out in the world, the fear 9 haunts us that we are really kids who cannot take care of ourselves. We cover that fear with acts of defiance and mimicked confidence. For allies to replace our parents, we turn to our contemporaries. They become conspirators. So long as their perspective meshes with our own, they are able to substitute for the sanctuary of the family. But that doesn't last very long. And the instant they diverge from the shaky ideals of "our group," they are seen as betrayers. Rebounds to the family are common between the ages of 18 and 22.

The tasks of this passage are to locate ourselves in a peer group role,   10
a sex role, an anticipated occupation, an ideology or world view. As a
result, we gather the impetus to leave home physically and the identity
to *begin* leaving home emotionally.

Even as one part of us seeks to be an individual, another part longs   11
to restore the safety and comfort of merging with another. Thus one of
the most popular myths of this passage is: We can piggyback our development by attaching to a Stronger One. But people who marry during
this time often prolong financial and emotional ties to the family and
relatives that impede them from becoming self-sufficient.

A stormy passage through the Pulling Up Roots years will probably   12
facilitate the normal progression of the adult life cycle. If one doesn't
have an identity crisis at this point, it will erupt during a later transition, when the penalties may be harder to bear.

The Trying Twenties

The Trying Twenties confront us with the question of how to take   13
hold in the adult world. Our focus shifts from the interior turmoils of
late adolescence — "Who am I?" "What is truth?" — and we become almost totally preoccupied with working out the externals. "How do I put
my aspirations into effect?" "What is the best way to start?" "Where do
I go?" "Who can help me?" "How did *you* do it?"

In this period, which is longer and more stable compared with the   14
passage that leads to it, the tasks are as enormous as they are exhilarating: To shape a Dream, that vision of ourselves which will generate energy, aliveness, and hope. To prepare for a lifework. To find a mentor if
possible. And to form the capacity for intimacy, without losing in the
process whatever consistency of self we have thus far mustered. The
first test structure must be erected around the life we choose to try.

Doing what we "should" is the most pervasive theme of the twen-   15
ties. The "shoulds" are largely defined by family models, the press of the
culture, or the prejudices of our peers. If the prevailing cultural instructions are that one should get married and settle down behind one's own
door, a nuclear family is born. If instead the peers insist that one should
do one's own thing, the 25-year-old is likely to harness himself onto a
Harley-Davidson and burn up Route 66 in the commitment to have no
commitments.

One of the terrifying aspects of the twenties is the inner conviction   16
that the choices we make are irrevocable. It is largely a false fear.
Change is quite possible, and some alteration of our original choices is
probably inevitable.

Two impulses, as always, are at work. One is to build a firm,   17
safe structure for the future by making strong commitments, to "be

set." Yet people who slip into a ready-made form without much self-examination are likely to find themselves locked in.

2 The other urge is to explore and experiment, keeping any structure   18
tentative and therefore easily reversible. Taken to the extreme, these
are people who skip from one trial job and one limited personal encounter to another, spending their twenties in the transient state.

Although the choices of our twenties are not irrevocable, they do   19
set in motion a Life Pattern. Some of us follow the lock-in pattern, others the transient pattern, the wunderkind pattern, the caregiver pattern, and there are a number of others. Such patterns strongly influence
the particular questions raised for each person during each passage....

Buoyed by powerful illusions and belief in the power of the will, we   20
commonly insist in our twenties that what we have chosen to do is the
one true course in life. Our backs go up at the merest hint that we are
like our parents, that two decades of parental training might be reflected in our current actions and attitudes.

"Not me," is the motto, "I'm different."   21

Catch-30

Impatient with devoting ourselves to the "shoulds," a new vitality   22
springs from within as we approach 30. Men and women alike speak of
feeling too narrow and restricted. They blame all sorts of things, but
what the restrictions boil down to are the outgrowth of career and personal choices of the twenties. They may have been choices perfectly
suited to that stage. But now the fit feels different. Some inner aspect
that was left out is striving to be taken into account. Important new
choices must be made, and commitments altered or deepened. The
work involves great change, turmoil, and often crisis—a simultaneous
feeling of rock bottom and the urge to bust out.

One common response is the tearing up of the life we spent most of   23
our twenties putting together. It may mean striking out on a secondary
road toward a new vision or converting a dream of "running for president" into a more realistic goal. The single person feels a push to find a
partner. The woman who was previously content at home with children chafes to venture into the world. The childless couple reconsiders
children. And almost everyone who is married, especially those married for seven years, feels a discontent.

If the discontent doesn't lead to a divorce, it will, or should, call for   24
a serious review of the marriage and of each partner's aspirations in
their Catch-30 condition. The gist of that condition was expressed by
a 29-year-old associate with a Wall Street law firm:

"I'm considering leaving the firm. I've been there four years now;   25
I'm getting good feedback, but I have no clients of my own. I feel weak.

If I wait much longer, it will be too late, too close to that fateful time of decision on whether or not to become a partner. I'm success-oriented. But the concept of being 55 years old and stuck in a monotonous job drives me wild. It drives me crazy now, just a little bit. I'd say that 85 percent of the time I thoroughly enjoy my work. But when I get a screwball case, I come away from court saying, 'What am I doing here?' It's a *visceral* reaction that I'm wasting my time. I'm trying to find some way to make a social contribution or a slot in city government. I keep saying, 'There's something more.'"

Besides the push to broaden himself professionally, there is a wish 26 to expand his personal life. He wants two or three more children. "The concept of a home has become very meaningful to me, a place to get away from troubles and relax. I love my son in a way I could not have anticipated. I never could live alone."

Consumed with the work of making his own critical life-steering 27 decisions, he demonstrates the essential shift at this age: an absolute requirement to be more self-concerned. The self has new value now that his competency has been proved.

His wife is struggling with her own age-30 priorities. She wants to 28 go to law school, but he wants more children. If she is going to stay home, she wants him to make more time for the family instead of taking on even wider professional commitments. His view of the bind, of what he would most like from his wife, is this:

"I'd like not to be bothered. It sounds cruel, but I'd like not to have 29 to worry about what she's going to do next week. Which is why I've told her several times that I think she should do something. Go back to school and get a degree in social work or geography or whatever. Hopefully that would fulfill her, and then I wouldn't have to worry about her line of problems. I want her to be decisive about herself."

The trouble with his advice to his wife is that it comes out of con- 30 cern with *his* convenience, rather than with *her* development. She quickly picks up on this lack of goodwill: He is trying to dispose of her. At the same time, he refuses her the same latitude to be "selfish" in making an independent decision to broaden her horizons. Both perceive a lack of mutuality. And that is what Catch-30 is all about for the couple.

Rooting and Extending

Life becomes less provisional, more rational and orderly in the 31 early thirties. We begin to settle down in the full sense. Most of us begin putting down roots and sending out new shoots. People buy houses and become very earnest about climbing career ladders. Men in particular concern themselves with "making it." Satisfaction with marriage generally goes downhill in the thirties (for those who have remained together) compared with the highly valued, vision-supporting marriage of the twenties. This coincides with the couple's reduced social life outside the family and the inturned focus on raising their children.

The Deadline Decade

In the middle of the thirties we come upon a crossroads. We have 32 reached the halfway mark. Yet even as we are reaching our prime, we begin to see there is a place where it finishes. Time starts to squeeze.

The loss of youth, the faltering of physical powers we have always 33 taken for granted, the fading purpose of stereotyped roles by which we have thus far identified ourselves, the spiritual dilemma of having no absolute answers—any or all of these shocks can give this passage the character of crisis. Such thoughts usher in a decade between 35 and 45 that can be called the Deadline Decade. It is a time of both danger and opportunity. All of us have the chance to rework the narrow identity by which we defined ourselves in the first half of life. And those of us who make the most of the opportunity will have a full-out authenticity crisis.

To come through this authenticity crisis, we must reexamine our 34 purposes and reevaluate how to spend our resources from now on. "Why am I doing all this? What do I really believe in?" No matter what we have been doing, there will be parts of ourselves that have been suppressed and now need to find expression. "Bad" feelings will demand acknowledgment along with the good.

It is frightening to step off onto the treacherous footbridge leading 35 to the second half of life. We can't take everything with us on this journey through uncertainty. Along the way, we discover that we are alone. We no longer have to ask permission because we are the providers of our own safety. We must learn to give ourselves permission. We stumble upon feminine or masculine aspects of our natures that up to this time have usually been masked. There is grieving to be done because an old self is dying. By taking in our suppressed and even our unwanted parts, we prepare at the gut level for the reintegration of an identity that is ours and ours alone—not some artificial form put together to please the culture or our mates. It is a hard passage at the beginning. But by disassembling ourselves, we can glimpse the light and gather our parts into a renewal.

Women sense this inner crossroads earlier than men do. The time 36 pinch often prompts a woman to stop and take an all-points survey at age 35. Whatever options she has already played out, she feels a "my last chance" urgency to review those options she has set aside and those that aging and biology will close off in the *now foreseeable* future. For all her qualms and confusion about where to start looking for a new future,

she usually enjoys an exhilaration of release. Assertiveness begins rising. There are so many firsts ahead.

Men, too, feel the time push in the mid-thirties. Most men respond   37
by pressing down harder on the career accelerator. It's "my last chance"
to pull away from the pack. It is no longer enough to be the loyal junior
executive, the promising young novelist, the lawyer who does a little
pro bono work on the side. He wants now to become part of top management, to be recognized as an established writer, or an active politician with his own legislative program. With some chagrin, he discovers
that he has been too anxious to please and too vulnerable to criticism.
He wants to put together his own ship.

During this period of intense concentration on external advance-   38
ment, it is common for men to be unaware of the more difficult, gut issues that are propelling them forward. The survey that was neglected at
35 becomes a crucible at 40. Whatever rung of achievement he has
reached, the man of 40 usually feels stale, restless, burdened, and unap-
preciated. He worries about his health. He wonders, "Is this all there
is?" He may make a series of departures from well-established lifelong
base lines, including marriage. More and more men are seeking second
careers in midlife. Some become self-destructive. And many men in
their forties experience a major shift of emphasis away from pouring all
their energies into their own advancement. A more tender, feeling side
comes into play. They become interested in developing an ethical self.

Renewal or Resignation

Somewhere in the mid-forties, equilibrium is regained. A new sta-   39
bility is achieved, which may be more or less satisfying.

If one has refused to budge through the midlife transition, the sense   40
of staleness will calcify into resignation. One by one, the safety and
supports will be withdrawn from the person who is standing still. Parents will become children; children will become strangers; a mate will
grow away or go away; the career will become just a job—and each of
these events will be felt as an abandonment. The crisis will probably
emerge again around 50. And although its wallop will be greater, the
jolt may be just what is needed to prod the resigned middle-ager toward
seeking revitalization.

On the other hand...   41

If we have confronted ourselves in the middle passage and found a   42
renewal of purpose around which we are eager to build a more authen-
tic life structure, these may well be the best years. Personal happiness
takes a sharp turn upward for partners who can now accept the fact: "I
cannot expect *anyone* to fully understand me." Parents can be forgiven
for the burdens of our childhood. Children can be let go without leav-

ing us in collapsed silence. At 50, there is a new warmth and mellowing. Friends become more important than ever, but so does privacy. Since it is so often proclaimed by people past midlife, the motto of this stage might be "No more bullshit."

QUESTIONS ON MEANING

1. In your own words, SUMMARIZE each of Sheehy's six predictable stages of adult life.
2. According to the author, what happens to people who fail to experience a given stage of growth at the usual time?
3. How would you characterize Sheehy's attitude toward growth and change in adult life?

QUESTIONS ON WRITING STRATEGY

1. Why does Sheehy employ the method of division or analysis? How does it serve her readers, too?
2. What, if anything, does the author gain by writing her essay in the first PERSON plural (*we, us*)?
3. What difficulties go along with making GENERALIZATIONS about human beings? To what extent does Sheehy surmount these difficulties?
4. How much knowledge of psychology does Sheehy expect of her AUDIENCE?
5. **OTHER METHODS.** Sheehy relies on CAUSE AND EFFECT to explain why needs and goals change at each stage of adulthood. Summarize the pattern of cause and effect in the "Catch-30" stage (paras. 22–30).

QUESTIONS ON LANGUAGE

1. Consult your dictionary if you need help in defining the following words: crustacean (para. 1); embryonic, tranquility, equilibrium (2); autonomy, primacy (3); plausible (4); inaccessible (8); sanctuary (9); impetus (10); exhilarating, mentor (14); pervasive (15); irrevocable (16); tentative (18); wunderkind (19); visceral (25); mutuality (30); dilemma (33); *pro bono*, chagrin, vulnerable (37); crucible (38); calcify (40).
2. What is a "nuclear family" (para. 15)?
3. The author coins a few phrases of her own. Refer to their context to help you define the following: step-style (para. 3); Stronger One (11); Catch-30 (24); authenticity crisis (33).

SUGGESTIONS FOR WRITING

1. **JOURNAL WRITING.** Did any of the stages outlined by Sheehy ring especially true for you? Describe some of the events in your life that place you in one of Sheehy's stages.

FROM JOURNAL TO ESSAY. Sheehy focuses each of her six stages on a "crisis." Does the word *crisis* seem appropriate or extreme to you? Choose one of Sheehy's stages that you know firsthand, and write an essay that EVALUATES her account of it. Use the details from your journal to support your evaluation.

2. Inspired by Sheehy's division of life after age eighteen into phases, look back on your own earlier life or that of a younger person you know, and detail a series of phases in it. Invent names for the phases.

3. CRITICAL WRITING. In popularizing scholarly research from developmental psychology, Sheehy eliminates such features as detailed analyses of researchers' methods and results, statistical correlations and other data, source citations, and specialized terminology. Write an essay EVALUATING the advantages and disadvantages of popularizations such as Sheehy's versus scholarly books and articles like those you read for courses in the sciences, social sciences, or humanities.

4. CONNECTIONS. You may have noticed the similarity between Sheehy's characterization of the Catch-30 couple (paras. 22–30) and Judy Brady's analysis in "I Want a Wife" (p. 274). Use the information provided by Sheehy (about other stages as well, if you like) to analyze the particular crisis of the "I" who wants a wife in Brady's essay. Support your ideas with EVIDENCE from both essays.

GAIL SHEEHY ON WRITING

With the recent publication of a sequel to *Passages*, the book containing "Predictable Crises of Adulthood," Gail Sheehy shows both how a writer's own situation can influence his or her ideas and how time can change those ideas. In the sequel, *New Passages*, Sheehy admits that when publishing *Passages* at the age of thirty-nine, she "couldn't imagine life beyond fifty. And I certainly couldn't bring myself to consider it a time of potential." But the intervening years have brought changes, and not just in Sheehy herself. "People," she writes, "are taking longer to grow up and much longer to die." Adolescence may now run through the twenties, marriage and children may not come until the forties, and life may not end until the nineties.

New Passages proposes three life stages: provisional adulthood, from ages eighteen to thirty; first adulthood, from ages thirty to forty-five; and second adulthood, from age forty-five to death. In an interview with Regina Weinreich of the *New York Times*, Sheehy said, "After years of interviews, it became apparent that all the age models were off. There were predictable stages but no predictable ages for when we go through them.... What I hope people will get out of the book is that there is a second adulthood. They can't carry the roles, identities, dreams of the first adulthood into the second.... They're going to live longer. Prepare by thinking what would be the new dream that will enliven the whole vast expanse of life."

FOR DISCUSSION

Should a writer's ideas be as vulnerable to change as Sheehy's were in *Passages*? Do Sheehy's recent observations about the stages of life invalidate "Predictable Crises of Adulthood"? Why, or why not?

JAMAICA KINCAID

JAMAICA KINCAID was born Elaine Potter Richardson in 1949 on the Caribbean island of Antigua. She attended school in Antigua and struggled to become independent of her mother and her place. "I was supposed to be full of good manners and good speech," she has recalled. "Where the hell I was going to go with it I don't know." Kincaid took it to New York, where she went at age seventeen to work as a family helper. She briefly attended Franconia College on a photography scholarship and did odd jobs in New York. In the early 1970s, she became friends with George Trow, a writer for *The New Yorker*. Soon she was contributing to the magazine, and in 1976 she became a staff writer. Soon after, she began writing fiction, producing a collection of stories, *At the Bottom of the River* (1983), and three novels, *Annie John* (1985), *Lucy* (1990), and *The Autobiography of My Mother* (1996)—all based on her own life on Antigua and as an immigrant. *A Small Place* (1988), also about Antigua, denounces the island's ruin by its colonial rulers.

Girl

This very short story was collected in *At the Bottom of the River*. Much like Judy Brady in "I Want a Wife" (p. 274), Kincaid analyzes the domain of the title girl, both the roles she is expected to fill and the condition of being her mother's daughter. The writer Stephanie Vaughn has said that Kincaid's story "spills out in a single breath.... Its exhilarating motion gives me the sense of a writer carried over the precipice by the energy of her own vision."

Wash the white clothes on Monday and put them on the stone heap; wash the color clothes on Tuesday and put them on the clothesline to dry; don't walk barehead in the hot sun; cook pumpkin fritters in very hot sweet oil; soak your little cloths right after you take them off; when buying cotton to make yourself a nice blouse, be sure that it doesn't have gum on it, because that way it won't hold up well after a wash; soak salt fish overnight before you cook it; is it true that you sing benna[1] in Sunday school?; always eat your food in such a way that it won't turn someone else's stomach; on Sundays try to walk like a lady and not like the slut you are so bent on becoming; don't sing benna in Sunday school; you mustn't speak to wharf-rat boys, not even to give directions; don't eat fruits on the street—flies will follow you; *but I don't sing benna on Sundays at all and never in Sunday school*; this is how to sew on a button; this

[1] Calypso music. —EDS.

304

is how to make a buttonhole for the button you have just sewed on; this is how to hem a dress when you see the hem coming down and so to prevent yourself from looking like the slut I know you are so bent on becoming; this is how you iron your father's khaki shirt so that it doesn't have a crease; this is how you iron your father's khaki pants so that they don't have a crease; this is how you grow okra—far from the house, because okra tree harbors red ants; when you are growing dasheen,[2] make sure it gets plenty of water or else it makes your throat itch when you are eating it; this is how you sweep a corner; this is how you sweep a whole house; this is how you sweep a yard; this is how you smile to someone you don't like too much; this is how you smile to someone you don't like at all; this is how you smile to someone you like completely; this is how you set a table for tea; this is how you set a table for dinner; this is how you set a table for dinner with an important guest; this is how you set a table for lunch; this is how you set a table for breakfast; this is how to behave in the presence of men who don't know you very well, and this way they won't recognize immediately the slut I have warned you against becoming; be sure to wash every day, even if it is with your own spit; don't squat down to play marbles—you are not a boy, you know; don't pick people's flowers—you might catch something; don't throw stones at blackbirds, because it might not be a blackbird at all; this is how to make a bread pudding; this is how to make doukona;[3] this is how to make pepper pot; this is how to make a good medicine for a cold; this is how to make a good medicine to throw away a child before it even becomes a child; this is how to catch a fish; this is how to throw back a fish you don't like, and that way something bad won't fall on you; this is how to bully a man; this is how a man bullies you; this is how to love a man, and if this doesn't work there are other ways, and if they don't work don't feel too bad about giving up; this is how to spit up in the air if you feel like it, and this is how to move quick so that it doesn't fall on you; this is how to make ends meet; always squeeze bread to make sure it's fresh; *but what if the baker won't let me feel the bread?*; you mean to say that after all you are really going to be the kind of woman who the baker won't let near the bread?

QUESTIONS ON MEANING

1. What are the CONNOTATIONS of the phrase "wharf-rat boys"? Why is the girl of the title supposed to avoid them?

[2] Taro, a tropical plant with an edible tuber. —EDS.
[3] A pudding made of plantains, a fruit similar to a banana. —EDS.

2. What does it mean to "be the kind of woman who the baker won't let near the bread" (last line)?
3. What do the elements of the mother's advice add up to: What kind of life does she depict for her daughter?

QUESTIONS ON WRITING STRATEGY

1. Why do you think Kincaid wrote her story as one long sentence? What does she achieve?
2. What does Kincaid convey through the one comment and one question in italics?
3. Toward the end of this story, the mother says, "this is how to spit up in the air if you feel like it, and this is how to move quick so that it doesn't fall on you." What is the EFFECT of this particular piece of advice? What effect would it have if it were the last line of the story?
4. **OTHER METHODS.** The many obligations of a girl/woman can be CLASSIFIED into groups of skills and behaviors. What categories do you see? How do they help organize the story?

QUESTIONS ON LANGUAGE

1. What do the repeated directions about how to "sweep," "smile," and "set a table" suggest?
2. What can you conclude about the girl from the mother's scolding, "don't squat down to play marbles—you are not a boy, you know"?
3. Make sure you know the meanings of the following words: fritters, khaki, okra.
4. The fiction writer Stephanie Vaughn advises reading "Girl" aloud. She says, "I find that it is best to stand up when you read this story aloud, and to take a breath from the deepest region of your belly. When your lungs are full, when your shoulders are back, you begin to speak the story, and then you find that you are singing." Try it yourself. How is reading the story aloud different from reading it to yourself?

SUGGESTIONS FOR WRITING

1. **JOURNAL WRITING.** What warnings or instructions were drilled into you when you were a young adolescent? Who took the responsibility for drilling you? In your journal, describe the advice you remember receiving.
   FROM JOURNAL TO ESSAY. "Adolescents' heads are stuffed with advice intended to make them conform to rigid cultural roles and values." Based on your own experience, do you agree or disagree with this statement? Write an essay explaining your position, using EXAMPLES from your journal entry as support.
2. It's fair to assume that "Girl" is at least partly autobiographical because Kincaid has often written or spoken about the influence of her mother. In "Jamaica Kincaid on Writing" (following), the author mentions rebelling against her mother's "magic." Elsewhere, she has said that her mother's

close attention made Kincaid's past "a kind of museum.... Clearly, the way I became a writer is that my mother wrote my life for me and told it to me." What adult has had a large influence on you? How are you different today because of him or her? Write an essay identifying the parts of yourself that you can attribute to this person — in other words, analyzing yourself as the product of this person's interest (or lack of interest) in you.

3. **CRITICAL WRITING.** The story's speaker repeatedly and gloomily connects her daughter and a "slut." Write an essay analyzing Kincaid's use of *slut*. How does the mother seem to be defining this word? Why does she repeat it so often? Should we ASSUME that the daughter actually is a "slut"? What might be the effect of this repetition on the daughter? What is the effect on you, the reader?

4. **CONNECTIONS.** Judy Brady, in "I Want a Wife" (p. 274), and Kincaid both analyze women's traditional roles, although they have different perspectives on those roles. How are the roles they describe similar? What do the speakers' TONES convey about their attitudes toward their roles? Write an essay explaining how Brady and Kincaid use word choice, sentence structures, repetition, and other elements of tone to clarify their speakers' values and feelings.

JAMAICA KINCAID ON WRITING

In a 1990 interview with Louise Kennedy in the *Boston Globe*, Jamaica Kincaid says that making sense of life is what motivates her writing. "I started out feeling alone," she remarks. "I grew up in a place where I was very alone. I didn't know then that I wanted to write; I didn't have that thought. But even if I had, I would have had no one to tell it to. They would have laughed before they threw me in a pond or something." With this beginning, Kincaid came to believe that the point of writing is not to please the reader. "Sometimes I feel — 'I'm pushed too far, I don't care, I don't care if you don't like this. I know it and it makes sense to me.'" The point, then, is to understand the world through the self. "I'm trying to discover the secret of myself.... For me everything passes through the self."

Kincaid's writing helps her come to terms with the conflicts in her life. "I could be dead or in jail. If you don't know how to make sense of what's happened to you, if you see things but can't express them — it's so painful." Part of Kincaid's pain growing up was the "magic" her mother held over her, a power that fueled Kincaid's rebellion. "That feeling of rebellion is doomed," she says. "You can't succeed. But it's worth trying because you find out that you can't. You have to try, or you die."

Although her native Antigua figures strongly in her writing, Kincaid cannot write there. "When I'm in the place where I'm from, I can't really think. I just absorb it; I take it all in. Then I come back and take it out and unpack it and walk through it." Her need for distance has led her to live in Vermont, "the opposite of where I come from. It changes. It's mountainous. It has seasons." As for Antigua, Kincaid says, "I don't know how to live there, but I don't know how to live without there."

FOR DISCUSSION

1. How can not caring about the reader's response liberate a writer?
2. What does Kincaid mean by "everything passes through the self"? Do you experience this process from time to time?
3. How does the author view her place of birth? Do you find her last statement contradictory?

ADDITIONAL WRITING TOPICS

Division or Analysis

Write an essay by the method of division or analysis using one of the following subjects (or choose your own subject). In your essay, make sure your purpose and your principle of division or analysis are clear to your readers. Explain the parts of your subject so that readers know how each relates to the others and contributes to the whole.

1. The slang or technical terminology of a group such as stand-up comedians or computer hackers
2. An especially bad movie, television show, or book
3. A doll, game, or other toy from childhood
4. A typical TV commercial for a product such as laundry soap, deodorant, beer, or an economy car
5. An appliance or machine, such as a stereo speaker, a motorcycle, a microwave oven, or a camera
6. An organization or association, such as a social club, a sports league, or a support group
7. The characteristic appearance of a rock singer or a classical violinist
8. A year in the life of a student
9. Your favorite poem
10. A short story, essay, or other work that made you think
11. The government of your community
12. The most popular bookstore (or other place of business) in town
13. The Bible
14. A band or orchestra
15. A famous painting or statue

7

week 6
311 - 316

CLASSIFICATION

Sorting into Kinds

337
323

THE METHOD

To CLASSIFY is to make sense of the world by arranging many units—trucks, chemical elements, wasps, students—into more manageable groups. Zoologists classify animals, botanists classify plants—and their classifications help us to understand a vast and complex subject: life on earth. To help us find books in a library, librarians classify books into categories: fiction, biography, history, psychology, and so forth. For the convenience of readers, newspapers run classified advertising, grouping many small ads into categories such as Help Wanted and Cars for Sale.

Subjects and Reasons for Classification

The subject of a classification is always a number of things, such as peaches or political systems. (In contrast, DIVISION OR ANALYSIS, the topic of the preceding chapter, usually deals with a solitary subject, a coherent whole, such as *a* peach or *a* political system.) The job of classification is to sort the things into groups or classes based on their similarities and differences. Say, for instance, you're going to write an essay about how people write. After interviewing a lot of writers, you determine that writers' processes differ widely, mainly in the amount of planning and rewriting they entail. (Notice that this determination involves analyzing the process of writing, separating it into steps. See Chap. 5.) On the basis of your findings, you create groups for planners, one-drafters, and rewriters. Once your groups are defined (and assuming they are valid), your subjects (the writers) almost sort themselves out.

Classification is done for a purpose. In a New York City guidebook, Joan Hamburg and Norma Ketay discuss low-priced hotels. (Notice that already they are examining the members of a group: low-priced as opposed to medium- and high-priced hotels.) They cast the low-priced hotels into categories: Rooms for Singles and Students, Rooms for Families, Rooms for Servicepeople, and Rooms for General Occupancy. Always their purpose is evident: to match up the visitor with a suitable kind of room. When a classification has no purpose, it seems a silly and hollow exercise.

Just as you can ANALYZE a subject (divide a pie) in many ways, you can classify a subject according to many principles. A different New York guidebook might classify all hotels according to price: grand luxury, luxury, commercial, low-priced (Hamburg and Ketay's category), fleabag, and flophouse. The purpose of this classification would be to match visitors to hotels fitting their pocketbooks. The principle you use in classifying things depends on your PURPOSE. A linguist might write an essay classifying the languages of the world according to their origins (Romance languages, Germanic languages, Coptic languages...), but a student battling with a college language requirement might write a humorous essay classifying them into three groups: hard to learn, harder to learn, and unlearnable.

Kinds of Classification

The simplest classification is binary (or two-part), in which you sort things out into (1) those with a certain distinguishing feature and (2) those without it. You might classify a number of persons, let's say, into smokers and nonsmokers, Madonna fans and nonfans, runners and nonrunners, believers and nonbelievers. Binary classification is most useful when your subject is easily divisible into positive and negative categories.

Classification can be complex as well. As Jonathan Swift reminds us,

> So, naturalists observe, a flea
> Hath smaller fleas that on him prey,
> And these have smaller yet to bite 'em.
> And so proceed *ad infinitum*.

In being faithful to reality, you will sometimes find that you have to sort out the members of categories into subcategories. Hamburg and Ketay did something of the kind when they subclassified the class of low-priced New York hotels. Writing about the varieties of one Germanic language, such as English, a writer could identify the subclasses of British English, North American English, Australian English, and so on.

As readers, we all enjoy watching a clever writer sort things into categories. We like to meet classifications that strike us as true and familiar. This pleasure may account for the appeal of magazine articles that classify things ("The Seven Common Garden Varieties of Moocher," "Five Embarrassing Types of Social Blunder"). Usefulness as well as pleasure may explain the popularity of classifications that EVALUATE things. In a survey of current movies, a newspaper critic might classify the films into categories: "Don't Miss," "Worth Seeing," "So-So," and "Never Mind." The magazine *Consumer Reports* uses this method of classifying in its comments on different brands of stereo speakers or canned tuna. Products are sorted into groups (excellent, good, fair, poor, and not acceptable), and the merits of each are discussed by the method of description. (Of a frozen pot pie: "Bottom crust gummy, meat spongy when chewed, with nondescript old-poultry and stale-flour flavor.")

THE PROCESS

Purposes and Theses

Classification will usually come into play when you want to impose order on a numerous and unwieldy subject. (In one essay in this chapter, Robert Reich classifies a huge subject, the people of the United States.) Sometimes you may use classification humorously, as Russell Baker does in another essay in this chapter, to give a charge to familiar experiences. Whichever use you make of classification, though, do it for a reason. The files of composition instructors are littered with student essays in which nothing was ventured and nothing gained by classification.

Things may be classified into categories that reveal truth, or into categories that don't tell us a thing. To sort out ten U.S. cities according to their relative freedom from air pollution, or their cost of living, or the degree of progress they have made in civil rights might prove highly informative and useful. Such a classification might even tell us where we'd want to live. But to sort out the cities according to a superficial feature such as the relative size of their cat and dog populations wouldn't interest anyone, probably, except a veterinarian looking for a job.

Your purpose, your THESIS, and your principle of classification will all overlap at the point where you find your interest in your subject. Say you're curious about how other students write. Is your interest primarily in the materials they use (word processor, typewriter, pencil), in where and when they write, or in how much planning and rewriting they do? Any of these could lead to a principle for sorting the students into groups. And that principle should be revealed in your THESIS SENTENCE (or sentences), letting readers know why you are classifying. Here, from the essays in this chapter, are a few examples of classification thesis sentences:

> Inanimate objects are classified into three major categories—those that don't work, those that break down and those that get lost. (Russell Baker, "The Plot Against People")

> They are revenge effects [of our technology], and they are less the malignant ironies of a spiteful world than the results of a lack of human foresight. They fall into five major categories: repeating, recomplicating, recongesting, regenerating and rearranging. (Edward Tenner, "Voice Mail and Fire Ants")

> In order to see in greater detail what is happening to American jobs, it helps to view the work that most Americans do in terms of new categories that reflect how U.S. workers fit into the global economy. Essentially, three broad categories are emerging. I call them (1) symbolic-analytic services, (2) routine production services, and (3) routine personal services. (Robert B. Reich, "Why the Rich Are Getting Richer and the Poor Poorer")

Categories

For a workable classification, make sure that the categories you choose don't overlap. If you were writing a survey of popular magazines for adults and you were sorting your subject into categories that included women's magazines and sports magazines, you might soon run into trouble. Into which category would you place *Women's Sports?* The trouble is that both categories take in the same item. To avoid this problem, you'll need to reorganize your classification on a different principle. You might sort out the magazines by their audiences: magazines mainly for women, magazines mainly for men, magazines for both women and men. Or you might group them according to subject matter: sports magazines, literary magazines, astrology magazines, fashion magazines, TV fan magazines, trade journals, and so on. *Women's Sports* would fit into either of those classification schemes, but into only *one* category in each scheme.

When you draw up a scheme of classification, be sure also that you include all essential categories. Omitting an important category can weaken the effect of your essay, no matter how well written it is. It would be a major oversight, for example, if you were to classify the residents of a dormitory according to their religious affiliations and not include a category for the numerous nonaffiliated. Your reader might wonder if your sloppiness in forgetting a category extended to your thinking about the topic as well.

Some form of outline can be helpful to keep the classes and their members straight as you develop ideas and write. You might experiment with a diagram in which you jot down headings for the groups, with plenty of space around them, and then let each heading accumulate members as you think of them, the way a magnet attracts paperclips. This kind of diagram offers more flexibility than a vertical list or outline, and it may be a better aid for keeping categories from overlapping or disappearing.

CHECKLIST FOR REVISING A CLASSIFICATION

✔ **PURPOSE.** Have you classified for a reason? Will readers see why you bothered?

✔ **PRINCIPLE OF CLASSIFICATION.** Will readers also see what rule or principle you have used for sorting individuals into groups? Is this principle apparent in your thesis sentence?

✔ **CONSISTENCY.** Does each representative of your subject fall into one category only, so that categories don't overlap?

✔ **COMPLETENESS.** Have you mentioned all the essential categories suggested by your principle of classification?

✔ **EVIDENCE.** Have you provided enough examples for each category so that readers can clearly distinguish one from another?

CLASSIFICATION IN A PARAGRAPH: TWO ILLUSTRATIONS

Using Classification to Write About Television

Most canned laughs produced by laugh machines fall into one of five reliable sounds. There are *titters*, light vocal laughs with which an imaginary audience responds to a comedian's least wriggle or grimace. Some producers rely heavily on *chuckles*, deeper, more chesty responses. Most profound of all, *belly laughs* are summoned to acclaim broader jokes and sexual innuendos. When provided at full level of sound and

Thesis sentence names principle of classification

Categories:
  1. Titters

  2. Chuckles
  3. Belly laughs

in longest duration, the belly laugh becomes the Big Boffola. There are also *wild howls* or *screamers*, extreme responses used not more than three times per show, lest they seem fake. These are crowd laughs, and yet the machine also offers *freaky laughs*, the piercing, eccentric screeches of solitary kooks. With them, a producer affirms that even a canned audience may include one thorny individualist.

4. Wild howls or screams

5. Freaky laughs

Examples clearly distinguish categories

Using Classification in an Academic Discipline

There are two distinct ways of holding and using tools: the *power grip* and the *precision grip*, as John Napier termed them. Human infants and children begin with the power grip and progress to the precision grip. Think of how a child holds a spoon: first in the power grip, in its fist or between its fingers and palm, and later between the tips of the thumb and first two fingers, in the precision grip. Many primates have the power grip also. It is the way they get firm hold of a tree branch. But neither a monkey nor an ape has a thumb long enough or flexible enough to be completely *opposable* through rotation at the wrist, able to reach comfortably to the tips of all the other fingers, as is required for our delicate yet strong precision grip. It is the opposability of our thumb and the independent control of our fingers that make possible nearly all the movements necessary to handle tools, to make clothing, to write with a pencil, to play a flute.
— Bernard Campbell, *Humankind Emerging*

Thesis sentence names principle of classificaton

Two categories explained side by side

Second category explained in greater detail

RUSSELL BAKER

RUSSELL BAKER is one of America's notable humorists and political satirists. He has written his "Observer" column for the *New York Times* for over thirty years, covering topics from the merely bothersome (unreadable menus) to the serious (the Vietnam War). Born in 1925 in Virginia, Baker was raised in New Jersey and Maryland by his widowed mother. After serving in the navy during World War II, he earned a B.A. from Johns Hopkins University in 1947. He became a reporter for the *Baltimore Sun* that year and then joined the *New York Times* in 1954. He covered the State Department, the White House, and Congress until 1962, when he began the column that is now syndicated in over four hundred newspapers. Baker has twice received the Pulitzer Prize, once for distinguished commentary and again for the first volume of his autobiography, *Growing Up* (1982). (The second volume, *The Good Times*, appeared in 1989.) Many of his columns have been collected in books, most recently *There's a Country in My Cellar* (1990). Baker has also written fiction and children's books and edited *Russell Baker's Book of American Humor* (1993). In 1993 he began his television career as host of PBS's *Masterpiece Theatre*.

The Plot Against People

The critic R. Z. Sheppard has commented that Baker can "best be appreciated for doing what a good humorist has always done: writing to preserve his sanity for at least one more day." In this piece from the *New York Times* in 1968, Baker takes aim, as he often does, at things.

Inanimate objects are classified into three major categories — those 1
that don't work, those that break down and those that get lost.

The goal of all inanimate objects is to resist man and ultimately to 2
defeat him, and the three major classifications are based on the method
each object uses to achieve its purpose. As a general rule, any object capable of breaking down at the moment when it is most needed will do
so. The automobile is typical of the category.

With the cunning typical of its breed, the automobile never breaks 3
down while entering a filling station with a large staff of idle mechanics. It waits until it reaches a downtown intersection in the middle of
the rush hour, or until it is fully loaded with family and luggage on the
Ohio Turnpike.

Thus it creates maximum misery, inconvenience, frustration and 4
irritability among its human cargo, thereby reducing its owner's life
span.

Washing machines, garbage disposals, lawn mowers, light bulbs, 5
automatic laundry dryers, water pipes, furnaces, electrical fuses, television tubes, hose nozzles, tape recorders, slide projectors—all are in
league with the automobile to take their turn at breaking down whenever life threatens to flow smoothly for their human enemies.

Many inanimate objects, of course, find it extremely difficult to 6
break down. Pliers, for example, and gloves and keys are almost totally
incapable of breaking down. Therefore, they have had to evolve a different technique for resisting man.

They get lost. Science has still not solved the mystery of how they 7
do it, and no man has ever caught one of them in the act of getting lost.
The most plausible theory is that they have developed a secret method
of locomotion which they are able to conceal the instant a human eye
falls upon them.

It is not uncommon for a pair of pliers to climb all the way from 8
the cellar to the attic in its single-minded determination to raise its
owner's blood pressure. Keys have been known to burrow three feet under mattresses. Women's purses, despite their great weight, frequently
travel through six or seven rooms to find hiding space under a couch.

Scientists have been struck by the fact that things that break down 9
virtually never get lost, while things that get lost hardly ever break
down.

A furnace, for example, will invariably break down at the depth of 10
the first winter cold wave, but it will never get lost. A woman's purse,
which after all does have some inherent capacity for breaking down,
hardly ever does; it almost invariably chooses to get lost.

Some persons believe this constitutes evidence that inanimate ob- 11
jects are not entirely hostile to man, and that a negotiated peace is possible. After all, they point out, a furnace could infuriate a man even
more thoroughly by getting lost than by breaking down, just as a glove
could upset him far more by breaking down than by getting lost.

Not everyone agrees, however, that this indicates a conciliatory at- 12
titude among inanimate objects. Many say it merely proves that furnaces, gloves and pliers are incredibly stupid.

The third class of objects—those that don't work—is the most cu- 13
rious of all. These include such objects as barometers, car clocks, cigarette lighters, flashlights and toy-train locomotives. It is inaccurate, of
course, to say that they never work. They work once, usually for the
first few hours after being brought home, and then quit. Thereafter,
they never work again.

In fact, it is widely assumed that they are built for the purpose of 14
not working. Some people have reached advanced ages without ever
seeing some of these objects—barometers, for example—in working
order.

Science is utterly baffled by the entire category. There are many 15
theories about it. The most interesting holds that the things that don't
work have attained the highest state possible for an inanimate object,
the state to which things that break down and things that get lost can
still only aspire.

They have truly defeated man by conditioning him never to expect 16
anything of them, and in return they have given man the only peace he
receives from inanimate society. He does not expect his barometer to
work, his electric locomotive to run, his cigarette lighter to light or his
flashlight to illuminate, and when they don't it does not raise his blood
pressure.

He cannot attain that peace with furnaces and keys and cars 17
and women's purses as long as he demands that they work for their
keep.

QUESTIONS ON MEANING

1. What is Baker's THESIS?
2. Why don't things that break down get lost, and vice versa?
3. Does Baker have any PURPOSE other than to make his readers smile?
4. How have inanimate objects "defeated man"?

QUESTIONS ON WRITING STRATEGY

1. What is the EFFECT of Baker's principle of classification? What categories are
   omitted here, and why?
2. Find three places where Baker uses HYPERBOLE. What is the EFFECT of this FIG-
   URE OF SPEECH?
3. How does the essay's INTRODUCTION help set its TONE? How does the CONCLU-
   SION reinforce the tone?
4. **OTHER METHODS.** How does Baker use NARRATION to portray inanimate objects in the act of "resisting" people? Discuss how these mini-narratives
   make his classification more persuasive.

QUESTIONS ON LANGUAGE

1. Look up any of these words that are unfamiliar: plausible, locomotion
   (para. 7); invariably, inherent (10); conciliatory (12).
2. What are the CONNOTATIONS of the word "cunning" (para. 3)? What is its effect in this context?
3. Why does Baker use such expressions as "man," "some people," and "their
   human enemies" rather than *I* to describe those who come into conflict
   with inanimate objects? How might the essay have been different if Baker
   had relied on *I*?

SUGGESTIONS FOR WRITING

1. **JOURNAL WRITING.** What other ways can you think of to classify inanimate objects? You may want to expand on Baker's categories or invent new ones of your own based on a different principle (for example, objects no student can live without, or objects no student would be caught dead with).

   FROM JOURNAL TO ESSAY. Write a brief, humorous essay based on one classification system from your journal entry. It may be helpful to use narration or DESCRIPTION in your classification. Figures of speech, especially hyperbole and UNDERSTATEMENT, can help you to establish a comic tone.

2. Think of a topic that would not generally be considered appropriate for a serious classification (some examples: game-show winners, body odors, stupid pet tricks, knock-knock jokes). Select a principle of classification and write a brief essay sorting the subject into categories. You may want to use a humorous tone; then again, you may want to approach the topic "seriously," counting on the contrast between subject and treatment to make your IRONY clear.

3. **CRITICAL WRITING.** In a short essay, discuss the likely AUDIENCE for "The Plot Against People." (Recall that it was first published in the *New York Times*.) What can you INFER from his EXAMPLES about Baker's own age and economic status? Does he ASSUME his audience is similar? How do the connections between author and audience help establish the essay's humor? Could this humor be seen as excluding some readers?

4. **CONNECTIONS.** Edward Tenner, in the next selection, "Voice Mail and Fire Ants," also talks about the "revenge" taken by inanimate objects, but he ultimately puts the blame on human beings. Compare Tenner's and Baker's essays. Which author creates a more persuasive classification? Which is more informative or more entertaining? Why?

RUSSELL BAKER ON WRITING

In "Computer Fallout," an essay from the October 11, 1987, *New York Times Magazine,* Baker sets out to prove that computers make a writer's life easier, but he ends up somewhere else entirely. The skillful way he takes us along with him is what makes the journey enjoyable — and perhaps familiar.

"The wonderful thing about writing with a computer instead of a typewriter or a lead pencil is that it's so easy to rewrite that you can make each sentence almost perfect before moving on to the next sentence.

"An impressive aspect of using a computer to write with

"One of the plusses about a computer on which to write

"Happily, the computer is a marked improvement over both the typewriter and the lead pencil for purposes of literary composition, due to the ease with which rewriting can be effectuated, thus enabling

"What a marked improvement the computer is for the writer over the typewriter and lead pencil

"The typewriter and lead pencil were good enough in their day, but if Shakespeare had been able to access a computer with a good writing program

"If writing friends scoff when you sit down at the computer and say, 'The lead pencil was good enough for Shakespeare

"One of the drawbacks of having a computer on which to write is the ease and rapidity with which the writing can be done, thus leading to the inclusion of many superfluous terms like 'lead pencil,' when the single word 'pencil' would be completely, entirely and utterly adequate.

"The ease with which one can rewrite on a computer gives it an advantage over such writing instruments as the pencil and typewriter by enabling the writer to turn an awkward and graceless sentence into one that is practically perfect, although it

"The writer's eternal quest for the practically perfect sentence may be ending at last, thanks to the computer's gift of editing ease and swiftness to those confronting awkward, formless, nasty, illiterate sentences such as

"Man's quest is eternal, but what specifically is it that he quests, and why does he

"Mankind's quest is

"Man's and woman's quest

"Mankind's and womankind's quest

"Humanity's quest for the perfect writing device

"Eternal has been humanity's quest

"Eternal have been many of humanity's quests

"From the earliest cave writing, eternal has been the quest for a device that will forever prevent writers from using the word 'quest,' particularly when modified by such adjectives as 'eternal,' 'endless,' 'tireless' and

"Many people are amazed at the ease

"Many persons are amazed by the ease

"Lots of people are astounded when they see the nearly perfect sentences I write since upgrading my writing instrumentation from pencil and typewriter to

"Listen, folks, there's nothing to writing almost perfect sentences with ease and rapidity provided you've given up the old horse-and-buggy writing mentality that says Shakespeare couldn't have written those great plays if he had enjoyed the convenience of electronic compositional instrumentation.

"Folks, have you ever realized that there's nothing to writing almost

"Have you ever stopped to think, folks, that maybe Shakespeare could have written even better if

"To be or not to be, that is the central focus of the inquiry.

"In the intrapersonal relationships played out within the mind as to the relative merits of continuing to exist as opposed to not continuing to exist

"Live or die, a choice as ancient as humanities' eternal quest, is a tough choice which has confounded mankind as well as womankind ever since the option of dreaming was first perceived as a potentially negating effect of the quiescence assumed to be obtainable through the latter course of action.

"I'm sick and tired of Luddites saying pencils and typewriters are just as good as computers for writing nearly perfect sentences when they—the Luddites, that is—have never experienced the swiftness and ease of computer writing which makes it possible to compose almost perfect sentences in practically no time at

"Folks, are you sick and tired of

"Are you, dear reader

"Good reader, are you

"A lot of you nice folks out there are probably just as sick and tired as I am of hearing people say they are sick and tired of this and that and

"Listen, people, I'm just as sick and tired as you are of having writers and TV commercial performers who oil me in cornpone politician prose addressed to 'you nice folks out

"A curious feature of computers, as opposed to pencils and typewriters, is that when you ought to be writing something more interesting than a nearly perfect sentence

"Since it is easier to revise and edit with a computer than with a typewriter or pencil, this amazing machine makes it very hard to stop editing and revising long enough to write a readable sentence, much less an entire newspaper column."

FOR DISCUSSION

1. What is Baker's unstated THESIS? Does he convince you?
2. Do you find yourself ever having the problem Baker finally admits to in the last paragraph?

EDWARD TENNER

Born in 1944 in Chicago, EDWARD TENNER is a scholar and writer who takes a special interest in the connections between technology and culture. He received a B.A. from Princeton University (1965) and an M.A. and Ph.D. from the University of Chicago (1967, 1972). From 1975 to 1991 Tenner worked as an editor at Princeton University Press, while also writing articles for the *Princeton Alumni Weekly*, *Harvard Magazine*, and other periodicals. He has published two general-interest books: *Tech Speak: Or, How to Talk High Tech* (1986) and *Why Things Bite Back: Technology and the Revenge of Unintended Consequences* (1996). Currently he is a visiting fellow at Princeton's Department of Geological and Geophysical Sciences.

Voice Mail and Fire Ants

Isn't technology grand? Not always, says Tenner, who sees our inventions taking revenge on us in unanticipated ways. In this essay from the *New York Times* in 1991, he offers a capsule version of his book *Why Things Bite Back*.

Why do the seats get smaller as the airplanes get larger? Why does 1 voice mail seem to double the time to complete a telephone call? Why do filter-tip cigarettes often fail to reduce nicotine intake? Why has the leisure society gone the way of the leisure suit?

The world seems to be getting even with mankind, twisting our 2 cleverness against us. Or we may be unconsciously twisting it ourselves. This is not a new phenomenon, but technology has magnified it. Wherever we look we face unintended consequences of mechanical, chemical, medical, social and financial ingenuity. They are revenge effects, and they are less the malignant ironies of a spiteful world than the results of a lack of human foresight. They fall into five major categories: repeating, recomplicating, recongesting, regenerating and rearranging.

Repeating occurs when a task is made easier or faster but becomes 3 required more often. In the 1980's, companies spent billions of dollars on personal computers, yet in 1989 the service sector showed its smallest productivity growth of the postwar era. For example, when making a spreadsheet was laborious, people did it as seldom and as cautiously as possible. Computers have simplified them, but bosses demand them more often.

Recomplicating is another consequence of computer simplification. 4 Touch-tone telephones were introduced to increase dialing speed, but now the time saved by punching has been consumed by systems built to

take advantage of it. Combining the telephone number, the carrier access code and credit card number, a call may require thirty digits—
more if a voice mail machine answers.

In *recongesting*, an updated function becomes slower and less com-   5
fortable than the original. Technological change opens new frontiers
only to clog them up again. Planners dreamed of the automobile-based
suburb as an antidote to the crowding of cities and the power of rail-
roads and urban landlords. But rapid traffic flow has turned out to be
unrealistic, as cars inch down roads bumper to bumper.

The historian and philosopher Ivan Illich estimates that the aver-   6
age American spends sixteen hundred hours driving or working to support transportation costs "to cover a year total of six thousand miles,
four miles per hour." He says, "This is just as fast as a pedestrian and
slower than a bicycle."

Regenerating appears after a problem seems to have been solved. In-   7
stead, the solution turns out to have revived or amplified the problem.

Pest control regenerates pests. In the 1950's and 1960's, the pesti-   8
cides heptachlor and Mirex killed the natural predators of fire ants,
which then moved into their rivals' territory. DDT devastated wasps,
the natural predators of Malaysian caterpillars, which flourished and
caused large-scale defoliation.

Finally, *rearranging* is the revenge effect that delays a problem or   9
moves it physically, usually magnifying its effect. The geologist W. Bar-
clay Kamb, in John McPhee's *The Control of Nature*, described efforts
to channel the flow of debris from the San Gabriel Mountains in California: "You're not changing the source of the sediment. Those crib-
works are less strong than nature's own constructs. . . . Sooner or later, a
flood will wipe out those small dams and scatter the debris. Everything
you store might come out in one event."

Likewise, suppressing forest fires builds up combustible materials   10
for even larger conflagrations. And disaster control and relief risk increasing casualties by encouraging occupation of unsafe areas.

The existence of revenge effects should not end the pursuit of con-   11
venience and increased productivity. We should bear in mind that
change never offers complete solutions, and be prepared to deal with its
negative consequences. Innovation involves both imperfect machines
and unpredictable people. Revenge effects don't mean that progress is
impossible, only that in planning for it we must look more to Rube
Goldberg than to Isaac Newton.[1]

---

[1] Rube Goldberg (1883–1970) was an American cartoonist known for drawings of
ridiculously complicated machines designed to complete simple tasks. Isaac Newton
(1642–1727) was an English mathematician and philosopher who sought universal
laws of science. He is most famous for discovering gravity. —Eds.

QUESTIONS ON MEANING

1. Locate Tenner's statement of THESIS.
2. Where does Tenner place the blame for the "unintended consequences" (para. 2) of technological advances?
3. Other than increased automobile traffic, what might be another example of "recongesting"?
4. Is Tenner entirely anti-technology? Support your answer with EVIDENCE from the essay.
5. What do you think Tenner's last sentence means?

QUESTIONS ON WRITING STRATEGY

1. What is the EFFECT of this essay's title?
2. Besides the five categories of revenge effects, what other classification does Tenner outline?
3. What is the TONE of the essay? Is it easy to characterize?
4. What is the effect of the statistics Tenner cites in paragraph 6? Do they weigh down the essay unnecessarily, or do they contribute to its persuasiveness?
5. **OTHER METHODS.** This essay demonstrates how the methods of classification and EXAMPLE often go hand in glove. How does Tenner integrate the two methods? How are they interdependent?

QUESTIONS ON LANGUAGE

1. Explain the IRONY at work in the first sentence of paragraph 4.
2. Why do you think that all five of Tenner's revenge effects start with *re-*?
3. Make sure you know the meanings of the following words: malignant (para. 2); spreadsheet (3); antidote (5); defoliation (8); sediment (9); combustible, conflagrations (10).

SUGGESTIONS FOR WRITING

1. **JOURNAL WRITING.** Think of all the ways that technology has improved your life. Write down as many instances as you can in which a new invention has, in your experience, caused a change for the better. You may want to divide your journal page into two columns in order to contrast clearly what things were like before and after the technological change.
   FROM JOURNAL TO ESSAY. Using classification, write an essay defending the view opposite Tenner's: that technological advances do more good than harm. Like Tenner, you will want to use examples (taken from your journal entry) and possibly NARRATION to illustrate your categories of technological improvement.
2. Think of a bad experience you have had with a technological "improvement." It could tie into one of Tenner's examples—troubles with computers or voice mail, for instance, or increased traffic congestion on a familiar

route—or it could be different. Write an essay in which you explain the problem and propose a solution for it. Your solution could be practical or fanciful, but it should be well detailed.

3. **CRITICAL WRITING.** Do you agree with Tenner's essentially pessimistic view of technological progress? Do you find his essay to be fair and balanced, or does he unfairly exaggerate the downside of technology to make his case? Write an EVALUATION of the essay, using specific passages as your evidence.

4. **CONNECTIONS.** "Russell Baker on Writing" (p. 320) details an example of Tenner's revenge effects: Computerized word processing makes revision so easy that we may not be able to stop revising and just write. (Tenner himself mentions the same effect toward the end of "Edward Tenner on Writing," below.) In an essay, explore your experiences with computerized word processing or with any other computerized function, such as preparing spreadsheets, conducting research, or communicating with others via electronic mail or bulletin boards. What are the advantages of the new technology? What are the disadvantages?

EDWARD TENNER ON WRITING

For *The Bedford Reader*, Edward Tenner reveals a number of surprising connections between the science he writes about and the writing he does about science.

"Before I became a full-time writer, I was a science book editor. Working with scientists changed my writing. Many scientists publish, but they usually write for limited audiences. Their papers present theories and experimental evidence concisely to colleagues who often scan graphs and tables before beginning the text. Few scientists write general-interest articles, let alone undertake what I was paid to find and to invite or incite: a book-length manuscript.

"At first, I was frustrated by the reluctance of most of my prospects to write for lay readers; then I learned to respect it. They were working long hours to say something significant and valid. There are few such ideas, whether in science or in the humanities and social sciences. They saw every writing project not necessarily as new knowledge but as a competitor for the limited time available to produce new knowledge. This is no less true in the humanities. For me, writing begins with decisions not to write about many plausible topics.

"It also starts with self-understanding. I am temperamentally an essayist rather than a reporter, just as some scientists are theorists and others experimentalists. Most of what I write starts with some powerful personal experience, as indeed scientific work often does. But once I begin an essay I work less from interviews and observations than from the published record of science, technology, and culture. Instead of explaining a single field, I look for hidden connections among diverse fields. My study of revenge effects began with my daily life, as when I saw more and more paper used in my computerized office. But it eventually drew on risk theory, transportation engineering, microbiology, population biology, and a dozen or more other recognized professions. Eagerness to bring in new theoretical perspectives is also a hallmark of good science.

"I relish the obvious. From scientists I learned that it can be more complex and challenging than anybody imagines. In the last twenty years the sciences of complexity have shown remarkable patterns in falling leaves and curling smoke. Not everything obvious is significant. But I look for a common experience or perception, like Murphy's law,[1] and try to discover what important issues are behind it.

"I use the past, just as biologists, earth scientists, and even astronomers do. My original field was history. But I avoid conventional divisions between past and present. I try to bring a historian's consciousness to the flow of daily culture. I read current newspapers and magazines as a historical record. I clip zealously. In my home office are twelve or more file drawers' worth of photocopies and notes. On my computer's hard drive and my university's file servers, I have many megabytes of electronic notes.

"As a result, I accept waste. Like most scientists and inventors, I am always contemplating multiple plausible ideas. Most of them I will never be able to use. They grow dated; my initial concepts prove wrong; other works appear and limit the market. Some materials are discarded, but others are recombined. Many of the sources of my book *Why Things Bite Back* originated in other files I kept. The more novel a project, the more wasteful it is likely to be.

"Before starting to write, I review my files. I have usually, and deliberately, overresearched, accumulating five to ten times more material than I need. This is another side of creative waste. I need the right quotation, the detail that drives the argument home. With materials at hand, I make a rough diagram linking ideas to each other in clusters. I take time to be sure I have included all major ideas and supporting evidence. Then I make a detailed outline and estimate the number of words per section. Each part is a building block, a module. I not only establish their relative importance; I pace myself and make a sometimes daunting job into a series of manageable ones.

"Once I begin writing, I realize how much I still don't know. Some pet ideas just don't work. If this happens to the greatest scientists and inventors, why shouldn't it happen to me? I persist. I often have to revise my thesis, even my structure. Whole paragraphs or sections are shunted to outtake files, perhaps to be used in future projects, as concepts often are in technology.

[1] Murphy's Law states that if something can go wrong, it will. —Eds.

"After a draft is complete, I tighten it. To bring the hard-won details of research into relief, I look for every word that can be cut or changed to make the essay or book chapter as concise, and precise, as I can make it. True, electronic composition and revision have pitfalls. It is easy to spend time making changes that are neutral at best: a revenge effect if ever there was one. I try to have a colleague's comments at hand as I revise to check my perceptions of what needs attention.

"Finally, I move on to other topics, other problems. It's hard to leave all those research materials in storage, but like so many of the scientists I have known, I find there are just too many new things to study. To me, as to them, writing is a search not only for answers but for new questions."

FOR DISCUSSION

1. What did working with scientists teach Tenner about writing?
2. How does Tenner decide what subjects to write about?
3. What, according to Tenner, is the value of waste in writing? Why is it "creative"?

DEBORAH TANNEN

DEBORAH TANNEN is a linguist who is best known for her popular studies of communication between men and women. Born and raised in New York City, Tannen earned a B.A. from Harpur College (now the State University of New York at Binghamton); M.A.s from Wayne State University and the University of California at Berkeley; and a Ph.D. in linguistics from Berkeley. She is University Professor at Georgetown University, has published many scholarly articles and books, and has lectured on linguistics all over the world. But her renown is more than academic: With television appearances ranging from *CBS News* to *Sally Jessy Raphael*, speeches to businesspeople and senators, scores of articles in newspapers and magazines, and best-selling books like *You Just Don't Understand* (1990) and *Talking from 9 to 5* (1994), Tannen has become, in the words of one reviewer, "America's conversational therapist."

But What Do You Mean?

Why do men and women so often communicate badly, if at all? This question motivates much of Tannen's research and writing, including the essay here. Excerpted in *Redbook* magazine from Tannen's book *Talking from 9 to 5*, "But What Do You Mean?" classifies the conversational areas where men and women have the most difficulty.

Conversation is a ritual. We say things that seem obviously the 1 thing to say, without thinking of the literal meaning of our words, any more than we expect the question "How are you?" to call forth a detailed account of aches and pains.

Unfortunately, women and men often have different ideas about 2 what's appropriate, different ways of speaking. Many of the conversational rituals common among women are designed to take the other person's feelings into account, while many of the conversational rituals common among men are designed to maintain the one-up position, or at least avoid appearing one-down. As a result, when men and women interact—especially at work—it's often women who are at the disadvantage. Because women are not trying to avoid the one-down position, that is unfortunately where they may end up.

Here, the biggest areas of miscommunication. 3

1. Apologies

Women are often told they apologize too much. The reason they're 4 told to stop doing it is that, to many men, apologizing seems synonymous with putting oneself down. But there are many times when "I'm sorry" isn't self-deprecating, or even an apology; it's an automatic way of keeping both speakers on an equal footing. For example, a well-known columnist once interviewed me and gave me her phone number in case I needed to call her back. I misplaced the number and had to go through the newspaper's main switchboard. When our conversation was winding down and we'd both made ending-type remarks, I added, "Oh, I almost forgot—I lost your direct number, can I get it again?" "Oh, I'm sorry," she came back instantly, even though she had done nothing wrong and *I* was the one who'd lost the number. But I understood she wasn't really apologizing; she was just automatically reassuring me she had no intention of denying me her number.

Even when "I'm sorry" *is* an apology, women often assume it will be the first step in a two-step ritual: I say "I'm sorry" and take half the blame, then you take the other half. At work, it might go something like this:

A: When you typed this letter, you missed this phrase I inserted.
B: Oh, I'm sorry. I'll fix it.
A: Well, I wrote it so small it was easy to miss.

When both parties share blame, it's a mutual face-saving device. But if one person, usually the woman, utters frequent apologies and the other doesn't, she ends up looking as if she's taking the blame for mishaps that aren't her fault. When she's only partially to blame, she looks entirely in the wrong.

I recently sat in on a meeting at an insurance company where the sole woman, Helen, said "I'm sorry" or "I apologize" repeatedly. At one point she said, "I'm thinking out loud. I apologize." Yet the meeting was intended to be an informal brainstorming session, and *everyone* was thinking out loud.

The reason Helen's apologies stood out was that she was the only person in the room making so many. And the reason I was concerned was that Helen felt the annual bonus she had received was unfair. When I interviewed her colleagues, they said that Helen was one of the best and most productive workers—yet she got one of the smallest bonuses. Although the problem might have been outright sexism, I suspect her speech style, which differs from that of her male colleagues, masks her competence.

Unfortunately, not apologizing can have its price too. Since so many women use ritual apologies, those who don't may be seen as hard-edged. What's important is to be aware of how often you say you're sorry (and why), and to monitor your speech based on the reaction you get.

2. Criticism

A woman who cowrote a report with a male colleague was hurt   10
when she read a rough draft to him and he leapt into a critical response
—"Oh, that's too dry! You have to make it snappier!" She herself
would have been more likely to say, "That's a really good start. Of
course, you'll want to make it a little snappier when you revise."

Whether criticism is given straight or softened is often a matter of   11
convention. In general, women use more softeners. I noticed this difference when talking to an editor about an essay I'd written. While going over changes she wanted to make, she said, "There's one more
thing. I know you may not agree with me. The reason I noticed the
problem is that your other points are so lucid and elegant." She went
on hedging for several more sentences until I put her out of her misery:
"Do you want to cut that part?" I asked—and of course she did. But I
appreciated her tentativeness. In contrast, another editor (a man) I
once called summarily rejected my idea for an article by barking, "Call
me when you have something new to say."

Those who are used to ways of talking that soften the impact of   12
criticism may find it hard to deal with the right-between-the-eyes style.
It has its own logic, however, and neither style is intrinsically better.
People who prefer criticism given straight are operating on an assumption that feelings aren't involved: "Here's the dope. I know you're good;
you can take it."

3. Thank-Yous

A woman manager I know starts meetings by thanking everyone   13
for coming, even though it's clearly their job to do so. Her "thank-you"
is simply a ritual.

A novelist received a fax from an assistant in her publisher's office;   14
it contained suggested catalog copy for her book. She immediately
faxed him her suggested changes and said, "Thanks for running this by
me," even though her contract gave her the right to approve all copy.
When she thanked the assistant, she fully expected him to reciprocate:
"Thanks for giving me such a quick response." Instead, he said, "You're
welcome." Suddenly, rather than an equal exchange of pleasantries, she
found herself positioned as the recipient of a favor. This made her feel
like responding, "Thanks for nothing!"

Many women use "thanks" as an automatic conversation starter   15
and closer; there's nothing literally to say thank you for. Like many rituals typical of women's conversation, it depends on the goodwill of the
other to restore the balance. When the other speaker doesn't reciprocate, a woman may feel like someone on a seesaw whose partner aban-

doned his end. Instead of balancing in the air, she has plopped to the ground, wondering how she got there.

4. Fighting

Many men expect the discussion of ideas to be a ritual fight— 16 explored through verbal opposition. They state their ideas in the strongest possible terms, thinking that if there are weaknesses someone will point them out, and by trying to argue against those objections, they will see how well their ideas hold up.

Those who expect their own ideas to be challenged will respond to 17 another's ideas by trying to poke holes and find weak links—as a way of *helping*. The logic is that when you are challenged you will rise to the occasion: Adrenaline makes your mind sharper; you get ideas and insights you would not have thought of without the spur of battle.

But many women take this approach as a personal attack. Worse, 18 they find it impossible to do their best work in such a contentious environment. If you're not used to ritual fighting, you begin to hear criticism of your ideas as soon as they are formed. Rather than making you think more clearly, it makes you doubt what you know. When you state your ideas, you hedge in order to fend off potential attacks. Ironically, this is more likely to *invite* attack because it makes you look weak.

Although you may never enjoy verbal sparring, some women find 19 it helpful to learn how to do it. An engineer who was the only woman among four men in a small company found that as soon as she learned to argue she was accepted and taken seriously. A doctor attending a hospital staff meeting made a similar discovery. She was becoming more and more angry with a male colleague who'd loudly disagreed with a point she'd made. Her better judgment told her to hold her tongue, to avoid making an enemy of this powerful senior colleague. But finally she couldn't hold it in any longer, and she rose to her feet and delivered an impassioned attack on his position. She sat down in a panic, certain she had permanently damaged her relationship with him. To her amazement, he came up to her afterward and said, "That was a great rebuttal. I'm really impressed. Let's go out for a beer after work and hash out our approaches to this problem."

5. Praise

A manager I'll call Lester had been on his new job six months 20 when he heard that the women reporting to him were deeply dissatisfied. When he talked to them about it, their feelings erupted; two said they were on the verge of quitting because he didn't appreciate their work, and they didn't want to wait to be fired. Lester was dumbfounded:

He believed they were doing a fine job. Surely, he thought, he had said nothing to give them the impression he didn't like their work. And indeed he hadn't. That was the problem. He had said *nothing*—and the women assumed he was following the adage "If you can't say something nice, don't say anything." He thought he was showing confidence in them by leaving them alone.

Men and women have different habits in regard to giving praise. 21 For example, Deirdre and her colleague William both gave presentations at a conference. Afterward, Deirdre told William, "That was a great talk!" He thanked her. Then she asked, "What did you think of mine?" and he gave her a lengthy and detailed critique. She found it uncomfortable to listen to his comments. But she assured herself that he meant well, and that his honesty was a signal that she, too, should be honest when he asked for a critique of his performance. As a matter of fact, she had noticed quite a few ways in which he could have improved his presentation. But she never got a chance to tell him because he never asked—and she felt put down. The worst part was that it seemed she had only herself to blame, since she *had* asked what he thought of her talk.

But had she really asked for his critique? The truth is, when she 22 asked for his opinion, she was expecting a compliment, which she felt was more or less required following anyone's talk. When he responded with criticism, she figured, "Oh, he's playing 'Let's critique each other' "—not a game she'd initiated, but one which she was willing to play. Had she realized he was going to criticize her and not ask her to reciprocate, she would never have asked in the first place.

It would be easy to assume that Deirdre was insecure, whether she 23 was fishing for a compliment or soliciting a critique. But she was simply talking automatically, performing one of the many conversational rituals that allow us to get through the day. William may have sincerely misunderstood Deirdre's intention—or may have been unable to pass up a chance to one-up her when given the opportunity.

6. Complaints

"Troubles talk" can be a way to establish rapport with a colleague. 24 You complain about a problem (which shows that you are just folks) and the other person responds with a similar problem (which puts you on equal footing). But while such commiserating is common among women, men are likely to hear it as a request to *solve* the problem.

One woman told me she would frequently initiate what she 25 thought would be pleasant complaint-airing sessions at work. She'd talk about situations that bothered her just to talk about them, maybe to understand them better. But her male office mate would quickly tell her how she could improve the situation. This left her feeling condescended to and frustrated. She was delighted to see this very impasse in a section in my book *You Just Don't Understand,* and showed it to him. "Oh," he said, "I see the problem. How can we solve it?" Then they both laughed, because it had happened again: He short-circuited the detailed discussion she'd hoped for and cut to the chase of finding a solution.

Sometimes the consequences of complaining are more serious: A   26
man might take a woman's lighthearted griping literally, and she can get a reputation as a chronic malcontent. Furthermore, she may be seen as not up to solving the problems that arise on the job.

7. Jokes

I heard a man call in to a talk show and say, "I've worked for two   27
women and neither one had a sense of humor. You know, when you work with men, there's a lot of joking and teasing." The show's host and the guest (both women) took his comment at face value and assumed the women this man worked for were humorless. The guest said, "Isn't it sad that women don't feel comfortable enough with authority to see the humor?" The host said, "Maybe when more women are in authority roles, they'll be more comfortable with power." But although the women this man worked for *may* have taken themselves too seriously, it's just as likely that they each had a terrific sense of humor, but maybe the humor wasn't the type he was used to. They may have been like the woman who wrote to me: "When I'm with men, my wit or cleverness seems inappropriate (or lost!) so I don't bother. When I'm with my women friends, however, there's no hold on puns or cracks and my humor is fully appreciated."

The types of humor women and men tend to prefer differ. Research   28
has shown that the most common form of humor among men is razzing, teasing, and mock-hostile attacks, while among women it's self-mocking. Women often mistake men's teasing as genuinely hostile. Men often mistake women's mock self-deprecation as truly putting themselves down.

Women have told me they were taken more seriously when they   29
learned to joke the way the guys did. For example, a teacher who went to a national conference with seven other teachers (mostly women) and a group of administrators (mostly men) was annoyed that the administrators always found reasons to leave boring seminars, while the teachers felt they had to stay and take notes. One evening, when the group met at a bar in the hotel, the principal asked her how one such seminar had turned out. She retorted, "As soon as you left, it got much better." He laughed out loud at her response. The playful insult ap-

pealed to the men—but there was a trade-off. The women seemed to back off from her after this. (Perhaps they were put off by her using joking to align herself with the bosses.)

There is no "right" way to talk. When problems arise, the culprit 30 may be style differences—and *all* styles will at times fail with others who don't share or understand them, just as English won't do you much good if you try to speak to someone who knows only French. If you want to get your message across, it's not a question of being "right"; it's a question of using language that's shared—or at least understood.

QUESTIONS ON MEANING

1. What is Tannen's PURPOSE in writing this essay? What does she hope it will accomplish?
2. What does Tannen mean when she writes, "Conversation is a ritual" (para. 1)?
3. What does Tannen see as the fundamental difference between men's and women's conversational strategies?
4. Why is "You're welcome" not always an appropriate response to "Thank you"?

QUESTIONS ON WRITING STRATEGY

1. This essay has a large cast of characters: twenty-three to be exact. What function do these characters serve? How does Tannen introduce them to the reader? Does she describe them in sufficient detail?
2. How does Tannen's DESCRIPTION of a columnist as "well-known" (para. 4) contribute to the effectiveness of her EXAMPLE?
3. Whom does Tannen see as her primary AUDIENCE? ANALYZE her use of the pronoun *you* in paragraphs 9 and 19. Whom does she seem to be addressing here? Why?
4. **OTHER METHODS.** For each of her seven areas of miscommunication, Tannen COMPARES AND CONTRASTS male and female communication styles and strategies. SUMMARIZE the main source of misunderstanding in each area.

QUESTIONS ON LANGUAGE

1. What is the EFFECT of "I put her out of her misery" (para. 11)? What does this phrase usually mean?
2. What does Tannen mean by a "right-between-the-eyes style" (para. 12)? What is the METAPHOR involved here?
3. What is the effect of Tannen's use of figurative verbs, such as "barking" (para. 11) and "erupted" (20)? Find at least one other example of the use of a verb in a nonliteral sense.

4. Look up any of the following words whose meanings you are unsure of: self-deprecating, synonymous (para. 4); lucid, tentativeness (11); intrinsically (12); reciprocate (14); adrenaline, spur (17); contentious, hedge (18); sparring, rebuttal (19); adage (20); soliciting (23); commiserating (24); initiate, condescended, impasse (25); chronic, malcontent (26); razzing (28); retorted (29).

SUGGESTIONS FOR WRITING

1. **JOURNAL WRITING.** Tannen's ANECDOTE about the newspaper columunist (para. 4) illustrates that much of what we say is purely automatic. Do you excuse yourself when you bump into inanimate objects? When someone says, "Have a good trip," do you answer, "You too," even if the other person isn't going anywhere? Do you find yourself overusing certain words or phrases such as "like" or "you know"? Pay close attention to these kinds of verbal tics in your own and others' speech. Over the course of a few days, note as many of them as you can in your journal.
   FROM JOURNAL TO ESSAY. Write an essay classifying the examples from your journal into categories of your own devising. You might sort out the examples by context ("phone blunders," "faulty farewells"), by purpose ("nervous tics," "space fillers"), or by some other principle of classification. Given your subject matter, you might want to adopt a humorous TONE.

2. How well does your STYLE of communication conform to that of your gender as described by Tannen? Write a short essay about a specific communication problem or misunderstanding you have had with someone of the opposite sex (sibling, friend, parent, significant other). How well does Tannen's differentiation of male and female communication styles account for your particular problem?

3. How true do you find Tannen's assessment of miscommunication between the sexes? Consider the conflicts you have observed between your parents, among fellow students or coworkers, in fictional portrayals in books and movies. Are Tannen's conclusions confirmed or called into question by your own observations and experiences? Write an essay confirming or questioning Tannen's GENERALIZATIONS, using your own examples.

4. **CRITICAL WRITING.** Tannen insists that "neither [communication] style is intrinsically better" (para. 12), that "There is no 'right' way to talk" (30). What do you make of this refusal to take sides in the battle of the sexes? Is Tannen always successful? Is absolute neutrality possible, or even desirable, when it comes to such divisive issues?

5. **CONNECTIONS.** What pictures of men and women emerge from Tannen's essay and from Dave Barry's "Batting Clean-Up and Striking Out" (p. 188)? In an essay, DEFINE each sex as portrayed by these two authors, and then agree or disagree with the definitions. Support your opinions with examples from your own observations and experience.

STEPHANIE ERICSSON

STEPHANIE ERICSSON is an insightful and frank writer who composes out of her own life. Her book on loss, *Companion Through the Darkness: Inner Dialogues on Grief* (1993), grew out of journal entries and extensive research into the grieving process following the sudden death of her husband while she was pregnant. Ericsson was born in 1953, grew up in San Francisco, and began writing at the age of fifteen. After studying filmmaking in college, she became a screenwriter's assistant and later a writer of situation comedies and advertising. During these years she struggled with substance abuse; after her recovery in 1980 she published *Shamefaced* and *Women of AA: Recovering Together* (both 1985). *Companion into the Dawn: Inner Dialogues on Loving* (1994) is Ericsson's most recent book. She lives in Minneapolis and Mexico with her two children.

The Ways We Lie

Ericsson wrote this essay from notes for *Companion into the Dawn*, and it was published in the *Utne Reader* for November/December 1992. We all lie, Ericsson finds; indeed, lying may be unavoidable and even sometimes beneficial. But then how do we know when to stop?

1   The bank called today and I told them my deposit was in the mail, even though I hadn't written a check yet. It'd been a rough day. The baby I'm pregnant with decided to do aerobics on my lungs for two hours, our three-year-old daughter painted the living-room couch with lipstick, the IRS put me on hold for an hour, and I was late to a business meeting because I was tired.

2   I told my client that traffic had been bad. When my partner came home, his haggard face told me his day hadn't gone any better than mine, so when he asked, "How was your day?" I said, "Oh, fine," knowing that one more straw might break his back. A friend called and wanted to take me to lunch. I said I was busy. Four lies in the course of a day, none of which I felt the least bit guilty about.

3   We lie. We all do. We exaggerate, we minimize, we avoid confrontation, we spare people's feelings, we conveniently forget, we keep secrets, we justify lying to the big-guy institutions. Like most people, I indulge in small falsehoods and still think of myself as an honest person. Sure I lie, but it doesn't hurt anything. Or does it?

4   I once tried going a whole week without telling a lie, and it was paralyzing. I discovered that telling the truth all the time is nearly impossible. It means living with some serious consequences: The bank

charges me $60 in overdraft fees, my partner keels over when I tell him about my travails, my client fires me for telling her I didn't feel like being on time, and my friend takes it personally when I say I'm not hungry. There must be some merit to lying.

But if I justify lying, what makes me any different from slick politicians or the corporate robbers who raided the S&L industry? Saying it's okay to lie one way and not another is hedging. I cannot seem to escape the voice deep inside me that tells me: When someone lies, someone loses.

What far-reaching consequences will I, or others, pay as a result of my lie? Will someone's trust be destroyed? Will someone else pay *my* penance because I ducked out? We must consider the *meaning of our actions*. Deception, lies, capital crimes, and misdemeanors all carry meanings. *Webster's* definition of *lie* is specific:

1: a false statement or action especially made with the intent to deceive; 2: anything that gives or is meant to give a false impression.

A definition like this implies that there are many, many ways to tell a lie. Here are just a few.

The White Lie

A man who won't lie to a woman has very little consideration for her feelings.
—Bergen Evans

The white lie assumes that the truth will cause more damage than a simple, harmless untruth. Telling a friend he looks great when he looks like hell can be based on a decision that the friend needs a compliment more than a frank opinion. But, in effect, it is the liar deciding what is best for the lied to. Ultimately, it is a vote of no confidence. It is an act of subtle arrogance for anyone to decide what is best for someone else.

Yet not all circumstances are quite so cut-and-dried. Take, for instance, the sergeant in Vietnam who knew one of his men was killed in action but listed him as missing so that the man's family would receive indefinite compensation instead of the lump-sum pittance the military gives widows and children. His intent was honorable. Yet for twenty years this family kept their hopes alive, unable to move on to a new life.

Façades

Et tu, Brute?
—Caesar

We all put up façades to one degree or another. When I put on a suit to go to see a client, I feel as though I am putting on another face, obeying the expectation that serious businesspeople wear suits rather than sweatpants. But I'm a writer. Normally, I get up, get the kid off to school, and sit at my computer in my pajamas until four in the afternoon. When I answer the phone, the caller thinks I'm wearing a suit (though the UPS man knows better).

But façades can be destructive because they are used to seduce others 11 into an illusion. For instance, I recently realized that a former friend was a liar. He presented himself with all the right looks and the right words and offered lots of new consciousness theories, fabulous books to read, and fascinating insights. Then I did some business with him, and the time came for him to pay me. He turned out to be all talk and no walk. I heard a plethora of reasonable excuses, including in-depth descriptions of the big break around the corner. In six months of work, I saw less than a hundred bucks. When I confronted him, he raised both eyebrows and tried to convince me that I'd heard him wrong, that he'd made no commitment to me. A simple investigation into his past revealed a crowded graveyard of disenchanted former friends.

Ignoring the Plain Facts

Well, you must understand that Father Porter is only human. . . .
— A Massachusetts priest

In the '60s, the Catholic Church in Massachusetts began hear- 12 ing complaints that Father James Porter was sexually molesting children. Rather than relieving him of his duties, the ecclesiastical authorities simply moved him from one parish to another between 1960 and 1967, actually providing him with a fresh supply of unsuspecting families and innocent children to abuse. After treatment in 1967 for pedophilia, he went back to work, this time in Minnesota. The new diocese was aware of Father Porter's obsession with children, but they needed priests and recklessly believed treatment had cured him. More children were abused until he was relieved of his duties a year later. By his own admission, Porter may have abused as many as a hundred children.

Ignoring the facts may not in and of itself be a form of lying, but 13 consider the context of this situation. If a lie is *a false action done with the intent to deceive,* then the Catholic Church's conscious covering for Porter created irreparable consequences. The church became a co-perpetrator with Porter.

Deflecting   *funioe*

When you have no basis for an argument, abuse the plaintiff.
— Cicero

I've discovered that I can keep anyone from seeing the true me by 14 being selectively blatant. I set a precedent of being up-front about intimate issues, but I never bring up the things I truly want to hide; I just let people assume I'm revealing everything. It's an effective way of hiding.

Any good liar knows that the way to perpetuate an untruth is to de-   15
flect attention from it. When Clarence Thomas exploded with accusations that the Senate hearings were a "high-tech lynching," he simply switched the focus from a highly charged subject to a radioactive subject.[1] Rather than defending himself, he took the offensive and accused the country of racism. It was a brilliant maneuver. Racism is now politically incorrect in official circles—unlike sexual harassment, which still rewards those who can get away with it.

Some of the most skilled deflectors are passive-aggressive people   16
who, when accused of inappropriate behavior, refuse to respond to the accusations. This you-don't-exist stance infuriates the accuser, who, understandably, screams something obscene out of frustration. The trap is sprung and the act of deflection successful, because now the passive-aggressive person can indignantly say, "Who can talk to someone as unreasonable as you?" The real issue is forgotten and the sins of the original victim become the focus. Feeling guilty of name-calling, the victim is fully tamed and crawls into a hole, ashamed. I have watched this fighting technique work thousands of times in disputes between men and women, and what I've learned is that the real culprit is not necessarily the one who swears the loudest.

Omission   *ispoustenje*

The cruelest lies are often told in silence.
—R. L. Stevenson

Omission involves telling most of the truth minus one or two key   17
facts whose absence changes the story completely. You break a pair of glasses that are guaranteed under normal use and get a new pair, without mentioning that the first pair broke during a rowdy game of basketball. Who hasn't tried something like that? But what about omission of information that could make a difference in how a person lives his or her life?

For instance, one day I found out that rabbinical legends tell of an-   18
other woman in the Garden of Eden before Eve. I was stunned. The omission of the Sumerian goddess Lilith from Genesis—as well as her demonization by ancient misogynists as an embodiment of female evil —felt like spiritual robbery. I felt like I'd just found out my mother was really my stepmother. To take seriously the tradition that Adam was created out of the same mud as his equal counterpart, Lilith, redefines all of Judeo-Christian history.

[1] Ericsson refers to the 1991 hearings to confirm Thomas for the Supreme Court, at which Thomas was accused by Anita Hill of sexual harassment.—EDS.

Some renegade Catholic feminists introduced me to a view of   19
Lilith that had been suppressed during the many centuries when this
strong goddess was seen only as a spirit of evil. Lilith was a proud goddess who defied Adam's need to control her, attempted negotiations,
and when this failed, said adios and left the Garden of Eden.

This omission of Lilith from the Bible was a patriarchal strategy to   20
keep women weak. Omitting the strong-woman archetype of Lilith
from Western religions and starting the story with Eve the Rib has
helped keep Christian and Jewish women believing they were the
lesser sex for thousands of years.

Stereotypes and Clichés

*Where opinion does not exist, the status quo becomes stereotyped and all
originality is discouraged.*

— Bertrand Russell

Stereotype and cliché serve a purpose as a form of shorthand. Our   21
need for vast amounts of information in nanoseconds has made the
stereotype vital to modern communication. Unfortunately, it often
shuts down original thinking, giving those hungry for the truth a candy
bar of misinformation instead of a balanced meal. The stereotype explains a situation with just enough truth to seem unquestionable.

All the "isms"—racism, sexism, ageism, et al.—are founded on   22
and fueled by the stereotype and the cliché, which are lies of exaggeration, omission, and ignorance. They are always dangerous. They take a
single tree and make it a landscape. They destroy curiosity. They close
minds and separate people. The single mother on welfare is assumed to
be cheating. Any black male could tell you how much of his identity
is obliterated daily by stereotypes. Fat people, ugly people, beautiful
people, old people, large-breasted women, short men, the mentally ill,
and the homeless all could tell you how much more they are like us than
we want to think. I once admitted to a group of people that I had a
mouth like a truck driver. Much to my surprise, a man stood up and said,
"I'm a truck driver, and I never cuss." Needless to say, I was humbled.

Groupthink

*Who is more foolish, the child afraid of the dark, or the man afraid of the
light?*

— Maurice Freehill

Irving Janis, in *Victims of Group Think*, defines this sort of lie as a   23
psychological phenomenon within decision-making groups in which
loyalty to the group has become more important than any other value,

with the result that dissent and the appraisal of alternatives are suppressed. If you've ever worked on a committee or in a corporation,
you've encountered groupthink. It requires a combination of other
forms of lying—ignoring facts, selective memory, omission, and denial,
to name a few.

The textbook example of groupthink came on December 7, 1941. 24
From as early as the fall of 1941, the warnings came in, one after another, that Japan was preparing for a massive military operation. The
Navy command in Hawaii assumed Pearl Harbor was invulnerable—
the Japanese weren't stupid enough to attack the United States' most
important base. On the other hand, racist stereotypes said the Japanese
weren't smart enough to invent a torpedo effective in less than 60 feet
of water (the fleet was docked in 30 feet); after all, U.S. technology
hadn't been able to do it.

On Friday, December 5, normal weekend leave was granted to all 25
the commanders at Pearl Harbor, even though the Japanese consulate
in Hawaii was busy burning papers. Within the tight, good-ole-boy
cohesiveness of the U.S. command in Hawaii, the myth of invul-
nerability stayed well entrenched. No one in the group considered the
alternatives. The rest is history.

Out-and-Out Lies

The only form of lying that is beyond reproach is lying for its own sake.
—Oscar Wilde

Of all the ways to lie, I like this one the best, probably because I get 26
tired of trying to figure out the real meanings behind things. At least I
can trust the bald-faced lie. I once asked my five-year-old nephew,
"Who broke the fence?" (I had seen him do it.) He answered, "The
murderers." Who could argue?

At least when this sort of lie is told it can be easily confronted. 27
As the person who is lied to, I know where I stand. The bald-faced lie
doesn't toy with my perceptions—it argues with them. It doesn't try to
refashion reality, it tries to refute it. *Read my lips*...No sleight of hand.
No guessing. If this were the only form of lying, there would be no such
things as floating anxiety or the adult-children-of-alcoholics movement.

Dismissal

Pay no attention to that man behind the curtain! I am the Great Oz!
—The Wizard of Oz

Dismissal is perhaps the slipperiest of all lies. Dismissing feelings, 28
perceptions, or even the raw facts of a situation ranks as a kind of

lie that can do as much damage to a person as any other kind of lie.

The roots of many mental disorders can be traced back to the dismissal of reality. Imagine that a person is told from the time she is a tot that her perceptions are inaccurate. *"Mommy, I'm scared."* "No you're not, darling." *"I don't like that man next door, he makes me feel icky."* "Johnny, that's a terrible thing to say, of course you like him. You go over there right now and be nice to him." 29

I've often mused over the idea that madness is actually a sane reaction to an insane world. Psychologist R. D. Laing supports this hypothesis in *Sanity, Madness and the Family,* an account of his investigation into the families of schizophrenics. The common thread that ran through all of the families he studied was a deliberate, staunch dismissal of the patient's perceptions from a very early age. Each of the patients started out with an accurate grasp of reality, which, through meticulous and methodical dismissal, was demolished until the only reality the patient could trust was catatonia. 30

Dismissal runs the gamut. Mild dismissal can be quite handy for forgiving the foibles of others in our day-to-day lives. Toddlers who have just learned to manipulate their parents' attention sometimes are dismissed out of necessity. Absolute attention from the parents would require so much energy that no one would get to eat dinner. But we must be careful and attentive about how far we take our "necessary" dismissals. Dismissal is a dangerous tool, because it's nothing less than a lie. 31

Delusion

We lie loudest when we lie to ourselves.
—Eric Hoffer

I could write the book on this one. Delusion, a cousin of dismissal, is the tendency to see excuses as facts. It's a powerful lying tool because it filters out information that contradicts what we want to believe. Alcoholics who believe that the problems in their lives are legitimate reasons for drinking rather than results of the drinking offer the classic example of deluded thinking. Delusion uses the mind's ability to see things in myriad ways to support what it wants to be the truth. 32

But delusion is also a survival mechanism we all use. If we were to fully contemplate the consequences of our stockpiles of nuclear weapons or global warming, we could hardly function on a day-to-day level. We don't want to incorporate that much reality into our lives because to do so would be paralyzing. 33

Delusion acts as an adhesive to keep the status quo intact. It shamelessly employs dismissal, omission, and amnesia, among other sorts of lies. Its most cunning defense is that it cannot see itself. 34

• • •

The liar's punishment . . . is that he cannot believe anyone else.
—George Bernard Shaw

These are only a few of the ways we lie. Or are lied to. As I said earlier, it's not easy to entirely eliminate lies from our lives. No matter how pious we may try to be, we will still embellish, hedge, and omit to lubricate the daily machinery of living. But there is a world of difference between telling functional lies and living a lie. Martin Buber once said, "The lie is the spirit committing treason against itself." Our acceptance of lies becomes a cultural cancer that eventually shrouds and reorders reality until moral garbage becomes as invisible to us as water is to a fish. 35

How much do we tolerate before we become sick and tired of being sick and tired? When will we stand up and declare our *right* to trust? When do we stop accepting that the real truth is in the fine print? Whose lips do we read this year when we vote for president? When will we stop being so reticent about making judgments? When do we stop turning over our personal power and responsibility to liars? 36

Maybe if I don't tell the bank the check's in the mail I'll be less tolerant of the lies told me every day. A country song I once heard said it all for me: "You've got to stand for something or you'll fall for anything." 37

QUESTIONS ON MEANING

1. What is Ericsson's THESIS?
2. Does Ericsson think it's possible to eliminate lies from our lives? What EVIDENCE does she offer?
3. If it were possible to eliminate lies from our lives, why would that be desirable?
4. What is this essay's PURPOSE?

QUESTIONS ON WRITING STRATEGY

1. Ericsson starts out by recounting her own four-lie day (paras. 1–2). What is the EFFECT of this INTRODUCTION?
2. At the beginning of each kind of lie, Ericsson provides an epigraph, a short quotation that forecasts a theme. Which of these epigraphs work best, do you think? What are your criteria for judgment?
3. What is the message of Ericsson's CONCLUSION? Does the conclusion work well? Why, or why not?
4. **OTHER METHODS.** Examine the way Ericsson uses DEFINITION and EXAMPLE to support her classification. Which definitions are clearest? Which examples are the most effective? Why?

QUESTIONS ON LANGUAGE

1. In paragraph 35, Ericsson writes, "Our acceptance of lies becomes a cultural cancer that eventually shrouds and reorders reality until moral garbage becomes as invisible to us as water is to a fish." How do the two METAPHORS in this sentence—cancer and garbage—relate to each other?
2. Occasionally Ericsson's anger shows through, as in paragraphs 12–13 and 18–20. Is the TONE appropriate in these cases? Why, or why not?
3. Look up any of these words you do not know: haggard (para. 2); travails (4); façades (10); plethora (11); ecclesiastical, pedophilia (12); irreparable, co-perpetrator (13); patriarchal, archetype (20); gamut (31); myriad (32); reticent (36).
4. Ericsson uses several words and phrases from the fields of psychology and sociology. Define: passive-aggressive (para. 16); floating anxiety, adult-children-of-alcoholics movement (27); schizophrenics, catatonia (30).

SUGGESTIONS FOR WRITING

1. **JOURNAL WRITING.** Ericsson says, "We lie. We all do" (para. 3), and that must mean you, too. Write about some of the lies you have told. Why did you lie? What were the consequences?
   FROM JOURNAL TO ESSAY. Develop one or more of the lies you've recalled into an essay. You may choose to elaborate on your lies by classifying according to some principle or by NARRATING the story of a particular lie and its outcome. Try to give your reader a sense of your motivation for lying in the first place.
2. Ericsson writes, "All the 'isms'—racism, sexism, ageism, et al.—are founded on and fueled by the stereotype and the cliché, which are lies of exaggeration, omission, and ignorance. They are always dangerous. They take a single tree and make it a landscape" (para. 22). Write an essay discussing stereotypes and how they work to encourage prejudice. Use Ericsson's definition as a base, and expand it to include stereotypes you find particularly injurious. How do these stereotypes oversimplify? How are they "dangerous"?
3. **CRITICAL WRITING.** EVALUATE the success of Ericsson's essay, considering especially how effectively her evidence supports her GENERALIZATIONS. Are there important categories she overlooks, exceptions she neglects to account for, gaps in definitions or examples? Offer specific evidence for your own view, whether positive or negative.
4. **CONNECTIONS.** Deborah Tannen, in "But What Do You Mean?" (p. 329), also writes about communication, but she emphasizes the differences in men's and women's styles. Read or reread Tannen's essay, and then in its light reconsider Ericsson's essay. Do you think some kinds of lies are more likely to be told by women or by men? (For instance, are women, in an effort to avoid conflict, more likely to tell white lies?) Or are gender distinctions irrelevant with lies? In an essay, express your opinion and support it with evidence from the essays and your own experience.

ROBERT B. REICH

ROBERT B. REICH was most recently secretary of labor in the administration of President Bill Clinton. Before his appointment, he was already well known as a writer, teacher, and leader of the "neoliberals"—those seeking ways for the United States to achieve economic strength without sacrificing social programs. Reich was born in 1946 in Scranton, Pennsylvania, and attended Dartmouth College, Oxford University (as a Rhodes Scholar), and Yale Law School. He was active in liberal politics in the late 1960s, worked in the federal government for some years, and taught at Harvard University's John F. Kennedy School of Government. Reich has contributed to the *Atlantic*, the *Harvard Business Review, The New Republic,* and other periodicals. He has written numerous books, among them *The Next American Frontier* (1983), *Tales of a New America* (1987), *The Work of Nations* (1991), and *American Competitiveness and American Brains* (1993). A collection of essays, *The Resurgent Liberal (and Other Unfashionable Prophesies),* was published in 1989.

Why the Rich Are Getting Richer and the Poor Poorer

This essay first appeared in May 1989 in *The New Republic*. Though Reich cites trends from the 1980s, his thesis is not dated: As he says, the changes he discusses are worldwide and far from over. What's needed for our country, Reich has said elsewhere, is a "true patriotism" that is based on "a common concern for, and investment in, the well-being of our future citizens." Reich's classification was reprinted in the January/February 1990 *Utne Reader*.

Between 1978 and 1987, the poorest fifth of American families became 8 percent poorer, and the richest fifth became 13 percent richer. That means the poorest fifth now have less than 5 percent of the nation's income, while the richest fifth have more than 40 percent.

This widening gap can't be blamed on the growth in single-parent lower-income families, which in fact slowed markedly after the late 1970s. Nor is it due mainly to the stingy social policies of the Reagan years. Granted, food stamp benefits have dropped 13 percent since 1981 (in real terms), and many states have failed to raise benefits for the poor and unemployed to keep up with inflation. But this doesn't come close to accounting for the growing persistence of economic inequality in the United States. Rather, this disturbing trend is connected to a profound change in the American economy as it merges with the global economy. And because the merging is far from complete, this trend will not stop all by itself anytime soon. It is significant that the growth of inequality can be seen most strikingly among Americans who have jobs. Through most of the postwar era, the wages of Americans at different income levels rose at about the same pace. Although different workers occupied different steps on the escalator, everyone moved up together. In those days poverty was the condition of *jobless* Americans, and the major economic challenge was to create enough jobs for everyone. Once people were safely in the work force, their problems were assumed to be over. Thus "full employment" became a liberal rallying cry.

But in recent years Americans with jobs have been traveling on 3
two escalators—one going up, the other going down. In 1987 the average hourly earnings of nonsupervisory workers (adjusted for inflation) were lower than in any year since 1966. Middle-level managers fared much better, although their median real earnings were only slightly above the levels of the 1970s. Executives, however, did spectacularly well. In 1988 alone, CEOs of the 100 largest publicly held industrial corporations received raises averaging almost 12 percent.

Between 1978 and 1987, as the real earnings of unskilled workers 4
were declining, the real incomes of investment bankers and other securities industry workers rose 21 percent. It is not unusual for a run-of-the-mill investment banker to bring home comfortably over a million dollars. Meanwhile, the number of impoverished *working* Americans climbed by nearly two million, or 23 percent, during those same years. Nearly 60 percent of the 20 million people who now fall below the Census Bureau's poverty line are from families with at least one member in full-time or part-time work.

The American economy now exhibits a wider gap between rich 5
and poor than it has at any other time since World War II. The most basic reason, put simply, is that America itself is ceasing to exist as an economic system separate from the rest of the world. One can no more meaningfully speak of an "American economy" than of a "Delaware economy." We are becoming but a region—albeit still a relatively wealthy region—of a global economy. This is a new kind of economy whose technologies, savings, and investments move effortlessly across borders, making it harder for individual nations to control their economic destinies.

We have yet to come to terms with the rise of the global corpora- 6
tion, whose managers, shareholders, and employees span the world. Our debates over the future of American jobs still focus on topics such as the competitiveness of the American automobile industry or the

future of American manufacturing. But these issues are increasingly irrelevant.

New technologies of worldwide communication and transporta-   7
tion have redrawn the economic playing field. American industries no
longer compete against Japanese or European industries. Rather, a
company with headquarters in the United States, production facilities
in Taiwan, and a marketing force spread across many nations competes
with another, similarly wide-ranging company. So when General Motors, say, is doing well, that probably is good news for a lot of executives
in Detroit, and for GM shareholders across the globe, but it isn't necessarily good news for a lot of assembly-line workers in Detroit, because
there may, in fact, be very few GM assembly-line workers in Detroit, or
anywhere else in America. The welfare of assembly-line workers in Detroit may depend, instead, on the health of corporations based in Japan
or Canada.

More to the point, even if those Canadian and Japanese corpora-   8
tions are doing well, those Detroit workers may be in trouble. For they
are increasingly part of an international labor market, encompassing
Asia, Africa, Western Europe, and, perhaps before long, Eastern Europe. With relative ease corporations can relocate their production
centers to take advantage of low wages. So American workers find
themselves settling for low wages in order to hold on to their jobs.
More and more, your "competitiveness" as a worker depends not on the
fortunes of any American corporation, or of any American industry,
but on what function you serve within the global economy.

In order to see in greater detail what is happening to American   9
jobs, it helps to view the work that most Americans do in terms of new
categories that reflect how U.S. workers fit into the global economy. Essentially, three broad categories are emerging. I call them (1) symbolic-
analytic services, (2) routine production services, and (3) routine personal services.

1. Symbolic-analytic services are based on the manipulation of   10
information: data, words, and oral and visual symbols. Symbolic analysis comprises some (but by no means all) of the work undertaken by
people who call themselves lawyers, investment bankers, commercial bankers, management consultants, research scientists, academics,
public-relations executives, real estate developers, and even a few creative accountants. Also, many advertising and marketing specialists,
art directors, design engineers, architects, writers and editors, musicians, and television and film producers.

Some of the manipulations of information performed by these sym-   11
bolic analysts offer ways of more efficiently deploying resources or shift-

ing financial assets, or of otherwise saving time and energy. Other manipulations grab money from people who are too slow or naive to protect themselves. Still others serve to entertain the public.

Most symbolic analysts work alone or in small teams. If they work 12
with others, they often have partners rather than bosses or supervisors. Their work environments tend to be quiet and tastefully decorated, often within tall steel-and-glass buildings. When they are not analyzing, designing, or strategizing, they are in meetings or on the telephone — giving advice or making deals. Many of them spend an inordinate amount of time in jet planes and hotels. They are generally articulate and well groomed. The vast majority are white males.

Symbolic analysis now accounts for more than 40 percent of America's gross national product, and almost 20 percent of our jobs. 13

The services performed by America's symbolic analysts are in high 14
demand around the world. The Japanese are buying up the insights and inventions of America's scientists and engineers (who are only too happy to sell them at a fat profit). The Europeans, meanwhile, are hiring our management consultants, business strategists, and investment bankers. Developing nations are hiring our civil and design engineers; and almost everyone is buying the output of our pop musicians, television stars, and film producers.

The same thing is happening with the global corporation. The 15
central offices of these sprawling entities, headquartered in America, are filled with symbolic analysts who manipulate information and then export their insights around the world via the corporation's far-flung operations. IBM, for instance, doesn't export machines from the United States; it manufactures its machines in factories all over the globe. IBM world headquarters, in Armonk, New York, exports just strategic planning and related management services.

Thus has the standard of living of America's symbolic analysts 16
risen. They increasingly find themselves part of a global labor market, not a national one. And because the United States has a highly developed economy, and an excellent university system, they find that the services they have to offer are in high demand around the whole world. This ensures that their salaries are quite high.

Those salaries are likely to go even higher in the years ahead, as the 17
world market for symbolic analysis continues to grow. Foreigners are trying to learn these skills and techniques, to be sure, but they still have a long way to go. No other country does a better job of preparing its most fortunate citizens for symbolic analysis than does the United States. None has surpassed America in providing experience and training, often with entire regions specializing in one or another kind of symbolic analysis (New York and Chicago for finance, Los Angeles for music and film, the San Francisco Bay area and greater Boston for sci-

ence and engineering). In this we can take pride. But for the second major category of American workers—the providers of routine production services—the future doesn't bode well.

2. Routine production services involve tasks that are repeated 18 over and over, as one step in a sequence of steps for producing a finished product. Although we tend to associate these jobs with manufacturing, they are becoming common in banking, insurance, wholesaling, retailing, health care—all industries employing millions of people who spend their days processing data, often putting information into computers or taking it out.

Most people involved in routine production services work with 19 many other people who do similar work, within large, centralized facilities. They are overseen by supervisors, who in turn are monitored by more senior supervisors. They are usually paid an hourly wage. Their jobs are often monotonous. Most of the workers do not have a college education. Those who deal with metal are mostly white males; those who deal with fabrics or information tend to be female and/or minorities.

Decades ago, those kinds of workers were relatively well paid. But 20 in recent years America's providers of routine production services have found themselves in direct competition with millions of foreign workers, most of whom work for a fraction of the pay American workers get. Through the miracle of satellite transmission, even routine data processing can now be undertaken in relatively poor nations, thousands of miles away from the skyscrapers where the data are finally used. This fact has given management ever greater power in bargaining talks. If routine production workers living in America don't agree to reduce their wages, then the work often goes abroad.

And it has. In 1950, routine production services constituted about 21 30 percent of our gross national product and well over half of American jobs. Today such services represent about 20 percent of the GNP and one fourth of jobs. And the scattering of foreign-owned factories placed here to circumvent American protectionism isn't going to reverse the trend. So the standard of living of America's routine production workers will likely keep declining. The dynamics behind the wage concessions, plant closings, and union-busting that have become commonplace won't be stopped without a major turnaround in labor organizing or political action.

3. Routine personal services also entail simple, repetitive work, 22 but, unlike routine production services, they are provided in person. Included in this employment category are restaurant and hotel workers, barbers and beauticians, retail sales personnel, cab drivers, household cleaners, day-care workers, hospital attendants and orderlies, truck drivers, and—among the fastest-growing of all careers—custodians and security guards.

Like production workers, providers of personal services are usually   23
paid by the hour. They are also carefully supervised and rarely have
more than a high school education. But unlike people in the other two
categories of work, they are in direct contact with the ultimate beneficiaries of what they do. And the companies they work for are often
small. In fact, some routine personal-service workers become entrepre-
neurs. (Most new businesses and new jobs in America come from this
sector—which now constitutes about 20 percent of GNP and 30 percent of jobs.) Women and minorities make up the bulk of routine
personal-service workers.

Apart from the small number who strike out on their own, these   24
workers are paid poorly. They are sheltered from the direct effects of
global competition, but not the indirect effects. They often compete
with undocumented workers willing to work for low wages, or with former or would-be production workers who can't find well-paying production jobs, or with labor-saving machinery (automated tellers,
self-service gas pumps) dreamed up by symbolic analysts in America
and manufactured in Asia. And because they tend to be unskilled and
dispersed among small businesses, personal-service workers rarely have
a union or a powerful lobby group to stand up for their interests. When
the economy turns sour, they are among the first to feel the effects.

These workers will continue to have jobs in the years ahead and   25
may experience some small increase in real wages. They will have demographics on their side, as the American work force shrinks. But for
all the foregoing reasons, the gap between their earnings and those of
the symbolic analysts will continue to grow if present economic trends
and labor conditions continue.

These three functional categories—symbolic analysis, routine pro-   26
duction services, and routine personal services—cover at least three
out of four American jobs. The rest of the nation's work force consists mainly of government employees (including public school teachers), employees in regulated industries (like utility workers), and
government-financed workers (engineers working on defense weapons
systems), many of whom are sheltered from global competition. One
further clarification: Some traditional job categories overlap several of
these categories. People called "secretaries," for example, include those
who actually spend their time doing symbolic analysis work closely al-
lied to what their bosses do; those who do routine data entry or re-
trieval of a sort that will eventually be automated or done overseas; and
those who provide routine personal services.

The important point is that workers in these three functional   27 categories are coming to have different competitive positions in the world economy. Symbolic analysts hold a commanding position in an increasingly global labor market. Routine production workers hold a relatively weak position in an increasingly global labor market. Routine personal service workers still find themselves in a national labor market, but for various reasons they suffer the indirect effects of competition from workers abroad.

How should we respond to these trends? One response is to accept them as inevitable consequences of change, but to try to offset their polarizing effects through a truly progressive income tax, coupled with more generous income assistance—including health insurance—for poor working Americans. (For a start, we might reverse the extraordinarily regressive Social Security amendments of 1983, through which poor working Americans are now financing the federal budget deficit, often paying more in payroll taxes than in income taxes.) 28

A more ambitious response would be to guard against class rigidities by ensuring that any talented American kid can become a symbolic analyst—regardless of family income or race. But America's gifted but poor children can't aspire to such jobs until the government spends substantially more than it does now to ensure excellent public schools in every city and region and ample financial help when they are ready to attend college. 29

Of course, it isn't clear that even under those circumstances there would be radical growth in the number of Americans who become research scientists, design engineers, musicians, management consultants, or (even if the world needed them) investment bankers and lawyers. So other responses are also needed. Perhaps the most ambitious would be to increase the numbers of Americans who could apply symbolic analysis to production and to personal services. 30

There is ample evidence, for example, that access to computerized information can enrich production jobs by enabling workers to alter the flow of materials and components in ways that increase efficiency. Production workers who have broader responsibilities and more control over how production is organized cease to be "routine" workers—becoming, in effect, symbolic analysts at a level very close to the production process. The same transformation can occur in personal-service jobs. Consider, for example, the checkout clerk whose computer enables her to control inventory and decide when to reorder items from the factory. 31

The number of such technologically empowered jobs, of course, is limited by the ability of workers to learn on the job. That means a far greater number of Americans will need a good grounding in mathematics, basic science, reading, and communication skills. So once again, comfortably integrating the American work force into the new 32 world economy turns out to rest heavily on education. (Better health care, especially prenatal and pediatric care, would also figure in here.)

Education and health care for poor children are apt to be costly. 33 Since poorer working Americans, already under a heavy tax load, can't afford it, the cost would have to be borne by wealthier Americans — who also would have to bear the cost of any income redistribution plans designed to neutralize the polarizing domestic effects of a globalized economy. Thus a central question is the willingness of the more fortunate American citizens — especially symbolic analysts, who constitute much of the most fortunate fifth, with 40 percent of the nation's income — to bear the burden. But here lies a catch-22. For as our economic fates diverge, the top fifth may be losing its sense of connectedness with the bottom fifth (or even the bottom half) that would elicit such generosity.

The conservative tide that has swept the land during the past 34 decade surely has many causes, but the fundamental changes in our economy should not be discounted as a major factor. It is now possible for the most fortunate fifth to sell their expertise directly in the global market, and thus maintain and enhance their standard of living, even as that of other Americans declines. There is less and less basis for a strong sense of interclass interdependence in America. Meanwhile, the fortunate fifth have also been able to insulate themselves from the less fortunate, by living in suburban enclaves far removed from the effects of poverty. Neither patriotism nor altruism may be sufficient to overcome these realities. Yet without the active support of at least some of the fortunate fifth, it will be more difficult to muster the political will necessary for change....

On withdrawing from the presidential race of 1988, Paul Simon of 35 Illinois said, "Americans instinctively know that we are one nation, one family, and when anyone in that family hurts, all of us hurt." Sadly, that is coming to be less and less the case.

QUESTIONS ON MEANING

1. What is Reich's PURPOSE in this essay? Is it the same as his reason for classifying the American labor force into three new categories?
2. In paragraphs 28 and 33, Reich speaks of "polarizing effects." What does he mean? How would polarization relate to his categories?
3. What responses does the author suggest to the problems he identifies? How does he rank these responses?
4. In Reich's opinion, what is needed to implement these responses?

QUESTIONS ON WRITING STRATEGY

1. What EVIDENCE does Reich use to define each of his categories? Does each category receive the same attention?
2. How does Reich deal with jobs that don't fit into his categories, or with more traditional categories that don't match his?
3. This essay first appeared in *The New Republic* and then in the *Utne Reader*, both magazines with a primarily educated, liberal AUDIENCE. Which of Reich's job categories do his readers most likely belong to? How might his audience have influenced Reich's purpose?
4. **OTHER METHODS.** As the essay's title indicates, Reich's classification is also an examination of CAUSES AND EFFECTS. What causes does Reich identify for the changes he sees?

QUESTIONS ON LANGUAGE

1. Define these key terms in Reich's essay: global economy (para. 2); inflation, median (3); impoverished (4); shareholders (7); symbolic (10); deploying (11); wholesaling (18); gross national product, protectionism (21); entre-preneurs (23); undocumented workers, lobby (24); demographics (25); progressive income tax, regressive (28); altruism (34).
2. What does the author think of investment bankers? Find language from the essay to support your opinion.
3. What does Reich mean by a *catch-22* (para. 33)? Where does the term come from? What has it come to mean?

SUGGESTIONS FOR WRITING

1. **JOURNAL WRITING.** If you have ever held a job Reich would classify as "rou-tine production" (paras. 18–21) or "routine personal" (22–25), what do you think of Reich's suggestion that such jobs might be enriched by giving workers more control over decisions (30–31)?
   FROM JOURNAL TO ESSAY. Write an essay proposing how a job you have held could be made more interesting and productive. First, explain the job as you experienced it. Then explain how you would change the job, focus-ing on training, decision making, communication, hours, and the like.
2. Reclassify the jobs in the help-wanted or employment section of your local newspaper into Reich's categories: symbolic-analytic, routine production, routine personal, and other (as in para. 26). Give reasons for your inclusion of each job opening in each of Reich's categories.
3. Reich's essay reclassifies a subject (jobs) that has been classified in other ways. Find a traditional classification of something, such as college courses, departments, or schools; staff positions; sections in the college bookstore or local supermarket—classification is everywhere. Reclassify the items ac-cording to an alternative principle of classification. You will have to state and perhaps defend your classification, and of course DEFINE and ILLUSTRATE your categories.
4. **CRITICAL WRITING.** What do you think of Reich's assessment of the discon-nectedness and responsibilities of the symbolic analysts? Write an essay

in which you agree or disagree with Reich, supporting your opinions with evidence from your own experience and reading as well as from Reich's essay.
5. **CONNECTIONS.** Like Reich, Barbara Lazear Ascher, in "On Compassion" (p. 145), is concerned about the growing gap between rich and poor, specifically about what she sees as an increasing lack of compassion for the poor on the part of middle-class Americans. How do the two authors' explanations for this gap differ? Which do you find more effective, Ascher's focus on particular people or Reich's "big picture" approach? What are the advantages and disadvantages of each strategy?

ROBERT B. REICH ON WRITING

In the introduction to his book *Tales of a New America*, Robert B. Reich explains why he finds it necessary to "probe the public consciousness and examine the reigning public philosophy": This is the terrain, he insists, "in which public problems are defined and public ideals are forged."

In seeking to map this terrain, Reich makes certain demands on his audience. "I am relying on you, the reader, to be an active explorer as well. You will need to ask yourself: How do these illustrations resonate with my experience? Are these interpretations plausible and meaningful to me? Do they help me better understand my own values, or lead me to question them?" In short, "examining what the prevailing vision has been, and what it might be" is a job not just for political scientists and government officials but for critical thinkers and readers as well.

FOR DISCUSSION

1. Why does writing on "public philosophy" demand critical reading of the sort Reich describes?
2. What other kinds of reading require the critical approach Reich asks of his readers?

ADDITIONAL WRITING TOPICS

Classification

Write an essay by the method of classification, in which you sort one of the following subjects into categories of your own. Make clear your PURPOSE in classifying and the basis of your classification. Explain each class with DEFINITIONS and EXAMPLES (you may find it helpful to make up a name for each group). Check your classes to be sure they neither gap nor overlap.

1. Commuters, or people who use public transportation
2. Environmental problems
3. Environmental solutions
4. Vegetarians
5. Talk shows
6. The ills or benefits of city life
7. The recordings you own
8. Families
9. Stand-up comedians
10. Present-day styles of marriage
11. Vacations
12. College students today
13. Paperback novels
14. Waiters you'd never tip
15. Comic strips
16. Movie monsters
17. Sports announcers
18. Inconsiderate people
19. Radio stations
20. Mall millers (people who mill around malls)

8

CAUSE AND EFFECT
Asking Why

THE METHOD

Press the button of a doorbell and, inside the house or apartment, chimes sound. Why? Because the touch of your finger on the button closed an electrical circuit. But why did you ring the doorbell? Because you were sent by your dispatcher: You are a bill collector calling on a customer whose payments are three months overdue.

The touch of your finger on the button is the *immediate cause* of the chimes: the event that precipitates another. That you were ordered by your dispatcher to go ring the doorbell is a *remote cause*: an underlying, more basic reason for the event, not apparent to an observer. Probably, ringing the doorbell will lead to some results: The door will open, and you may be given a check—or a kick in the teeth.

To figure out reasons and results is to use the method of CAUSE AND EFFECT. You try to answer the question "Why did something happen?" or the question "What were the consequences?" As part of answering either question, you use DIVISION or ANALYSIS (Chap. 6) to separate the flow of events into causes or effects.

Seeking causes, you can ask, for example, "Why did Yugoslavia

357

break apart?" "For what reason or reasons do birds migrate?" "What has caused sales of Detroit-made cars to pick up (or decline) lately?" Looking for effects, you can ask "What have been the effects of the birth-control pill on the typical American family?" "What impact has the personal computer had on the nursing profession?" You can look to a possible future and ask "Of what use might a course in psychology be to me if I become an office manager?" "Suppose a new comet the size of Halley's were to strike Philadelphia—what would be the probable consequences?" Essay exams in history and economics courses tend often to ask for either causes or effects: "What were the principal causes of America's involvement in the war in Vietnam?" "What were the immediate effects on the world monetary system of Franklin D. Roosevelt's removing the United States from the gold standard?"

Don't, by the way, confuse cause and effect with the method of PROCESS ANALYSIS (Chap. 5). Some process analysis essays, too, deal with happenings; but they focus more on repeatable events (rather than unique ones) and they explain *how* (rather than why) something happened. If you were explaining the process by which the doorbell rings, you might break the happening into stages—(1) the finger presses the button; (2) the circuit closes; (3) the current travels the wire; (4) the chimes make music—and you'd set forth the process in detail. But why did the finger press the button? What happened because the doorbell rang? To answer those questions, you need cause and effect.

In trying to explain why things happen, you can expect to find a whole array of causes—interconnected, perhaps, like the strands of a spiderweb. You'll want to do an honest job of unraveling, and this may take time. For a jury to acquit or convict an accused slayer, weeks of testimony from witnesses, detectives, and psychiatrists may be required, then days of deliberation. It took a great historian, Jakob Burckhardt, most of his lifetime to set forth a few reasons for the dawn of the Italian Renaissance. To be sure, juries must take great care when a life hangs in the balance; and Burckhardt, after all, was writing an immense book. To produce a college essay, you don't have forty years; but before you start to write, you will need to devote extra time and thought to seeing which facts are the causes, and which matter most.

To answer the questions "Why?" and "What followed as a result?" may sometimes be hard, but it can be satisfying—even illuminating. Indeed, to seek causes and effects is one way for the mind to discover order in a reality that otherwise might seem (as life came to seem to Macbeth) "a tale told by an idiot, full of sound and fury, signifying nothing."

THE PROCESS

Subjects for Cause and Effect

In writing an essay that seeks causes or one that seeks effects, first make sure that your subject is manageable. Choose a subject you can get to the bottom of, given the time and information you have. For a 500-word essay due Thursday, the causes of teenage rebellion would be a more unwieldy topic than why a certain thirteen-year-old you know ran away from home.

Excellent papers may be written on small, personal subjects. You can ask yourself, for instance, why you behaved in a certain way at a certain moment. You can examine the reasons for your current beliefs and attitudes. Such a paper might be rewarding: You might happen upon a truth you hadn't realized before. In fact, both you and your reader may profit from an essay that seeks causes along the lines of these: "Why I Espouse Nudism," or "Why I Quit College and Why I Returned." Such a paper, of course, takes thought. It isn't easy to research your own motivations. A thoughtful, personal paper that discerns *effects* might follow from a topic such as "Where Nudism Led Me" or "What Happened When I Quit College."

Causal Relations

Your toughest job in writing a cause-and-effect essay may be figuring out what caused what. Sometimes one event will appear to trigger another, and it in turn will trigger yet another, and another still, in an order we call a *causal chain*. A classic example of such a chain is set forth in a Mother Goose rhyme:

> For want of a nail the shoe was lost,
> For want of a shoe the horse was lost,
> For want of a horse the rider was lost,
> For want of a rider the battle was lost,
> For want of a battle the kingdom was lost —
> And all for the want of a nail.

In reality, causes are seldom so easy to find as that missing nail: They tend to be many and complicated. A battle may be lost for more than one reason. Perhaps the losing general had fewer soldiers, and had a blinding hangover the morning he mapped out his battle strategy. Perhaps winter set in, expected reinforcements failed to arrive, and a Joan of Arc inspired the winning army. The downfall of a kingdom is not to be explained as though it were the toppling of the last domino in a file. Still, one event precedes another in time, and in discerning causes you don't ignore chronological order; you pay attention to it.

When you can see a number of apparent causes, weigh them and assign each a relative importance. Which do you find matter most? Often, you will see that causes are more important or less so: major or minor. If Judd acquires a heavy drug habit and also takes up residence in a video arcade, and as a result finds himself penniless, it is probably safe to assume that the drug habit is the major cause of his going broke and his addiction to video games a minor one. If you were writing about his sad case, you'd probably emphasize the drug habit by giving it most of your space, perhaps touching on video games in a brief sentence.

When seeking remote causes, look only as far back as necessary. Explaining why a small town has fallen on hard times, you might confine yourself to the immediate cause of the hardship: the closing of a factory. You might explain what caused the shutdown: a dispute between union and management. You might even go back to the cause of the dispute (announced firings) and the cause of the firings (loss of sales to a Japanese competitor). For a short essay, that might be far enough back in time to go; but if you were writing a whole book (*Pottsville in the 1990s: Its Glorious Past and Its Present Agony*), you might look to causes still more remote. You could trace the beginning of the decline of Pottsville back to the discovery, in Kyoto in 1845, of a better carrot grater. A manageable short paper showing effects might work in the other direction, moving from the factory closing to its impact on the town: unemployment, the closing of stores and the only movie house, people packing up and moving away.

Two cautions about causal relations are in order here. One is to beware of confusing coincidence with cause. In the logical fallacy called *post hoc* (short for Latin *post hoc, ergo propter hoc,* "after this, therefore because of this"), one assumes, erroneously, that because A happened before B, A must have caused B. This is the error of the superstitious man who decides that he lost his job because a black cat walked in front of him. Another error is to oversimplify causes by failing to recognize their full number and complexity—claiming, say, that violent crime is simply a result of "all those gangster shows on TV." Avoid such wrong turns in reasoning by patiently looking for evidence before you write, and by giving it careful thought. (For a fuller list of such LOGICAL FALLACIES, or errors in reasoning, see pp. 449–51.)

Discovery of Causes

To help find causes of action and events, you can ask yourself a few searching questions. These have been suggested by the work of the literary critic Kenneth Burke:

1. *What act am I trying to explain?*
2. *What is the character, personality, or mental state of whoever acted?*
3. *In what scene or location did the act take place, and in what circumstances?*
4. *What instruments or means did the person use?*
5. *For what purpose did the person act?*

Burke calls these elements a *pentad* (or set of five): the *act*, the *actor*, the *scene*, the *agency*, and the *purpose*. If you are trying to explain, for instance, why a person burned down a liquor shop, it will be revealing to ask about his character and mental state. Was the act committed by the shop's worried, debt-ridden owner? a mentally disturbed anti-alcohol crusader? a drunk who had been denied a purchase? The scene of the burning, too, might tell you something. Was the shop near a church, a mental hospital, or a fireworks factory? And what was the agency (or means of the act): a flaming torch or a flipped-away cigarette butt? To learn the purpose might be illuminating, whether it was to collect insurance on the shop, to get revenge, or to work what the actor believed to be the will of the Lord. You can further deepen your inquiry by seeing relationships between the terms of the pentad. Ask, for instance, what does the actor have to do with this scene? (Is he or she the preacher in the church across the street, who has been staring at the liquor shop resentfully for the past twenty years?)[1]

You can use Burke's pentad to help explain the acts of groups as well as those of individuals. Why, for instance, did the sophomore class revel degenerate into a brawl? Here are some possible answers:

1. *Act:* the brawl
2. *Actors:* the sophs were letting off steam after exams, and a mean, tense spirit prevailed
3. *Scene:* a keg-beer party outdoors in the quad at midnight on a sticky and hot May night
4. *Agencies:* fists and sticks
5. *Purpose:* the brawlers were seeking to punish whoever kicked over the keg

Don't worry if not all the questions apply, if not all the answers are immediately forthcoming. Bring the pentad to bear on the sad case

---

[1] If you are interested and care to explore the possibilities of Burke's pentad, you can pair up its five terms in ten different ways: act to actor, actor to scene, actor to agency, actor to purpose, act to scene, act to agency, act to purpose, scene to agency, scene to purpose, agency to purpose. This approach can go profoundly deep. We suggest you try writing ten questions (one for each pair) in the form "What does act have to do with actor?" Ask them of some act you'd like to explain.

of Judd, the drug addict, and probably only the question about his character and mental state would help you much. Even a single hint,
though, can help you write. Burke's pentad isn't meant to be a grim
rigmarole; it is a means of discovery, to generate a lot of possible material for you—insights, observations, hunches to pursue. It won't solve
each and every human mystery, but sometimes it will helpfully deepen
your thought.

Purpose and Thesis

Because cause-and-effect writing often starts with a question, it
tends to be purposeful. Still, you don't want to leave your reader asking
his or her own question: "Why did this writer bother to analyze causes
and effects?" Forestall such a question by *telling* why: Assert your main
idea in a THESIS SENTENCE or sentences.

Three essays in this chapter provide good examples of thesis sentences that put across, concisely, what the subject is and why the author is bothering to analyze causes or effects.

> It is possible to stop most drug addiction in the United States within
> a very short time. Simply make all drugs available and sell them at
> cost. (Gore Vidal, "Drugs")

> My suspicion is, in fact, that very few of us...have really responded
> to the AIDS crisis the way the Federal Government and educators
> would like us to believe. My guess is that we're all but ignoring it and
> that almost anyone who claims otherwise is lying. (Meghan Daum,
> "Safe-Sex Lies")

> Consider three ideas, proposed in perfect seriousness to explain that
> greatest of all titillating puzzles—the extinction of dinosaurs....I
> want to show why two of them rank as silly speculation, while the
> other represents science at its grandest and most useful. (Stephen Jay
> Gould, "Sex, Drugs, Disasters, and the Extinction of Dinosaurs")

Final Word

In stating what you believe to be causes and effects, don't be afraid
to voice a well-considered hunch. Your instructor doesn't expect you to
write, in a short time, a definitive account of the causes of an event or
a belief or a phenomenon—only to write a coherent and reasonable
one. To discern all causes—including remote ones—and all effects is
beyond the power of any one human mind. Still, admirable and well-
informed writers on matters such as politics, economics, and world and
national affairs are often canny guessers and brave drawers of inferences. At times, even the most cautious and responsible writer has to

leap boldly over a void to strike firm ground on the far side. Consider your evidence. Focus your thinking. Look well before leaping. Then take off.

CHECKLIST FOR REVISING A CAUSE-AND-EFFECT ESSAY

✔ **SUBJECT.** Have you been able to cover your subject adequately in the time and space available? Should you perhaps narrow the subject so that you can fairly address the important causes and/or effects?

✔ **COMPLETENESS.** Have you included all relevant causes or effects? Does your analysis reach back for remote causes or forward for remote effects?

✔ **CAUSAL RELATIONS.** Have you presented a clear pattern of causes or effects? Have you distinguished the remote from the immediate, the major from the minor?

✔ **ACCURACY AND FAIRNESS.** Have you avoided the *post hoc* fallacy, assuming that A caused B just because it preceded B? Have you also avoided over-simplifying and instead covered causes or effects in all their complexity?

✔ **FOCUS.** For your readers' benefit, have you focused your analysis by stating your main idea succinctly in a thesis sentence or sentences?

CAUSE AND EFFECT IN A PARAGRAPH: TWO ILLUSTRATIONS

Using Cause and Effect to Write About Television

Why is it that, despite a growing interest in soccer among American athletes, and despite its ranking as the most popular sport in the world, commercial television all but ignores it? Granted, soccer sometimes makes it to cable, as during the World Cup, but mostly it's shut out. The reason stems partly from the basic nature of commercial television, which exists not to inform and entertain but to sell. During most major sporting events on television—football, baseball, basketball, boxing—producers can take advantage of natural interruptions in the action to broadcast sales pitches; or, if the natural breaks occur too infrequently, the producers can contrive time-outs for the sole purpose of airing lucrative commercials. But soccer is played in two solid halves of forty-five minutes each; not even injury to a player is cause for a time-out. How, then, to insert the requisite number of commercial breaks without resorting to false fouls or other questionable tactics? After CBS aired a soccer match, on May 27,

Topic sentence: question to be answered

Analysis of causes

Commercial TV requires commercial breaks

Soccer is played with only one break

Example of failed attempt to adapt soccer to TV

1967, players reported, according to Stanley Frank, that before the game the referee had instructed them "to stay down every nine minutes." The resulting hue and cry rose all the way to the House Communications Subcommittee. From that day to this, no one has been able to figure out how to screen advertising jingles during a televised soccer game. The result is that commercial television has treated soccer almost as if it didn't exist.

Result: little soccer on TV

Using Cause and Effect
in an Academic Discipline

Many factors played a role in [President Lyndon] Johnson's fateful decision [to escalate the Vietnam War]. But the most obvious explanation is that the new president faced many pressures to expand the American involvement and only a very few to limit it. As the untested successor to a revered and martyred president, he felt obliged to prove his worthiness for the office by continuing the policies of his predecessor. Aid to South Vietnam had been one of the most prominent of those policies. Johnson also felt it necessary to retain in his administration many of the important figures of the Kennedy years. In doing so, he surrounded himself with a group of foreign policy advisers—Secretary of State Dean Rusk, Secretary of Defense Robert McNamara, National Security Adviser McGeorge Bundy—who strongly believed not only that the United States had an important obligation to resist communism in Vietnam, but that it possessed the ability and resources to make that resistance successful. As a result, Johnson seldom had access to information making clear how difficult the new commitment might become. A compliant Congress raised little protest to, and indeed at one point openly endorsed, Johnson's use of executive powers to lead the nation into war. And for several years at least, public opinion remained firmly behind him—in part because Barry Goldwater's bellicose remarks about the war during the 1964 campaign made Johnson seem by comparison to be a moderate on the issue. Above all, intervention in South Vietnam was fully consistent with nearly twenty years of American foreign policy. An anticommunist ally was appealing to the United States for assistance; all the assumptions of the containment doctrine seemed to require the nation to oblige. Johnson seemed unconcerned that the government of South Vietnam existed only because the United States had put it there, and that the regime had never succeeded in acquiring the loyalty of its people. Vietnam, he believed, provided a test of American willingness to fight communist aggression, a test he was determined not to fail.

—Richard N. Current et al., *American History: A Survey*

Topic sentence: summary of causes to be discussed

Causes:

Need to prove worthiness

Advisers urging involvement and shutting off alternative views

Congressional cooperation

Support of public opinion

Consistency with American foreign policy against communism

GORE VIDAL

GORE VIDAL was born in 1925 at the U.S. Military Academy at West Point, where his father was an instructor. At the age of nineteen, he wrote his first novel, *Williwaw* (1946), while serving as a warrant officer aboard an army supply ship. Among the more recent of his twenty-one novels are *Duluth* (1983), *Lincoln* (1984), *Empire* (1987), and *Hollywood* (1989). He has also written mysteries under the pen name Edgar Box. As a playwright, he is best known for *Visit to a Small Planet* (1957), which was made into a film. The grandson of Senator T. P. Gore, who represented Oklahoma for thirty years, Vidal twice ran unsuccessfully for Congress, but in 1992 he portrayed a senator in the movie *Bob Roberts*. A provocative and perceptive literary and social critic, Vidal is a frequent contributor to *The New York Review of Books* and other magazines, and he has published several collections of essays, most recently *United States Essays, 1951–1991* (1993). His latest book is a memoir, *Palimpsest* (1995). Vidal divides his time between Italy and America.

Drugs

Vidal, whom some critics have called America's finest living essayist, first published "Drugs" in 1970 on the *New York Times's* op-ed page and then included the essay in *Homage to Daniel Shays: Collected Essays 1952–1972*. "Drugs" addresses a problem that has worsened since it was first published. Lately, an increasing number of social scientists, medical professionals, and politicians have urged that we consider just such a radical solution as Vidal proposes. (For an opposing view, see A. M. Rosenthal's "The Case for Slavery," p. 370.)

It is possible to stop most drug addiction in the United States 1 within a very short time. Simply make all drugs available and sell them at cost. Label each drug with a precise description of what effect — good and bad — the drug will have on the taker. This will require heroic honesty. Don't say that marijuana is addictive or dangerous when it is neither, as millions of people know — unlike "speed," which kills most unpleasantly, or heroin, which is addictive and difficult to kick.

For the record, I have tried — once — almost every drug and liked 2 none, disproving the popular Fu Manchu theory that a single whiff of opium will enslave the mind. Nevertheless many drugs are bad for certain people to take and they should be told why in a sensible way.

Along with exhortation and warning, it might be good for our cit- 3

izens to recall (or learn for the first time) that the United States was the
creation of men who believed that each man has the right to do what
he wants with his own life as long as he does not interfere with his
neighbor's pursuit of happiness. (That his neighbor's idea of happiness
is persecuting others does confuse matters a bit.)

This is a startling notion to the current generation of Americans.   4
They reflect a system of public education which has made the Bill of
Rights, literally, unacceptable to a majority of high school graduates
(see the annual Purdue reports) who now form the "silent majority"—
a phrase which that underestimated wit Richard Nixon took from
Homer, who used it to describe the dead.

Now one can hear the warning rumble begin: If everyone is al-   5
lowed to take drugs everyone will and the GNP will decrease, the Com-
mies will stop us from making everyone free, and we shall end up a race
of zombies, passively murmuring "groovy" to one another. Alarming
thought. Yet it seems most unlikely that any reasonably sane person
will become a drug addict if he knows in advance what addiction is going to be like.

Is everyone reasonably sane? No. Some people will always become   6
drug addicts just as some people will always become alcoholics, and it is
just too bad. Every man, however, has the power (and should have the
legal right) to kill himself if he chooses. But since most men don't, they
won't be mainliners either. Nevertheless, forbidding people things they
like or think they might enjoy only makes them want those things all
the more. This psychological insight is, for some mysterious reason,
perennially denied our governors.

It is a lucky thing for the American moralist that our country has   7
always existed in a kind of time-vacuum: We have no public memory of
anything that happened before last Tuesday. No one in Washington today recalls what happened during the years alcohol was forbidden to
the people by a Congress that thought it had a divine mission to stamp
out Demon Rum—launching, in the process, the greatest crime wave
in the country's history, causing thousands of deaths from bad alcohol,
and creating a general (and persisting) contempt among the citizenry
for the laws of the United States.

The same thing is happening today. But the government has   8
learned nothing from past attempts at prohibition, not to mention re-
pression.

Last year when the supply of Mexican marijuana was slightly   9
curtailed by the Feds, the pushers got the kids hooked on heroin
and deaths increased dramatically, particularly in New York. Whose
fault? Evil men like the Mafiosi? Permissive Dr. Spock? Wild-eyed Dr.
Leary? No.

The government of the United States was responsible for those   10 deaths. The bureaucratic machine has a vested interest in playing cops and robbers. Both the Bureau of Narcotics and the Mafia want strong laws against the sale and use of drugs because if drugs are sold at cost there would be no money in it for anyone.

If there was no money in it for the Mafia, there would be no 11 friendly playground pushers, and addicts would not commit crimes to pay for the next fix. Finally, if there was no money in it, the Bureau of Narcotics would wither away, something they are not about to do without a struggle.

Will anything sensible be done? Of course not. The American 12 people are as devoted to the idea of sin and its punishment as they are to making money—and fighting drugs is nearly as big a business as pushing them. Since the combination of sin and money is irresistible (particularly to the professional politician), the situation will only grow worse.

QUESTIONS ON MEANING

1. What do you take to be Vidal's main PURPOSE in writing this essay? How well does he accomplish it?
2. For what reasons, according to Vidal, is it unlikely that our drug laws will be eased? Can you suggest other possible reasons why the Bureau of Narcotics favors strict drug laws?
3. Vidal's essay was first published almost three decades ago. Do you find the views expressed in it still timely, or out of date?

QUESTIONS ON WRITING STRATEGY

1. How would you characterize Vidal's humor? Find some examples of it.
2. Where in the essay does Vidal appear to anticipate the response of his AUDIENCE? How can you tell?
3. What function do the essay's RHETORICAL QUESTIONS perform?
4. **OTHER METHODS.** Study Vidal's use of EXAMPLE in paragraphs 8–10. Does the example of the U.S. government's role in heroin deaths effectively support Vidal's point that restricting drug use does not work? Is Vidal guilty here of oversimplification (p. 360)?

QUESTIONS ON LANGUAGE

1. Know the definitions of the following terms: exhortation (para. 3); GNP (5); mainliners, perennially (6); curtailed (9).
2. How do you interpret Vidal's use of the phrase "underestimated wit" to describe Richard Nixon?

SUGGESTIONS FOR WRITING

1. **JOURNAL WRITING.** Vidal is convinced that the best way to combat the drug problem in this country is to "make all drugs available and sell them at cost." Does this seem like a good idea to you? What do you think would be the practical effects—positive or negative—of legalizing drugs?
   FROM JOURNAL TO ESSAY. Now that you have considered the effects of legalizing drugs, look back at Vidal's explanations for why they have *not* been legalized. In an essay, explain why you think the United States resists legalizing drugs. You may support Vidal's moral and economic arguments, you may oppose one or several of his claims, or you may propose new reasons of your own. In any case, be sure to make clear, as Vidal does, the connection between the foreseeable effects of legalization and the reasoning that keeps drugs illegal.

2. Research the situation reported by Vidal in paragraphs 9 and 10. (Begin with the *New York Times Index* for the years 1969 and 1970.) Write an essay that clearly and objectively analyzes the causes of the situation.

3. **CRITICAL WRITING.** How readily do you accept Vidal's statement that "each man has a right to do what he wants with his own life"—including, presumably, to be a drug addict—"as long as he does not interfere with his neighbor's pursuit of happiness" (para. 3)? Do you accept Vidal's implicit ASSUMPTION that people with easy access to drugs are not necessarily threats to their neighbors? Back up your answers with EVIDENCE from your experience and reading.

4. **CONNECTIONS.** In an essay, compare Vidal's essay with A. M. Rosenthal's "The Case for Slavery" (p. 370). Focus especially on the main assertions of each—the advantages and disadvantages of drug legalization—and on the evidence each provides. Conclude with a statement, backed by reasons, about which essay you think is the more effective.

GORE VIDAL ON WRITING

"Do you find writing easy?" Gerald Clark asked Gore Vidal for the *Paris Review.* "Do you enjoy it?"

"Oh, yes, of course I enjoy it," Vidal shot back. "I wouldn't do it if I didn't. Whenever I get up in the morning, I write for about three hours. I write novels in longhand on yellow pads, exactly like the First Criminal Nixon. For some reason I write plays and essays on the typewriter. The first draft usually comes rather fast. One oddity: I never reread a text until I have finished the first draft. Otherwise it's too discouraging. Also, when you have the whole thing in front of you for the first time, you've forgotten most of it and see it fresh. Rewriting, however, is a slow, grinding business.

"When I first started writing, I used to plan everything in advance, not only chapter to chapter but page to page. Terribly constricting—like doing a film from someone else's meticulous treatment. About the time of *The Judgment of Paris* [a novel published in 1952] I started improvising. I began with a mood. A sentence. The first sentence is all-important. [My novel] *Washington, D.C.* began with a dream, a summer storm at night in a garden above the Potomac — that was Merrywood, where I grew up.

"The most interesting thing about writing is the way that it obliterates time. Three hours seem like three minutes. Then there is the business of surprise. I never know what is coming next. The phrase that sounds in the head changes when it appears on the page. Then I start probing it with a pen, finding new meanings. Sometimes I burst out laughing at what is happening as I twist and turn sentences. Strange business, all in all. One never gets to the end of it. That's why I go on, I suppose. To see what the next sentences I write will be."

FOR DISCUSSION

1. What is it that Vidal seems to enjoy most about writing?
2. What advantage does he find in not planning every page in advance?

A. M. ROSENTHAL

Abraham Michael Rosenthal, born in 1922 in Ontario, Canada, came to the United States as a child and attended City College in New York City (B.S., 1944). His long association with the *New York Times* began the year he graduated from college. He served the newspaper as correspondent at the United Nations and in India, Poland, Switzerland, and Japan; as managing editor; and as executive editor. Since formally retiring from the *Times* in 1988, he has written a regular op-ed column for the paper. Rosenthal is the author of *38 Witnesses* (1964) and coauthor (with Arthur Gelb) of several other books, including those in the series "The Sophisticated Traveller." He has written articles for the *New York Times Magazine, Saturday Evening Post*, and *Foreign Affairs*. In 1960 his reporting of international news won him a Pulitzer Prize.

The Case for Slavery

Like Gore Vidal's "Drugs" (p. 365), this essay was first published on the op-ed page of the *New York Times*. But there the similarity ends. Rosenthal's piece appeared in 1989, almost two decades after Vidal's, and it forcefully opposes what Vidal proposes.

Across the country, a scattered but influential collection of intellectuals is intensely engaged in making the case for slavery. 1

With considerable passion, these Americans are repeatedly expounding the benefits of not only tolerating slavery but legalizing it: 2

It would make life less dangerous for the free. It would save a great deal of money. And since the economies could be used to improve the lot of the slaves, in the end they would be better off. 3

The new antiabolitionists, like their predecessors in the nineteenth century, concede that those now in bondage do not themselves see the benefits of legalizing their status. 4

But in time they will, we are assured, because the beautiful part of legalization is that slavery would be designed so as to keep slaves pacified with the very thing that enslaves them! 5

The form of slavery under discussion is drug addiction. It does not have every characteristic of more traditional forms of bondage. But they have enough in common to make the comparison morally valid—and the campaign for drug legalization morally disgusting. 6

Like the plantation slavery that was a foundation of American so- 7 ciety for so long, drug addiction largely involves specifiable groups of people. Most of the enchained are children and adolescents of all colors and black and Hispanic adults.

Like plantation slavery, drug addiction is passed on from genera-   8
tion to generation. And this may be the most important similarity: Like plantation slavery, addiction can destroy among its victims the social resources most valuable to free people for their own betterment—family life, family traditions, family values.

In plantation-time America, mothers were taken from their chil-   9
dren. In drug-time America, mothers abandon their children. Do the children suffer less, or the mothers?

Antiabolitionists argue that legalization would make drugs so   10
cheap and available that the profit for crime would be removed. Well-supplied addicts would be peaceful addicts. We would not waste billions for jails and could spend some of the savings helping the addicted become drug-free.

That would happen at the very time that new millions of Ameri-   11
cans were being enticed into addiction by legalization—somehow.

Are we really foolish enough to believe that tens of thousands of   12
drug gang members would meekly steal away, foiled by the marvels of the free market?

Not likely. The pushers would cut prices, making more money than   13
ever from the ever-growing mass market. They would immediately increase the potency and variety beyond anything available at any government-approved narcotics counters.

Crime would increase. Crack produces paranoid violence. More   14
permissiveness equals more use equals more violence.

And what will legalization do to the brains of Americans drawn   15
into drug slavery by easy availability?

Earlier this year, an expert drug pediatrician told me that after only   16
a few months babies born with crack addiction seemed to recover. Now we learn that stultifying behavioral effects last at least through early childhood. Will they last forever?

How long will crack affect neurological patterns in the brains of   17
adult crack users? Dr. Gabriel G. Nahas of Columbia University argues in his new book, *Cocaine: The Great White Plague*, that the damage may be irreversible. Would it not be an act of simple intelligence to drop the legalization campaign until we find out?

Then why do a number of writers and academicians, left to right,   18
support it? I have discussed this with antidrug leaders like Jesse Jackson, Dr. Mitchell Rosenthal of Phoenix House, and William J. Bennett, who search for answers themselves.

Perhaps the answer is that the legalizers are not dealing with real-   19
ity in America. I think the reason has to do with class.

Crack is beginning to move into the white middle and upper   20
classes. That is a tragedy for those addicted.

However, it has not yet destroyed the communities around which   21
their lives revolve, not taken over every street and doorway. It has not
passed generation to generation among them, killing the continuity of
family.

But in ghetto communities poverty and drugs come together in a   22
catalytic reaction that is reducing them to social rubble.

The antiabolitionists, virtually all white and well-to-do, do not see   23
or do not care. Either way they show symptoms of the callousness of
class. That can be a particularly dangerous social disorder.

QUESTIONS ON MEANING

1. On what grounds does Rosenthal claim that the ANALOGY between drug addiction and slavery is valid? How does he say the two are alike?
2. Rosenthal records two sets of possible results from the legalization of drugs:
   one from those who favor legalization, the other his own. Summarize the
   two sides.
3. Explain what Rosenthal means when he says that support of drug legalization "has to do with class" (para. 19).
4. What is Rosenthal's PURPOSE in writing this essay? Does he fulfill it?

QUESTIONS ON WRITING STRATEGY

1. Would you say Rosenthal is more interested in the causes and effects of
   drug addiction or in the causes and effects of the legalization argument?
   Why?
2. When does Rosenthal first introduce his topic? Why does he delay it so
   long?
3. Analyze the TONE of this essay. Why do you think Rosenthal takes this
   tone?
4. On what EVIDENCE does Rosenthal's argument principally depend? Is his evidence adequate?
5. **OTHER METHODS.** Rosenthal uses cause and effect to further an ARGUMENT.
   Examine the APPEALS he relies on: Are they mainly rational or emotional?
   Find examples of each.

QUESTIONS ON LANGUAGE

1. What does Rosenthal achieve by repeatedly calling drug legalization advocates "antiabolitionists"?
2. Typically for newspaper writers, Rosenthal uses very short paragraphs, some
   only a sentence. In a newspaper's narrow columns, this approach keeps

paragraphs short. What is its EFFECT in the wider columns of a book? As an exercise, connect related paragraphs of Rosenthal's into larger paragraphs.
3. Consult your dictionary for the meanings of any unfamiliar words: expounding (para. 2); concede, predecessors (4); pacified (5); specifiable, enchained (7); enticed (11); foiled (12); paranoid (14); stultifying (16); irreversible (17); academicians (18); catalytic (22); callousness (23).

SUGGESTIONS FOR WRITING

1. **JOURNAL WRITING.** The end of Rosenthal's essay suggests that people who support the legalization of drugs must have a certain "callousness of class"—in other words, they can afford to make glib pronouncements about drugs because drugs are not yet entrenched in their middle- and upper-class communities. Does this assertion seem accurate to you? Have you had any personal experiences that support or refute it?
   FROM JOURNAL TO ESSAY. Write an essay in which you argue a specific assertion about the role of socioeconomic class in the debate over drugs— not just legalizing them, necessarily, but also other ways of combating them, such as preventing smuggling, curtailing street dealing, imprisoning users, or funding drug treatment facilities. Support your assertion with evidence from your experience, observations, and reading.
2. Choose a controversy that you know something about—it could be local (a college issue such as parking regulations, financial aid, or race relations), national (tax increases, bilingual education), or international (global warming, human rights violations). Take issue with one side in the controversy by analyzing the possible effects of that position.
3. **CRITICAL WRITING.** ANALYZE Rosenthal's analogy between drug addiction and slavery and, by extension, between legalization and antiabolition. In your analysis, go beyond Rosenthal to spell out all the similarities and differences you can see. Be specific. All told, how effective do you find the analogy?
4. **CONNECTIONS.** After reading Gore Vidal's "Drugs" (p. 365) and Rosenthal's "The Case for Slavery," write an essay in which you take sides for or against the legalization of drugs. You may argue from your own experience and observations, using Vidal or Rosenthal as a backup, or you could do some library research to test, extend, and support your opinions.

A. M. ROSENTHAL ON WRITING

In "Learning on the Job," a memoir of his forty years as a newspaper reporter and editor, A. M. Rosenthal has recalled a lesson he learned at the start of his career. "The very first day I was on the job as a reporter—a real reporter, with a press card in my pocket and a light in my heart—I learned all about the First Amendment. It was a Saturday and I was sitting in the *Times*'s newsroom when an assistant editor walked over, told me that there had been a murder or a suicide at the

Mayflower Hotel in midtown, and why didn't I go over and see what it was all about. Yes, sir! I rushed out, jumped on a bus, got to the hotel, asked an elevator operator where the trouble was. Ninth floor, he told me, and up I went. A push of the buzzer and the door opened. Standing there was a police detective. He was twelve and a half feet tall. I started to walk in and he put his hand into my face. That hand was just a bit larger than a basketball.

" 'Where are you going, kid?' he said.

" 'I'm a reporter,' I said. '*Times*. I want to see the body.'

"He looked at me, up and down, slowly. 'Beat it,' he proposed.

"Beat it? I hadn't realized anybody talked to *Times* reporters that way. I knew there had to be some misunderstanding. So I smiled, pulled out my press card, and showed it to him. He took it, read it carefully front and back, handed it back, and said: 'Shove it in your ear.'

"Shove it in my ear? I could not comprehend what was taking place. 'But I'm from the *Times*,' I explained. 'A reporter from the *New York Times*. Don't you want me to get the story right?'

" 'Listen, Four Eyes,' he said, 'I don't care if you drop dead.' Then he slammed the door in my face and there I stood, staring at that door. I slunk off to a pay phone in the lobby and called the special reporters' number that had been confided to me—LAckawanna 4-1090, I've never forgotten it—and confessed to the clerk on the city desk that I had not only been unable to crack the case but had never even seen the corpse.

" 'Don't worry about it kid,' he said. 'We got it already from the A.P.[1] They called the police headquarters and got the story. Come on in.'

"Right there at the Mayflower I learned my first lesson about the First Amendment. The First Amendment means I have the right to ask anybody any question I wish. And anybody has the right to tell me to shove it in my ear. I have been involved in First Amendment cases for more than twenty years, but when I began as a reporter I was not answering any call to protect and defend the Constitution of the United States. I was not even thinking about the Constitution of the United States. All I was thinking about was the pleasure and joy of newspapering, of the wonderful zest of being able to run around, see things, find out what was going on, write about it.... That was what the newspaper business meant to me then and mostly still does—the delight of discovery, the exhilaration of writing a story and the quick gratification of seeing it in the paper; ink, ink, ink, even if it does rub off on your fingers just a tiny bit.

"We newspaper people are given to talking and writing about jour-

[1] Associated Press. —EDS.

nalistic philosophy and I certainly have done my share.... But newspapering is not a philosophy, it is a way of spending a lifetime, and most
of us in it know that if you really don't love it, love the whole mixture
of searching, finding, and telling, love the strange daily rhythm where
you have to climb higher and higher during the day instead of slacken-
ing off as the day goes on as normal people do, if you don't have a sensation of apprehension when you set out to find a story and a swagger
when you sit down to write it, you are in the wrong business. You can
make more money as a dentist and cops won't tell you to shove it in
your ear."

FOR DISCUSSION

1. What is the First Amendment to the Constitution, and exactly what did
   Rosenthal learn about it?
2. What aspects of being a reporter have the greatest appeal for Rosenthal?
3. As Rosenthal recounts the joys of a reporter's life, he also reveals, directly
   or indirectly, some of the disadvantages. What are they?

THOMAS SOWELL

THOMAS SOWELL has been called "perhaps the leading black scholar among conservatives." His support for free markets and corresponding disdain for government regulations and social programs has endeared him to those on the right of center, while his logic and clarity have earned him respect from those on the left. Born in North Carolina in 1930, Sowell attended a segregated high school and went on to earn three degrees in economics: a B.A. from Harvard College (1958), an M.A. from Columbia University (1959), and a Ph.D. from the University of Chicago (1968). He has taught at Harvard, Cornell University, Amherst College, and other schools; served as an economist in government and business; and held positions at several research centers, since 1980 at the Hoover Institution at Stanford University. Sowell writes a syndicated newspaper column and has published over two dozen books on economics, education, and race.

Student Loans

In this essay from *Is Reality Optional?* (1993), a collection of his columns and essays, Sowell demonstrates both the free-market conservatism and the wry tone for which he is known. His question: Why should the government fund loans for college students when the loans are not only unnecessary but actually bad for education?

The first lesson of economics is scarcity: There is never enough of 1 anything to fully satisfy all those who want it.

The first lesson of politics is to disregard the first lesson of econom- 2 ics. When politicians discover some group that is being vocal about not having as much as they want, the "solution" is to give them more. Where do politicians get this "more"? They rob Peter to pay Paul.

After a while, of course, they discover that Peter doesn't have 3 enough. Bursting with compassion, politicians rush to the rescue. Needless to say, they do not admit that robbing Peter to pay Paul was a dumb idea in the first place. On the contrary, they now rob Tom, Dick, and Harry to help Peter.

The latest chapter in this long-running saga is that politicians have 4 now suddenly discovered that many college students graduate heavily in debt. To politicians it follows, as the night follows the day, that the government should come to their rescue with the taxpayers' money.

How big is this crushing burden of college students' debt that we 5 hear so much about from politicians and media deep thinkers? For those students who graduate from public colleges owing money, the debt averages a little under $7,000. For those who graduate from private colleges owing money, the average debt is a little under $9,000.

Buying a very modestly priced automobile involves more debt than 6
that. And a car loan has to be paid off faster than the ten years that college graduates get to repay their student loans. Moreover, you have to keep buying cars every several years, while one college education lasts a lifetime.

College graduates of course earn higher incomes than other people. 7
Why, then, should we panic at the thought that they have to repay loans for the education which gave them their opportunities? Even graduates with relatively modest incomes pay less than 10 percent of their annual salary on the loan the first year — with declining percentages in future years, as their pay increases.

Political hysteria and media hype may focus on the low-income 8
student with a huge debt. That is where you get your heart-rending stories — even if they are not at all typical. In reality, the soaring student loans of the past decade have resulted from allowing high-income people to borrow under government programs.

Before 1978, college loans were available through government pro- 9
grams only to students whose family income was below some cut-off level. That cut-off level was about double the national average income, but at least it kept out the Rockefellers and the Vanderbilts. But, in an era of "compassion," Congress took off even those limits.

That opened the floodgates. No matter how rich you were, it still 10
paid to borrow money through the government at low interest rates. The money you had set aside for your children's education could be invested somewhere else, at higher interest rates. Then, when the student loan became due, parents could pay it off with the money they had set aside — pocketing the difference in interest rates.

To politicians and the media, however, the rapidly growing loans 11
showed what a great "need" there was. The fact that many students welshed when time came to repay their loans showed how "crushing" their burden of debt must be. In reality, those who welsh typically have smaller loans, but have dropped out of college before finishing. People who are irresponsible in one way are often irresponsible in other ways.

No small amount of the deterioration of college standards has been 12
due to the increasingly easy availability of college to people who are not very serious about getting an education. College is not a bad place to hang out for a few years, if you have nothing better to do, and if someone else is paying for it. Its costs are staggering, but the taxpayers carry much of that burden, not only for state universities and city colleges, but also to an increasing extent even for "private" institutions.

Numerous government subsidies and loan programs make it pos- 13
sible for many people to use vast amounts of society's resources at low

cost to themselves. Whether in money terms or in real terms, federal aid to higher education has increased several hundred percent since 1970. That has enabled colleges to raise their tuition by leaps and bounds and enabled professors to be paid more and more for doing less and less teaching.

Naturally all these beneficiaries are going to create hype and hysteria to keep more of the taxpayers' money coming in. But we would be fools to keep on writing blank checks for them.   14

When you weigh the cost of things, in economics that's called "trade-offs." In politics, it's called "mean-spirited." Apparently, if we just took a different attitude, scarcity would go away.   15

QUESTIONS ON MEANING

1. Explain the conflict Sowell sees between the realities of economics and the interests of politicians.
2. What is meant by the expression "robbing Peter to pay Paul"?
3. Explain the distinction Sowell makes in paragraph 13 between "money terms" and "real terms."
4. What is Sowell's PURPOSE in this essay? What are the implications of his cause-and-effect analysis?

QUESTIONS ON WRITING STRATEGY

1. PARAPHRASE Sowell's cause-and-effect analysis as summed up in paragraphs 13 and 14.
2. What is the EFFECT of the COMPARISON Sowell makes in paragraphs 5–6? How does it contribute to his ARGUMENT?
3. How would you characterize Sowell's TONE?
4. Locate examples of Sowell's use of statistics to back up his argument. What is their effect?
5. **OTHER METHODS.** As it often does, the method of cause and effect here helps to develop an argument. SUMMARIZE Sowell's argument in a sentence.

QUESTIONS ON LANGUAGE

1. Make sure you are familiar with the following words: saga (para. 4); hype (8); floodgates (10); welshed (11); deterioration (12); beneficiaries (14).
2. What is the effect of Sowell's use of the phrase "hang out" in paragraph 12? Can you find another example of surprising DICTION in this essay?
3. Why does Sowell use quotation marks around these words: "more" (para. 2); "compassion" (9); "need," "crushing" (11); and "private" (12)? Does he overuse this device?

SUGGESTIONS FOR WRITING

1. **JOURNAL WRITING.** Choose a problem that interests you and that you know quite a bit about. It might be local (such as the quality of food on campus, participation in student government, traffic on the interstate), or more removed (the sale of a sports team, a failed attempt to protect computer data). Whatever issue you choose, it should be small enough and specific enough to tackle in a short essay. Divide a page or two of your journal into two columns. On the right side, list the characteristics of the situation as it stands today: the effects. On the left side, list all the factors that have helped create this situation: the causes.

   FROM JOURNAL TO ESSAY. Shape the notes from your journal into a coherently reasoned cause-and-effect essay, explaining why the situation you have chosen has come about. As a guide to developing your essay, you may want to ask the five questions in Kenneth Burke's pentad (p. 361).

2. As a college student, you are in a good position to EVALUATE the claims Sowell makes in this essay. Identify his GENERALIZATIONS, such as that cases of low-income students going into debt are "not at all typical" (para. 8) or that students who "welsh" on their loans are irresponsible (para. 11) or that student loans contribute to the "deterioration of college standards" (para. 12). How true is Sowell's portrayal of college students and their performance? How fair are his accusations?

3. **CRITICAL WRITING.** Underlying all of Sowell's arguments is a stated ASSUMPTION: "There is never enough of anything to fully satisfy all those who want it" (para. 1). Do you agree with this notion of scarcity of resources in the United States? How would calling this central assumption into question affect Sowell's argument?

4. **CONNECTIONS.** Compare this essay with Robert B. Reich's "Why the Rich Are Getting Richer and the Poor Poorer" (p. 346). How much emphasis does each writer place on individual as opposed to societal/governmental responsibility for ensuring success in life? Can the two writers' points of view be labeled "conservative" and "liberal" or "Republican" and "Democratic," or are the differences between their philosophies of government more subtle?

MEGHAN DAUM

Born in 1970 in Palo Alto, California, MEGHAN DAUM is a writer who specializes in the communications media. Daum graduated from Vassar College with a B.A. in English (1992) and from Columbia University with an M.A. in writing (1996). She worked on the staffs of *Allure* magazine and Columbia University Press. Now writing full-time, Daum has published articles in the *New York Times Book Review*, *GQ*, and *New York Magazine*. She lives in New York City.

Safe-Sex Lies

This essay from the *New York Times Magazine* caused a stir when it was published in January 1996. Daum deftly portrays the anxiety, mistrust, and dishonesty that she and others of her generation experience in the age of AIDS.

I have been tested for HIV three times. I've gone to clinics and 1 stuck my arm out for those disposable needles, each time forgetting the fear and nausea that descend upon me before the results come back, those minutes spent in a publicly financed waiting room staring at a video loop about "living with" this thing that kills you. These tests have taken place over five years, and the results have always been negative—not surprisingly in restrospect, since I am not a member of a "high-risk group," don't sleep around and don't take pity on heroin-addicted bass players by going to bed with them in the hopes of being thanked in the liner notes of their first major independent release. Still, getting tested always seemed like the thing to do. Despite my demographic profile, despite the fact that I grew up middle class, attended an elite college and do not personally know any women or straight men within that demographic profile who have the AIDS virus, I am terrified of this disease. I went to a college where condoms and dental dams lay in baskets in dormitory lobbies, where it seemed incumbent on health service counselors to give us the straight talk, to tell us never, ever to have sex without condoms unless we wanted to die; that's right, *die*, shrivel overnight, vomit up our futures, pose a threat to others. (And they'd seen it happen, oh, yes, they had.) They gave us pamphlets, didn't quite explain how to use dental dams, told us where we could get tested, threw us more fistfuls of condoms (even some glow-in-the-dark brands, just for variety). This can actually be fun, they said, if only we'd adopt a better attitude.

We're told we can get this disease and we believe it and vow to pro- 2 tect ourselves, and intend (really, truly) to stick by this rule, until we don't because we just can't, because it's just not fair, because our sense of entitlement exceeds our sense of vulnerability. So we blow off precaution again and again, and then we get scared and get tested, and when it comes out O.K., we run out of the clinic, pamphlets in hand, eyes cast upward, promising ourselves we'll never be stupid again. But of course we are stupid, again and again. And the testing is always for the same reasons and with the same results, and soon it becomes more like fibbing about SAT scores ten years after the fact than lying about whether we practice unsafe sex, a lie that sounds like such a breach of contract with ourselves that we might as well be talking about putting a loaded gun under our pillow every night.

Still, I've gone into more than a few relationships with the safest of   3 intentions and discarded them after the fourth or fifth encounter. Perhaps this is a shocking admission, but my hunch is that I'm not the only one doing it. My suspicion is, in fact, that very few of us—"us" being the demographic profile frequently charged with thinking we're immortal, the population accused of being cynical and lazy and weak— have really responded to the AIDS crisis the way the Federal Government and educators would like us to believe. My guess is that we're all but ignoring it and that almost anyone who claims otherwise is lying.

It seems there is a lot of lying going around. One of the main tenets   4 of the safe sex message is that ageless mantra "you don't know where he's been," meaning that everyone is a potential threat, that we're all either scoundrels or ignoramuses. "He didn't tell me he was shooting drugs," says an HIV-positive woman on a public-service advertisement. Safe sex "documentaries" on MTV and call-in radio shows on pop stations give us woman after woman whose boyfriend "claimed he loved me but was sleeping around." The message we receive is that trusting anyone is itself an irresponsible act, that having faith in an intimate partner, particularly women in relation to men, is a symptom of such profound naïveté that we're obviously not mature enough to be having sex anyway.

I find this reasoning almost more troubling than the disease itself.   5 It flies in the face of the social order from which I, as someone born in 1970, was supposed to benefit. That this reasoning runs counter to almost any feminist ideology—the ideology that proclaimed, at least back in the seventies, that women should feel free to ask men on dates and wear jeans and have orgasms—is an admission that no AIDS-concerned citizen is willing to make. Two decades after *The Joy of Sex* made sexual pleasure permissible for both sexes and three decades after the pill put a government-approved stamp on premarital sex, we're still told not to trust each other. We've entered a period where mistrust equals responsibility, where fear signifies health.

Since I spent all of the seventies under the age of ten, I've never 6
known a significantly different sexual and social climate. Supposedly
this makes it easier to live with the AIDS crisis. Health educators and
AIDS activists like to think that people of my generation can be made
to unlearn what we never knew, to break the reckless habits we didn't
actually form. But what we have learned thoroughly is how not to enjoy ourselves. Just like our mothers, whose adolescences were haunted
by the abstract taboo against being "bad" girls, my contemporaries and
I are discouraged from doing what feels good. As it did with our mothers, the onus falls largely on the women. We know that it's much easier
for women to contract HIV from a man than the other way around. We
know that an "unsafe" man generally means someone who has shot
drugs or slept with other men, or possibly slept with prostitutes. We
find ourselves wondering about these things over dinner dates. We look
for any hints of homosexual tendencies, any references to a hypodermic
moment. We try to catch him in the lie we've been told he'll tell.

What could be sadder? We're not allowed to believe anyone any- 7
more. And the reason we're not isn't so much because of AIDS but because of the anxiety that ripples around the disease. The information
about AIDS that is supposed to produce "awareness" has been subsumed into the aura of style. AIDS awareness has become so much a
part of the pop culture that not only is it barely noticeable, it is largely
ineffectual. MTV runs programs about safe sex that are barely distin-
guishable from documentaries about Madonna. A print advertisement
for Benetton features a collage of hundreds of tiny photographs of
young people, some of whom are shaded with the word AIDS written
across their faces. Many are white and blond and have the tousled,
moneyed look common to more traditional fashion spreads or even
yearbooks from colleges like the one I attended. There is no text other
than the company's slogan. There is no explanation of how these faces
were chosen, no public statement of whether these people actually
have the disease or not. I called Benetton for clarification and was told
that the photographs were supposed to represent people from all over
the world and that no one was known to be HIV-positive — just as I
suspected. The advertisement was a work of art, which meant I could
interpret the image any way I liked. This is how the deliverers of the
safe-sex message shoot themselves in the foot. Confronted with arty effects instead of actual information, people like me are going to believe
what we want to believe, which, of course, is whatever isn't too scary.
So we turn the page.

Since I am pretty sure I do not sleep with bisexual men or IV drug 8
users, my main personal concern about AIDS is that men can get the
virus from women and subsequently pass it on to other women. According to the Centers for Disease Control's National AIDS Clearing-

house surveillance report, less than three-quarters of 1 percent of white non-Hispanic men with HIV infection contracted the virus through heterosexual sex with a non–IV drug–using woman. (Interestingly, the CDC labels this category as "risk not specified.") But this statistic seems too dry for MTV and campus health brochures, whose eye-catching "sex kills" rhetoric tells us nothing other than to ignore what we don't feel like thinking about. Obviously, there are still too many cases of HIV; there is a deadly risk in certain kinds of sexual behavior and therefore reason to take precautions. But until more people appear on television, look into the camera and tell me that they contracted HIV through heterosexual sex with someone who had no risk factors, I will continue to disregard the message.

Besides, the very sophistication that allows people like me to filter out much of the hype behind music videos, fashion magazines and television talk shows is what we use to block out the safe-sex message. We are not a population that makes personal decisions based on the public service work of a rock star. We're not going to sacrifice the thing we believe we deserve, the experiences we waited for, because Levi Strauss is a major sponsor of MTV's coverage of World AIDS Day.

So the inconsistent behavior continues, as do the confessions among friends and the lies to health care providers during routine exams, because we just can't bear the terrifying lectures that ensue when we confess to not always protecting ourselves. Life in your twenties is fraught not only with financial and professional uncertainty, but also with a specter of death that floats above the pursuit of a sex life. And there is no solution, only the conclusion that invariably finishes the hushed conversations: the whole thing simply "sucks." It's a bummer on a grand scale.

Heterosexuals are receiving vague signals. We're told that if we are sufficiently vigilant, we will probably be all right. We're being told to assume the worst and to not invite disaster by hoping for the best. We're being encouraged to keep our fantasies on a tight rein, otherwise we'll lose control of the whole buggy, and no one can say we weren't warned. So for us AIDS remains a private hell, smoldering beneath intimate conversations among friends and surfacing on those occasional sleepless nights when it occurs to us to wonder about it, upon which that dark hysteria sets in, and those catalogues of whom we've done it with and whom they might have done it with and oh-my-God-I'll-surely-die seem to project themselves onto the ceiling, the way fanged monsters did when we were children. But we fall asleep and then we wake up. And nothing has changed except our willingness to forget about it, which has become the ultimate survival mechanism. What my peers and I are left with is a generalized anxiety, a low-grade fear and anger that resides at the core of everything we do. Our attitudes have been affected by the disease by leaving us scared, but our behavior has stayed largely the same. One result is a corrosion of the soul, a chronic dishonesty and fear that will most likely damage us more than the disease itself. In this world, peace of mind is a utopian concept.

QUESTIONS ON MEANING

1. What is Daum's PURPOSE in writing this essay? On whom, or what, is she placing blame? Does she offer any solutions in the essay, or is she merely outlining a problem previously unacknowledged?
2. What is Daum's THESIS? Where is it stated?
3. What does Daum mean when she says, "Our sense of entitlement exceeds our sense of vulnerability" (para. 2)?
4. Explain how AIDS awareness has become "part of the pop culture" (para. 7).
5. Why does it make a difference to Daum that the people represented in the Benetton ad are not known to be HIV-positive?
6. Explain the title's double meaning: What are the two kinds of "Safe-Sex Lies" discussed in the essay?

QUESTIONS ON WRITING STRATEGY

1. Daum asserts that the media exaggerate the prevalence of AIDS among heterosexuals who are not IV drug users. Explain the chain of causes and effects that she sees as leading from this exaggeration.
2. What is the TONE of the essay?
3. What is the EFFECT of Daum's confession in the second paragraph?
4. What AUDIENCE do you think Daum had in mind when she was writing this essay? Is she targeting all readers of the *New York Times* or a more specific subset of them?

QUESTIONS ON LANGUAGE

1. Look up any of the following words you don't already know: retrospect, demographic, incumbent (para. 1); entitlement, breach (2); cynical (3); mantra, scoundrels, ignoramuses, naïveté (4); ideology (5); abstract, contemporaries, onus (6); subsumed, aura, tousled (7); surveillance (8); fraught, specter (10); vigilant, smoldering, generalized, low-grade (11).
2. What is the effect of the word *those* in "those disposable needles" and "those minutes spent in a publicly financed waiting room" (para. 1)?
3. Daum's language is often quite informal, as in conversation—for instance, "unless we wanted to die; that's right, *die*" and "they'd seen it happen, oh, yes, they had" (para. 1); "It seems there is a lot of lying going around" (4); or "It's a bummer on a grand scale" (10). What is the effect of this language? Is it appropriate to Daum's subject and purpose? Why, or why not?

SUGGESTIONS FOR WRITING

1. **JOURNAL WRITING.** Daum is part of an ever-expanding group of writers representing what has been called "Generation X." What do you think are the characteristics of this generation? In your journal, make a list of the specific qualities and concerns that distinguish Generation X from its predecessors. **FROM JOURNAL TO ESSAY.** Write an essay DEFINING Generation X, drawing on your journal entry, Daum's essay, and any other sources that offer ideas. Keep in mind that characterization of such a large and diverse group will require GENERALIZATION on your part. How does your definition compare with other definitions you have heard in the media? Does any attempt to characterize a generation necessarily oversimplify? Do you find some value or interest in the exercise?

2. Write an essay about how AIDS has (or hasn't) changed your life, considering the following questions: Is AIDS something you think about often, or is it something "out there" that happens to other people? How do the media influence your attitudes toward the disease? If a cure for AIDS were discovered tomorrow, would your approach to sexuality and relationships change, or has AIDS permanently affected your attitudes?

3. **CRITICAL WRITING.** Analyze how Daum's "demographic profile" (para. 1) determines her perspective on AIDS. Do you find this limited perspective appropriate, or do you think Daum should have mentioned other views as well—perhaps of those who urge sexual abstinence or who care for AIDS patients or who have AIDS themselves? To what extent does Daum's limited perspective weaken or strengthen her essay?

4. **CONNECTIONS.** Daum and Armin A. Brott, in "Not All Men Are Sly Foxes" (p. 278), are both concerned about the subtle effects of words and pictures on an audience: Daum is interested in the way safe sex is marketed, the face advertising puts on AIDS; Brott is troubled by the negative stereotyping of fathers in books for children. Write an essay criticizing what you consider to be inaccurate or inappropriate media representation of a given group (for example, single mothers, gays and lesbians, lawyers, football players, fashion models). What message do these portrayals send to members of that group and to those outside the group? How might the portrayals be improved?

STEPHEN JAY GOULD

A paleontologist and collector of snails, STEPHEN JAY GOULD was born in New York City in 1941, went to Antioch College, and took a doctorate from Columbia University. Since the age of twenty-five, Gould has taught biology, geology, and the history of science at Harvard, where his courses are among the most popular. Although he has written for specialists (*Ontogeny and Phylogeny*, 1977), Gould is best known for essays that explore science in prose a layperson can enjoy. He writes a monthly column for *Natural History* magazine, and these and other essays have been collected in eight books, including *The Panda's Thumb* (1980), *Hens' Teeth and Horses' Toes* (1983), *Eight Little Piggies* (1993), and *Dinosaur in a Haystack* (1995). His latest book is *Full House* (1996), which holds that the best measure of evolution is not progress or complexity but variety. In 1981, Gould received $200,000 (popularly called a "genius grant") from the MacArthur Foundation, which subsidizes the work of original artists and thinkers.

Sex, Drugs, Disasters, and the Extinction of Dinosaurs

In this essay, Stephen Jay Gould tackles one of the greatest mysteries in the evolution of life on this planet: the extinction of dinosaurs. Working backward from this concrete effect (the fact that dinosaurs are extinct), Gould employs both scholarship and wit to analyze several possible causes. The essay originally appeared in *Discover* magazine in March 1984, and it is included in Gould's fourth collection of essays, *The Flamingo's Smile*.

Science, in its most fundamental definition, is a fruitful mode of inquiry, not a list of enticing conclusions. The conclusions are the consequence, not the essence. 1

My greatest unhappiness with most popular presentations of science concerns their failure to separate fascinating claims from the methods that scientists use to establish the facts of nature. Journalists, and the public, thrive on controversial and stunning statements. But science is, basically, a way of knowing—in P. B. Medawar's apt words, "the art of the soluble." If the growing corps of popular science writers would focus on *how* scientists develop and defend those fascinating claims, they would make their greatest possible contribution to public understanding. 2

Consider three ideas, proposed in perfect seriousness to explain that greatest of all titillating puzzles—the extinction of dinosaurs. Since these three notions invoke the primally fascinating themes of 3 our culture—sex, drugs, and violence—they surely reside in the category of fascinating claims. I want to show why two of them rank as silly speculation, while the other represents science at its grandest and most useful.

Science works with testable proposals. If, after much compilation 4 and scrutiny of data, new information continues to affirm a hypothesis, we may accept it provisionally and gain confidence as further evidence mounts. We can never be completely sure that a hypothesis is right, though we may be able to show with confidence that it is wrong. The best scientific hypotheses are also generous and expansive: They suggest extensions and implications that enlighten related, and even far distant, subjects. Simply consider how the idea of evolution has influenced virtually every intellectual field.

Useless speculation, on the other hand, is restrictive. It generates 5 no testable hypothesis, and offers no way to obtain potentially refuting evidence. Please note that I am not speaking of truth or falsity. The speculation may well be true; still, if it provides, in principle, no material for affirmation or rejection, we can make nothing of it. It must simply stand forever as an intriguing idea. Useless speculation turns in on itself and leads nowhere; good science, containing both seeds for its potential refutation and implications for more and different testable knowledge, reaches out. But, enough preaching. Let's move on to dinosaurs, and the three proposals for their extinction.

1. *Sex.*   Testes function only in a narrow range of temperature (those of mammals hang externally in a scrotal sac because internal body temperatures are too high for their proper function). A worldwide rise in temperature at the close of the Cretaceous period caused the testes of dinosaurs to stop functioning and led to their extinction by sterilization of males.

2. *Drugs.*   Angiosperms (flowering plants) first evolved toward the end of the dinosaurs' reign. Many of these plants contain psychoactive agents, avoided by mammals today as a result of their bitter taste. Dinosaurs had neither means to taste the bitterness nor livers effective enough to detoxify the substances. They died of massive overdoses.

3. *Disasters.*   A large comet or asteroid struck the earth some 65 million years ago, lofting a cloud of dust into the sky and blocking sunlight, thereby suppressing photosynthesis and so drastically lowering world temperatures that dinosaurs and hosts of other creatures became extinct.

Before analyzing these three tantalizing statements, we must establish a basic ground rule often violated in proposals for the dinosaurs' demise.

There is no separate problem of the extinction of dinosaurs. Too often we divorce specific events from their wider contexts and systems of cause and effect. The fundamental fact of dinosaur extinction is its synchrony with the demise of so many other groups across a wide range of habitats, from terrestrial to marine.

The history of life has been punctuated by brief episodes of mass   6
extinction. A recent analysis by University of Chicago paleontologists Jack Sepkoski and Dave Raup, based on the best and most exhaustive tabulation of data ever assembled, shows clearly that five episodes of mass dying stand well above the "background" extinctions of normal times (when we consider all mass extinctions, large and small, they seem to fall in a regular 26-million-year cycle). The Cretaceous debacle, occurring 65 million years ago and separating the Mesozoic and Cenozoic eras of our geological time scale, ranks prominently among the five. Nearly all the marine plankton (single-celled floating creatures) died with geological suddenness; among marine invertebrates, nearly 15 percent of all families perished, including many previously dominant groups, especially the ammonites (relatives of squids in coiled shells). On land, the dinosaurs disappeared after more than 100 million years of unchallenged domination.

In this context, speculations limited to dinosaurs alone ignore the   7
larger phenomenon. We need a coordinated explanation for a system of events that includes the extinction of dinosaurs as one component. Thus it makes little sense, though it may fuel our desire to view mammals as inevitable inheritors of the earth, to guess that dinosaurs died because small mammals ate their eggs (a perennial favorite among untestable speculations). It seems most unlikely that some disaster peculiar to dinosaurs befell these massive beasts—and that the debacle happened to strike just when one of history's five great dyings had enveloped the earth for completely different reasons.

The testicular theory, an old favorite from the 1940s, had its root   8
in an interesting and thoroughly respectable study of temperature tolerances in the American alligator, published in the staid *Bulletin of the American Museum of Natural History* in 1946 by three experts on living and fossil reptiles—E. H. Colbert, my own first teacher in paleontology; R. B. Cowles; and C. M. Bogert.

The first sentence of their summary reveals a purpose beyond alliga-   9
tors: "This report describes an attempt to infer the reactions of extinct reptiles, especially the dinosaurs, to high temperatures as based upon reactions observed in the modern alligator." They studied, by rectal thermometry, the body temperatures of alligators under changing conditions of heating and cooling. (Well, let's face it, you wouldn't want to try sticking a thermometer under a 'gator's tongue.) The predictions under test go way back to an old theory first stated by Galileo in the 1630s—the

unequal scaling of surfaces and volumes. As an animal, or any object, grows (provided its shape doesn't change), surface areas must increase more slowly than volumes—since surfaces get larger as length squared, while volumes increase much more rapidly, as length cubed. Therefore, small animals have high ratios of surface to volume, while large animals cover themselves with relatively little surface.

Among cold-blooded animals lacking any physiological mecha-   10
nism for keeping their temperatures constant, small creatures have a hell of a time keeping warm—because they lose so much heat through their relatively large surfaces. On the other hand, large animals, with their relatively small surfaces, may lose heat so slowly that, once warm, they may maintain effectively constant temperatures against ordinary fluctuations of climate. (In fact, the resolution of the "hot-blooded dinosaur" controversy that burned so brightly a few years back may simply be that, while large dinosaurs possessed no physiological mechanism for constant temperature, and were not therefore warm-blooded in the technical sense, their large size and relatively small surface area kept them warm.)

Colbert, Cowles, and Bogert compared the warming rates of small   11
and large alligators. As predicted, the small fellows heated up (and cooled down) more quickly. When exposed to a warm sun, a tiny 50-gram (1.76-ounce) alligator heated up one degree Celsius every minute and a half, while a large alligator, 260 times bigger at 13,000 grams (28.7 pounds), took seven and a half minutes to gain a degree. Extrapolating up to an adult 10-ton dinosaur, they concluded that a one-degree rise in body temperature would take eighty-six hours. If large animals absorb heat so slowly (through their relatively small surfaces), they will also be unable to shed any excess heat gained when temperatures rise above a favorable level.

The authors then guessed that large dinosaurs lived at or near their   12
optimum temperatures; Cowles suggested that a rise in global temperatures just before the Cretaceous extinction caused the dinosaurs to heat up beyond their optimal tolerance—and, being so large, they couldn't shed the unwanted heat. (In a most unusual statement within a scientific paper, Colbert and Bogert then explicitly disavowed this speculative extension of their empirical work on alligators.) Cowles conceded that this excess heat probably wasn't enough to kill or even to enervate the great beasts, but since testes often function only within a narrow range of temperature, he proposed that this global rise might have sterilized all the males, causing extinction by natural contraception.

The overdose theory has recently been supported by UCLA psy-   13
chiatrist Ronald K. Siegel. Siegel has gathered, he claims, more than 2,000 records of animals who, when given access, administer various drugs to themselves—from a mere swig of alcohol to massive doses of

the big H. Elephants will swill the equivalent of twenty beers at a time, but do not like alcohol in concentrations greater than 7 percent. In a silly bit of anthropocentric speculation, Siegel states that "elephants drink, perhaps, to forget...the anxiety produced by shrinking rangeland and the competition for food."

Since fertile imaginations can apply almost any hot idea to the ex-   14
tinction of dinosaurs, Siegel found a way. Flowering plants did not evolve until late in the dinosaurs' reign. These plants also produced an array of aromatic, amino-acid-based alkaloids—the major group of psychoactive agents. Most mammals are "smart" enough to avoid these potential poisons. The alkaloids simply don't taste good (they are bitter); in any case, we mammals have livers happily supplied with the capacity to detoxify them. But, Siegel speculates, perhaps dinosaurs could neither taste the bitterness nor detoxify the substances once ingested. He recently told members of the American Psychological Association: "I'm not suggesting that all dinosaurs OD'd on plant drugs, but it certainly was a factor." He also argued that death by overdose may help explain why so many dinosaur fossils are found in contorted positions. (Do not go gently into that good night.)

Extraterrestrial catastrophes have long pedigrees in the popular lit-   15
erature of extinction, but the subject exploded again in 1979, after a long lull, when the father-son, physicist-geologist team of Luis and Walter Alvarez proposed that an asteroid, some 10 km in diameter, struck the earth 65 million years ago (comets, rather than asteroids, have since gained favor. Good science is self-corrective).

The force of such a collision would be immense, greater by far than   16
the megatonnage of all the world's nuclear weapons. In trying to reconstruct a scenario that would explain the simultaneous dying of dinosaurs on land and so many creatures in the sea, the Alvarezes proposed that a gigantic dust cloud, generated by particles blown aloft in the impact, would so darken the earth that photosynthesis would cease and temperatures drop precipitously. (Rage, rage against the dying of the light.) The single-celled photosynthetic oceanic plankton, with life cycles measured in weeks, would perish outright, but land plants might survive through the dormancy of their seeds (land plants were not much affected by the Cretaceous extinction, and any adequate theory must account for the curious pattern of differential survival). Dinosaurs would die by starvation and freezing; small, warm-blooded mammals, with more modest requirements for food and better regulation of body temperature, would squeak through. "Let the bastards freeze in the dark," as bumper stickers of our chauvinistic neighbors in sunbelt states proclaimed several years ago during the Northeast's winter oil crisis.

All three theories, testicular malfunction, psychoactive overdos-   17 ing, and asteroidal zapping, grab our attention mightily. As pure phenomenology, they rank about equally high on any hit parade of primal fascination. Yet one represents expansive science, the others restrictive and untestable speculation. The proper criterion lies in evidence and methodology; we must probe behind the superficial fascination of particular claims.

How could we possibly decide whether the hypothesis of testicular 18 frying is right or wrong? We would have to know things that the fossil record cannot provide. What temperatures were optimal for dinosaurs? Could they avoid the absorption of excess heat by staying in the shade, or in caves? At what temperatures did their testicles cease to function? Were late Cretaceous climates ever warm enough to drive the internal temperatures of dinosaurs close to this ceiling? Testicles simply don't fossilize, and how could we infer their temperature tolerances even if they did? In short, Cowles's hypothesis is only an intriguing speculation leading nowhere. The most damning statement against it appeared right in the conclusion of Colbert, Cowles, and Bogert's paper, when they admitted: "It is difficult to advance any definite arguments against this hypothesis." My statement may seem paradoxical — isn't a hypothesis really good if you can't devise any arguments against it? Quite the contrary. It is simply untestable and unusable.

Siegel's overdosing has even less going for it. At least Cowles ex 19 trapolated his conclusion from some good data on alligators. And he didn't completely violate the primary guideline of siting dinosaur extinction in the context of a general mass dying — for rise in temperature could be the root cause of a general catastrophe, zapping dinosaurs by testicular malfunction and different groups for other reasons. But Siegel's speculation cannot touch the extinction of ammonites or oceanic plankton (diatoms make their own food with good sweet sunlight; they don't OD on the chemicals of terrestrial plants). It is simply a gratuitous, attention-grabbing guess. It cannot be tested, for how can we know what dinosaurs tasted and what their livers could do? Livers don't fossilize any better than testicles.

The hypothesis doesn't even make any sense in its own context. An 20 giosperms were in full flower ten million years before dinosaurs went the way of all flesh. Why did it take so long? As for the pains of a chemical death recorded in contortions of fossils, I regret to say (or rather I'm pleased to note for the dinosaurs' sake) that Siegel's knowledge of geology must be a bit deficient: Muscles contract after death and geological strata rise and fall with motions of the earth's crust after burial — more than enough reason to distort a fossil's pristine appearance.

The impact story, on the other hand, has a sound basis in evidence. 21 It can be tested, extended, refined, and, if wrong, disproved. The

Alvarezes did not just construct an arresting guess for public consumption. They proposed their hypothesis after laborious geochemical studies with Frank Asaro and Helen Michael had revealed a massive increase of iridium in rocks deposited right at the time of extinction. Iridium, a rare metal of the platinum group, is virtually absent from indigenous rocks of the earth's crust; most of our iridium arrives on extraterrestrial objects that strike the earth.

The Alvarez hypothesis bore immediate fruit. Based originally on   22
evidence from two European localities, it led geochemists throughout the world to examine other sediments of the same age. They found abnormally high amounts of iridium everywhere — from continental rocks of the western United States to deep sea cores from the South Atlantic.

Cowles proposed his testicular hypothesis in the mid-1940s. Where   23
has it gone since then? Absolutely nowhere, because scientists can do nothing with it. The hypothesis must stand as a curious appendage to a solid study of alligators. Siegel's overdose scenario will also win a few press notices and fade into oblivion. The Alvarezes' asteroid falls into a different category altogether, and much of the popular commentary has missed this essential distinction by focusing on the impact and its attendant results, and forgetting what really matters to a scientist — the iridium. If you talk just about asteroids, dust, and darkness, you tell stories no better and no more entertaining than fried testicles or terminal trips. It is the iridium — the source of testable evidence — that counts and forges the crucial distinction between speculation and science.

The proof, to twist a phrase, lies in the doing. Cowles's hypothesis   24
has generated nothing in thirty-five years. Since its proposal in 1979, the Alvarez hypothesis has spawned hundreds of studies, a major conference, and attendant publications. Geologists are fired up. They are looking for iridium at all other extinction boundaries. Every week exposes a new wrinkle in the scientific press. Further evidence that the Cretaceous iridium represents extraterrestrial impact and not indigenous volcanism continues to accumulate. As I revise this essay in November 1984 (this paragraph will be out of date when [it] is published), new data include chemical "signatures" of other isotopes indicating unearthly provenance, glass spherules of a size and sort produced by impact and not by volcanic eruptions, and high-pressure varieties of silica formed (so far as we know) only under the tremendous shock of impact.

My point is simply this: Whatever the eventual outcome (I suspect   25
it will be positive), the Alvarez hypothesis is exciting, fruitful science because it generates tests, provides us with things to do, and expands outward. We are having fun, battling back and forth, moving toward a resolution, and extending the hypothesis beyond its original scope.

As just one example of the unexpected, distant cross-fertilization   26
that good science engenders, the Alvarez hypothesis made a major con-

tribution to a theme that has riveted public attention in the past few months—so-called nuclear winter. In a speech delivered in April 1982, Luis Alvarez calculated the energy that a ten-kilometer asteroid would release on impact. He compared such an explosion with a full nuclear exchange and implied that all-out atomic war might unleash similar consequences.

This theme of impact leading to massive dust clouds and falling 27 temperatures formed an important input to the decision of Carl Sagan and a group of colleagues to model the climatic consequences of nuclear holocaust. Full nuclear exchange would probably generate the same kind of dust cloud and darkening that may have wiped out the dinosaurs. Temperatures would drop precipitously and agriculture might become impossible. Avoidance of nuclear war is fundamentally an ethical and political imperative, but we must know the factual consequences to make firm judgments. I am heartened by a final link across disciplines and deep concerns—another criterion, by the way, of science at its best: A recognition of the very phenomenon that made our evolution possible by exterminating the previously dominant dinosaurs and clearing a way for the evolution of large mammals, including us, might actually help to save us from joining those magnificent beasts in contorted poses among the strata of the earth.

QUESTIONS ON MEANING

1. According to Gould, what constitutes a scientific hypothesis? What constitutes useless speculation? Where in the essay do you find his DEFINITIONS of these terms?
2. State, in your own words, the THESIS of this essay.
3. What does Gould perceive to be the major flaws in the testicular malfunction and drug overdose theories about the extinction of dinosaurs? Cite his specific reasons for discrediting each theory.
4. What is the connection between nuclear holocaust and the extinction of dinosaurs? (See the essay's last paragraph.)

QUESTIONS ON WRITING STRATEGY

1. How do you understand the phrases "hit parade of primal fascination" (para. 17) and "the hypothesis of testicular frying" (18)? Is the TONE here somber, silly, whimsical, ironic, or what?
2. Paragraphs 14 and 16 both contain references to Dylan Thomas's poem "Do Not Go Gentle into That Good Night." (The poem's title is used in para. 14; "Rage, rage against the dying of the light," one of the poem's refrains, appears in para. 16.) If you are not familiar with the poem, look it

up. Is it necessary to know the poem to understand Gould's use of these lines? What is the EFFECT of these ALLUSIONS?

3. In explaining the Alvarezes' hypothesis about the dinosaurs, Gould outlines a causal chain. Draw a diagram to illustrate this chain.

4. **OTHER METHODS.** The methods of EXAMPLE, COMPARISON AND CONTRAST, PROCESS ANALYSIS, and DIVISION or ANALYSIS are all at work in this essay. Identify instances of each, and discuss the function each performs in the essay.

QUESTIONS ON LANGUAGE

1. What do you take the sentence "There is no separate problem of the extinction of dinosaurs" (para. 5) to mean? Separate from what? According to Gould, then, what *is* the problem being discussed?

2. Be sure you can define the following words: enticing (para. 1); hypothesis (4); psychoactive, photosynthesis, synchrony (5); paleontology (8); extrapolating (11); empirical (12); gratuitous (19).

SUGGESTIONS FOR WRITING

1. **JOURNAL WRITING.** Gould's essay is interesting partly because he proposes several possible causes for the same effect. We all do the same thing daily (if more informally) when we try to solve puzzles like "Why is my bike tire flat?" (it was slashed; I rode over glass; I haven't ridden the bike in weeks) or "Why do little siblings ask so many questions?" (to annoy us; because they're curious; because someone puts them up to it). In your journal, try to work out the probable cause(s) of a situation in which you are directly involved—working in the school cafeteria, taking a psychology course offered only on Wednesday evenings, riding to school with a person you detest, dating your former best friend, whatever. What are all the causes you can think of—both immediate and remote?

   FROM JOURNAL TO ESSAY. Once you have a number of ideas about the causes of your situation, write a formal essay that explains the causes in detail. Make sure to give your AUDIENCE a clear sense of the situation. You may want to rely on NARRATION, telling the story of the circumstances.

2. As Gould himself predicts (para. 24), his summary of the research into the Alvarez hypothesis is now dated: More data have accumulated; the hypothesis has been challenged, tested, revised. Consult the *Readers' Guide to Periodical Literature* or *InfoTrac* for the past several years to find articles on the extinction of the dinosaurs. Write an essay updating Gould's in which you summarize the significant EVIDENCE for and against the Alvarez hypothesis.

3. **CRITICAL WRITING.** Apply Gould's distinction between hypothesis and speculation (paras. 4–5) in an area you know well—for instance, Civil War battles, dance, basketball, waste recycling, carpentry, nursing. What, in your area, is the equivalent of the useful hypothesis? What is the equivalent of the useless speculation? Be as specific as possible so that a reader outside the field can understand you.

4. **CONNECTIONS.** Gould's is one of several essays in this book written by specialists for an audience of nonspecialists; others include Bruce Catton's

"Grant and Lee" (p. 193), Horace Miner's "Body Ritual Among the Nacirema" (p. 239), Edward Tenner's "Voice Mail and Fire Ants" (p. 323), Deborah Tannen's "But What Do You Mean?" (p. 329), and Robert B. Reich's "Why the Rich Are Getting Richer and the Poor Poorer" (p. 346). In an essay, compare Gould's essay with one of the others listed in terms of complexity of material, use and explanation of technical vocabulary, and clarity of explanation. Overall, which essay do you find more effective in explaining a technical subject?

STEPHEN JAY GOULD ON WRITING

In his prologue to *The Flamingo's Smile,* Stephen Jay Gould positions himself in a long and respectable tradition of writers who communicate scientific ideas to a general audience. To popularize, he says, does not mean to trivialize, cheapen, or adulterate. "I follow one cardinal rule in writing these essays," he insists. "No compromises. I will make language accessible by defining or eliminating jargon; I will not simplify concepts. I can state all sorts of highfalutin, moral justifications for this approach (and I do believe in them), but the basic reason is simple and personal. I write these essays primarily to aid my own quest to learn and understand as much as possible about nature in the short time allotted."

In his own view, Gould is lucky: He is a writer carried along by a single, fascinating theme. "If my volumes work at all, they owe their reputation to coherence supplied by the common theme of evolutionary theory. I have a wonderful advantage among essayists because no other theme so beautifully encompasses both the particulars that fascinate and the generalities that instruct....Each essay is both a single long argument and a welding together of particulars."

FOR DISCUSSION

1. What differences would occur naturally between the work of a scientist writing for other scientists and the work of Gould, who writes about science for a general AUDIENCE?
2. How does the author defend himself against the possible charge that, as a popularizer of science, he trivializes his subject?

ADDITIONAL WRITING TOPICS

Cause and Effect

1. In a short essay, explain *either* the causes *or* the effects of a situation that concerns you. Narrow your topic enough to treat it in some detail, and provide more than a mere list of causes or effects. If seeking causes, you will have to decide carefully how far back to go in your search for remote causes. If stating effects, fill your essay with examples. Here are some topics to consider:

Labor strikes in professional sports
Children searching for pornography on the Internet
State laws mandating the use of seat belts in cars (or the wearing of helmets on motorcycles)
Friction between two roommates, or two friends
The pressure on students to get good grades
Some quirk in your personality, or a friend's
The increasing need for more than one breadwinner per family
The temptation to do something dishonest to get ahead
The popularity of a particular television program, comic strip, rock group, or pop singer
The steady increase in college costs
The scarcity of people in training for employment as skilled workers: plumbers, tool and die makers, electricians, masons, carpenters, to name a few
A decision to enter the ministry or a religious order
The fact that cigarette advertising is banned from television
The absence of a peacetime draft
The fact that more couples are choosing to have only one child, or none
The growing popularity of private elementary and high schools
The fact that most Americans can communicate in no language other than English
Being "born again"
The fact that women increasingly are training for jobs formerly regarded as men's only
The pressure on young people to conform to the standards of their peers
The emphasis on competitive sports in high school and college

2. In *Blue Highways* (1982), an account of his rambles around America, William Least Heat Moon explains why Americans, and not the British, settled the vast tract of northern land that lies between the Mississippi and the Rockies. He traces what he believes to be the major cause in this paragraph:

> Were it not for a web-footed rodent and a haberdashery fad in eighteenth-century Europe, Minnesota might be a Canadian province today. The beaver, almost as much as the horse, helped

396

shape the course of early American history. Some *Mayflower* colonists paid their passage with beaver pelts; and a good fur could bring an Indian three steel knives or a five-foot stack could bring a musket. But even more influential were the trappers and fur traders penetrating the great Northern wilderness between the Mississippi River and the Rocky Mountains, since it was their presence that helped hold the Near West against British expansion from the north; and it was their explorations that opened the heart of the nation to white settlement. These men, by making pelts the currency of the wilds, laid the base for a new economy that quickly overwhelmed the old. And all because European men of mode simply had to wear a beaver hat.

In a Least Heat Moon–like paragraph of your own, explain how a small cause produced a large effect. You might generate ideas by browsing in a history book — where you might find, for instance, that a cow belonging to Mrs. Patrick O'Leary is believed to have started the Great Chicago Fire of 1871 by kicking over a lighted lantern — or in a collection of *Ripley's Believe It or Not*. If some small event in your life has had large consequences, you might care to write instead from personal experience.

9

Week Gight

DEFINITION
Tracing a Boundary

THE METHOD

As a rule, when we hear the word DEFINITION, we immediately think of a dictionary. In that helpful storehouse—a writer's best friend—we find the literal and specific meaning (or meanings) of a word. The dictionary supplies this information concisely: in a sentence, in a phrase, or even in a *synonym*—a single word that means the same thing ("**narrative** [năr-e-tĭv] *n.* **1**: story...").

Stating such a definition is often a good way to begin an essay when basic terms may be in doubt. A short definition can clarify your subject to your reader, and perhaps help you to limit what you have to say. If, for instance, you are going to discuss a demolition derby, explaining such a spectacle to readers who may never have seen one, you might offer at the outset a short definition of *demolition derby*, your subject and your key term.

In constructing a short definition, the usual procedure is to state the general class to which the subject belongs and then add any particular features that distinguish it. You could say: "A demolition derby is a contest"—that is its general class—"in which drivers ram old cars into one another until only one car is left running." Short definitions may

399

be useful at *any* moment in an essay, whenever you introduce a technical term that readers may not know. When a term is really central to your essay and likely to be misunderstood, a *stipulative definition* may be helpful. This fuller explanation stipulates, or specifies, the particular way you are using a term. The paragraph on page 405, defining *TV addiction*, is a stipulative definition from a much longer essay on the causes and cures of the addiction.

In this chapter, we are mainly concerned with *extended definition*, a kind of expository writing that relies on a variety of other methods. Suppose you wanted to write an essay to make clear what *poetry* means. You would specify its elements—rhythm, IMAGES, and so on—by using DIVISION or ANALYSIS. You'd probably provide EXAMPLES of each element. You might COMPARE AND CONTRAST poetry with prose. You might discuss the EFFECT of poetry on the reader. (Emily Dickinson, a poet herself, once stated the effect that reading a poem had on her: "I feel as if the top of my head were taken off.") In fact, extended definition, unlike other methods of writing discussed in this book, is perhaps less a method in itself than the application of a variety of methods to clarify a purpose. Like DESCRIPTION, extended definition tries to *show* a reader its subject. It does so by establishing boundaries, for its writer tries to differentiate a subject from anything that might be confused with it. When Tom Wolfe, in his essay in this chapter, seeks to define a certain trend he has noticed in newspapers, books, and television, he describes exactly what he sees happening, so that we, too, will understand what he calls "the pornography of violence." In an extended definition, a writer studies the nature of a subject, carefully sums up its chief characteristics, and strives to answer the question "What is this?" or "What makes this what it is, not something else?"

An extended definition can *define* (from the Latin, "to set bounds to") a word, or it can define a thing (a laser beam), a concept (male chauvinism), or a general phenomenon (the popularity of the demolition derby). Unlike a sentence definition, or any you would find in a standard dictionary, an extended definition takes room: at least a paragraph, perhaps an entire volume. The subject may be as large as the concepts of "holocaust" and "pornography."

Outside an English course, how is this method of writing used? In a newspaper feature, a sportswriter defines what makes a *great team* great. In a journal article, a physician defines the nature of a previously unknown syndrome or disease. In a written opinion, a judge defines not only a word but a concept, *obscenity*. In a book review, a critic defines a newly prevalent kind of poem. In a letter to a younger brother or sister contemplating college, a student might define a *gut course* and how to recognize one.

Unlike a definition in a dictionary that sets forth the literal meaning of a word in an unimpassioned manner, some definitions imply biases. In his extended definition of *pornoviolence*, Tom Wolfe is biased, even jaundiced, in his view of American media. In defining *patron* to the earl of Chesterfield, who had tried to befriend him after ignoring his petitions for aid during his years of grinding poverty, Samuel Johnson wrote scornfully: "Is not a Patron, my Lord, one who looks with unconcern on a man struggling for life in the water, and, when he has reached the ground, encumbers him with help?" IRONY, METAPHOR, and short definition have rarely been wielded with such crushing power. (*Encumbers*, by the way, is a wonderfully physical word in its context: It means "to burden with dead weight.") In having many methods of writing at their disposal, writers of extended definitions have ample freedom and wide latitude.

THE PROCESS

Discovery of Meanings

Say you're preparing to write an extended definition. To discover points about your subject worth noticing, you may find it useful to ask yourself a series of questions. These questions may be applied both to individual subjects, such as a basketball superstar or a comet, and to collective subjects: institutions (like the American family, a typical savings bank, a university, the Church of Jesus Christ of Latter-Day Saints) and organizations (IBM, the Mafia, a heavy-metal band, a Little League baseball team). To illustrate how the questions might work, at least in one instance, let's say you plan to write a paper defining a male chauvinist.[1]

1. *Is this subject unique, or are there others of its kind? If it resembles others, in what ways? How is it different?* As you can see, these last two questions invite you to compare and contrast. Applied to the concept of male chauvinism, these questions might remind you that male chauvinists come in different varieties—middle-aged and college-aged, for instance—and you might care to compare and contrast the two kinds.
2. *In what different forms does it occur, while keeping its own identity?* Specific examples might occur to you: your Uncle George, who won't hire any "damned females" in his auto repair shop; some

---

[1] The six questions that follow are freely adapted from those first stated by Richard E. Young, Alton L. Becker, and Kenneth L. Pike, who have applied insights from psychology and linguistics to the writing process. Their procedure for generating ideas and discovering information is called *tagmemics*. To investigate subjects in greater depth, their own six questions may be used in nine possible combinations, as they explain in detail in *Rhetoric: Discovery and Change* (New York: Harcourt, 1970).

college-aged male acquaintance who regards women as nothing but *Penthouse* centerfolds. Each form—Uncle George and the would-be stud—might rate a description.

3. *When and where do we find it? Under what circumstances and in what situations?* Well, where have you been lately? At any parties where male chauvinism reared its ugly head? In any classroom discussions? Consider other areas of your experience: Did you meet any such males while holding a part-time summer job?

4. *What is it at the present moment?* Perhaps you might make the point that a few years ago male chauvinists used to be blatant tyrants and harsh critics of women. Today, wary of being recognized, they appear as ordinary citizens who now and then slip in a little tyranny, or make a nasty remark. You might care to draw examples from life.

5. *What does it do? What are its functions and activities?* Male chauvinists try to keep women in what they imagine to be women's place. These questions might even invite you to reply with a process analysis. You might show how some male chauvinist you know goes about implementing his views: how a personnel director you met, who determines pay scales, systematically eliminates women from better-paying jobs; how the *Penthouse* reader plots a seduction.

6. *How is it put together? What parts make it up? What holds these parts together?* You could apply analysis to the various beliefs and assumptions that, all together, make up a male chauvinist's attitude. This question might work well in writing about some organization: the personnel director's company, for instance, with its unfair hiring policies.

Not all these questions will fit every subject under the sun, and some may lead nowhere, but you will usually find them well worth asking. They can make you aware of points to notice, remind you of facts you already know. They can also suggest interesting points you need to find out more about.

Methods of Development

The preceding questions will give you a good start on using whatever method or methods of writing can best answer the overall question "What is the nature of this subject?" You will probably find yourself making use of much that you have learned earlier from this book. A short definition like the one for *demolition derby* on page 399 may be a good start for your essay, especially if you think your readers need a quick grounding in the subject or in your view of it. (But feel no duty to place a dictionaryish definition in the INTRODUCTION of every essay you write: The device is overused.) In explaining a demolition derby, if your readers already have at least a vague idea of the meaning of the term and need no short, formal definition of it, you might open your extended definition with the aid of NARRATION. You could relate the events at a typical demolition derby, starting with a description of the lineup of old beat-up vehicles:

> One hundred worthless cars—everything from a 1940 Cadillac to a Dodge Dart to a recently wrecked Thunderbird, their glass removed, their radiators leaking—assemble on a racetrack or an open field. Their drivers, wearing crash helmets, buckle themselves into their seats, some pulling at beer cans to soften the blows to come.

You might proceed by example, listing demolition derbies you have known ("The great destruction of 184 vehicles took place at the Orleans County Fair in Barton, Vermont, in the summer of '91..."). If you have enough examples, you might wish to CLASSIFY them; or perhaps you might analyze a demolition derby, dividing it into its components of cars, drivers, judges, first-aid squad, and spectators, and discussing each. You could compare and contrast a demolition derby with that amusement park ride known as Bumper Cars or Dodge-'ems, in which small cars with rubber bumpers bash one another head-on, but (unlike cars in the derby) harmlessly. A PROCESS ANALYSIS of a demolition derby might help your readers understand the nature of the spectacle: how in round after round, cars are eliminated until one remains. You might ask "What causes the owners of old cars to want to smash them?" or "What causes people to watch the destruction?" or "What are the consequences?" To answer such questions in an essay, you would apply the method of CAUSE AND EFFECT.

Thesis

Opening up your subject with questions and developing it with various methods are good ways to see what your subject has to offer, but they can also leave you with a welter of ideas and a blurred focus. As in description, when all your details build to a dominant impression, so in definition you want to center all your thoughts and evidence about the subject on a single controlling idea, a THESIS. It's not essential to state this idea in a THESIS SENTENCE, although doing so can be a service to your readers. What is essential is that the idea govern.

Here, from the essays in this chapter, are several thesis sentences. Notice how each focuses the broad subject to an assertion about the subject, and how we can detect the author's bias toward the subject.

The word *chink* may have been created to harm, ridicule, and humiliate, but for us [Chinese Americans] it may have done the exact opposite. (Christine Leong, "Being a Chink")

In the new pornography [of violence], the theme is not sex. The new pornography depicts practitioners acting out another, murkier drive: people staving teeth in, ripping guts open, blowing brains out, and getting even with all those bastards. (Tom Wolfe, "Pornoviolence")

We should give [the murder of the Jews] its true designation and not hide it behind polite, erudite terms [such as *holocaust*] created out of classical words. (Bruno Bettelheim, "The Holocaust")

Evidence

Writing an extended definition, you are like a mapmaker charting a territory, taking in some of what lies within the boundaries and ignoring what lies outside. The boundaries, of course, may be wide; and for this reason, the writing of an extended definition sometimes tempts a writer to sweep across a continent airily and to soar off into abstract clouds. Like any other method of expository writing, though, definition will work only for the writer who remembers the world of the senses and supports every generalization with concrete evidence.

There may be no finer illustration of the perils of definition than the scene, in Charles Dickens's novel *Hard Times*, of the grim schoolroom of a teacher named Gradgrind, who insists on facts but who completely ignores living realities. When a girl whose father is a horse trainer is unable to define a horse, Gradgrind blames her for not knowing what a horse is; and he praises the definition of a horse supplied by a pet pupil: "Quadruped. Graminivorous. Forty teeth, namely twenty-four grinders, four eye-teeth, and twelve incisive. Sheds coat in the spring; in marshy countries, sheds hoofs, too. Hoofs hard, but requiring to be shod with iron. Age known by marks in mouth." To anyone who didn't already know what a horse is, this enumeration of facts would prove of little help. In writing an extended definition, never lose sight of the reality you are attempting to bound, even if its frontiers are as inclusive as those of *psychological burnout* or *human rights*. Give your reader examples, narrate an illustrative story, bring in specific description — in whatever method you use, keep coming down to earth. Without your eyes on the world, you will define no reality. You might define *animal husbandry* till the cows come home and never make clear what it means.

CHECKLIST FOR REVISING A DEFINITION

✔ **MEANINGS.** Have you explored your subject fully, turning up both its obvious and its not-so-obvious meanings?

✔ **METHODS OF DEVELOPMENT.** Have you used an appropriate range of other methods to develop your subject?

✔ **THESIS.** Have you focused your definition and kept within that focus, drawing clear boundaries around your subject?

✔ **EVIDENCE.** Is your definition specific? Do examples, anecdotes, and concrete details both pin the subject down and make it vivid for readers?

DEFINITION IN A PARAGRAPH: TWO ILLUSTRATIONS

Using Definition to Write About Television

But who is addicted to TV? According to Marie Winn, author of *The Plug-in Drug: Television, Children, and the Family,* TV addicts are similar to drug or alcohol addicts: They seek a more pleasurable experience than they can get from normal life; they depend on the source of this pleasure; and their lives are damaged by their dependency. TV addicts, says Winn, use TV to screen out the real world of feelings, worries, demands. They watch compulsively—four, five, even six hours on a work day. And they reject (usually passively, sometimes actively) interaction with family or friends, diverting or productive work at hobbies or chores, and chances for change and growth.

A stipulative definition of TV addiction from an essay on its causes and cures

Comparison with drug or alcohol addiction

Analysis is of TV addicts' characteristics

(Note that the extended definition summarized here—Marie Winn's "TV Addiction"—appears on p. 420.)

Using Definition in an Academic Discipline

When the character traits found in any two species owe their resemblance to a common ancestry, taxonomists say the states are *homologous,* or are *homologues* of each other. *Homology* is defined as correspondence between two structures due to inheritance from a common ancestor. Homologous structures can be identical in appearance and can even be based on identical genes. However, such structures can diverge until they become very different in both appearance and function. Nevertheless, homologous structures usually retain certain basic features that betray a common ancestry. Consider the forelimbs of vertebrates. It is easy to make a detailed, bone-by-bone, muscle-by-muscle comparison of the forearm of a person and a monkey and to conclude that the forearms, as well as the various parts of the forearm, are homologous. The forelimb of a dog, however, shows marked

Definition of homology and related words

Short definition

Refined definition

Examples:

Similar appearance, function, and structure

differences from those of primates in both structure and
function. The forelimb is used for locomotion by dogs but
for grasping and manipulation by people and monkeys. Even
so, all of the bones can still be matched. The wing of a bird
and the flipper of a seal are even more different from each
other or from the human forearm, yet they too are constructed around bones that can be matched on a nearly perfect one-to-one basis.

> —William K. Purves and Gordon H. Orians,
> *Life: The Science of Biology*

*Dissimilar appearance
and function, but
similar structure*

GLORIA NAYLOR

GLORIA NAYLOR describes herself as "just a girl from Queens who can turn a sentence," but she is well known for bringing African American women vividly within the fold of American literature. She was born in 1950 in New York City and served for some years as a missionary for the Jehovah's Witnesses, working "for better world conditions." While in college she made her living as a telephone operator. She graduated from Brooklyn College in 1981 and received an M.A. in African American literature from Yale University in 1983. While teaching at several universities and publishing numerous stories and essays, Naylor has written four interconnected novels: *The Women of Brewster Place* (1982), *Linden Hills* (1985), *Mama Day* (1988), and *Bailey's Cafe* (1992). *The Women of Brewster Place* won the American Book Award for best first novel, and Naylor has also received fellowships from the National Endowment for the Arts and the Guggenheim Foundation. She lives in New York City.

The Meanings of a Word

When she was in third grade, Naylor was stung by a word that seemed new. Only later did she realize she'd been hearing the word all her life, but in an entirely different context. "The Meanings of a Word" (editors' title) first appeared in the *New York Times* in 1986.

Language is the subject. It is the written form with which I've 1 managed to keep the wolf away from the door and, in diaries, to keep my sanity. In spite of this, I consider the written word inferior to the spoken, and much of the frustration experienced by novelists is the awareness that whatever we manage to capture in even the most transcendent passages falls far short of the richness of life. Dialogue achieves its power in the dynamics of a fleeting moment of sight, sound, smell, and touch.

I'm not going to enter the debate here about whether it is language 2 that shapes reality or vice versa. That battle is doomed to be waged whenever we seek intermittent reprieve from the chicken and egg dispute. I will simply take the position that the spoken word, like the written word, amounts to a nonsensical arrangement of sounds or letters without a consensus that assigns "meaning." And building from the meanings of what we hear, we order reality. Words themselves are innocuous; it is the consensus that gives them true power.

I remember the first time I heard the word *nigger*. In my third-grade ₃
class, our math tests were being passed down the rows, and as I handed
the papers to a little boy in back of me, I remarked that once again he had
received a much lower mark than I did. He snatched his test from me and
spit out that word. Had he called me a nymphomaniac or a necrophiliac,
I couldn't have been more puzzled. I didn't know what a nigger was, but
I knew that whatever it meant, it was something he shouldn't have called
me. This was verified when I raised my hand, and in a loud voice repeated what he had said and watched the teacher scold him for using a
"bad" word. I was later to go home and ask the inevitable question that
every black parent must face—"Mommy, what does *nigger* mean?"

And what exactly did it mean? Thinking back, I realize that this ₄
could not have been the first time the word was used in my presence. I
was part of a large extended family that had migrated from the rural
South after World War II and formed a close-knit network that gravitated around my maternal grandparents. Their ground-floor apartment
in one of the buildings they owned in Harlem was a weekend mecca for
my immediate family, along with countless aunts, uncles, and cousins
who brought along assorted friends. It was a bustling and open house
with assorted neighbors and tenants popping in and out to exchange
bits of gossip, pick up an old quarrel, or referee the ongoing checkers
game in which my grandmother cheated shamelessly. They were all
there to let down their hair and put up their feet after a week of labor
in the factories, laundries, and shipyards of New York.

Amid the clamor, which could reach deafening proportions—two ₅
or three conversations going on simultaneously, punctuated by the
sound of a baby's crying somewhere in the back rooms or out on the
street—there was still a rigid set of rules about what was said and how.
Older children were sent out of the living room when it was time to get
into the juicy details about "you-know-who" up on the third floor who
had gone and gotten herself "p-r-e-g-n-a-n-t!" But my parents, knowing that I could spell well beyond my years, always demanded that I follow the others out to play. Beyond sexual misconduct and death, everything else was considered harmless for our young ears. And so
among the anecdotes of the triumphs and disappointments in the various workings of their lives, the word *nigger* was used in my presence, but
it was set within contexts and inflections that caused it to register in my
mind as something else.

In the singular, the word was always applied to a man who had dis- ₆
tinguished himself in some situation that brought their approval for his
strength, intelligence, or drive:

"Did Johnny *really* do that?"   ₇

"I'm telling you, that nigger pulled in $6,000 of overtime last year. ₈
Said he got enough for a down payment on a house."

When used with a possessive adjective by a woman—"my nig-   9
ger"—it became a term of endearment for her husband or boyfriend.
But it could be more than just a term applied to a man. In their mouths
it became the pure essence of manhood—a disembodied force that
channeled their past history of struggle and present survival against the
odds into a victorious statement of being: "Yeah, that old foreman
found out quick enough—you don't mess with a nigger."

In the plural, it became a description of some group within the   10
community that had overstepped the bounds of decency as my family
defined it. Parents who neglected their children, a drunken couple who
fought in public, people who simply refused to look for work, those
with excessively dirty mouths or unkempt households were all "trifling
niggers." This particular circle could forgive hard times, unemployment, the occasional bout of depression—they had gone through all of
that themselves—but the unforgivable sin was a lack of self-respect.

A woman could never be a "nigger" in the singular, with its con-   11
notation of confirming worth. The noun *girl* was its closest equivalent
in that sense, but only when used in direct address and regardless of the
gender doing the addressing. *Girl* was a token of respect for a woman.
The one-syllable word was drawn out to sound like three in recognition
of the extra ounce of wit, nerve, or daring that the woman had shown
in the situation under discussion.

"G-i-r-l, stop. You mean you said that to his face?"   12

But if the word was used in a third-person reference or shortened so   13
that it almost snapped out of the mouth, it always involved some element of communal disapproval. And age became an important factor
in these exchanges. It was only between individuals of the same generation, or from any older person to a younger (but never the other way
around), that *girl* would be considered a compliment.

I don't agree with the argument that use of the word *nigger* at this   14
social stratum of the black community was an internalization of racism.
The dynamics were the exact opposite: the people in my grandmother's
living room took a word that whites used to signify worthlessness or
degradation and rendered it impotent. Gathering there together, they
transformed *nigger* to signify the varied and complex human beings
they knew themselves to be. If the word was to disappear totally from
the mouths of even the most liberal of white society, no one in that
room was naive enough to believe it would disappear from white
minds. Meeting the word head-on, they proved it had absolutely nothing to do with the way they were determined to live their lives.

So there must have been dozens of times that *nigger* was spoken in   15
front of me before I reached the third grade. But I didn't "hear" it until
it was said by a small pair of lips that had already learned it could be a

way to humiliate me. That was the word I went home and asked my mother about. And since she knew that I had to grow up in America, she took me in her lap and explained.

QUESTIONS ON MEANING

1. Why does Naylor think that written language is inferior to spoken language (para. 1)?
2. In paragraph 15, Naylor says that although the word *nigger* had been used in her presence many times, she didn't really "hear" the word until a mean little boy said it. How do you explain this contradiction?
3. Naylor says that "the people in my grandmother's living room...transformed *nigger*" (para. 14). How?
4. What is Naylor's primary PURPOSE in this essay?

QUESTIONS ON WRITING STRATEGY

1. In her first two paragraphs, Naylor discusses language in the ABSTRACT. How are these paragraphs connected to her stories about the word *nigger*? Why do you think she begins the essay this way? Is this INTRODUCTION effective or not? Why?
2. Look back at the last two sentences of Naylor's essay. What is the EFFECT of ending on this idea?
3. Go through Naylor's essay and note which paragraphs discuss the racist uses of *nigger* and which discuss the nonracist uses. How do Naylor's organization and the space she devotes to each use help Naylor make her point?
4. **OTHER METHODS.** After each DEFINITION of the words *nigger* and *girl*, Naylor gives an EXAMPLE in the form of a quotation. These examples are in paragraphs 7–10 (for instance, "'Yeah, that old foreman found out quick enough—you don't mess with a nigger'" [9]) and paragraph 12 ("'G-i-r-l, stop. You mean you said that to his face?'"). What do such examples add to Naylor's definitions?

QUESTIONS ON LANGUAGE

1. What is "the chicken and egg dispute" (para. 2)? What does this dispute say about the relationship between language and reality?
2. What do the words *nymphomaniac* and *necrophiliac* CONNOTE in paragraph 3?
3. If you don't know the meanings of the following words, look them up in a dictionary: transcendent, dynamics (para. 1); intermittent, reprieve, consensus, innocuous (2); verified (3); gravitated, mecca (4); clamor, inflections (5); endearment, disembodied (9); unkempt, trifling (10); communal (13); stratum, internalization, degradation, rendered, impotent, naive (14).

SUGGESTIONS FOR WRITING

1. **JOURNAL WRITING.** As Naylor shows, the language of stereotypes can be powerful and painful to encounter. Have you ever experienced or witnessed this kind of labeling? What were your reactions? (Keep in mind that race is but one object of stereotypes. Consider income, marital status, sexual preference, weight, height, education, and neighborhood, for just a few other characteristics.)

   FROM JOURNAL TO ESSAY. Using your own experiences as examples, write an essay modeled on Naylor's in which you define "the meanings of a word" (or words). Do you find, too, that meaning varies with context? If so, make the variations clear.

2. Can you think of other labels that may be defined in more than one way? (These might include *smart, childish, old-fashioned, artistic, proud, attractive, heroic,* and so on.) Choose one such label, and write one paragraph for each possible definition. Be sure to explain the contexts for each definition and to give enough examples so that the meanings are clear.

3. **CRITICAL WRITING.** Naylor claims that words are "nonsensical...without a consensus that assigns 'meaning'" (para. 2). If so, how do we understand the meaning of a word like *nigger,* when Naylor has shown us that there is more than one consensus about its meaning? Does Naylor contradict herself? Write an essay that either supports or refutes Naylor's claim about meaning and context. You will need to consider how she and you define consensus.

4. **CONNECTIONS.** The next essay, Christine Leong's "Being a Chink," identifies a moment when Leong was first struck by the negative power of racist language. Write an essay that COMPARES AND CONTRASTS these two women's reactions to a derogatory label. How did the context help shape their reactions?

GLORIA NAYLOR ON WRITING

Studying literature in college was somewhat disappointing for Gloria Naylor. "What I wanted to see," she told William Goldstein of *Publishers Weekly,* "were reflections of me and my existence and experience." Then, reading African American literature in graduate school, she discovered that "blacks have been writing in this country since this country has been writing and have a literary heritage of their own. Unfortunately, they haven't had encouragement or recognition for their efforts.... What had happened was that when black people wrote, it wasn't quite [considered] serious work—it was race work or protest work."

For Naylor this discovery was a turning point. "I wanted to become a writer because I felt that my presence as a black woman and my perspective as a woman in general had been underrepresented." Her work tries to "articulate experiences that want articulating—for those readers who reflect the subject matter, black readers, and for those who don't, basically white middle-class readers."

FOR DISCUSSION

1. What does Naylor mean when she says that she tries to "articulate experiences that want articulating"?
2. Naylor is motivated to write by a consciousness of herself as an African American and a woman. How do you see this motivation driving her essay "The Meanings of a Word"?

CHRISTINE LEONG

Asked for information about herself, CHRISTINE LEONG e-mailed us a brief autobiography. "I was born in Manhattan in February 1976. I graduated from Stuyvesant High School in June 1994, and I can look back and honestly say that those were the best days of my life (so far). I am currently a sophomore at the Stern School of Business at New York University, majoring in finance and information systems and thinking about a psychology or communications minor. In preparation of my future career in the financial markets, I've been interning at Merrill Lynch for almost a year. My hobbies include writing, reading suspense/horror novels, going to museums, photography, and anything outdoors. The one thing I couldn't live without is music."

Being a Chink

Leong wrote this essay for her freshman composition class at NYU, and it was published in *Mercer Street, 1995–96,* a collection of NYU students' essays. As you'll see, Leong was inspired by Gloria Naylor's "The Meanings of a Word" (p. 407) to report her own experiences with a word either hurtful or warm, depending on the speaker.

The power of language is something that people often underestimate. It is the one thing that allows people to communicate with each other, to be understood, to be heard. It gives us identity, personality, social status, and it also creates communities, defining both insiders and outsiders. Language has the ability to heal or to harm, to praise or belittle to promote peace or even to glorify hate. But perhaps most important, language is the tool used to define us and differentiate us from the next person. Names and labels are what separate us from each other. Sometimes these things are innocuous, depending on the particular word and the context in which it is used. Often they serve to ridicule and humiliate.

I remember the first time I saw the word *chink*. I used to work over the summers at my father's Chinese restaurant, the Oriental, to earn a few extra dollars of spending money. It was a warm, sunny Friday morning, and I was busy performing my weekly task of cleaning out the storage area under the cash register at the front of the store. Armed with a large can of Pledge furniture polish and an old cloth, I started attacking the old oak shelves, sorting through junk mail that had accumulated over the last week, separating the bills and other important things that had to be set aside for later, before wiping each wooden panel clean. It was a pretty uneventful chore, that is, until I got to the bottom shelf, the last of three. I always hated cleaning this particular shelf because it required me to get down on my hands and knees behind the counter and reach all the way back into the compartment to dig out all the stuff that managed to get wedged against the wall.

After bending to scoop all the papers out of that third cubicle, I be- 3
gan to sort through them haphazardly. A few old menus, a gum wrapper (I always wondered how little things like that got stuffed in there), some promotional flyers, two capless pens, a dusty scratch pad, and something that appeared to be a little white envelope. Nothing seemed unusual until I examined that last item more closely. It was an old Mid-Lantic envelope from the bank across the street. I was just about to crumple it up and throw it into the trash can when I decided to check if there was any money left in it. Too lazy to deal with the actual "chore" of opening the envelope, I held it up to the light.

As the faint yellow glow from the antique light fixture above me 4
shone through the envelope, turning it transparent, my suspicion that it was empty was confirmed. However, what I found was more shocking than anything I could have imagined. There, outlined by the light, was the word *chink* written backwards. I quickly lowered my arm onto the cool, smooth surface of the counter and flipped the envelope onto its other side, refusing to believe what I had just read. On the back, in dark blue ink with a large circle drawn around it, was the word CHINK written in my father's handwriting.

Up until that moment, I hadn't known that my father knew such 5
words, and thinking again, perhaps he didn't know this one either. After all, it was a habit of his to write down English words he did not know when he heard them and look them up in the dictionary later that day, learning them and adding them to his vocabulary. My mind began spinning with all the possible reasons he had written this particular word down. I wondered if an angry patron who had come in earlier had called him that.

I was shocked at that possibility, but I was not surprised. Being one 6
of only two Asian families living and running a business in a small suburban town predominately inhabited by old Caucasian people was bound to breed some kind of discrimination, if not hatred. I know that my father might not have known exactly what the word *chink* meant, but he must have had a good idea, because he never came to ask me about it as he did with all the other slang words that couldn't be found in the dictionary. It's funny, though, I do not remember the first time I was called a *chink*. I only remember the pain and outrage I felt the first time I saw it in writing, perhaps the first time I discovered that someone had used that hateful word to degrade my father.

In her essay "The Meanings of a Word," Gloria Naylor examines 7
the various meanings of the word *nigger*, definitions that have consen-

sual meanings throughout society and others that vary according to how and when the word is used. In this piece, Naylor uses personal examples to describe how "the people in [her] grandmother's living room took a word that whites used to signify worthlessness or degradation and rendered it impotent," by transforming *nigger* into a word signifying "the varied and complex human beings that they knew themselves to be." Naylor goes on to add that although none of these people were foolish enough to believe that the word *nigger* would magically be erased from the minds of all humankind, they were convinced that their "head-on" approach of dealing with the label that society had put on them "proved that it had absolutely nothing to do with the way they were determined to live their lives."

It has been nearly eight years since that day I stumbled across the   8
bank envelope. Since then we have moved from that suburb in New Jersey to New York City, where the Asian population is much larger, and the word *chink*, although still heard, is either heard less frequently or in a rather "harmless" manner between myself and fellow Chinese (Asian) teenage friends. I do not remember how it happened exactly. I just know that we have been calling each other *chink* for quite a long while now. The word has never been used to belittle or degrade, but rather as a term of endearment, a loving insult between friends, almost but not quite exactly the way *nigger* is sometimes used among black people. It is a practice that we still engage in today, and although we know that there are times when the use of the word *chink* is very inappropriate, it is an accepted term within our circle.

Do not misunderstand us, we are all intelligent Asian youths, all   9
graduating from New York City's top high school, all college students, and we know what the word *chink* truly means. We know, because over the years we have heard it countless times, from strangers on the streets and in stores, from fellow students and peers, and in some instances even from teachers, although it might not have been meant for us to hear.

So you see, even though we may use the term *chink* rather casually,   10
it is only used that way amongst ourselves because we know that when we say it to each other it is truly without malice or harmful intent. I do not think that any of us knows exactly why we do it, but perhaps it is our own way, like the characters in Naylor's piece, of dealing with a label that can never be removed. It is not determined by who we are on the inside, or what we are capable of accomplishing, but instead by what we look like—the shape of our eyes, the color of our skin, the texture of our hair, and our delicate features. Perhaps we intentionally misuse the word as a symbol of our overcoming the stereotypes that American society has imposed upon us, a way of showing that although others have tried to make us feel small, weak, and insignificant, we are

the opposite. We are strong, we are determined, we are the voices of the future, and we refuse to let a simple word paralyze us, belittle us, or control us.

The word *chink* may have been created to harm, ridicule, and hu-   11 miliate, but for us it may have done the exact opposite. In some ways it has helped us find a certain comfort in each other, each of us knowing what the other has gone through, a common thread of racism binding us all together, a strange union born from the word *chink* that was used against us, and a shared goal of perseverance.

QUESTIONS ON MEANING

1. In paragraph 9 Leong says that she and her friends "know what the word *chink* truly means." Where in her essay does she explain this "true" meaning?
2. What has the word *chink* come to mean when Leong and her friends use it? Where in the essay does Leong explain this?
3. One might argue that the THESIS of Leong's essay is that language is not absolute. Is her PURPOSE, then, to propose a new DEFINITION for a word, to teach the reader something about how labels work, or to explain how adapting a racist term can be a form of gaining power? How do you know?

QUESTIONS ON WRITING STRATEGY

1. Look carefully at Gloria Naylor's essay "The Meanings of a Word" (p. 407). What structural similarities do you notice between it and Leong's? Why do you think Leong adapts these features of Naylor's essay?
2. In paragraph 3 Leong details all the forgotten items she finds under the counter. What is the EFFECT of ending with the "old MidLantic envelope from the bank across the street"?
3. What is the main purpose of the extended example from Naylor's essay in paragraph 7?
4. Why is Leong so careful to explain that she and her friends are all intelligent and educated (para. 9)?
5. **OTHER METHODS.** Leong suggests CAUSE AND EFFECT when she expresses "outrage" at seeing the word *chink* in writing (para. 3). Why does Leong react so strongly to the writing on the envelope?

QUESTIONS ON LANGUAGE

1. In paragraph 10 Leong explains that she and her friends are "dealing with a label that can never be removed." What other words does she use in this paragraph to suggest the potential helplessness of being permanently labeled?
2. What do the CONNOTATIONS of "term of endearment" (para. 8) indicate about the way Leong and her friends have redefined *chink*?

3. Make sure you know the meanings of the following words: status, belittle, innocuous (para. 1); cubicle, haphazardly (3); Caucasian, degrade (6); consensual, rendered, impotent (7); malice (10); perseverance (11).

SUGGESTIONS FOR WRITING

1. **JOURNAL WRITING.** Although children often assume they will be protected by their parents, Leong presents a situation in which she wanted to protect her father. Have you ever felt particularly angry or defensive on behalf of a parent? Why? What did you do about it?

   FROM JOURNAL TO ESSAY. Write an essay that explores why and how children might feel compelled to act like parents toward their own parents. Is this a shift that comes with age? with specific circumstances? out of the blue? Make some GENERALIZATIONS about this process, but feel free to use the personal recollections from your journal entry as EVIDENCE.

2. As Leong explains in her INTRODUCTION, not all labels are intended to be hurtful. Often they are shorthand ways for our families and friends to identify us, perhaps reflecting something about our appearance ("Red," "Slim") or our interests ("Sport," "Chef"). What do your family or friends call you? Write several paragraphs giving a careful definition of this label. Where did it come from? Why is it appropriate (or not)?

3. **CRITICAL WRITING.** In her opening paragraph Leong says that "language is the tool used to define us." But she goes on to explain how she and her friends *refuse* to be defined by racist language. Does this apparent contradiction weaken her essay? Why, or why not? (To answer this question, consider the purpose of Leong's essay. See "Meaning" question 3.)

4. **CONNECTIONS.** Both Leong and Gloria Naylor, in "The Meanings of a Word" (p. 407), show that racist language can be taken over by those against whom it is directed. They also show that for groups or communities to redefine, and thus to own, these racist slurs can be empowering. Do you find their ARGUMENTS convincing, or do these redefinitions reveal what Naylor denies—namely, "an internalization of racism" (para. 14)? In an essay, explain your opinion on this issue, using as evidence passages from Naylor's and Leong's essays as well as insights and EXAMPLES from your own observations and experience.

CHRISTINE LEONG ON WRITING

For *The Bedford Reader,* Christine Leong commented on the difficulties of writing and the rewards that can ensue.

"Writing is something that comes easily for many people, but unfortunately I am not one of them. For me the writing process is one of the hardest and quite possibly is *the* most nerve wracking thing that I have ever experienced. I can't even begin to count all the hours I have spent throughout the course of my life staring at a blank computer screen, trying desperately to come up with the right combination of words to express my thoughts and feelings, and although after many hours of frustration I eventually end up with something, I am never happy with it because I am undoubtedly my own worst critic. Perhaps my mentality of 'it's not good enough yet' stems from my belief that writing can never really be completed; to me it has no beginning and no end but is rather a small representation of who I am at a given moment in time, and I believe that the more things I experience in life, the more I am able to contribute to my writing. Thus, whatever I write always has the potential of being better; there's always room for improvement via more revisions, greater insight, and about a hundred more drafts.

"I used to believe that writing always had to make sense, but since then I have learned that there are many things in this life that do not adhere to this 'rule.' I now realize that writing doesn't necessarily have to be grammatically correct or even sensible, and the only thing that really matters is that whatever is written is truly inspired. Passion comes through very clearly in a writer's words, and the more emotion that goes into a piece, the more impact it will ultimately have on the reader. In recent years I have learned that there are no real writing guidelines, and that writing is much like any other art form: it can be abstract or it can follow more traditional 'themes.' However, in order for a piece of writing to be effective, in the sense that it can differentiate itself from any other writing sample and hopefully have some significance to the reader, I believe that it has to come from within.

"The majority of what I write about, and that which I feel is worth reading, is inspired by actual experiences that I have had. For example, 'Being a Chink' began as an assignment in a freshman writing workshop class in college. When first presented with the task of writing it, I was at a complete loss for words and had absolutely no clue where to start. However, after reading Gloria Naylor's 'The Meanings of a Word,' I was reminded of one of the most traumatic and memorable events in my life. The piece triggered a very strong memory, and before long I found myself writing down anything that came into my head, letting my thoughts and emotions flow freely in the form of words without thinking about whether or not they made any kind of sense. Many hours later I discovered that I had written the basic structure of what would eventually be my final product. I must honestly say that I can't really recall the actual process of writing 'Being a Chink'; it was just an essay that seemed to take on a life and form of its own. Perhaps that, along with its universal theme, is what makes it such a strong piece. It not only is a recollection from my adolescence but is something that defines the very essence of the person that I have become since then.

"In retrospect, I now realize that writing 'Being a Chink' was not only about completing an essay and fulfilling a writing requirement; it was also about the acknowledgment of my own growth as a person. In many ways, without my initially being aware of it, the piece has helped me come to terms with one of the most controversial issues that I have ever been faced with."

FOR DISCUSSION

1. Does Leong's characterization of writing as "nerve wracking" ring bells with you? How do you overcome writer's block?
2. What do you think about Leong's statement that "writing doesn't necessarily have to be grammatically correct or even sensible, and the only thing that really matters is that whatever is written is truly inspired"? In your experience with writing, what are the roles of correctness, sense, and inspiration? What matters most to you? What matters most to readers?

MARIE WINN

Marie Winn was born in Czechoslovakia in 1936. As a child she immigrated with her family to New York City, where she attended the public schools. She graduated from Radcliffe College and went on to Columbia University for further study. She has contributed articles to the *New York Times Magazine*, the *New York Times Book Review*, *Smithsonian*, and the *Wall Street Journal*. She is also the author of eleven books for both adults and children, including *The Fireside Book of Fun and Game Songs* (1974). Three of her books for adults raise difficult issues of child rearing and have attracted much attention: *The Plug-In Drug: Television, Children, and the Family* (1977, revised 1985), *Children Without Childhood* (1983), and *Unplugging the Plug-In Drug* (1987).

TV Addiction

Do you know someone who can't stop watching television? In this excerpt from *The Plug-In Drug*, Winn defines the troubling malady named in the title. The essay actually performs double duty as a definition, first explaining *addiction*, then *TV addiction*.

The word "addiction" is often used loosely and wryly in conversation. People will refer to themselves as "mystery book addicts" or "cookie addicts." E. B. White[1] writes of his annual surge of interest in gardening: "We are hooked and are making an attempt to kick the habit." Yet nobody really believes that reading mysteries or ordering seeds by catalogue is serious enough to be compared with addictions to heroin or alcohol. The word "addiction" is here used jokingly to denote a tendency to overindulge in some pleasurable activity.

People often refer to being "hooked on TV." Does this, too, fall into the lighthearted category of cookie eating and other pleasures that people pursue with unusual intensity, or is there a kind of television viewing that falls into the more serious category of destructive addiction?

When we think about addiction to drugs or alcohol, we frequently focus on negative aspects, ignoring the pleasures that accompany drinking or drug-taking. And yet the essence of any serious addiction is a pursuit of pleasure, a search for a "high" that normal life does not supply. It is only the inability to function without the addictive substance that is dismaying, the dependence of the organism upon a certain ex-

[1] See page 104. —Eds.

420

perience and an increasing inability to function normally without it. Thus a person will take two or three drinks at the end of the day not merely for the pleasure drinking provides, but also because he "doesn't feel normal" without them.

An addict does not merely pursue a pleasurable experience and need to experience it in order to function normally. He needs to *repeat* it again and again. Something about that particular experience makes life without it less than complete. Other potentially pleasurable experiences are no longer possible, for under the spell of the addictive experience, his life is peculiarly distorted. The addict craves an experience and yet he is never really satisfied. The organism may be temporarily sated, but soon it begins to crave again.

Finally, a serious addiction is distinguished from a harmless pursuit of pleasure by its distinctly destructive elements. A heroin addict, for instance, leads a damaged life: His increasing need for heroin in increasing doses prevents him from working, from maintaining relationships, from developing in human ways. Similarly an alcoholic's life is narrowed and dehumanized by his dependence on alcohol.

Let us consider television viewing in the light of the conditions that define serious addictions.

Not unlike drugs or alcohol, the television experience allows the participant to blot out the real world and enter into a pleasurable and passive mental state. The worries and anxieties of reality are as effectively deferred by becoming absorbed in a television program as by going on a "trip" induced by drugs or alcohol. And just as alcoholics are only inchoately aware of their addiction, feeling that they control their drinking more than they really do ("I can cut it out any time I want — I just like to have three or four drinks before dinner"), people similarly overestimate their control over television watching. Even as they put off other activities to spend hour after hour watching television, they feel they could easily resume living in a different, less passive style. But somehow or other while the television set is present in their homes, the click doesn't sound. With television pleasures available, those other experiences seem less attractive, more difficult somehow.

A heavy viewer (a college English instructor) observes: "I find television almost irresistible. When the set is on, I cannot ignore it. I can't turn it off. I feel sapped, will-less, enervated. As I reach out to turn off the set, the strength goes out of my arms. So I sit there for hours and hours."

The self-confessed television addict often feels he "ought" to do other things — but the fact that he doesn't read and doesn't plant his garden or sew or crochet or play games or have conversations means that those activities are no longer as desirable as television viewing. In a way a heavy viewer's life is as imbalanced by his television "habit" as a drug addict's or an alcoholic's. He is living in a holding pattern, as it were, passing up the activities that lead to growth or development or a sense of accomplishment. This is one reason people talk about their television viewing so ruefully, so apologetically. They are aware that it is an unproductive experience, that almost any other endeavor is more worthwhile by any human measure.

Finally, it is the adverse effect of television viewing on the lives of so many people that defines it as a serious addiction. The television habit distorts the sense of time. It renders other experiences vague and curiously unreal while taking on a greater reality for itself. It weakens relationships by reducing and sometimes eliminating normal opportunities for talking, for communicating.

And yet television does not satisfy, else why would the viewer continue to watch hour after hour, day after day? "The measure of health," writes Lawrence Kubie, "is flexibility...and especially the freedom to cease when sated." But the television viewer can never be sated with his television experiences—they do not provide the true nourishment that satiation requires—and thus he finds that he cannot stop watching.

10

11

QUESTIONS ON MEANING

1. What distinction does Winn make between the "harmless pursuit of pleasure" and addiction?
2. In paragraph 2, Winn poses the question that leads to her THESIS. What is the answer to this question? Do you find it explicitly stated anywhere?
3. What does Winn think are the main problems caused by excessive TV viewing?
4. Does Winn think there can be anything good about watching television? How do you know?

QUESTIONS ON WRITING STRATEGY

1. Why does Winn take such care to define *addiction* (paras. 3–5)? What does this stipulative definition do for the essay?
2. Winn does not answer her thesis question immediately after she asks it (para. 2). Why, do you think? What is the EFFECT of this delay?
3. Throughout her essay, Winn puts a number of words and phrases in quotation marks—for example, "hooked on TV" (para. 2), "high" (3), "trip" (7), "ought" (9). What does this punctuation contribute to Winn's essay?
4. **OTHER METHODS.** Study Winn's COMPARISON between drug and alcohol addiction and TV addiction. How are the two similar? Are they different in any way?

QUESTIONS ON LANGUAGE

1. Winn uses several METAPHORS of eating to explain addiction (see paras. 4 and 11, especially). If you do not know the meanings of *craves, sated, nourishment,* and *satiated,* look them up in a dictionary. What is the effect of using such terms to define addiction?
2. What does Winn mean when she describes addiction as "living in a holding pattern" (para. 9)?
3. Consult a dictionary if you don't know the meanings of any of the following words: wryly, denote (para. 1); dismaying, organism (3); dehumanized (5); inchoately (7); sapped, enervated (8); ruefully, apologetically, endeavor (9); adverse, renders, vague (10).

SUGGESTIONS FOR WRITING

1. **JOURNAL WRITING.** If you like to watch television, Winn's essay may seem exaggerated. After all, isn't turning on the TV a great way to unwind or to be entertained? Write about your own relationship to television. How often do you watch? Does TV viewing interfere with your life, or do you have it under control? What does TV viewing do for (or to) you?
   FROM JOURNAL TO ESSAY. Would Winn consider you a television addict? Do you consider yourself one? Write an essay that compares and contrasts your relationship with TV to Winn's definition of *TV addiction.* Would you revise her claims about the effects of TV addiction, or do you think she is accurate? Is it possible to watch a lot of television without being an addict?
2. As Winn's opening paragraph points out, people often claim to be "addicted" to all kinds of things. From your experience, you probably know that such addictions can include everything from spy novels to Snickers candy bars to driving dangerously. Write an essay in which you define an addiction (but not to cigarettes, drugs, alcohol, or television). Your essay's TONE may be serious or humorous, but you should give your readers a sense of the addiction's CAUSES AND EFFECTS as well as EXAMPLES of its sufferers.
3. **CRITICAL WRITING.** "Finally it is the adverse effect of television viewing on the lives of so many people that defines it as a serious addiction" (para. 10). Do you agree with this statement: Does the number of people affected define an addiction as "serious"? If fewer people suffered the "adverse effect" of TV viewing, would it not be a serious addiction? Or, in contrast, do the huge numbers of TV viewers remove the behavior from addicted to normal? Write an essay that either confirms or refutes Winn's assertion, using examples to support your opinion.
4. **CONNECTIONS.** Gore Vidal's "Drugs" (p. 365) proposes legalizing drugs as a solution to the problem of drug addiction and its effects on our society. Following Vidal's model (though not his precise recommendations, of course, since television is already legal), propose a solution to the problem of TV addiction. Your solution may be serious or humorous, and it may approach the problem at the level of the individual addict or at the level of society as a whole.

MARIE WINN ON WRITING

For Marie Winn, the most enjoyable part of writing is making improvements. "I love spending an hour or two with a dictionary and a thesaurus looking for a more nearly perfect word," she declares in an account of her working habits written for *The Bedford Reader*. "Or taking my pen and ruthlessly pruning all the unnecessary adjectives (a practice I can wholeheartedly recommend to you), or fooling around with the rhythm of a sentence or a paragraph by changing a verb into a participle, or making any number of little changes that a magazine editor I work with ruefully calls 'mouse milking.'"

But the proportion of time Winn spends at this "delightful occupation" is small. "For me, the pleasure and pain of writing go on simultaneously. Once I have finally forced myself to bite the bullet and get to work, as soon as the flow of writing stops — after a few sentences or paragraphs or, if I am extraordinarily lucky, a few pages — then, as a little reward for having actually written something and also as a procrastinating measure to delay the painful necessity of having to write something again, I play with the words and sentences on the page.

"That's the trouble, of course: There have to be words and sentences on the page before I can enjoy the pleasure of playing with them. Somehow I have to transform the vague and confused tangle of ideas in my head into an orderly and logical sequence on a blank piece of paper. That's the real hell of writing: the inescapable need to think clearly. . . . You have to figure it out, make it all hang together, consider the implications, the alternatives, eliminate the contradictions, the extraneous thoughts, the illogical conclusions. I *hate* that part of writing and I have a feeling you know perfectly well what I'm talking about."

FOR DISCUSSION

1. For Winn, what is the most difficult part of the writing process? What part does she most enjoy?
2. What does the author see as the role that thinking plays in writing?

TOM WOLFE

Tom Wolfe, author, journalist, and cartoonist, was born in 1931 in Richmond, Virginia, and went to Washington and Lee University. After taking a Ph.D. in American Studies at Yale, he decided against an academic career and instead worked as a reporter for the *Springfield Union* and the *Washington Post*. Early in the 1960s, Wolfe began writing his electrifying, satiric articles on the American scene (with special, mocking attention to subcultures and trendsetters), which have enlivened *New York*, *Esquire*, *Rolling Stone*, *Harper's*, and other magazines. Among his books are *The Electric Kool-Aid Acid Test* (1965), a memoir of LSD-spaced-out hippies; *The Pump House Gang* (1968), a study of California surfers; *The Right Stuff* (1979), a chronicle of America's first astronauts, which won the American Book Award and was made into a movie; and *From Bauhaus to Our House* (1981), a complaint against modern architecture. Though the movie made from it bombed, Wolfe's first novel, *The Bonfire of the Vanities* (1987), was both controversial and hugely popular.

Pornoviolence

This essay, from a collection raking over the 1970s, *Mauve Gloves & Madmen, Clutter & Vine* (1976), is vintage Tom Wolfe. He played a large part in the invention of "the new journalism" (a brand of reporting that tells the truth excitedly, as if it were fiction), and his essay is marked by certain breathless features of style: long sentences full of parenthetical asides, ellipses (...), generous use of italics. Wolfe here coins a term to fit the blend of pornography and pandering to bloodlust that he finds in the media. Although not recent, his remarks have dated little since they first appeared.

"*Keeps His Mom-in-law in Chains*, meet *Kills Son and Feeds Corpse to Pigs*." 1

"Pleased to meet you." 2

"*Teenager Twists Off Corpse's Head... to Get Gold Teeth*, meet *Strangles Girl Friend, Then Chops Her to Pieces*." 3

"How you doing?" 4

"*Nurse's Aide Sees Fingers Chopped Off in Meat Grinder*, meet *I Left My Babies in the Deep Freeze*." 5

"It's a pleasure." 6

It's a pleasure! No doubt about that! In all these years of journalism I have covered more conventions than I care to remember. Podiatrists, theosophists, Professional Budget Finance dentists, oyster farmers, 7 mathematicians, truckers, dry cleaners, stamp collectors, Esperantists, nudists, and newspaper editors—I have seen them all, together, in vast assemblies, sloughing through the wall-to-wall of a thousand hotel lobbies (the nudists excepted) in their shimmering gray-metal suits and pajama-stripe shirts with white Plasti-Coat name cards on their chests, and I have sat through their speeches and seminars (the nudists included) and attentively endured ear baths such as you wouldn't believe. And yet none has ever been quite like the convention of the stringers for the *National Enquirer*.

The *Enquirer* is a weekly newspaper that is probably known by sight 8 to millions more than know it by name. No one who ever came face-to-face with the *Enquirer* on a newsstand in its wildest days is likely to have forgotten the sight: a tabloid with great inky shocks of type all over the front page saying something on the order of *Gouges Out Wife's Eyes to Make Her Ugly, Dad Hurls Hot Grease in Daughter's Face, Wife Commits Suicide After 2 Years of Poisoning Fails to Kill Husband...*

The stories themselves were supplied largely by stringers, i.e., corre- 9 spondents, from all over the country, the world, for that matter, mostly copy editors and reporters on local newspapers. Every so often they would come upon a story, usually via the police beat, that was so grotesque the local sheet would discard it or run it in a highly glossed form rather than offend or perplex its readers. The stringers would preserve them for the *Enquirer*, which always rewarded them well and respectfully.

One year the *Enquirer* convened and feted them at a hotel in Man- 10 hattan. This convention was a success in every way. The only awkward moment was at the outset when the stringers all pulled in. None of them knew each other. Their hosts got around the problem by introducing them by the stories they had supplied. The introductions went like this:

"Harry, I want you to meet Frank here. Frank did that story, you re- 11 member that story, *Midget Murderer Throws Girl Off Cliff After She Refuses to Dance with Him.*"

"Pleased to meet you. That was some story." 12

"And Harry did the one about *I Spent Three Days Trapped at Bottom* 13 *of Forty-Foot-Deep Mine Shaft and Was Saved by a Swarm of Flies.*"

"Likewise, I'm sure." 14

And *Midget Murderer Throws Girl Off Cliff* shakes hands with *I* 15 *Spent Three Days Trapped at Bottom of Forty-Foot-Deep Mine Shaft*, and *Buries Her Baby Alive* shakes hands with *Boy, Twelve, Strangles Two-Year-Old Girl*, and *Kills Son and Feeds Corpse to Pigs* shakes hands with *He Strangles Old Woman and Smears Corpse with Syrup, Ketchup, and Oatmeal...*and...

...There was a great deal of esprit about the whole thing. These 16 men were, in fact, the avant-garde of a new genre that since then has become institutionalized throughout the nation without anyone knowing its proper name. I speak of the new pornography, the pornography of violence.

Pornography comes from the Greek word *porne*, meaning "harlot," [17] and pornography is literally the depiction of the acts of harlots. In the new pornography, the theme is not sex. The new pornography depicts practitioners acting out another, murkier drive: people staving teeth in, ripping guts open, blowing brains out, and getting even with all those bastards...

The success of the *Enquirer* prompted many imitators to enter the [18] field, *Midnight*, the *Star Chronicle*, the *National Insider*, *Inside News*, the *National Close-up*, the *National Tattler*, the *National Examiner*. A truly competitive free press evolved, and soon a reader could go to the newspaper of his choice for *Kill the Retarded!* (*Won't You Join My Movement?*) and *Unfaithful Wife? Burn Her Bed!*, *Harem Master's Mistress Chops Him with Machete*, *Babe Bites Off Boy's Tongue*, and *Cuts Buddy's Face to Pieces for Stealing His Business and Fiancée*.

And yet the last time I surveyed the Violence press, I noticed a cu- [19] rious thing. These pioneering journals seem to have pulled back. They seem to be regressing to what is by now the Redi-Mix staple of literate Americans, mere sex. *Ecstasy and Me* (*by Hedy Lamarr*),[1] says the *National Enquirer*. *I Run a Sex Art Gallery*, says the *National Insider*. What has happened, I think, is something that has happened to avant-gardes in many fields, from William Morris and the Craftsmen to the Bauhaus group.[2] Namely, their discoveries have been preempted by the Establishment and so thoroughly dissolved into the mainstream they no longer look original.

Robert Harrison, the former publisher of *Confidential*, and later [20] publisher of the aforementioned *Inside News*, was perhaps the first person to see it coming. I was interviewing Harrison early in January 1964 for a story in *Esquire* about six weeks after the assassination of President Kennedy, and we were in a cab in the West Fifties in Manhattan, at a stoplight, by a newsstand, and Harrison suddenly pointed at the newsstand and said, "Look at that. They're doing the same thing the *Enquirer* does."

There on the stand was a row of slick-paper, magazine-size publica- [21] tions, known in the trade as one-shots, with titles like *Four Days That*

---

[1] *Ecstasy*, an early, European-made Hedy Lamarr film, was notorious for its scenes of soft-core lovemaking. Later, paired with Charles ("Come with me to the Casbah") Boyer, Lamarr rose to Hollywood stardom in *Algiers* (1938). — Eds.

[2] Morris (1834–96), an English artist, poet, printer, and socialist, founded a company of craftspeople to bring tasteful design to furniture (the Morris chair) and other implements of everyday life. The Bauhaus, an influential art school in Germany (1919–33), taught crafts and brought new ideas of design to architecture and to goods produced in factories. — Eds.

Shook the World, Death of a President, An American Tragedy, or just *John Fitzgerald Kennedy (1921–1963).* "You want to know why people buy those things?" said Harrison. "People buy those things to see a man get his head blown off."

And, of course, he was right. Only now the publishers were in   22 many cases the pillars of the American press. Invariably, these "special coverages" of the assassination bore introductions piously commemorating the fallen President, exhorting the American people to strength and unity in a time of crisis, urging greater vigilance and safeguards for the new President, and even raising the nice metaphysical question of collective guilt in "an age of violence."

In the years since then, of course, there has been an incessant re-   23 play, with every recoverable clinical detail, of those less than five seconds in which a man got his head blown off. And throughout this deluge of words, pictures, and film frames, I have been intrigued with one thing: The point of view, the vantage point, is almost never that of the victim, riding in the Presidential Lincoln Continental. What you get is…the view from Oswald's rifle. You can step right up here and look point-blank right through the very hairline cross in Lee Harvey Oswald's Optics Ordinance in weaponry four-power Japanese telescope sight and watch, frame by frame by frame by frame, as that man there's head comes apart. Just a little History there before your very eyes.

The television networks have schooled us in the view from Os-   24 wald's rifle and made it seem a normal pastime. The TV viewpoint is nearly always that of the man who is going to strike. The last time I watched *Gunsmoke,* which was not known as a very violent Western in TV terms, the action went like this: The Wellington agents and the stagecoach driver pull guns on the badlands gang leader's daughter and Kitty, the heart-of-gold saloonkeeper, and kidnap them. Then the badlands gang shoots two Wellington agents. Then they tie up five more and talk about shooting them. Then they desist because they might not be able to get a hotel room in the next town if the word got around. Then one badlands gang gunslinger attempts to rape Kitty while the gang leader's younger daughter looks on. Then Kitty resists, so he slugs her one in the jaw. Then the gang leader slugs him. Then the gang leader slugs Kitty. Then Kitty throws hot stew in a gang member's face and hits him over the back of the head with a revolver. Then he knocks her down with a rock. Then the gang sticks up a bank. Here comes the marshal, Matt Dillon. He shoots a gang member and breaks it up. Then the gang leader shoots the guy who was guarding his daughter and the woman. Then the marshal shoots the gang leader. The final exploding bullet signals The End.

It is not the accumulated slayings and bone crushings that make   25 this pornoviolence, however. What makes it pornoviolence is that in almost every case the camera angle, therefore the viewer, is with the gun, the fist, the rock. The pornography of violence has no point of view in the old sense that novels do. You do not live the action through the hero's eyes. You live with the aggressor, whoever he may be. One moment you are the hero. The next you are the villain. No matter whose side you may be on consciously, you are in fact with the muscle, and it is you who disintegrate all comers, villains, lawmen, women, anybody. On the rare occasions in which the gun is emptied into the camera—i.e., into your face—the effect is so startling that the pornography of violence all but loses its fantasy charm. There are not nearly so many masochists as sadists among those little devils whispering into one's ears.

In fact, sex—"sadomasochism"—is only a part of the pornography 26 of violence. Violence is much more wrapped up, simply, with status. Violence is the simple, ultimate solution for problems of status competition, just as gambling is the simple, ultimate solution for economic competition. The old pornography was the fantasy of easy sexual delights in a world where sex was kept unavailable. The new pornography is the fantasy of easy triumph in a world where status competition has become so complicated and frustrating.

Already the old pornography is losing its kick because of overexpo- 27 sure. In the late thirties, Nathanael West published his last and best-regarded novel, *The Day of the Locust*, and it was a terrible flop commercially, and his publisher said if he ever published another book about Hollywood it would "have to be *My Thirty-nine Ways of Making Love by Hedy Lamarr*." He thought he was saying something that was funny because it was beyond the realm of possibility. Less than thirty years later, however, Hedy Lamarr's *Ecstasy and Me* was published. Whether she mentions thirty-nine ways, I'm not sure, but she gets off to a flying start: "The men in my life have ranged from a classic case history of impotence, to a whip-brandishing sadist who enjoyed sex only after he tied my arms behind me with the sash of his robe. There was another man who took his pleasure with a girl in my own bed, while he thought I was asleep in it."

Yet she was too late. The book very nearly sank without a trace. 28 The sin itself is wearing out. Pornography cannot exist without certified taboo to violate. And today Lust, like the rest of the Seven Deadly Sins—Pride, Sloth, Envy, Greed, Anger, and Gluttony—is becoming a rather minor vice. The Seven Deadly Sins, after all, are only sins against the self. Theologically, the idea of Lust—well, the idea is that if you seduce some poor girl from Akron, it is not a sin because you are ruining her, but because you are wasting your time and your energies and damaging your own spirit. This goes back to the old work ethic, when the idea was to keep every able-bodied man's shoulder to the wheel. In an age of riches for all, the ethic becomes more nearly: Let him do anything he pleases, as long as he doesn't get in my way. And if he does get in my way, or even if he doesn't ... well ... we have *new* fantasies for that. *Put hair on the walls.*

"Hair on the walls" is the invisible subtitle of Truman Capote's   29
book *In Cold Blood.* The book is neither a who-done-it nor a will-they-be-caught, since the answers to both questions are known from the outset. It does ask why-did-they-do-it, but the answer is soon as clear as it is going to be. Instead, the book's suspense is based largely on a totally new idea in detective stories: the promise of gory details, and the withholding of them until the end. Early in the game one of the two murderers, Dick, starts promising to put "plenty of hair on them-those walls" with a shotgun. So read on, gentle readers, and on and on; you are led up to the moment before the crime on page 60—yet the specifics, what happened, the gory details, are kept out of sight, in grisly dangle, until page 244.

But Dick and Perry, Capote's killers, are only a couple of Low Rent   30
bums. With James Bond the new pornography reached a dead center, the bureaucratic middle class. The appeal of Bond has been explained as the appeal of the lone man who can solve enormously complicated, even world problems through his own bravery and initiative. But Bond is not a lone man at all, of course. He is not the Lone Ranger. He is much easier to identify than that. He is a salaried functionary in a bureaucracy. He is a sport, but a believable one; not a millionaire, but a bureaucrat on an expense account. He is not even a high-level bureaucrat. He is an operative. This point is carefully and repeatedly made by having his superiors dress him down for violations of standard operating procedure. Bond, like the Lone Ranger, solves problems with guns and fists. When it is over, however, the Lone Ranger leaves a silver bullet. Bond, like the rest of us, fills out a report in triplicate.

Marshall McLuhan[3] says we are in a period in which it will become   31
harder and harder to stimulate lust through words and pictures—i.e., the old pornography. In the latest round of pornographic movies the producers have found it necessary to introduce violence, bondage, torture, and aggressive physical destruction to an extraordinary degree. The same sort of bloody escalation may very well happen in the pure pornography of violence. Even such able craftsmen as Truman Capote, Ian Fleming, NBC, and CBS may not suffice. Fortunately, there are historical models to rescue us from this frustration. In the latter days of

---

[3] Canadian English professor, author of *Understanding Media* (1964), *The Medium Is the Message* (1967), and other books, McLuhan (1911–80) analyzed the effects on world society of television and other electronic media.—EDS.

the Roman Empire, the Emperor Commodus became jealous of the celebrity of the great gladiators. He took to the arena himself, with his sword, and began dispatching suitably screened cripples and hobbled fighters. Audience participation became so popular that soon various *illuminati* of the Commodus set, various boys and girls of the year, were out there, suited up, gaily cutting a sequence of dwarfs and feebles down to short ribs. Ah, swinging generations, what new delights await?

QUESTIONS ON MEANING

1. Which of the following statements comes closest to summing up Tom Wolfe's main PURPOSE in writing "Pornoviolence"?

   Wolfe writes to define a word.
   Wolfe writes to define a trend in society.
   Wolfe writes to define a trend in the media that reflects a trend in society.
   Wolfe writes to explain how John F. Kennedy was assassinated.
   Wolfe writes to entertain us by mocking Americans' latest foolishness.

   (If you don't find any of these statements adequate, compose your own.)

2. If you have ever read the *National Enquirer* or any of its imitators, test the accuracy of Wolfe's reporting. What is the purpose of a featured article in the *Enquirer*?
3. According to Wolfe, what POINT OF VIEW does the writer or producer of pornoviolence always take? What other examples of this point of view (in violent incidents on films or TV shows) can you supply? (Did you ever see a replay of Jack Ruby's shooting of Oswald, for instance?)
4. "Violence is the simple, ultimate solution for problems of status competition" (para. 26). What does Wolfe mean?
5. Wolfe does not explicitly pass judgment on Truman Capote's book *In Cold Blood* (para. 29). But what is his opinion of it? How can you tell?
6. "No advocate of change for the sake of change, Tom Wolfe writes as a conservative moralist who rankles with savage indignation." Does this critical remark fit this particular essay? What, in Wolfe's view, appears to be happening to America and Americans?

QUESTIONS ON WRITING STRATEGY

1. On first reading, what did you make of Wolfe's opening sentence, "'*Keeps His Mom-in-law in Chains*, meet *Kills Son and Feeds Corpse to Pigs*'"? At what point did you first tumble to what the writer was doing? What IRONY do you find in the convention hosts' introducing people by the headlines of their gory stories? What advantage is it to Wolfe's essay that his INTRODUCTION (with its odd introductions) keeps you guessing for a while?
2. What is Wolfe's point in listing (in para. 7) some of the other conventions he has reported—gatherings of nudists, oyster farmers, and others?

3. At what moment does Wolfe give us his short definition of *pornoviolence*, or the new pornography? Do you think he would have done better to introduce his short definition of the word in paragraph 1? Why, or why not?
4. What is the TONE or attitude of Wolfe's CONCLUSION (para. 31)? Note in particular the closing line.
5. **OTHER METHODS.** Typically for a writer of extended definition, Wolfe draws on many methods of development, including NARRATION, DIVISION or ANALYSIS, and CAUSE AND EFFECT. What is the purpose of the COMPARISON AND CONTRAST in paragraph 30?

QUESTIONS ON LANGUAGE

1. What help to the reader does Wolfe provide by noting the source of the word *pornography* (para. 17)?
2. "The television networks have schooled us in the view from Oswald's rifle" (para. 24). What CONNOTATIONS enlarge the meaning of *schooled*?
3. Define *masochist* and *sadist* (para. 25). What kind of DICTION do you find in these terms? In "plenty of hair on them-those walls" (29)?
4. How much use does Wolfe make of COLLOQUIAL EXPRESSIONS? Point to examples.
5. What does Wolfe mean in noting that the fighters slain by the Emperor Commodus were "hobbled" and the cripples were "suitably screened" (para. 31)? What unflattering connotations does this emperor's very name contain? (If you don't get this, look up *commode* in your desk dictionary.)

SUGGESTIONS FOR WRITING

1. **JOURNAL WRITING.** Write about some recent examples of pornoviolence you have seen in the movies or on television or in newspapers or magazines. What, if anything, should be done about such examples?

   FROM JOURNAL TO ESSAY. Write an essay ARGUING why we should or should not try to regulate or otherwise censor pornoviolence in the media. Take into account who would set the standards, what the standards would be, and who would enforce the regulations. You might also research some of the heated debates on regulating sexual pornography on the Internet. A look in the *Readers' Guide to Periodical Literature* or *InfoTrac* could lead you to sources of ideas and support for your argument about pornoviolence.
2. Write an essay defining some current trend you've noticed in films or TV, popular music, sports, consumer buying, or some other large arena of life. Like Wolfe, invent a name for it. Use plenty of examples to make your definition clear.
3. **CRITICAL WRITING.** Analyze Wolfe's distinctive journalistic style. In the note on the essay, we mention parenthetical asides (they appear between dashes as well as parentheses), three-dot ellipsis marks, and italics. Consider also his use of *I*, his piling up of detail (as in paras. 7 and 24), his informal diction ("losing its kick," "got his head blown off"), his choice of quotations, and any other features that strike you. What is the overall EFFECT of this style? What does it say about Wolfe?
4. **CONNECTIONS.** Read or reread Barbara Ehrenreich's "In Defense of Talk Shows" (p. 282). How is the problem she describes—exploiting people for

entertainment—similar to or different from Wolfe's idea of pornoviolence? Write an essay comparing television talk shows and pornoviolence, considering their respective purposes, their methods (for instance, reliance on exploitation or spectacle), and their effects on their audiences.

TOM WOLFE ON WRITING

"What about your writing techniques and habits?" Tom Wolfe was asked by Joe David Bellamy for *Writer's Digest*. "The actual writing I do very fast," Wolfe said. "I make a very tight outline of everything I write before I write it. And often, as in the case of *The Electric Kool-Aid Acid Test*, the research, the reporting, is going to take me much longer than the writing. By writing an outline you really are writing in a way, because you're creating the structure of what you're going to do. Once I really know what I'm going to write, I don't find the actual writing takes all that long.

"*The Electric Kool-Aid Acid Test* in manuscript form was about 1,100 pages, triple-spaced, typewritten. That means about 200 words a page, and, you know, some of that was thrown out or cut eventually; but I wrote all of that in three and a half months. I had never written a full-length book before, and at first I decided I would treat each chapter as if it were a magazine article—because I *had* done that before. So I would set an artificial deadline, and I'd make myself meet it. And I did that for three chapters.

"But after I had done this three times and then I looked ahead and I saw that there were *twenty-five* more times I was going to have to do this, I couldn't face it anymore. I said, 'I cannot do this, even one more time, because there's no end to it.' So I completely changed my system, and I set up a quota for myself—of ten typewritten pages a day. At 200 words a page that's 2,000 words, which is not, you know, an overwhelming amount. It's a good clip, but it's not overwhelming. And I found this worked much better. I had my outline done, and sometimes ten pages would get me hardly an eighth-of-an-inch along the outline. It didn't bother me. Just like working in a factory—end of ten pages, I'd close my lunch pail."

FOR DISCUSSION

1. In what way is outlining really writing, according to Wolfe? (In answering, consider the implications of his statement about "creating a structure.")
2. What strategy did the author finally settle on to get himself through the toil of his first book? What made this strategy superior to the one he had used earlier?

BRUNO BETTELHEIM

Described in his *New York Times* obituary as "a psychoanalyst of great impact" and "a gifted writer...with a great literary and moral sensibility," BRUNO BETTELHEIM was born in Austria in 1903 and died in the United States in 1990. Growing up in the Vienna of Sigmund Freud, Bettelheim became interested in psychoanalysis as a young teenager and trained as a psychologist at the University of Vienna. He had already earned a wide reputation when he was imprisoned by the Nazis in the Buchenwald and Dachau concentration camps. When released because of American intervention in 1939, Bettelheim emigrated to Chicago. After several research and teaching positions, in 1944 he began teaching at the University of Chicago and continued there until his retirement in 1973. Bettelheim's work concentrated on children with severe emotional disorders such as autism and psychosis, and many of his theories were provocative and controversial. Some of his well-known books, all on children, are *Love Is Not Enough* (1950), *Truants from Life* (1955), *The Children of the Dream* (1969), and *The Uses of Enchantment* (1976).

The Holocaust

In two books, *The Informed Heart* (1960) and *Surviving, and Other Essays* (1979), Bettelheim probed his and others' experiences in the Nazis' concentration camps. What follows is a freestanding slice of a much longer essay, "The Holocaust—One Generation After," from *Surviving*. Here Bettelheim, with cool passion, dissects a loaded word.

To begin with, it was not the hapless victims of the Nazis who 1 named their incomprehensible and totally unmasterable fate the "holocaust." It was the Americans who applied this artificial and highly technical term to the Nazi extermination of the European Jews. But while the event when named as mass murder most foul evokes the most immediate, most powerful revulsion, when it is designated by a rare technical term, we must first in our minds translate it back into emotionally meaningful language. Using technical or specially created terms instead of words from our common vocabulary is one of the best-known and most widely used distancing devices, separating the intellectual from the emotional experience. Talking about "the holocaust" permits us to manage it intellectually where the raw facts, when given their ordinary names, would overwhelm us emotionally—because it was catastrophe beyond comprehension, beyond the limits of our imagination, unless we force ourselves against our desire to extend it to encompass these terrible events.

This linguistic circumlocution began while it all was only in the   2
planning stage. Even the Nazis — usually given to grossness in language
and action — shied away from facing openly what they were up to and
called this vile mass murder "the final solution of the Jewish problem."
After all, solving a problem can be made to appear like an honorable
enterprise, as long as we are not forced to recognize that the solution
we are about to embark on consists of the completely unprovoked, vicious murder of millions of helpless men, women, and children. The
Nuremberg judges of these Nazi criminals followed their example of
circumlocution by coining a neologism out of one Greek and one Latin
root: genocide. These artificially created technical terms fail to connect with our strongest feelings. The horror of murder is part of our
most common human heritage. From earliest infancy on, it arouses violent abhorrence in us. Therefore in whatever form it appears we
should give such an act its true designation and not hide it behind polite, erudite terms created out of classical words.

To call this vile mass murder "the holocaust" is not to give it a spe-   3
cial name emphasizing its uniqueness which would permit, over time,
the word becoming invested with feelings germane to the event it
refers to. The correct definition of *holocaust* is "burnt offering." As such,
it is part of the language of the psalmist, a meaningful word to all who
have some acquaintance with the Bible, full of the richest emotional
connotations. By using the term "holocaust," entirely false associations
are established through conscious and unconscious connotations between the most vicious of mass murders and ancient rituals of a deeply
religious nature.

Using a word with such strong unconscious religious connotations   4
when speaking of the murder of millions of Jews robs the victims of this
abominable mass murder of the only thing left to them: their uniqueness. Calling the most callous, most brutal, most horrid, most heinous
mass murder a burnt offering is a sacrilege, a profanation of God and
man.

Martyrdom is part of our religious heritage. A martyr, burned at the   5
stake, is a burnt offering to his god. And it is true that after the Jews
were asphyxiated, the victims' corpses were burned. But I believe we
fool ourselves if we think we are honoring the victims of systematic
murder by using this term, which has the highest moral connotations.
By doing so, we connect for our own psychological reasons what happened in the extermination camps with historical events we deeply regret, but also greatly admire. We do so because this makes it easier for
us to cope; only in doing so we cope with our distorted image of what
happened, not with the events the way they did happen.

By calling the victims of the Nazis martyrs, we falsify their fate.   6
The true meaning of *martyr* is: "One who voluntarily undergoes the

penalty of death for refusing to renounce his faith" (*Oxford English Dictionary*). The Nazis made sure that nobody could mistakenly think that their victims were murdered for their religious beliefs. Renouncing their faith would have saved none of them. Those who had converted to Christianity were gassed, as were those who were atheists, and those who were deeply religious Jews. They did not die for any conviction, and certainly not out of choice.

Millions of Jews were systematically slaughtered, as were untold 7 other "undesirables," not for any convictions of theirs, but only because they stood in the way of the realization of an illusion. They neither died for their convictions, nor were they slaughtered because of their convictions, but only in consequence of the Nazis' delusional belief about what was required to protect the purity of their assumed superior racial endowment, and what they thought necessary to guarantee them the living space they believed they needed and were entitled to. Thus while these millions were slaughtered for an idea, they did not die for one.

Millions—men, women, and children—were processed after they 8 had been utterly brutalized, their humanity destroyed, their clothes torn from their bodies. Naked, they were sorted into those who were destined to be murdered immediately, and those others who had a short-term usefulness as slave labor. But after a brief interval they, too, were to be herded into the same gas chambers into which the others were immediately piled, there to be asphyxiated so that, in their last moments, they could not prevent themselves from fighting each other in vain for a last breath of air.

To call these most wretched victims of a murderous delusion, of de- 9 structive drives run rampant, martyrs or a burnt offering is a distortion invented for our comfort, small as it may be. It pretends that this most vicious of mass murders had some deeper meaning; that in some fashion the victims either offered themselves or at least became sacrifices to a higher cause. It robs them of the last recognition which could be theirs, denies them the last dignity we could accord them: to face and accept what their death was all about, not embellishing it for the small psychological relief this may give us.

We could feel so much better if the victims had acted out of choice. 10 For our emotional relief, therefore, we dwell on the tiny minority who did exercise some choice: the resistance fighters of the Warsaw ghetto, for example, and others like them. We are ready to overlook the fact that these people fought back only at a time when everything was lost, when the overwhelming majority of those who had been forced into the ghettos had already been exterminated without resisting. Certainly those few who finally fought for their survival and their convictions, risking and losing their lives in doing so, deserve our admiration; their deeds give us a moral lift. But the more we dwell on these few, the more unfair are we to the memory of the millions who were slaughtered—who gave in, did not fight back—because we deny them the only thing which up to the very end remained uniquely their own: their fate.

QUESTIONS ON MEANING

1. Why does Bettelheim feel that *holocaust* is an inappropriate term for the mass murder of Jews during World War II? Why does he say this sort of "linguistic circumlocution" is used? (What is a "linguistic circumlocution"?)
2. What is Bettelheim's PURPOSE here?
3. According to Bettelheim, what do we do besides using unemotional terms to distance ourselves from the murder of the Jews?
4. Does Bettelheim suggest an alternative term for *holocaust*?

QUESTIONS ON WRITING STRATEGY

1. Where does Bettelheim stress etymologies, or word histories, and dictionary definitions? What is their EFFECT?
2. What does Bettelheim accomplish with paragraph 8? Why is this paragraph essential?
3. How would you characterize Bettelheim's TONE? What creates it? Is it appropriate, do you think?
4. In several places Bettelheim repeats or restates passages—for instance, "By doing so...We do so...only in doing so" (para. 5), or "stood in the way of the realization of an illusion...in consequence of the Nazis' delusional belief...slaughtered for an idea" (7). Do you think such repetition and restatement is deliberate on Bettelheim's part? Why, or why not?
5. **OTHER METHODS.** Bettelheim's definition is an ARGUMENT. What is the THESIS of his argument? What EVIDENCE supports the thesis?

QUESTIONS ON LANGUAGE

1. ANALYZE the words Bettelheim uses to refer to the murder of the Jews. How do the words support his argument?
2. What is the effect of Bettelheim's use of *we*—for instance, in paragraphs 5 and 10?
3. Look up any unfamiliar words: hapless (para. 1); neologism, abhorrence, erudite (2); germane, psalmist (3); abominable, callous, heinous, sacrilege, profanation (4); asphyxiated (5); delusional, endowment (7); rampant, embellishing (9).

SUGGESTIONS FOR WRITING

1. **JOURNAL WRITING.** Sports, dance, music, business, medicine, cooking, auto mechanics, and parenting—these are just a few activities with lan-

guages of "technical or specially created terms" (para. 1) that work often like shorthand for insiders and sound like code to outsiders. In an activity or field you know well, how did you move from outsider to insider? Where, when, and how did you learn the meanings of specialized terms?

FROM JOURNAL TO ESSAY. Write an essay in which you define and discuss the specialized terms in the activity or field you wrote of in your journal. What are the most important and common terms? What do they mean? How did you learn their meanings? What purpose do these terms serve— or what problems do they cause?

2. Although Bettelheim does not use the term, he is objecting to the use of a EUPHEMISM, or inoffensive word, in place of a word that might wound or offend. Euphemisms abound in the speech of politicians: The economy undergoes a "slowdown" or a "downturn"; people who are laid off are "downsized"; lying is "misspeaking." Drawing on Bettelheim's arguments as you see fit, write an essay about one or more euphemisms appearing in a daily newspaper. What do the euphemisms accomplish, and for whom? What do they conceal, and who is hurt?

3. **CRITICAL WRITING.** Research the word *holocaust* in a dictionary of word histories (an etymological dictionary) and an interpretation of the Bible. (A librarian can direct you to these sources.) On the basis of your research, do you agree or disagree with Bettelheim's rejection of the word? (In your answer, consider whether the word's wide use for the Nazi murders has provided it with new meanings.)

4. **CONNECTIONS.** Read "I Have a Dream," by Martin Luther King, Jr. (p. 502). Compare it with Bettelheim's essay on the purposeful use of repetition and restatement. How does each author use this device? For what aim? What is the EFFECT? If you like, you can narrow your comparison to one representative passage of each essay. Just be sure to use quotations to support your comparison.

ADDITIONAL WRITING TOPICS

Definition

1. Write an essay in which you define an institution, trend, phenomenon, or abstraction as specifically and concretely as possible. Following are some suggestions designed to stimulate ideas. Before you begin, limit your subject.

   Responsibility
   Fun
   Sorrow
   Unethical behavior
   The environment
   Education
   Progress
   Advertising
   Happiness
   Fads
   Feminism
   Marriage
   Sportsmanship
   Leadership
   Leisure
   Originality
   Character
   Imagination
   Democracy
   A smile
   A classic (of music, literature, art, or film)
   Dieting
   Meditation
   Friendship

2. In a brief essay, define one of the following. In each instance, you have a choice of something good or something bad to talk about.

   A good or bad boss
   A good or bad parent
   A good or bad host
   A good or bad TV newscaster
   A good or bad physician
   A good or bad nurse
   A good or bad minister, priest, or rabbi
   A good or bad roommate
   A good or bad driver
   A good or bad disk jockey

3. In a paragraph, define one of the following for someone who has never heard the term: *dis, wigged out, dweeb, awesome, fool around, wimp, druggie, snob, freak, loser, loner, freeloader, burnout, soul, quack,* "*chill,*" *pig-out, gross out, winging it,* "*bad,*" "*sweet.*"

10

ARGUMENT AND PERSUASION

Stating Opinions and Proposals

THE METHOD

Practically every day, we try to persuade ourselves or someone else. We usually attempt such persuasion without being aware that we follow any special method at all. Often, we'll state an *opinion*: We'll tell someone our own way of viewing things. We say to a friend, "I'm starting to like Senator Clark. Look at all she's done to help people with disabilities. Look at her voting record on toxic waste." And, having stated these opinions, we might go on to make a *proposal*, to recommend that some action be taken. Addressing our friend, we might suggest, "Hey, Senator Clark is talking on campus at four-thirty. Want to come with me and listen to her?"

Sometimes you try to convince yourself that a certain way of interpreting things is right. You even set forth an opinion in writing—as in a letter to a friend who has asked, "Now that you're at New Age College, how do you like the place?" You may write a letter of protest to a landlord who wants to raise your rent, pointing out that the bathroom hot water faucet doesn't work. As a concerned citizen, you may wish to speak your mind in an occasional letter to a newspaper or to your elected representatives.

If you should enter certain professions, you will be expected to persuade people in writing. Before arguing a case in court, a lawyer prepares briefs setting forth all the points in favor of his or her side. Business executives regularly put in writing their ideas for new products and ventures, for improvements in cost control and job efficiency. Researchers write proposals for grants to obtain money to support their work. Scientists write and publish papers to persuade the scientific community that their findings are valid, often stating hypotheses, or tentative opinions.

Even if you never produce a single persuasive work (which is very unlikely), you will certainly encounter such works directed at you. In truth, we live our lives under a steady rain of opinions and proposals. Organizations that work for causes campaign with posters and direct mail, all hoping that we will see things their way. Moreover, we are bombarded with proposals from people who wish us to act. Religious leaders urge us to lead more virtuous lives. Advertisers urge us to rush right out and buy the large economy size.

Small wonder, then, that argument and persuasion—and CRITICAL READING of argument and persuasion—may be among the most useful skills a college student can acquire. Time and again, your instructors will ask you to criticize or to state opinions, either in class or in writing. You may be asked to state your view of anything from the electoral college to animal experimentation. You may be asked to judge the desirability or undesirability of compulsory testing for AIDS, or the revision of existing immigration laws. On an examination in, say, sociology, you may be asked, "Suggest three practical approaches to the most pressing needs of disadvantaged people in urban areas." Critically reading other people's arguments and composing your own, you will find, helps you discover what you think, refine it, and share what you believe.

Is there a difference between argument and persuasion? It is, admittedly, not always clear. Strictly speaking, PERSUASION aims to influence readers' actions, or their support for an action, by engaging their beliefs and feelings, while ARGUMENT aims to win readers' agreement with an assertion or claim by engaging their powers of reasoning. But most effective persuasion or argument contains elements of both methods; hence the confusion. In this book we tend to use the terms interchangeably. And one other point: We tend to talk here about *writing* argument and persuasion, but most of what we say has to do with *reading* them as well. When we discuss your need, as a writer, to support your assertions, we are also discussing your need, as a reader, to question the support other authors provide for their assertions. In reading arguments critically, you apply the critical reading skills we discussed in the book's Introduction—ANALYSIS, INFERENCE, SYNTHESIS, EVALUATION—to a particular kind of writing.

Basic Considerations

Writer and Reader

Unlike some television advertisers, responsible writers of argument and persuasion do not try to storm people's minds. In writing a paper for a course, you persuade by gentler means: by sharing your view with a reader willing to consider it. You'll want to learn how to express your view clearly and vigorously. But to be fair and persuasive, it is important to understand your reader's view as well.

In stating your opinion, you present the truth as you see it: "The immigration laws discourage employers from hiring non-native workers" or "The immigration laws protect legal aliens." To persuade your readers that your view makes sense, you need not begin by proclaiming that, by Heaven, your view is absolutely right and should prevail. Instead, you might begin by trying to state what your reader probably thinks, as best you can infer it. You don't consider views that differ from your own merely to flatter your reader. You do so to correct your own view and make it more accurate. Regarded in this light, argument and persuasion aren't cynical ways to pull other people's strings. Writer and reader become two sensible people trying to find a common ground. This view will relieve you, whenever you have to state your opinions in writing, of the terrible obligation to be 100 percent right at all times.

Thesis Sentences

In an argument you champion or defend your opinion about something. This opinion is the THESIS, or *claim*, of your argument, and it will probably appear in your essay as your THESIS SENTENCE or sentences. Usually, but not always, you'll state your thesis sentence at the beginning of your essay, making a play for readers' attention and clueing them in to your purpose. But if you think readers may have difficulty accepting your thesis until they've heard some or all of your argument, then you might save the thesis sentence for the middle or end.

The essays in this chapter provide a variety of thesis sentences as models. The three examples below come from arguments about American cultural diversity:

> Multiculturalism is not a grassroots movement. It was created, nurtured, and expanded through government policy. Without the expenditure of vast sums of money, it would wither away and die. (Linda Chavez, "Demystifying Multiculturalism")

> Such blurring of cultural styles occurs in everyday life in the United States. . . . [Y]et members of the nation's present educational and cultural Elect still cling to the notion that the United States belongs to

some vaguely defined entity they refer to as "Western civilization."...
(Ishmael Reed, "America: The Multinational Society")

[The myth that Asian-Americans are a Model Minority] distorts
Asian-Americans' true status and ignores our racial handicaps. And
the Model Minority's ideology ... attempts to justify the existing system of racial inequality by blaming the victims rather than the system itself. (Curtis Chang, "Streets of Gold")

Evidence and Appeals

To support the thesis of your argument, you need EVIDENCE—anything that demonstrates what you're claiming. Evidence may include
facts, statistics (facts expressed in numbers), expert opinions, examples,
reported experience. Linda Chavez, for instance, supports the thesis
quoted on page 443 with statistics about the racial composition of the
American workforce and intermarriage among ethnic groups, quotations from a scholarly study of minority students and from prominent
multiculturists with whom she disagrees, and examples of what she perceives as the damaging effects of multiculturalism on education.

Like other writers of argument, Chavez also appeals to readers'
intelligence and to their feelings. In appealing to reason—a RATIONAL
APPEAL—Chavez relies on conventional methods of reasoning (see the
facing page) and supplies the evidence cited above, much of which she
believes will be new to her readers. In appealing to feelings—an EMO-
TIONAL APPEAL—she sometimes simply restates what she believes readers already know well, such as the historical ability of the United States
"to incorporate so many disparate groups, creating a new whole from
the many parts." Editorials in publications for special audiences (such
as members of religious denominations, or people whose political views
are far to the left or right) tend to contain few factual surprises for their
subscribers, who presumably read to have their views reinforced. In
spoken discourse, you can hear emotional appeals in a commencement
day speech or a Fourth of July oration. An impressive example of emotional appeal is included in this chapter: the speech by Martin Luther
King, Jr., "I Have a Dream." Dr. King's speech did not tell its audience
anything new to them, for the listeners were mostly African Americans
disappointed in the American Dream. The speaker appeals primarily
not to reason but to feelings—and to the willingness of his listeners to
be inspired.

Emotional argument, to be sure, can sometimes be cynical manipulation. It can mean selling a sucker a bill of shoddy goods by appealing to pride or shame—"Do you really want to deprive your children of
what's best for them?" But emotional argument can also stir readers to
constructive action by fair means. It recognizes that we are not intel-

lectual robots but creatures with feelings. Indeed, in any effective argument, a writer had better engage the feelings of readers or they may reply, "True enough, but who cares?" Argument, to succeed in persuading, makes us feel that a writer's views are close to our own.

Yet another resource in argument is ETHICAL APPEAL: impressing your reader that you are a well-informed person of good will, good sense, and good moral character—and, therefore, to be believed. You make such an appeal by reasoning carefully, writing well, and collecting ample evidence. You can also cite or quote respected authorities. If you don't know whether an authority is respected, you can ask a reference librarian for tips on finding out, or talk to an instructor who is a specialist in that field.

In arguing, you don't prove your assertion in the same irrefutable way in which a chemist demonstrates that hydrogen will burn. If you say, "AIDS should be given first priority among health issues," that kind of claim isn't clearly either true or false. Argument takes place in areas that invite more than one opinion. In writing an argument, you help your reader see and understand just one open-eyed, open-minded view of reality.

Reasoning

When we argue rationally, we reason—that is, we make statements that lead to a conclusion. From the time of the ancient Greeks down to our own day, distinctly different methods of proceeding from statements to conclusions have been devised. This section will tell you of a recent, informal method of reasoning and also of two traditional methods. Understanding these methods, knowing how to use them, and being able to recognize when they are misused will make you a better writer *and* reader.

Data, Claim, and Warrant

In recent decades, a simple, practical method of reasoning has been devised by the British philosopher Stephen Toulmin.[1] Helpfully, Toulmin has divided a typical argument into three parts:

1. The DATA: *the evidence to prove something*
2. The CLAIM: *what you are proving with the data*
3. The WARRANT: *the assumption or principle that connects the data to the claim*

---

[1] *The Uses of Argument* (1969) sets forth Toulmin's system in detail. His views are further explained and applied by Douglas Ehninger and Wayne Brockriede in *Decision by Debate* (2nd ed., 1978) and by Toulmin himself, with Richard Rieke and Allan Janik, in *An Introduction to Reasoning* (2nd ed., 1984).

Any clear, explicit argument has to have all three parts. Toulmin's own example of such an argument is this:

Harry was born in Bermuda ———┬——— Harry is a British subject
(*Data*)   (*Claim*)

Since a man born in Bermuda
will be a British subject
(*Warrant*)

Of course, the data for a larger, more controversial claim will be more extensive. Here are some claims that would call for many more data, perhaps thousands of words.

> The war on drugs is not winnable.
> The United States must help to destroy drug production in South
>   America.
> Drug addiction is a personal matter.

The warrant, that middle term, is often crucially important. It is usually an ASSUMPTION or a GENERALIZATION that explains *why* the claim follows from the data. Often a writer won't bother to state a warrant because it is obvious: "In his bid for reelection, Mayor Perkins failed miserably. Out of 5,000 votes cast for both candidates, he received only 200." The warrant might be stated, "To make what I would consider a strong showing, he would have had to receive 2,000 votes or more," but it is clear that 200 out of 5,000 is a small minority, and no further explanation seems necessary.

A flaw in many arguments, though, is that the warrant is not clear. A clear warrant is essential. To be persuaded, a reader needs to understand your assumptions and the thinking that follows from them. If you were to argue, "Drug abuse is a serious problem in the United States. Therefore, the United States must help to destroy drug production in Latin America," then your reader might well be left wondering why the second statement follows from the first. But if you were to add, between the statements, "As long as drugs are manufactured in Latin America, they will be smuggled into the United States, and drug abuse will continue," then you supply a warrant. You show why your claim follows from your data—which, of course, you must also supply to make your case.

The unstated warrant can pitch an argument into trouble—whether your own or another writer's. Since warrants are usually assumptions or generalizations, rather than assertions of fact, they are valid only if readers accept or agree that they are valid. With stated warrants, any weaknesses are more likely to show. Suppose someone asserts that a certain woman should not be elected mayor because women cannot form ideas independently of their husbands and this woman's

husband has bad ideas on how to run the city. At least the warrant—
that women cannot form ideas independently of their husbands—is
out there on the table, exposed for all to inspect. But unstated warrants
can be just as absurd, or even just doubtful, and pass unnoticed because
they are not exposed. Here's the same argument without its warrant:
"She shouldn't be elected mayor because her husband has bad ideas on
how to run the city."

Here's another argument with an unstated warrant, this one
adapted from a magazine advertisement: "Scientists have no proof, just
statistical correlations, linking smoking and heart disease, so you
needn't worry about the connection." Now, the fact that this ad was
placed by a cigarette manufacturer would tip off any reasonably alert
reader to beware of bias in the claim. To discover the slant, we need to
examine the unstated warrant, which runs something like this: "Since
they are not proof, statistical correlations are worthless as guides to behavior." It is true that statistical correlations are not scientific proof, by
which we generally mean repeated results obtained under controlled
laboratory conditions—the kind of conditions to which human beings
cannot ethically be subjected. But statistical correlations *can* establish
connections and in fact inform much of our healthful behavior, such as
getting physical exercise, avoiding fatty foods, brushing our teeth, and
not driving while intoxicated. The advertiser's unstated warrant isn't
valid, so neither is the argument.

Let's look at how Toulmin's scheme can work in constructing an argument. In an assignment for her course in English composition, Maire
Flynn was asked to produce a condensed argument in three short paragraphs. The first paragraph was to set forth some data; the second, a
claim; and the third, a warrant. The result became a kind of outline
that the writer could then expand into a whole essay. Here is Flynn's argument.

DATA
Over the past five years, assistance in the form of food stamps has had
the effect of increasing the number of people on welfare instead of reducing it. Despite this help, 95 percent of long-term recipients remain below the poverty line today.

CLAIM
I maintain that the present system of distributing food stamps is a dis-
mal failure, a less effective way to help the needy than other possible
ways.

WARRANT
No one is happy to receive charity. We need to encourage people
to quit the welfare rolls; we need to make sure that government
aid goes only to the deserving. More effective than giving out food
might be to help untrained young people learn job skills; to help

single mothers with small children to obtain child care, freeing them
for the job market; and to enlarge and improve our state employment
counseling and job-placement services. The problem of poverty will
be helped only if more people will find jobs and become self-
sufficient.

In her warrant paragraph, Flynn spells out her reasons for holding her
opinion—the one she states in her claim. "The warrant," she found,
"was the hardest part to write," but hers turned out to be clear. Like any
good warrant, hers expresses those thoughts that her data set in motion. Another way of looking at the warrant: It is the thinking that led
the writer on to the opinion she holds. In this statement of her warrant,
Flynn makes clear her assumptions: that people who can support themselves don't deserve food stamps and that a person is better off (and
happier) holding a job than receiving charity. By generating more ideas
and evidence, she was easily able to expand both the data paragraph
and the warrant paragraph, and the result was a coherent essay of seven
hundred words.

How, by the way, would someone who didn't accept Flynn's warrant argue with her? What about old, infirm, or disabled persons who
cannot work? What quite different assumptions about poverty might be
possible?

Deductive and Inductive Reasoning

Stephen Toulmin's method of argument is a fairly recent—and
very helpful—way to analyze and construct arguments. Two other reliable methods date back to the Greek philosopher Aristotle, who identified the complementary processes of INDUCTIVE REASONING (induction)
and DEDUCTIVE REASONING (deduction). In *Zen and the Art of Motorcycle
Maintenance*, Robert M. Pirsig gives examples of deductive and inductive reasoning:

> If the cycle goes over a bump and the engine misfires, and then
> goes over another bump and the engine misfires, and then goes over
> another bump and the engine misfires, and then goes over a long
> smooth stretch of road and there is no misfiring, and then goes over a
> fourth bump and the engine misfires again, one can logically con-
> clude that the misfiring is caused by the bumps. That is induction:
> reasoning from particular experiences to general truths.
>
> Deductive inferences do the reverse. They start with general
> knowledge and predict a specific observation. For example if, from
> reading the hierarchy of facts about the machine, the mechanic
> knows the horn of the cycle is powered exclusively by electricity from
> the battery, then he can logically infer that if the battery is dead the
> horn will not work. That is deduction.

In inductive reasoning, the method of the sciences, we collect bits of evidence on which to base generalizations. From interviews with a hundred self-identified conservative Republicans (the evidence), you might conclude that conservative Republicans favor less government regulation of business (the generalization). The more evidence you have, the more trustworthy your generalization is, but it would never be airtight unless you talked to every conservative Republican in the country. Since such thoroughness is impractical if not impossible, inductive reasoning involves making a so-called inductive leap from the evidence to the conclusion. The smaller the leap—the more evidence you have—the better.

Deductive reasoning works the other way, from a general statement to particular cases. The basis of deduction is the SYLLOGISM, a three-step form of reasoning practiced by Aristotle:

> All men are mortal.
> Socrates is a man.
> Therefore, Socrates is mortal.

The first statement (the major premise) is a generalization about a large group: It is the result of inductive reasoning. The second statement (the minor premise) says something about a particular member of that large group. The third statement (the conclusion) follows inevitably from the premises and applies the generalization to the particular: If the premises are true, then the conclusion must be true. Here is another syllogism:

> MAJOR PREMISE: Conservative Republicans favor less government regulation of business.
> MINOR PREMISE: William F. Buckley, Jr., is a conservative Republican.
> CONCLUSION: Therefore, William F. Buckley, Jr., favors less government regulation of business.

Problems with deductive reasoning start in the premises. In 1633, Scipio Chiaramonti, professor of philosophy at the University of Pisa, came up with this untrustworthy syllogism: "Animals, which move, have limbs and muscles. The earth has no limbs and muscles. Hence, the earth does not move." This is bad deductive reasoning, and its flaw is to assume that all things need limbs and muscles to move—ignoring raindrops, rivers, and many other moving things. In the next few pages, we'll look at some of the things that can go wrong with any kind of reasoning.

Logical Fallacies

In arguments we read and hear, we often meet LOGICAL FALLACIES: errors in reasoning that lead to wrong conclusions. From the time when you start thinking about your proposition or claim and planning your paper, you'll need to watch out for them. To help you recognize logical fallacies when you see them or hear them, and so guard against them when you write, here is a list of the most common.

- *Non sequitur* (from the Latin, "it does not follow"): stating a conclusion that doesn't follow from the first premise or premises. "I've lived in this town a long time — why, my grandfather was the first mayor — so I'm against putting fluoride in the drinking water."
- *Oversimplification:* supplying neat and easy explanations for large and complicated phenomena. "No wonder drug abuse is out of control. Look at how the courts have hobbled police officers." Oversimplified solutions are also popular: "All these teenage kids that get in trouble with the law — why, they ought to ship 'em over to China. That would straighten 'em out!"
- *Hasty generalization:* leaping to a generalization from inadequate or faulty evidence. The most familiar hasty generalization is the stereotype: "Men aren't sensitive enough to be day-care providers." "Women are too emotional to fight in combat."
- *Either/or reasoning:* assuming that a reality may be divided into only two parts or extremes; assuming that a given problem has only one of two possible solutions. "What's to be done about the trade imbalance with Japan? Either we ban all Japanese imports, or American industry will collapse." Obviously, either/or reasoning is a kind of extreme oversimplification.
- *Argument from doubtful or unidentified authority:* "We ought to castrate all sex offenders; Uncle Oswald says we should." Or: "According to reliable sources, my opponent is lying."
- *Argument ad hominem* (from the Latin, "to the man"): attacking a person's views by attacking his or her character. "Mayor Burns is divorced and estranged from his family. How can we listen to his pleas for a city nursing home?"
- *Begging the question:* taking for granted from the start what you set out to demonstrate. When you reason in a *logical* way, you state that because something is true, then, as a result, some other truth follows. When you beg the question, however, you repeat that what is true is true. If you argue, for instance, that dogs are a menace to people because they are dangerous, you don't prove a thing, since the idea that dogs are dangerous is already assumed in the statement that they are a menace. Beggars of questions often just repeat what they already believe, only in different words. This fallacy sometimes takes the form of arguing in a circle, or demonstrating a premise by a conclusion and a conclusion by a premise: "I am in college because that is the right thing to do. Going to college is the right thing to do because it is expected of me."

- *Post hoc, ergo propter hoc* (from the Latin, "after this, therefore because of this"), or *post hoc* for short: assuming that because B follows A, B was caused by A. "Ever since the city suspended height restrictions on skyscrapers, the city budget has been balanced." (See also p. 360.)
- *False analogy:* the claim of persuasive likeness when no significant likeness exists. An ANALOGY asserts that because two things are comparable in some respects, they are comparable in other respects as well. Analogies cannot serve as evidence in a rational argument because the differences always outweigh the similarities; but analogies can reinforce such arguments *if* the subjects are indeed similar in some ways. If they aren't, the analogy is false. Many observers see the "war on drugs" as a false and damaging analogy because warfare aims for clear victory over a specific, organized enemy, whereas the complete eradication of illegal drugs is probably unrealistic and, in any event, the "enemy" isn't well defined: the drugs themselves? users? sellers? producers? the producing nations? (These critics urge approaching drugs as a social problem to be skillfully managed and reduced.)

THE PROCESS

In stating an opinion, you set forth and support a claim—a truth you believe. You may find such a truth by thinking and feeling, by talking to your instructors or fellow students, by scanning a newspaper or reading books and magazines, by listening to a discussion of some problem or controversy.

In stating a proposal, you already have an opinion in mind, and from there, you go on to urge an action or a solution to a problem. Usually, these two statements will take place within the same piece of writing: A writer will first set forth a view ("Compact disks are grossly overpriced") and then go right on to a proposal ("Compact disks should be discounted in the college store").

Whether your essay states an opinion, a proposal, or both, it is likely to contain similar ingredients. One essential is your thesis—the proposition or claim you are going to defend. As we noted earlier (p. 443), the likeliest spot for your thesis statement is near the start of your essay, where you might also explain why you think the thesis worth upholding, perhaps showing how it concerns your readers. If you plan to include both an opinion and a proposal in your essay, you may wish to set forth your opinion first, saving your proposal for later, perhaps for your conclusion.

Your thesis stated, introduce your least important point first. Then build in a crescendo to the strongest point you have. This structure will lend emphasis to your essay, and perhaps make your chain of ideas more persuasive as the reader continues to follow it.

For every point, give evidence: facts, figures, examples, expert opinions. If you introduce statistics, make sure that they are up to date and fairly represented. In an essay advocating a law against smoking, it would be unfair to declare that "in Pottsville, Illinois, last year, 50 percent of all deaths were caused by lung cancer" if only two people died in Pottsville last year — one of them struck by a car.

If you are arguing fairly, you should be able to face potential criticisms fairly, and give your critics due credit, by recognizing the objections you expect your assertion will meet. This is the strategy H. L. Mencken uses in "The Penalty of Death," and he introduces it in his essay right at the beginning. (You might also tackle the opposition at the end of your essay or at relevant points throughout.) Notice that Mencken takes pains to dispense with his opponents: He doesn't just dismiss them; he reasons with them.

In your conclusion, briefly restate your claim, if possible in a fresh, pointed way. (For example, see the concluding sentence in the essay by William F. Buckley, Jr., in this chapter.) In emotionally persuasive writing, you may want to end with a strong appeal. (See "I Have a Dream" by Martin Luther King, Jr.)

Finally, don't forget the power of humor in argument. You don't have to crack gratuitous jokes, but there is often an advantage in having a reader or listener who laughs on your side. When Abraham Lincoln debated Stephen Douglas, he triumphed in his reply to Douglas's snide remark that Lincoln had once been a bartender. "I have long since quit my side of the bar," Lincoln declared, "while Mr. Douglas clings to his as tenaciously as ever."

In arguing — doing everything you can to bring your reader around to your view — you can draw on any method of writing discussed in this book. Arguing for or against welfare funding, you might give EXAMPLES of wasteful spending, or of neighborhoods where welfare funds are needed. You might analyze the CAUSES of social problems that call for welfare funds, or foresee the likely EFFECTS of cutting welfare programs or of keeping them. You might COMPARE AND CONTRAST the idea of slashing welfare funds with the idea of increasing them. You could use NARRATION to tell a pointed story; you could use DESCRIPTION to portray certain welfare recipients and their neighborhoods. If you wanted to, you could employ several of these methods in writing a single argument.

You will rarely find, when you begin to write a persuasive paper, that you have too much evidence to support your claim. But unless you're writing a term paper and have months to spend on it, you're limited in how much evidence you can gather. Begin by stating your claim. Make it narrow enough to support in the time you have available. For a paper due a week from now, the opinion that "our city's downtown area has a serious litter problem" can probably be backed up in part by your own eyewitness reports. But to support the claim "Litter is one of the worst environmental problems of North American cities," you would surely need to spend time in a library.

In rewriting, you may find yourself tempted to keep all the evidence you have collected with such effort. Of course, some of it may not support your claim; some may seem likely to persuade the reader only to go to sleep. If so, throw it out. A stronger argument will remain.

CHECKLIST FOR REVISING ARGUMENT OR PERSUASION

✔ **AUDIENCE.** Have you taken account of your readers' probable views? Have you reasoned with readers, not attacked them? Are your emotional appeals appropriate to readers' likely feelings? Do you acknowledge opposing views?

✔ **THESIS.** Does your argument have a thesis, a claim about how your subject is or should be? Is the thesis narrow enough to argue convincingly in the space and time available? Is it stated clearly? Is it reasonable?

✔ **EVIDENCE.** Is your thesis well supported with facts, statistics, expert opinions, and examples? Is your evidence recent and fair?

✔ **WARRANT.** Have you made sound connections between your evidence and your thesis or claim?

✔ **LOGICAL FALLACIES.** Have you avoided common errors in reasoning, such as oversimplifying or begging the question? (See pp. 450–51 for a list of fallacies.)

✔ **STRUCTURE.** Does your organization lead readers through your argument step by step, building to your strongest ideas and frequently connecting your evidence to your central claim?

ARGUMENT AND PERSUASION IN A PARAGRAPH: TWO ILLUSTRATIONS

Arguing About Television

Television news has a serious failing: It's show business. *Topic sentence: the claim* Unlike a newspaper, its every image has to entertain the average beer drinker. To score high ratings and win advertisers, the visual medium favors the spectacular: riots, tornados, air crashes. Now that satellite transmission invites live cover- *Evidence:* age, newscasters go for the fast-breaking story at the expense of thoughtful analysis. "The more you can get data out in- *Expert opinion* stantly," says media critic Jeff Greenfield, "the more you rely

on instant data to define the news." TV zooms in on people
who make news, but, to avoid boredom, won't let them argue or explain. (How can they, in speeches limited to fifteen
seconds?) On NBC late news for September 12, 1987, Pres-   *Facts and examples*
ident Reagan blasted a plan to end war in Nicaragua. His ad-
dress was clipped to sixty seconds, then an anchorwoman
digested the opposition in one quick line: "Democrats to-
night were critical of the president's remarks." During the
1992 presidential election, all three candidates sometimes
deliberately packaged bad news so that it could not be dis-
tilled to a sound bite on the evening news—and thus would
not make the evening news at all. Americans who rely on
television for their news (two-thirds, according to recent   *Statistic*
polls) exist on a starvation diet.

Arguing in an Academic Discipline

   Although the public stereotypes a lobbyist as a fast-   *Topic sentence: the claim*
talking person twisting an elected official's arm to get special
concessions, the reality is quite different. Today's lobbyist,
who may be fully employed by one industry or represent a
variety of clients, is often a quiet-spoken, well-educated   *Evidence:*
man or woman armed with statistics and research reports.
Robert Gray, former head of Hill and Knowlton's Washing-   *Expert opinion*
ton office and a public affairs expert for thirty years, adds,
"Lobbying is no longer a booze and buddies business. It's presenting honest facts and convincing Congress that your side
has more merit than the other." He rejects lobbying as being
simply "influence peddling and button-holing" top administration officials. Although the public has the perception
that lobbying is done only by big business, Gray correctly
points out that a variety of special interests also do it. These   *Facts and examples*
may include such groups as the Sierra Club, Mothers
Against Drunk Driving, National Association of Social
Workers, American Civil Liberties Union, and the American Federation of Labor. Even the American Society of
Plastic and Reconstructive Surgeons hired a Washington
public relations firm in their battle against restrictions on
breast implants. Lobbying, quite literally, is an activity in
which widely diverse groups and organizations engage as an
exercise of free speech and representation in the marketplace of ideas. Lobbyists often balance each other and work
toward legislative compromises that not only benefit their
self-interests but society as a whole.
                              —Dennis L. Wilcox, Phillip H. Ault,
                                   and Warren K. Agee, *Public
                                   Relations: Strategies and Tactics*

H. L. MENCKEN

HENRY LOUIS MENCKEN (1880–1956) was a native of Baltimore, where
for four decades he worked as newspaper reporter, editor, and columnist. In the 1920s, his boisterous, cynical observations on American
life, appearing regularly in *The Smart Set* and later in *The American
Mercury* (which he founded and edited), made him probably the
most widely quoted writer in the country. As an editor and literary
critic, Mencken championed Sinclair Lewis, Theodore Dreiser, and
other realistic writers. As a social critic, he leveled blasts at pomp,
hypocrisy, and the middle classes (whom he labeled "the booboisie").
(The publication of *The Diary of H. L. Mencken* in 1989 revealed its
author's outspoken opinions and touched off a controversy: Was
Mencken a bigot? The debate goes on.) In 1933, when Mencken's attempts to laugh off the Depression began to ring hollow, his magazine
died. He then devoted himself to revising and supplementing *The
American Language* (4th ed., 1948), a learned and highly entertaining
survey of a nation's speech habits and vocabulary. Two dozen of
Mencken's books are now in print, including *A Mencken Chrestomathy* (1949), a representative selection of his best writings of various
kinds; and *A Choice of Days* (1980), a selection from his memoirs.

The Penalty of Death

Above all, Mencken was a humorist whose thought had a serious
core. He argues by first making the reader's jaw drop, then inducing a
laugh, and finally causing the reader to ponder, "Hmmmm—what if
he's right?" The following still-controversial essay, from *Prejudices,
Fifth Series* (1926), shows Mencken the persuader in top form.
Michael Kroll takes a different approach to capital punishment in the
essay following Mencken's.

Of the arguments against capital punishment that issue from up- 1
lifters, two are commonly heard most often, to wit:

1. That hanging a man (or frying him or gassing him) is a dreadful
   business, degrading to those who have to do it and revolting to
   those who have to witness it.
2. That it is useless, for it does not deter others from the same crime.

The first of these arguments, it seems to me, is plainly too weak to 2
need serious refutation. All it says, in brief, is that the work of the
hangman is unpleasant. Granted. But suppose it is? It may be quite

necessary to society for all that. There are, indeed, many other jobs that
are unpleasant, and yet no one thinks of abolishing them—that of the
plumber, that of the soldier, that of the garbageman, that of the priest
hearing confessions, that of the sandhog, and so on. Moreover, what
evidence is there that any actual hangman complains of his work? I
have heard none. On the contrary, I have known many who delighted
in their ancient art, and practiced it proudly.

In the second argument of the abolitionists there is rather more   3
force, but even here, I believe, the ground under them is shaky. Their
fundamental error consists in assuming that the whole aim of punishing criminals is to deter other (potential) criminals—that we hang or
electrocute A simply in order to so alarm B that he will not kill C. This,
I believe, is an assumption which confuses a part with the whole. Deterrence, obviously, is *one* of the aims of punishment, but it is surely not
the only one. On the contrary, there are at least a half dozen, and some
are probably quite as important. At least one of them, practically considered, is *more* important. Commonly, it is described as revenge, but
revenge is really not the word for it. I borrow a better term from the late
Aristotle: *katharsis*. *Katharsis*, so used, means a salubrious discharge of
emotions, a healthy letting off of steam. A schoolboy, disliking his
teacher, deposits a tack upon the pedagogical chair; the teacher jumps
and the boy laughs. This is *katharsis*. What I contend is that one of the
prime objects of all judicial punishments is to afford the same grateful
relief (*a*) to the immediate victims of the criminal punished, and (*b*) to
the general body of moral and timorous men.

These persons, and particularly the first group, are concerned only   4
indirectly with deterring other criminals. The thing they crave primarily is the satisfaction of seeing the criminal actually before them suffer
as he made them suffer. What they want is the peace of mind that goes
with the feeling that accounts are squared. Until they get that satisfaction they are in a state of emotional tension, and hence unhappy. The
instant they get it they are comfortable. I do not argue that this yearn-
ing is noble; I simply argue that it is almost universal among human beings. In the face of injuries that are unimportant and can be borne
without damage it may yield to higher impulses; that is to say, it may
yield to what is called Christian charity. But when the injury is serious
Christianity is adjourned, and even saints reach for their sidearms. It is
plainly asking too much of human nature to expect it to conquer so
natural an impulse. A keeps a store and has a bookkeeper, B. B steals
$700, employs it in playing at dice or bingo, and is cleaned out. What
is A to do? Let B go? If he does so he will be unable to sleep at night.
The sense of injury, of injustice, of frustration will haunt him like pruritus. So he turns B over to the police, and they hustle B to prison.
Thereafter A can sleep. More, he has pleasant dreams. He pictures B

chained to the wall of a dungeon a hundred feet underground, devoured by rats and scorpions. It is so agreeable that it makes him forget his $700. He has got his *katharsis*.

The same thing precisely takes place on a larger scale when there is 5 a crime which destroys a whole community's sense of security. Every law-abiding citizen feels menaced and frustrated until the criminals have been struck down—until the communal capacity to get even with them, and more than even, has been dramatically demonstrated. Here, manifestly, the business of deterring others is no more than an afterthought. The main thing is to destroy the concrete scoundrels whose act has alarmed everyone, and thus made everyone unhappy. Until they are brought to book that unhappiness continues; when the law has been executed upon them there is a sigh of relief. In other words, there is *katharsis*.

I know of no public demand for the death penalty for ordinary 6 crimes, even for ordinary homicides. Its infliction would shock all men of normal decency of feeling. But for crimes involving the deliberate and inexcusable taking of human life, by men openly defiant of all civilized order—for such crimes it seems, to nine men out of ten, a just and proper punishment. Any lesser penalty leaves them feeling that the criminal has got the better of society—that he is free to add insult to injury by laughing. That feeling can be dissipated only by a recourse to *katharsis*, the invention of the aforesaid Aristotle. It is more effectively and economically achieved, as human nature now is, by wafting the criminal to realms of bliss.

The real objection to capital punishment doesn't lie against the ac- 7 tual extermination of the condemned, but against our brutal American habit of putting it off so long. After all, every one of us must die soon or late, and a murderer, it must be assumed, is one who makes that sad fact the cornerstone of his metaphysic. But it is one thing to die, and quite another thing to lie for long months and even years under the shadow of death. No sane man would choose such a finish. All of us, despite the Prayer Book, long for a swift and unexpected end. Unhappily, a murderer, under the irrational American system, is tortured for what, to him, must seem a whole series of eternities. For months on end he sits in prison while his lawyers carry on their idiotic buffoonery with writs, injunctions, mandamuses, and appeals. In order to get his money (or that of his friends) they have to feed him with hope. Now and then, by the imbecility of a judge or some trick of juridic science, they actually justify it. But let us say that, his money all gone, they finally throw up their hands. Their client is now ready for the rope or the chair. But he must still wait for months before it fetches him.

That wait, I believe, is horribly cruel. I have seen more than one 8 man sitting in the death-house, and I don't want to see any more.

Worse, it is wholly useless. Why should he wait at all? Why not hang him the day after the last court dissipates his last hope? Why torture him as not even cannibals would torture their victims? The common answer is that he must have time to make his peace with God. But how long does that take? It may be accomplished, I believe, in two hours quite as comfortably as in two years. There are, indeed, no temporal limitations upon God. He could forgive a whole herd of murderers in a millionth of a second. More, it has been done.

QUESTIONS ON MEANING

1. Identify Mencken's main reasons for his support of capital punishment. What is his THESIS?
2. In paragraph 3, Mencken asserts that there are at least half a dozen reasons for punishing offenders. In his essay, he mentions two, deterrence and revenge. What others can you supply?
3. For which class of offenders does Mencken advocate the death penalty?
4. What is Mencken's "real objection" to capital punishment?

QUESTIONS ON WRITING STRATEGY

1. How would you characterize Mencken's humor? Point to examples of it. In the light of the grim subject, do you find the humor funny?
2. In his first paragraph, Mencken pares his subject down to manageable size. What techniques does he employ for this purpose?
3. At the start of paragraph 7, Mencken shifts his stance from concern for the victims of crime to concern for prisoners awaiting execution. Does the shift help or weaken the effectiveness of his earlier justification for capital punishment?
4. Do you think the author expects his AUDIENCE to agree with him? At what points does he seem to recognize the fact that some readers may see things differently?
5. In paragraphs 2 and 3, Mencken uses ANALOGIES in an apparent attempt to strengthen his argument. What are the analogies? Do they seem false to you? (See p. 451 for a discussion of false analogy.) Do you think Mencken would agree with your judgment?
6. **OTHER METHODS.** To explain what he sees as the most important aim of capital punishment, Mencken uses DEFINITION. What does he define, and what techniques does he use to make the definition clear?

QUESTIONS ON LANGUAGE

1. Mencken opens his argument by referring to those who reject capital punishment as "uplifters." What CONNOTATIONS does this word have for you? Does the use of this "loaded" word strengthen or weaken Mencken's position? Explain.

2. Be sure you know the meanings of the following words: refutation, sandhog (para. 2); salubrious, pedagogical, timorous (3); pruritus (4); wafting (6); mandamuses, juridic (7).
3. What emotional overtones can you detect in Mencken's reference to the hangman's job as an "ancient art" (para. 2)?
4. Writing at a time when there was no debate over the usage, Mencken often uses "man" and "he" for examples that could be either a man or a woman (such as A in para. 4) and uses "men" to mean people in general ("all men of normal decency of feeling," para. 6). Does this usage date the essay or otherwise weaken it? Why?

SUGGESTIONS FOR WRITING

1. **JOURNAL WRITING.** Although Mencken supports capital punishment, he condemns "our brutal American habit" of delaying executions for court appeals (paras. 7–8). What do you think of our methods of trying, sentencing, or appealing the sentences of criminals in this country? Does our system seem just to you?

   FROM JOURNAL TO ESSAY. Develop a focused and persuasive thesis from the opinions you expressed in your journal entry, and support it with EVIDENCE from your reading and observations. (You may also wish to do library research among the many books and articles written on the criminal justice system.) Rather than take on the entire administration of justice, follow Mencken's model and narrow your thesis to one aspect of the system.
2. In a brief essay, argue for or against humor as a technique of argument or persuasion. Use examples from Mencken's essay as EVIDENCE.
3. **CRITICAL WRITING.** Write an essay refuting Mencken's argument; or take Mencken's side but supply any additional reasons you can think of. In either case, begin your argument with an ANALYSIS of Mencken's argument, and use examples (real or hypothetical) to support your view.
4. **CONNECTIONS.** Compare this essay with the following one by Michael Kroll, "The Unquiet Death of Robert Harris." Imagine a debate between the two writers. How would Kroll respond to Mencken's argument that fallible human beings can't do without *katharsis*? How would Mencken answer Kroll's charge that turning death into a public spectacle is barbarous? On what point do they agree?

H. L. MENCKEN ON WRITING

"All my work hangs together," wrote H. L. Mencken in a piece called "Addendum on Aims," "once the main ideas under it are discerned. Those ideas are chiefly of a skeptical character. I believe that nothing is unconditionally true, and hence I am opposed to every statement of positive truth and to every man who states it. Such men seem to me to be either idiots or scoundrels. To one category or the other belong all theologians, professors, editorial writers, right-thinkers, etc.... Whether [my work] appears to be burlesque, or serious criticism, or mere casual controversy, it is always directed against one thing: unwarranted pretension."

Mencken cheerfully acknowledged his debts to his teachers: mostly writers he read as a young man and newspaper editors he worked under. "My style of writing is chiefly grounded upon an early enthusiasm for Huxley,[1] the greatest of all masters of orderly exposition. He taught me the importance of giving to every argument a simple structure. As for the fancy work on the surface, it comes chiefly from an anonymous editorial writer in the *New York Sun*, circa 1900. He taught me the value of apt phrases. My vocabulary is pretty large; it probably runs to 25,000 words. It represents much labor. I am constantly expanding it. I believe that a good phrase is better than a Great Truth — which is usually buncombe. I delight in argument, not because I want to convince, but because argument itself is an end."

In another essay, "The Fringes of Lovely Letters," Mencken wrote that "what is in the head infallibly oozes out of the nub of the pen. If it is sparkling Burgundy the writing is full of life and charm. If it is mush the writing is mush too." He recalls the example of President Warren G. Harding, who once sent a message to Congress that was quite incomprehensible. "Why? Simply because Dr. Harding's thoughts, on the high and grave subjects he discussed, were so muddled that he couldn't understand them himself. But on matters within his range of customary meditation he was clear and even charming, as all of us are....Style cannot go beyond the ideas which lie at the heart of it. If they are clear, it too will be clear. If they are held passionately, it will be eloquent."

FOR DISCUSSION

1. According to Mencken, what PURPOSE animates his writing?
2. What relationship does Mencken see between a writer's thought and his or her STYLE?
3. Where in his views on writing does Mencken use FIGURES OF SPEECH to advantage?

---

[1] Thomas Henry Huxley (1825–95), English biologist and educator, who wrote many essays popularizing science. In Victorian England, Huxley was the leading exponent and defender of Charles Darwin's theory of evolution. — EDS.

MICHAEL KROLL

MICHAEL KROLL is a writer and investigator specializing in the criminal justice system. Born in 1943 and raised in rural California, Kroll graduated in 1965 from the University of California at Berkeley with a B.A. in political science. For almost a decade he was a journalist and editor with the Pacific News Service, writing about juvenile justice, capital punishment, and prisons. His articles have appeared in periodicals such as the *Los Angeles Times*, the *New York Times*, *California Lawyer*, and *The Progressive*, and he has been a guest on talk shows. With a special interest in capital punishment, Kroll has also run the Death Penalty Information Center in Washington, D.C., and he is currently director of a project to uncover evidence that might strengthen the court appeals of individuals sentenced to death in California.

The Unquiet Death of Robert Harris

Kroll met Robert Alton Harris in 1984, when Harris was awaiting execution for the 1978 murders of two teenagers. The two men became friends, giving Kroll a uniquely personal view of Harris's long journey to the gas chamber and to death on April 21, 1992. Harris's execution was controversial: It was the first in California in twenty-five years. Kroll's account appeared in *The Nation* magazine a few months later.

"Ladies and gentlemen. Please stay in your places until your escort 1 comes for you. Follow your escort, as instructed. Thank you."

The words were spoken in the manner of the operator of the 2 Jungle Cruise at Disneyland: well-rehearsed and "professional." They were spoken by the public information officer of California's San Quentin penitentiary, Vernell Crittendon, as we waited to be ushered out of the gas chamber where my friend Robert Harris was slumped over, dead, in Chair B.

When not conveying us to and from the gas chamber, our "escorts" 3 guarded us in a small, tidy office with barred windows facing the east gate, where a circus of media lights lit up the night sky, letting us see silhouettes in the darkness. There were two desks, the exact number of straight-backed chairs needed to accommodate us, some nineteen-cent bags of potato chips, a couple of apples and bananas, and bad coffee.

We—a psychologist and lawyer who knew Robert Harris profes- 4 sionally, his brother Randy, whom he had designated to witness the gassing, and I, a close friend for nearly a decade—had entered at the west gate at 10 P.M. as instructed to present our credentials (a written invitation from Warden Daniel Vasquez himself) and submit to a thorough pat-down search and a metal detector. Our escorts took us in a prison van to the front of the old fortress and escorted us up a few steps into the office of one G. Mosqueda, program administrator. Then we began what we thought at the time would be a short vigil. It turned out to be eight hours.

We'd been there only a few minutes when another staff person arrived wearing a civilian suit and a name tag that identified him as Martinez. He walked up to Randy, pointed his finger, and said, "Randall Harris. Come with me!" Randy smiled, got up, and followed him out. (Randy thought they were taking him for counseling. It was a fair assumption; counselors had been provided to advise members of the victims' families who had come to witness the execution. This was to insure, Warden Vasquez told them, that "there is only one casualty in that room.")   5

When they brought him back, he told his own horror story. He had been ordered to submit to a full body-cavity search. "We have learned from a reliable source that you are planning something," Martinez had said. Randy was ordered to open his mouth for inspection, take his clothes off, bend over, lift his testicles, pull back his foreskin. "If you try anything," Martinez had threatened, "you'll be sorry, and so will your brother."   6

His brother was waiting just a few feet from the gas chamber.   7

After Randy rejoined us, shaken and humiliated, our escort gave us our marching orders. "When the phone rings and I get the order to go, stand and follow me quickly." The phone, which had the kind of clanging ring that scares you to death even when you are not already scared to death, rang many times that night, and each time our hearts stopped. But *the* call did not come at midnight. It did not come for a long time. With no television to inform us, we waited, hour after hour, wondering what was happening, drinking bad coffee and asking to be escorted to the bathroom.   8

Later, we learned that in those hours the U.S. Court of Appeals for the Ninth Circuit had granted three stays of execution. One concerned newly discovered evidence that Robert's brother Danny, who had participated in the crime but served fewer than four years in exchange for his testimony against Robert, had actually fired the first shot. The two other stays — including one signed by ten judges — were based on the pending suit challenging the constitutionality of cyanide gas as a method of execution. Each of the three stays was dissolved by the U.S. Supreme Court.   9

Finally, a little after three o'clock, the call came and Mendez said, "Now."   10

We followed him into the freezing, brilliant night, but Mendez   11
stopped us just short of the entrance to the gas chamber. Shivering, we
watched the other witnesses being led out of the cold—the media into
one building opposite the gas chamber and the victims' family members into the East Block visiting room just beyond it. After a while, responding to words coming over his walkie-talkie that I could not hear,
Mendez led us into the main visiting room to our immediate right. I
had been in this room many times, but never at night, and never, as
now, was it deserted of staff and inmates.

Finally the wait was over. Mendez spoke into his walkie-talkie.   12
"Okay," he said, and then turned his attention to us. "Let's go."

We, the family and friends of the condemned, were led to risers   13
along a wall behind and to the left of the chamber. Three burly guards
brought Robert in and strapped him quickly to Chair B. His back was
to us. He could see us only by craning his neck and peering over his left
shoulder. From behind him, I looked over his right shoulder into the
unblinking red eye of the video camera that was trained on his face
in order to assist U.S. District Judge Marilyn Patel in determining
whether death by lethal gas is cruel and unusual punishment. He
peered around the room, making eye contact, smiling and nodding at
people he knew. I held my breath. A guard's digital watch started beep-
ing. She smiled sheepishly and covered it with her sleeve.

Minutes passed. Some people whispered. Some smiled. And then   14
the phone rang. The phone to the gas chamber rings for only one reason: A stay of execution has been granted. But nothing happened. Nobody moved—nobody except Robert, that is, who twisted and turned
trying to figure out what was happening. He peered down between his
legs to see if he could see the vat of acid beneath him. He sniffed the air
and mouthed the words, "Pull it." More minutes passed. He peered over
his left shoulder where I was just out his line of vision. "Where's Mike?"
he mouthed.

I jumped down to the lower riser and walked over to the window.   15
A female guard ordered me back to my place, but not before Robert saw
me, smiled, and settled down.

Ten minutes after the phone rang, the gas chamber door was   16
opened and the three guards unfastened Robert and took him from the
chamber. Nothing like that had ever happened in the history of the gas
chamber. (I later learned that during that eternity, California's attorney
general, Dan Lungren, had been on the phone to the clerk of the U.S.
Supreme Court informing him that Robert was in the chamber. Lungren begged the justices to overturn the stay. But the court wanted to
read what circuit court Judge Harry Pregerson had written in the fourth
and last stay of execution, so Lungren was told to take Robert from the
chamber.)

We were escorted back to Mosqueda's office to continue waiting. I 17
shook uncontrollably for a long time, and cried openly. My escort suggested I needed medical attention, hinting I might have to leave. I
forced back my tears and pulled myself together, although I could not
stop trembling.

We resumed the grim vigil, cut off from the outside world. Just af- 18
ter six in the morning, I saw the witnesses from the victims' families being led past our window toward the chamber. Some were laughing. As
honored guests, they had been playing video games, napping in the
warden's home, and eating specially prepared food. My heart stopped.
Something was happening. Karen, the lawyer with us, called the office
where lawyers who supported Harris had gathered, and was told the
stay of execution was still in place. But, as with the aborted execution
attempt, they were the last to know.

Within fifteen seconds, the phone clattered to life, and Mendez 19
told us the stay had been dissolved. (He did not tell us the Supreme
Court had ordered all federal courts to enter no more stays of execution
regardless of the issues.) We were going again.

Quickly we moved through the chill dawn air toward the chamber. 20
Randy whispered in my ear, "Slow down." Near the entrance, Vernell
Crittendon stood watching the procession move smoothly into the
chamber. He pumped his upturned fist three times, the way football
players do when their team has scored.

When they brought Robert in, he was grim-faced, tired and ashen. 21
Beyond the horror of having stood at the brink of the abyss just two and
a half hours before, he had been up for several days and nights. He was
under horrific pressure. Again, he nodded to acquaintances. He did not
smile. He faced to his right and said "I'm sorry" to the father of murder
victim Michael Baker. He craned his neck left once more and nodded
quickly toward us. "It's all right," he reassured us. After about two minutes, he sniffed the air, then breathed deeply several times.

His head began to roll and his eyes closed, then opened again. His 22
head dropped, then came up with an abrupt jerk, and rolled some more.
It was grotesque and hideous, and I looked away. When I looked back,
his head came up again, and I covered my mouth. Randy was whim-
pering in pain next to me, and we clutched each other. The lawyer,
sobbing audibly, put her arms around us and tried to comfort us. I could
not stop shivering. Reverend Harris, Robert's second cousin and spiritual adviser, who had been with Robert in the holding cell almost until the moment they took him away, whispered, "He's ready. He was
tired. It's all right. His punishment is over."

He writhed for seven minutes, his head falling on his chest, saliva 23
drooling from his open mouth. He lifted his head again and again.
Seven minutes. A lifetime. Nine more minutes passed with his head

slumped on his chest. His heart, a survivor's heart, had kept pumping for nine more minutes, while we held each other. Some of the witnesses laughed. I thought of the label "Laughing Killer," affixed to Robert by the media, and knew these good people would never be described as laughing killers.

We were in the middle of something indescribably ugly. Not just   24
the cold-blooded killing of a human being, and not even the fact that we happened to love him—but the ritual of it, the participation of us, the witnesses, the witnessing itself of this most private and personal act. It was nakedly barbaric. Nobody could say this had anything to do with justice, I thought. Yet this medieval torture chamber is what a large majority of my fellow Californians, including most in the room with me, believe in. The implications of this filled me with fear—fear for myself and for all of us, a fear I am ashamed to confess—while my friend was being strangled slowly to death in front me.

Some witnesses began shuffling nervously. People looked at their   25
watches. Then a guard stepped forward and announced that Robert Al-ton Harris, C.D.C. Prisoner B-66883, had expired in the gas chamber at 6:21 A.M., sixteen minutes after the cyanide had been gently lowered into the sulfuric acid.

It was the moment Crittendon had been waiting for. He stepped   26
into the middle of the quiet room, his Jheri-Kurls reflecting the eerie green light from the gas chamber where my friend lay dead, slumped forward against the straps in Chair B.

"Ladies and gentlemen. Please stay in your places until your escort   27
comes for you. Follow your escort, as instructed. Thank you."

Our guard came and we followed him out. The eighteen media wit-   28
nesses, who had stood against the wall opposite us scribbling on paper provided by the prison, preceded us out of the room. As they had been for weeks, they were desperate for a Harris family member to say some-thing to them. "Is this a Harris? Is this a Harris?" a reporter standing just outside the door shouted, pointing at each of us as we emerged into the first light of morning over San Francisco Bay.

My god, it was a beautiful day.   29

QUESTIONS ON MEANING

1. Is Kroll's PURPOSE merely to serve as a witness to his friend's execution, or is there an unstated proposal in the essay? If so, what is it?
2. Why did the execution take so long? What was taking place behind the scenes?

3. What can you INFER about Kroll's opinion of the Supreme Court's decision to dissolve all three of the Court of Appeals' stays of execution (para. 9)? How does he indirectly make this opinion known?
4. How do you read the last sentence of the essay? Is it merely IRONIC?
5. Do you think Kroll is against the death penalty, or merely against the way it was carried out in this case?

QUESTIONS ON WRITING STRATEGY

1. At what three points does Kroll pause in the story of the execution? What does he accomplish each time?
2. What is the TONE of the essay? How does it contribute to Kroll's ETHICAL APPEAL (see p. 445)?
3. Is Kroll's approach generally based on a RATIONAL or an EMOTIONAL APPEAL (see pp. 444–45)?
4. What is the EFFECT of Kroll's DESCRIPTION of the victims' families in paragraphs 18 and 23? How does Kroll's POINT OF VIEW shape this description?
5. Why does Kroll describe Harris's death in such detail (paras. 22–23)?
6. **OTHER METHODS.** This essay is an example of NARRATION being used in the service of an argument. What advantage does Kroll gain by presenting his argument in the form of a personal account?

QUESTIONS ON LANGUAGE

1. Make sure you know the meanings of the following words: silhouettes (para. 3); vigil (4); stays (9); burly (13); ashen, abyss (21); grotesque (22); barbaric (24).
2. What is Kroll's objection to Vernell Crittendon's tone (paras. 1–2)? What do you make of his job title: "public information officer"?
3. What is the tone of the phrase "a written invitation from Warden Daniel Vasquez himself" (para. 4)?
4. How does Kroll's use of reported speech contribute to his portrait of the prison officials?

SUGGESTIONS FOR WRITING

1. **JOURNAL WRITING.** What do you think of the death penalty? Write down as many reasons both for and against it as you can. Your reasons may be moral, emotional, or purely pragmatic. You may know of statistics or historical precedents that support the existence or abolition of the death penalty. Write down whatever comes to mind.
   FROM JOURNAL TO ESSAY. Write an essay in which you argue either for or against the death penalty. Support your argument with the EVIDENCE in favor of your position that you developed in your journal writing. As for the evidence that contradicts your opinion, use it to try to anticipate, and respond to, readers' likely objections to your view.
2. What is your opinion on televising public executions? How would a televised account of an execution differ from the kind of written narrative Kroll provides? What are the advantages of each method of narration, visual and written?

3. **CRITICAL WRITING.** Kroll's THESIS about the barbarity of staging executions as public spectacle comes nearly at the end of the essay (para. 24), yet he hints throughout the essay that this is the aspect of his friend's execution that disturbs him the most. How does Kroll prepare the reader for his statement of thesis? What details emphasize the packaging of the execution as public entertainment?

4. **CONNECTIONS.** In "The Penalty of Death" (p. 455), H. L. Mencken approaches the death penalty quite differently from Kroll. Not only do their opinions differ fundamentally, but Mencken's view is broad and ABSTRACT, while Kroll's is intensely personal; and Mencken's appeal is largely rational, while Kroll's is largely emotional. In an essay, discuss the effectiveness of these two essays apart from the opinions they support — that is, focus on the authors' strategies of argument rather than on the arguments themselves. What are the advantages and disadvantages of each strategy?

LINDA CHAVEZ

An outspoken voice on issues of civil rights and affirmative action, LINDA CHAVEZ has held high positions in government, written extensively for the national press, and served as a commentator on television and radio. She was born in 1947 in Albuquerque, New Mexico, to a Spanish American family long established in the Southwest. She graduated from the University of Colorado (B.A., 1970) and did graduate work at the University of California, Los Angeles, and at the University of Maryland. In the early 1970s Chavez began working for government agencies in Washington, D.C. From 1983 to 1985 she was executive director of the U.S. Commission on Civil Rights, where she questioned "affirmative action policies that operate on the assumption"—which she considers false—"that racism and sexism are ingrained in American society." In 1985 President Ronald Reagan appointed Chavez as director of the White House Office of Public Liaison. She is currently a fellow at the Manhattan Institute for Policy Research and has written a book, *Out of the Barrio: Toward a New Politics of Hispanic Assimilation* (1991).

Demystifying Multiculturalism

In this essay published in *The National Review* in 1994, Chavez condemns the multicultural movement in the United States. It is, she says, a destructive solution to a problem that would otherwise solve itself.

Multiculturalism is on the advance, everywhere from President Clinton's cabinet to corporate boardrooms to public-school classrooms. If you believe the multiculturalists' progaganda, whites are on the verge of becoming a minority in the United States. The multiculturalists predict that this demographic shift will fundamentally change American culture—indeed destroy the very idea that America *has* a single, unified culture. They aren't taking any chances, however. They have enlisted the help of government, corporate leaders, the media, and the education establishment in waging a cultural revolution. But has America truly become a multicultural nation? And if not, will those who capitulate to these demands create a self-fulfilling prophecy?

At the heart of the argument is the assumption that the white population is rapidly declining in relation to the nonwhite population. A 1987 Hudson Institute report helped catapult this claim to national prominence. The study, *Workforce 2000*, estimated that by the turn of the century only 15 percent of new workers would be white males. The figure was widely interpreted to mean that whites were about to be-come a minority in the workplace—and in the country.

In fact, white males will still constitute about 45 percent—a plu- 3
rality—of the workforce in the year 2000. The proportion of white men in the workforce *is* declining—it was nearly 51 percent in 1980—but primarily because the proportion of white women is growing. They will make up 39 percent of the workforce within ten years, according to government projections, up from 36 percent in 1980. Together, white men and women will account for 84 percent of all workers by 2000—hardly a minority share.

But the business world is behaving as if a demographic tidal wave is 4
about to hit. A whole new industry of "diversity professionals" has emerged to help managers cope with the expected deluge of nonwhite workers. These consultants are paid as much as $10,000 a day to train managers to "value diversity," a term so ubiquitous that it has appeared in more than seven hundred articles in major newspapers in the last three years. According to Heather MacDonald in *The New Republic*, about half of Fortune 500 corporations now employ someone respon-sible for "diversity."

What precisely does valuing diversity mean? The underlying as- 5
sumptions seem to be that nonwhites are so different from whites that employers must make major changes to accommodate them, and that white workers will be naturally resistant to including nonwhites in their ranks. Public-opinion polls don't bear out the latter. They show that sup-port among whites for equal job opportunity for blacks is extraordinarily high, exceeding 90 percent as early as 1975. As for accommodating dif-ferent cultures, the problem is not culture—or race, or ethnicity—but education. Many young people, in particular, are poorly prepared for work, and the problem is most severe among those who attended inner-city schools, most of them blacks and Hispanics.

Nevertheless, multiculturalists insist on treating race and ethnicity 6
as if they were synonymous with culture. They presume that skin color and national origin, which are immutable traits, determine values, mores, language, and other cultural attributes, which, of course, are learned. In the multiculturalists' world view, African-Americans, Puerto Ricans, or Chinese-Americans living in New York City have more in common with persons of their ancestral group living in Lagos or San Juan or Hong Kong than they do with other New Yorkers who are white. Culture becomes a fixed entity, transmitted, as it were, in the genes, rather than through experience. Thus, "Afrocentricity," a vari-ant of multiculturalism, is "a way of being," its exponents claim. Ac-cording to a leader of the Afrocentric education movement, Molefi Kete Asante, there is "one African Cultural System manifested in

diversities," whether one speaks of Afro-Brazilians, Cubans, or Nigerians (or, presumably, African-Americans). Exactly how this differs from the traditional racist notion that all blacks (Jews, Mexicans, Chinese, etc.) think alike is unclear. What is clear is that the multiculturalists have abandoned the ideal that all persons should be judged by the content of their character, not the color of their skin. Indeed, the multiculturalists seem to believe that a person's character is *determined* by the color of his skin and by his ancestry.

Such convictions lead multiculturalists to conclude that, again in   7
the words of Asante, "[T]here is no common American culture." The logic is simple, but wrong-headed: Since Americans (or more often, their forebears) hail from many different places, each of which has its own specific culture, the argument goes, America must be multicultural. And it is becoming more so every day as new immigrants bring their cultures with them.

Indeed, multiculturalists hope to ride the immigrant wave to   8
greater power and influence. They have certainly done so in education. Some 2.3 million children who cannot speak English well now attend public school, an increase of 1 million in the last seven years. Multicultural advocates cite the presence of such children to demand bilingual education and other multicultural services. The Los Angeles Unified School District alone currently offers instruction in Spanish, Armenian, Korean, Cantonese, Tagalog, Russian, and Japanese. Federal and state governments now spend literally billions of dollars on these programs.

Ironically, the multiculturalists' emphasis on education undercuts   9
their argument that culture is inextricable from race or national origin. They are acutely aware just how fragile cultural identification is; why else are they so adamant about reinforcing it? Multiculturalists insist on teaching immigrant children in their native language, instructing them in the history and customs of their native land and imbuing them with reverence for their ancestral heroes, lest these youngsters be seduced by American culture. Far from losing faith in the power of assimilation, they seem to believe that without a heavy dose of multicultural indoctrination, immigrants won't be able to resist it. And they're right, though it remains to be seen whether anything, including the multiculturalists' crude methods, will ultimately detour immigrants from the assimilation path.

The urge to assimilate has traditionally been overpowering in the   10
United States, especially among the children of immigrants. Only groups that maintain strict rules against intermarriage with persons outside the group, such as Orthodox Jews and the Amish, have ever succeeded in preserving distinct, full-blown cultures within American society. (It is interesting to note that religion seems to be a more effec-

tive deterrent to full assimilation than the secular elements of culture, including language.) Although many Americans worry that Hispanic immigrants, for example, are not learning English and will therefore fail to assimilate into the American mainstream, little evidence supports the case. By the third generation in the United States, a majority of Hispanics, like other ethnic groups, speak only English and are closer to other Americans on most measures of social and economic status than they are to Hispanic immigrants. On one of the most rigorous gauges of assimilation—intermarriage—Hispanics rank high. About one-third of young third-generation Hispanics marry non-Hispanic whites, a pattern similar to that of young Asians. Even for blacks, exogamy rates, which have been quite low historically, are going up; about 3 percent of blacks now marry outside their group.

The impetus for multiculturalism is not coming from immigrants, 11 but from their more affluent and assimilated native-born counterparts. The proponents are most often the elite—the best educated and most successful members of their respective racial and ethnic groups. College campuses, where the most radical displays of multiculturalism take place, are fertile recruiting grounds. Last May, for example, a group of Mexican-American students at UCLA, frustrated that the university would not elevate the school's 23-year-old Chicano-studies program to full department status, stormed the faculty center, breaking windows and furniture and causing half a million dollars in damage. The same month, a group of Asian-American students at UC Irvine went on a hunger strike to pressure administrators into hiring more professors of Asian-American studies. These were not immigrants, or even, by and large, disadvantaged students, but middle-class beneficiaries of their parents' or grandparents' successful assimilation to the American mainstream.

The protestors' quest had almost nothing to do with any effort to 12 maintain their ethnic identity. For the most part, such students probably never thought of themselves as anything but American before they entered college. A recent study of minority students at the University of California at Berkeley found that most Hispanic and Asian students "discovered" their ethnic identity after they arrived on campus—when they also discovered that they were victims of systematic discrimination. As one Mexican-American freshman summed it up, she was "unaware of the things that have been going on with our people, all the injustice we've suffered, how the world really is. I thought racism didn't exist and here, you know, it just comes to light." The researchers added that "students of color" had difficulty pinpointing exactly what constituted this "subtle form of the new racism.... There was much talk about certain facial expressions, or the way people look, and how white students 'take over the class' and speak past you."

Whatever their new-found victim status, these students look amaz-   13
ingly like other Americans on most indices. For example, the median
family income of Mexican-American students at Berkeley in 1989 was
$32,500, slightly above the national median for all Americans that
year, $32,191; and 17 percent of those students came from families that
earned more than $75,000 a year, even though they were admitted to
the university under affirmative-action programs (presumably because
they suffered some educational disadvantage attributed to their ethnicity).

Affirmative-action programs make less and less sense as discrimi-   14
nation diminishes in this society—which it indisputably has—and as
minorities improve their economic status. Racial and ethnic identity,
too, might wane if there weren't such aggressive efforts to ensure that
this not happen. The multiculturalists know they risk losing their constituency if young blacks, Hispanics, Asians, and others don't maintain
strong racial and ethnic affiliations. Young generations must be *trained*
to think of themselves as members of oppressed minority groups entitled to special treatment. And the government provides both the incentives and the money to ensure that this happens. Meanwhile, the
main beneficiaries are the multicultural professionals, who often earn
exorbitant incomes peddling identity.

One particularly egregious example occurred in the District of Co-   15
lumbia last fall. The school system paid $250,000 to a husband-and-
wife consultant team to produce an Afrocentric study guide to be used
in a single public elementary school. Controversy erupted after the two
spent three years and produced only a five-page outline. Although the
husband had previously taught at Howard University, the wife's chief
credential was a master's degree from an unaccredited "university"
which she and her husband had founded. When the *Washington Post*
criticized the school superintendent for his handling of the affair, he
called a press conference to defend the couple, who promptly claimed
they were the victims of a racist vendetta.

D.C. students rank lowest in the nation in math and fourth-lowest   16
in verbal achievement; one can only wonder what $250,000 in tutor-
ing at one school might have done. Instead, the students were treated
to bulletin boards in the classrooms proclaiming on their behalf: "We
are the sons and daughters of The Most High. We are the princes and
princesses of African kings and queens. We are the descendants of our
black ancestors. We are black and we are proud." This incident is not
unique. Thousands of consultants with little or no real expertise sell
feel-good programs to school systems across the nation.

Multiculturalism is not a grassroots movement. It was created, nur-   17
tured, and expanded through government policy. Without the expen-

diture of vast sums of public money, it would wither away and die. That is not to say that ethnic communities would disappear from the American scene or that groups would not retain some attachment to their ancestral roots. American assimilation has always entailed some give and take, and American culture has been enriched by what individual groups brought to it. The distinguishing characteristic of American culture is its ability to incorporate so many disparate groups, creating a new whole from the many parts. What could be more American, for example, than jazz and film, two distinctive art forms created, respectively, by blacks and immigrant Jews but which all Americans think of as their own? But in the past, government—especially public schools —saw it as a duty to try to bring newcomers into the fold by teaching them English, by introducing them to the great American heroes as their own, by instilling respect for American institutions. Lately, we have nearly reversed course, treating each group, new and old, as if what is most important is to preserve its separate identity and space.

It is easy to blame the ideologues and radicals who are pushing the disuniting of America, to use Arthur Schlesinger's phrase, but the real culprits are those who provide multiculturalists the money and the access to press their cause. Without the acquiescence of policy-makers and ordinary citizens, multiculturalism would be no threat. Unfortunately, most major institutions have little stomach for resisting the multicultural impulse—and many seem eager to comply with whatever demands the muliculturalists make. Americans should have learned by now that policy matters. We have only to look at the failure of our welfare and crime policies to know that providing perverse incentives can change the way individuals behave—for the worse. Who is to say that if we pour enough money into dividing Americans we won't succeed? 18

QUESTIONS ON MEANING

1. What is Chavez's PURPOSE in writing this essay? Whose behavior is she trying to influence?
2. PARAPHRASE the distinction Chavez makes in paragraph 6 between race or ethnicity and culture.
3. What similarity does Chavez see between multiculturalism and racism (para. 6)?
4. Explain in your own words the contradiction Chavez finds between multiculturalists' sense of the fragility of racial and ethnic identity (their fear that if not fostered it will be assimilated into the mainstream) and their belief that "culture is inextricable from race or national origin" (para. 9).

QUESTIONS ON WRITING STRATEGY

1. How does the first paragraph of the essay function in relation to Chavez's argument?
2. In paragraphs 2 and 3 Chavez calls into question what she considers to be the fundamental assumption or warrant of her opponents' argument. How does she refute what would appear to be a straightforward statistic?
3. What surprising shift in Chavez's argument takes place in the last paragraph?
4. **OTHER METHODS.** Point out a few places where Chavez uses specific EXAMPLES to back up her arguments. What point does each example support? How effective is it?

QUESTIONS ON LANGUAGE

1. What does language such as "on the advance" and "propaganda" (para. 1) and "demystifying" (title) tell us about Chavez's opinion of multiculturalism? Find other examples of word choice that help convey her political views.
2. Why does Chavez put words such as "diversity" (para. 4) and "Afrocentricity" (6) in quotation marks?
3. When Chavez speaks of the "ideal that all persons should be judged by the content of their character, not the color of their skin" (para. 6), she ALLUDES to "I Have a Dream," by Martin Luther King, Jr. (see p. 504, para. 14). What is the EFFECT of this allusion? Why do you think Chavez doesn't name King?
4. Look up any of the following words that are unfamiliar to you: propaganda, capitulate (para. 1); catapult (2); plurality (3); demographic, deluge, ubiquitous (4); synonymous, immutable, variant, exponents (6); advocates (8); inextricable, acutely, adamant, imbuing, reverence, assimilation, indoctrination (9); deterrent, secular, gauges, exogamy (10); impetus, fertile, beneficiaries (11); constituency, incentives, exorbitant (14); egregious, vendetta (15); grassroots, disparate (17); ideologues, culprits, acquiescence, perverse (18).

SUGGESTIONS FOR WRITING

1. **JOURNAL WRITING.** What is an American? Make a list of qualities, attitudes, or behaviors that you consider to be inherently American, either in yourself or in others.
   FROM JOURNAL TO ESSAY. Shape your journal notes into an essay in which you DEFINE the American character. Is there an Americanness that transcends race and ethnicity?
2. Chavez has an assimilationist ideal of American identity: She sees the nation as a melting pot. What are the advantages of the kind of cultural fusion Chavez advocates? Is abandoning one's cultural heritage, which the melting pot entails (at least in part), too high a price to pay for a unified national identity? Are the assimilation success stories Chavez cites in paragraph 17 the rule or the exception?

3. Write an argument agreeing or disagreeing with Chavez's views on multicultural education. Do you think there is too much emphasis on racial and ethnic identification in the classroom today? Not enough? How has your own experience in school and college contributed to your opinion on this issue? Support your claims with EVIDENCE.

4. **CRITICAL WRITING.** Like any argument, Chavez's is based on certain AS-SUMPTIONS that are open to debate. Do you agree with her characterization (for example, in para. 6) of the opposition? with her dismissal of multiculturalism on the grounds that it is not a grassroots, lower-class movement? with her use of the example cited in paragraph 15 as representative of multiculturalists on the whole? Defend or refute these or any other stated or unstated assumptions you find behind her argument. You might use the list of logical fallacies from the introduction to this chapter (pp. 450–51) as a guide.

5. **CONNECTIONS.** Chavez and Ishmael Reed, in "America: The Multinational Society" (next page), have very different perspectives on the status of minorities in America today. While Chavez claims that discrimination has "indisputably" diminished (para. 14), Reed finds the "paranoid" stance of the Puritans still figuring strongly in contemporary attitudes toward minorities (paras. 9–12). With which of these authors do you agree? Support your answer with examples from your experience or reading.

ISHMAEL REED

Born in Chattanooga, Tennessee, in 1938 and raised in Buffalo, New York, ISHMAEL REED began writing in elementary school and as a teenager had work published. He attended the State University of New York at Buffalo. In the years since, Reed has become known as a writer given to experimentation and provocation. He has produced nine novels, four volumes of poetry, three plays, and countless songs. Some notable works include the poetry collections *catechism of d neoamerican hoodoo church* (1971) and *Conjure* (1972); the novels *The Free-Lance Pallbearers* (1967), *Mumbo Jumbo* (1972), *The Terrible Threes* (1989), *Japanese by Spring* (1993), and *Airing Dirty Laundry* (1993); and the essay collection *Writin' Is Fightin'* (1988). Reed has also edited the *Before Columbus Foundation Fiction Anthology* (1992), a collection of stories published under the auspices of the foundation he created and chairs. He teaches at the University of California at Berkeley.

America:
The Multinational Society

As its title suggests, this essay holds that Americans need not be afraid of immigrants and others who may seem to threaten unity and stability: The transformation to a multicultural society is already occurring, and, Reed thinks, it is making us a stronger nation. Reed's opinion is perhaps unsurprising from one whose own ancestry is part African American, part Native American, part French, and part Irish. The essay was first published in a periodical, *San Francisco Focus*, and was then collected in *Writin' Is Fightin'*.

At the annual Lower East Side Jewish Festival yesterday, a Chinese woman ate a pizza slice in front of Ty Thuan Duc's Vietnamese grocery store. Beside her a Spanish-speaking family patronized a cart with two signs: "Italian Ices" and "Kosher by Rabbi Alper." And after the pastrami ran out, everybody ate knishes.

—*New York Times*, 23 June 1983

On the day before Memorial Day, 1983, a poet called me to describe a city he had just visited. He said that one section included mosques, built by the Islamic people who dwelled there. Attending his reading, he said, were large numbers of Hispanic people, forty thousand of whom lived in the same city. He was not talking about a fabled city located in some mysterious region of the world. The city he'd visited was Detroit.

A few months before, as I was leaving Houston, Texas, I heard it announced on the radio that Texas's largest minority was Mexican-American, and though a foundation recently issued a report critical of bilingual education, the taped voice used to guide the passengers on the air trams connecting terminals in Dallas Airport is in both Spanish and English. If the trend continues, a day will come when it will be difficult to travel through some sections of the country without hearing commands in both English and Spanish; after all, for some western states, Spanish was the first written language and the Spanish style lives on in the western way of life.

Shortly after my Texas trip, I sat in an auditorium located on the   3 campus of the University of Wisconsin at Milwaukee as a Yale professor—whose original work on the influence of African cultures upon those of the Americas has led to his ostracism from some monocultural intellectual circles—walked up and down the aisle, like an old-time southern evangelist, dancing and drumming the top of the lectern, illustrating his points before some serious Afro-American intellectuals and artists who cheered and applauded his performance and his mastery of information. The professor was "white." After his lecture, he joined a group of Milwaukeeans in a conversation. All of the participants spoke Yoruban, though only the professor had ever traveled to Africa.

One of the artists told me that his paintings, which included   4 African and Afro-American mythological symbols and imagery, were hanging in the local McDonald's restaurant. The next day I went to McDonald's and snapped pictures of smiling youngsters eating hamburgers below paintings that could grace the walls of any of the country's leading museums. The manager of the local McDonald's said, "I don't know what you boys are doing, but I like it," as he commissioned the local painters to exhibit in his restaurant.

Such blurring of cultural styles occurs in everyday life in the   5 United States to a greater extent than anyone can imagine and is probably more prevalent than the sensational conflict between people of different backgrounds that is played up and often encouraged by the media. The result is what the Yale professor Robert Thompson referred to as a cultural bouillabaisse, yet members of the nation's present educational and cultural Elect still cling to the notion that the United States belongs to some vaguely defined entity they refer to as "Western civilization," by which they mean, presumably, a civilization created by the people of Europe, as if Europe can be viewed in monolithic terms. Is Beethoven's Ninth Symphony, which includes Turkish marches, a part of Western civilization, or the late nineteenth- and twentieth-century French paintings, whose creators were influenced by Japanese art? And what of the Cubists, through whom the influence of African art changed modern painting, or the Surrealists, who were so impressed with the art of the Pacific Northwest Indians that, in their map of North America, Alaska dwarfs the lower forty-eight in size?

Are the Russians, who are often criticized for their adoption of "Western" ways by Tsarist dissidents in exile, members of Western civilization? And what of the millions of Europeans who have black African and Asian ancestry, black Africans having occupied several countries for hundreds of years? Are these "Europeans" members of Western civilization, or the Hungarians, who originated across the Urals in a place called Greater Hungary, or the Irish, who came from the Iberian Peninsula?

Even the notion that North America is part of Western civilization because our "system of government" is derived from Europe is being challenged by Native American historians who say that the founding fathers, Benjamin Franklin especially, were actually influenced by the system of government that had been adopted by the Iroquois hundreds of years prior to the arrival of large numbers of Europeans.

Western civilization, then, becomes another confusing category like Third World, or Judeo-Christian culture, as man attempts to impose his small-screen view of political and cultural reality upon a complex world. Our most publicized novelist recently said that Western civilization was the greatest achievement of mankind, an attitude that flourishes on the street level as scribbles in public restrooms: "White Power," "Niggers and Spics Suck," or "Hitler was a prophet," the latter being the most telling, for wasn't Adolf Hitler the archetypal monoculturalist who, in his pigheaded arrogance, believed that one way and one blood was so pure that it had to be protected from alien strains at all costs? Where did such an attitude, which has caused so much misery and depression in our national life, which has tainted even our noblest achievements, begin? An attitude that caused the incarceration of Japanese-American citizens during World War II, the persecution of Chicanos and Chinese-Americans, the near-extermination of the Indians, and the murder and lynchings of thousands of Afro-Americans.

Virtuous, hardworking, pious, even though they occasionally would wander off after some fancy clothes, or rendezvous in the woods with the town prostitute, the Puritans are idealized in our schoolbooks as "a hardy band" of no-nonsense patriarchs whose discipline razed the forest and brought order to the New World (a term that annoys Native American historians). Industrious, responsible, it was their "Yankee ingenuity" and practicality that created the work ethic. They were simple folk who produced a number of good poets, and they set the tone for the American writing style, of lean and spare lines, long before Hemingway. They worshiped in churches whose colors blended in with the New England snow, churches with simple structures and ornate lecterns.

The Puritans were a daring lot, but they had a mean streak. They 10
hated the theater and banned Christmas. They punished people in a
cruel and inhuman manner. They killed children who disobeyed their
parents. When they came in contact with those whom they considered
heathens or aliens, they behaved in such a bizarre and irrational manner that this chapter in the American history comes down to us as a
late-movie horror film. They exterminated the Indians, who taught
them how to survive in a world unknown to them, and their encounter
with the calypso culture of Barbados resulted in what the tourist guide
in Salem's Witches' House refers to as the Witchcraft Hysteria.

The Puritan legacy of hard work and meticulous accounting led to 11
the establishment of a great idustrial society; it is no wonder that the
American industrial revolution began in Lowell, Massachusetts. But
there was the other side, the strange and paranoid attitudes toward
those different from the Elect.

The cultural attitudes of that early Elect continue to be voiced in 12
everyday life in the United States: the president of a distinguished university, writing a letter to the *Times*, belittling the study of African civ-
ilizations; the television network that promoted its show on the
Vatican art with the boast that this art represented "the finest achievements of the human spirit." A modern up-tempo state of complex
rhythms that depends upon contacts with an international community
can no longer behave as if it dwelled in a "Zion Wilderness" surrounded
by beasts and pagans.

When I heard a schoolteacher warn the other night about the in- 13
vasion of the American educational system by foreign curriculums, I
wanted to yell at the television set, "Lady, they're already here." It has
already begun because the world is here. The world has been arriving at
these shores for at least ten thousand years from Europe, Africa, and
Asia. In the late nineteenth and early twentieth centuries, large numbers of Europeans arrived, adding their cultures to those of the European, African, and Asian settlers who were already here, and recently
millions have been entering the country from South America and the
Caribbean, making Yale Professor Bob Thompson's bouillabaisse richer
and thicker.

One of our most visionary politicians said that he envisioned a 14
time when the United States could become the brain of the world, by
which he meant the respository of all of the latest advanced information systems. I thought of that remark when an enterprising poet friend
of mine called to say that he had just sold a poem to a computer magazine and that the editors were delighted to get it because they didn't
carry fiction or poetry. Is that the kind of world we desire? A humdrum
homogeneous world of all brains and no heart, no fiction, no poetry; a
world of robots with human attendants bereft or imagination, of cul-

ture? Or does North America deserve a more exciting destiny? To become a place where the cultures of the world crisscross. This is possible because the United States is unique in the world: The world is here.

QUESTIONS ON MEANING

1. How does Reed see *Western civilization* being defined by those who champion it as the dominant culture? In his eyes, what is wrong with this definition?
2. What do you take to be Reed's PURPOSE in this essay?
3. What does Reed mean by the two key and contrasting terms *monocultural* (paras. 3, 8) and *bouillabaisse* (5, 13)?
4. How does Reed interpret the notion that "the United States could become the brain of the world" (para. 14)? What is his objection?

QUESTIONS ON WRITING STRATEGY

1. Why does Reed wait until the fifth paragraph to present his THESIS? Does he arrive at it through INDUCTION or DEDUCTION?
2. How does Reed's CONCLUSION promote his argument?
3. What ASSUMPTIONS does the author make about the attitudes and beliefs of his AUDIENCE? How do his use of EVIDENCE and his TONE support your answer?
4. **OTHER METHODS.** In paragraphs 8–12, Reed examines CAUSES AND EFFECTS. What is the point of this ANALYSIS in his argument?

QUESTIONS ON LANGUAGE

1. Look up the definitions of any words below that you are unfamiliar with: mosques (para. 1); ostracism (3); Elect (noun), Cubists, Surrealists (5); dissidents (6); archetypal, incarceration, lynchings (8); razed (9); repository, bereft (14).
2. What is the EFFECT of the "scribbles in public restrooms" (para. 8)? What do they represent to Reed?
3. Analyze Reed's use of language in discussing the Puritans (paras. 9–11). What attitude(s) toward the Puritans does the language convey?

SUGGESTIONS FOR WRITING

1. **JOURNAL WRITING.** Reed suggests that we can often find out what a society thinks by reading the "scribbles in public restrooms" (para. 8). What do you think we can learn by reading the writing on public walls, school desks, and other places where graffiti flourishes?
   FROM JOURNAL TO ESSAY. Does graffiti accurately represent the community where it exists — or at least some part of the community? If a stranger to the community saw and read the graffiti, what impression would he or she have? Write an essay in which you explain how significant you think the

writing on the walls is. Be sure to back up your ideas with EXAMPLES of graffiti you have seen.

2. Reed calls Western civilization "another confusing category like Third World, or Judeo-Christian culture" (para. 8). How confusing are these other terms? In social-science encyclopedias, dictionaries of culture, and other library references (but not abridged dictionaries), find at least three definitions of either term. Write a brief essay that specifies the similarities and differences in the definitions.

3. **CRITICAL WRITING.** Reed asserts that a "blurring of cultural styles...is probably more prevalent [in the United States] than the sensational conflict between people of different backgrounds that is played up and often encouraged by the media." Is this true in your experience? Support or refute Reed's assertion by COMPARING AND CONTRASTING the image and reality of a community you either live in or visit. Support your essay with examples.

4. **CONNECTIONS.** Compare Reed's essay with "Demystifying Multiculturalism," by Linda Chavez (p. 468). Where do the authors agree? Where do they disagree? As clearly as possible, SUMMARIZE and analyze the two arguments, using quotations and PARAPHRASES from them to support your ideas.

ISHMAEL REED ON WRITING

Ishmael Reed describes himself as someone with a "prolific writing jab"—a knack for starting fights, or at least stirring up controversy, with his pen. In fiction and nonfiction, he has taken on governments, literary intellectuals, the media, feminists—any person or any group he felt needed correcting. As he told the writer William C. Brisick, he sees himself as part "trickster," a term he learned from Native Americans for a figure common to many folk traditions who exposes pretension and dishonesty. Essays for Reed are a means of "talking back, a way of including in the national dialogue another point of view, one not present in the media."

Reed does not disdain using his talents for even more practical purposes. To publicize the deterioration of his crack-infested neighborhood in Oakland, California, Reed wrote an article for a local newspaper that gained wide attention, both pro and con. In addition to this piece, Reed composed press releases for the neighborhood association —writing that "really moved the community," he says. "It's become functional art."

FOR DISCUSSION

1. Would you say that writing that has a practical goal (a press release, for instance) can be valued for its own sake as writing? Is it art?

2. What of the "trickster" do you see in Reed's essay "America: The Multinational Society"?

CURTIS CHANG

A 1990 graduate of Harvard University, Curtis Chang majored in government. He was born in Taiwan and immigrated to the United States in 1971 with his family. He attended public school near Chicago. At Harvard, Chang helped found the Minority Student Alliance, belonged to the debating society, wrote for the *Harvard Political Review*, and was a leader of the Harvard-Radcliffe Christian Fellowship. Winner of the Michael C. Rockefeller Fellowship for Travel Abroad, Chang spent 1992 in Soweto, South Africa. He was a teaching fellow in Harvard's government department and is now a campus minister at Tufts University.

Streets of Gold:
The Myth of the Model Minority

This essay, like Brad Manning's (p. 113) and Linnea Saukko's (p. 246), won a Bedford Prize in Student Writing and was published in *Student Writers at Work*, edited by Nancy Sommers and Donald Mc-Quade. Written when Chang was a freshman at Harvard, the essay grew out of his friendship with black students, his increasing interest in issues of racial identity, and his realization that Asian Americans had at best an ambiguous position in American society. "Streets of Gold" states and supports an opinion forcefully and, we think, convincingly. And it has something else to recommend it as well: It provides a model of research writing and documentation. The documentation style is that of the Modern Language Association, explained on pages 658–67.

Over one hundred years ago, an American myth misled many of 1 my ancestors. Seeking cheap labor, railroad companies convinced numerous Chinese that American streets were paved with gold. Today, the media portray Asian-Americans as finally mining those golden streets. Major publications like *Time, Newsweek, U.S. News & World Report, Fortune, The New Republic,* the *Wall Street Journal,* and the *New York Times Magazine* have all recently published congratulatory "Model Minority" headline stories with such titles as

America's Super Minority
An American Success Story
A "Model Minority"
Why They Succeed
The Ultimate Assimilation
The Triumph of Asian-Americans.

But the Model Minority is another "Streets of Gold" tale. It distorts 2
Asian-Americans' true status and ignores our racial handicaps. And
the Model Minority's ideology is even worse than its mythology. It attempts to justify the existing system of racial inequality by blaming the
victims rather than the system itself.

The Model Minority myth introduces us as an ethnic minority that 3
is finally "making it in America," as stated in *Time* (Doerner 42). The
media consistently define "making it" as achieving material wealth,
wealth that flows from our successes in the workplace and the schoolroom. This economic achievement allegedly proves a minority can, as
Fortune says, "lay claim to the American dream" (Ramirez 149).

Trying to show how "Asian-Americans present a picture of afflu- 4
ence and economic success," as the *New York Times Magazine* puts it
(Oxnam 72), nine out of ten of the major Model Minority stories of the
last four years relied heavily on one statistic: the family median income. The median Asian-American family income, according to the
U.S. Census Survey of Income and Education data, is $22,713 com-
pared to $20,800 for white Americans. Armed with that figure, na-
tional magazines such as *Newsweek* have trumpeted our "remarkable,
ever-mounting achievements" (Kasindorf et al. 51).

Such assertions demonstrate the truth of the aphorism "Statistics 5
are like a bikini. What they reveal is suggestive, but what they conceal
is vital." The family median income statistic conceals the fact that
Asian-American families generally (1) have more children and live-in
relatives and thus have more mouths to feed; (2) are often forced by necessity to have everyone in the family work, averaging *more* than two
family income earners (whites only have 1.6) (Cabezas 402); and (3)
live disproportionately in high cost of living areas (i.e., New York,
Chicago, Los Angeles, and Honolulu) which artificially inflate income
figures. Dr. Robert S. Mariano, professor of economics at the University
of Pennsylvania, has calculated that

> when such appropriate adjustments and comparisons are made, a dif-
> ferent and rather disturbing picture emerges, showing indeed a
> clearly disadvantaged group.... Filipino and Chinese men *are no bet-*
> *ter off than black men with regard to median incomes.* (55)[1]

Along with other racial minorities, Asian-Americans are still scraping
for the crumbs of the economic pie.

Throughout their distortion of our status, the media propagate two 6
crucial assumptions. First, they lump all Asian-Americans into one

[1] The picture becomes even more disturbing when one realizes the higher income
figures do not necessarily equal higher quality of life. For instance, in New York Chi-
natown, more than 1 out of 5 work more than 57 hours per week, almost 1 out of 10 elderly must labor more than 55 hours per week (Nishi 503).

monolithic, homogeneous, yellow-skinned mass. Such a view ignores the existence of an incredibly disadvantaged Asian-American underclass. Asians work in low-income and low-status jobs two to three times more than whites (Cabezas 438). Recent Vietnamese refugees in California are living like the Appalachian poor. While going to his Manhattan office, multimillionaire architect I. M. Pei's car passes Chinese restaurants and laundries where 72% of all New York Chinese men still work (U.S. Bureau of the Census qtd. in Cabezas 443).

But the media make an even more dangerous assumption. They   7
suggest that (alleged) material success is the same thing as basic racial equality. Citing that venerable family median income figure, magazines claim Asian-Americans are "obviously nondisadvantaged folks," as stated in *Fortune* (Seligman 64). Yet a 1979 United States Equal Employment Opportunity Commission study on Asian-Americans discovered widespread anti-Asian hiring and promotion practices. Asian-Americans "in the professional, technical, and managerial occupations" often face "modern racism—the subtle, sophisticated, systemic patterns and practices...which function to effect and to obscure the discriminatory outcomes" (Nishi 398). One myth simply does not prove another: Neither our "astonishing economic prosperity" (Ramirez 152) nor a racially equal America exist.

An emphasis on material success also pervades the media's stress on   8
Asian-Americans' educational status at "the top of the class" ("Asian Americans" 4). Our "march into the ranks of the educational elite," as *U.S. News & World Report* puts it (McBee et al. 41), is significant, according to *Fortune*, because "all that education is paying off spectacularly" (Ramirez 149). Once again, the same fallacious assumptions plague this "whiz kids" image of Asian-Americans.

The media again ignore the fact that class division accounts for   9
much of the publicized success. Until 1976, the U.S. Immigration Department only admitted Asian immigrants that were termed "skilled" workers. "Skilled" generally meant college educated, usually in the sciences since poor English would not be a handicap. The result was that the vast majority of pre-1976 Asian immigrants came from already well-educated, upper-class backgrounds—the classic "brain drain" syndrome (Hirschman and Wong 507–10).

The post-1976 immigrants, however, come generally from the   10
lower, less educated classes (Kim 24). A study by Professor Elizabeth Ahn Toupin of Tufts University matched similar Asian and non-Asian students *along class lines* and found that Asian-Americans "did not perform at a superior academic level to non-Asian students. Asian-Americans were more likely to be placed on academic probation than their white counterparts.... Twice as many Asian-American students withdrew from the university" (12).

Thus, it is doubtful whether the perceived widespread educational 11
success will continue as the Asian-American population eventually
balances out along class lines. When 16.2% of all Chinese have less
than four years of schooling (*four times* the percentage of whites)
(Azores 73), it seems many future Asian-Americans will worry more
about being able to read a newspaper rather than a Harvard acceptance
letter.

Most important, the media assume once again that achieving a cer- 12
tain level of material or educational success means achieving real
equality. People easily forget that to begin with, Asians invest heavily
in education since other means of upward mobility are barred to them
by race. Until recently, for instance, Asian-Americans were barred
from unions and traditional lines of credit (Yun 23–24).[2] Other "white"
avenues to success, such as the "old boy network," are still closed to
Asian-Americans.

When *Time* claims "as a result of their academic achievement 13
Asians are climbing the economic ladder with remarkable speed," it
glosses over an inescapable fact: There is a white ladder and then there
is a yellow one. Almost all of the academic studies on the *actual returns
Asians receive* from their education point to prevalent discrimination.
A striking example of this was found in a City University of New York
research project which constructed résumés with equivalent educational backgrounds. Applications were then sent to employers, one
group under an Asian name and a similar group under a Caucasian
name. Whites received interviews five times more than Asians (Nishi
399). The media never headline even more shocking data that can be
easily found in the U.S. Census. For instance, Chinese and Filipino
males only earned respectively 74% and 52% as much as their *equally
educated* white counterparts. Asian females fared even worse. Their
salaries were only 44% to 54% as large as equivalent white males' paychecks (Cabezas 391). Blacks suffer from this same statistical disparity.
We Asian-Americans are indeed a Model Minority—a perfect model
of racial discrimination in America.

Yet this media myth encourages neglect of our pressing needs. 14
"Clearly, many Asian-Americans and Pacific peoples are invisible to
the governmental agencies," reported the California State Advisory
Committee to the U.S. Commission on Civil Rights. "Discrimination
against Asian-Americans and Pacific peoples is as much the result of
omission as commission" (qtd. in Chun 7). In 1979, while the president praised Asian-Americans' "successful integration into American
society," his administration revoked Asian-Americans' eligibility for

---

[2] For further analysis on the role racism plays in Asian-Americans' stress on education and certain technical and scientific fields, see Suzuki (44).

minority small business loans, devastating thousands of struggling, newly arrived small businessmen. Hosts of other minority issues, ranging from reparations for the Japanese-American internment to the ominous rise of anti-Asian violence, are widely ignored by the general public.

The media, in fact, insist to the general populace that we are not a   15 true racial minority. In an attack on affirmative action, the *Boston Globe* pointed out that universities, like many people, "obviously feel that Asian-Americans, especially those of Chinese and Japanese descent, are brilliant, privileged, and wrongly classified as minorities" ("Affirmative Non-actions" 10). Harvard Dean Henry Rosovsky remarked in the same article that "It does not seem to me that as a group, they are disadvantaged.... Asian-Americans appear to be in an odd category among other protected minorities."

The image that we Asians aren't like "other minorities" is funda-   16 mental to the Model Minority ideology. Any elementary-school student knows that the teacher designates one student the model, the "teacher's pet," in order to set an example for others to follow. One only sets up a "model minority" in order to communicate to the other "students," the blacks and Hispanics, "Why can't you be like that?" The media, in fact, almost admit to "grading" minorities as they headline Model Minority stories "Asian-Americans: Are They Making the Grade?" (McBee et al.). And Asians have earned the highest grade by fulfilling one important assignment: identifying with the white majority, with its values and wishes.

Unlike blacks, for instance, we Asian-Americans have not vig-   17 orously asserted our ethnic identity (a.k.a. Black Power). And the American public has historically demanded assimilation over racial pluralism.[3] Over the years, *Newsweek* has published titles from "Success Story: Outwhiting the Whites" to "The Ultimate Assimilation," which lauded the increasing number of Asian-white marriages as evidence of Asian-Americans' "acceptance into American society" (Kantrowitz et al. 80).

Even more significant is the public's approval of how we have suc-   18 ceeded in the "American tradition" (Ramirez 164). Unlike the blacks and Hispanics, we "Puritan-like" Asians (Oxnam 72) disdain governmental assistance. A *New Republic* piece, "The Triumph of Asian-Americans," similarly applauded how "Asian-Americans pose no problems at all" (Bell 30). The media consistently compare the crime-

---

[3] A full discussion of racial pluralism versus assimilation is impossible here. But suffice it to say that pluralism accepts ethnic cultures as equally different; assimilation asks for a "melting" into the majority. An example of the assimilation philosophy is the massive "Americanization" programs of the late 1880s, which successfully erased Eastern Europe immigrants' customs in favor of Ango-Saxon ones.

ridden image of other minorities with the picture of law-abiding Asian
parents whose "well-behaved kids" hit books and not the streets
("Asian Americans" 4).

Some insist there is nothing terrible about whites conjuring up our   19
"tremendous" success, divining from it model American traits, then
preaching, "Why can't you blacks and Hispanics be like that?" After
all, one might argue, aren't those traits desirable?

Such a view, as mentioned, neglects Asian-Americans' true and   20
pressing needs. Moreover, this view completely misses the Model Minority image's fundamental ideology, an ideology meant to falsely grant
America absolution from its racial barriers.

David O. Sears and Donald R. Kinder, two social scientists, have   21
recently published significant empirical studies on the underpinnings
of American racial attitudes. They consistently discovered that Americans' stress on "values, such as 'individualism and self-reliance, the
work ethic, obedience, and discipline'...can be invoked, however per-
versely, to feed racist appetites" (qtd. in Kennedy 88). In other words,
the Model Minority image lets Americans' consciences rest easy. They
can think: "It's not our fault those blacks and Hispanics can't make it.
They're just too lazy. After all, look at the Asians."[4] Consequently,
American society never confronts the systemic racial and economic
factors underlying such inequality. The victims instead bear the blame.

This ideology behind the Model Minority image is best seen when   22
we examine one of the first Model Minority stories, which suddenly appeared in the mid-1960s. It is important to note that the period was
marked by newfound, strident black demands for equality and power.

> At a time when it is being proposed that hundreds of billions be spent
> to uplift Negroes and other minorities, the nation's 300,000 Chinese-
> Americans are moving ahead on their own — with no help from any-
> one else.... Few Chinese-Americans are getting welfare handouts —
> or even want them.... They don't sit around moaning. ("Success
> Story of One Minority Group" 73)

The same article then concludes that the Chinese-American history
and accomplishment "would shock those now complaining about the
hardships endured by today's Negroes."

Not surprisingly, the dunce-capped blacks and Hispanics resent us   23
apple-polishing, "well-behaved" teacher's pets. Black comedian Richard

---

[4]This phenomenon of blaming the victim for racial inequality is as old as America itself. For instance, southerners once eased their consciences over slavery by labeling blacks as animals lacking humanity. Today, America does it by labeling them as
inferior people lacking "desirable" traits. For an excellent further analysis of this ideology, actually widespread among American intellectuals, see *Iron Cages: Race and Culture in 19th-Century America* by Ronald T. Takaki.

Pryor performs a revealing routine in which new Asian immigrants learn from whites their first English word: "Nigger." And Asian-Americans themselves succumb to the Model Minority's deceptive mythology and racist ideology.[5] "I made it without help," one often hears among Asian circles; "why can't they?" In a 1986 nationwide poll, only 27% of Asian-American students rated "racial understanding" as "essential." The figure plunged 9% in the last year alone (a year marked by a torrent of Model Minority stories) (Hune). We "whitewashed" Asians have simply lost our identity as a fellow, disadvantaged minority.

But we don't even need to look beyond the Model Minority stories   24
themselves to realize that whites see us as "whiter" than blacks — but not quite white enough. For instance, citing that familiar median family income figure, *Fortune* magazine of 17 May 1982 complained that the Asian-American community is in fact "getting *more* than its share of the pie" (Seligman 64). For decades, when white Americans were leading the nation in every single economic measure, editorials arguing that whites were getting more than *their* share of the pie were rather rare.

No matter how "well-behaved" we are, Asian-Americans are still   25
excluded from the real pie, the "positions of institutional power and political power" (Kuo 289). Professor Harry Kitano of UCLA has written extensively on the plight of Asian-Americans as the "middle-man minority," a minority supposedly satisfied materially but forever racially barred from a true, *significant* role in society. Empirical studies indicate that Asian-Americans "have been channeled into lower-echelon white-collar jobs having little or no decision making authority" (Suzuki 38). For example, in *Fortune*'s 1,000 largest companies, Asian-American nameplates rest on a mere half of one percent of all officers' and directors' desks (a statistical disparity worsened by the fact that most of the Asians founded their companies) (Ramirez 152). While the education of the upper-class Asians may save them from the bread lines, their race still keeps them from the boardroom.

Our docile acceptance of such exclusion is actually one of our   26
"model" traits. When Asian-Americans in San Francisco showed their first hint of political activism and protested Asian exclusion from city boards, the *Washington Monthly* warned in a long Asian-American article, "Watch out, here comes another group to pander to" ("The Wrong Way" 21). *The New Republic* praised Asian-American political movements because

---

[5] America has a long history of playing off one minority against the other. During the early 1900s, for instance, mining companies in the west often hired Asians solely as scabs against striking black miners. Black versus Asian hostility and violence usually followed. This pattern was repeated in numerous industries. In a larger historical sense, almost every immigrant group has assimilated, to some degree, the culture of antiblack racism.

Unlike blacks or Hispanics, Asian-American politicians have the luxury of not having to devote the bulk of their time to an "Asian-American agenda," and thus escape becoming prisoners of such an agenda.... The most important thing for Asian-Americans ... is simply "being part of the process." (Bell 31)

This is strikingly reminiscent of another of the first Model Minority stories: 27

As the Black and Brown communities push for changes in the present system, the Oriental is set forth as an example to be followed—a minority group that has achieved success through adaptation rather than confrontation. (*Gidra* qtd. in Chun 7)

But it is precisely this "present system," this system of subtle, per-   28
sistent racism that we all must confront, not adapt to. For example, we Asians gained our right to vote from the 1964 Civil Rights Act that blacks marched, bled, died, and, in the words of that original Model Minority story, "sat around moaning for." Unless we assert our true identity as a minority and challenge racial misconceptions and inequalities, we will be nothing more than techno-coolies—collecting our wages but silently enduring basic political and economic inequality.

This country perpetuated a myth once. Today, no one can afford to   29
dreamily chase after that gold in the streets, oblivious to the genuine treasure of racial equality. When racism persists, can one really call any minority a "model"?

Works Cited

"Affirmative Non-actions." Op-ed. *Boston Globe* 14 Jan. 1985: 10.

"Asian Americans, The Drive to Excel." *Newsweek on Campus* April 1984: 4–13.

Asian American Studies: Contemporary Issues. Proc. from East Coast Asian American Scholars Conference. 1986.

Azores, Fortunata M. "Census Methodology and the Development of Social Indicators for Asian and Pacific Americans." United States Commission on Civil Rights 70–79.

Bell, David A. "The Triumph of Asian-Americans." *New Republic* 15 & 22 July 1985: 24–31.

Cabezas, Armado. "Employment Issues of Asian Americans." United States Commission on Civil Rights.

Chun, Ki-Taek. "The Myth of Asian American Success and Its Educational Ramifications." *IRCD Bulletin* Winter/Spring 1980.

Doerner, William R. "To America with Skills." *Time* 8 July 1985: 42–44.

Dutta, Manoranjan. "Asian/Pacific American Employment Profile: Myth and Reality—Issues and Answers." United States Commission on Civil Rights 445–89.

Hirschman, Charles, and Morrison G. Wong. "Trends in Socioeconomic Achievement Among Immigrants and Native-Born Asian-Americans, 1960–1976." *Sociological Quarterly* 22.4 (1981): 495–513.

Hune, Shirley. Keynote address. East Coast Asian Student Union Conference. Boston University. 14 Feb. 1987.

Kahng, Anthony. "Employment Issues." United States Commission on Civil Rights 1980.

Kantrowitz, Barbara, et al. "The Ultimate Assimilation." *Newsweek* 24 Nov. 1986: 80.

Kasindorf, Martin, et al. "Asian-Americans: A 'Model Minority.'" *Newsweek* 6 Dec. 1982: 39–51.

Kennedy, David M. "The Making of a Classic. Gunnar Myrdal and Black-White Relations: The Use and Abuse of *An American Dilemma*." *Atlantic* May 1987: 86–89.

Kiang, Peter. Personal interview. 1 May 1987.

Kim, Illsoo. "Class Division Among Asian Immigrants: Its Implications for Social Welfare Policy." *Asian American Studies* 24–25.

Kuo, Wen H. "On the Study of Asian-Americans: Its Current State and Agenda." *Sociological Quarterly* 20.2 (1979): 279–90.

Mariano, Robert S. "Census Issues." United States Commission on Civil Rights 54–59.

McBee, Susanna, et al. "Asian-Americans: Are They Making the Grade?" *U.S. News & World Report* 2 Apr. 1984: 41–47.

Nishi, Setsuko Matsunaga. "Asian American Employment Issues: Myths and Realities." United States Commission on Civil Rights 397–99, 495–507.

Oxnam, Robert B. "Why Asians Succeed Here." *New York Times Magazine* 30 Nov. 1986: 72+.

Ramirez, Anthony. "America's Super Minority." *Fortune* 24 Nov. 1986: 148–49.

Seligman, Daniel. "Keeping Up: Working Smarter." *Fortune* 17 May 1982: 64.

"Success Story of One Minority Group in the U.S." *U.S. News & World Report* 26 Dec. 1966: 73–76.

"Success Story: Outwhiting the Whites." *Newsweek* 21 June 1971: 24–25.

Sung, Betty Lee. *A Survey of Chinese American Manpower and Employment.* New York: Praeger, 1976.

Suzuki, Bob H. "Education and the Socialization of Asian Americans: A Revisionist Analysis of the 'Model Minority' Thesis." *Amerasia Journal* 4.2 (1977): 23–51.

Toupin, Elizabeth Ahn. "A Model University for a Model Minority." *Asian American Studies* 10–12.

United States Commission on Civil Rights. *Civil Rights Issues of Asian and Pacific Americans: Myths and Realities.* 1980.

"The Wrong Way to Court Ethnics." *Washington Monthly* May 1986: 21–26.

Yun, Grace. "Notes from Discussions on Asian American Education." *Asian American Studies* 20–24.

QUESTIONS ON MEANING

1. What is Chang's THESIS? Why does he introduce it where he does?
2. What "two crucial assumptions" do the media mistakenly propagate about Asian Americans?
3. What exactly does Chang mean by the "pressing needs" of Asian Americans?
4. SUMMARIZE Chang's ideas about the "Model Minority ideology" (beginning in para. 16). What is an *ideology*? What does this one do?

QUESTIONS ON WRITING STRATEGY

1. Is Chang's argument based more on EMOTIONAL APPEAL or on RATIONAL APPEAL? Why do you say so?
2. Try to summarize Chang's argument in a SYLLOGISM (as demonstrated on p. 449). What part of the syllogism corresponds to Chang's thesis?
3. What types of EVIDENCE does Chang base his argument on? Is the evidence adequate?
4. ANALYZE Chang's POINT OF VIEW. With whom does he ally himself? How does his position affect the essay?
5. Where does Chang acknowledge and address possible objections to his argument?
6. **OTHER METHODS.** How does Chang use DIVISION or ANALYSIS to develop his argument?

QUESTIONS ON LANGUAGE

1. What is the "old boy network" (para. 12)? What are the implications of this phrase?
2. In paragraph 28, Chang uses the term "techno-coolies." What ALLUSION is he making? Why is it especially suitable at this point in the essay?
3. Chang refers in paragraphs 5, 24, and 25 to an "economic pie." What images does this METAPHOR evoke?
4. Consult your dictionary if any of the following words are unfamiliar: allegedly (para. 3); median (4); aphorism (5); propagates, monolithic (6); venerable, systemic (7); fallacious (8); prevalent, disparity (13); reparations, internment (14); assimilation, lauded (17); absolution (20); empirical (21); succumb, torrent (23); lower-echelon (25); docile, pander (26); perpetuated (29).

SUGGESTIONS FOR WRITING

1. **JOURNAL WRITING.** Chang's essay suggests how important it is to view newspapers, television, and other media critically. Can you think of an incident when the media distorted or omitted facts? The subject may be as local or as national as you like: a neighborhood fire, a demonstration, an arrest, a legislative debate, anything. Write about the distortion in your journal.
   FROM JOURNAL TO ESSAY. Write an essay in which you analyze and correct

the media record of the incident you wrote of in your journal. To convince your readers of how and why the media record was inaccurate, you'll need to provide lots of details comparing what really happened and what the media reported.

2. Take Chang's essay further: Write a concrete proposal for correcting the situation he describes.

3. **CRITICAL WRITING.** Number 4 under "Questions on Meaning" asked you to summarize Chang's assertions about the "Model Minority ideology" (paras. 16–29). In an essay, analyze and EVALUATE these assertions. What ASSUMPTIONS is Chang making—for instance, about the existence or denial of racial barriers in the United States? Do you agree or disagree with Chang's assumptions and with his argument about the Model Minority ideology? Why?

4. **CONNECTIONS.** Chang, Linda Chavez ("Demystifying Multiculturalism," p. 468), and Ishmael Reed (" America: The Multinational Society," p. 476) are all members of an ethnic minority, but the three authors use this status very differently in their writing. To what extent does each writer identify with or claim to represent his or her ethnic group? How central is each one's own identity to the argument he or she makes? When you write, do you have a sense of representing a larger group or an expectation that you will be read as doing so? If so, how does this influence your writing? Does it tend to liberate or constrain you?

CURTIS CHANG ON WRITING

For Curtis Chang, a word processor is an "essential" writing tool. Once he completes and outlines his research, he explains in *Student Writers at Work,* "I must see my thoughts on the computer screen. I find it difficult to manipulate thoughts unless I can physically manipulate the words that represent them."

But the word processor can be a mixed blessing, for it supports Chang's "urge to perfect each sentence as I am writing. One is especially vulnerable when working on a word processor. I often have to force myself to continue getting the basic facts out first." Once he does have his thoughts on screen, Chang turns to global revision, an important part of his writing process. Although he strives for perfect sentences, Chang thinks of revision as "more than just the usual forms of correcting grammar and spelling and using one adjective instead of another." For Chang, "Revising means acting as devil's advocate and trying to pick apart my paper's argument. Then I have to answer to those criticisms."

Like many writers, Chang is rarely satisfied with his work. For each paper, he reports, "I average about three drafts, but it is usually determined by time constraints. I never really finish an essay; I just tire of tinkering with it."

FOR DISCUSSION

1. Why does Chang try not to perfect his sentences until the entire essay is written? What is the advantage of "getting the basic facts out first"?
2. Chang considers the word processor essential for writing. Would his extensive revisions be possible without one?

WILLIAM F. BUCKLEY, JR.

Born in New York in 1925, WILLIAM FRANK BUCKLEY, JR., is one of the most articulate proponents of American conservatism. Shortly after his graduation from Yale, he published *God and Man at Yale* (1951), a memoir espousing conservative political values and traditional Christian principles. Since then, he has written more than twenty works on politics and government, published a syndicated newspaper column, and founded and edited *The National Review*, a magazine of conservative opinion. His most recent nonfiction book is *Happy Days Were Here Again: Reflections of a Libertarian Journalist* (1993), but he has also written several books on sailing and many spy novels. In 1991 Buckley was awarded the Presidential Medal of Freedom. With all his publications and honors, however, Buckley is probably best known for his weekly television debate program, *Firing Line*. As the program's several million viewers know, he is a man of wry charm. When he was half-seriously running for mayor of New York City in 1965, someone asked him what he would do if elected. "Demand a recount," he replied.

Why Don't We Complain?

Most people riding in an overheated commuter train would perspire quietly. For Buckley, this excess of warmth sparks an indignant essay, first published in *Esquire* in 1961, in which he takes to task both himself and his fellow Americans. Does the essay appeal mainly to reason or to emotion? And what would happen if everyone were to do as Buckley urges?

It was the very last coach and the only empty seat on the entire train, so there was no turning back. The problem was to breathe. Outside, the temperature was below freezing. Inside the railroad car the temperature must have been about 85 degrees. I took off my overcoat, and a few minutes later my jacket, and noticed that the car was flecked with the white shirts of the passengers. I soon found my hand moving to loosen my tie. From one end of the car to the other, as we rattled through Westchester County, we sweated; but we did not moan.

I watched the train conductor appear at the head of the car. "Tickets, all tickets, please!" In a more virile age, I thought, the passengers would seize the conductor and strap him down on a seat over the radiator to share the fate of his patrons. He shuffled down the aisle, picking up tickets, punching commutation cards. *No one addressed a word to him.* He approached my seat, and I drew a deep breath of resolution.

"Conductor," I began with a considerable edge to my voice....Instantly the doleful eyes of my seatmate turned tiredly from his newspaper to fix me with a resentful stare: What question could be so important as to justify my sibilant intrusion into his stupor? I was shaken by those eyes. I am incapable of making a discreet fuss, so I mumbled a question about what time we were due in Stamford (I didn't even ask whether it would be before or after dehydration could be expected to set in), got my reply, and went back to my newspaper and to wiping my brow.

The conductor had nonchalantly walked down the gauntlet of 3 eighty sweating American freemen, and not one of them had asked him to explain why the passengers in that car had been consigned to suffer. There is nothing to be done when the temperature *outdoors* is 85 degrees, and indoors the air conditioner has broken down; obviously when that happens there is nothing to do, except perhaps curse the day that one was born. But when the temperature outdoors is below freezing, it takes a positive act of will on somebody's part to set the temperature *indoors* at 85. Somewhere a valve was turned too far, a furnace overstocked, a thermostat maladjusted: something that could easily be remedied by turning off the heat and allowing the great outdoors to come indoors. All this is so obvious. What is not obvious is what has happened to the American people.

It isn't just the commuters, whom we have come to visualize as a 4 supine breed who have got on to the trick of suspending their sensory faculties twice a day while they submit to the creeping dissolution of the railroad industry. It isn't just they who have given up trying to rectify irrational vexations. It is the American people everywhere.

A few weeks ago at a large movie theater I turned to my wife and 5 said, "The picture is out of focus." "Be quiet," she answered. I obeyed. But a few minutes later I raised the point again, with mounting impatience. "It will be all right in a minute," she said apprehensively. (She would rather lose her eyesight than be around when I make one of my infrequent scenes.) I waited. It was *just* out of focus — not glaringly out, but out. My vision is 20-20, and I assume that is the vision, adjusted, for most people in the movie house. So, after hectoring my wife throughout the first reel, I finally prevailed upon her to admit that it *was* off, and very annoying. We then settled down, coming to rest on the presumption that: a) someone connected with the management of the theater must soon notice the blur and make the correction; or b) that someone seated near the rear of the house would make the complaint in behalf of those of us up front; or c) that — any minute now — the entire house would explode into catcalls and foot stamping, calling dramatic attention to the irksome distortion.

What happened was nothing. The movie ended, as it had begun 6 *just* out of focus, and as we trooped out, we stretched our faces in a variety of contortions to accustom the eye to the shock of normal focus.

I think it is safe to say that everybody suffered on that occasion. 7
And I think it is safe to assume that everyone was expecting someone else to take the initiative in going back to speak to the manager. And it is probably true even that if we had supposed the movie would run right through the blurred image, someone surely would have summoned up the purposive indignation to get up out of his seat and file his complaint.

But notice that no one did. And the reason no one did is because 8
we are all increasingly anxious in America to be unobtrusive, we are reluctant to make our voices heard, hesitant about claiming our rights; we are afraid that our cause is unjust, or that if it is not unjust, that it is ambiguous; or if not even that, that it is too trivial to justify the horrors of a confrontation with Authority; we will sit in an oven or endure a racking headache before undertaking a head-on, I'm-here-to-tell-you complaint. That tendency to passive compliance, to a heedless endurance, is something to keep one's eyes on—in sharp focus.

I myself can occasionally summon the courage to complain, but I 9
cannot, as I have intimated, complain softly. My own instinct is so strong to let the thing ride, to forget about it—to expect that someone will take the matter up, when the grievance is collective, in my behalf —that it is only when the provocation is at a very special key, whose vibrations touch simultaneously a complexus of nerves, allergies, and passions, that I catch fire and find the reserves of courage and assertiveness to speak up. When that happens, I get quite carried away. My blood gets hot, my brow wet, I become unbearably and unconscionably sarcastic and bellicose; I am girded for a total showdown.

Why should that be? Why could not I (or anyone else) on that rail- 10
road coach have said simply to the conductor, "Sir"—I take that back: that sounds sarcastic—"Conductor, would you be good enough to turn down the heat? I am extremely hot. In fact, I tend to get hot every time the temperature reaches 85 degr—." Strike that last sentence. Just end it with the simple statement that you are extremely hot, and let the conductor infer the cause.

Every New Year's Eve I resolve to do something about the Milque- 11
toast in me and vow to speak up, calmly, for my rights, and for the betterment of our society, on every appropriate occasion. Entering last New Year's Eve I was fortified in my resolve because that morning at breakfast I had had to ask the waitress three times for a glass of milk. She finally brought it—after I had finished my eggs, which is when I don't want it anymore. I did not have the manliness to order her to take the milk back, but settled instead for a cowardly sulk, and ostentatiously refused to drink the milk—though I later paid for it—rather

than state plainly to the hostess, as I should have, why I had not drunk it, and would not pay for it.

So by the time the New Year ushered out the Old, riding in on my 12
morning's indignation and stimulated by the gastric juices of resolution that flow so faithfully on New Year's Eve, I rendered my vow. Henceforward I would conquer my shyness, my despicable disposition to supineness. I would speak out like a man against the unnecessary annoyances of our time.

Forty-eight hours later, I was standing in line at the ski repair store 13
in Pico Peak, Vermont. All I needed, to get on with my skiing, was the loan, for one minute, of a small screwdriver, to tighten a loose binding. Behind the counter in the workshop were two men. One was industriously engaged in servicing the complicated requirements of a young lady at the head of the line, and obviously he would be tied up for quite a while. The other—"Jiggs," his workmate called him—was a middle-aged man, who sat in a chair puffing a pipe, exchanging small talk with his working partner. My pulse began its telltale acceleration. The minutes ticked on. I stared at the idle shopkeeper, hoping to shame him into action, but he was impervious to my telepathic reproof and continued his small talk with his friend, brazenly insensitive to the nervous demands of six good men who were raring to ski.

Suddenly my New Year's Eve resolution struck me. It was now or 14
never. I broke from my place in line and marched to the counter. I was going to control myself. I dug my nails into my palms. My effort was only partially successful.

"If you are not too busy," I said icily, "would you mind handing me 15
a screwdriver?"

Work stopped and everyone turned his eyes on me, and I experi- 16
enced that mortification I always feel when I am the center of centripetal shafts of curiosity, resentment, perplexity.

But the worst was yet to come. "I am sorry, sir," said Jiggs deferen- 17
tially, moving the pipe from his mouth. "I am not supposed to move. I have just had a heart attack." That was the signal for a great whirring noise that descended from heaven. We looked, stricken, out the window, and it appeared as though a cyclone had suddenly focused on the snowy courtyard between the shop and the ski lift. Suddenly a gigantic army helicopter materialized, and hovered down to a landing. Two men jumped out of the plane carrying a stretcher, tore into the ski shop, and lifted the shopkeeper onto the stretcher. Jiggs bade his companion good-bye and was whisked out the door, into the plane, up to the heavens, down—we learned—to a nearby army hospital. I looked up manfully—into a score of man-eating eyes. I put the experience down as a reversal.

As I write this, on an airplane, I have run out of paper and need to 18 reach into my briefcase under my legs for more. I cannot do this until my empty lunch tray is removed from my lap. I arrested the stewardess as she passed empty-handed down the aisle on the way to the kitchen to fetch the lunch trays for the passengers up forward who haven't been served yet. "Would you please take my tray?" "Just a *moment*, sir!" she said, and marched on sternly. Shall I tell her that since she is headed for the kitchen *anyway*, it could not delay the feeding of the other passengers by more than two seconds necessary to stash away my empty tray? Or remind her that not fifteen minutes ago she spoke unctuously into the loudspeaker the words undoubtedly devised by the airline's highly paid public relations counselor: "If there is anything I or Miss French can do for you to make your trip more enjoyable, *please* let us—" I have run out of paper.

I think the observable reluctance of the majority of Americans to 19 assert themselves in minor matters is related to our increased sense of helplessness in an age of technology and centralized political and economic power. For generations, Americans who were too hot, or too cold, got up and did something about it. Now we call the plumber, or the electrician, or the furnace man. The habit of looking after our own needs obviously had something to do with the assertiveness that characterized the American family familiar to readers of American literature. With the technification of life goes our direct responsibility for our material environment, and we are conditioned to adopt a position of helplessness not only as regards the broken air conditioner, but as regards the overheated train. It takes an expert to fix the former, but not the latter; yet these distinctions, as we withdraw into helplessness, tend to fade away.

Our notorious political apathy is a related phenomenon. Every 20 year, whether the Republican or the Democratic Party is in office, more and more power drains away from the individual to feed vast reservoirs in far-off places; and we have less and less say about the shape of events which shape our future. From this alienation of personal power comes the sense of resignation with which we accept the political dispensations of a powerful government whose hold upon us continues to increase.

An editor of a national weekly news magazine told me a few years 21 ago that as few as a dozen letters of protest against an editorial stance of his magazine was enough to convene a plenipotentiary meeting of the board of editors to review policy. "So few people complain, or make their voices heard," he explained to me, "that we assume a dozen letters represent the inarticulated views of thousands of readers." In the past ten years, he said, the volume of mail has noticeably decreased, even though the circulation of his magazine has risen.

When our voices are finally mute, when we have finally suppressed 22 the natural instinct to complain, whether the vexation is trivial or grave, we shall have become automatons, incapable of feeling. When Premier Khrushchev first came to this country late in 1959 he was primed, we are informed, to experience the bitter resentment of the American people against his tyranny, against his persecutions, against the movement which is responsible for the great number of American deaths in Korea, for billions in taxes every year, and for life everlasting on the brink of disaster; but Khrushchev was pleasantly surprised, and reported back to the Russian people that he had been met with over-whelming cordiality (read: apathy), except, to be sure, for "a few fascists who followed me around with their wretched posters, and should be horsewhipped."

I may be crazy, but I say there would have been lots more posters in   23
a society where train temperatures in the dead of winter are not allowed to climb to 85 degrees without complaint.

QUESTIONS ON MEANING

1. How does Buckley account for his failure to complain to the train conductor? What reasons does he give for not taking action when he notices that the movie he is watching is out of focus?
2. Where does Buckley finally place the blame for the average American's reluctance to try to "rectify irrational vexations"?
3. By what means does the author bring his argument around to the subject of political apathy?
4. What THESIS does Buckley attempt to support? How would you state it?

QUESTIONS ON WRITING STRATEGY

1. In taking to task not only his fellow Americans but also himself, does Buckley strengthen or weaken his charge that, as a people, Americans do not complain enough?
2. Judging from the vocabulary displayed in this essay, would you say that Buckley is writing for a highly specialized AUDIENCE or an educated but non-specialized general audience?
3. As a whole, is Buckley's essay an example of appeal to emotion or reasoned argument or both? Give EVIDENCE for your answer.
4. **OTHER METHODS.** Buckley includes as evidence four NARRATIVES of his personal experiences. What is the point of the narrative about Jiggs (paras. 13–17)?

QUESTIONS ON LANGUAGE

1. Define the following words: virile, doleful, sibilant (para. 2); supine (4); hectoring (5); unobtrusive, ambiguous (8); intimated, unconscionably,

bellicose (9); ostentatiously (11); despicable (12); impervious (13); mortification, centripetal (16); deferentially (17); unctuously (18); notorious,
dispensations (20); plenipotentiary, inarticulated (21); automatons (22).

2. What does Buckley's use of the capital A in *Authority* (para. 8) contribute
to the sentence in which he uses it?

3. What is Buckley talking about when he alludes to "the Milquetoast in me"
(para. 11)? (Notice how well the ALLUSION fits into the paragraph, with its
emphasis on breakfast and a glass of milk.)

SUGGESTIONS FOR WRITING

1. **JOURNAL WRITING.** One reason we don't complain, Buckley says, is that we
expect someone else to. Do you ever "take the initiative" (para. 7) to complain about big or little hassles, or do you, too, sit in silent annoyance?
Why?
   FROM JOURNAL TO ESSAY. Write an essay about one moment when you either spoke up against an annoyance or didn't complain when you should
   have. Narrate this incident, also using the information from your journal
   entry to help explain why you did or did not act.

2. Think of some disturbing incident you have witnessed, or some annoying
treatment you have received in a store or other public place, and write a
letter of complaint to whomever you believe responsible. Be specific in
your evidence, be temperate in your language, make clear what you would
like to come of your complaint (your proposal), and be sure to put your letter in the mail.

3. **CRITICAL WRITING.** Write a paper in which you ANALYZE and EVALUATE any
one of Buckley's ideas. For instance: Do we feel as helpless as Buckley says
(para. 19)? Are we politically apathetic, and if so should the government be
blamed (para. 20)? For that matter, do we not complain? Support your view
with evidence from your experience, observation, or reading.

4. **CONNECTIONS.** Both Buckley and Barbara Huttmann, in "A Crime of
Compassion" (p. 83), make a strong ETHICAL APPEAL (see p. 445), going out
of their way to convince readers of their goodwill, reasonableness, and authority. Write an essay in which you analyze the ethical appeal of both authors, using quotations and PARAPHRASES from both essays to support your
analysis.

WILLIAM F. BUCKLEY, JR., ON WRITING

In the autobiographical *Overdrive*, Buckley recalls a conversation
with a friend and fellow columnist: "George Will once told me how
deeply he loves to write. 'I wake in the morning,' he explained to me,
'and I ask myself: Is this one of the days I have to write a column? And
if the answer is yes, I rise a happy man.' I, on the other hand, wake neither particularly happy nor unhappy, but to the extent that my mood is
affected by the question whether I need to write a column that morning, the impact of Monday-Wednesday-Friday"—the days when he

must write a newspaper column—"is definitely negative. Because I do not like to write, for the simple reason that writing is extremely hard work, and I do not 'like' extremely hard work."

Still, in the course of a "typical year," Buckley estimates that he produces not only 150 newspaper columns, but also a dozen longer articles, eight or ten speeches, fifty introductions for his television program, various editorial pieces for the magazine he edits, *The National Review*, and a book or two. "Why do I do so much?...It is easier to stay up late working for hours than to take one tenth the time to inquire into the question whether the work is worth performing."

In the introduction to another book, *A Hymnal: The Controversial Arts*, Buckley states an attitude toward writing that most other writers would not share. "I have discovered, in sixteen years of writing columns," he declares, "that there is no observable difference in the quality of that which is written at very great speed (twenty minutes, say), and that which takes three or four times as long....Pieces that take longer to write sometimes, on revisiting them, move along grumpily."

FOR DISCUSSION

1. Given that he so dislikes writing, why does Buckley do it?
2. Buckley's attitude toward giving time to writing is unusual. What is the more usual view of writing?

MARTIN LUTHER KING, JR.

MARTIN LUTHER KING, JR. (1929–68), was born in Atlanta, the son of a Baptist minister, and was himself ordained in the same denomination. Stepping to the forefront of the civil rights movement in 1955, King led African Americans in a boycott of segregated city buses in Montgomery, Alabama; became first president of the Southern Christian Leadership Conference; and staged sit-ins and mass marches that helped bring about the Civil Rights Act passed by Congress in 1964 and the Voting Rights Act of 1965. He received the Nobel Peace Prize in 1964. While King preached "nonviolent resistance," he was himself the target of violence. He was stabbed in New York, pelted with stones in Chicago; his home in Montgomery was bombed; and finally in Memphis he was assassinated by a sniper. On his tombstone near Atlanta's Ebenezer Baptist Church are these words from the spiritual he quotes at the conclusion of "I Have a Dream": "Free at last, free at last, thank God almighty, I'm free at last." Martin Luther King's birthday, January 15, is now a national holiday.

I Have a Dream

In Washington, D.C., on August 28, 1963, King's campaign of nonviolent resistance reached its historic climax. On that date, commemorating the centennial of Lincoln's Emancipation Proclamation freeing the slaves, King led a march of 200,000 persons, black and white, from the Washington Monument to the Lincoln Memorial. Before this throng, and to millions who watched on television, he delivered this unforgettable speech.

Five score years ago, a great American, in whose symbolic shadow 1 we stand, signed the Emancipation Proclamation. This momentous decree came as a great beacon light of hope to millions of Negro slaves who had been seared in the flames of withering injustice. It came as a joyous daybreak to end the long night of captivity.

But one hundred years later, we must face the tragic fact that the 2 Negro is still not free. One hundred years later, the life of the Negro is still sadly crippled by the manacles of segregation and the chains of discrimination. One hundred years later, the Negro lives on a lonely island of poverty in the midst of a vast ocean of material prosperity. One hundred years later, the Negro is still languishing in the corners of American society and finds himself in exile in his own land. So we have come here today to dramatize an appalling condition.

In a sense we have come to our nation's capital to cash a check. 3

When the architects of our republic wrote the magnificent words of the Constitution and the Declaration of Independence, they were signing a promissory note to which every American was to fall heir. This note was a promise that all men would be guaranteed the unalienable rights of life, liberty, and the pursuit of happiness. *a promise*

It is obvious today that America has defaulted on this promissory 4 note insofar as her citizens of color are concerned. Instead of honoring this sacred obligation, America has given the Negro people a bad check; a check which has come back marked "insufficient funds." But we refuse to believe that the bank of justice is bankrupt. We refuse to believe that there are insufficient funds in the great vaults of opportunity of this nation. So we have come to cash this check—a check that will give us upon demand the riches of freedom and the security of justice. We have also come to this hallowed spot to remind America of the fierce urgency of *now*. This is no time to engage in the luxury of cooling off or to take the tranquilizing drugs of gradualism. *Now* is the time to make real the promises of Democracy. *Now* is the time to rise from the dark and desolate valley of segregation to the sunlit path of racial justice. *Now* is the time to open the doors of opportunity to all of God's children. *Now* is the time to lift our nation from the quicksands of racial injustice to the solid rock of brotherhood.

It would be fatal for the nation to overlook the urgency of the mo- 5 ment and to underestimate the determination of the Negro. This sweltering summer of the Negro's legitimate discontent will not pass until there is an invigorating autumn of freedom and equality; 1963 is not an end, but a beginning. Those who hope that the Negro needed to blow off steam and will now be content will have a rude awakening if the nation returns to business as usual. There will be neither rest nor tranquillity in America until the Negro is granted his citizenship rights. The whirlwinds of revolt will continue to shake the foundations of our nation until the bright day of justice emerges.

But there is something that I must say to my people who stand 6 on the warm threshold which leads into the palace of justice. In the process of gaining our rightful place we must not be guilty of wrongful deeds. Let us not seek to satisfy our thirst for freedom by drinking from the cup of bitterness and hatred. We must forever conduct our struggle on the high plane of dignity and discipline. We must not allow our creative protest to degenerate into physical violence. Again and again we must rise to the majestic heights of meeting physical force with soul force. The marvelous new militancy which has engulfed the Negro community must not lead us to a distrust of all white people, for many of our white brothers, as evidenced by their presence here today, have come to realize that their destiny is tied up with our destiny and their freedom is inextricably bound to our freedom. We cannot walk alone.

And as we walk, we must make the pledge that we shall march 7
ahead. We cannot turn back. There are those who are asking the devo-
tees of civil rights, "When will you be satisfied?" We can never be satisfied as long as the Negro is the victim of the unspeakable horrors of
police brutality. We can never be satisfied as long as our bodies, heavy
with the fatigue of travel, cannot gain lodging in the motels of the
highways and the hotels of the cities. We cannot be satisfied as long as
the Negro's basic mobility is from a smaller ghetto to a larger one. We
can never be satisfied as long as a Negro in Mississippi cannot vote and
a Negro in New York believes he has nothing for which to vote. No,
no, we are not satisfied, and we will not be satisfied until justice rolls
down like waters and righteousness like a mighty stream.

I am not unmindful that some of you have come here out of great 8
trials and tribulations. Some of you have come fresh from narrow jail
cells. Some of you have come from areas where your quest for freedom
left you battered by the storms of persecution and staggered by the
winds of police brutality. You have been the veterans of creative suffering. Continue to work with the faith that unearned suffering is redemptive.

Go back to Mississippi, go back to Alabama, go back to South Car- 9
olina, go back to Georgia, go back to Louisiana, go back to the slums
and ghettos of our northern cities, knowing that somehow this situation can and will be changed. Let us not wallow in the valley of despair.

I say to you today, my friends, that in spite of the difficulties and 10
frustrations of the moment I still have a dream. It is a dream deeply
rooted in the American dream.

I have a dream that one day this nation will rise up and live out the 11
true meaning of its creed: "We hold these truths to be self-evident; that
all men are created equal."

I have a dream that one day on the red hills of Georgia the sons of 12
former slaves and the sons of former slaveowners will be able to sit
down together at the table of brotherhood.

I have a dream that one day even the state of Mississippi, a desert 13
state sweltering with the heat of injustice and oppression, will be transformed into an oasis of freedom and justice.

I have a dream that my four little children will one day live in a na- 14
tion where they will not be judged by the color of their skin but by the
content of their character.

I have a dream today. 15

I have a dream that one day the state of Alabama, whose governor's 16
lips are presently dripping with the words of interposition and nullification, will be transformed into a situation where little black boys and
black girls will be able to join hands with little white boys and white
girls and walk together as sisters and brothers.

I have a dream today.   17

I have a dream that one day every valley shall be exalted, every hill   18
and mountain shall be made low, the rough places will be made plain,
and the crooked places will be made straight, and the glory of the Lord
shall be revealed, and all flesh shall see it together.

This is our hope. This is the faith with which I return to the South.   19
With this faith we will be able to hew out of the mountain of despair a
stone of hope. With this faith we will be able to transform the jangling
discords of our nation into a beautiful symphony of brotherhood. With
this faith we will be able to work together, to pray together, to struggle
together, to go to jail together, to stand up for freedom together, knowing that we will be free one day.

This will be the day when all of God's children will be able to sing   20
with new meaning

> My country, 'tis of thee,
> Sweet land of liberty,
>   Of thee I sing:
> Land where my fathers died,
> Land of the pilgrims' pride,
> From every mountainside
>   Let freedom ring.

He uses the mountains as a way takes to climb over the obstacle & racism. This can be fixed.

And if America is to be a great nation this must become true. So let   21
freedom ring from the prodigious hilltops of New Hampshire. Let freedom ring from the mighty mountains of New York. Let freedom ring
from the heightening Alleghenies of Pennsylvania!

Let freedom ring from the snowcapped Rockies of Colorado!   22

Let freedom ring from the curvaceous peaks of California!   23

But not only that; let freedom ring from Stone Mountain of Geor-   24
gia!

Let freedom ring from Lookout Mountain of Tennessee!   25

Let freedom ring from every hill and molehill of Mississippi. From   26
every mountainside, let freedom ring.

When we let freedom ring, when we let it ring from every village   27
and every hamlet, from every state and every city, we will be able to
speed up that day when all of God's children, black men and white
men, Jews and Gentiles, Protestants and Catholics, will be able to join
hands and sing in the words of the old Negro spiritual, "Free at last! free
at last! thank God almighty, we are free at last!"

QUESTIONS ON MEANING

1. What is the apparent PURPOSE of this speech?
2. What THESIS does King develop in his first four paragraphs?
3. What does King mean by the "marvelous new militancy which has engulfed the Negro community" (para. 6)? Does this contradict King's non-violent philosophy?
4. In what passages of his speech does King notice events of history? Where does he acknowledge the historic occasion on which he is speaking?

QUESTIONS ON WRITING STRATEGY

1. Analyze King's ETHICAL APPEAL (see p. 445). Where in the speech, for instance, does he present himself as reasonable despite his passion? To what extent does his personal authority lend power to his words?
2. What indicates that King's words were meant primarily for an AUDIENCE of listeners, and only secondarily for a reading audience? To hear these indications, try reading the speech aloud. What uses of PARALLELISM do you notice?
3. Where in the speech does King acknowledge that not all of his listeners are African American?
4. How much EMPHASIS does King place on the past? How much does he place on the future?
5. **OTHER METHODS.** What EXAMPLES does King offer of particular injustices (para. 7)? In his speech as a whole, do his observations tend to be GENERAL or SPECIFIC?

QUESTIONS ON LANGUAGE

1. In general, is the language of King's speech ABSTRACT or CONCRETE? How is this level appropriate to the speaker's message and to the span of history with which he deals?
2. Point to memorable FIGURES OF SPEECH.
3. Define momentous (para. 1); manacles, languishing (2); promissory note, unalienable (3); defaulted, hallowed, gradualism (4); inextricably (6); mobility, ghetto (7); tribulations, redemptive (8); interposition, nullification (16); prodigious (21); curvaceous (23); hamlet (27).

SUGGESTIONS FOR WRITING

1. **JOURNAL WRITING.** Do you think we have moved closer to fulfilling King's dream in the decades since he gave this famous speech? Why, or why not? **FROM JOURNAL TO ESSAY.** Write an essay that explains your sense of how well the United States has progressed toward realizing King's dream. You may choose to focus on America as a whole or on your particular community, but you should use specific EVIDENCE to support your opinion.
2. Propose some course of action in a situation that you consider an injustice. Racial injustice is one possible area, or unfairness to any minority, or to women, children, the old, ex-convicts, the handicapped, the poor. If pos-

sible, narrow your subject to a particular incident or a local situation on which you can write knowledgeably.

3. **CRITICAL WRITING.** What can you INFER from this speech about King's own attitudes toward oppression and injustice? Does he follow his own injunction not "to satisfy our thirst for freedom by drinking from the cup of bitterness and hatred" (para. 6)? Explain your answer, using evidence from the speech.

4. **CONNECTIONS.** King's "I Have a Dream" and Jonathan Swift's "A Modest Proposal" (the following essay) both seek to arouse an audience to action, and yet they take very different approaches to achieve this purpose. COMPARE AND CONTRAST the authors' persuasive strategies, considering especially their effectiveness for the situation each writes about and the audience each addresses.

JONATHAN SWIFT

JONATHAN SWIFT (1667–1745), the son of English parents who had settled in Ireland, divided his energies among literature, politics, and
the Church of England. Dissatisfied with the quiet life of an Anglican
parish priest, Swift spent much of his time in London hobnobbing
with writers and producing pamphlets in support of the Tory Party.
In 1713 Queen Anne rewarded his political services with an assignment the London-loving Swift didn't want: to supervise St. Patrick's
Cathedral in Dublin. There, as Dean Swift, he ended his days—
beloved by the Irish, whose interests he defended against the English
government. Although Swift's chief works include the remarkable
satires *The Battle of the Books* and *A Tale of a Tub* (both 1704) and
scores of fine poems, he is best remembered for *Gulliver's Travels*
(1726), an account of four imaginary voyages. This classic is always
abridged when it is given to children because of its frank descriptions
of human filth and viciousness. In *Gulliver's Travels*, Swift pays tribute
to the reasoning portion of "that animal called man," and delivers a
stinging rebuke to the rest of him.

A Modest Proposal

Three consecutive years of drought and sparse crops had worked
hardship upon the Irish when Swift wrote this ferocious essay in the
summer of 1729. At the time, there were said to be thirty-five thousand wandering beggars in the country: Whole families had quit their
farms and had taken to the roads. Large landowners, of English ancestry, preferred to ignore their tenants' sufferings and lived abroad to
dodge taxes and payment of church duties. Swift had no special fondness for the Irish, but he hated the inhumanity he witnessed.

Although printed as a pamphlet in Dublin, Swift's essay is clearly
meant for English readers as well as Irish ones. When circulated, the
pamphlet caused a sensation in both Ireland and England and had to
be reprinted seven times in the same year. Swift is an expert with
plain, vigorous English prose, and "A Modest Proposal" is a masterpiece of SATIRE and IRONY. (If you are uncertain what Swift argues for,
see the discussion of these devices in Useful Terms.)

> For Preventing the Children of Poor People in Ireland
> from Being a Burden to Their Parents or Country,
> and for Making Them Beneficial to the Public

It is a melancholy object to those who walk through this great 1
town[1] or travel in the country, when they see the streets, the roads, and

---

[1] Dublin. —EDS.

cabin doors, crowded with beggars of the female sex, followed by three, four, or six children, all in rags and importuning every passenger for an alms. These mothers, instead of being able to work for their honest livelihood, are forced to employ all their time in strolling to beg sustenance for their helpless infants, who, as they grow up, either turn thieves for want of work, or leave their dear native country to fight for the Pretender in Spain, or sell themselves to the Barbados.[2]

I think it is agreed by all parties that this prodigious number of chil- 2 dren in the arms, or on the backs, or at the heels of their mothers, and frequently of their fathers, is in the present deplorable state of the kingdom a very great additional grievance; and therefore whoever could find out a fair, cheap, and easy method of making these children sound, useful members of the commonwealth would deserve so well of the public as to have his statue set up for a preserver of the nation.

But my intention is very far from being confined to provide only for 3 the children of professed beggars; it is of a much greater extent, and shall take in the whole number of infants at a certain age who are born of parents in effect as little able to support them as those who demand our charity in the streets.

As to my own part, having turned my thoughts for many years 4 upon this important subject, and maturely weighed the several schemes of other projectors,[3] I have always found them grossly mistaken in their computation. It is true, a child just dropped from its dam may be supported by her milk for a solar year, with little other nourishment; at most not above the value of two shillings, which the mother may certainly get, or the value in scraps, by her lawful occupation of begging; and it is exactly at one year that I propose to provide for them in such a manner as instead of being a charge upon their parents or the parish, or wanting food and raiment for the rest of their lives, they shall on the contrary contribute to the feeding, and partly to the clothing, of many thousands.

There is likewise another great advantage in my scheme, that it 5 will prevent those voluntary abortions, and that horrid practice of women murdering their bastard children, alas, too frequent among us, sacrificing the poor innocent babes, I doubt, more to avoid the expense than the shame, which would move tears and pity in the most savage and inhuman breast.

The number of souls in this kingdom being usually reckoned one 6 million and a half, of these I calculate there may be about two hundred

[2] The Pretender was James Stuart, exiled in Spain; in 1718 many Irishmen had joined an army seeking to restore him to the English throne. Others wishing to emigrate had signed papers as indentured servants, agreeing to work for a number of years in the Barbados or other British colonies in exchange for their ocean passage. —EDS.

[3] Planners. —EDS.

thousand couples whose wives are breeders; from which number I subtract thirty thousand couples who are able to maintain their own children, although I apprehend there cannot be so many under the present
distress of the kingdom; but this being granted, there will remain an
hundred and seventy thousand breeders. I again subtract fifty thousand
for those women who miscarry, or whose children die by accident or
disease within the year. There only remain an hundred and twenty
thousand children of poor parents annually born. The question therefore is, how this number shall be reared and provided for, which, as I
have already said, under the present situation of affairs, is utterly impossible by all the methods hitherto proposed. For we can neither employ them in handicraft or agriculture; we neither build houses (I mean
in the country) nor cultivate land. They can very seldom pick up a
livelihood stealing till they arrive at six years old, except where they
are of towardly parts;[4] although I confess they learn the rudiments
much earlier, during which time they can however be looked upon only
as probationers, as I have been informed by a principal gentleman in
the country of Cavan, who protested to me that he never knew above
one or two instances under the age of six, even in a part of the kingdom
so renowned for the quickest proficiency in that art.

I am assured by our merchants that a boy or a girl before twelve   7
years old is no salable commodity; and even when they come to this age
they will not yield above three pounds, or three pounds and half a
crown at most on the Exchange; which cannot turn to account either
to the parents or the kingdom, the charge of nutriment and rags having
been at least four times that value.

I shall now therefore humbly propose my own thoughts, which I   8
hope will not be liable to the least objection.

I have been assured by a very knowing American of my acquain-   9
tance in London, that a young healthy child well nursed is at a year old
a most delicious, nourishing, and wholesome food, whether stewed,
roasted, baked, or boiled; and I make no doubt that it will equally serve
in a fricassee or a ragout.[5]

I do therefore humbly offer it to public consideration that of the   10
hundred and twenty thousand children, already computed, twenty
thousand may be reserved for breed, whereof only one fourth part to be
males, which is more than we allow to sheep, black cattle, or swine;
and my reason is that these children are seldom the fruits of marriage,
a circumstance not much regarded by our savages, therefore one male
will be sufficient to serve four females. That the remaining hundred
thousand may at a year old be offered in sale to the persons of quality

---

[4] Teachable wits, innate abilities. — EDS.
[5] Stew. — EDS.

and fortune through the kingdom, always advising the mother to let them suck plentifully in the last month, so as to render them plump and fat for a good table. A child will make two dishes at an entertainment for friends; and when the family dines alone, the fore or hind quarter will make a reasonable dish, and seasoned with a little pepper or salt will be very good boiled on the fourth day, especially in winter.

I have reckoned upon a medium that a child just born will weigh 11 twelve pounds, and in a solar year it tolerably nursed increaseth to twenty-eight pounds.

I grant this food will be somewhat dear, and therefore very proper 12 for landlords, who, as they have already devoured most of the parents, seem to have the best title to the children.

Infant's flesh will be in season throughout the year, but more plen- 13 tiful in March, and a little before and after. For we are told by a grave author, an eminent French physician,[6] that fish being a prolific diet, there are more children born in Roman Catholic countries about nine months after Lent than at any other season; therefore, reckoning a year after Lent, the markets will be more glutted than usual, because the number of popish infants is at least three to one in this kingdom; and therefore it will have one other collateral advantage, by lessening the number of Papists among us.

I have already computed the charge of nursing a beggar's child (in 14 which list I reckon all cottagers, laborers, and four-fifths of the farmers) to be about two shillings per annum, rags included; and I believe no gentleman would repine to give ten shillings for the carcass of a good fat child, which, as I have said, will make four dishes of excellent nutritive meat, when he hath only some particular friend or his own family to dine with him. Thus the squire will learn to be a good landlord, and grow popular among the tenants; the mother will have eight shillings net profit, and be fit for work till she produces another child.

Those who are more thrifty (as I must confess the times require) 15 may flay the carcass; the skin of which artificially[7] dressed will make admirable gloves for ladies, and summer boots for fine gentlemen.

As to our city of Dublin, shambles[8] may be appointed for this pur- 16 pose in the most convenient parts of it, and butchers we may be assured will not be wanting; although I rather recommend buying the children alive, and dressing them hot from the knife as we do roasting pigs.

A very worthy person, a true lover of his country, and whose virtues 17 I highly esteem, was lately pleased in discoursing on this matter to offer a refinement upon my scheme. He said that many gentlemen of his

[6] Swift's favorite French writer, François Rabelais, sixteenth-century author; not "grave" at all, but a broad humorist. — EDS.

[7] With art or craft. — EDS.

[8] Butcher shops or slaughterhouses. — EDS.

kingdom, having of late destroyed their deer, he conceived that the want of venison might be well supplied by the bodies of young lads and maidens, not exceeding fourteen years of age nor under twelve, so great a number of both sexes in every county being now ready to starve for want of work and service; and these to be disposed of by their parents, if alive, or otherwise by their nearest relations. But with due deference to so excellent a friend and so deserving a patriot, I cannot be altogether in his sentiments; for as to the males, my American acquaintance assured me from frequent experience that their flesh was generally tough and lean, like that of our schoolboys, by continual exercise, and their taste disagreeable; and to fatten them would not answer the charge. Then as to the females, it would, I think with humble submission, be a loss to the public, because they soon would become breeders themselves; and besides, it is not improbable that some scrupulous people might be apt to censure such a practice (although indeed very unjustly) as a little bordering upon cruelty; which, I confess, hath always been with me the strongest objection against any project, how well soever intended.

But in order to justify my friend, he confessed that this expedient   18 was put into his head by the famous Psalmanazar,[9] a native of the island Formosa, who came from thence to London above twenty years ago, and in conversation told my friend that in his country when any young person happened to be put to death, the executioner sold the carcass to persons of quality as a prime dainty; and that in his time the body of a plump girl of fifteen, who was crucified for an attempt to poison the emperor, was sold to his Imperial Majesty's prime minister of state, and other great mandarins of the court, in joints from the gibbet, at four hundred crowns. Neither indeed can I deny that if the same use were made of several plump young girls in this town, who without one single groat to their fortunes cannot stir abroad without a chair, and appear at the playhouse and assemblies in foreign fineries which they never will pay for, the kingdom would not be the worse.

Some persons of a desponding spirit are in great concern about that   19 vast number of poor people who are aged, diseased, or maimed, and I have been desired to employ my thoughts what course may be taken to ease the nation of so grievous an encumbrance. But I am not in the least pain upon that matter, because it is very well known that they are every day dying and rotting by cold and famine, and filth and vermin, as fast as can be reasonably expected. And as to the younger laborers, they are now in almost as hopeful a condition. They cannot get work, and consequently pine away for want of nourishment to a degree that if

[9] Georges Psalmanazar, a Frenchman who pretended to be Japanese, author of a completely imaginary *Description of the Isle Formosa* (1705), had become a well-known figure in gullible London society. — EDS.

any time they are accidentally hired to common labor, they have not strength to perform it; and thus the country and themselves are happily delivered from the evils to come.

I have too long digressed, and therefore shall return to my subject. 20 I think the advantages by the proposal which I have made are obvious and many, as well as of the highest importance.

For first, as I have already observed, it would greatly lessen the 21 number of Papists, with whom we are yearly overrun, being the principal breeders of the nation as well as our most dangerous enemies; and who stay at home on purpose to deliver the kingdom to the Pretender, hoping to take their advantage by the absence of so many good Protestants, who have chosen rather to leave their country than to stay at home and pay tithes against their conscience to an Episcopal curate.

Secondly, the poorer tenants will have something valuable of their 22 own, which by law may be made liable to distress,[10] and help to pay their landlord's rent, their corn and cattle being already seized and money a thing unknown.

Thirdly, whereas the maintenance of an hundred thousand chil- 23 dren, from two years old and upwards, cannot be computed at less than ten shillings a piece per annum, the nation's stock will be thereby increased fifty thousand pounds per annum, besides the profit of a new dish introduced to the tables of all gentlemen of fortune in the kingdom who have any refinement in taste. And the money will circulate among ourselves, the goods being entirely of our own growth and manufacture.

Fourthly, the constant breeders, besides the gain of eight shillings 24 sterling per annum by the sale of their children, will be rid of the charge of maintaining them after the first year.

Fifthly, this food would likewise bring great custom to taverns, 25 where the vintners will certainly be so prudent as to procure the best receipts for dressing it to perfection, and consequently have their houses frequented by all the fine gentlemen, who justly value themselves upon their knowledge in good eating; and a skillful cook, who understands how to oblige his guests, will contrive to make it as expensive as they please.

Sixthly, this would be a great inducement to marriage, which all 26 wise nations have either encouraged by rewards or enforced by laws and penalties. It would increase the care and tenderness of mothers toward their children, when they were sure of a settlement for life to the poor babes, provided in some sort by the public, to their annual profit instead of expense. We should see an honest emulation among the married women, which of them could bring the fattest child to the market.

[10] Subject to seizure by creditors. — EDS.

Men would become as fond of their wives during the time of their pregnancy as they are now of their mares in foal, their cows in calf, or sows when they are ready to farrow; nor offer to beat or kick them (as is too frequent a practice) for fear of a miscarriage.

Many other advantages might be enumerated. For instance, the addition of some thousand carcasses in our exportation of barreled beef, the propagation of swine's flesh, and improvements in the art of making good bacon, so much wanted among us by the great destruction of pigs, too frequent at our tables, which are no way comparable in taste or magnificence to a well-grown, fat, yearling child, which roasted whole will make a considerable figure at a lord mayor's feast or any other public entertainment. But this and many others I omit, being studious of brevity.   27

Supposing that one thousand families in this city would be constant customers for infants' flesh, besides others who might have it at merry meetings, particularly weddings and christenings, I compute that Dublin would take off annually about twenty thousand carcasses, and the rest of the kingdom (where probably they will be sold somewhat cheaper) the remaining eighty thousand.   28

I can think of no one objection that will possibly be raised against this proposal, unless it should be urged that the number of people will be thereby much lessened in the kingdom. This I freely own, and it was indeed one principal design in offering it to the world. I desire the reader will observe, that I calculate my remedy for this one individual kingdom of Ireland and for no other that ever was, is, or I think ever can be upon earth. Therefore let no man talk to me of other expedients: of taxing our absentees at five shillings a pound: of using neither clothes nor household furniture except what is of our own growth and manufacture: of utterly rejecting the materials and instruments that promote foreign luxury: of curing the expensiveness of pride, vanity, idleness, and gaming in our women: of introducing a vein of parsimony, prudence, and temperance: of learning to love our country, in the want of which we differ even from Laplanders and the inhabitants of Topinamboo:[11] of quitting our animosities and factions, nor acting any longer like the Jews, who were murdering one another at the very moment their city was taken:[12] of being a little cautious not to sell our country and conscience for nothing: of teaching landlords to have at least one degree of mercy toward their tenants: lastly, of putting a spirit of honesty, industry, and skill into our shopkeepers; who, if a resolution could now be taken to buy only our native goods, would immediately   29

---

[11] A district of Brazil.—Eds.

[12] During the Roman siege of Jerusalem (A.D. 70), prominent Jews were executed on the charge of being in league with the enemy.—Eds.

unite to cheat and exact upon us in the price, the measure, and the goodness, nor could ever yet be brought to make one fair proposal of just dealing, though often and earnestly invited to it.

Therefore I repeat, let no man talk to me of these and the like ex- 30 pedients, till he hath at least some glimpse of hope that there will ever be some hearty and sincere attempt to put them in practice.

But as to myself, having been wearied out for many years with of- 31 fering vain, idle, visionary thoughts, and at length utterly despairing of success, I fortunately fell upon this proposal, which, as it is wholly new, so it hath something solid and real, of no expense and little trouble, full in our own power, and whereby we can incur no danger in disobliging England. For this kind of commodity will not bear exportation, the flesh being of too tender a consistence to admit a long continuance in salt, although perhaps I could name a country which would be glad to eat up our whole nation without it.

After all, I am not so violently bent upon my own opinion as to re- 32 ject any offer proposed by wise men, which shall be found equally innocent, cheap, easy, and effectual. But before something of that kind shall be advanced in contradiction to my scheme, and offering a better, I desire the author or authors will be pleased maturely to consider two points. First, as things now stand, how they will be able to find food and raiment for an hundred thousand useless mouths and backs. And secondly, there being a round million of creatures in human figure throughout this kingdom, whose sole subsistence put into a common stock would leave them in debt two millions of pounds sterling, adding those who are beggars by profession to the bulk of farmers, cottagers, and laborers, with their wives and children who are beggars in effect; I desire those politicians who dislike my overture, and may perhaps be so bold to attempt an answer, that they will first ask the parents of these mortals whether they would not at this day think it a great happiness to have been sold for food at a year old in this manner I prescribe, and thereby have avoided such a perpetual scene of misfortunes as they have since gone through by the oppression of landlords, the impossibility of paying rent without money or trade, the want of common sustenance, with neither house nor clothes to cover them from the inclemencies of the weather, and the most inevitable prospect of entailing the like or greater miseries upon their breed forever.

I profess, in the sincerity of my heart, that I have not the least per- 33 sonal interest in endeavoring to promote this necessary work, having no other motive than the public good of my country, by advancing our trade, providing for infants, relieving the poor, and giving some pleasure to the rich. I have no children by which I can propose to get a single penny; the youngest being nine years old, and my wife past childbearing.

QUESTIONS ON MEANING

1. On the surface, what is Swift proposing?
2. Beneath his IRONY, what is Swift's argument?
3. What do you take to be the PURPOSE of Swift's essay?
4. How does the introductory paragraph serve Swift's purpose?
5. Comment on the statement, "I can think of no one objection that will possibly be raised against this proposal" (para. 29). What objections can you think of?

QUESTIONS ON WRITING STRATEGY

1. Describe the mask of the personage through whom Swift writes.
2. By what means does the writer attest to his reasonableness?
3. At what point in the essay did it become clear to you that the proposal isn't modest but horrible?
4. As an essay in argument, does "A Modest Proposal" appeal primarily to reason or to emotion?
5. **OTHER METHODS.** Although not serious, Swift's proposal is worked out in detailed paragraphs of PROCESS ANALYSIS. What is the EFFECT of paragraphs 10–16? Why do you think Swift took such trouble with the process?

QUESTIONS ON LANGUAGE

1. How does Swift's choice of words enforce the monstrousness of his proposal? Note especially words from the vocabulary of breeding and butchery.
2. Consult your dictionary for the meanings of any of the following words not yet in your vocabulary: importuning, sustenance (para. 1); prodigious, commonwealth (2); computation, raiment (4); apprehend, rudiments, probationers (6); nutriment (7); fricassee (9); repine (14); flay (15); scrupulous, censure (17); mandarins (18); desponding, encumbrance (19); per annum (23); vintners (25); emulation, foal, farrow (26); expedients, parsimony, animosities (29); disobliging, consistence (31); overture, inclemencies (32).

SUGGESTIONS FOR WRITING

1. **JOURNAL WRITING.** Swift's proposal is aimed at a serious social problem of his day. What problems can you think of today that—like the poverty and starvation Swift describes—seem to require drastic action? You might consider groups of people whom you regard as mistreated or victimized. Look at the newspaper if nothing leaps to mind.
   FROM JOURNAL TO ESSAY. Write an essay in which you propose a solution to one of the problems raised in your journal. Your essay may be either of the following:
   a. A straight argument, giving EVIDENCE, in which you set forth possible solutions to the problem.
   b. An ironic proposal in the manner of Swift. If you do this one, find a de-

vice other than cannibalism to eliminate the victims or their problems. You don't want to imitate Swift too closely; he is probably inimitable.

2. In an encyclopedia, look into what has happened in Ireland since Swift wrote. Choose a specific contemporary aspect of Irish-English relations, research it in books and periodicals, and write a report on it.

3. **CRITICAL WRITING.** Choose several examples of irony in "A Modest Proposal" that you find particularly effective. In a brief essay, ANALYZE Swift's use of irony. Do your examples of irony depend on understating, overstating, or saying the opposite of what is meant? How do they improve on literal statements? What is the value of irony in argument?

4. **CONNECTIONS.** Analyze the ways Swift and Martin Luther King, Jr., in "I Have a Dream" (p. 502), create sympathy for the oppressed groups they are concerned about. Concentrate not only on what they say but on the words they use and their TONE. Then write a process analysis explaining techniques for portraying oppression so as to win the reader's sympathy. Use quotations or PARAPHRASES from Swift's and King's essays as examples. If you can think of other techniques that neither author uses, by all means include and illustrate them as well.

JONATHAN SWIFT ON WRITING

Although surely one of the most inventive writers in English literature, Swift voiced his contempt for writers of his day who bragged of their newness and originality. In *The Battle of the Books*, he compares such a self-professed original to a spider who "spins and spits wholly from himself, and scorns to own any obligation or assistance from without." Swift has the fable-writer Aesop praise that writer who, like a bee gathering nectar, draws from many sources.

> Erect your schemes with as much method and skill as you please; yet if the materials be nothing but dirt, spun out of your own entrails (the guts of modern brains), the edifice will conclude at last in a cobweb.... As for us Ancients, we are content, with the bee, to pretend to nothing of our own beyond our wings and our voice, that is to say, our flights and our language. For the rest, whatever we have got has been by infinite labor and search and ranging through every corner of nature; the difference is, that, instead of dirt and poison, we have rather chosen to fill our hives with honey and wax, thus furnishing mankind with the two noblest of things, which are sweetness and light.

Swift's advice for a writer would seem to be: Don't just invent things out of thin air; read the best writers of the past. Observe and converse. Do legwork.

Interestingly, when in *Gulliver's Travels* Swift portrays his ideal beings, the Houyhnhnms, a race of noble and intelligent horses, he in-

cludes no writers at all in their society. "The Houyhnhnms have no letters," Gulliver observes, "and consequently their knowledge is all traditional." Still, "in poetry they must be allowed to excel all other mortals;
wherein the justness of their description are indeed inimitable."
(Those very traits—striking comparisons and detailed descriptions—
make much of Swift's own writing memorable.)

In his great book, in "A Modest Proposal," and in virtually all he
wrote, Swift's purpose was forthright and evident. He declared in
"Verses on the Death of Dr. Swift,"

> As with a moral view designed
> To cure the vices of mankind:...
> Yet malice never was his aim;
> He lashed the vice but spared the name.
> No individual could resent,
> Where thousands equally were meant.
> His satire points at no defect
> But what all mortals may correct.

FOR DISCUSSION

1. Try applying Swift's parable of the spider and the bee to our own day. How
   much truth is left in it?
2. Reread thoughtfully the quotation from Swift's poem. According to the
   poet, what faults or abuses can a satiric writer fall into? How may these be
   avoided?
3. What do you take to be Swift's main PURPOSE as a writer? In your own words,
   SUMMARIZE it.

ADDITIONAL WRITING TOPICS

Argument and Persuasion

1. Write a persuasive essay in which you express a deeply felt opinion. In it, address a particular person or audience. For instance, you might direct your essay

    To a friend unwilling to attend a ballet performance (or a wrestling match) with you on the grounds that such an event is for the birds

    To a teacher who asserts that more term papers, and longer ones, are necessary

    To a state trooper who intends to give you a ticket for speeding

    To a male employer skeptical of hiring women

    To a developer who plans to tear down a historic house

    To someone who sees no purpose in studying a foreign language

    To a high-school class whose members don't want to go to college

    To an older generation skeptical of the value of "all that noise" (meaning current popular music)

    To an atheist who asserts that religion is a lot of pie-in-the-sky

    To the members of a library board who want to ban a certain book

2. Write a letter to your campus newspaper, or to a city newspaper, in which you argue for or against a certain cause or view. You may wish to object to a particular feature, column, or editorial in the paper. Send your letter and see if it is published.

3. Write a short letter to your congressional or state representative, arguing in favor of (or against) the passage of some pending legislation. See a news magazine or a newspaper for a worthwhile bill to write about. Or else write in favor of some continuing cause: for instance, saving whales, reducing (or increasing) armaments, or providing (or reducing) aid to the arts.

4. Write an essay arguing that something you feel strongly about should be changed, removed, abolished, enforced, repeated, revised, reinstated, or reconsidered. Be sure to propose some plan for carrying out whatever suggestions you make. Possible topics, listed to start you thinking, are these:

    The drinking age
    Gun laws
    Low-income housing
    Graduation requirements
    The mandatory retirement age
    ROTC programs in schools and colleges
    Movie ratings (G, PG, PG-13, R, NC-17, X)
    School prayer
    Fraternities and sororities

Dress codes
TV advertising

5. On the model of Maire Flynn's three-part condensed argument on pages 447–48, write a condensed argument in three paragraphs demonstrating data, claim, and warrant. For a topic, consider any problem or controversy in this morning's newspaper and form an opinion on it.

PART TWO

MIXING THE METHODS

Everywhere in this book, we have tried to prove how flexible the methods of development are. All the preceding essays offer superb examples of DESCRIPTION or CLASSIFICATION or DEFINITION or ARGUMENT, but every one also illustrates other methods, too—description in PROCESS ANALYSIS, ANALYSIS and NARRATION in COMPARISON, EXAMPLES and CAUSE AND EFFECT in argument.

In the next five chapters we take this point even further by abandoning the individual methods. The authors represented here *combine* methods to discover ideas and think critically about their subjects. Rather than illustrating a single method, then, each chapter focuses on a common theme: language, family, gender roles, communities, and the new cybercommunities created through the medium of computers. While two or three authors write on each of these subjects, their approaches, including their use of methods, could not be more varied. Each writer draws on whatever methods, at whatever length, will help him or her get a point across to readers.

You have already begun to attain this same command by focusing on the individual methods, making each a part of your kit of writing tools. Now, when you face a writing assignment, you can consider whether and how each method may help you develop your subject. Indeed, as we noted in this book's introduction (pp. 25–26), one way to approach a subject is to apply each method to it, one by one. Following is a list of questions derived from the methods, along with examples from George Orwell's "Politics and the English Language," the selection opening the next chapter. Treating the degraded condition of the English language and thus of thought and truth, Orwell uses every single method of development. (For a more graphic illustration of Orwell's creative use of the methods, we have annotated the essay itself. See p. 526.)

1. *Narration: Can you tell a story about the subject?* Orwell tells several brief stories about real and imaginary abuses of the language.
2. *Description: Can you use your senses to illuminate the subject?* Using vivid IMAGES of people and the effect of their words, Orwell freshens his narratives and other passages.
3. *Example: Can you point to instances that will make the subject concrete and specific?* Orwell uses innumerable specific examples — passages of prose, particular phrases, dishonest people, political lies.
4. *Comparison and contrast: Will setting the subject alongside another generate useful information?* Comparison lets Orwell show concrete differences between the prose he despises and the prose he trusts.
5. *Process analysis: Will a step-by-step explanation add to the reader's understanding?* Orwell explains several processes, most notably how to defend the English language by writing freshly, concretely, simply.
6. *Division or analysis: Can slicing the subject into its parts produce a clearer vision of it?* "Politics and the English Language" is studded with analyses of prose passages by other writers.
7. *Classification: Is it worthwhile to sort the subject into kinds or groups?* A key section of Orwell's essay classifies the "tricks" of bad prose writers, such as "pretentious diction" and "meaningless words."
8. *Cause and effect: Does it add to the subject to ask why it happened or what its results are?* Orwell answers both of these questions, examining the causes and the effects of the language's decline.
9. *Definition: Can you trace a boundary that will clarify the subject's meaning?* In one definition after another, Orwell pins down exactly what he means by terms such as "dying metaphor" and "false verbal limb."
10. *Argument and persuasion: Can you state an opinion or make a proposal about the subject?* "Politics and the English Language" is an extended argument against one kind of writing and in favor of another. Orwell states his opinion early on and supports it with the kinds of EVIDENCE we've noted above.

Rarely will every one of these questions produce fruit for a given essay, but inevitably two or three or four will. Try the whole list when you're stuck at the beginning of an assignment or when you're snagged in the middle of a draft. You'll find the questions are as good at removing obstacles as they are at generating ideas.

11

LANGUAGE AND TRUTH

How many ways can we lie to each other? Why don't we just tell the truth? The authors in this chapter grapple with such questions. George Orwell, in his famous diatribe "Politics and the English Language," rails against abuses of the language that, he believes, undermine the way we think and even threaten our liberty. David Segal, in "Excuuuse Me," bemoans the eclipse of ethnic and other "off-color" humor, a necessary form of truth telling, he thinks, that releases tension in a diverse culture. And finally, Marco Wilkinson, in "Exposing Truth for the Lie That It Is," seeks the very nature of "Truth" in his own experience as a gay man.

GEORGE ORWELL

GEORGE ORWELL was the pen name of Eric Blair (1903–50), born in Bengal, India, the son of an English civil servant. After attending Eton on a scholarship, he joined the British police in Burma, where he acquired a distrust for the methods of the empire. Then followed years of tramping, odd jobs, and near-starvation—recalled in *Down and Out in Paris and London* (1933). From living on the fringe of society and from his reportorial writing about English miners and factory workers, Orwell deepened his sympathy with underdogs. Severely wounded while fighting in the Spanish Civil War, he wrote a memoir, *Homage to Catalonia* (1938), voicing disillusionment with Loyalists who, he claimed, sought not to free Spain but to exterminate their political enemies. A socialist by conviction, Orwell kept pointing to the dangers of a collective state run by totalitarians. In *Animal Farm* (1945), he satirized Soviet bureaucracy; and in his famous novel *1984* (1949), he foresaw a regimented England whose government perverts truth and spies on citizens by two-way television. (The motto of the state and its leader: Big Brother Is Watching You.)

Politics and
the English Language

In Orwell's novel *1984*, a dictatorship tries to replace spoken and written English with Newspeak, an official language that limits thought by reducing its users' vocabulary. (The words *light* and *bad*, for instance, are suppressed in favor of *unlight* and *unbad*.) This concern with language and with its importance to society is constant in George Orwell's work. First published in 1946, "Politics and the English Language" still stands as one of the most devastating attacks on muddy writing and thinking ever penned. Orwell's six short rules for writing responsible prose are well worth remembering.

Perhaps more than any other essay in this book, Orwell's shows the flexibility and the power of the methods of development in concert: As we noted on pages 522–23, he draws on every method in constructing his case. In proof, we have annotated this essay to highlight the more notable uses of the methods. The only one we don't identify is ARGUMENT, because the entire essay argues a THESIS.

Most people who bother with the matter at all would admit that the English language is in a bad way, but it is generally assumed that we cannot by conscious action do anything about it. Our civilization is decadent and our language

—so the argument runs—must inevitably share in the general collapse. It follows that any struggle against the abuse of language is a sentimental archaism, like preferring candles to electric light or hansom cabs to airplanes. Underneath this lies the half-conscious belief that language is a natural growth and not an instrument which we shape for our own purposes.

Now, it is clear that the decline of a language must ultimately have political and economic causes: It is not due simply to the bad influence of this or that individual writer. But an effect can become a cause, reinforcing the original cause and producing the same effect in an intensified form, and so on indefinitely. A man may take a drink because he feels himself to be a failure, and then fail all the more completely because he drinks. It is rather the same thing that is happening to the English language. It becomes ugly and inaccurate because our thoughts are foolish, but the slovenliness of our language makes it easier for us to have foolish thoughts. The point is that the process is reversible. Modern English, especially written English, is full of bad habits which spread by imitation and which can be avoided if one is willing to take the necessary trouble. If one gets rid of these habits one can think more clearly, and to think clearly is a necessary first step toward political regeneration: so that the fight against bad English is not frivolous and is not the exclusive concern of professional writers. I will come back to this presently, and I hope that by that time the meaning of what I have said here will have become clearer. Meanwhile, here are five specimens of the English language as it is now habitually written.

These five passages have not been picked out because they are especially bad—I could have quoted far worse if I had chosen—but because they illustrate various of the mental vices from which we now suffer. They are a little below the average, but are fairly representative samples. I number them so that I can refer back to them when necessary:

> (1) I am not, indeed, sure whether it is not true to say that the Milton who once seemed not unlike a seventeenth-century Shelley had not become, out of an experience ever more bitter in each year, more alien [sic] to the founder of that Jesuit sect which nothing could induce him to tolerate.
> Professor Harold Laski (Essay in *Freedom of Expression*).

2

Cause/ effect

Comparison

3

Example

(2) Above all, we cannot play ducks and drakes with a native battery of idioms which prescribes such egregious collocations of vocables as the Basic *put up with* for *tolerate* or *put at a loss* for *bewilder*.

Example

> Professor Lancelot Hogben (*Interglossa*).

(3) On the one side we have the free personality: By definition it is not neurotic, for it has neither conflict nor dream. Its desires, such as they are, are transparent, for they are just what institutional approval keeps in the forefront of consciousness; another institutional pattern would alter their number and intensity; there is little in them that is natural, irreducible, or culturally dangerous. But *on the other side*, the social bond itself is nothing but the mutual reflection of these self-secure integrities. Recall the definition of love. Is not this the very picture of a small academic? Where is there a place in this hall of mirrors for either personality or fraternity?

> Essay on psychology in *Politics* (New York).

(4) All the "best people" from the gentlemen's clubs, and all the frantic fascist captains, united in common hatred of Socialism and bestial horror of the rising tide of the mass revolutionary movement, have turned to acts of provocation, to foul incendiarism, to medieval legends of poisoned wells, to legalize their own destruction of proletarian organizations, and rouse the agitated petty-bourgeoisie to chauvinistic fervor on behalf of the fight against the revolutionary way out of the crisis.

> Communist pamphlet.

(5) If a new spirit *is* to be infused into this old country, there is one thorny and contentious reform which must be tackled, and that is the humanization and galvanization of the B.B.C. Timidity here will bespeak cancer and atrophy of the soul. The heart of Britain may be sound and of strong beat, for instance, but the British lion's roar at present is like that of Bottom in Shakespeare's *Midsummer Night's Dream* — as gentle as any sucking dove. A virile new Britain cannot continue indefinitely to be traduced in the eyes or rather ears, of the world by the effete languors of Langham Place, brazenly masquerading as "standard English." When the Voice of Britain is heard at nine o'clock, better far and infinitely less ludicrous to hear aitches honestly dropped than the present priggish, inflated, inhibited, school-ma'amish arch braying of blameless bashful mewing maidens!

> Letter in *Tribune*.

Each of these passages has faults of its own, but, quite apart from avoidable ugliness, two qualities are common to

Division/ analysis

4

all of them. The first is staleness of imagery: The other is lack of precision. The writer either has a meaning and cannot express it, or he inadvertently says something else, or he is almost indifferent as to whether his words mean anything or not. The mixture of vagueness and sheer incompetence is the most marked characteristic of modern English prose, and especially of any kind of political writing. As soon as certain topics are raised, the concrete melts into the abstract and no one seems to think of turns of speech that are not hackneyed: Prose consists less and less of *words* chosen for the sake of their meaning, and more and more of *phrases* tacked together like the sections of a prefabricated henhouse. I list below, with notes and examples, various of the tricks by means of which the work of prose-construction is habitually dodged:

Division/ analysis

Description

Dying Metaphors. A newly invented metaphor assists thought by evoking a visual image, while on the other hand a metaphor which is technically "dead" (e.g., *iron resolution*) has in effect reverted to being an ordinary word and can generally be used without loss of vividness. But in between these two classes there is a huge dump of worn-out metaphors which have lost all evocative power and are merely used because they save people the trouble of inventing phrases for themselves. Examples are: *Ring the changes on, take up the cudgels for, toe the line, ride roughshod over, stand shoulder to shoulder with, play into the hands of, no axe to grind, grist to the mill, fishing in troubled waters, rift within the lute, on the order of the day, Achilles' heel, swan song, hotbed.* Many of these are used without knowledge of their meaning (what is a "rift," for instance?), and incompatible metaphors are frequently mixed, a sure sign that the writer is not interested in what he is saying. Some metaphors now current have been twisted out of their original meaning without those who use them even being aware of the fact. For example, *toe the line* is sometimes written *tow the line.* Another example is *the hammer and the anvil,* now always used with the implication that the anvil gets the worst of it. In real life it is always the anvil that breaks the hammer, never the other way about: A writer who stopped to think what he was saying would be aware of this, and would avoid perverting the original phrase.

5

Classification

Definition

Example

Operators or Verbal False Limbs. These save the trouble of picking out appropriate verbs and nouns, and at the same

6

Definition

time pad each sentence with extra syllables which give it an
appearance of symmetry. Characteristic phrases are: *render
inoperative, militate against, make contact with, be subjected to,
give rise to, give grounds for, have the effect of, play a leading
part (role) in, make itself felt, take effect, exhibit a tendency to,
serve the purpose of,* etc., etc. The keynote is the elimination
of simple verbs. Instead of being a single word, such as *break,
stop, spoil, mend, kill,* a verb becomes a *phrase,* made up of a
noun or adjective tacked on to some general-purpose verb
such as *prove, serve, form, play, render.* In addition, the passive voice is wherever possible used in preference to the active, and noun constructions are used instead of gerunds (*by
examination of* instead of *by examining*). The range of verbs is
further cut down by means of the *-ize* and *de-* formation, and
the banal statements are given an appearance of profundity
by means of the *not un-* formation. Simple conjunctions and
prepositions are replaced by such phrases as *with respect to,
having regard to, the fact that, by dint of, in view of, in the interests of, on the hypothesis that;* and the ends of sentences are
saved from anticlimax by such resounding commonplaces as
*greatly to be desired, cannot be left out of account, a develop-
ment to be expected in the near future, deserving of serious consideration, brought to a satisfactory conclusion,* and so on and
so forth.

Classification

*Example
and
process
analysis*

   Pretentious Diction. Words like *phenomenon, element, individual* (as noun), *objective, categorical, effective, virtual,
basic, primary, promote, constitute, exhibit, exploit, utilize,
eliminate, liquidate,* are used to dress up simple statements
and give an air of scientific impartiality to biased judgments.
Adjectives like *epoch-making, epic, historic, unforgettable, tri-
umphant, age-old, inevitable, inexorable, veritable,* are used to
dignify the sordid processes of international politics, while
writing that aims at glorifying war usually takes on an archaic color, its characteristic words being: *realm, throne,
chariot, mailed fist, trident, sword, shield, buckler, banner, jackboot, clarion.* Foreign words and expressions such as *cul de
sac, ancien régime, deus ex machina, mutatis mutandis, status
quo, gleichschaltung, weltanschauung,* are used to give an air
of culture and elegance. Except for the useful abbreviations
i.e., e.g., and *etc.,* there is no real need for any of the hundreds of foreign phrases now current in English. Bad writers,
and especially scientific, political, and sociological writers,
are nearly always haunted by the notion that Latin or Greek

7

Example

words are grander than Saxon ones, and unnecessary words like *expedite, ameliorate, predict, extraneous, deracinated, clandestine, subaqueous* and hundreds of others constantly gain ground from their Anglo-Saxon opposite numbers.[1] The jargon peculiar to Marxist writing (*hyena, hangman, cannibal, petty bourgeois, these gentry, lackey, flunkey, mad dog, White Guard,* etc.) consists largely of words and phrases translated from Russian, German, or French; but the normal way of coining a new word is to use a Latin or Greek root with the appropriate affix and, where necessary, the *-ize* formation. It is often easier to make up words of this kind (*deregionalize, impermissible, extramarital, nonfragmentatory,* and so forth) than to think up the English words that will cover one's meaning. The result, in general, is an increase in slovenliness and vagueness.

Classification

Example

Meaningless Words. In certain kinds of writing, particularly in art criticism and literary criticism, it is normal to come across long passages which are almost completely lacking in meaning.[2] Words like *romantic, plastic, values, human, dead, sentimental, natural, vitality,* as used in art criticism, are strictly meaningless in the sense that they not only do not point to any discoverable object, but are hardly ever expected to do so by the reader. When one critic writes, "The outstanding feature of Mr. X's work is its living quality," while another writes, "The immediately striking thing about Mr. X's work is its peculiar deadness," the reader accepts this as a simple difference of opinion. If words like *black* and *white* were involved, instead of the jargon words *dead* and *living,* he would see at once that language was being used in an improper way. Many political words are similarly abused. The word *fascism* has now no meaning except in so far as it signifies "something not desirable." The words *democracy, socialism, freedom, patriotic, realistic, justice,* have each of them

8

Example

---

[1] An interesting illustration of this is the way in which the English flower names which were in use till very recently are being ousted by Greek ones, *snapdragon* becoming *antirrhinum, forget-me-not* becoming *myosotis,* etc. It is hard to see any practical reason for this change of fashion: It is probably due to an instinctive turning-away from the more homely word and a vague feeling that the Greek word is scientific.

[2] Example: "Comfort's catholicity of perception and image, strangely Whitmanesque in range, almost the exact opposite in aesthetic compulsion, continues to evoke that trembling atmospheric accumulative hinting at a cruel, an inexorably serene timelessness. . . . Wrey Gardiner scores by aiming at simple bull's-eyes with precision. Only they are not so simple, and through this contented sadness runs more than the surface bitter-sweet of resignation." (*Poetry Quarterly.*)

several different meanings which cannot be reconciled with one another. In the case of a word like *democracy*, not only is there no agreed definition, but the attempt to make one is resisted from all sides. It is almost universally felt that when we call a country democratic we are praising it: Consequently the defenders of every kind of regime claim that it is a democracy, and fear that they might have to stop using the word if it were tied down to any one meaning. Words of this kind are often used in a consciously dishonest way. That is, the person who uses them has his own private definition, but allows his hearer to think he means something quite different. Statements like *Marshal Pétain was a true patriot, The Soviet Press is the freest in the world, The Catholic Church is opposed to persecution*, are almost always made with intent to deceive. Other words used in variable meanings, in most cases more or less dishonestly, are: *class, totalitarian, science, progressive, reactionary, bourgeois, equality*.

Classification

Example

Now that I have made this catalog of swindles and perversions, let me give another example of the kind of writing that they lead to. This time it must of its nature be an imaginary one. I am going to translate a passage of good English into modern English of the worst sort. Here is a well-known verse from *Ecclesiastes*:

9

> I returned and saw under the sun, that the race is not to the swift, nor the battle to the strong, neither yet bread to the wise, nor yet riches to men of understanding, nor yet favor to men of skill; but time and chance happeneth to them all.

Example, comparison, and division/ analysis

Here it is in modern English:

> Objective consideration of contemporary phenomena compels the conclusion that success or failure in competitive activities exhibits no tendency to be commensurate with innate capacity, but that a considerable element of the unpredictable must invariably be taken into account.

This is a parody, but not a very gross one. Exhibit (3), above, for instance, contains several patches of the same kind of English. It will be seen that I have not made a full translation. The beginning and ending of the sentence follow the original meaning fairly closely, but in the middle the concrete illustrations—race, battle, bread—dissolve into the vague phrase "success or failure in competitive activi-

10

ties." This had to be so, because no modern writer of the kind I am discussing—no one capable of using phrases like "objective consideration of contemporary phenomena"— would ever tabulate his thoughts in that precise and detailed way. The whole tendency of modern prose is away from concreteness. Now analyze these two sentences a little more closely. The first contains forty-nine words but only sixty syllables, and all its words are those of everyday life. The second contains thirty-eight words of ninety syllables: eighteen of its words are from Latin roots, and one from Greek. The first sentence contains six vivid images, and only one phrase ("time and chance") that could be called vague. The second contains not a single fresh, arresting phrase, and in spite of its ninety syllables it gives only a shortened version of the meaning contained in the first. Yet without a doubt it is the second kind of sentence that is gaining ground in modern English. I do not want to exaggerate. This kind of writing is not yet universal, and outcrops of simplicity will occur here and there in the worst-written page. Still, if you or I were told to write a few lines on the uncertainty of human fortunes, we should probably come much nearer to my imaginary sentence than to the one from *Ecclesiastes*.

Examples, comparison, and division/ analysis

As I have tried to show, modern writing at its worst does not consist in picking out words for the sake of their meaning and inventing images in order to make the meaning clearer. It consists in gumming together long strips of words which have already been set in order by someone else, and making the results presentable by sheer humbug. The attraction of this way of writing is that it is easy. It is easier— even quicker once you have the habit—to say *In my opinion it is a not unjustifiable assumption that* than to say *I think*. If you use ready-made phrases, you not only don't have to hunt about for words; you also don't have to bother with the rhythms of your sentences, since these phrases are generally so arranged as to be more or less euphonious. When you are composing in a hurry—when you are dictating to a stenographer, for instance, or making a public speech—it is natural to fall into a pretentious, Latinized style. Tags like *a consideration which we should do well to bear in mind* or *a conclusion to which all of us would readily assent* will save many a sentence from coming down with a bump. By using stale metaphors, similes, and idioms, you save much mental effort, at the cost of leaving your meaning vague, not only for your reader but for yourself. This is the significance of mixed

11

Process analysis

Example

Example

metaphors. The sole aim of a metaphor is to call up a visual image. When these images clash — as in *The Fascist octopus has sung its swan song, the jackboot is thrown into the melting pot* — it can be taken as certain that the writer is not seeing a mental image of the objects he is naming; in other words he is not really thinking. Look again at the examples I gave at the beginning of this essay. Professor Laski (1) uses five negatives in fifty-three words. One of these is superfluous, making nonsense of the whole passage, and in addition there is the slip *alien* for akin, making further nonsense, and several avoidable pieces of clumsiness which increase the general vagueness. Professor Hogben (2) plays ducks and drakes with a battery which is able to write prescriptions, and, while disapproving of the everyday phrase *put up with*, is unwilling to look *egregious* up in the dictionary and see what it means. (3), if one takes an uncharitable attitude toward it, is simply meaningless: Probably one could work out its intended meaning by reading the whole of the article in which it occurs. In (4), the writer knows more or less what he wants to say, but an accumulation of stale phrases chokes him like tea leaves blocking a sink. In (5), words and meaning have almost parted company. People who write in this manner usually have a general emotional meaning — they dislike one thing and want to express solidarity with another — but they are not interested in the detail of what they are saying. A scrupulous writer, in every sentence that he writes, will ask himself at least four questions, thus: What am I trying to say? What words will express it? What image or idiom will make it clearer? Is this image fresh enough to have an effect? And he will probably ask himself two more: Could I put it more shortly? Have I said anything that is avoidably ugly? But you are not obliged to go to all this trouble. You can shirk it by simply throwing your mind open and letting the ready-made phrases come crowding in. They will construct your sentences for you — even think your thoughts for you, to a certain extent — and at need they will perform the important service of partially concealing your meaning even from yourself. It is at this point that the special connection between politics and the debasement of language becomes clear.

> *Example*
>
> *Process analysis*
>
> *Example and division/ analysis*
>
> *Comparison*

In our time it is broadly true that political writing is bad writing. Where it is not true, it will generally be found that the writer is some kind of rebel, expressing his private opinions and not a "party line." Orthodoxy, of whatever color,

seems to demand a lifeless, imitative style. The political dialects to be found in pamphlets, leading articles, manifestos,
White Papers, and the speeches of under-secretaries do, of *Comparison*
course, vary from party to party, but they are all alike in that
one almost never finds in them a fresh, vivid, homemade
turn of speech. When one watches some tired hack on the
platform mechanically repeating the familiar phrases — *bestial atrocities, iron heel, bloodstained tyranny, free peoples of the
world, stand shoulder to shoulder* — one often has a curious *Description
and
example*
feeling that one is not watching a live human being but
some kind of dummy; a feeling which suddenly becomes
stronger at moments when the light catches the speaker's
spectacles and turns them into blank discs which seem to
have no eyes behind them. And this is not altogether fanciful. A speaker who uses that kind of phraseology has gone
some distance toward turning himself into a machine. The
appropriate noises are coming out of his larynx, but his brain
is not involved as it would be if he were choosing his words
for himself. If the speech he is making is one that he is accustomed to make over and over again, he may be almost
unconscious of what he is saying, as one is when one utters
the responses in church. And this reduced state of consciousness, if not indispensable, is at any rate favorable to *Cause/
effect*
political conformity.

    In our time, political speech and writing are largely the   13
defense of the indefensible. Things like the continuance of
British rule in India, the Russian purges and deportations,
the dropping of the atom bombs on Japan, can indeed be defended, but only by arguments which are too brutal for most
people to face, and which do not square with the professed
aims of political parties. Thus political language has to consist largely of euphemism, question-begging and sheer
cloudy vagueness. Defenseless villages are bombarded from
the air, the inhabitants driven out into the countryside, the *Example*
cattle machine-gunned, the huts set on fire with incendiary
bullets: This is called *pacification*. Millions of peasants are *Description*
robbed of their farms and sent trudging along the roads with
no more than they can carry: This is called *transfer of population* or *rectification of frontiers*. People are imprisoned for
years without trial, or shot in the back of the neck or sent to
die of scurvy in Arctic lumber camps: This is called *elimination of unreliable elements*. Such phraseology is needed if one
wants to name things without calling up mental pictures of
them. Consider for instance some comfortable English pro-

fessor defending Russian totalitarianism. He cannot say out-right, "I believe in killing off your opponents when you can get good results by doing so." Probably, therefore, he will say something like this:

"While freely conceding that the Soviet régime exhibits certain features which the humanitarian may be inclined to deplore, we must, I think, agree that a certain curtailment of the right to political opposition is an unavoidable concomi-tant of transitional periods, and that the rigors which the Russian people have been called upon to undergo have been amply justified in the sphere of concrete achievement."

14

The inflated style is itself a kind of euphemism. A mass of Latin words fall upon the facts like soft snow, blurring the outlines and covering up all the details. The great enemy of clear language is insincerity. When there is a gap between one's real and one's declared aims, one turns as it were in-stinctively to long words and exhausted idioms, like a cut-tlefish squirting out ink. In our age there is no such thing as "keeping out of politics." All issues are political issues, and politics itself is a mass of lies, evasions, folly, hatred, and schizophrenia. When the general atmosphere is bad, lan-guage must suffer. I should expect to find—this is a guess which I have not sufficient knowledge to verify—that the German, Russian, and Italian languages have all deterio-rated in the last ten or fifteen years, as a result of dictator-ship.

15

Description

Cause/effect

Description

But if thought corrupts language, language can also cor-rupt thought. A bad usage can spread by tradition and imi-tation, even among people who should and do know better. The debased language that I have been discussing is in some ways very convenient. Phrases like *a not unjustifiable assump-tion, leaves much to be desired, would serve no good purpose, a consideration which we should do well to bear in mind,* are a continuous temptation, a packet of aspirins always at one's elbow. Look back through this essay, and for certain you will find that I have again and again committed the very faults I am protesting against. By this morning's post I have received a pamphlet dealing with conditions in Germany. The au-thor tells me that he "felt impelled" to write it. I open it at random, and here is almost the first sentence that I see: "(The Allies) have an opportunity not only of achieving a radical transformation of Germany's social and political structure in such a way as to avoid a nationalistic reaction in Germany itself, but at the same time of laying the founda-

16

Example

Description

Narration

tions of a co-operative and unified Europe." You see, he "feels impelled" to write—feels, presumably, that he has something new to say—and yet his words, like cavalry horses answering the bugle, group themselves automatically into the familiar dreary pattern. This invasion of one's mind by ready-made phrases (*lay the foundations, achieve a radical transformation*) can only be prevented if one is constantly on guard against them, and every such phrase anesthetizes a portion of one's brain.

Cause/ effect

Description

I said earlier that the decadence of our language is probably curable. Those who deny this would argue, if they produced an argument at all, that language merely reflects existing social conditions, and that we cannot influence its development by any direct tinkering with words and constructions. So far as the general tone or spirit of a language goes, this may be true, but it is not true in detail. Silly words and expressions have often disappeared, not through any evolutionary process but owing to the conscious action of a minority. Two recent examples were *explore every avenue* and *leave no stone unturned*, which were killed by the jeers of a few journalists. There is a long list of flyblown metaphors which could similarly be got rid of if enough people would interest themselves in the job; and it should also be possible to laugh the *not un-* formation out of existence,[3] to reduce the amount of Latin and Greek in the average sentence, to drive out foreign phrases and strayed scientific words, and, in general, to make pretentiousness unfashionable. But all these are minor points. The defense of the English language implies more than this, and perhaps it is best to start by saying what it does *not* imply.

17

Example

Definition

To begin with it has nothing to do with archaism, with the salvaging of obsolete words and turns of speech, or with the setting up of a "standard English" which must never be departed from. On the contrary, it is especially concerned with the scrapping of every word or idiom which has outworn its usefulness. It has nothing to do with correct grammar and syntax, which are of no importance so long as one makes one's meaning clear, or with the avoidance of Americanisms, or with having what is called a "good prose style." On the other hand it is not concerned with fake simplicity and the attempt to make written English colloquial. Nor

18

[3] One can cure oneself of the *not un-* formation by memorizing this sentence: A *not unblack dog was chasing a not unsmall rabbit across a not ungreen field.*

does it even imply in every case preferring the Saxon word to the Latin one, though it does imply using the fewest and shortest words that will cover one's meaning. What is above all needed is to let the meaning choose the word, and not the other way about. In prose, the worst thing one can do with words is to surrender to them. When you think of a concrete object, you think wordlessly, and then, if you want to describe the thing you have been visualizing you probably hunt about till you find the exact words that seem to fit. When you think of something abstract you are more inclined to use words from the start, and unless you make a conscious effort to prevent it, the existing dialect will come rushing in and do the job for you, at the expense of blurring or even changing your meaning. Probably it is better to put off using words as long as possible and get one's meaning as clear as one can through pictures or sensations. Afterwards one can choose — not simply *accept* — the phrases that will best cover the meaning, and then switch round and decide what impression one's words are likely to make on another person. This last effort of the mind cuts out all stale or mixed images, all prefabricated phrases, needless repetitions, and humbug and vagueness generally. But one can often be in doubt about the effect of a word or phrase, and one needs rules that one can rely on when instinct fails. I think the following rules will cover most cases:

Process analysis

Comparison

 (i) Never use a metaphor, simile, or other figure of speech which you are used to seeing in print.
 (ii) Never use a long word where a short one will do.
 (iii) If it is possible to cut a word out, always cut it out.
 (iv) Never use the passive where you can use the active.
 (v) Never use a foreign phrase, a scientific word or a jargon word if you can think of an everyday English equivalent.
 (vi) Break any of these rules sooner than say anything outright barbarous.

These rules sound elementary, and so they are, but they demand a deep change in attitude in anyone who has grown used to writing in the style now fashionable. One could keep all of them and still write bad English, but one could not write the kind of stuff that I quoted in those five specimens at the beginning of this article.

I have not here been considering the literary use of language, but merely language as an instrument for expressing and not for concealing or preventing thought. Stuart Chase and others have come near to claiming that all abstract

19

words are meaningless, and have used this as a pretext for advocating a kind of political quietism. Since you don't know what Fascism is, how can you struggle against Fascism? One need not swallow such absurdities as this, but one ought to recognize that the present political chaos is connected with the decay of language, and that one can probably bring about some improvement by starting at the verbal end. If you simplify your English, you are freed from the worst follies of orthodoxy. You cannot speak any of the necessary dialects, and when you make a stupid remark its stupidity will be obvious, even to yourself. Political language — and with variations this is true of all political parties, from Conservatives to Anarchists — is designed to make lies sound truthful and murder respectable, and to give an appearance of solidity to pure wind. One cannot change this all in a moment, but one can at least change one's own habits, and from time to time one can even, if one jeers loudly enough, send some worn-out and useless phrase — some *jackboot, Achilles' heel, hotbed, melting pot, acid test, veritable inferno,* or other lump of verbal refuse — into the dustbin where it belongs.

Cause/effect

Example

QUESTIONS ON MEANING

1. Orwell states his THESIS early in his essay. What is it?
2. What two common faults does Orwell find in all five of his horrible examples (paras. 3–4)?
3. What questions does Orwell provide for scrupulous writers to ask themselves?
4. How does Orwell support his contention that there is a direct relationship between bad writing and political injustice? Why, in his view, is vague and misleading language necessary to describe acts of oppression?
5. What, according to Orwell, can *you* do to combat the decay of the English language?

QUESTIONS ON WRITING STRATEGY

1. Identify Orwell's AUDIENCE.
2. Taking his own advice, Orwell seeks fresh phrases and colorful, concrete FIGURES OF SPEECH. Point to some of these.
3. Examine the organization of this essay. (Following the order of the essay, list the topics covered.) Is the structure clear to you? Why, or why not?

4. **MIXED METHODS.** Orwell makes his case with many, many EXAMPLES of bad prose, some of which he ANALYZES to show just what is wrong (see especially paras. 3–4, 9–11). Some of Orwell's examples are dated, such as a few dying metaphors (5) that have mercifully disappeared or the British rule of India (13), which ended in 1947. Does the age of the essay weaken it? Can you think of examples (and corresponding analysis) to replace any of Orwell's that are dated?

5. **MIXED METHODS.** Orwell musters not only example and analysis but also every other method to develop his ARGUMENT. Locate uses of CLASSIFICATION and PROCESS ANALYSIS. What do these contribute to the essay?

QUESTIONS ON LANGUAGE

1. In plainer words than Lancelot Hogben's, what are "egregious collocations of vocables" (in Orwell's second example in para. 3)?
2. Mixed METAPHORS, such as "the fascist octopus has sung its swan song" (para. 11), can be unintentionally funny. Recall or invent some more examples. What, according to Orwell, is the cause of such verbal snafus?
3. Does Orwell agree that "all abstract words are meaningless" (para. 20)?
4. Define decadent, archaism (para. 1); slovenliness, regeneration, frivolous (2); inadvertently, hackneyed, prefabricated (4); evocative (5); symmetry, banal, profundity (6); sordid (7); reconciled (8); parody, tabulate (10); euphonious, superfluous, scrupulous, debasement (11); orthodoxy, phraseology (12); purges, euphemism, totalitarianism (13); curtailment, concomitant (14); impelled (16); colloquial, barbarous (18); quietism (19).

SUGGESTIONS FOR WRITING

1. **JOURNAL WRITING.** Choose two familiar objects, places, or people to describe—your favorite item of clothing, the bathroom sink, the corner store, whatever. Giving yourself ten minutes for each one (twenty minutes in all) and using complete sentences, write down as many details about these subjects as you can—as though describing them to someone who has never seen them.

   FROM JOURNAL TO ESSAY. Considering Orwell's objections to vague, meaningless language and "dying metaphors," look carefully at the descriptions you wrote in your journal. Did you fall into any of the writing traps Orwell identifies? Are there places where you are wordy or too general? Have you written sentences like "She is really beautiful" instead of describing your subject's features so that readers can *see* it for themselves? Choose one of your descriptions and revise it until it is as precise and vivid as you can make it. (You may need to write several paragraphs to achieve this precision.)

2. From browsing in current newspapers and magazines, find a few passages of writing as bad as the ones George Orwell quotes and condemns in "Politics and the English Language." Analyze what you find wrong with them.

3. Like Orwell, who in "Politics and the English Language" deliberately worsens a verse from Ecclesiastes (para. 9), take a passage of excellent prose and try rewriting it in words as abstract and colorless as possible. For passages to

work on, try paragraph 14 from Bruce Catton's "Grant and Lee" (p. 196), paragraph 12 from Martin Luther King's "I Have a Dream" (p. 504), or any other passage you admire. If you choose an unfamiliar passage, supply a copy of it along with your finished paper. What does your experiment demonstrate?

4. **CRITICAL WRITING.** Does Orwell do as Orwell says? Apply his *do's* and *don't's* to his own writing, choosing one or two paragraphs to analyze. Use quotations from the essay to explain and support your analysis.

5. **CONNECTIONS (PART ONE).** Orwell points out that much political speech and writing is deliberately vague because blunt, truthful words would reveal arguments "too brutal for most people to face" (para. 13). Stephanie Ericsson, in "The Ways We Lie" (p. 337), proposes that some lying seems justified to protect ourselves from exposure or to avoid offending people or hurting their feelings. Is this the kind of lying Orwell means? Write an essay discussing the harm or harmlessness of political evasions, using examples from Orwell, if you like, and from recent news. (It may help to work with some classmates to generate examples that you can all use.)

6. **CONNECTIONS (PART TWO).** Like Orwell, David Segal, in "Excuuuse Me" (p. 544), warns against EUPHEMISM as a way of ducking a reality we don't want to face. Do you see the kind of euphemism Segal mentions (for example, "the differently abled," para. 5) as similar to the propaganda Orwell discusses in paragraphs 13–15? Does the difference in intention behind these two forms of euphemism ("defending the indefensible," 13, versus protecting others' feelings) render one more acceptable, or should all euphemism be avoided? Answer these questions in an essay, using examples from Orwell's and Segal's essays as well as from your own reading and observation.

GEORGE ORWELL ON WRITING

Orwell explains the motives for his own writing in the essay "Why I Write" (1946):

"What I have most wanted to do throughout the past ten years is to make political writing into an art. My starting point is always a feeling of partisanship, a sense of injustice. When I sit down to write a book, I do not say to myself, 'I am going to produce a work of art.' I write it because there is some lie that I want to expose, some fact to which I want to draw attention, and my initial concern is to get a hearing. But I could not do the work of writing a book, or even a long magazine article, if it were not also an esthetic experience. Anyone who cares to examine my work will see that even when it is downright propaganda it contains much that a full-time politician would consider irrelevant. I am not able, and I do not want, completely to abandon the worldview that I acquired in childhood. So long as I remain alive and well I shall continue to feel strongly about prose style, to love the surface of the earth, and to take a pleasure in solid objects and scraps of useless information. It is no use trying to suppress that side of myself. The job is to reconcile my ingrained likes and dislikes with the essentially public, nonindividual activities that this age forces on all of us.

"It is not easy. It raises problems of construction and of language, and it raises in a new way the problem of truthfulness. Let me give just one example of the cruder kind of difficulty that arises. My book about the Spanish civil war, *Homage to Catalonia*, is, of course, a frankly political book, but in the main it is written with a certain detachment and regard for form. I did try very hard in it to tell the whole truth without violating my literary instincts. But among other things it contains a long chapter, full of newspaper quotations and the like, defending the Trotskyists who were accused of plotting with Franco. Clearly such a chapter, which after a year or two would lose its interest for any ordinary reader, must ruin the book. A critic whom I respect read me a lecture about it. 'Why did you put in all that stuff?' he said. 'You've turned what might have been a good book into journalism.' What he said was true, but I could not have done otherwise. I happened to know, what very few people in England had been allowed to know, that innocent men were being falsely accused. If I had not been angry about that I should never have written the book.

"In one form or another this problem comes up again. The problem of language is subtler and would take too long to discuss. I will only say that of late years I have tried to write less picturesquely and more exactly. In any case I find that by the time you have perfected any style of writing, you have always outgrown it. *Animal Farm* was the first book in which I tried, with full consciousness of what I was doing, to fuse political purpose and artistic purpose into the whole....

"Looking back through the last page or two, I see that I have made it appear as though my motives in writing were wholly public-spirited. I don't want to leave that as the final impression. All writers are vain, selfish, and lazy, and at the very bottom of their motives there lies a mystery. Writing a book is a horrible, exhausting struggle, like a long bout of some painful illness. One would never undertake such a thing if one were not driven on by some demon whom one can neither resist nor understand. For all one knows that demon is simply the same instinct that makes a baby squall for attention. And yet it is also true that one can write nothing readable unless one constantly struggles to efface one's own personality. Good prose is like a windowpane. I cannot say with certainty which of my motives are the strongest, but I know which of them deserve to be followed. And looking back through my work, I see that it is invariably where I lacked a *political* purpose that I wrote lifeless books and was betrayed into purple passages, sentences without meaning, decorative adjectives, and humbug generally."

FOR DISCUSSION

1. What does Orwell mean by his "political purpose" in writing? By his "artistic purpose"? How did he sometimes find it hard to fulfill both purposes?
2. Think about Orwell's remark that "one can write nothing readable unless one constantly struggles to efface one's own personality." From your own experience, have you found any truth in this observation, or any reason to think otherwise?

DAVID SEGAL

Born in Boston in 1964, DAVID SEGAL graduated from Harvard University in 1986 and received a master's degree in politics from Oxford University in 1989. His journalism and essays have appeared in *The New Republic*, *Harper's*, the *Washington Post*, and the *Wall Street Journal*. He has worked as a speechwriter for the Israeli ambassador to the United States and as an editor of *The Washington Monthly*. He is now a reporter for the business section of the *Washington Post*. Segal says he is "happiest," however, "when singing and playing rhythm guitar for the Bremmers, a D.C.-based rock and blues band which makes up in enthusiasm what it lacks in precision."

Excuuuse Me

In this essay for *The New Republic* in May 1992, Segal argues that exaggerated efforts not to offend people's feelings—what has been called "political correctness"—are robbing our tense multicultural society of an essential "safety valve": ethnic and other off-color humor.

"Excuuuse Me" is a strong ARGUMENT for reviving such humor, an argument backed by ANALYSIS of off-color jokes and an examination of their CAUSES AND EFFECTS. Throughout, Segal peppers his essay with EXAMPLES of the kind of humor he has in mind.

It was inevitable that the chill of sensitivity now felt in public discourse and academic life would eventually come to comedy. But P.C.[1] humor has arrived more swiftly—and completely—than even ardent activists could have hoped. Take three films written and directed by David and Jerry Zucker and Jim Abrahams. *Airplane*, released in 1980, has a slew of gay bits, two black men speaking indecipherable jive over subtitles, close to a minyan of Jewish jokes, drug gags, references to bestiality, nun jokes, five obscenities, and one gratuitous front shot of a naked woman. *Naked Gun*, released in 1989, contains only one drug joke, one obscenity, no nudity, not a single Jewish joke, and three gay lines. In 1991 and *Naked Gun 2½*, there were no obscenities, no frontal nudity, just two ethnic slurs, three tentative gay jokes, and one muttered "mazel-tov." Moreover, an earnest stripe of environmentalism is painted down the movie's middle. At the end of the film the protagonist says, "Love is like the ozone layer: you only miss it once it's gone" without a hint of irony.

[1] Politically correct. —EDS.

It's been a long slide downhill. Like the deficit, off-color humor   2
touches everyone but has no constituency, and neither politicians nor
pundits will be clamoring for its return anytime soon. But there are
good reasons to lament its passing. Let me count the ways.

Risqué humor defuses tensions. Lenny Bruce used to do a stand-up   3
routine in which he'd gesture to each ethnic minority in the room and
call them the most offensive names in the book: "I got a nigger here,
two spics there...." When his audience was ready to assault him, he'd
reveal his point: that epithets get at least part of their sting precisely by
being placed off-limits. By spreading the abuse about, you take the sting
out of it. (The caveat, of course, is that if you're going to use ethnic humor, you should avoid singling out any particular group for derision.)
Today's puritans, in contrast, are a drag on our culture, impeding frank
talk about race, sex, class, and sexuality, and deadening our public wit
at the same time. It's no coincidence that in the 1980s, before multiculturalism killed racial jokes, productive discussions of race were more
common.

Risqué humor educates. The experience of American Jews in this   4
country may be the best example of how this works. For decades the
capacity of Jewish comedians to poke fun at the peculiar tics of their
people helped make Jewish otherness, a quality that aroused suspicion
and hatred in bygone eras, something disarming. It's a safe bet that
the films of Mel Brooks and Woody Allen did more to stymie anti-
Semitism in the past twenty years than all the wide-eyed vigilance and
arm-waving of the Anti-Defamation League. When a quick cut-away
shot in *Annie Hall* reveals that the grandmother of Allen's WASPy
girlfriend sees him as a bearded and yarmulked rabbi, we laugh even
as we empathize with his discomfort. Gays have used humor the same
way. You'd be hard-pressed to watch *La Cage Aux Folles*, a musical
about a troupe of mincing gay entertainers, and have your homophobia
strengthened. *Airplane* had a character—John, an air traffic controller
—whose jokes, improvised by gay actor and activist Steve Stucco,
made fun of gay sensibility without attacking it. When someone hands
him a piece of paper and asks what he can make of it, Stucco begins
folding it and says, "Oh a brooch, or a hat, or a pterodactyl."

Risqué humor disarms. A classic—and rare—modern example is *In*   5
Living Color, which showcases merciless skits about black culture. (The
reason it survives the P.C. police is that it's largely written and acted by
blacks.) Witness a *Star Trek* spoof, "The Wrath of Farrakhan," a vicious
lampoon of the black Muslim leader; or a sketch making fun of West
Indians' hard-work habits. The feature "Men on Films," starring
Damon Wayans and David Alan Grier (a.k.a. Antoine and Blaine),
breaks taboos and wows both gay and straight audiences—while en-
raging the humorless activists. One regular skit centers on "Handi

Man," a caped, spastic superhero who foils villains with his dwarf side-kick. To believe this hardens prejudice against people with disabilities is to believe that people are fundamentally barbaric; and assuming the handicapped are too tender a subject for humor is more patronizing than outright disdain. Indeed, there may be no better way to perpetrate a myth of disabled otherness than coming up with euphemisms like "the differently abled" and making irreverent utterances off-limits.

Risqué humor undermines prejudices. A black comic I recently saw   6
had the right idea: He said he got so mad when a grocery clerk snick-ered about his purchase of frozen fried chicken that "I just grabbed my watermelon and tap danced on out of there." The joke both played with stereotypes and ridiculed them: Sometimes the best offense is of-fense. The major problem with ethnic humor—that it is often de-ployed by the powerful against the powerless—is best answered not by silencing the powerful (that hardly takes away their power) but by un-leashing the humorous abilities of the powerless. Allowing ethnic hu-mor means that blacks are allowed to make fun of whites (Eddie Murphy), gays are allowed to make fun of straights (Harvey Fierstein), and women are allowed to make fun of men (Roseanne Barr). In to-day's more ethnically and sexually diverse media, little of this opportu-nity for humor is being realized. Diversity is being achieved; and the result, ironically, is more piety. This is not only a bore, but an insult to the rich traditions of gay, black, Jewish, female, fat, ugly, disabled hu-mor—and a boon to society's wealthy, powerful, and largely unfunny elites.

Risqué humor is funny. Ethnic humor's final defense is that it makes   7
people laugh. In a free society, this is an irrepressible—and admirable —activity, and one I suspect we did more of some years back. Ask your-self: Were you laughing harder a decade ago? When Buck Henry hosted *Saturday Night Live* in the 1970s he'd do a skit in which he played a pe-dophilic baby sitter who got his jollies by playing games with his two nieces, like "find the pocket with the treat" and "show me your dirty laundry." In 1967 Mel Brooks won a best screenplay Academy Award for *The Producers*, which was full of Jewish, gay, and Nazi jokes and is now a confirmed classic. Brooks's 1991 offering was *Life Stinks*, which was bereft of anything off-color and was rightly panned.

As we've pushed the risqué off-stage, we've brought violent slap-   8
stick back on as a means of keeping the audience's attention. *Saturday Night Live* has abandoned racy material in favor of skits like "Horrible Headwound Harry," which features Dana Carvey as a party guest bleed-ing from the head. And last year *Home Alone*, the story of a little boy, played by Macaulay Culkin, who fends off two burglars from his house by, among other things, dropping a hot iron on their heads, became the most lucrative comedy of movie history, grossing more than $285 mil-

lion. The violence was far more explicit than anything the Three Stooges ever came up with, and all of it was done by a 12-year-old. Compare this with *Animal House,* which used to be the top-grossing comedy; it was filled with sexist — and hilarious — moments like the one in which the conscience of Tom Hulce's character advises him to take advantage of his passed-out, underage date.

In a multicultural society like ours, humor is not a threat, it's a crit- ical support. It keeps us sane, and it's a useful safety valve. If we can't be cruel about each other in jest, we might end up being cruel to each other in deadly seriousness. The politically correct war against insensitive humor might end up generating the very social and racial tension it is trying to defuse. 9

QUESTIONS ON MEANING

1. What does Segal mean by the "chill of sensitivity" that he feels has "come to comedy"?
2. Why does Segal believe comedy has become more physically violent?
3. Why does Segal say that "political correctness" in humor is a "boon to society's wealthy, powerful, and largely unfunny elites"?
4. What is Segal's THESIS? Where does he state it?
5. What is Segal's PURPOSE?

QUESTIONS ON WRITING STRATEGY

1. From the EVIDENCE of the essay itself, whom does Segal see as his AUDIENCE? How old are they? What are their attitudes toward his subject?
2. What is Segal's TONE? In this essay on humor, does he try to be funny? Why, or why not?
3. **MIXED METHODS.** Segal's ARGUMENT is supported mainly by ANALYSIS of off-color humor and of its EFFECTS. List the elements he identifies in such humor and the effects of each.
4. **MIXED METHODS.** Consider the EXAMPLES Segal uses to support his argument. Do they convince you? Can you think of other examples that might undermine Segal's thesis?

QUESTIONS ON LANGUAGE

1. Segal uses several words and phrases from show business. Can you give meanings for these: bits (para. 1); routine (3); cut-away shot, improvised (4); skits (5); panned (7); slapstick, grossing (8)?
2. What are the CONNOTATIONS of the word "puritans" (para. 3)? Why does Segal apply it to advocates of "political correctness"? How is its use IRONIC here?

3. What does Segal mean by "a myth of disabled otherness" (para. 5)?
4. Supply definitions for the following words: gratuitous (para. 1); pundits (2); risqué, epithets, caveat (3); tics, stymie (4); piety (6); pedophilic, bereft (7).

SUGGESTIONS FOR WRITING

1. **JOURNAL WRITING.** Almost everyone has been the butt of someone else's joke. Write about a time when you found yourself in this position, either as an individual or as a member of a group being stereotyped. What happened? How did you react?

   FROM JOURNAL TO ESSAY. Develop your experience of being the butt of a joke into a NARRATIVE essay that reveals why this experience was or was not funny. Lots of vivid details will bring this experience alive for your readers.

2. Argue in favor of some widely criticized media content. Examples: religious television programming, "feelings"-oriented children's songs and videos, violent horror movies, sexy music videos. Why are the critics wrong? How does this entertainment contribute to society?

3. **CRITICAL WRITING.** Write an essay in which you agree or disagree with Segal. If you agree with him, extend his argument in some way, such as discussing how other supposed insensitivities actually benefit our culture. If you disagree with Segal, refute his claims one by one. In either case, be as careful as Segal is to supply clear reasons and specific examples.

4. **CONNECTIONS (PART ONE).** COMPARE this essay with Michiko Kakutani's "The Word Police" (p. 287). How do the authors conceive of "political correctness" in similar ways? How do their conceptions differ? Which author would give free speech greater leeway? What do *you* think of their arguments?

5. **CONNECTIONS (PART TWO).** Consider this essay in the light of George Orwell's "Politics and the English Language" (p. 526). On what points do the two writers seem to agree? On what do they disagree? If Orwell were alive today, what stance do you think he would take on the issue of "politically correct" humor? Support your claim with evidence from his essay.

DAVID SEGAL ON WRITING

For *The Bedford Reader,* David Segal provided some good pointers on writing arguments.

"Every opinion essay, like a springboard dive, comes with a degree-of-difficulty factor—the more outrageous the argument, the more points you get for simply trying to make it. 'What's Right with Mother Teresa' would no doubt be a tale of noble sentiments and heart-warming anecdotes, but it promises all the flair of a pool-side two-hand cannonball. 'The Case Against Mother Teresa,' on the other hand, is a full-twisting triple back flip off the three-meter board. And probably a lot of fun to read.

"Ideally, a piece like 'Excuuuse Me' convinces a reader of something that he or she didn't believe at the start, and that means some finesse work is necessary. I like to imagine when I write an argument like 'Excuuuse Me' that I have my arm slung chummily around a friend—a college roommate perhaps—and I'm quietly and earnestly talking as we walk.

"Usually my strategy is to make an argument that carries him along a seamless path. 'You believe this, right?' 'Well, yeah,' I hear back. 'Then you also have to believe this,' I reply. 'I guess,' he replies. 'In that case you also agree that...' And so on until by the end of our walk he's in some place that he never thought he'd be, allowing, with a hint of resignation, that we actually are of one mind on an issue he thought we disagreed about.

"For 'Excuuuse Me' I used a variant of that strategy: Instead of linking the ideas, I simply piled one on top of the other. In this case, I'm saying to my reader, 'Look, here's a mass of evidence to support my idea. You might not buy all the evidence, but you'll probably buy some of it.' When your reader agrees with enough of what you've written, you win. And if your point is sufficiently outlandish, winning is just like nailing that triple back flip and getting a 9.9 from the competitor's toughest judge."

FOR DISCUSSION

1. How does Segal conceive of his AUDIENCE? What does he have to do to achieve his PURPOSE with this audience?
2. Segal doesn't mention whether he cares about his subject in addition to finding it challenging. Judging from "Excuuuse Me," do you think he does? Why?
3. Consider Segal's comments about the structure and the use of EVIDENCE in "Excuuuse Me." Were you aware of these strategies when reading the essay?
4. Out of ten possible points, what score would *you* give Segal's essay? Why?

MARCO WILKINSON

MARCO WILKINSON was born on July 1, 1976, in West Warwick, Rhode Island, and grew up there. He attended La Salle Academy in nearby Providence, where he was involved in the theater, an after-school writing workshop, and a student group committed to community issues and service. Wilkinson graduated from La Salle in 1994 and won a National Merit Scholarship. He is currently a junior at New York University, where he is majoring in English and is one of his college's Presidential Scholars. In addition to academic papers, Wilkinson writes poetry and short fiction. He is considering graduate school in English, possibly concentrating on literature and gender.

Exposing Truth
for the Lie That It Is

Wilkinson wrote this essay as a student in NYU's freshman composition program, and it was reprinted in Mercer Street, an NYU collection. Witnessing a lively festival and reading another writer, Wilkinson reinterprets his own life and the very meaning of reality.

Overall, this essay is an ARGUMENT in favor of a certain view of language and reality, but within paragraphs Wilkinson uses DIVISION or ANALYSIS, CAUSE AND EFFECT, and DEFINITION. Through NARRATION and DESCRIPTION Wilkinson depicts particular incidents and scenes. With EXAMPLE he brings abstractions to earth.

Cheerleaders with beards strolled arm in arm down the street. 1 "Women" with three-foot-high green bee-hives giggled at silver-lamé suited space boys. Six-foot-five divas draped in sequins and heels and attitudes that extended around them like magical auras sauntered along, too beautiful, too glamorous, to even notice the ordinary people around them. But if a camera, glinting in the sunlight, caught their eyes, they turned fiercely, like dragons with glittering scales, not to attack, but to pose. Some over nine feet tall in full regalia, they were totems of defiance against any attempt at definition. This was Wigstock, a festival of drag and a window into the recent disappearance of "Truth" from the West's intellectual landscape.

I walked into this wonderland unassumingly and was sucked into 2 its surreal reality. It turned out to be the perfect introduction to my studies at NYU because it showed me just how slippery and ultimately untenable "Truth" can be. I came to this city and this school for many reasons, but one of them was because I am gay, and I wanted to live in an environment that was not only tolerant but actively accepting of that part of myself. I had gone to a Catholic high school, where, surprisingly enough, I received the most support as I began to work out for myself a definition for my sexuality. In high school I embraced what I suppose is our society's mainstream pro-gay stance: "Sexual orientation and gender are natural, maybe even biological, and not a matter of choice; thus homosexuality should not be condemned." In the spirit of this position even my religion teachers took on the issue of homosexuality in classes on morality, teaching tolerance and acceptance. And yet, after my experiences in New York, starting with Wigstock, I can see how simplistic and even demeaning the argument really is. Coming in the form of a justification, it amounts to little more than an excuse for my existence. "Marco is gay, but it can't be helped."

"Well, honey, are you gonna take my picture or are you gonna let   3 all this beauty go to waste?"

I just stood there for several seconds in awe. What was I to make of   4 a seven-foot-tall Diana Ross with an impossibly deep voice and a dress of purple sequins that trailed forever behind her on the soft summer breeze? This, contrary to everything I ever believed in support of my sexuality, was certainly not natural. The lush purple eyeshadow and the glittering lipstick still moist on her smile were certainly chosen, not forced by mysterious natural forces onto this person's face. And though it was all unnatural, it was still beautiful. This utterly unreal vision before me evoked a sense of liberty that made the "natural, biological" argument that had once wrapped around me like a warm coat, protecting me from the cold barbs of my high school peers, seem more like a straitjacket—restraining, uncomfortable, and untrue.

This new sense of discomfort over my own sense of self-definition   5 stayed with me, through experience and study, until this semester when I was introduced to Stanley Fish, whose ideas clarified for me issues that were quickly dismantling that old "natural" argument before my eyes. In his essay, "How To Recognize A Poem When You See One," Fish, a prominent literary theorist, discusses the ability of words to take on multiple meanings and examines the source of those meanings. He proposes that meaning rests not in the object of interpretation but in the method by which the object is interpreted.

He recounts how he taught two classes in very different subjects,   6 linguistics and religious poetry, and how the same words, a list of names on the chalkboard, could have very different meanings. In his linguistics class the list of names was for a reading assignment. In his religious poetry class he found that his students easily understood the list of names as a poem, finding lucid and appropriate meanings within the context of religious poetry. Fish presents us with a problem here of one object containing multiple meanings whose answer, while addressed to the literary community, begs for application in wider and wider circles of understanding life, including understanding of one's own sexuality.

How can the same word or words explode with an infinity of mean-   7
ings without creating meaninglessness? How can something as complex as gender and desire be crystallized into stasis and objectivity? The
answer is in the act of recognition, simple enough at first glance but a
complex process under Fish's keen eye. Fish writes that while we may
believe we recognize poetry by its distinguishing features, with his students "it was the act of recognition that came first . . . and the distinguishing features that followed." Meaning rises up after the interpreter
is able to name what she or he sees. This naming allows for a construction of parts to fit the interpreter's idea of a pre-supposed whole. "Definitions," Fish writes, "instruct them [the interpreters] in ways of
looking that will produce what they expect to see." Thus, a series of
words, as in Fish's example, can be both an assignment and a poem, depending upon the name or blueprint according to which the parts are
arranged and viewed.

In my own life, as I look back, I can see clearly now that moment   8
when, standing in the middle of my kitchen at the age of fifteen, I
thought to myself, "I am gay." The sentence raced faster and faster
through my head, organizing all of the emotions, thoughts, and experiences that I had until that moment been unable to name. I can see
now how from that moment on I began rearranging the parts of my
life to fit this definition. My mistake was in thinking that I had discovered a "fact," when now I realize that no such thing can objectively exist.

Fish goes on in his essay to explain that we do not notice this   9
process of definition and construction because the definitions, the
blueprints by which we organize and understand our lives, have been
inculcated in us by society so deeply that they appear to be natural
facts. At once creating a mask of reality which veils our constructs, it
also holds all of our individual constructs of "reality" together so that
life doesn't disintegrate into meaninglessness. In a world where each
person constructs her or his own reality there is surprisingly less variety
than one would think, Fish points out, because we all get our supply of
definitions and categories by which to interpret the world from the
same reservoir of information. As parts of the same society we see the
world in remarkably similar ways.

When the thought "I am gay" occurred to me, I was working with   10
a definition that, for better or worse, I received, like everybody else,
from the society in which I was raised. Thus, just as I was reconstructing my life in the image of a definition I shared with everyone around
me, they were all interpreting this newly reconstructed self using the
same definition I was using. I was making myself "gay" and they were

seeing someone who was "gay." The fact that both the viewer and the viewed share the same definition from society works to create the veneer of naturalness. But there are problems with the "naturalness" that is created, because it reduces the complexity of the process by which we understand reality to mere objectivity. Although it seems so, nothing has inherent meaning. It is precisely the inherency implicit in a "natural" approach to reality that makes it so unnatural.

This unnaturalness sometimes allows for cracks to form in the mask   11
of a "natural" reality, creating a sense of unease which offers a chance at insight. In my own experience I could never construct a perfect mask of real "gayness" to fit over my face. I always felt a subtle sense of alienation from myself because I could never quite get the parts of my life to fit the mold of "gayness" which I knew, even though I was supposed to be "naturally" gay.

"Honey, a goddess is a rare thing. Are you just gonna stand there or   12
are you gonna take my picture?" The drag queen's immaculately tweezed eyebrows arched up and her sparkling lips puckered inquisitively. I smiled and snapped a quick shot before she moved on to other admirers.

Looking back on Wigstock I can see that it was but the first foray   13
into a world of illusion and artifice that has grown larger and larger as my studies show me just how complex a problem "reality" can be. The drag queens are transformed. No longer otherworldly divas, their wigs have become helmets, their dresses armor. In my mind now they stand as warriors who fight not on the side of "Truth," but, in fact, to expose the lie that "Truth" is. I thank them and Stanley Fish for helping me loose myself from the straitjacket of "naturalness." I am unnatural. I am queer.

QUESTIONS ON MEANING

1. What is Wilkinson's objection to what he sees as "society's mainstream pro-gay stance" (para. 2)?
2. Why does Wilkinson choose drag queens to symbolize the "slipperiness" of truth?
3. What similarity does Wilkinson see between the drag queens at Wigstock and the list of words on Stanley Fish's blackboard?
4. In a sentence or two, SUMMARIZE Wilkinson's ARGUMENT about the relativity of truth. How is truth a "lie"?
5. What is Wilkinson's PURPOSE? Is the essay more a DEFINITION of truth or more an argument seeking to change behaviors or attitudes?

QUESTIONS ON WRITING STRATEGY

1. What is the EFFECT of Wilkinson's opening DESCRIPTION?
2. Who, other than the professor for whom it was originally written, might be an appropriate AUDIENCE for this essay?
3. **MIXED METHODS.** Wilkinson combines NARRATION, description, and EXAMPLE to support an argument. Explain the structure of the essay. What is the advantage of its narrative frame?
4. **MIXED METHODS.** How does the example in paragraph 8 illustrate the CAUSE-AND-EFFECT relationship outlined in paragraph 7?

QUESTIONS ON LANGUAGE

1. How does the language Wilkinson uses to describe the drag queens at Wigstock emphasize their "unnaturalness"?
2. Wilkinson uses several SIMILES and METAPHORS in this essay. Give a few examples.
3. Explain the IRONY of the last sentence. What meaning does it take on in the context of the essay?
4. Make sure you know the meanings of the following words: lamé, regalia, totems (para. 1); unassumingly, surreal, untenable, demeaning (2); barbs (4); lucid (6); crystallized, stasis (7); inculcated, constructs (noun), reservoir (9); immaculately, inquisitively (12); foray, artifice, divas (13).

SUGGESTIONS FOR WRITING

1. **JOURNAL WRITING.** Wilkinson talks about his "sense of discomfort over my own sense of self-definition" (para. 5), about "rearranging the parts of my life to fit this definition" (8). Consider the categories that you use to define yourself or that others place you in. Are you known as a "straight-A student," a "jock," a "slacker," a "popular kid"? Even if you don't match any of these types, spend some time writing about how you think about yourself.

   FROM JOURNAL TO ESSAY. Write an essay about your sense of self. How do your own or others' expectations of you shape your behavior? To what extent are you created by your own or others' definition of you, and what happens when, as in Wilkinson's case, that definition is called into question? Do you take comfort in being able to categorize yourself as a type, or do you resist any attempt at such GENERALIZATION?
2. What do you think of Wilkinson's pronouncement of "the recent disappearance of 'Truth' from the West's intellectual landscape" (para. 1)? What are the implications of his refusal to accept the "veneer of naturalness" (10) that most people rely on to cope with the complexity of reality? Is it possible never to generalize or to label anyone or anything? Would this lead to freedom or to "meaninglessness" (9)?
3. **CRITICAL WRITING.** In an essay, ANALYZE Wilkinson's STYLE and DICTION. To what extent, in your opinion, are they influenced by the fact that the essay was originally written for a class? Does the essay's somewhat academic style add to or detract from its persuasiveness? How might an essay on the same

subject be different if it appeared in a mainstream magazine such as *Time,
Newsweek, Esquire,* or *Vogue?*

4. **CONNECTIONS (PART ONE).** This essay and Annie Dillard's "The Chase" (p.
   59) both describe moments of epiphany, when truths previously unrecognized immediately become apparent. For Wilkinson, the realization that he
   was gay immediately explained "all the emotions, thoughts, and experiences that I had until that moment been unable to name." In Dillard's case,
   a simple childhood experience taught her a lifelong lesson about human
   nature. Write a NARRATIVE essay about an epiphany you have experienced.
   What were the circumstances surrounding it, and what did it teach you?

5. **CONNECTIONS (PART TWO).** How does Wilkinson's belief about the instability of truth compare with George Orwell's ASSUMPTIONS about truth in
   "Politics and the English Language" (p. 526)? How would Orwell respond
   to Wilkinson's claim that "no such thing [as a fact] can objectively exist"
   (para. 8)? What would Wilkinson have to say about Orwell's discussion of
   abstract words (19)? Are their two sets of assumptions about the nature of
   truth compatible?

MARCO WILKINSON ON WRITING

For *The Bedford Reader,* Marco Wilkinson offered these insights
into writing, language, and truth:

"The blank computer screen, the blinking cursor, the emptiness
calling out to be filled: They still inspire a terror in me, even now as I'm
writing these words. What if I write the wrong thing? Or worse, what if
I don't have anything at all to write? The writing process is such a mysterious thing. You feel something: a thought, an emotion, something
you can't even name. You try to express this thing, to exhume it and
look at it in the light of day, by writing it. You share this expression of
yourself with others. Do they see it, this wonder you've dug out of yourself? 'No, it's not *that,*' they say, 'it's *this,*' and each of them produces a
different thing, their own prized objects, dug up out of the fertile
ground of their own experience.

"This shouldn't be discouraging, though. It's only if you hold on to
the idea that there's any such thing as a 'truth' that can be communicated to others that writing will fail you. Sure, you're holding it in your
hands, this feeling, this thought, this 'thing' that is you, and it's 'true'
for you, but writing will never truly express this thing to another person. I think writing at its best is a kind of mirror. The prize you find
might be valuable only for yourself, but by writing it down you also
write the process by which you retrieved it. This process is perhaps
more important because those who read will hear in it an echo of a road
they need to take to find their own prizes. Holding up your 'truth' for
others allows them to see their own 'truths.'

"Writing for me is a conversation between idea and experience. Experiences trigger ideas. Ideas give meaning to experiences. Experiences embody ideas and ideas wrap meaning around experiences. This reciprocal relationship constructs a kind of 'truth' that creates a whole out of the two parts for the reader. For me as a writer an idea and an experience are two totally separate events. In 'Exposing Truth for the Lie That It Is,' my description of Wigstock evolved out of a sketch I had written some six months before I had even read anything by Stanley Fish. I think it's important to write down experiences, no matter how trivial, banal, or unintelligible they might seem at the time. If they strike a chord in you, then hold on to them through writing. One day, weeks, months, or years later, some idea will come and shape that experience and others, constructing out of them a whole, a 'truth.' Likewise an idea that at first seems elusive, untenable, or downright ridiculous may just need an experience to give it life, to take the word and make it flesh.

"I don't think there's anything 'natural' about writing. Inspired words dropped like rose petals from some muse up above seems like an idealistic wish that sets the writer up for disappointment. The yoking of idea and experience to each other is a craft, an unnatural process of interpretation that is deliberate and calculated. But then again I know that whenever I sit down to write and finally overcome that terror of the blank screen, I write but something strange happens. I start with an intention, a goal of expression, but by the time the words reach the screen they are different. They've metamorphosed, slid sideways into some unforeseen tangent that often takes me in a different, but ultimately better, direction. Maybe this loss of control between the mind and the hand is really just an illustration of the immediacy of the mind's ability to reconstruct, reconfigure, reality into some kind of sense. All interpretation, even our perception of 'reality,' is an unnatural and artificial process. So when you can't express exactly what you want to, don't see this as failure. Don't clamp down on your thoughts but let go of the reins and see what treasures come to the surface. Later on you can always refine what you've written.

"The writing (and reading) process has a lot to do with finding your 'truth' but also with seeing how that 'truth' came about. We live in a world where meanings mount and collapse. The writer negotiates the borders, following that thin line called 'truth.' Walking that line is a dance, a game to be played, a joke to be laughed at."

FOR DISCUSSION

1. What benefits does Wilkinson see in keeping notes on one's experiences? How did such journal keeping help him with "Exposing Truth for the Lie That It Is"?

2. Wilkinson often discovers that words have "metamorphosed"—changed utterly—traveling from his mind to his computer screen. Have you ever experienced the "loss of control between the mind and the hand" that Wilkinson writes of? Have you found it productive or not? Why?

12

THE POWER OF FAMILY

What is the hold, for good or ill, that family members have on one another? What do our families do for, or to, us? The essays in this chapter can only begin to answer such questions, but they are so varied that just about everyone will hear in them a familiar chord or two. In "Stone Soup," Barbara Kingsolver explores what makes a family today, when the traditional model is but one of many options. In "Aria: A Memoir of a Bilingual Childhood," Richard Rodriguez recalls the loss he experienced when English supplanted Spanish in his Mexican American family. And in "No Name Woman," Maxine Hong Kingston tries to imagine what pressures of family led her Chinese aunt to drown herself in the household well.

BARBARA KINGSOLVER

A writer of fiction, poetry, and nonfiction and a self-described "human rights activist," BARBARA KINGSOLVER was born in Annapolis, Maryland, in 1955 and grew up in eastern Kentucky. She studied biology at De Pauw University (B.A., 1977) and the University of Arizona (M.S., 1981) and worked in the field as a researcher and technical writer. A full-time writer since 1985, Kingsolver has published the novels *The Bean Trees* (1988), *Animal Dreams* (1990), and *Pigs in Heaven* (1993); a story collection, *Homeland and Other Stories* (1989); a poetry collection, *Another America* (1990); and an essay collection, *High Tide in Tucson* (1995). She lives in Tucson, a desert setting that she prefers because it "makes you pay attention to color and contrast and hard edges, in terms of both physical landscape and human landscape."

Stone Soup

This essay on the contemporary family relies on part on Kingsolver's own experiences, because, she says, "You can't just put the ideas there. You have to put clothes on them and make them walk around." One of the essays collected in *High Tide in Tucson*, "Stone Soup" originally appeared in *Parenting* magazine in 1995.

"Stone Soup" is an ARGUMENT in favor of a DEFINITION — a broader definition of *family* than "mother, father, two kids." Kingsolver supports her argument mainly with NARRATIVES of her own and others' experiences, which she uses as EXAMPLES, with COMPARISON of traditional and nontraditional families, and with analysis of the CAUSES AND EFFECTS of various family arrangements.

In the catalog of family values, where do we rank an occasion like 1 this? A curly-haired boy who wanted to run before he walked, age seven now, a soccer player scoring a winning goal. He turns to the bleachers with his fists in the air and a smile wide as a gap-toothed galaxy. His own cheering section of grown-ups and kids all leap to their feet and hug each other, delirious with love for this boy. He's Andy, my best friend's son. The cheering section includes his mother and her friends, his brother, his father and stepmother, a stepbrother and stepsister, and a grandparent. Lucky is the child with this many relatives on hand to hail a proud accomplishment. I'm there too, witnessing a family fortune. But in spite of myself, defensive words take shape in my head. I am thinking: I dare *anybody* to call this a broken home.

Families change, and remain the same. Why are our names for 2 home so slow to catch up to the truth of where we live?

When I was a child, I had two parents who loved me without cease. 3
One of them attended every excuse for attention I ever contrived, and
the other made it to the ones with higher production values, like piano
recitals and appendicitis. So I was a lucky child too. I played with a set
of paper dolls called "The Family of Dolls," four in number, who came
with the factory-assigned names of Dad, Mom, Sis, and Junior. I think
you know what they looked like, at least before I loved them to death
and their heads fell off.

Now I've replaced the dolls with a life. I knit my days around my 4
daughter's survival and happiness, and am proud to say her head is still
on. But we aren't the Family of Dolls. Maybe you're not, either. And if
not, even though you are statistically no oddity, it's probably been suggested to you in a hundred ways that yours isn't exactly a real family, but
an impostor family, a harbinger of cultural ruin, a slapdash substitute —
something like counterfeit money. Here at the tail end of our century,
most of us are up to our ears in the noisy business of trying to support and
love a thing called family. But there's a current in the air with ferocious
moral force that finds its way even into political campaigns, claiming
there is only one right way to do it, the Way It Has Always Been.

In the face of a thriving, particolored world, this narrow view is so 5
pickled and absurd I'm astonished that it gets airplay. And I'm astonished that it still stings.

Every parent has endured the arrogance of a child-unfriendly 6
grump sitting in judgment, explaining what those kids of ours really
need (for example, "a good licking"). If we're polite, we move our crew
to another bench in the park. If we're forthright (as I am in my mind,
only, for the rest of the day), we fix them with a sweet imperious stare
and say, "Come back and let's talk about it after you've changed a thousand diapers."

But it's harder somehow to shrug off the Family-of-Dolls Family 7
Values crew when they judge (from their safe distance) that divorced
people, blended families, gay families, and single parents are failures.
That our children are at risk, and the whole arrangement is messy and
embarrassing. A marriage that ends is not called "finished," it's called
failed. The children of this family may have been born to a happy
union, but now they are called *the children of divorce*.

I had no idea how thoroughly these assumptions overlaid my cul- 8
ture until I went through divorce myself. I wrote to a friend: "This
might be worse than being widowed. Overnight I've suffered the same
losses — companionship, financial and practical support, my identity as
a wife and partner, the future I'd taken for granted. I am lonely, grieving, and hard-pressed to take care of my household alone. But instead
of bringing casseroles, people are acting like I had a fit and broke up the
family china."

Once upon a time I held these beliefs about divorce: That everyone   9
who does it could have chosen not to do it. That it's a lazy way out of
marital problems. That it selfishly puts personal happiness ahead of
family integrity. Now I tremble for my ignorance. It's easy, in fortunate
times, to forget about the ambush that could leave your head reeling:
serious mental or physical illness, death in the family, abandonment, financial calamity, humiliation, violence, despair.

I started out like any child, intent on being the Family of Dolls. I   10
set upon young womanhood believing in most of the doctrines of my
generation: I wore my skirts four inches above the knee. I had that Barbie with her zebra-striped swimsuit and a figure unlike anything found
in nature. And I understood the Prince Charming Theory of Marriage,
a quest for Mr. Right that ends smack dab where you find him. I did not
completely understand that another whole story *begins* there, and no
fairy tale prepared me for the combination of bad luck and persistent
hope that would interrupt my dream and lead me to other arrangements. Like a cancer diagnosis, a dying marriage is a thing to fight, to
deny, and finally, when there's no choice left, to dig in and survive.
Casseroles would help. Likewise, I imagine it must be a painful reckoning in adolescence (or later on) to realize one's own true love will never
look like the soft-focus fragrance ads because Prince Charming (surprise!) is a princess. Or vice versa. Or has skin the color your parents
didn't want you messing with, except in the Crayola box.

It's awfully easy to hold in contempt the straw broken home, and   11
that mythical category of persons who toss away nuclear family for the
sheer fun of it. Even the legal terms we use have a suggestion of caprice.
I resent the phrase "irreconcilable differences," which suggests a stubborn refusal to accept a spouse's little quirks. This is specious. Every happily married couple I know has loads of irreconcilable differences.
Negotiating where to set the thermostat is not the point. A nonfunc-
tioning marriage is a slow asphyxiation. It is waking up despised each
morning, listening to the pulse of your own loneliness before the radio
begins to blare its raucous gospel that you're nothing if you aren't loved.
It is sharing your airless house with the threat of suicide or other kinds of
violence, while the ghost that whispers, "Leave here and destroy your
children," has passed over every door and nailed it shut. Disassembling
a marriage in these circumstances is as much *fun* as amputating your own
gangrenous leg. You do it, if you can, to save a life—or two, or more.

I know of no one who really went looking to hoe the harder row,   12
especially the daunting one of single parenthood. Yet it seems to be the
most American of customs to blame the burdened for their destiny.
We'd like so desperately to believe in freedom and justice for all, we
can hardly name that rogue bad luck, even when he's a close enough
snake to bite us. In the wake of my divorce, some friends (even a few

close ones) chose to vanish, rather than linger within striking distance of misfortune.

But most stuck around, bless their hearts, and if I'm any the wiser 13 for my trials, it's from having learned the worth of steadfast friendship. And also, what not to say. The least helpful question is: "Did you want the divorce, or didn't you?" Did I want to keep that gangrenous leg, or not? How to explain, in a culture that venerates choice: Two terrifying options are much worse than none at all. Give me any day the quick hand of cruel fate that will leave me scarred but blameless. As it was, I kept thinking of that wicked third-grade joke in which some boy comes up behind you and grabs your ear, starts in with a prolonged tug, and asks, "Do you want this ear any longer?"

Still, the friend who holds your hand and says the wrong thing is 14 made of dearer stuff than the one who stays away. And generally, through all of it, you live. My favorite fictional character, Kate Vaiden (in the novel by Reynolds Price), advises: "Strength just comes in one brand — you stand up at sunrise and meet what they send you and keep your hair combed."

Once you've weathered the straits, you get to cross the tricky junc- 15 ture from casualty to survivor. If you're on your feet at the end of a year or two, and have begun putting together a happy new existence, those friends who were kind enough to feel sorry for you when you needed it must now accept you back to the ranks of the living. If you're truly blessed, they will dance at your second wedding. Everybody else, for heaven's sake, should stop throwing stones.

Arguing about whether nontraditional families deserve pity or tol- 16 erance is a little like the medieval debate about left-handedness as a mark of the devil. Divorce, remarriage, single parenthood, gay parents, and blended families simply are. They're facts of our time. Some of the reasons listed by sociologists for these family reconstructions are: the idea of marriage as a romantic partnership rather than a pragmatic one; a shift in women's expectations, from servility to self-respect and inde- pendence; and longevity (prior to antibiotics no marriage was expected to last many decades — in Colonial days the average couple lived to be married less than twelve years). Add to all this, our growing sense of entitlement to happiness and safety from abuse. Most would agree these are all good things. Yet their result — a culture in which serial monogamy and the consequent reshaping of families are the norm — gets diagnosed as "failing."

For many of us, once we have put ourselves Humpty-Dumpty-wise 17 back together again, the main problem with our reorganized family is that other people think we have a problem. My daughter tells me the only time she's uncomfortable about being the child of divorced parents is when her friends say they feel sorry for her. It's a bizarre sympathy, given that half the kids in her school and nation are in the same boat, pursuing childish happiness with the same energy as their married-parent peers. When anyone asks how *she* feels about it, she spontaneously lists the benefits: Our house is in the country and we have a dog, but she can go to her dad's neighborhood for the urban thrills of a pool and sidewalks for roller-skating. What's more, she has three sets of grandparents!

Why is it surprising that a child would revel in a widened family 18 and the right to feel at home in more than one house? Isn't it the opposite that should worry us—a child with no home at all, or too few resources to feel safe? The child at risk is the one whose parents are too immature themselves to guide wisely; too diminished by poverty to nurture; too far from opportunity to offer hope. The number of children in the U.S. living in poverty at this moment is almost unfathomably large: 20 percent. There are families among us that need help all right, and by no means are they new on the landscape. The rate at which teenage girls had babies in 1957 (ninety-six per thousand) was twice what it is now. That remarkable statistic is ignored by the religious right—probably because the teen birth rate was cut in half mainly by legalized abortion. In fact, the policy gatekeepers who coined the phrase "family values" have steadfastly ignored the desperation of too-small families, and since 1979 have steadily reduced the amount of financial support available to a single parent. But, this camp's most outspoken attacks seem aimed at the notion of families getting too complex, with add-ons and extras such as a gay parent's partner, or a remarried mother's new husband and his children.

To judge a family's value by its tidy symmetry is to purchase a book 19 for its cover. There's no moral authority there. The famous family comprised of Dad, Mom, Sis, and Junior living as an isolated economic unit is not built on historical bedrock. In *The Way We Never Were,* Stephanie Coontz writes, "Whenever people propose that we go back to the traditional family, I always suggest that they pick a ballpark date for the family they have in mind." Colonial families were tidily disciplined, but their members (meaning everyone but infants) labored incessantly and died young. Then the Victorian family adopted a new division of labor, in which women's role was domestic and children were allowed time for study and play, but this was an upper-class construct supported by myriad slaves. Coontz writes, "For every nineteenth-century middle-class family that protected its wife and child within the family circle, there was an Irish or German girl scrubbing floors...a Welsh boy mining coal to keep the home-baked goodies warm, a black girl doing the family laundry, a black mother and child picking cotton to be made into clothes for the family, and a Jewish or an Italian daugh-

ter in a sweatshop making 'ladies' dresses or artificial flowers for the
family to purchase."

The abolition of slavery brought slightly more democratic arrange- 20
ments, in which extended families were harnessed together in cottage
industries; at the turn of the century came a steep rise in child labor in
mines and sweatshops. Twenty percent of American children lived in
orphanages at the time; their parents were not necessarily dead, but
couldn't afford to keep them.

During the Depression and up to the end of World War II, many 21
millions of U.S. households were more multigenerational than nuclear.
Women my grandmother's age were likely to live with a fluid assort-
ment of elderly relatives, in-laws, siblings, and children. In many cases
they spent virtually every waking hour working in the company of
other women — a companionable scenario in which it would be easier,
I imagine, to tolerate an estranged or difficult spouse. I'm reluctant to
idealize a life of so much hard work and so little spousal intimacy, but
its advantage may have been resilience. A family so large and varied
would not easily be brought down by a single blow: It could absorb a
death, long illness, an abandonment here or there, and any number of
irreconcilable differences.

The Family of Dolls came along midcentury as a great American 22
experiment. A booming economy required a mobile labor force and demanded that women surrender jobs to returning soldiers. Families came
to be defined by a single breadwinner. They struck out for single-family
homes at an earlier age than ever before, and in unprecedented numbers they raised children in suburban isolation. The nuclear family was
launched to sink or swim.

More than a few sank. Social historians corroborate that the sub- 23
urban family of the postwar economic boom, which we have recently
selected as our definition of "traditional," was no panacea. Twenty-five
percent of Americans were poor in the mid-1950s, and as yet there
were no food stamps. Sixty percent of the elderly lived on less than
$1,000 a year, and most had no medical insurance. In the sequestered
suburbs, alcoholism and sexual abuse of children were far more widespread than anyone imagined.

Expectations soared, and the economy sagged. It's hard to depend 24
on one other adult for everything, come what may. In the last three
decades, that amorphous, adaptable structure we call "family" has been
reshaped once more by economic tides. Compared with fifties families,
mothers are far more likely now to be employed. We are statistically
more likely to divorce, and to live in blended families or other extranuclear arrangements. We are also more likely to plan and space our
children, and to rate our marriages as "happy." We are less likely to suffer abuse without recourse, or to stare out at our lives through a glaze of

prescription tranquilizers. Our aged parents are less likely to be destitute, and we're half as likely to have a teenage daughter turn up a mother herself. All in all, I would say that if "intact" in modern family-values jargon means living quietly desperate in the bell jar,[1] then hip-hip-hooray for "broken." A neat family model constructed to service the Baby Boom economy seems to be returning gradually to a grand, lumpy shape that human families apparently have tended toward since they first took root in the Olduvai Gorge.[2] We're social animals, deeply fond of companionship, and children love best to run in packs. If there is a *normal* for humans, at all, I expect it looks like two or three Families of Dolls, connected variously by kinship and passion, shuffled like cards and strewn over several shoeboxes.

The sooner we can let go the fairy tale of families functioning perfectly in isolation, the better we might embrace the relief of community. Even the admirable parents who've stayed married through thick and thin are very likely, at present, to incorporate other adults into their families—household help and baby-sitters if they can afford them, or neighbors and grandparents if they can't. For single parents, this support is the rock-bottom definition of family. And most parents who have split apart, however painfully, still manage to maintain family continuity for their children, creating in many cases a boisterous phenomenon that Constance Ahrons in her book *The Good Divorce* calls the "binuclear family." Call it what you will—when ex-spouses beat swords into plowshares and jump up and down at a soccer game together, it makes for happy kids.   25

Cinderella, look, who needs her? All those evil stepsisters? That story always seemed like too much cotton-picking fuss over clothes. A childhood tale that fascinated me more was the one called "Stone Soup," and the gist of it is this: Once upon a time, a pair of beleaguered soldiers straggled home to a village empty-handed, in a land ruined by war. They were famished, but the villagers had so little they shouted evil words and slammed their doors. So the soldiers dragged out a big kettle, filled it with water, and put it on a fire to boil. They rolled a clean round stone into the pot, while the villagers peered through their curtains in amazement.   26

"What kind of soup is that?" they hooted.   27

"Stone soup," the soldiers replied. "Everybody can have some when it's done."   28

---

[1] A glass vessel shaped like a bell, used to contain a delicate object or a controlled experiment. — Eds.

[2] A site in Tanzania, East Africa, where remains of some of the earliest human ancestors have been discovered. — Eds.

"Well, thanks," one matron grumbled, coming out with a shriveled   29
carrot. "But it'd be better if you threw this in."

And so on, of course, a vegetable at a time, until the whole suspi-   30
cious village managed to feed itself grandly.

Any family is a big empty pot, save for what gets thrown in. Each   31
stew turns out different. Generosity, a resolve to turn bad luck into
good, and respect for variety—these things will nourish a nation of
children. Name-calling and suspicion will not. My soup contains a rock
or two of hard times, and maybe yours does too. I expect it's a heck of a
bouillabaisse.

QUESTIONS ON MEANING

1. Kingsolver uses the phrase "family values" in her first line and refers to the
   idea many times throughout. What are the CONNOTATIONS of this phrase?
   What is the connection between this phrase and Kingsolver's PURPOSE?
2. What is Kingsolver trying to suggest with the RHETORICAL QUESTION in paragraph 2: "Why are our names for home so slow to catch up with the truth
   of where we live?"
3. Kingsolver claims that the "Way It Has Always Been" has a "ferocious
   moral force," but then immediately labels this a "narrow...pickled" view of
   the world (paras. 4–5). What does each interpretation mean? What does
   this contrast suggest?
4. What is the ALLUSION in the line "Everybody else, for heaven's sake, should
   stop throwing stones" (para. 15)?
5. Kingsolver writes, "All in all, I would say that if 'intact' in modern family-
   values jargon means lying quietly desperate in the bell jar, then hip-hip-
   hooray for 'broken'" (para. 24). How does her contrast of "intact" with
   "broken" reveal the THESIS of her essay?

QUESTIONS ON WRITING STRATEGY

1. Kingsolver tells us that we know what the Family of Dolls looks like (para.
   3). Can you describe them? Why does she ASSUME we know this?
2. Why does Kingsolver present us with a "revised" arrangement of the Family of Dolls (para. 24)? How does the advice about strength given by Kingsolver's favorite fictional character (14) serve a similar purpose?
3. What conclusions are we supposed to draw from Kingsolver's statistics in
   paragraph 18 and her suggestions about the children who are "at risk"?
4. **MIXED METHODS.** Locate Kingsolver's DESCRIPTIONS of marriage failure and
   divorce. What overall impression do they add up to?
5. **MIXED METHODS.** In paragraphs 19–24, Kingsolver uses CAUSE AND EFFECT to
   outline the history of the American family. What key changes does Kingsolver identify? Why does she provide this history? Why does she bring up
   the Olduvai Gorge at the end of this discussion?

QUESTIONS ON LANGUAGE

1. Kingsolver contrasts the "nuclear" family with the "blended" family that may have "extranuclear arrangements" (para. 24). What are the meanings of each of these terms?
2. In paragraph 4 Kingsolver uses a string of negative terms ("impostor," "harbinger of cultural ruin," "slapdash," "counterfeit") to describe how the nontraditional family "isn't exactly a real family." Look up any of these words you don't know. How do they support Kingsolver's idea that the real problem divorced families face is that others think there is a problem (para. 17)?
3. In paragraph 8 Kingsolver contrasts two possible reactions to news of a divorce. What do the IMAGES of bringing over a casserole versus acting like she's broken up the family china suggest?
4. If any of the following words are unfamiliar, look them up in a dictionary: delirious (para. 1); particolored (5); imperious (6); integrity, calamity (9); doctrines, reckoning (10); caprice, irreconcilable, specious, asphyxiation, raucous, disassembling, gangrenous (11); daunting, rogue (12); venerates (13); straits, casualty (15); pragmatic, longevity, entitlement (16); revel, unfathomably (18); symmetry, bedrock, incessantly, myriad (19); abolition (20); companionable, scenario, spousal, resilience (21); unprecedented (22); corroborate, panacea, sequestered (23); amorphous, recourse, destitute (24); boisterous (25); beleaguered (26); bouillabaisse (31).

SUGGESTIONS FOR WRITING

1. **JOURNAL WRITING.** In Kingsolver's terms, what kind of family did you grow up in, traditional or not? What experiences or events from your childhood highlight that family structure? (Examples: differences in your mother's and father's styles of discipline; taking on extra chores when one of your parents moved out; watching your parents argue; getting along with a stepsibling.) **FROM JOURNAL TO ESSAY.** Based on some of the experiences you recalled in your journal, what conclusions can you draw about the "healthiness" of your family structure versus another one? What are the advantages and disadvantages of making GENERALIZATIONS about "nuclear" and "blended" families?
2. Analyze Kingsolver's uses of the tales "Cinderella" (paras. 10, 26) and "Stone Soup" (paras. 26–30). What is the EFFECT of these tales? What does Kingsolver gain by merely ALLUDING to "Cinderella" rather than spelling out the tale? How do the details of both stories (whether repeated or not) add to Kingsolver's argument?
3. **CRITICAL WRITING.** Kingsolver contrasts the independent, isolated family (which she calls a "fairy tale") with the support network of an extended family (para. 25). Do you agree with her preference for the second kind? Is it any more realistic than the first? Write an essay supporting or refuting Kingsolver's views of family, drawing on your own experiences and observations.
4. **CONNECTIONS (PART ONE).** Ishmael Reed, in "America: The Multinational Society" (p. 476), quotes a description of America as a "cultural bouillabaisse" (para. 5). Similarly, Kingsolver describes the contemporary family

as "a heck of a bouillabaisse" (para. 31). (If you do not know what a bouillabaisse is, look the word up in a dictionary.) How is a bouillabaisse an appropriate METAPHOR for both authors? How do their visions overlap? Where, if at all, do they diverge?

5. **CONNECTIONS (PART TWO).** Kingsolver claims that it "seems to be the most American of customs to blame the burdened for their destiny" (para. 12). Maxine Hong Kingston's "No Name Woman" (p. 585) shows how Chinese villagers punished a whole family for one member's mistakes. Write an essay COMPARING these two selections' ideas on the justice of blame and punishment endured by families. Are the families at fault? What role do traditional values play in each situation?

BARBARA KINGSOLVER ON WRITING

"People think it's sort of funny," Barbara Kingsolver says, "that I went to graduate school as a biologist and then became a writer." In a 1996 interview with Robin Epstein of *The Progressive* magazine, Kingsolver explains that the processes of science and writing are very similar. "What I learned [in science] is how to formulate or identify a new question that hasn't been asked before, and then to set about solving it, to do original research to find the way to an answer. And that's what I do when I write a book."

Asked if she ever has doubts about her "abilities as a writer," Kingsolver replies, "I still have them. Beginning a book is really hard. I'm trying to begin one now and I just keep throwing stuff away and thinking, 'Can I do this? I don't think I'm smart enough.' You have to have a reverence for the undertaking. And I think reverence implies a certain lack of self-esteem.... You feel daunted and unworthy. But in this age of glorifying the individual and self-esteem, I think there's something healthy about being daunted. Cockiness doesn't lend itself to good writing. It really doesn't."

FOR DISCUSSION

1. Many writers, including experienced ones, often feel hampered by a lack of confidence in their abilities. How then could an excess of confidence harm a writer's work?
2. Kingsolver is like Edward Tenner (p. 326) in seeing parallels between scientific inquiry and writing. What similarities does each writer see? Are Tenner's and Kingsolver's insights about writing potentially helpful to nonscientists?

RICHARD RODRIGUEZ

The son of Spanish-speaking Mexican Americans, RICHARD RODRIGUEZ was born in 1944 in San Francisco. After graduation from Stanford in 1967, he earned an M.A. from Columbia, studied at the Warburg Institute in London, and received a Ph.D. in English literature from the University of California at Berkeley. He once taught but now devotes himself to writing and lecturing. Rodriguez's essays have appeared in *The American Scholar, Change,* and many other magazines. He is a contributing editor for *U.S. News & World Report* and *Harper's* magazines, and he is an on-air essayist for PBS's *Newshour with Jim Lehrer*. In 1982 he published *Hunger of Memory,* a widely discussed book of autobiographical essays. *Mexico's Children* (1991) is a study of Mexicans in America, and *Days of Obligation: An Argument with My Mexican Father* (1992) is also a memoir.

Aria: A Memoir of a Bilingual Childhood

"Aria: A Memoir of a Bilingual Childhood" is taken from *Hunger of Memory*. First published in *The American Scholar* in 1981, this poignant memoir sets forth the author's views of bilingual education. To the child Rodriguez, Spanish was a private language, English a public one. Would the boy have learned faster and better if his teachers had allowed him the use of his native language in school?

In this essay, four methods of development predominate. Rodriguez uses NARRATION and DESCRIPTION to evoke his childhood experiences with language. He uses COMPARISON AND CONTRAST to distinguish home and school, Spanish and English, the private and the public realms. And the whole essay is an ARGUMENT against bilingual education.

I remember, to start with, that day in Sacramento, in a California 1 now nearly thirty years past, when I first entered a classroom—able to understand about fifty stray English words. The third of four children, I had been preceded by my older brother and sister to a neighborhood Roman Catholic school. But neither of them had revealed very much about their classroom experiences. They left each morning and returned each afternoon, always together, speaking Spanish as they climbed the five steps to the porch. And their mysterious books, wrapped in brown shopping-bag paper, remained on the table next to the door, closed firmly behind them.

An accident of geography sent me to a school where all my class- 2 mates were white and many were the children of doctors and lawyers and business executives. On that first day of school, my classmates must certainly have been uneasy to find themselves apart from their families, in the first institution of their lives. But I was astonished. I was fated to be the "problem student" in class.

The nun said, in a friendly but oddly impersonal voice: "Boys and 3 girls, this is Richard Rodriguez." (I heard her sound it out: *Rich-heard Road-ree-guess.*) It was the first time I had heard anyone say my name in English. "Richard," the nun repeated more slowly, writing my name down in her book. Quickly I turned to see my mother's face dissolve in a watery blur behind the pebbled-glass door.

Now, many years later, I hear of something called "bilingual edu- 4 cation"—a scheme proposed in the late 1960s by Hispanic-American social activists, later endorsed by a congressional vote. It is a program that seeks to permit non–English-speaking children (many from lower class homes) to use their "family language" as the language of school. Such, at least, is the aim its supporters announce. I hear them, and am forced to say no: It is not possible for a child, any child, ever to use his family's language in school. Not to understand this is to misunderstand the public uses of schooling and to trivialize the nature of intimate life.

Memory teaches me what I know of these matters. The boy re- 5 minds the adult. I was a bilingual child, but of a certain kind: "socially disadvantaged," the son of working-class parents, both Mexican immigrants.

In the early years of my boyhood, my parents coped very well in 6 America. My father had steady work. My mother managed at home. They were nobody's victims. When we moved to a house many blocks from the Mexican-American section of town, they were not intimidated by those two or three neighbors who initially tried to make us unwelcome. ("Keep your brats away from my sidewalk!") But despite all they achieved, or perhaps because they had so much to achieve, they lacked any deep feeling of ease, of belonging in public. They regarded the people at work or in crowds as being very distant from us. Those were the others, *los gringos*. That term was interchangeable in their speech with another, even more telling: *los americanos*.

I grew up in a house where the only regular guests were my rela- 7 tions. On a certain day, enormous families of relatives would visit us, and there would be so many people that the noise and the bodies would spill out to the backyard and onto the front porch. Then for weeks no one would come. (If the doorbell rang, it was usually a salesman.) Our house stood apart—gaudy yellow in a row of white bungalows. We were the people with the noisy dog, the people who raised chickens. We were the foreigners on the block. A few neighbors would smile and wave at us. We waved back. But until I was seven years old, I did not know the name of the old couple living next door or the names of the kids living across the street.

In public, my father and mother spoke a hesitant, accented, and not always grammatical English. And then they would have to strain, their bodies tense, to catch the sense of what was rapidly said by *los gringos*. At home, they returned to Spanish. The language of their Mexican past sounded in counterpoint to the English spoken in public. The words would come quickly, with ease. Conveyed through those sounds was the pleasing, soothing, consoling reminder that one was at home. 8

During those years when I was first learning to speak, my mother and father addressed me only in Spanish; in Spanish I learned to reply. By contrast, English (*inglés*) was the language I came to associate with gringos, rarely heard in the house. I learned my first words of English overhearing my parents speaking to strangers. At six years of age, I knew just enough words for my mother to trust me on errands to stores one block away—but no more. 9

I was then a listening child, careful to hear the very different sounds of Spanish and English. Wide-eyed with hearing, I'd listen to sounds more than to words. First, there were English (gringo) sounds. So many words still were unknown to me that when the butcher or the lady at the drugstore said something, exotic polysyllabic sounds would bloom in the midst of their sentences. Often the speech of people in public seemed to me very loud, booming with confidence. The man behind the counter would literally ask, "What can I do for you?" But by being so firm and clear, the sound of his voice said that he was a gringo; he belonged in public society. There were also the high, nasal notes of middle-class American speech—which I rarely am conscious of hearing today because I hear them so often, but could not stop hearing when I was a boy. Crowds at Safeway or at bus stops were noisy with the birdlike sounds of *los gringos*. I'd move away from them all—all the chirping chatter above me. 10

My own sounds I was unable to hear, but I knew that I spoke English poorly. My words could not extend to form complete thoughts. And the words I did speak I didn't know well enough to make distinct sounds. (Listeners would usually lower their heads to hear better what I was trying to say.) But it was one thing for *me* to speak English with difficulty; it was more troubling to hear my parents speaking in public: their high-whining vowels and guttural consonants; their sentences that got stuck with "eh" and "ah" sounds; the confused syntax; the hesitant rhythm of sounds so different from the way gringos spoke. I'd notice, moreover, that my parents' voices were softer than those of gringos we would meet. 11

I am tempted to say now that none of this mattered. (In adulthood 12

I am embarrassed by childhood fears.) And, in a way, it didn't matter
very much that my parents could not speak English with ease. Their
linguistic difficulties had no serious consequences. My mother and father made themselves understood at the county hospital clinic and at
government offices. And yet, in another way, it mattered very much. It
was unsettling to hear my parents struggle with English. Hearing them,
I'd grow nervous, and my clutching trust in their protection and power
would be weakened.

There were many times like the night at a brightly lit gasoline sta-   13
tion (a blaring white memory) when I stood uneasily hearing my father
talk to a teenage attendant. I do not recall what they were saying, but I
cannot forget the sounds my father made as he spoke. At one point his
words slid together to form one long word—sounds as confused as the
threads of blue and green oil in the puddle next to my shoes. His voice
rushed through what he had left to say. Toward the end, he reached
falsetto notes, appealing to his listener's understanding. I looked away
at the lights of passing automobiles. I tried not to hear any more. But I
heard only too well the attendant's reply, his calm, easy tones. Shortly
afterward, headed for home, I shivered when my father put his hand on
my shoulder. The very first chance that I got, I evaded his grasp and ran
on ahead into the dark, skipping with feigned boyish exuberance.

But then there was Spanish: *español*, the language rarely heard   14
away from the house; *español*, the language which seemed to me therefore a private language, my family's language. To hear its sounds was to
feel myself specially recognized as one of the family, apart from *los otros*.
A simple remark, an inconsequential comment could convey that assurance. My parents would say something to me and I would feel embraced by the sounds of their words. Those sounds said: *I am speaking
with ease in Spanish. I am addressing you in words I never use with los gringos. I recognize you as someone special, close, like no one outside. You belong with us. In the family. Ricardo.*

At the age of six, well past the time when most middle-class chil-   15
dren no longer notice the difference between sounds uttered at home
and words spoken in public, I had a different experience. I lived in a
world compounded of sounds. I was a child longer than most. I lived in
a magical world, surrounded by sounds both pleasing and fearful. I
shared with my family a language enchantingly private—different
from that used in the city around us.

Just opening or closing the screen door behind me was an impor-   16
tant experience. I'd rarely leave home all alone or without feeling reluctance. Walking down the sidewalk, under the canopy of tall trees,
I'd warily notice the (suddenly) silent neighborhood kids who stood
warily watching me. Nervously, I'd arrive at the grocery store to hear
there the sounds of the gringo, reminding me that in this so-big world

I was a foreigner. But if leaving home was never routine, neither was coming back. Walking toward our house, climbing the steps from the sidewalk, in summer when the front door was open, I'd hear voices beyond the screen door talking in Spanish. For a second or two I'd stay, linger there listening. Smiling, I'd hear my mother call out, saying in Spanish, "Is that you, Richard?" Those were her words, but all the while her sounds would assure me: *You are home now. Come close inside. With us.* "*Sí,*" I'd reply.

Once more inside the house, I would resume my place in the family. The sounds would grow harder to hear. Once more at home, I would grow less conscious of them. It required, however, no more than the blurt of the doorbell to alert me all over again to listen to sounds. The house would turn instantly quiet while my mother went to the door. I'd hear her hard English sounds. I'd wait to hear her voice turn to soft-sounding Spanish, which assured me, as surely as did the clicking tongue of the lock on the door, that the stranger was gone.   17

Plainly it is not healthy to hear such sounds so often. It is not healthy to distinguish public from private sounds so easily. I remained cloistered by sounds, timid and shy in public, too dependent on the voices at home. I remember many nights when my father would come back from work, and I'd hear him call out to my mother in Spanish, sounding relieved. In Spanish, his voice would sound the light and free notes that he never could manage in English. Some nights I'd jump up just hearing his voice. My brother and I would come running into the room where he was with our mother. Our laughing (so deep was the pleasure!) became screaming. Like others who feel the pain of public alienation, we transformed the knowledge of our public separateness into a consoling reminder of our intimacy. Excited, our voices joined in a celebration of sounds. *We are speaking now the way we never speak out in public—we are together,* the sounds told me. Some nights no one seemed willing to loosen the hold that sounds had on us. At dinner we invented new words that sounded Spanish, but made sense only to us. We pieced together new words by taking, say, an English verb and giving it Spanish endings. My mother's instructions at bedtime would be lacquered with mock-urgent tones. Or a word like *sí,* sounded in several notes, would convey added measures of feeling. Tongues lingered around the edges of words, especially fat vowels, and we happily sounded that military drum roll, the twirling roar of the Spanish *r.* Family language, my family's sounds: the voices of my parents and sisters and brother. Their voices insisting: *You belong here. We are family members. Related. Special to one another. Listen!* Voices singing and sighing, rising and straining, then surging, teeming with pleasure which burst syllables into fragments of laughter. At times it seemed there was steady quiet only   18

when, from another room, the rustling whispers of my parents faded
and I edged closer to sleep.

Supporters of bilingual education imply today that students like me   19
miss a great deal by not being taught in their family's language. What
they seem not to recognize is that, as a socially disadvantaged child, I
regarded Spanish as a private language. It was a ghetto language that
deepened and strengthened my feeling of separateness. What I needed
to learn in school was that I had the right, and the obligation, to speak
the public language. The odd truth is that my first-grade classmates
could have become bilingual, in the conventional sense of the word,
more easily than I. Had they been taught early (as upper-middle-class
children often are taught) a "second language" like Spanish or French,
they could have regarded it simply as another public language. In my
case, such bilingualism could not have been so quickly achieved. What
I did not believe was that I could speak a single public language.

Without question, it would have pleased me to have heard my   20
teachers address me in Spanish when I entered the classroom. I would
have felt much less afraid. I would have imagined that my instructors
were somehow "related" to me; I would indeed have heard their Spanish as my family's language. I would have trusted them and responded
with ease. But I would have delayed — postponed for how long? — having to learn the language of public society. I would have evaded — and
for how long? — learning the great lesson of school: that I had a public
identity.

Fortunately, my teachers were unsentimental about their responsi-   21
bility. What they understood was that I needed to speak public English.
So their voices would search me out, asking me questions. Each time I
heard them I'd look up in surprise to see a nun's face frowning at me.
I'd mumble, not really meaning to answer. The nun would persist.
"Richard, stand up. Don't look at the floor. Speak up. Speak to the entire class, not just to me!" But I couldn't believe English could be my
language to use. (In part, I did not want to believe it.) I continued to
mumble. I resisted the teacher's demands. (Did I somehow suspect that
once I learned this public language my family life would be changed?)
Silent, waiting for the bell to sound, I remained dazed, different, afraid.

Because I wrongly imagined that English was intrinsically a public   22
language and Spanish was intrinsically private, I easily noted the difference between classroom language and the language at home. At
school, words were directed to a general audience of listeners. ("Boys
and girls...") Words were meaningfully ordered. And the point was not
self-expression alone, but to make oneself understood by many others.
The teacher quizzed: "Boys and girls, why do we use that word in this
sentence? Could we think of a better word to use there? Would the

sentence change its meaning if the words were differently arranged? Isn't there a better way of saying much the same thing?" (I couldn't say. I wouldn't try to say.)

Three months passed. Five. A half year. Unsmiling, ever watchful, 23 my teachers noted my silence. They began to connect my behavior with the slow progress my brother and sisters were making. Until, one Saturday morning, three nuns arrived at the house to talk to our parents. Stiffly they sat on the blue living-room sofa. From the doorway of another room, spying on the visitors, I noted the incongruity, the clash of two worlds, the faces and voices of school intruding upon the familiar setting of home. I overheard one voice gently wondering, "Do your children speak only Spanish at home, Mrs. Rodriguez?" While another voice added, "That Richard especially seems so timid and shy."

That Rich-heard! 24

With great tact, the visitors continued, "Is it possible for you and 25 your husband to encourage your children to practice their English when they are home?" Of course my parents complied. What would they not do for their children's well-being? And how could they question the Church's authority which those women represented? In an instant they agreed to give up the language (the sounds) which had revealed and accentuated our family's closeness. The moment after the visitors left, the change was observed. "*Ahora,* speak to us only *en inglés,*" my father and mother told us.

At first, it seemed a kind of game. After dinner each night, the family 26 gathered together to practice "our" English. It was still then *inglés,* a language foreign to us, so we felt drawn to it as strangers. Laughing, we would try to define words we could not pronounce. We played with strange English sounds, often overanglicizing our pronunciations. And we filled the smiling gaps of our sentences with familiar Spanish sounds. But that was cheating, somebody shouted, and everyone laughed.

In school, meanwhile, like my brother and sisters, I was required to 27 attend a daily tutoring session. I needed a full year of this special work. I also needed my teachers to keep my attention from straying in class by calling out, "*Rich-heard*"—their English voices slowly loosening the ties to my other name, with its three notes, *Ri-car-do.* Most of all, I needed to hear my mother and father speak to me in a moment of seriousness in "broken"—suddenly heartbreaking—English. This scene was inevitable. One Saturday morning I entered the kitchen where my parents were talking, but I did not realize that they were talking in Spanish until, the moment they saw me, their voices changed and they began speaking English. The gringo sounds they uttered startled me.

Pushed me away. In that moment of trivial misunderstanding and profound insight, I felt my throat twisted by unsounded grief. I simply
turned and left the room. But I had no place to escape to where I could
grieve in Spanish. My brother and sisters were speaking English in another part of the house.

Again and again in the days following, as I grew increasingly angry,   28
I was obliged to hear my mother and father encouraging me: "Speak to
us *en inglés*." Only then did I determine to learn classroom English.
Thus, sometime afterward it happened: One day in school, I raised my
hand to volunteer an answer to a question. I spoke out in a loud voice
and I did not think it remarkable when the entire class understood.
That day I moved very far from being the disadvantaged child I had
been only days earlier. Taken hold at last was the belief, the calming assurance, that I *belonged* in public.

Shortly after, I stopped hearing the high, troubling sounds of *los*   29
gringos. A more and more confident speaker of English, I didn't listen
to how strangers sounded when they talked to me. With so many
English-speaking people around me, I no longer heard American accents. Conversations quickened. Listening to persons whose voices
sounded eccentrically pitched, I might note their sounds for a few seconds, but then I'd concentrate on what they were saying. Now when I
heard someone's tone of voice — angry or questioning or sarcastic or
happy or sad — I didn't distinguish it from the words it expressed.
Sound and word were thus tightly wedded. At the end of each day I was
often bemused, and always relieved, to realize how "soundless," though
crowded with words, my day in public had been. An eight-year-old boy,
I finally came to accept what had been technically true since my birth:
I was an American citizen.

But diminished by then was the special feeling of closeness at   30
home. Gone was the desperate, urgent, intense feeling of being at
home among those with whom I felt intimate. Our family remained a
loving family, but one greatly changed. We were no longer so close, no
longer bound tightly together by the knowledge of our separateness
from *los gringos*. Neither my older brother nor my sisters rushed home
after school anymore. Nor did I. When I arrived home, often there
would be neighborhood kids in the house. Or the house would be
empty of sounds.

Following the dramatic Americanization of their children, even   31
my parents grew more publicly confident — especially my mother. First
she learned the names of all the people on the block. Then she decided
we needed to have a telephone in our house. My father, for his part,
continued to use the word gringo, but it was no longer charged with
bitterness or distrust. Stripped of any emotional content, the word
simply became a name for those Americans not of Hispanic descent.

Hearing him, sometimes, I wasn't sure if he was pronouncing the Spanish word *gringo*, or saying gringo in English.

There was a new silence at home. As we children learned more and 32 more English, we shared fewer and fewer words with our parents. Sentences needed to be spoken slowly when one of us addressed our mother or father. Often the parent wouldn't understand. The child would need to repeat himself. Still the parent misunderstood. The young voice, frustrated, would end up saying, "Never mind"—the subject was closed. Dinners would be noisy with the clinking of knives and forks against dishes. My mother would smile softly between her remarks; my father, at the other end of the table, would chew and chew his food while he stared over the heads of his children.

My mother! My father! After English became my primary lan- 33 guage, I no longer knew what words to use in addressing my parents. The old Spanish words (those tender accents of sound) I had earlier used—*mamá* and *papá*—I couldn't use anymore. They would have been all-too-painful reminders of how much had changed in my life. On the other hand, the words I heard neighborhood kids call their parents seemed equally unsatisfactory. "Mother" and "father," "ma," "pa," "dad," "pop" (how I hated the all-American sound of that last word)— all these I felt were unsuitable terms of address for *my* parents. As a result, I never used them at home. Whenever I'd speak to my parents, I would try to get their attention by looking at them. In public conversations, I'd refer to them as my "parents" or my "mother" and "father."

My mother and father, for their part, responded differently, as their 34 children spoke to them less. My mother grew restless, seemed troubled and anxious at the scarceness of words exchanged in the house. She would question me about my day when I came home from school. She smiled at my small talk. She pried at the edges of my sentences to get me to say something more. ("What...?") She'd join conversations she overheard, but her intrusions often stopped her children's talking. By contrast, my father seemed to grow reconciled to the new quiet. Though his English somewhat improved, he tended more and more to retire into silence. At dinner he spoke very little. One night his children and even his wife helplessly giggled at his garbled English pronunciation of the Catholic "Grace Before Meals." Thereafter he made his wife recite the prayer at the start of each meal, even on formal occasions when there were guests in the house.

Hers became the public voice of the family. On official business it 35 was she, not my father, who would usually talk to strangers on the phone or in stores. We children grew so accustomed to his silence that years later we would routinely refer to his "shyness." (My mother often tried to explain: Both of his parents died when he was eight. He was raised by an uncle who treated him as little more than a menial servant.

He was never encouraged to speak. He grew up alone—a man of few words.) But I realized my father was not shy whenever I'd watch him speaking Spanish with relatives. Using Spanish, he was quickly effusive. Especially when talking with other men, his voice would spark, flicker, flare alive with varied sounds. In Spanish he expressed ideas and feelings he rarely revealed when speaking English. With firm Spanish sounds he conveyed a confidence and authority that English would never allow him.

The silence at home, however, was not simply the result of fewer   36
words passing between parents and children. More profound for me was the silence created by my inattention to sounds. At about the time I no longer bothered to listen with care to the sounds of English in public, I grew careless about listening to the sounds made by the family when they spoke. Most of the time I would hear someone speaking at home and didn't distinguish his sounds from the words people uttered in public. I didn't even pay much attention to my parents' accented and ungrammatical speech—at least not at home. Only when I was with them in public would I become alert to their accents. But even then their sounds caused me less and less concern. For I was growing increasingly confident of my own public identity.

I would have been happier about my public success had I not re-   37
called, sometimes, what it had been like earlier, when my family conveyed its intimacy through a set of conveniently private sounds. Sometimes in public, hearing a stranger, I'd hark back to my lost past. A Mexican farm worker approached me one day downtown. He wanted directions to some place. "*Hijito,...*" he said. And his voice stirred old longings. Another time I was standing beside my mother in the visiting room of a Carmelite convent, before the dense screen which rendered the nuns shadowy figures. I heard several of them speaking Spanish in their busy, singsong, overlapping voices, assuring my mother that, yes, yes, we were remembered, all our family was remembered, in their prayers. Those voices echoed faraway family sounds. Another day a dark-faced old woman touched my shoulder lightly to steady herself as she boarded a bus. She murmured something to me I couldn't quite comprehend. Her Spanish voice came near, like the face of a never-before-seen relative in the instant before I was kissed. That voice, like so many of the Spanish voices I'd hear in public, recalled the golden age of my childhood.

Bilingual educators say today that children lose a degree of "indi-   38
viduality" by becoming assimilated into public society. (Bilingual schooling is a program popularized in the seventies, that decade when middle-class "ethnics" began to resist the process of assimilation—the "American melting pot.") But the bilingualists oversimplify when they

scorn the value and necessity of assimilation. They do not seem to realize that a person is individualized in two ways. So they do not realize that, while one suffers a diminished sense of *private* individuality by being assimilated into public society, such assimilation makes possible the achievement of *public* individuality.

Simplistically again, the bilingualists insist that a student should be 39 reminded of his difference from others in mass society, of his "heritage." But they equate mere separateness with individuality. The fact is that only in private—with intimates—is separateness from the crowd a prerequisite for individuality; an intimate "tells" me that I am unique, unlike all others, apart from the crowd. In public, by contrast, full individuality is achieved, paradoxically, by those who are able to consider themselves members of the crowd. Thus it happened for me. Only when I was able to think of myself as an American, no longer an alien in gringo society, could I seek the rights and opportunities necessary for full public individuality. The social and political advantages I enjoy as a man began on the day I came to believe that my name is indeed *Richheard Road-ree-guess*. It is true that my public society today is often impersonal; in fact, my public society is usually mass society. But despite the anonymity of the crowd, and despite the fact that the individuality I achieve in public is often tenuous—because it depends on my being one in a crowd—I celebrate the day I acquired my new name. Those middle-class ethnics who scorn assimilation seem to me filled with decadent self-pity, obsessed by the burden of public life. Dangerously, they romanticize public separateness and trivialize the dilemma of those who are truly socially disadvantaged.

If I rehearse here the changes in my private life after my Ameri- 40 canization, it is finally to emphasize a public gain. The loss implies the gain. The house I returned to each afternoon was quiet. Intimate sounds no longer greeted me at the door. Inside there were other noises. The telephone rang. Neighborhood kids ran past the door of the bedroom where I was reading my schoolbooks—covered with brown shopping-bag paper. Once I learned the public language, it would never again be easy for me to hear intimate family voices. More and more of my day was spent hearing words, not sounds. But that may only be a way of saying that on the day I raised my hand in class and spoke loudly to an entire roomful of faces, my childhood started to end.

QUESTIONS ON MEANING

1. Rodriguez's essay is both memoir and ARGUMENT. What is the thrust of the author's argument? Where in the essay does he set it forth?
2. How did the child Rodriguez react when, in his presence, his parents had to struggle to make themselves understood by "*los gringos*"?
3. What does the author mean when he says, "I was a child longer than most" (para. 15)?
4. According to the author, what impact did the Rodriguez children's use of English have on relationships within the family?
5. Contrast the child Rodriguez's view of the nuns who insisted he speak English with his adult view.

QUESTIONS ON WRITING STRATEGY

1. How effective an INTRODUCTION is Rodriguez's first paragraph?
2. Several times in his essay Rodriguez shifts from memoir to argument and back again. What is the overall EFFECT of these shifts? Do they strengthen or weaken the author's stance against bilingual education?
3. Twice in his essay (in paras. 1 and 40) the author mentions schoolbooks wrapped in shopping-bag paper. How does the use of this detail enhance his argument?
4. What AUDIENCE probably would not like this essay? Why would they not like it?
5. **MIXED METHODS.** Examine how Rodriguez uses DESCRIPTION to COMPARE AND CONTRAST the sounds of Spanish and English (paras. 10, 11, 13, 14, 18, 33, 37). What sounds does he evoke? What are the differences among them?
6. **MIXED METHODS.** Rodriguez's essay is an argument supported mainly by personal NARRATIVE—Rodriguez's own experience. What kind of ETHICAL APPEAL does the narrative make? What can we INFER about Rodriguez's personality, intellect, fairness, and trustworthiness?

QUESTIONS ON LANGUAGE

1. Consult the dictionary if you need help defining these words: counterpoint (para. 8); polysyllabic (10); guttural, syntax (11); falsetto, exuberance (13); inconsequential (14); cloistered, lacquered (18); diffident (21); intrinsically (22); incongruity (23); bemused (29); effusive (35); assimilated (38); paradoxically, tenuous, decadent (39).
2. In Rodriguez's essay, how do the words *public* and *private* relate to the issue of bilingual education? What important distinction does the author make between *individuality* and *separateness* (para. 39)?
3. What exactly does the author mean when he says, "More and more of my day was spent hearing words, not sounds" (para. 40)?

SUGGESTIONS FOR WRITING

1. **JOURNAL WRITING.** Rodriguez remembers thinking as a child, "We are speaking now the way we never speak out in public—we are together" (para. 18). Was there language in your childhood home that was similarly private? Did you and your family speak a language other than the dominant one, or did you share tones of voice, slang words, ALLUSIONS, inside jokes, or other kinds of language that were different from what you heard in public? **FROM JOURNAL TO ESSAY.** Write an essay DEFINING the distinctive quality of the language spoken in your home when you were a child. What effect, if any, did this language have on you when you went out into public? Does it influence your memories of childhood? Do you revert to this private language when you are with your family?

2. Bilingual education is a controversial issue with EVIDENCE and strong feelings on both sides. In a page or so of preliminary writing, respond to Rodriguez's essay with your own gut feelings on the issue. Then do some library research to extend, support, or refute your views. (Consult the *Readers' Guide to Periodical Literature* as a first step.) In a well-reasoned and well-supported essay, give your opinion on whether or not public schools should teach children in their "family language."

3. **CRITICAL WRITING.** In his argument against bilingual education, Rodriguez offers no data from studies, no testimony from education experts, indeed no evidence at all except his personal experience. In an essay, ANALYZE and EVALUATE this evidence: How convincing do you find it? Is it adequate to support the argument? (In your essay consider Rodriguez's ethical appeal, the topic of the sixth question on writing strategy, previous page.)

4. **CONNECTIONS (PART ONE).** Rodriguez's mother and father seem to have had a definite idea of their parental obligations to their children. Look at Jamaica Kincaid's story "Girl" (p. 304) and write a COMPARISON between that mother's sense of parental obligations and the Rodriguezes'. What, for example, is the connection between good parenting and teaching one's child to conform? In both cases, you will have to infer the parents' values from their actions and words. Use evidence from both works to support your inferences.

5. **CONNECTIONS (PART TWO).** Though it apparently included relatives outside the nucleus of parents and children, Rodriguez's family seems to have been quite isolated by culture and language from the rest of American society. In "Stone Soup" (p. 560), Barbara Kingsolver also explores the isolation of the independent nuclear family, but she does not focus on culture and language as much as on physical and emotional separation from others, including extended family. Write an essay about the differences between these two kinds of isolation. What are their possible disadvantages? possible advantages? Which might be more harmful to family members? For evidence, draw on Rodriguez's and Kingsolver's essays and your own experiences.

RICHARD RODRIGUEZ ON WRITING

For *The Bedford Reader*, Richard Rodriguez has described the writing of "Aria":

"From grammar school to college, my teachers offered perennial encouragement: 'Write about what you know.' Every year I would respond with the student's complaint: 'I have nothing to write about ... I haven't done anything.' (Writers, real writers, I thought, lived in New York or Paris; they smoked on the back jackets of library books, their chores done.)

"Stories die for not being told.... My story got told because I had received an education; my teachers had given me the skill of stringing words together in a coherent line. But it was not until I was a man that I felt any need to write my story. A few years ago I left graduate school, quit teaching for political reasons (to protest affirmative action). But after leaving the classroom, as the months passed, I grew desperate to talk to serious people about serious things. In the great journals of the world, I noticed, there was conversation of a sort, glamorous company of a sort, and I determined to join it. I began writing to stay alive — not as a job, but to stay alive.

"Even as you see my essay now, in cool printer's type, I look at some pages and cannot remember having written them. Or else I can remember earlier versions — unused incident, character, description (rooms, faces) — crumbled and discarded. Flung from possibility. They hit the wastebasket, those pages, and yet, defying gravity with a scratchy, starchy resilience, tried to reopen themselves. Then they fell silent. I read certain other sentences now and they recall the very day they were composed — the afternoon of rain or the telephone call that was to come a few moments after, the house, the room where these sentences were composed, the pattern of the rug, the wastebasket. (In all there were about thirty or forty versions that preceded this final 'Aria.') I tried to describe my experiences exactly, at once to discover myself and to reveal myself. Always I had to write against the fear I felt that no one would be able to understand what I was saying.

"As a reader, I have been struck by the way those novels and essays that are most particular, most particularly about one other life and time (Hannibal, Missouri; one summer; a slave; the loveliness of a muddy river) most fully achieve universality and call to be cherished. It is a paradox apparently: The more a writer unearths the detail that makes a life singular, the more a reader is led to feel a kind of sharing. Perhaps the reason we are able to respond to the life that is so different is because we all, each of us, think privately that we are different from one another. And the more closely we examine another life in its misery or wisdom or foolishness, the more it seems we take some version of ourselves.

"It is, in any case, finally you that I end up having to trust not to laugh, not to snicker. Even as you regard me in these lines, I try to imagine your face as you read. You who read 'Aria,' especially those of you with your theme-divining yellow felt pen poised in your hand, you for whom this essay is yet another assignment, please do not forget that it is my life I am handing you in these pages—memories that are as personal for me as family photographs in an old cigar box."

FOR DISCUSSION

1. What seems to be Rodriguez's attitude toward his AUDIENCE when he writes? Do you think he writes chiefly for his readers, or for himself? Defend your answer.
2. Rodriguez tells us what he said when, as a student, he was told, "Write about what you know." What do you think he would say now?

MAXINE HONG KINGSTON

MAXINE HONG KINGSTON grew up caught between two complex and very different cultures: the China of her parents and the America of her surroundings. In her first two books, *The Woman Warrior: Memoirs of a Girlhood Among Ghosts* (1979) and *China Men* (1980), Kingston combines Chinese myth and history with family tales to create a dreamlike world that shifts between reality and fantasy. Born in 1940 in Stockton, California, Kingston was the first American-born child of a scholar and a medical practitioner who became laundry workers in this country. After graduating from the University of California at Berkeley (B.A., 1962), Kingston taught English at California and Hawaii high schools and at the University of Hawaii. She now lives in Oakland, California, and teaches at U.C. Berkeley. Kingston has contributed essays, poems, and stories to *The New Yorker*, the *New York Times Magazine*, *Ms.*, and other periodicals. Her most recent book is the novel *Tripmaster Monkey: His Fake Book* (1989), and she is reconstructing a manuscript she lost in a fire.

No Name Woman

"No Name Woman" is part of *The Woman Warrior*. Like much of Kingston's writing, it blends the "talk-stories" of Kingston's elders, her own vivid imaginings, and the reality of her experience—this time to discover why her Chinese aunt drowned herself in the family well.

"No Name Woman" thus seeks CAUSES, and it does so by COMPARING two NARRATIVES—that told by Kingston's mother and that invented by Kingston herself. Besides these three methods of development, DESCRIPTION and EXAMPLE are also pervasive.

"You must not tell anyone," my mother said, "what I am about to 1 tell you. In China your father had a sister who killed herself. She jumped into the family well. We say that your father has all brothers because it is as if she had never been born.

"In 1924 just a few days after our village celebrated seventeen 2 hurry-up weddings—to make sure that every young man who went 'out on the road' would responsibly come home—your father and his brothers and your grandfather and his brothers and your aunt's new husband sailed for America, the Gold Mountain. It was your grandfather's last trip. Those lucky enough to get contracts waved good-bye from the decks. They fed and guarded the stowaways and helped them off in Cuba, New York, Bali, Hawaii. 'We'll meet in California next year,' they said. All of them sent money home.

"I remember looking at your aunt one day when she and I were ³
dressing; I had not noticed before that she had such a protruding melon
of a stomach. But I did not think, 'She's pregnant,' until she began to
look like other pregnant women, her shirt pulling and the white tops of
her black pants showing. She could not have been pregnant, you see,
because her husband had been gone for years. No one said anything.
We did not discuss it. In early summer she was ready to have the child,
long after the time when it could have been possible.

"The village had also been counting. On the night the baby was ⁴
to be born the villagers raided our house. Some were crying. Like a
great saw, teeth strung with lights, files of people walked zigzag across
our land, tearing the rice. Their lanterns doubled in the disturbed
black water, which drained away through the broken bunds. As the
villagers closed in, we could see that some of them, probably men and
women we knew well, wore white masks. The people with long hair
hung it over their faces. Women with short hair made it stand up on
end. Some had tied white bands around their foreheads, arms, and
legs.

"At first they threw mud and rocks at the house. Then they threw ⁵
eggs and began slaughtering our stock. We could hear the animals
scream their deaths—the roosters, the pigs, a last great roar from the
ox. Familiar wild heads flared in our night windows; the villagers en-
circled us. Some of the faces stopped to peer at us, their eyes rushing
like searchlights. The hands flattened against the panes, framed heads,
and left red prints.

"The villagers broke in the front and the back doors at the same ⁶
time, even though we had not locked the doors against them. Their
knives dripped with the blood of our animals. They smeared blood on
the doors and walls. One woman swung a chicken, whose throat she
had slit, splattering blood in red arcs about her. We stood together in
the middle of our house, in the family hall with the pictures and tables
of the ancestors around us, and looked straight ahead.

"At that time the house had only two wings. When the men came ⁷
back, we would build two more to enclose our courtyard and a third one
to begin a second courtyard. The villagers pushed through both wings,
even your grandparents' rooms, to find your aunt's, which was also mine
until the men returned. From this room a new wing for one of the
younger families would grow. They ripped up her clothes and shoes and
broke her combs, grinding them underfoot. They tore her work from
the loom. They scattered the cooking fire and rolled the new weaving
in it. We could hear them in the kitchen breaking our bowls and bang-
ing the pots. They overturned the great waist-high earthenware jugs;
duck eggs, pickled fruits, vegetables burst out and mixed in acrid tor-
rents. The old woman from the next field swept a broom through the

air and loosed the spirits-of-the-broom over our heads. 'Pig.' 'Ghost.' 'Pig,' they sobbed and scolded while they ruined our house.

"When they left, they took sugar and oranges to bless themselves.   8
They cut pieces from the dead animals. Some of them took bowls that were not broken and clothes that were not torn. Afterward we swept up the rice and sewed it back up into sacks. But the smells from the spilled preserves lasted. Your aunt gave birth in the pigsty that night. The next morning when I went up for the water, I found her and the baby plugging up the family well.

"Don't let your father know that I told you. He denies her. Now   9
that you have started to menstruate, what happened to her could happen to you. Don't humiliate us. You wouldn't like to be forgotten as if you had never been born. The villagers are watchful."

Whenever she had to warn us about life, my mother told stories   10
that ran like this one, a story to grow up on. She tested our strength to establish realities. Those in the emigrant generations who could not reassert brute survival died young and far from home. Those of us in the first American generations have had to figure out how the invisible world the emigrants built around our childhoods fit in solid America.

The emigrants confused the gods by diverting their curses, mis-   11
leading them with crooked streets and false names. They must try to confuse their offspring as well, who, I suppose, threaten them in similar ways—always trying to get things straight, always trying to name the unspeakable. The Chinese I know hide their names; sojourners take new names when their lives change and guard their real names with silence.

Chinese-Americans, when you try to understand what things in   12
you are Chinese, how do you separate what is peculiar to childhood, to poverty, insanities, one family, your mother who marked your growing with stories, from what is Chinese? What is Chinese tradition and what is the movies?

If I want to learn what clothes my aunt wore, whether flashy or or-   13
dinary, I would have to begin, "Remember Father's drowned-in-the-well sister?" I cannot ask that. My mother has told me once and for all the useful parts. She will add nothing unless powered by Necessity, a riverbank that guides her life. She plants vegetable gardens rather than lawns; she carries the odd-shaped tomatoes home from the fields and eats food left for the gods.

Whenever we did frivolous things, we used up energy; we flew high   14
kites. We children came up off the ground over the melting cones our parents brought home from work and the American movie on New Year's Day—*Oh, You Beautiful Doll* with Betty Grable one year, and *She Wore a Yellow Ribbon* with John Wayne another year. After the one car-

nival ride each, we paid in guilt; our tired father counted his change on the dark walk home.

Adultery is extravagance. Could people who hatch their own   15
chicks and eat the embryos and the heads for delicacies and boil the
feet in vinegar for party food, leaving only the gravel, eating even the
gizzard lining—could such people engender a prodigal aunt? To be a
woman, to have a daughter in starvation time was a waste enough. My
aunt could not have been the lone romantic who gave up everything
for sex. Women in the old China did not choose. Some man had com-
manded her to lie with him and be his secret evil. I wonder whether he
masked himself when he joined the raid on her family.

Perhaps she encountered him in the fields or on the mountain   16
where the daughters-in-law collected fuel. Or perhaps he first noticed
her in the marketplace. He was not a stranger because the village
housed no strangers. She had to have dealings with him other than sex.
Perhaps he worked an adjoining field, or he sold her the cloth for the
dress she sewed and wore. His demand must have surprised, then terrified her. She obeyed him; she always did as she was told.

When the family found a young man in the next village to be her   17
husband, she stood tractably beside the best rooster, his proxy, and
promised before they met that she would be his forever. She was lucky
that he was her age and she would be the first wife, an advantage secure
now. The night she first saw him, he had sex with her. Then he left for
America. She had almost forgotten what he looked like. When she
tried to envision him, she only saw the black and white face in the
group photograph the men had had taken before leaving.

The other man was not, after all, much different from her husband.   18
They both gave orders: she followed. "If you tell your family, I'll beat
you. I'll kill you. Be here again next week." No one talked sex, ever.
And she might have separated the rapes from the rest of living if only
she did not have to buy her oil from him or gather wood in the same
forest. I want her fear to have lasted just as long as rape lasted so that
the fear could have been contained. No drawn-out fear. But women at
sex hazarded birth and hence lifetimes. The fear did not stop but per-
meated everywhere. She told the man, "I think I'm pregnant." He organized the raid against her.

On nights when my mother and father talked about their life back   19
home, sometimes they mentioned an "outcast table" whose business
they still seemed to be settling, their voices tight. In a commensal tradition, where food is precious, the powerful older people made wrong-
doers eat alone. Instead of letting them start separate new lives like the
Japanese, who could become samurais and geishas, the Chinese family,
faces averted but eyes glowering sideways, hung on to the offenders and
fed them leftovers. My aunt must have lived in the same house as my

parents and eaten at an outcast table. My mother spoke about the raid as if she had seen it, when she and my aunt, a daughter-in-law to a different household, should not have been living together at all. Daughters-in-law lived with their husbands' parents, not their own; a synonym for marriage in Chinese is "taking a daughter-in-law." Her husband's parents could have sold her, mortgaged her, stoned her. But they had sent her back to her own mother and father, a mysterious act hinting at disgraces not told me. Perhaps they had thrown her out to deflect the avengers.

She was the only daughter; her four brothers went with her father, husband, and uncles "out on the road" and for some years became western men. When the goods were divided among the family, three of the brothers took land, and the youngest, my father, chose an education. After my grandparents gave their daughter away to her husband's family, they had dispensed all the adventure and all the property. They expected her alone to keep the traditional ways, which her brothers, now among the barbarians, could fumble without detection. The heavy, deep-rooted women were to maintain the past against the flood, safe for returning. But the rare urge west had fixed upon our family, and so my aunt crossed boundaries not delineated in space. 20

The work of preservation demands that the feelings playing about in one's guts not be turned into action. Just watch their passing like cherry blossoms. But perhaps my aunt, my forerunner, caught in a slow life, let dreams grow and fade and after some months or years went toward what persisted. Fear at the enormities of the forbidden kept her desires delicate, wire and bone. She looked at a man because she liked the way the hair was tucked behind his ears, or she liked the question-mark line of a long torso curving at the shoulder and straight at the hip. For warm eyes or a soft voice or a slow walk—that's all—a few hairs, a line, a brightness, a sound, a pace, she gave up family. She offered us up for a charm that vanished with tiredness, a pigtail that didn't toss when the wind died. Why, the wrong lighting could erase the dearest thing about him. 21

It could very well have been, however, that my aunt did not take subtle enjoyment of her friend, but, a wild woman, kept rollicking company. Imagining her free with sex doesn't fit, though. I don't know any women like that, or men either. Unless I see her life branching into mine, she gives me no ancestral help. 22

To sustain her being in love, she often worked at herself in the mirror, guessing at the colors and shapes that would interest him, changing them frequently in order to hit on the right combination. She wanted him to look back. 23

On a farm near the sea, a woman who tended her appearance reaped a reputation for eccentricity. All the married women blunt-cut 24 their hair in flaps about their ears or pulled it back in tight buns. No nonsense. Neither style blew easily into heart-catching tangles. And at their weddings they displayed themselves in their long hair for the last time. "It brushed the backs of my knees," my mother tells me. "It was braided, and even so, it brushed the backs of my knees."

At the mirror my aunt combed individuality into her bob. A bun   25 could have been contrived to escape into black streamers blowing in the wind or in quiet wisps about her face, but only the older women in our picture album wear buns. She brushed her hair back from her forehead, tucking the flaps behind her ears. She looped a piece of thread, knotted into a circle between her index fingers and thumbs, and ran the double strand across her forehead. When she closed her fingers as if she were making a pair of shadow geese bite, the string twisted together catching the little hairs. Then she pulled the thread away from her skin, ripping the hairs out neatly, her eyes watering from the needles of pain. Opening her fingers, she cleaned the thread, then rolled it along her hairline and the tops of her eyebrows. My mother did the same to me and my sisters and herself. I used to believe that the expression "caught by the short hairs" meant a captive held with a depilatory string. It especially hurt at the temples, but my mother said we were lucky we didn't have to have our feet bound when we were seven. Sisters used to sit on their beds and cry together, she said, as their mothers or their slave removed the bandages for a few minutes each night and let the blood gush back into their veins. I hope that the man my aunt loved appreciated a smooth brow, that he wasn't just a tits-and-ass man.

Once my aunt found a freckle on her chin, at a spot that the al-   26 manac said predestined her for unhappiness. She dug it out with a hot needle and washed the wound with peroxide.

More attention to her looks than these pullings of hairs and pick-   27 ings at spots would have caused gossip among the villagers. They owned work clothes and good clothes, and they wore good clothes for feasting the new seasons. But since a woman combing her hair hexes beginnings, my aunt rarely found an occasion to look her best. Women looked like great sea snails—the corded wood, babies, and laundry they carried were the whorls on their backs. The Chinese did not admire a bent back; goddesses and warriors stood straight. Still there must have been a marvelous freeing of beauty when a worker laid down her burden and stretched and arched.

Such commonplace loveliness, however, was not enough for my   28 aunt. She dreamed of a lover for the fifteen days of New Year's, the time for families to exchange visits, money, and food. She plied her secret comb. And sure enough she cursed the year, the family, the village, and herself.

Even as her hair lured her imminent lover, many other men looked   29
at her. Uncles, cousins, nephews, brothers would have looked, too, had
they been home between journeys. Perhaps they had already been restraining their curiosity, and they left, fearful that their glances, like a
field of nesting birds, might be startled and caught. Poverty hurt, and
that was their first reason for leaving. But another, final reason for leaving the crowded house was the never-said.

She may have been unusually beloved, the precious only daughter,   30
spoiled and mirror gazing because of the affection the family lavished
on her. When her husband left, they welcomed the chance to take her
back from the in-laws; she could live like the little daughter for just a
while longer. There are stories that my grandfather was different from
other people, "crazy ever since the little Jap bayoneted him in the
head." He used to put his naked penis on the dinner table, laughing.
And one day he brought home a baby girl, wrapped up inside his brown
western-style greatcoat. He had traded one of his sons, probably my father, the youngest, for her. My grandmother made him trade back.
When he finally got a daughter of his own, he doted on her. They must
have all loved her, except perhaps my father, the only brother who
never went back to China, having once been traded for a girl.

Brothers and sisters, newly men and women, had to efface their   31
sexual color and present plain miens. Disturbing hair and eyes, a smile
like no other, threatened the ideal of five generations living under one
roof. To focus blurs, people shouted face to face and yelled from room
to room. The immigrants I know have loud voices, unmodulated to
American tones even after years away from the village where they
called their friendships out across the fields. I have not been able to
stop my mother's screams in public libraries or over telephones. Walking erect (knees straight, toes pointed forward, not pigeon-toed, which
is Chinese-feminine) and speaking in an inaudible voice, I have tried
to turn myself American-feminine. Chinese communication was loud,
public. Only sick people had to whisper. But at the dinner table, where
the family members came nearest one another, no one could talk, not
the outcasts nor any eaters. Every word that falls from the mouth is a
coin lost. Silently they gave and accepted food with both hands. A preoccupied child who took his bowl with one hand got a sideways glare.
A complete moment of total attention is due everyone alike. Children
and lovers have no singularity here, but my aunt used a secret voice, a
separate attentiveness.

She kept the man's name to herself throughout her labor and dy-   32
ing; she did not accuse him that he be punished with her. To save her
inseminator's name she gave silent birth.

He may have been somebody in her own household, but inter-   33
course with a man outside the family would have been no less abhor-

rent. All the village were kinsmen, and the titles shouted in loud country voices never let kinship be forgotten. Any man within visiting distance would have been neutralized as a lover—"brother," "younger brother," "older brother"—one hundred and fifteen relationship titles. Parents researched birth charts probably not so much to assure good fortune as to circumvent incest in a population that has but one hundred surnames. Everybody has eight million relatives. How useless then sexual mannerisms, how dangerous.

As if it came from an atavism deeper than fear, I used to add 34 "brother" silently to boys' names. It hexed the boys, who would or would not ask me to dance, and made them less scary and as familiar and deserving of benevolence as girls.

But, of course, I hexed myself also—no dates. I should have stood 35 up, both arms waving, and shouted out across libraries, "Hey, you! Love me back." I had no idea, though, how to make attraction selective, how to control its direction and magnitude. If I made myself American-pretty so that the five or six Chinese boys in the class fell in love with me, everyone else—the Caucasian, Negro, and Japanese boys—would too. Sisterliness, dignified and honorable, made much more sense.

Attraction eludes control so stubbornly that whole societies de- 36 signed to organize relationships among people cannot keep order, not even when they bind people to one another from childhood and raise them together. Among the very poor and the wealthy, brothers married their adopted sisters, like doves. Our family allowed some romance, paying adult brides' prices and providing dowries so that their sons and daughters could marry strangers. Marriage promises to turn strangers into friendly relatives—a nation of siblings.

In the village structure, spirits shimmered among the live crea- 37 tures, balanced and held in equilibrium by time and land. But one human being flaring up into violence could open up a black hole, a maelstrom that pulled in the sky. The frightened villagers, who depended on one another to maintain the real, went to my aunt to show her a personal, physical representation of the break she made in the "roundness." Misallying couples snapped off the future, which was to be embodied in true offspring. The villagers punished her for acting as if she could have a private life, secret and apart from them.

If my aunt had betrayed the family at a time of large grain yields 38 and peace, when many boys were born, and wings were being built on many houses, perhaps she might have escaped such severe punishment. But the men—hungry, greedy, tired of planting in dry soil, cuckolded—had been forced to leave the village in order to send food-money home. There were ghost plagues, bandit plagues, wars with the Japanese, floods. My Chinese brother and sister had died of an unknown sickness.

Adultery, perhaps only a mistake during good times, became a crime when the village needed food.

The round moon cakes and round doorways, the round tables of 39 graduated size that fit one roundness inside another, round windows and rice bowls — these talismans had lost their power to warn this family of the law: A family must be whole, faithfully keeping the descent line by having sons to feed the old and the dead who in turn look after the family. The villagers came to show my aunt and lover-in-hiding a broken house. The villagers were speeding up the circling of events because she was too shortsighted to see that her infidelity had already harmed the village, that waves of consequences would return unpredictably, sometimes in disguise, as now, to hurt her. This roundness had to be made coin-sized so that she would see its circumference: punish her at the birth of her baby. Awaken her to the inexorable. People who refused fatalism because they could invent small resources insisted on culpability. Deny accidents and wrest fault from the stars.

After the villagers left, their lanterns now scattering in various di- 40 rections toward home, the family broke their silence and cursed her. "Aiaa, we're going to die. Death is coming. Death is coming. Look what you've done. You've killed us. Ghost! Dead Ghost! Ghost! You've never been born." She ran out into the fields, far enough from the house so that she could no longer hear their voices, and pressed herself against the earth, her own land no more. When she felt the birth coming, she thought that she had been hurt. Her body seized together. "They've hurt me too much," she thought. "This is gall, and it will kill me." With forehead and knees against the earth, her body convulsed and then relaxed. She turned on her back, lay on the ground. The black well of sky and stars went out and out and out forever; her body and her complexity seemed to disappear. She was one of the stars, a bright dot in blackness, without home, without a companion, in eternal cold and silence. An agoraphobia rose in her, speeding higher and higher, bigger and bigger; she would not be able to contain it; there would be no end to fear.

Flayed, unprotected against space, she felt pain return, focusing her 41 body. This pain chilled her — a cold, steady kind of surface pain. Inside, spasmodically, the other pain, the pain of the child, heated her. For hours she lay on the ground, alternately body and space. Sometimes a vision of normal comfort obliterated reality: she saw the family in the evening gambling at the dinner table, the young people massaging their elders' backs. She saw them congratulating one another, high joy on the mornings the rice shoots came up. When these pictures burst, the stars drew out further apart. Black space opened.

She got to her feet to fight better and remembered that old- 42 fashioned women gave birth in their pigsties to fool the jealous, pain-dealing gods, who do not snatch piglets. Before the next spasms could stop her, she ran to the pigsty, each step a rushing out into emptiness. She climbed over the fence and knelt in the dirt. It was good to have a fence enclosing her, a tribal person alone.

Laboring, this woman who had carried her child as a foreign 43 growth that sickened her every day, expelled it at last. She reached down to touch the hot, wet, moving mass, surely smaller than anything human, and could feel that it was human after all — fingers, toes, nails, nose. She pulled it up on to her belly, and it lay curled there, butt in the air, feet precisely tucked one under the other. She opened her loose shirt and buttoned the child inside. After resting, it squirmed and thrashed and she pushed it up to her breast. It turned its head this way and that until it found her nipple. There, it made little snuffling noises. She clenched her teeth at its preciousness, lovely as a young calf, a piglet, a little dog.

She may have gone to the pigsty as a last act of responsibility: she 44 would protect this child as she had protected its father. It would look after her soul, leaving supplies on her grave. But how would this tiny child without family find her grave when there would be no marker for her anywhere, neither in the earth nor the family hall? No one would give her a family hall name. She had taken the child with her into the wastes. At its birth the two of them had felt the same raw pain of separation, a wound that only the family pressing tight could close. A child with no descent line would not soften her life but only trail after her, ghost-like, begging her to give it purpose. At dawn the villagers on their way to the fields would stand around the fence and look.

Full of milk, the little ghost slept. When it awoke, she hardened 45 her breasts against the milk that crying loosens. Toward morning she picked up the baby and walked to the well.

Carrying the baby to the well shows loving. Otherwise abandon it. 46 Turn its face into the mud. Mothers who love their children take them along. It was probably a girl; there is some hope of forgiveness for boys.

"Don't tell anyone you had an aunt. Your father does not want to 47 hear her name. She has never been born." I have believed that sex was unspeakable and words so strong and fathers so frail that "aunt" would do my father mysterious harm. I have thought that my family, having settled among immigrants who had also been their neighbors in the ancestral land, needed to clean their name, and a wrong word would incite the kinspeople even here. But there is more to this silence: they want me to participate in her punishment. And I have.

In the twenty years since I heard this story I have not asked for de- 48 tails nor said my aunt's name; I do not know it. People who comfort the dead can also chase after them to hurt them further—a reverse ancestor worship. The real punishment was not the raid swiftly inflicted by the villagers, but the family's deliberately forgetting her. Her betrayal so maddened them, they saw to it that she would suffer forever, even after death. Always hungry, always needing, she would have to beg food from other ghosts, snatch and steal it from those whose living descendants give them gifts. She would have to fight the ghosts massed at crossroads for the buns a few thoughtful citizens leave to decoy her away from village and home so that the ancestral spirits could feast unharassed. At peace, they could act like gods, not ghosts, their descent lines providing them with paper suits and dresses, spirit money, paper houses, paper automobiles, chicken, meat, and rice into eternity—essences delivered up in smoke and flames, steam and incense rising from each rice bowl. In an attempt to make the Chinese care for people outside the family, Chairman Mao encourages us now to give our paper replicas to the spirits of outstanding soldiers and workers, no matter whose ancestors they may be. My aunt remains forever hungry. Goods are not distributed evenly among the dead.

My aunt haunts me—her ghost drawn to me because now, after 49 fifty years of neglect, I alone devote pages of paper to her, though not origamied into houses and clothes. I do not think she always means me well. I am telling on her, and she was a spite suicide, drowning herself in the drinking water. The Chinese are always very frightened of the drowned one, whose weeping ghost, wet hair hanging and skin bloated, waits silently by the water to pull down a substitute.

QUESTIONS ON MEANING

1. What PURPOSE does Kingston have in telling her aunt's story? How does this differ from her mother's purpose in relating the tale?
2. According to Kingston, who could have been the father of her aunt's child? Who could not?
3. Kingston says that her mother told stories "to warn us about life." What warning does this story provide?
4. Why is Kingston so fascinated by her aunt's life and death?

QUESTIONS ON WRITING STRATEGY

1. Whom does Kingston seem to include in her AUDIENCE: her family and other older Chinese? second-generation Chinese Americans like herself? other Americans? How might she expect each of these groups to respond to her essay?

2. Why is Kingston's opening line—her mother's "You must not tell any-one"—especially fitting for this essay? What secrets are being told? Why does Kingston divulge them?

3. As Kingston tells her tale of her aunt, some events are based on her mother's story or her knowledge of Chinese customs, and some are wholly imaginary. What is the EFFECT of blending these several threads of reality, perception, and imagination?

4. **MIXED METHODS.** Kingston COMPARES AND CONTRASTS various versions of her aunt's story, trying to find the CAUSES that led her aunt to drown in the well. In the end, what causes does Kingston seem to accept?

5. **MIXED METHODS.** Examine the DESCRIPTION in the two contrasting NARRA-TIVES of how Kingston's aunt became pregnant: one in paragraphs 15–18 and the other in paragraphs 21–28. How do the details create different re-alities? Which version does Kingston seem more committed to? Why?

QUESTIONS ON LANGUAGE

1. How does Kingston's language—lyrical, poetic, full of IMAGES and METAPHORS—reveal her relationship to her Chinese heritage? Find phrases that are especially striking.

2. Look up any of these words you do not know: bunds (para. 4); acrid (7); frivolous (14); tractably, proxy (17); hazarded (18); commensal (19); de-lineated (20); depilatory (25); plied (28); miens (31); abhorrent, circum-vent (33); atavism (34); maelstrom (37); talismans, inexorable, fatalism, culpability (39); gall, agoraphobia (40); spasmodically (41).

3. Sometimes Kingston indicates that she is reconstructing or imagining events through verbs like "would have" and words like "maybe" and "per-haps" ("Perhaps she encountered him in the fields," para. 16). Other times she presents obviously imaginary events as if they actually happened ("Once my aunt found a freckle on her chin," 26). What effect does Kingston achieve with these apparent inconsistencies?

SUGGESTIONS FOR WRITING

1. **JOURNAL WRITING.** Most of us have heard family stories that left lasting impressions—ghost stories like Kingston's, or superstitions, traditions, bi-ographies of ancestors, and so on. What family stories do you remember vividly from your childhood?

   FROM JOURNAL TO ESSAY. Develop one of your family stories in a narrative essay. Build in the context of the story as well: Who told it to you? What purpose did he or she have in telling it to you? How does it illustrate your family's beliefs and values?

2. Write an essay explaining the role of ancestors in Chinese family and reli-gious life, supplementing what Kingston says with research in the library or (if you are Chinese American) drawing on your own experiences.

3. **CRITICAL WRITING.** ANALYZE the ideas about gender roles revealed in "No Name Woman," both in China and in the Chinese American culture Kingston grew up in. How have these ideas affected Kingston? Do you per-ceive any semblance of them in contemporary American culture?

4. **CONNECTIONS (PART ONE).** Read or reread E. B. White's "Once More to the Lake" (p. 104). While White explores bonds between fathers and sons in his family, Kingston explores family bonds among women. Write an essay examining the kinds of communication that each author describes between generations. What lessons do parents pass to children? What role do conversation and ritual play in teaching and learning these lessons?

5. **CONNECTIONS (PART TWO).** Richard Rodriguez's "Aria" (p. 570) and Kingston's "No Name Woman" both address the conflicts between traditions and change in terms of language: what can and cannot be spoken about, who can speak, what language is used when. However, the two authors come to different conclusions about the relevance of such traditions to today's world. Write an essay detailing the similarities and differences between their views of tradition and change.

MAXINE HONG KINGSTON ON WRITING

In an interview with Jean W. Ross published in *Contemporary Authors* in 1984, Maxine Hong Kingston discusses the writing and revising of *The Woman Warrior*. Ross asks Kingston to clarify an earlier statement that she had "no idea how people who don't write endure their lives." Kingston replies: "When I said that, I was thinking about how words and stories create order. Some of the things that happen to us in life seem to have no meaning, but when you write them down you find the meanings for them; or, as you translate life into words, you force a meaning. Meaning is intrinsic in words and stories."

Ross then asks if Kingston used an outline and planned to blend fact with legend in *The Woman Warrior*. "Oh no, no," Kingston answers. "What I have at the beginning of a book is not an outline. I have no idea of how stories will end or where the beginning will lead. Sometimes I draw pictures. I draw a blob and then I have a little arrow and it goes to this other blob, if you want to call that an outline. It's hardly even words; it's like a doodle. Then when it turns into words, I find the words lead me to various scenes and stories which I don't know about until I get there. I don't see the order until very late in the writing and sometimes the ending just comes. I just run up against it. All of a sudden the book's over and I didn't know it would be over."

A question from Ross about whether her emotions enter her writing leads Kingston to talk about revision. "Well, when I first set something down I feel the emotions I write about. But when I do a second draft, third draft, ninth draft, then I don't feel very emotional. The rewriting is very intellectual; all my education and reading and intellect are involved. The mechanics of sentences, how one phrase or word goes with another one — all that happens in later drafts. There's a very emotional first draft and a very technical last draft."

FOR DISCUSSION

1. Do you agree with Kingston that when you write things down you find their meaning? Give examples of when the writing process has or hasn't clarified an experience for you.
2. Kingston doodles as a way to discover her material. How do you discover what you have to say?
3. What does Kingston mean by "the mechanics of sentences"? Do you consider this element as you revise?

13

BOYS AND GIRLS, MEN AND WOMEN

How do biology and upbringing—nature and nurture—make men men and women women? How many of the differences between the sexes are desirable, and which should we—or even *can* we—change? The authors in this chapter view questions like these through the filters of their own experiences. John Updike, in "The Disposable Rocket," finds, not unhappily, that many of the distinctions between the sexes do indeed originate with their bodies. Emily Prager, in "Our Barbies, Ourselves," sees in the world's most popular doll a dubious model for little girls. And Katha Pollitt, in "Why Boys Don't Play with Dolls," explores how children's taste in toys is influenced, maybe even formed, by the adults in their lives.

JOHN UPDIKE

The esteemed and widely popular writer JOHN UPDIKE has published about forty books of fiction, poetry, and essays, all of them distinctively lyrical and evocative. He was born in 1932 in Shillington, Pennsylvania, grew up in that small town, and carried it with him into his writing. "My subject," he has said, "is the American Protestant small-town middle class." Updike graduated from Harvard University (B.A., 1954) and attended art school in England. He worked for a couple of years at *The New Yorker* and has published many of his short stories and book reviews in that magazine. His awards include the Pulitzer Prize, the National Book Award, the American Book Award, and the Howells Medal of the American Academy and Institute of Arts and Letters, of which he is also a member. Updike's seventeen novels, for which he is best known, include the linked stories *Rabbit, Run* (1960), *Rabbit Redux* (1971), *Rabbit Is Rich* (1981), and *Rabbit at Rest* (1990); the most recent novel is *In the Beauty of the Lilies* (1996).

The Disposable Rocket

Is anatomy destiny? Perhaps not entirely, holds Updike in this essay, but the body does significantly affect the mind it carries. Whether male or female, any reader will find this piece engaging and perhaps provocative. It was first published in the *Michigan Quarterly Review* in 1993 and appeared in that year's *Best American Essays*.

"The Disposable Rocket" is at once a DEFINITION of the male body, an inquiry into the EFFECTS of anatomy, and a COMPARISON AND CONTRAST between male and female bodies. It is full of EXAMPLES, injects bits of NARRATION, and sings with DESCRIPTION.

Inhabiting a male body is much like having a bank account; as long 1 as it's healthy, you don't think much about it. Compared to the female body, it is a low-maintenance proposition: a shower now and then, trim the fingernails every ten days, a haircut once a month. Oh yes, shaving—scraping or buzzing away at your face every morning. Byron,[1] in *Don Juan*, thought the repeated nuisance of shaving balanced out the periodic agony, for females, of childbirth. Women are, his lines tell us,

Condemn'd to child-bed, as men for their sins
Have shaving too entail'd upon their chins, —

A daily plague, which in the aggregate
 May average on the whole with parturition.

---

[1] George Gordon Byron (1788–1824) was an English poet. *Don Juan* (1819–24) was left unfinished at Lord Byron's death. —EDS.

From the standpoint of reproduction, the male body is a delivery system, as the female is a mazy device for retention. Once the delivery is
made, men feel a faint but distinct falling-off of interest. Yet against the
enduring female heroics of birth and nurture should be set the male's
superhuman frenzy to deliver his goods: He vaults walls, skips sleep,
risks wallet, health, and his political future all to ram home his seed
into the gut of the chosen woman. The sense of the chase lives in him
as the key to life. His body is, like a delivery rocket that falls away in
space, a disposable means. Men put their bodies at risk to experience
the release from gravity.

When my tenancy of a male body was fairly new—of six or so   2
years' duration—I used to jump and fall just for the joy of it. Falling—
backwards, downstairs—became a specialty of mine, an attention-
getting stunt I was practicing into my thirties, at suburban parties.
Falling is, after all, a kind of flying, though of briefer duration than
would be ideal. My impulse to hurl myself from high windows and the
edges of cliffs belongs to my body, not my mind, which resists the siren
call of the chasm with all its might; the interior struggle knocks the
wind from my lungs and tightens my scrotum and gives any trip to Europe, with its Alps, castle parapets, and gargoyled cathedral lookouts, a
flavor of nightmare. Falling, strangely, no longer figures in my dreams,
as it often did when I was a boy and my subconscious was more honest
with me. An airplane, that necessary evil, turns the earth into a map so
quickly the brain turns aloof and calm; still, I marvel that there is no
end of young men willing to become jet pilots.

Any accounting of male-female differences must include the male's   3
superior recklessness, a drive not, I think, toward death, as the darker
feminist cosmogonies would have it, but to test the limits, to see what
the traffic will bear—a kind of mechanic's curiosity. The number of
men who do lasting damage to their young bodies is striking; war and
car accidents aside, secondary-school sports, with the approval of parents and the encouragement of brutish coaches, take a fearful toll of
skulls and knees. We were made for combat, back in the post-simian,
East African days, and the bumping, the whacking, the breathlessness,
the pain-smothering adrenaline rush, form a cumbersome and unfashionable bliss, but bliss nevertheless. Take your body to the edge, and see
if it flies.

The male sense of space must differ from that of the female, who   4
has such interesting, active, and significant inner space. The space that
interests men is outer. The fly ball high against the sky, the long pass
spiraling overhead, the jet fighter like a scarcely visible pinpoint nozzle
laying down its vapor trail at forty thousand feet, the gazelle haunch
flickering just beyond arrow-reach, the uncountable stars sprinkled on
their great black wheel, the horizon, the mountaintop, the quasar—

these bring portents with them, and awaken a sense of relation with the invisible, with the empty. The ideal male body is taut with lines of potential force, a diagram extending outward; the ideal female body curves around centers of repose. Of course, no one is ideal, and the sexes are somewhat androgynous subdivisions of a species: Diana the huntress is a more trendy body-type nowadays than languid, overweight Venus, and polymorphous Dionysus poses for more underwear ads than Mars. Relatively, though, men's bodies, however elegant, are designed for covering territory, for moving on.

An erection, too, defies gravity, flirts with it precariously. It extends 5 the diagram of outward direction into downright detachability—objective in the case of the sperm, subjective in the case of the testicles and penis. Men's bodies, at this juncture, feel only partly theirs; a demon of sorts has been attached to their lower torsos, whose performance is erratic and whose errands seem, at times, ridiculous. It is like having a (much) smaller brother toward whom you feel both fond and impatient; if he is you, it is you in curiously simplified and ignoble form. This sense, of the male body being two of them, is acknowledged in verbal love play and erotic writing, where the penis is playfully given its own name, an individuation not even the rarest rapture grants a vagina. Here, where maleness gathers to a quintessence of itself, there can be no insincerity, there can be no hiding; for sheer nakedness, there is nothing like a hopeful phallus; its aggressive shape is indivisible from its tender-skinned vulnerability. The act of intercourse, from the point of view of a consenting female, has an element of mothering, of enwrapment, of merciful concealment, even. The male body, for the interval, is tucked out of harm's way.

To inhabit a male body, then, is to feel somewhat detached from it. 6 It is not an enemy, but not entirely a friend. Our essence seems to lie not in cells and muscles but in the traces our thoughts and actions inscribe on the air. The male body skims the surface of nature's deep, wherein the blood and pain and mysterious cravings of women perpetuate the species. Participating less in nature's processes than the female body, the male body gives the impression—false—of being exempt from time. Its powers of strength and reach descend in early adolescence, along with acne and sweaty feet, and depart, in imperceptible increments, after thirty or so. It surprises me to discover, when I remove my shoes and socks, the same paper-white hairless ankles that struck me as pathetic when I observed them on my father. I felt betrayed when, in some tumble of touch football twenty years ago, I heard my tibia snap; and when, between two reading engagements in Cleveland, my appendix tried to burst; and when the other day, not for the first time, there arose to my nostrils out of my own body the musty attic smell my grandfather's body had.

A man's body does not betray its tenant as rapidly as a woman's.   7
Never as fine and lovely, it has less distance to fall; what rugged beauty
it has is wrinkle-proof. It keeps its capability of procreation indecently
long. Unless intense athletic demands are made on it, the thing serves
well enough to sixty, which is my age now. From here on, it's chancy.
There are no breasts or ovaries to admit cancer to the male body, but
the prostate, that awkwardly located little source of seminal fluid,
shows the strain of sexual function with fits of hysterical cell replica-
tion, and all that beer and potato chips add up in the coronary arteries.
A writer, whose physical equipment can be minimal, as long as it gets
him to the desk, the lectern, and New York City once in a while, cannot but be grateful to his body, especially to his eyes, those tender and
intricate sites where the brain extrudes from the skull, and to his hands,
which hold the pen or tap the keyboard. His body has been, not himself exactly, but a close pal, pot-bellied and balding like most of his
other pals now. A man and his body are like a boy and the buddy who
has a driver's license and the use of his father's car for the evening; he
goes along, gratefully, for the ride.

QUESTIONS ON MEANING

1. In the first line of this essay, Updike compares the male body to a bank account. What does he mean by this COMPARISON? How is this comparison
   used or modified throughout his essay?
2. Consider what the title of this essay says about the male desire Updike
   identifies, to "experience the release from gravity" (para. 1). Explain Updike's THESIS in terms of this connection.
3. Updike says the impulse to hurl himself into the air from high places "belongs to my body, not my mind" (para. 2). What does he mean by this distinction? Why is it important?
4. What is it that Updike labels both a "demon" and a "smaller brother" in
   paragraph 5? What do these labels—and the contrast between them—
   suggest?

QUESTIONS ON WRITING STRATEGY

1. What is the point of paragraph 2? What is Updike saying about youth versus adulthood?
2. In paragraph 4 Updike uses sports METAPHORS and nature ANALOGIES in the
   same sentence to help explain the male sense of space. How does each contribute to the point he is trying to make? Why does he use so many different IMAGES to explain this point?
3. What EFFECT does Updike achieve with his ALLUSIONS to the ancient Greek
   gods Diana, Venus, Dionysus, and Mars (para. 4)?

4. **MIXED METHODS.** Updike relies on IMAGES to compare and contrast women's and men's bodies. Locate some of these comparisons.
5. **MIXED METHODS.** What, in a nutshell, is Updike's DEFINITION of the male body? How does he use CAUSE AND EFFECT to develop it?

QUESTIONS ON LANGUAGE

1. Updike quotes from Lord Byron's epic poem *Don Juan* as his first suggestion of how the male body can be trouble. Look up any of the following words in the poem if they are unfamiliar: entail'd (entailed), aggregate, parturition. How serious or IRONIC do you think the comparison between shaving and giving birth is supposed to be on either Byron's or Updike's part?
2. Updike contrasts the "enduring female heroics" of being a mother versus the "male's superhuman frenzy to deliver his goods" (para. 1). What are the CONNOTATIONS of "heroics" as opposed to "frenzy"? How does Updike's choice of these words influence our understanding of his contrast?
3. At the end of paragraph 6 Updike refers to "the musty attic smell my grandfather's body had." What does this image suggest? Why does Updike mention this smell?
4. Consult your dictionary for any of the following words you do not know: tenancy, siren, chasm, scrotum, parapets, gargoyled, aloof (para. 2); cosmogonies, post-simian, adrenaline (3); gazelle, haunch, quasar, portents, taut, androgynous, languid (4); precariously, juncture, torsos, erratic, ignoble, individuation, phallus, enwrapment (5); perpetuate, imperceptible, increments, tibia (6); procreation, ovaries, prostate, seminal, coronary (7).

SUGGESTIONS FOR WRITING

1. **JOURNAL WRITING.** Updike's essay invites readers to consider their relationship to their own bodies. How do you feel about your body? What makes you happy about it? What frustrates you? How would you define your own "maleness" or "femaleness," both in physical and in mental terms? **FROM JOURNAL TO ESSAY.** Using your sense of your own body as an example, write an essay defining your own sense of the "male experience" or the "female experience" in terms of the body. Consider what the body is, does, wants, allows, or restricts; how the body changes over time; what is consistent or unique from one person's body to another's; and the extent to which one can reasonably make GENERALIZATIONS about the sexes.
2. Write an essay examining the significance of Updike's images of flying. Your thesis should make a claim about why these images are or are not a particularly effective way for Updike to explain his ideas. For EVIDENCE, ANALYZE several of the flight images, explaining what they mean and what information Updike conveys with them.
3. **CRITICAL WRITING.** No doubt you can think of exceptions to some of Updike's generalizations about men and women. Write an analysis of this essay, whether you agree with it or not. Where do you think Updike makes reasonable assertions, and why? Where do you think he goes too far, and why? Does he subscribe to stereotypes of men and women?

4. **CONNECTIONS (PART ONE)**. Like Updike, Brad Manning, in "Arm Wrestling with My Father" (p. 113), reflects on the psychological effect of recognizing the physical changes that accompany aging. Do the two authors reach similar conclusions about the significance of these changes? Write an essay that explores each author's attitude toward his body and the process of "growing up."

5. **CONNECTIONS (PART TWO)**. Updike's essay asserts that innate physical differences cause many of the differences in men's and women's attitudes, motivations, and behaviors. His is the nature side of the nature-versus-nurture debate. Katha Pollitt, in contrast, argues in "Why Boys Don't Play with Dolls" (p. 612) that biology has little to do with the differences between men and women. Instead, she points to society (or nurture) for creating these differences. Write an essay that ARGUES which of these two authors is more convincing. To do this, you will need to take a stand on the nature-nurture debate and then compare and EVALUATE the evidence these authors present.

JOHN UPDIKE ON WRITING

A famously meticulous writer, John Updike nonetheless claims to write quickly. Fairly early in his career, in 1967, he explained to Charles Thomas Samuels of *The Paris Review* just what's to be gained from speed.

"There may be some reason," he said, "to question the whole idea of fineness and care in writing. Maybe something can get into sloppy writing that would elude careful writing. I'm not terribly careful myself, actually. I write fairly rapidly if I get going, and don't change much, and have never been one for making outlines or taking out whole paragraphs or agonizing much. If a thing goes, it goes for me, and if it doesn't go, I eventually stop and get off."

Updike was asked what "gets into sloppy writing that eludes more careful prose."

"It comes down to what is language," Updike replied. "Up to now, until this age of mass literacy, language has been something spoken. In utterance there's a minimum of slowness. In trying to treat words as chisel strokes, you run the risk of losing the quality of utterance, the rhythm of utterance, the happiness. A phrase out of Mark Twain—he describes a raft hitting a bridge and says that it 'went all to smash and scatteration like a box of matches struck by lightning.' The beauty of 'scatteration' could only have occurred to a talkative man, a man who had been brought up among people who were talking and who loved to talk himself. I'm aware myself of a certain dryness of this reservoir, this backlog of spoken talk. A Rumanian once said to me that Americans are always telling stories. I'm not sure this is as true as it once was.

Where we once used to spin yarns, now we sit in front of the TV and receive pictures. I'm not sure the younger generation even knows how to gossip. But, as for a writer, if he has something to tell, he should perhaps type it almost as fast as he could talk it. We must look to the organic world, not the inorganic world, for metaphors; and just as the organic world has periods of repose and periods of great speed and exercise, so I think the writer's process should be organically varied. But there's a kind of tautness that you should feel within yourself no matter how slow or fast you're spinning out the reel."

FOR DISCUSSION

1. To what extent do you think Updike's ideas about feeling "a kind of tautness" while composing apply to academic as well as to fiction writing? What might *you* gain by writing fast?
2. What might be the advantage to a writer—any kind of writer—of talk? Do you agree with Updike that to "sit in front of the TV and receive pictures" rather than "gossip" could deprive a writer of essential experience? Why, or why not?

EMILY PRAGER

EMILY PRAGER was first published at age five when the *Houston Post* released her novel *Cinderella Goes to the Ball and Breaks Her Leg*. Born in 1952, she grew up in Houston, Asia, and New York City and graduated from Barnard College with a degree in anthropology. She wrote for *The National Lampoon Magazine*, cowrote and acted in the films *Mr. Mike's Mondo* and *Arena Brains*, and starred for four years in the soap opera *The Edge of Night*. Prager has written humor and social satire for numerous periodicals, and she has published three books of fiction: *A Visit from the Footbinder and Other Stories* (1982), *Clea and Zeus Divorce* (1987), and *Eve's Tattoo* (1991).

Our Barbies, Ourselves

The Barbie doll is just a harmless plaything for little girls, right? Prager suspected not, even when she was a child, and recently some new information confirmed her hunch. This essay first appeared in *Interview* magazine in 1991.

"Our Barbies, Ourselves" is notably an ANALYSIS of Barbie and her boyfriend, Ken. Prager also uses DESCRIPTION to portray both dolls, COMPARISON to set Barbie alongside her predecessors and Ken, and CAUSE AND EFFECT to explain the consequences of such toys for their owners.

I read an astounding obituary in *The New York Times* not too long 1 ago. It concerned the death of one Jack Ryan. A former husband of Zsa Zsa Gabor, it said, Mr. Ryan had been an inventor and designer during his lifetime. A man of eclectic creativity, he designed Sparrow and Hawk missiles when he worked for the Raytheon Company, and, the notice said, when he consulted for Mattel he designed Barbie.[1]

If Barbie was designed by a man, suddenly a lot of things made 2 sense to me, things I'd wondered about for years. I used to look at Barbie and wonder, What's wrong with this picture? What kind of woman designed this doll? Let's be honest: Barbie looks like someone who got her start at the Playboy Mansion. She could be a regular guest on *The Howard Stern Show*. It is a fact of Barbie's design that her breasts are so out of proportion to the rest of her body that if she were a human woman, she'd fall flat on her face.

[1] After Prager wrote this essay, Barbie's thirty-fifth birthday was the occasion for a "biography" asserting that Ryan did not design the doll from scratch but supervised its evolution from a sophisticated adult doll made in Germany. —EDS.

If it's true that a woman didn't design Barbie, you don't know how 3
much saner that makes me feel. Of course, that doesn't ameliorate the
damage. There are millions of women who are subliminally sure that
a thirty-nine-inch bust and a twenty-three-inch waist are the epitome
of lovability. Could this account for the popularity of breast implant
surgery?

I don't mean to step on anyone's toes here. I loved my Barbie. Se- 4
cretly, I still believe that neon pink and turquoise blue are the only colors in which to decorate a duplex condo. And like many others of my
generation, I've never married, simply because I cannot find a man who
looks as good in clam diggers as Ken.

The question that comes to mind is, of course, Did Mr. Ryan design 5
Barbie as a weapon? Because it *is* odd that Barbie appeared about the
same time in my consciousness as the feminist movement—a time
when women sought equality and small breasts were king. Or is Barbie
the dream date of weapons designers? Or perhaps it's simpler than that:
Perhaps Barbie is Zsa Zsa if she were eleven inches tall. No matter
what, my discovery of Jack Ryan confirms what I have always felt:
There is something indescribably masculine about Barbie—dare I say
it, phallic. For all her giant breasts and high-heeled feet, she lacks a certain softness. If you asked a little girl what kind of doll she wanted for
Christmas, I just don't think she'd reply, "Please, Santa, I want a hard-
body."

On the other hand, you could say that Barbie, in feminist terms, is 6
definitely her own person. With her condos and fashion plazas and
pools and beauty salons, she is definitely a liberated woman, a gal
on the move. And she has always been sexual, even totemic. Before
Barbie, American dolls were flat-footed and breastless, and ineffably
dignified. They were created in the image of little girls or babies.
Madame Alexander was the queen of doll makers in the '50s, and her
dollies looked like Elizabeth Taylor in *National Velvet*. They represented the kind of girls who looked perfect in jodhpurs, whose hair
was never out of place, who grew up to be Jackie Kennedy—before
she married Onassis. Her dolls' boyfriends were figments of the imagination, figments with large portfolios and three piece suits and presidential aspirations, figments who could keep dolly in the style to
which little girls of the '50s were programmed to become accustomed,
a style that spasm-ed with the '60s and the appearance of Barbie. And
perhaps what accounts for Barbie's vast popularity is that she was also
a '60s woman: into free love and fun colors, anti-class, and possessed
of a real, molded boyfriend, Ken, with whom she could chant a
mantra.

But there were problems with Ken. I always felt weird about him. 7
He had no genitals, and, even at age ten, I found that ominous. I mean,

here was Barbie with these humongous breasts, and that was O.K. with the toy company. And then, there was Ken with that truncated, unidentifiable lump at his groin. I sensed injustice at work. Why, I wondered, was Barbie designed with such obvious sexual equipment and Ken not? Why was his treated as if it were more mysterious than hers? Did the fact that it was treated as such indicate that somehow his equipment, his essential maleness, was considered more powerful than hers, more worthy of the dignity of concealment? And if the issue in the mind of the toy company was obscenity and its possible damage to children, I still object. How do they think I felt, knowing that no matter how many water beds they slept in, or hot tubs they romped in, or swimming pools they lounged by under the stars, Barbie and Ken could never make love? No matter how much sexuality Barbie possessed, she would never turn Ken on. He would be forever withholding, forever detached. There was a loneliness about Barbie's situation that was always disturbing. And twenty-five years later, movies and videos are still filled with topless women and covered men. As if we're all trapped in Barbie's world and can never escape.

QUESTIONS ON MEANING

1. Why does Prager say that "suddenly a lot of things made sense" when she discovered that Barbie was designed by a man? Is she referring here only to Barbie's looks?
2. Are we supposed to believe the claims that Prager makes in paragraph 4? What is the point she is trying to make?
3. What is Prager's DEFINITION of a *feminist* in this essay? Where do you find this definition?
4. What is Prager's THESIS?

QUESTIONS ON WRITING STRATEGY

1. Prager refers to four famous women by name. What does each reference suggest? What is the EFFECT of her using these famous names?
2. Prager poses several RHETORICAL QUESTIONS, such as "Could this account for the popularity of breast implant surgery?" (para. 3), "Or is Barbie the dream date of weapons designers?" (5), and "Why...was Barbie designed with such obvious sexual equipment and Ken not?" (7). What is the PURPOSE of these rhetorical questions?
3. **MIXED METHODS.** Prager's ANALYSIS of Barbie relies on DESCRIPTION of the doll's appearance. What are Barbie's main attributes, according to Prager?
4. **MIXED METHODS.** In her last paragraph Prager COMPARES AND CONTRASTS the ways the toy company depicted the sexuality of Barbie and Ken. What

are the differences? What ideas of CAUSE AND EFFECT emerge from this comparison?

QUESTIONS ON LANGUAGE

1. Prager notes that Barbie is a product of a time when "small breasts were king" (para. 5). What is the significance of the word *king* in this context?
2. Why does Prager call Barbie "masculine" in paragraph 5? Does this description contradict Prager's view of Barbie as an unattainable and inappropriate feminine ideal?
3. Prager describes dolls' boyfriends before Barbie's Ken as "figments with large portfolios and three-piece suits and presidential aspirations" (para. 6). What are the CONNOTATIONS of this description?
4. Consult your dictionary if any of the following words are unfamiliar: eclectic (para. 1); ameliorate, subliminally, epitome (3); phallic (5); totemic, ineffably, jodhpurs (6); humongous, truncated (7).

SUGGESTIONS FOR WRITING

1. **JOURNAL WRITING.** Did you play with Barbie or another kind of doll as a child (for instance, Ken, G.I. Joe, *Star Wars* action figures)? Describe your relationship with this doll, or explain why you never owned one.
   FROM JOURNAL TO ESSAY. Using your own experiences as EVIDENCE, write an essay that explains the influence of a particular doll or of dolls in general. Your essay may be serious or humorous, but it should include plenty of description and focus on cause and effect.
2. Prager asserts that knowing a man designed Barbie *explains* a lot of problems she always had with Barbie, but it does not *excuse* or *solve* the problems. What new knowledge can you think of that provided a reasonable explanation for a personal problem, while doing nothing to repair the situation? For instance, did you come to understand why your taxes or your rent increased, why you received a disappointing grade in a course, why someone dislikes you, or why a friend is depressed? In an essay, explain the situation, what you now understand about it, and finally, what it would take, in addition to the new information, to solve the problem.
3. **CRITICAL WRITING.** In paragraph 6 Prager suggests, with a tinge of IRONY, several ways to think of Barbie as contributing to the liberation rather than the oppression of women. What do *you* think of Barbie as a role model for girls? Write an essay supporting or refuting Prager's thesis. (If you haven't seen a Barbie doll in a while, you might visit a toy store or borrow a child's.) Is Barbie damaging, as Prager maintains, or liberating, or neither?
4. **CONNECTIONS (PART ONE).** Prager says that "movies and videos are still filled with topless women and covered men," perpetuating the same double standard as that illustrated by Barbie and Ken (para. 7). To what extent do Prager's views on this double standard resemble Judy Brady's views in "I Want a Wife" (p. 274)? Using evidence from Prager's and Brady's essays, analyze the two authors' attitudes toward relationships between men and women.

5. **CONNECTIONS (PART TWO).** "John Updike's 'The Disposable Rocket' (p. 600) appeals to men who can relate to his claims about the male body, while Prager's essay appeals to women who reject men's stereotypes about the female body." Do you agree with this statement? Why, or why not? Who do you think is the intended AUDIENCE for each of these essays? Write an essay connecting each author's TONE and evidence to the audience he or she is addressing.

KATHA POLLITT

KATHA POLLITT is a poet and essayist. Her poetry has been praised for its "serious charm" and "spare delicacy" in capturing thought and feeling. Her essays have contained strong and convincing commentary on such topics as surrogate motherhood and women in the media. Pollitt was born in New York City in 1949 and earned a B.A. from Radcliffe College in 1972. Her verse began appearing in the 1970s in such magazines as *The New Yorker* and *Atlantic Monthly*; it was collected in the book *Antarctic Traveler* (1982), which won the National Book Critics Circle award in 1983. Pollitt has received several other awards as well, including a grant from the National Endowment for the Arts and a Guggenheim fellowship. Her essays and criticism have appeared in *Mother Jones*, the *New York Times*, *The New Yorker*, and *The Nation*, where she is currently an associate editor writing a regular column. *Reasonable Creatures: Essays on Women and Feminism* appeared in 1994. Pollitt lives in New York City.

Why Boys Don't Play with Dolls

This essay, first published in the *New York Times Magazine* in 1995, responds to studies emphasizing the biological causes of sex differences. To Pollitt, these studies are irrelevant: What counts is social conditioning.

A model of CAUSE AND EFFECT in the service of ARGUMENT, "Why Boys Don't Play with Dolls" also uses brief NARRATIVES, EXAMPLES of children's toys and parents' attitudes, and ANALYSIS and COMPARISON of children's and parents' behaviors.

It's twenty-eight years since the founding of NOW,[1] and boys still   1
like trucks and girls still like dolls. Increasingly, we are told that the source of these robust preferences must lie outside society—in prenatal hormonal influences, brain chemistry, genes—and that feminism has reached its natural limits. What else could possibly explain the love of preschool girls for party dresses or the desire of toddler boys to own more guns than Mark from Michigan?

True, recent studies claim to show small cognitive differences be-   2
tween the sexes: He gets around by orienting himself in space; she does it by remembering landmarks. Time will tell if any deserve the hoopla with which each is invariably greeted, over the protests of the researchers themselves. But even if the results hold up (and the history of such research is not encouraging), we don't need studies of sex-

[1] National Organization for Women. —EDS.

differentiated brain activity in reading, say, to understand why boys and girls still seem so unalike.

The feminist movement has done much for some women, and something for every woman, but it has hardly turned America into a playground free of sex roles. It hasn't even got women to stop dieting or men to stop interrupting them.

Instead of looking at kids to "prove" that differences in behavior by sex are innate, we can look at the ways we raise kids as an index to how unfinished the feminist revolution really is, and how tentatively it is embraced even by adults who fully expect their daughters to enter previously male-dominated professions and their sons to change diapers.

I'm at a children's birthday party. "I'm sorry," one mom silently mouths to the mother of the birthday girl, who has just torn open her present — Tropical Splash Barbie. Now, you can love Barbie or you can hate Barbie, and there are feminists in both camps. But *apologize* for Barbie? Inflict Barbie, against your own convictions, on the child of a friend you know will be none too pleased?

Every mother in that room had spent years becoming a person who had to be taken seriously, not least by herself. Even the most attractive, I'm willing to bet, had suffered over her body's failure to fit the impossible American ideal. Given all that, it seems crazy to transmit Barbie to the next generation. Yet to reject her is to say that what Barbie represents — being sexy, thin, stylish — is unimportant, which is obviously not true, and children know it's not true.

Women's looks matter terribly in this society, and so Barbie, however ambivalently, must be passed along. After all, there are worse toys. The Cut and Style Barbie styling head, for example, a grotesque object intended to encourage "hair play." The grown-ups who give that probably apologize, too.

How happy would most parents be to have a child who flouted sex conventions? I know a lot of women, feminists, who complain in a comical, eyeball-rolling way about their sons' passion for sports: the ruined weekends, obnoxious coaches, macho values. But they would not think of discouraging their sons from participating in this activity they find so foolish. Or do they? Their husbands are sports fans, too, and they like their husbands a lot.

Could it be that even sports-resistant moms see athletics as part of manliness? That if their sons wanted to spend the weekend writing up their diaries, or reading, or baking, they'd find it disturbing? Too antisocial? Too lonely? Too gay?

Theories of innate differences in behavior are appealing. They let parents off the hook — no small recommendation in a culture that holds moms, and sometimes even dads, responsible for their children's every misstep on the road to bliss and success.

They allow grown-ups to take the path of least resistance to the   11
dominant culture, which always requires less psychic effort, even if it
means more actual work: Just ask the working mother who comes home
exhausted and nonetheless finds it easier to pick up her son's socks than
make him do it himself. They let families buy for their children, without *too* much guilt, the unbelievably sexist junk that the kids, who have
been watching commercials since birth, understandably crave.

But the thing the theories do most of all is tell adults that the *adult*   12
world—in which moms and dads still play by many of the old rules
even as they question and fidget and chafe against them—is the way
it's supposed to be. A girl with a doll and a boy with a truck "explain"
why men are from Mars and women are from Venus, why wives do
housework and husbands just don't understand.

The paradox is that the world of rigid and hierarchical sex roles   13
evoked by determinist theories is already passing away. Three-year-olds
may indeed insist that doctors are male and nurses female, even if their
own mother is a physician. Six-year-olds know better. These days,
something like half of all medical students are female, and male applications to nursing school are inching upward. When tomorrow's three-
year-olds play doctor, who's to say how they'll assign the roles?

With sex roles, as in every area of life, people aspire to what is pos-   14
sible, and conform to what is necessary. But these are not fixed, especially today. Biological determinism may reassure some adults about
their present, but it is feminism, the ideology of flexible and converging sex roles, that fits our children's future. And the kids, somehow,
know this.

That's why, if you look carefully, you'll find that for every kid who   15
fits a stereotype, there's another who's breaking one down. Sometimes
it's the same kid—the boy who skateboards *and* takes cooking in his af-
terschool program; the girl who collects stuffed animals *and* A-pluses in
science.

Feminists are often accused of imposing their "agenda" on chil-   16
dren. Isn't that what adults always do, consciously and unconsciously?
Kids aren't born religious, or polite, or kind, or able to remember where
they put their sneakers. Inculcating these behaviors, and the values behind them, is a tremendous amount of work, involving many adults.
We don't have a choice, really, about *whether* we should give our children messages about what it means to be male and female—they're
bombarded with them from morning till night.

QUESTIONS ON MEANING

1. What does Pollitt imply by pointing out that despite the existence of the National Organization for Women, "boys still like trucks and girls still like dolls" (para. 1)?
2. Does Pollitt believe that gender differences develop because of or despite the influences of society? How do you know?
3. Where do you find the THESIS of Pollitt's essay? Why do you think she placed it there?
4. Pollitt says that the "path of least resistance...requires less psychic effort, even if it means more actual work" (para. 11). What does she mean?

QUESTIONS ON WRITING STRATEGY

1. Pollitt admits that theories of gender differences based on biological differences can be attractive (paras. 10–12). Does this admission weaken her argument? Why, or why not?
2. This easy originally appeared in the *New York Times Magazine*. In what ways does Pollitt direct her essay to readers of that periodical? How might the essay have differed if Pollitt had written it for *Seventeen* or another magazine for young women?
3. **MIXED METHODS.** Look at the EXAMPLES Pollitt gives to illustrate how parents support gender differences, even when they would like to resist them (paras. 8–9). Why does she choose these particular examples? What do her RHETORICAL QUESTIONS add to her examples?
4. **MIXED METHODS.** In paragraphs 5–7 Pollitt uses CAUSE AND EFFECT to explore why mothers give Barbie dolls as gifts and what the consequences are. SUMMARIZE this part of the ARGUMENT.

QUESTIONS ON LANGUAGE

1. What does Pollitt mean when she explains that America is not yet "a playground free of sex roles" (para. 3)? What is the significance of the word *playground* in this context?
2. In her last paragraph Pollitt talks about "inculcating" behaviors in children, through messages with which they're constantly "bombarded." What are the CONNOTATIONS of these words? Why does Pollitt choose them to describe the process of learning values?
3. What is the TONE of the question that ends paragraph 13? What is Pollitt's point in asking it?
4. If any of the following words are unfamiliar, look them up: prenatal (para. 1); cognitive, hoopla, sex-differentiated (2); innate (4); ambivalently, grotesque (7); flouted, obnoxious (8); psychic (11); chafe (12); hierarchical, determinist (13); converging (14).

SUGGESTIONS FOR WRITING

1. **JOURNAL WRITING.** Pollitt asserts that adults have some "agenda" of values they impose on their children. What was your parents' agenda for you when you were growing up? What lessons do you remember being drummed into your head?
   FROM JOURNAL TO ESSAY. Choose one or two lessons recorded in your journal entry, and write a NARRATIVE essay that reveals your family's value system. Was the agenda made obvious to you or kept hidden? Did you eventually learn the things your parents tried to teach, or did you resist them? How important are these lessons or values to you today?

2. "With sex roles, as in every area of life, people aspire to what is possible, and conform to what is necessary" (para. 14). Pollitt suggests here that we can rarely, if ever, achieve our ideals. Do you agree or disagree with this statement? Choosing one or two specific "areas of life" that provide you with lots of examples, write an essay explaining why you do or don't buy Pollitt's claim.

3. **CRITICAL WRITING.** Pollitt proposes a "feminist" approach to child rearing that emphasizes "flexible and converging sex roles" (para. 14). Do you agree with her that this agenda "fits our children's future," or do you see value in traditional sex roles that makes these roles appropriate for the future? In an essay, agree or disagree with Pollitt, using as EVIDENCE your own experiences and observations as well as Pollitt's assertions and examples.

4. **CONNECTIONS (PART ONE).** Read or reread Margaret Atwood's poem "Bored" (p. 132), attending to the way the child did what "he" (her father) expected of her. Could the child have resisted? Using evidence from Atwood's poem and Pollitt's essay as you see fit, but also drawing on your own observations and experiences, write an essay explaining your view of how parents determine their children's behavior. What is the connection between social roles and parents' expectations? How can children act against the values of their parents? Once children are grown, how free are they, or should they be, from the patterns and values their parents set for them?

5. **CONNECTIONS (PART TWO).** Pollitt and Emily Prager, in "Our Barbies, Ourselves" (p. 607), both use the Barbie doll as a symbol of how stereotypes affect our ideas about femininity. Is Barbie a useful example in both of these essays? Would other toys or additional examples of toys have been more effective, or are toys too trivial for such arguments? How convincing are the two authors' claims about gender roles, based on Barbie?

KATHA POLLITT ON WRITING

Katha Pollitt began writing early. "I started writing poetry when I was in about sixth grade," she told Ruth Coniff of *The Progressive* magazine in 1994. "I used to come home from school and go up to my room and sit on my bed and write my poems. And I was writing angry letters to the newspaper. . . . I recently came across a letter I had written when I was twelve years old to the *New York Times*. It was about some complicated legal case involving someone who was accused of being a spy, but I have absolutely no memory of writing this letter or of what this case was. It was actually like something I would write today. I thought, ... have I been doing this for that long?"

Coniff observed that Pollitt's poetry is not political and asked why. "Well," Pollitt replied, "I was always a two-track writer. I always wrote poetry and prose.... I have to say that I see poetry and political writing as different endeavors. What I want in a poem is not an argument, it's not a statement, it has to do with language. I'm looking for a kind of energized, fresh, alive perception.... To me it's much more interesting to read that than to read a poem with whose politics I would agree, but that doesn't have a lot of depth of language and imagination in it.... What I like about poetry is the verbal concentration and levels of meaning. A poem with only one level of meaning is not a very interesting poem."

FOR DISCUSSION

1. What are your earliest memories of writing? When have you written on your own (that is, not for a school assignment)? What moves you to write?
2. Explore Pollitt's ideas about poetry versus political prose by comparing two works earlier in this book: Margaret Atwood's poem "Bored" (p. 132) and Armin A. Brott's essay "Not All Men Are Sly Foxes" (p. 278). Both are about men, particularly fathers, but how do they differ in their use of language? Does this difference make one "better" than the other? Why?

14

THE NATURE OF
COMMUNITY

All of us live in communities, from neighborhoods or dormitories to towns or cities. According to *The American Heritage Dictionary*, the word *community* means "a group of people living in the same locality and under the same government" or "a group of people having common interests." The selections in this chapter pursue this concept very differently. In his essay "The Web of Life," Scott Russell Sanders emphasizes how the sharing of aims and interests can sustain the residents of a small city. In her short story "The Lottery," Shirley Jackson fixes her attention, and ours, on the conformity demanded of those who would dwell together in harmony.

The essays in the chapter after this one (p. 639) broach a new kind of community, cyberspace, in which the members do not dwell together at all but communicate through computers.

SCOTT RUSSELL SANDERS

SCOTT RUSSELL SANDERS writes stories, novels, and essays about plain people who, in his words, "are neither literary nor intellectual." He was born in 1945 in Memphis, Tennessee, and reports a somewhat nomadic childhood. He attended Brown University (B.A., 1967) and Cambridge University (Ph.D., 1971) and for more than twenty-five years has taught English at Indiana University in Bloomington. His books include stories for children, such as *Aurora Means Dawn* (1989); novels for adults, such as *Terrarium* (1985) and *The Invisible Company* (1989); collections of short stories, such as *Fetching the Dead* (1984) and *Hear the Wind Blow* (1985); and collections of essays, such as *Secrets of the Universe* (1991) and *Staying Put: Making a Home in a Restless World* (1993).

The Web of Life

Moving around as a child led Sanders to seek roots in early adulthood, and he has lived since then in Bloomington, Indiana. His concern "with the life people make together" is evident in this essay, which appeared first in *The Georgia Review* in 1994 and then in the *Utne Reader* in 1995.

"The Web of Life" is a DEFINITION of *community* and an ARGUMENT for its ties. Sanders uses other methods as well: Through NARRATION and DESCRIPTION he conveys his experience of living in a community. Through COMPARISON AND CONTRAST he illuminates two opposing traditions of American culture. Through CAUSE AND EFFECT he explains what we gain from communities and what we lose without them.

A woman who recently moved from Los Angeles to Bloomington, 1 Indiana, told me that she would not be able to stay here long, because she was already beginning to recognize people in the grocery stores, on the sidewalks, in the library. Being surrounded by familiar faces made her nervous, after years in a city where she could range about anonymously. Every traveler knows the sense of liberation that comes from journeying to a place where nobody expects anything of you. Everyone who has gone to college knows the exhilaration of slipping away from the watchful eyes of Mom and Dad. We all need seasons of withdrawal from responsibility. But if we make a career of being unaccountable, we have lost something essential to our humanity, and we may well become a burden or a threat to those around us.

Ever since the eclipse of our native cultures, the dominant Ameri- 2 can view has been that we should cultivate the self rather than the community; that we should look to the individual as the source of hope and the center of value, while expecting hindrance and harm from society. We have understood freedom for the most part negatively rather than positively, as release from constraints rather than as a condition for making a decent life in common. Hands off, we say; give me elbow room; good fences make good neighbors; my home is my castle; don't tread on me. I'm looking out for number one, we say; I'm doing my own thing. We have a Bill of Rights, which protects each of us from a bullying society, but no Bill of Responsibilities, which would oblige us to answer the needs of others.

What other view could have emerged from our history? The first 3 Europeans to reach America were daredevils and treasure seekers, as were most of those who mapped the interior. Many colonists were renegades of one stripe or another, some of them religious nonconformists, some political rebels, more than a few of them fugitives from the law. The trappers, hunters, traders, and freebooters who pushed the frontier westward seldom recognized any authority beyond the reach of their own hands. Coast to coast, our land has been settled and our cities have been filled by generations of immigrants more intent on leaving behind old tyrannies than on seeking new social bonds.

The cult of the individual shows up everywhere in American lore, 4 which celebrates drifters, rebels, and loners while pitying or reviling the pillars of the community. The backwoods explorer like Daniel Boone, the riverboat rowdy like Mike Fink, the lumberjack, the prospector, the rambler and gambler, the daring crook like Jesse James or the resourceful killer like Billy the Kid, along with countless lonesome cowboys, all wander, unattached, through the great spaces of our imagination.

Fortunately, while our tradition is heavily tilted in favor of private 5 life, we also inherit a tradition of caring for the community. Writing about what he had seen in the 1830s, Alexis de Tocqueville[1] judged Americans to be avaricious, self-serving, and aggressive; but he was also amazed by our eagerness to form clubs, to raise barns or town halls, to join together in one cause or another: "In no country in the world," he wrote, "do the citizens make such exertions for the common weal. I know of no people who have established schools so numerous and efficacious, places of public worship better suited to the wants of the inhabitants, or roads kept in better repair."

Today we might revise Tocqueville's estimate of our schools or 6 roads, but we can still see all around us the fruits of that concern for the common weal—the libraries, museums, courthouses, hospitals,

---

[1]Tocqueville (1805–59) was a French writer who traveled to the young United States in 1831 and wrote memorably of its people and institutions in *Democracy in America* (1835, 1840).—EDS.

orphanages, universities, parks, on and on. No matter where we live, our home places have also benefited from the Granges and unions, the volunteer fire brigades, the art guilds and garden clubs, the charities, food kitchens, homeless shelters, soccer and baseball teams, the Scouts and 4-H, the Girls and Boys Clubs, the Lions and Elks and Rotarians, the countless gatherings of people who saw a need and responded to it.

This history of local care hardly ever makes it into our literature, for it is less glamorous than rebellion, yet it is a crucial part of our heritage. Any of us could cite examples of people who dug in and joined with others to make our home places better places. Women and men who invest themselves in their communities, fighting for good schools or green spaces, paying attention to where they are, seem to me as worthy of celebration as those adventurous loners who keep drifting on, prospecting for pleasure.

The words *community*, *communion*, and *communicate* all derive from *common*, and the two syllables of *common* grow from separate roots, the first meaning "together" or "next to," the second having to do with barter or exchange. Embodied in that word is a sense of our shared life as one of giving and receiving—music, touch, ideas, recipes, stories, medicine, tools, the whole range of artifacts and talents. After twenty-five years with my wife, Ruth, that is how I have come to understand marriage, as a constant exchange of labor and love. We do not calculate who gives how much; if we had to, the marriage would be in trouble. Looking outward from this community of two, I see my life embedded in ever larger exchanges—those of family and friendship, neighborhood and city, countryside and country—and on every scale there is giving and receiving, calling and answering.

Many people shy away from community out of a fear that it may become suffocating, confining, even vicious; and of course it may, if it grows rigid or exclusive. A healthy community is dynamic, stirred up by the energies of those who already belong, open to new members and fresh influences, kept in motion by the constant bartering of gifts. It is fashionable just now to speak of this open quality as "tolerance," but that word sounds too grudging to me—as though, to avoid strife, we must grit our teeth and ignore whatever is strange to us. The community I desire is not grudging; it is exuberant, joyful, grounded in affection, pleasure, and mutual aid. Such a community arises not from duty or money but from the free interchange of people who share a place, share work and food, sorrows and hope. Taking part in the common life means dwelling in a web of relationships, the many threads tugging at you while also holding you upright.

I have told elsewhere the story of a man who lived in the Ohio township where I grew up, a builder who refused to join the volunteer fire department. Why should he join, when his house was brick, properly wired, fitted out with new appliances? Well, one day that house caught fire. His wife dialed the emergency number, the siren wailed, and pretty soon the volunteer firemen, my father among them, showed up with the pumper truck. But they held back on the hoses, asking the builder if he still saw no reason to join, and the builder said he could see a pretty good reason to join right there and then, and the volunteers let the water loose.

I have also told before the story of a family from that township 11
whose house burned down. The local people sheltered the family, then built them a new house. This was a poor township. But nobody thought to call in the government or apply to a foundation. These were neighbors in a fix, and so you helped them, just as you would harvest corn for an ailing farmer or pull a flailing child from the creek or put your arm around a weeping friend.

My daughter Eva and I recently went to a concert in Bloomington's 12
newly opened arts center. The old limestone building had once been the town hall, then a fire station and jail, then for several years an abandoned shell. Volunteers bought the building from the city for a dollar and renovated it with materials, labor, and money donated by local people. Now we have a handsome facility that is in constant use for pottery classes, theater productions, puppet shows, art exhibits, poetry readings, and every manner of musical event.

The music Eva and I heard was *Hymnody of Earth*, for hammer dul- 13
cimer, percussion, and children's choir. Composed by our next-door neighbor Malcolm Dalglish and featuring lyrics by our Ohio Valley neighbor Wendell Berry, it was performed that night by Malcolm, percussionist Glen Velez, and the Bloomington Youth Chorus. As I sat there with Eva in a sellout crowd—about a third of whom I knew by name, another third by face—I listened to music that had been elaborated within earshot of my house, and I heard my friend play his instrument, and I watched those children's faces shining with the colors of the human spectrum, and I felt the restored building clasping us like the cupped hands of our community. I knew once more that I was in the right place, a place created and filled and inspired by our lives together.

I am not harking back to some idyllic past, like the one embalmed 14
in the *Saturday Evening Post* covers by Norman Rockwell or the prints of Currier and Ives. The past was never golden. As a people, we still need to unlearn some of the bad habits we formed during the long period of settlement. One good habit we might reclaim, however, is looking after those who live nearby. For much of our history, neighbors have

kept one another going, kept one another sane. Still today, in town and country, in apartment buildings and barrios, even in suburban estates, you are certain to lead a narrower life without the steady presence of neighbors. It is neither quaint nor sentimental to advocate neighborliness; it is far more sentimental to suggest that we can do without such mutual aid.

Even Emerson,[2] preaching self-reliance, knew the necessity of 15 neighbors. He lived in a village, gave and received help, and delivered his essays as lectures for fellow citizens whom he hoped to sway. He could have left his ideas in his journals, where they first took shape, but he knew those ideas would only have effect when they were shared. I like to think he would have agreed with the Lakota shaman Black Elk,[3] who said, "A man who has a vision is not able to use the power of it until after he has performed the vision on earth for the people to see." If you visit Emerson's house in Concord, you will find leather buckets hanging near the door, for he belonged to the village fire brigade, and even in the seclusion of his study, in the depths of thought, he kept his ears open for the the alarm bell.

We should not have to wait until our houses are burning before we 16 see the wisdom of facing our local needs by joining in common work. We should not have to wait until gunfire breaks out in our schools, rashes break out on our skin, dead fish float in our streams, or beggars sleep on our streets before we act on behalf of the community. On a crowded planet, we had better learn how to live well together, or we will live miserably apart.

QUESTIONS ON MEANING

1. What is the THESIS of this essay? Where does Sanders state it?
2. How does Sanders explain the traditional American DEFINITION of freedom (para. 2)? How does this definition help support his thesis?
3. Why does Sanders dislike the word *tolerance* as applied to a community (para. 9)?
4. What does *sentimental* mean? Why does Sanders believe it is sentimental to suggest that we can do without each other (para. 14)?

---

[2] Ralph Waldo Emerson (1803–82) was an influential American philosopher and essayist who stressed individualism. — EDS.

[3] Black Elk was a shaman, or spiritual medium, of the Oglala Lakota branch of the Sioux Indian nation. His autobiography, *Black Elk Speaks* (1932), is a record of the culture and struggles of the Plains Indians in the nineteenth century. — EDS.

QUESTIONS ON WRITING STRATEGY

1. What is the EFFECT of the series of familiar sayings in paragraph 2?
2. Why does Sanders give the etymology—the history—of the word *community* (para. 8)?
3. **MIXED METHODS.** Sanders relates three NARRATIVES of community in paragraphs 10–13 as EXAMPLES of how communities work. What do these stories do that straight explanation would not?
4. **MIXED METHODS.** In paragraphs 2–7 Sanders COMPARES AND CONTRASTS two threads of American thought and action. What are these threads? What effects do they have on us today?

QUESTIONS ON LANGUAGE

1. What does Sanders suggest by saying that "we all need seasons of withdrawal from responsibility" (para. 1)? How does the word *seasons* shape his point?
2. Explain the METAPHOR of the essay's title.
3. Familiarize yourself with the meanings of any of the following words you do not already know: exhilaration, unaccountable (para 1); eclipse, hindrance (2); renegades, nonconformists, freebooters, tyrannies (3); reviling, prospector (4); avaricious, weal, efficacious (5); Granges, brigades, guilds (6); barter, artifacts (8); grudging, exuberant (9); dulcimer, percussion, lyrics (13); idyllic, barrios (14).

SUGGESTIONS FOR WRITING

1. **JOURNAL WRITING.** What are the characteristics of the community you live in? Is it filled with individuals who act independently, or do its members cooperate extensively, or is the reality somewhere in between? What incidents can you recall that illustrate the philosophy of the members of your community?

   FROM JOURNAL TO ESSAY. Sanders presents two models of community life: one based on individual interests, one based on cooperation. Which do you think is more common in America today? Using examples from your own community, write an essay that defines your sense of the typical American community. (You may reject the notion of "typical," too, claiming that there is no such thing. Or you may believe that your community is the exception rather than the rule.) However you decide to approach this essay, provide EVIDENCE from real life to support your points.
2. Sanders ends his essay with a call for Americans to "learn how to live well together." What would achieving this aim entail? Write an essay with concrete suggestions for what Americans need to learn and do to "live well together."
3. **CRITICAL WRITING.** How convincing is Sanders's ARGUMENT? Write a critical ANALYSIS of "The Web of Life," considering some or all of the following questions: How effective is Sanders's use of historical precedents as evidence? Are his narratives of particular community situations persuasive? Does Sanders at least implicitly acknowledge opposing views by giving

adequate attention to the value of individualism? What APPEALS does he make
— rational, emotional, and ethical?

4. **CONNECTIONS (PART ONE).** Read or reread Bruce Catton's "Grant and Lee:
   A Study in Contrasts" (p. 193). Like Sanders, Catton identifies two traditions in American history, which he locates in the great Civil War generals. To what extent do Sanders's and Catton's traditions overlap? Write an
   essay that compares and contrasts the two authors' views of American history.

5. **CONNECTIONS (PART TWO).** Sanders holds that a community must be flexible and dynamic in order to succeed (para. 9). The next selection, Shirley
   Jackson's short story "The Lottery," depicts a community that is particularly
   inflexible, adhering to traditions it barely understands. Does Jackson's story
   support Sanders's point about flexibility, or does it reveal value in preserving tradition at all costs? Write an essay that analyzes "The Lottery" in light
   of Sanders's argument.

SCOTT RUSSELL SANDERS ON WRITING

In exchanges with *Contemporary Authors* over the years, Scott Russell Sanders has connected writing and community in a way that extends the ideas of "The Web of Life":

"I do not much value experimentation in form and style, if it is not
engendered by new insights into human experience. I do value clarity
of language and vision.... I believe that a writer should be a servant of
language, community, and nature. Language is the creation and sustenance of community; and any community, if it is to be healthy and
durable, must be respectful of the natural order which makes life possible. Because there is no true human existence apart from family and
community, I feel a deep commitment to my region, to the land, to the
people and all other living things with which I share this place. My
writing is driven by a deep regard for particular places and voices, persons and tools, plants and animals, for human skills and stories, for the
small change of daily life — a regard compounded of grief and curiosity
and love. If my writing does not help my neighbors to live more alertly,
pleasurably, or wisely, then it is worth little."

FOR DISCUSSION

1. What does Sanders mean by "Language is the creation and sustenance of
   community"? What does language do for a community? Could a community exist without some form of language?

2. Do you think "The Web of Life" achieves the goal Sanders states in his last
   sentence: Will he help *you* "live more alertly, pleasurably, or wisely"? Why,
   or why not?

SHIRLEY JACKSON

SHIRLEY JACKSON was a fiction writer best known for horror stories that probe the dark side of human nature and social behavior. But she also wrote humorously about domestic life, a subject she knew well as a wife and the mother of four children. Born in 1919 in California, Jackson moved as a teenager to Syracuse, New York, and graduated from Syracuse University in 1940. She started writing as a young girl and was highly disciplined and productive all her life. She began publishing stories in 1941, and eventually her fiction appeared in *The New Yorker, Harper's, Good Housekeeping*, and many other magazines. Her tales of family life appeared in two books, *Life Among the Savages* (1953) and *Raising Demons* (1957). Her more popular (and to her more significant) suspense novels included *The Haunting of Hill House* (1959) and *We Have Always Lived in the Castle* (1962). After Jackson's death in 1965, her husband, the literary critic Stanley Edgar Hyman, published two volumes of her stories, novels, and lectures, *The Magic of Shirley Jackson* (1966) and *Come Along with Me* (1968).

The Lottery

By far Jackson's best-known work and indeed one of the best-known short stories ever, "The Lottery" first appeared in *The New Yorker* in 1948 to loud applause and louder cries of outrage. Jackson's husband, denying that her work purveyed "neurotic fantasies," argued instead that it was fitting "for our distressing world of concentration camps and The Bomb." See if you agree.

"The Lottery," being fiction, is primarily NARRATION. But Jackson uses DESCRIPTION to depict the characters, PROCESS ANALYSIS to explain how the lottery works, and CAUSE AND EFFECT to explore the reasons for the lottery.

The morning of June 27th was clear and sunny, with the fresh 1 warmth of a full-summer day; the flowers were blossoming profusely and the grass was richly green. The people of the village began to gather in the square, between the post office and the bank, around ten o'clock; in some towns there were so many people that the lottery took two days and had to be started on June 26th, but in this village, where there were only about three hundred people, the whole lottery took less than two hours, so it could begin at ten o'clock in the morning and still be through in time to allow the villagers to get home for noon dinner.

The children assembled first, of course. School was recently over 2 for the summer, and the feeling of liberty sat uneasily on most of them; they tended to gather together quietly for a while before they broke into boisterous play, and their talk was still of the classroom and the teacher, of books and reprimands. Bobby Martin had already stuffed his pockets full of stones, and the other boys soon followed his example, selecting the smoothest and roundest stones; Bobby and Harry Jones and Dickie Delacroix—the villagers pronounced this name "Dellacroy"—eventually made a great pile of stones in one corner of the square and guarded it against the raids of the other boys. The girls stood aside, talking among themselves, looking over their shoulders at the boys, and the very small children rolled in the dust or clung to the hands of their older brothers or sisters.

Soon the men began to gather, surveying their own children, speaking of planting and rain, tractors and taxes. They stood together, away from the pile of stones in the corner, and their jokes were quiet and they smiled rather than laughed. The women, wearing faded house dresses and sweaters, came shortly after their menfolk. They greeted one another and exchanged bits of gossip as they went to join their husbands. Soon the women, standing by their husbands, began to call to their children, and the children came reluctantly, having to be called four or five times. Bobby Martin ducked under his mother's grasping hand and ran, laughing, back to the pile of stones. His father spoke up sharply, and Bobby came quickly and took his place between his father and his oldest brother.

The lottery was conducted—as were the square dances, the teenage club, the Halloween program—by Mr. Summers, who had time and energy to devote to civic activities. He was a round-faced, jovial man and he ran the coal business, and people were sorry for him, because he had no children and his wife was a scold. When he arrived in the square, carrying the black wooden box, there was a murmur of conversation among the villagers, and he waved and called, "Little late today, folks." The postmaster, Mr. Graves, followed him, carrying a three-legged stool, and the stool was put in the center of the square and Mr. Summers set the black box down on it. The villagers kept their distance, leaving a space between themselves and the stool, and when Mr. Summers said, "Some of you fellows want to give me a hand?" there was a hesitation before two men, Mr. Martin and his oldest son, Baxter, came forward to hold the box steady on the stool while Mr. Summers stirred up the papers inside it.

The original paraphernalia for the lottery had been lost long ago, and the black box now resting on the stool had been put into use even before Old Man Warner, the oldest man in town, was born. Mr. Summers spoke frequently to the villagers about making a new box, but no one liked to upset even as much tradition as was represented by the black box. There was a story that the present box had been made with some pieces of the box that had preceded it, the one that had been constructed when the first people settled down to make a village here. Every year, after the lottery, Mr. Summers began talking again about a new box, but every year the subject was allowed to fade off without anything's being done. The black box grew shabbier each year; by now it was no longer completely black but splintered badly along one side to show the original wood color, and in some places faded or stained.

Mr. Martin and his oldest son, Baxter, held the black box securely on the stool until Mr. Summers had stirred the papers thoroughly with his hand. Because so much of the ritual had been forgotten or discarded, Mr. Summers had been successful in having slips of paper substituted for the chips of wood that had been used for generations. Chips of wood, Mr. Summers had argued, had been all very well when the village was tiny, but now that the population was more than three hundred and likely to keep on growing, it was necessary to use something that would fit more easily into the black box. The night before the lottery, Mr. Summers and Mr. Graves made up the slips of paper and put them in the box, and it was then taken to the safe of Mr. Summers' coal company and locked up until Mr. Summers was ready to take it to the square next morning. The rest of the year, the box was put away, sometimes one place, sometimes another; it had spent one year in Mr. Graves's barn and another year underfoot in the post office, and sometimes it was set on a shelf in the Martin grocery and left there.

There was a great deal of fussing to be done before Mr. Summers declared the lottery open. There were the lists to make up — of heads of families, heads of households in each family, members of each household in each family. There was the proper swearing-in of Mr. Summers by the postmaster, as the official of the lottery; at one time, some people remembered, there had been a recital of some sort, performed by the official of the lottery, a perfunctory, tuneless chant that had been rattled off duly each year; some people believed that the official of the lottery used to stand just so when he said or sang it, others believed that he was supposed to walk among the people, but years and years ago this part of the ritual had been allowed to lapse. There had been, also, a ritual salute, which the official of the lottery had had to use in addressing each person who came up to draw from the box, but this also had changed with time, until now it was felt necessary only for the official to speak to each person approaching. Mr. Summers was very good at all this; in his clean white shirt and blue jeans, with one hand resting carelessly on the black box, he seemed very proper and important as he talked interminably to Mr. Graves and the Martins.

Just as Mr. Summers finally left off talking and turned to the assembled villagers, Mrs. Hutchinson came hurriedly along the path to the square, her sweater thrown over her shoulders, and slid into place in the back of the crowd. "Clean forgot what day it was," she said to

Mrs. Delacroix, who stood next to her, and they both laughed softly. "Thought my old man was out back stacking wood," Mrs. Hutchinson went on, "and then I looked out the window and the kids was gone, and then I remembered it was the twenty-seventh and came a-running." She dried her hands on her apron, and Mrs. Delacroix said, "You're in time, though. They're still talking away up there."

Mrs. Hutchinson craned her neck to see through the crowd and found her husband and children standing near the front. She tapped Mrs. Delacroix on the arm as a farewell and began to make her way through the crowd. The people separated good-humoredly to let her through, two or three people said, in voices just loud enough to be heard across the crowd, "Here comes your Missus, Hutchinson," and "Bill, she made it after all." Mrs. Hutchinson reached her husband, and Mr. Summers, who had been waiting, said cheerfully, "Thought we were going to have to get on without you, Tessie." Mrs. Hutchinson said, grinning, "Wouldn't have me leave m'dishes in the sink, now, would you, Joe?" and soft laughter ran through the crowd as the people stirred back into position after Mrs. Hutchinson's arrival. 9

"Well now," Mr. Summers said soberly, "guess we better get started, get this over with, so's we can go back to work. Anybody ain't here?" 10

"Dunbar," several people said. "Dunbar, Dunbar." 11

Mr. Summers consulted his list. "Clyde Dunbar," he said. "That's right. He's broke his leg, hasn't he? Who's drawing for him?" 12

"Me, I guess," a woman said, and Mr. Summers turned to look at her. "Wife draws for her husband," Mr. Summers said. "Don't you have a grown boy to do it for you, Janey?" Although Mr. Summers and everyone else in the village knew the answer perfectly well, it was the business of the official of the lottery to ask such questions formally. Mr. Summers waited with an expression of polite interest while Mrs. Dunbar answered. 13

"Horace's not but sixteen yet," Mrs. Dunbar said regretfully. "Guess I gotta fill in for the old man this year." 14

"Right," Mr. Summers said. He made a note on the list he was holding. Then he asked, "Watson boy drawing this year?" 15

A tall boy in the crowd raised his hand. "Here," he said. "I'm drawing for m'mother and me." He blinked his eyes nervously and ducked his head as several voices in the crowd said things like "Good fellow, Jack," and "Glad to see your mother's got a man to do it." 16

"Well," Mr. Summers said, "guess that's everyone. Old Man Warner make it?" 17

"Here," a voice said, and Mr. Summers nodded. 18

A sudden hush fell on the crowd as Mr. Summers cleared his throat and looked at the list. "All ready?" he called. "Now, I'll read the names 19

—heads of families first—and the men come up and take a paper out of the box. Keep the paper folded in your hand without looking at it until everyone has had a turn. Everything clear?"

The people had done it so many times that they only half listened to   20
the directions, most of them were quiet, wetting their lips, not looking around. Then Mr. Summers raised one hand high and said, "Adams." A man disengaged himself from the crowd and came forward. "Hi, Steve," Mr. Summers said, and Mr. Adams said, "Hi, Joe." They grinned at one another humorlessly and nervously. Then Mr. Adams reached into the black box and took out a folded paper. He held it firmly by one corner as he turned and went hastily back to his place in the crowd, where he stood a little apart from his family, not looking down at his hand.

"Allen," Mr. Summers said, "Anderson.... Bentham."   21

"Seems like there's no time at all between lotteries any more," Mrs.   22
Delacroix said to Mrs. Graves in the back row. "Seems like we got through with the last one only last week."

"Time sure goes fast," Mrs. Graves said.   23

"Clark.... Delacroix."   24

"There goes my old man," Mrs. Delacroix said. She held her breath   25
while her husband went forward.

"Dunbar," Mr. Summers said, and Mrs. Dunbar went steadily to the   26
box while one of the women said, "Go on Janey," and another said, "There she goes."

"We're next," Mrs. Graves said. She watched while Mr. Graves   27
came around from the side of the box, greeted Mr. Summers gravely, and selected a slip of paper from the box. By now, all through the crowd there were men holding the small folded papers in their large hands, turning them over and over nervously. Mrs. Dunbar and her two sons stood together, Mrs. Dunbar holding the slip of paper.

"Harburt.... Hutchinson."   28

"Get up there, Bill," Mrs. Hutchinson said, and the people near her   29
laughed.

"Jones."   30

"They do say," Mr. Adams said to Old Man Warner, who stood   31
next to him, "that over in the north village they're talking of giving up the lottery."

Old Man Warner snorted. "Pack of crazy fools," he said. "Listening   32
to the young folks, nothing's good enough for *them*. Next thing you know, they'll be wanting to go back to living in caves, nobody work any more, live *that* way for a while. Used to be a saying about 'Lottery in June, corn be heavy soon.' First thing you know, we'd all be eating stewed chickweed and acorns. There's *always* been a lottery," he added petulantly. "Bad enough to see young Joe Summers up there joking with everybody."

"Some places have already quit lotteries," Mrs. Adams said. 33

"Nothing but trouble in *that*," Old Man Warner said stoutly. "Pack 34 of young fools."

"Martin." And Bobby Martin watched his father go forward. 35 "Overdyke.... Percy."

"I wish they'd hurry," Mrs. Dunbar said to her older son. "I wish 36 they'd hurry."

"They're almost through," her son said. 37

"You get ready to run tell Dad," Mrs. Dunbar said. 38

Mr. Summers called his own name and then stepped forward pre- 39 cisely and selected a slip from the box. Then he called, "Warner."

"Seventy-seventh year I been in the lottery," Old Man Warner said 40 as he went through the crowd. "Seventy-seventh time."

"Watson." The tall boy came awkwardly through the crowd. Some- 41 one said, "Don't be nervous, Jack," and Mr. Summers said, "Take your time, son."

"Zanini." 42

After that, there was a long pause, a breathless pause, until Mr. 43 Summers, holding his slip of paper in the air, said, "All right, fellows." For a minute, no one moved, and then all the slips of paper were opened. Suddenly, all the women began to speak at once, saying, "Who is it?" "Who's got it?" "Is it the Dunbars?" "Is it the Watsons?" Then the voices began to say, "It's Hutchinson. It's Bill," "Bill Hutchinson's got it."

"Go tell your father," Mrs. Dunbar said to her older son. 44

People began to look around to see the Hutchinsons. Bill Hutchin- 45 son was standing quiet, staring down at the paper in his hand. Sud- denly, Tessie Hutchinson shouted to Mr. Summers, "You didn't give him time enough to take any paper he wanted. I saw you. It wasn't fair!"

"Be a good sport, Tessie," Mrs. Delacroix called, and Mrs. Graves 46 said, "All of us took the same chance."

"Shut up, Tessie," Bill Hutchinson said. 47

"Well, everyone," Mr. Summers said, "that was done pretty fast, 48 and now we've got to be hurrying a little more to get done in time." He consulted his next list. "Bill," he said, "you draw for the Hutchinson family. You got any other households in the Hutchinsons?"

"There's Don and Eva," Mrs. Hutchinson yelled. "Make *them* take 49 their chance!"

"Daughters drew with their husband's families, Tessie," Mr. Sum- 50 mers said gently. "You know that as well as anyone else."

"It wasn't *fair*," Tessie said. 51

"I guess not, Joe," Bill Hutchinson said regretfully. "My daughter 52 draws with her husband's family, that's only fair. And I've got no other family except the kids."

"Then, as far as drawing for families is concerned, it's you," Mr. 53 Summers said in explanation, "and as far as drawing for households is concerned, that's you, too. Right?"

"Right," Bill Hutchinson said. 54

"How many kids, Bill?" Mr. Summers asked formally. 55

"Three," Bill Hutchinson said. "There's Bill, Jr., and Nancy, and 56 little Dave. And Tessie and me."

"All right, then," Mr. Summer said. "Harry, you got their tickets 57 back?"

Mr. Graves nodded and held up the slips of paper. "Put them in the 58 box, then," Mr. Summers directed. "Take Bill's and put it in."

"I think we ought to start over," Mrs. Hutchinson said, as quietly as 59 she could. "I tell you it wasn't *fair*. You didn't give him time enough to choose. *Everybody* saw that."

Mr. Graves had selected the five slips and put them in the box, and 60 he dropped all the papers but those onto the ground, where the breeze caught them and lifted them off.

"Listen, everybody," Mrs. Hutchinson was saying to the people 61 around her.

"Ready, Bill?" Mr. Summers asked, and Bill Hutchinson, with one 62 quick glance around at his wife and children, nodded.

"Remember," Mr. Summers said, "take the slips and keep them 63 folded until each person has taken one. Harry, you help little Dave." Mr. Graves took the hand of the little boy, who came willingly with him up to the box. "Take a paper out of the box, Davy," Mr. Summers said. Davy put his hand into the box and laughed. "Take just *one* paper," Mr. Summers said. "Harry, you hold it for him." Mr. Graves took the child's hand and removed the folded paper from the tight fist and held it while little Dave stood next to him and looked up at him wonderingly.

"Nancy next," Mr. Summers said. Nancy was twelve, and her 64 school friends breathed heavily as she went forward, switching her skirt, and took a slip daintily from the box. "Bill, Jr.," Mr. Summers said, and Billy, his face red and his feet overlarge, nearly knocked the box over as he got a paper out. "Tessie," Mr. Summers said. She hesitated for a minute, looking around defiantly, and then set her lips and went up to the box. She snatched a paper out and held it behind her.

"Bill," Mr. Summers said, and Bill Hutchinson reached into the 65 box and felt around, bringing his hand out at last with the slip of paper in it.

The crowd was quiet. A girl whispered, "I hope it's not Nancy," and 66 the sound of the whisper reached the edges of the crowd.

"It's not the way it used to be," Old Man Warner said clearly. "People ain't the way they used to be." 67

"All right," Mr. Summers said. "Open the papers. Harry, you open little Dave's." 68

Mr. Graves opened the slip of paper and there was a general sigh through the crowd as he held it up and everyone could see that it was blank. Nancy and Bill, Jr., opened theirs at the same time, and both beamed and laughed, turning around to the crowd and holding their slips of paper above their heads. 69

"Tessie," Mr. Summers said. There was a pause, and then Mr. Summers looked at Bill Hutchinson, and Bill unfolded his paper and showed it. It was blank. 70

"It's Tessie," Mr. Summers said, and his voice was hushed. "Show us her paper, Bill." 71

Bill Hutchinson went over to his wife and forced the slip of paper out of her hand. It had a black spot on it, the black spot Mr. Summers had made the night before with the heavy pencil in the coal-company office. Bill Hutchinson held it up and there was a stir in the crowd. 72

"All right, folks," Mr. Summers said. "Let's finish quickly." 73

Although the villagers had forgotten the ritual and lost the original black box, they still remembered to use stones. The pile of stones the boys had made earlier was ready; there were stones on the ground with the blowing scraps of paper that had come out of the box. Mrs. Delacroix selected a stone so large she had to pick it up with both hands and turned to Mrs. Dunbar. "Come on," she said. "Hurry up." 74

Mrs. Dunbar had small stones in both hands, and she said, gasping for breath, "I can't run at all. You'll have to go ahead and I'll catch up with you." 75

The children had stones already, and someone gave little Davy Hutchinson a few pebbles. 76

Tessie Hutchinson was in the center of a cleared space by now, and she held her hands out desperately as the villagers moved in on her. "It isn't fair," she said. A stone hit her on the side of the head. 77

Old Man Warner was saying, "Come on, come on, everyone." Steve Adams was in front of the crowd of villagers, with Mrs. Graves beside him. 78

"It isn't fair, it isn't right," Mrs. Hutchinson screamed and then they were upon her. 79

QUESTIONS ON MEANING

1. The PURPOSE of all fiction might be taken as entertainment or self-expression. Does Jackson have any other purpose in "The Lottery"?
2. When does the reader know what is actually going to occur?
3. Describe this story's community on the basis of what Jackson says of it.
4. What do the villagers' attitudes toward the black box indicate about their feelings toward the lottery?

QUESTIONS ON WRITING STRATEGY

1. On your first reading of the story, what did you make of the references to rocks in paragraphs 2–3? Do you think they effectively forecast the ending?
2. Jackson has a character introduce a controversial notion in paragraph 31. Why does she do this?
3. **MIXED METHODS.** In this NARRATIVE Jackson uses the third PERSON (*he, she, it, they*) and does not enter the minds of her characters. Why do you think she keeps this distant POINT OF VIEW?
4. **MIXED METHODS.** Jackson is exploring — or inviting us to explore — CAUSES AND EFFECTS. Why do the villagers participate in the lottery every year? What does paragraph 32 hint might have been the original reason for it?

QUESTIONS ON LANGUAGE

1. Dialogue provides much information not stated elsewhere in the story. Give three EXAMPLES of such information about the community and its interactions.
2. Check a dictionary for definitions of the following words: profusely (para. 1); boisterous, reprimand (2); jovial, scold, paraphernalia (4); perfunctory, duly, interminably (7); petulantly (32).
3. Jackson admits to setting the story in her Vermont village in the present time (that is, 1948). Judging from the names of the villagers, where did these people's ancestors originally come from? What do you make of the names Delacroix and Zanini? What is their significance?
4. Unlike much fiction, "The Lottery" contains few FIGURES OF SPEECH. Why do you think this is?

SUGGESTIONS FOR WRITING

1. **JOURNAL WRITING.** What rituals do you participate in, either in your family or in your community? Who else participates? What is the significance of the ritual? (Keep in mind that a ritual may be religious or not and may be as common as washing the dinner dishes together or as infrequent as a celebration of the new year.)
   FROM JOURNAL TO ESSAY. Write a narrative essay about one of the rituals you participate in. Provide your readers with enough details to make the

ritual come alive and to give a clear sense of its purpose or significance for those who perform it.

2. Write an imaginary narrative, perhaps set in the future, of a ritual that demonstrates something about the people who participate in it. The ritual can be but need not be as sinister as Jackson's lottery; yours could concern bathing, eating, dating, going to school, driving, growing older.

3. In his 1974 book *Obedience to Authority*, the psychologist Stanley Milgram reported and analyzed the results of a study he had conducted that caused a furor among psychologists and the general public. Under orders from white-coated "experimenters," many subjects administered what they believed to be life-threatening electric shocks to other people whom they could hear but not see. In fact, the "victims" were actors and received no shocks, but the subjects thought otherwise and many continued to administer stronger and stronger "shocks" when ordered to do so. Find *Obedience to Authority* in the library and COMPARE AND CONTRAST the circumstances of Milgram's experiment with those of Jackson's lottery. For instance, who or what is the order-giving authority in the lottery? What is the significance of seeing or not seeing one's victim?

4. **CRITICAL WRITING.** In a 1960 lecture (which we quote more from in "Shirley Jackson on Writing"), Jackson said that a common response she received to "The Lottery" was "What does this story mean?" (She never answered the question.) In an essay, interpret the meaning of the story as *you* understand it. (What does it say, for instance, about social customs, conformity, guilt, obliviousness, or good and evil?) You will have to INFER meaning from such features as Jackson's own TONE as narrator, the tone of the villagers' dialogue, and, of course, the events of the story. Your essay should be supported with specific EVIDENCE from the story.

5. **CONNECTIONS (PART ONE).** While both are short stories, Shirley Jackson's "The Lottery" and Edgar Allan Poe's "The Tell-Tale Heart" (p. 88) differ in two techniques of narration: use of dialogue (heavy in Jackson, light in Poe) and point of view of the narrator (OBJECTIVE, third-person in Jackson; SUBJECTIVE, first-person in Poe). Write an essay on the effects of these techniques in each story, using examples from the stories as your evidence.

6. **CONNECTIONS (PART TWO).** Scott Russell Sanders's "The Web of Life" (p. 620) claims that people living together in community rely on mutual compassion and concern for each other. Jackson's story suggests that such attitudes may break down, with terrible consequences. Have you ever known a small community to turn its back on or even attack an innocent person or family in its midst? Write an essay explaining how reliable Sanders's sense of community concern is. Use examples from your own observations and experience as evidence.

SHIRLEY JACKSON ON WRITING

Come Along with Me, a posthumous collection of her work, contains a lecture by Shirley Jackson titled "Biography of a Story"—specifically, a biography of "The Lottery." Far from being born in cruelty or cynicism, the story had quite benign origins. Jackson wrote the story, she recalled, "on a bright June morning when summer seemed to have come at last, with blue skies and warm sun and no heavenly signs to warn me that my morning's work was anything but just another story. The idea had come to me while I was pushing my daughter up the hill in her stroller—it was, as I say, a warm morning, and the hill was steep, and beside my daughter the stroller held the day's groceries—and perhaps the effort of that last fifty yards up the hill put an edge on the story; at any rate, I had the idea fairly clearly in my mind when I put my daughter in her playpen and the frozen vegetables in the refrigerator, and, writing the story, I found that it went quickly and easily, moving from beginning to end without pause. As a matter of fact, when I read it over later I decided that except for one or two minor corrections, it needed no changes, and the story I finally typed up and sent off to my agent the next day was almost word for word the original draft. This, as any writer of stories can tell you, is not a usual thing. All I know is that when I came to read the story over I felt strongly that I didn't want to fuss with it. I didn't think it was perfect, but I didn't want to fuss with it. It was, I thought, a serious, straightforward story, and I was pleased and a little surprised at the ease with which it had been written; I was reasonably proud of it, and hoped that my agent would sell it to some magazine and I would have the gratification of seeing it in print."

After the story was published, however, Jackson was surprised to find both it and herself the subject of "bewilderment, speculation, and plain old-fashioned abuse." She wrote that "one of the most terrifying aspects of publishing stories and books is the realization that they are going to be read, and read by strangers. I had never fully realized this before, although I had of course in my imagination dwelt lovingly upon the thought of the millions and millions of people who were going to be uplifted and enriched and delighted by the stories I wrote. It had simply never occurred to me that these millions and millions of people might be so far from being uplifted that they would sit down and write me letters I was downright scared to open; of the three-hundred-odd letters that I received that summer I can count only thirteen that spoke kindly to me, and they were mostly from friends."

Jackson's favorite letter was one concluding, "Our brothers feel that Miss Jackson is a true prophet and disciple of the true gospel of the redeeming light. When will the next revelation be published?" Jackson's answer: "Never. I am out of the lottery business for good."

FOR DISCUSSION

1. What lesson can we draw about creative inspiration from Jackson's anecdote about the origins of "The Lottery"?
2. What seems to have alarmed Jackson about readers' reactions to her story? Do you think she was naive in expecting otherwise?

15

THE FUTURE OF CYBERCOMMUNITY

Even those who aren't online themselves can't have missed the constant buzz about the "information superhighway" and the Internet (or Net for short). The consensus seems to be that computers are changing our lives; the question is "For better or for worse?" In the two essays reprinted here, the authors probe the kind of community we can expect in cyberspace. (*Cyber* comes from *cybernetics*, the study of communications in various kinds of systems, including electronic. The prefix now usually refers to computer-based systems.) Esther Dyson, in "Cyberspace for All," sees happy possibilities for individual choice and affiliation, free of the constraints of geography and governments. M. Kadi, in "Welcome to Cyberbia," sees societies of like-minded people isolated from those who are different from themselves.

What future do you see?

ESTHER DYSON

Esther Dyson, born in 1951, is a prominent spokesperson for the information superhighway. In 1972 she received a B.A. in economics from Harvard University, where she wrote for the *Harvard Crimson*. After college she reported for *Forbes* magazine and then worked as a securities analyst. She now serves as president of EDventure Holdings, a company specializing in information technology, and she edits EDventure's influential newsletter *Release 1.0*. Dyson has written for the *Harvard Business Review*, the *New York Times*, and *Wired* magazine, among other periodicals. She lectures widely and serves on the boards of international corporations and networks. She lives in New York City.

Cyberspace for All

Recent debates about legislation to regulate the Internet, especially to restrict or ban "indecent" material, prompted Dyson to write "Cyberspace for All" (editors' title). While defending cyberspace from what she sees as intrusive and damaging regulation, Dyson also depicts a future in which everyone can find at least one comfortable, supportive community.

This essay is an ARGUMENT developed by a number of other methods. Dyson uses ANALOGY, a special form of COMPARISON, to DEFINE what *cyberspace* is, and she explains how it works with PROCESS ANALYSIS. She uses CAUSE AND EFFECT to project the characteristics of an unregulated Internet. And throughout she gives EXAMPLES to make her ideas clear.

Something in the American psyche loves new frontiers. We hanker after wide-open spaces; we like to explore; we like to make rules instead of follow them. But in this age of political correctness and other intrusions on our national cult of independence, it's hard to find a place where you can go and be yourself without worrying about the neighbors.

There is such a place: cyberspace. Lost in the furor over porn on the Net is the exhilarating sense of freedom that this new frontier once promised—and still does in some quarters. Formerly a playground for computer nerds and techies, cyberspace now embraces every conceivable constituency: schoolchildren, flirtatious singles, Hungarian-Americans, accountants—along with pederasts and porn fans. Can they all get along? Or will our fear of kids surfing for cyberporn behind their bedroom doors provoke a crackdown?

The first order of business is to grasp what cyberspace *is*. It might help to leave behind metaphors of highways and frontiers and to think instead of real estate. Real estate, remember, is an intellectual, legal, artificial environment constructed *on top of* land. Real estate recognizes the difference between parkland and shopping mall, between red-light zone and school district, between church, state and drugstore.

In the same way, you could think of cyberspace as a giant and un-   4
bounded world of virtual real estate. Some property is privately owned and rented out; other property is common land; some places are suitable for children, and others are best avoided by all but the kinkiest citizens. Unfortunately, it's those places that are now capturing the popular imagination: places that offer bomb-making instructions, pornography, advice on how to procure stolen credit cards. They make cyberspace sound like a nasty place. Good citizens jump to a conclusion: better regulate it....

Regardless of how many laws or lawsuits are launched, regulation   5
won't work.

Aside from being unconstitutional, using censorship to counter in-   6
decency and other troubling "speech" fundamentally misinterprets the nature of cyberspace. Cyberspace isn't a frontier where wicked people can grab unsuspecting children, nor is it a giant television system that can beam offensive messages at unwilling viewers. In this kind of real estate, users have to *choose* where they visit, what they see, what they do. It's optional, and it's much easier to bypass a place on the Net than it is to avoid walking past an unsavory block of stores on the way to your local 7-11.

Put plainly, cyberspace is a voluntary destination—in reality,   7
many destinations. You don't just get "onto the Net"; you have to go someplace in particular. That means that people can choose where to go and what to see. Yes, community standards should be enforced, but those standards should be set by cyberspace communities themselves, not by the courts or by politicians in Washington. What we need isn't Government control over all these electronic communities: We need self-rule.

What makes cyberspace so alluring is precisely the way in which   8
it's *different* from shopping malls, television, highways and other terrestrial jurisdictions. But let's define the territory:

First, there are private e-mail conversations, akin to the conversa-   9
tions you have over the telephone or voice mail. These are private and consensual and require no regulation at all.

Second, there are information and entertainment services, where   10
people can download anything from legal texts and lists of "great new restaurants" to game software or dirty pictures. These places are like bookstores, malls and movie houses—places where you go to buy something. The customer needs to request an item or sign up for a sub-

scription; stuff (especially pornography) is not sent out to people who don't ask for it. Some of these services are free or included as part of a broad service like Compuserve or America Online; others charge and may bill their customers directly.

Third, there are "real" communities—groups of people who com- 11
municate among themselves. In real-estate terms, they're like bars or restaurants or bathhouses. Each active participant contributes to a general conversation, generally through posted messages. Other participants may simply listen or watch. Some are supervised by a moderator; others are more like bulletin boards—anyone is free to post anything. Many of these services started out unmoderated but are now imposing rules to keep out unwanted advertising, extraneous discussions or increasingly rude participants. Without a moderator, the decibel level often gets too high.

Ultimately, it's the rules that determine the success of such places. 12
Some of the rules are determined by the supplier of content; some of the rules concern prices and membership fees. The rules may be simple: "Only high-quality content about oil-industry liability and pollution legislation: $120 an hour." Or: "This forum is unmoderated, and restricted to information about copyright issues. People who insist on posting advertising or unrelated material will be asked to desist (and may eventually be barred)." Or: "Only children 8 to 12, on school-related topics and only clean words. The moderator will decide what's acceptable."

Cyberspace communities evolve just the way terrestrial communi- 13
ties do: People with like-minded interests band together. Every cyberspace community has its own character. Overall, the communities on Compuserve tend to be more techy or professional; those on America Online, affluent young singles; Prodigy, family oriented. Then there are independents like Echo, a hip, downtown New York service, or Women's Wire, targeted to women who want to avoid the male culture prevalent elsewhere on the Net. There's SurfWatch, a new program allowing access only to locations deemed suitable for children. On the Internet itself, there are lots of passionate noncommercial discussion groups on topics ranging from Hungarian politics (Hungary-Online) to copyright law.

And yes, there are also porn-oriented services, where people share 14
dirty pictures and communicate with one another about all kinds of practices, often anonymously. Whether these services encourage the fantasies they depict is subject to debate—the same debate that has raged about pornography in other media. But the point is that no one is forcing this stuff on anybody.

What's unique about cyberspace is that it liberates us from the 15 tyranny of government, where everyone lives by the rule of the majority. In a democracy, minority groups and minority preferences tend to get squeezed out, whether they are minorities of race and culture or minorities of individual taste. Cyberspace allows communities of any size and kind to flourish; in cyberspace, communities are chosen by the users, not forced on them by accidents of geography. This freedom gives the rules that preside in cyberspace a moral authority that rules in terrestrial environments don't have. Most people are stuck in the country of their birth, but if you don't like the rules of a cyberspace community, you can just sign off. Love it or leave it. Likewise, if parents don't like the rules of a given cyberspace community, they can restrict their children's access to it.

What's likely to happen in cyberspace is the formation of new communities, free of the constraints that cause conflict on earth. Instead of a global village, which is a nice dream but impossible to manage, we'll have invented another world of self-contained communities that cater to their own members' inclinations without interfering with anyone else's. The possibility of a real market-style evolution of governance is at hand. In cyberspace, we'll be able to test and evolve rules governing what needs to be governed—intellectual property, content and access control, rules about privacy and free speech. Some communities will allow anyone in; others will restrict access to members who qualify on one basis or another. Those communities that prove self-sustaining will prosper (and perhaps grow and split into subsets with ever-more-particular interests and identities). Those that can't survive—either because people lose interest or get scared off—will simply wither away. 16

In the near future, explorers in cyberspace will need to get better at defining and identifying their communities. They will need to put in place—and accept—their own local governments, just as the owners of expensive real estate often prefer to have their own security guards rather than call in the police. But they will rarely need help from any terrestrial government. 17

Of course, terrestrial governments may not agree. What to do, for instance, about pornography? The answer is labeling—not banning—questionable material. In order to avoid censorship and lower the political temperature, it makes sense for cyberspace participants themselves to agree on a scheme for questionable items, so that people or automatic filters can avoid them. In other words, posting pornography in "alt.sex.bestiality" would be O.K.; it's easy enough for software manufacturers to build an automatic filter that would prevent you—or your child—from ever seeing that item on a menu. (It's as if all the items were wrapped, with labels on the wrapper.) Someone who posted the 18 same material under the title "Kid-Fun" could be sued for mislabeling.

Without a lot of fanfare, private enterprises and local groups are al- 19
ready producing a variety of labeling and ranking services, along with
kid-oriented sites like Kidlink, EdWeb and Kids' Space. People differ in
their tastes and values and can find services or reviewers on the Net
that suit them in the same way they select books and magazines. Or
they can wander freely if they prefer, making up their own itinerary.

In the end, our society needs to grow up. Growing up means un- 20
derstanding that there are no perfect answers, no all-purpose solutions,
no government-sanctioned safe havens. We haven't created a perfect
society on earth and we won't have one in cyberspace either. But at
least we can have individual choice—and individual responsibility.

QUESTIONS ON MEANING

1. What are the two main reasons Dyson gives for saying that "regulation [of
   cyberspace] won't work"?
2. Is Dyson opposed to any kind of regulation, or just censorship? How do you
   know?
3. Why does Dyson reject censorship of cyberspace? What is her solution to
   "indecency and other 'troubling' speech" in cyberspace?
4. In your own words, state the THESIS of Dyson's essay.

QUESTIONS ON WRITING STRATEGY

1. Dyson frequently acknowledges that there is objectionable content on the
   Internet—in paragraphs 2, 4, 10, 14, and 18. Do these admissions undermine her ARGUMENT against censorship? Why, or why not?
2. What is the main similarity between cybercommunities and terrestrial (or
   earthbound) communities? What is the main difference? Why is this contrast important to Dyson's thesis?
3. Dyson introduces the traditional IMAGE of cyberspace as a frontier (para. 2),
   only to discard this METAPHOR in the next paragraph. Why does Dyson prefer the metaphor of real estate for cyberspace?
4. **MIXED METHODS.** Dyson CLASSIFIES the sites available on the Internet and
   COMPARES each group to something familiar (paras. 9–15). What groups does
   she identify? What important attributes of cyberspace emerge from this
   comparison?
5. **MIXED METHODS.** In some of the same paragraphs cited above, Dyson uses
   PROCESS ANALYSIS to explain how parts of the Internet work. Why do you
   think she devotes attention to the workings of cyberspace? How does this
   attention support her argument?

QUESTIONS ON LANGUAGE

1. How does Dyson's DEFINITION of *democracy* (para. 15) refine our usual sense of this term?
2. Dyson assumes that her AUDIENCE is familiar with the vocabulary of computers. Although she clearly defines *cyberspace*, she leaves other terms undefined. If any of the following are unfamiliar to you, find out what they mean in a book such as *The Internet for Dummies* or *Student's Guide to the Internet:* surfing (para. 2); virtual (4); e-mail (9); download, software (10); posted, bulletin boards (11); sign off (15).
3. Why does Dyson describe the many Internet sites available in terms of their "constituencies"? How do the CONNOTATIONS of that word help Dyson make her point about self-rule?
4. If you need help with the meanings of any of the following words, look them up in the dictionary: psyche, exhilarating, pederasts (para. 2); procure (4); unsavory (6); alluring (8); akin, consensual (9); extraneous, decibel (11); liability, forum, desist (12); terrestrial, prevalent (13); cater (16); itinerary (19); sanctioned, havens (20).

SUGGESTIONS FOR WRITING

1. **JOURNAL WRITING.** What is your personal experience of the Internet? What kind of role does it play in your life? How would censorship of the Internet affect you or the quality or quantity of the information you receive? **FROM JOURNAL TO ESSAY.** Do you agree with Dyson's argument that censorship of the Internet will cause more harm than good? Write a brief essay that explains why or why not, using your own experience as EVIDENCE. Or, if you are not an Internet user, write a brief essay that explains how you think censorship might affect your ability to become one.
2. Dyson says that "our society needs to grow up" (para. 20). What does she mean by this? In an essay, explain another problem or issue in our society that you think might be solved if we just "grew up." Be sure to spell out not just the details of the problem but also how "growing up" would help solve it.
3. **CRITICAL WRITING.** Dyson's solution to the problem of potentially offensive material in cyberspace is to advocate user responsibility and mandatory classification and labeling of sites. Are you convinced that her solution would work? Is it practical to implement? Write an essay in which you argue either for or against self-government as a solution to this Internet problem. Consider how responsible users could or would really be, who would make decisions about labeling, and how rule-breakers would be discovered and stopped.
4. **CONNECTIONS (PART ONE).** Read or reread Michiko Kakutani's "The Word Police" (p. 287). How does Kakutani's argument about the obstacles created by "political correctness" in language inform Dyson's argument about the obstacles to individualism created by censorship (in the name of "political correctness") in cyberspace? Write an essay explaining the connections between these two authors' ideas. (You do not have to agree with the authors' conclusions; instead, you can explain their arguments in order to refute them.)

5. **CONNECTIONS (PART TWO).** Dyson's view of the Internet's future is mostly optimistic, while M. Kadi, in "Welcome to Cyberbia" (p. 648), takes a much dimmer view. Write an essay that compares and contrasts these two authors' attitudes toward the Internet. What is the substance of each author's argument? What does each base her opinion on? Use evidence from both essays to support your comparison.

ESTHER DYSON ON WRITING

We asked Esther Dyson to tell us about her writing process. She responded by telling us how she wrote "Esther Dyson on Writing."

"How did I write this essay? (And how do I write most things?) First of all, I *avoided* writing it for weeks, while I thought about it from time to time. 'How do I write?' That's an easy topic: All I have to do is describe my actual experience—with a little overview of tactics, strategy, psychological motivation.

"When I finally resolved to do it, I thought about it at length in the swimming pool—which is where I spend an hour thinking every day. Thinking in the pool is effective. When I'm actually writing, it's hard to think broadly; instead I move from sentence to sentence, detail to detail, nits of grammar and clever transitions. But in the pool, with no way to write things down (other than jumping out of the pool for a particularly felicitous phrase), I can think about structure, basic points, what I'm trying to accomplish with a particular piece of work.

"It's easier to produce the words once I've got the broad idea.

"Writing a 500-word essay, of course, is different from writing a 20,000-word newsletter or the ultimate challenge—a book. It's a question of scale, yes, but a newsletter is not simply 40 essays strung together, nor is a book just a series of essays. You have to construct any piece of writing as a coherent work, with sequence, cross-references, a flow of arguments, and a conclusion that draws everything together ... ideally.

"In fact, the writing often starts with paragraphs. Just get the thoughts out, and then you can organize them later. (I believe that word-processing has been a huge boon to writing—although it has probably encouraged a lot of redundant prose.) You can start work without starting The Work: You can begin in the middle, so that you don't face the fear of starting wrong. Often, I leave the beginning until the end; the process of writing helps me figure out what I was saying and how to present it. In the case of this essay, however, I began with the beginning, partly because it is so short. I wanted to write something clever, an example of itself.

"Often, I've written so much material that by the time I actually 'start,' most of the writing is already done. The task is to organize all the material, provide the links, and often get rid of redundancies. One of the toughest parts of editing is when you've said the same thing twice, both times very elegantly, and have to decide which to sacrifice.

"I faced this challenge once as a high-school student, when I was doing an assigned paper explaining the theory of relativity. I wrote it in the form of a two-person play, a cocktail-party conversation between a Sweet Young Thing and an elderly professor who was delighted to explain it to her over and over. Yes, it was an outrageous set of stereotypes. The young lady was a bit dim, so the professor got to explain things several times, each time with wit and elegance. I don't remember what grade I got, but I do remember I had a wonderful time writing it. (There—that was a colorful, embellishing anecdote.)

"Now, how to end this? What did I really say? I always have the most trouble with endings..."

FOR DISCUSSION

1. What is the advantage for Dyson of thinking about writing while she is swimming? How do you think best about a writing project—while occupied with something else or with pencil or keyboard at hand?
2. How do you get started on a writing project? Have you ever tried skipping the beginning and starting in the middle instead?

M. KADI

A self-described "cyberjunkie," M. KADI is a computer consultant and a writer on computer subjects. She was born in 1968 and grew up in San Francisco. She attended the University of California at Berkeley, graduating in 1990 with a B.A. in philosophy. Her essays have appeared in the *Utne Reader*, *h2so4*, *bOING bOING*, and *hotWired* (the online *Wired* magazine). As an independent consultant, Kadi designs pages for the World Wide Web. She lives in San Francisco.

Welcome to Cyberbia

With her work and, she says, all her hobbies centering on computers, Kadi is well positioned to probe the pluses and minuses of the latest technology. In this essay from a 1995 *Utne Reader* (originally printed in *h2so4*), Kadi skewers the "fabulous, wonderful, limitless world of communication" promised on the Internet.

"Welcome to Cyberbia" is an ARGUMENT developed largely by PROCESS ANALYSIS: Kadi explains how someone is likely to use the Internet. The entire analysis is an EXAMPLE, and leads to a conclusion about the EFFECTS of Internet use.

> *Computer networking offers the soundest basis for world peace that has yet been presented. Peace must be created on the bulwark of understanding. International computer networks will knit together the peoples of the world in bonds of mutual respect; its possibilities are vast, indeed.*
> —*Scientific American*, June 1994

Computer bulletin board services offer up the glories of e-mail, the thought provocation of newsgroups, the sharing of ideas implicit in public posting, and the interaction of real-time chats. The fabulous, wonderful, limitless world of communication is just waiting for you to log on. Sure. Yeah. Right. What this whole delirious, interconnected, global community of a world needs is a little reality check.

Let's face facts. The U.S. government by and large foots the bill for the Internet, through maintaining the structural (hardware) backbone, including, among other things, funding to major universities. As surely as the Department of Defense started this whole thing, AT&T or Ted Turner[1] is going to end up running it, so I don't think it's too unrealistic to take a look at the Net as it exists in its commercial form in order to expose some of the realities lurking behind the regurgitated media rhetoric and the religious fanaticism of Net junkies.

---

[1] Ted Turner owned a conglomerate of media companies that is now part of Time Warner. —EDS.

The average person, J. Individual, has an income. How much of 3
J. Individual's income is going to be spent on computer connectivity?
Does $120 a month sound reasonable? Well, you may find that a bit too
steep for your pocketbook, but the brutal fact is that $120 is a "reason-
able" monthly amount. The major on-line services have a monthly service charge of approximately $15. Fifteen dollars to join the global
community, communicate with a diverse group of people, and access
the world's largest repository of knowledge since the Alexandrian library[2] doesn't seem unreasonable, does it? But don't overlook the average per-hour connection rate of $3 (which can skyrocket upwards of
$10, depending on your modem speed and service). You might think
that you are a crack whiz with your communications software—that
you are rigorous and stringent and never, ever respond to e-mail or a forum while you're on-line—but let me tell you that no one is capable of
logging on efficiently every time. Thirty hours per month is a realistic
estimate for on-line time spent by a single user engaging in activities
beyond primitive e-mail. Now consider that the average, one-step-
above-complete-neophyte user has at least two distinct BBS [bulletin
board system] accounts, and do the math. Total monthly cost: $120.
Most likely, that's already more than the combined cost of your utility
bills. How many people are prepared to double their monthly bills for
the sole purpose of connectivity?

In case you think 30 hours a month is an outrageous estimate, 4
think of it in terms of television. Thirty hours a month in front of a
television is simply the evening news plus a weekly *Seinfield/Frasier*
hour. Thirty hours a month is less time than the average car-phone
owner spends on the phone while commuting. Even a conscientious
geek, logging on for e-mail and the up-to-the-minute news that only
the Net services can provide, is probably going to spend 30 hours a
month on-line. And, let's be truthful here, 30 hours a month ignores
shareware downloads, computer illiteracy, real-time chatting, interactive game playing, and any serious forum following, which by nature
entail a significant amount of scrolling and/or downloading time.

If you are really and truly going to use the Net services to connect 5
with the global community, the hourly charges are going to add up
pretty quickly. Take out a piece of paper, pretend you're writing a
check, and print out "One hundred and twenty dollars—" and tell me
again, how diverse is the on-line community?

That scenario aside, let's pretend that you have as much time and 6
as much money to spend on-line as you damn well want. What do you
actually do on-line?

---

[2] This ancient library in what is now Egypt was said to contain 700,000 volumes.
—EDS.

Well, you download some cool shareware, you post technical ques-   7
tions in the computer user group forums, you check your stocks, you
read the news and maybe some reviews—hey, you've already passed
that 30-hour limit! But, of course, since computer networks are supposed to make it easy to reach out and touch strangers who share a
particular obsession or concern, you are participating in the on-line
forums, discussion groups, and conferences.

Let's review the structure of forums. For the purposes of this essay,   8
we will examine the smallest of the major user-friendly commercial services—America Online (AOL).[3] There is no precise statistic available
(at least none that the company will reveal—you have to do the research by HAND!!!) on exactly how many subject-specific discussion
areas (folders) exist on America Online. Any on-line service is going to
have zillions of posts—contributions from users—pertaining to computer usage (the computer games area of America Online, for example,
breaks into 500 separate topics with over 100,000 individual posts), so
let's look at a less popular area: the "Lifestyles and Interests" department.

For starters, as I write this, there are 57 initial categories within the   9
Lifestyles and Interests area. One of these categories in Ham Radio. Ham
Radio? How can there possibly be 5,909 separate, individual posts about
Ham Radio? There are 5,865 postings in the Biking (and that's just bi-
cycles, not motorcycles) category. Genealogy—22,525 posts. The Gay
and Lesbian category is slightly more substantial—36,333 posts. There
are five separate categories for political and issue discussion. The big
catchall topic area, the Exchange, has over 100,000 posts. Servicewide
(on the smallest service, remember) there are over a million posts.

You may want to join the on-line revolution, but obviously you   10
can't wade through everything that's being discussed—you need to decide which topics interest you, which folders to browse. Within the Exchange alone (one of 57 subdivisions within one of another 50 higher
divisions) there are 1,492 separate topic-specific folders—each containing a rough average of 50 posts, but many containing closer to 400.
(Note: America Online automatically empties folders when their post
totals reach 400, so total post numbers do not reflect the overall historical totals for a given topic. Sometimes the posting is so frequent that
the "shelf life" of a given post is no more than four weeks.)

So, there you are, J. Individual, ready to start interacting with folks,   11
sharing stories and communicating. You have narrowed yourself into a
single folder, three tiers down in the America Online hierarchy, and now
you must choose between nearly 1,500 folders. Of course, once you
choose a few of these folders, you will then have to read all the posts in
order to catch up, be current, and not merely repeat a previous post.

---

[3] America Online is now the largest commercial service. —EDS.

A polite post is no more than two paragraphs long (a screenful of 12
text, which obviously has a number of intellectually negative implications). Let's say you choose 10 folders (out of 1,500). Each folder contains an average of 50 posts. Five hundred posts, at, say, one paragraph
each, and you're now looking at the equivalent of a 200-page book.

Enough with the stats. Let me back up a minute and present you 13
with some very disturbing, but rational, assumptions. J. Individual
wants to join the on-line revolution, to connect and communicate. But
J. is not going to read all one million posts on AOL. (After all, J. has a
second on-line service.) Exercising choice is J. Individual's God-given
right as an American, and, by gosh, J. Individual is going to make some
decisions. So J. is going to ignore all the support groups — after all, J. is
a normal, well-adjusted person, and all of J.'s friends are normal, well-
adjusted people; what does J. need to know about alcoholism or incest
victims? J. Individual is white. So J. Individual is going to ignore all the
multicultural folders. J. couldn't give a hoot about gender issues and
does not want to discuss religion or philosophy. Ultimately, J. Individual does not engage in topics that do not interest J. Individual. So who
is J. meeting? Why, people who are *just like* J.

J. Individual has now joined the electronic community. Surfed the 14
Net. Found some friends. *Tuned in, turned on, and geeked out.* Traveled
the Information Highway and, just a few miles down that great democratic expressway, J. Individual has settled into an electronic suburb.

Are any of us so very different? It's my time and my money and I am 15
not going to waste any of it reading posts by disgruntled Robert-Bly
drum-beating men's-movement boys who think that they should have
some say over, for instance, whether or not I choose to carry a child to
term simply because a condom broke. I know where I stand. I'm an
adult. I know what's up and I am not going to waste my money arguing
with a bunch of neanderthals.

Oh yeah; I am so connected, so enlightened, so open to the oppos- 16
ing viewpoint. I'm out there, meeting all kinds of people from different
economic backgrounds (who have $120 a month to burn), from all re-
ligions (yeah, right, like anyone actually discusses religion anymore
from a user standpoint), from all kinds of different ethnic backgrounds
and with all kinds of sexual orientations (as if any of this ever comes up
outside of the appropriate topic folder).

People are drawn to topics and folders that interest them and 17
therefore people will only meet people who are interested in the same
topics in the same folders. Rarely does anyone venture into a random
folder just to see what others (the Other?) are talking about.

Basically, between the monetary constraints and the sheer number 18
of topics and individual posts, the great Information Highway is not a
place where you will enter an "amazing web of new people, places, and

ideas." One does not encounter people from "all walks of life" because there are too many people and too many folders. Diversity might be out there (and personally I don't think it is), but the simple fact is that the average person will not encounter it because with one brain, one job, one partner, one family, and one life, no one has the time!

Just in case these arguments based on time and money aren't com-   19
pletely convincing, let me bring up a historical reference. Please take another look at the opening quote of this essay, from *Scientific American*. It was featured in their "50 Years Ago Today" column. Where you read "computer networking," the quote originally contained the word *television*. Amusing, isn't it?

QUESTIONS ON MEANING

1. What does "Cyberbia" in Kadi's title refer to? How does this word capture Kadi's main idea?
2. What is Kadi's THESIS? Where does she state it?
3. Why does Kadi say that the Internet community needs "a little reality check" (para. 1)?
4. What does Kadi mean to imply by mentioning the Department of Defense, AT&T, and Ted Turner in paragraph 2?
5. Reread paragraph 5. What is Kadi getting at?

QUESTIONS ON WRITING STRATEGY

1. What is the TONE of this essay? Is it effective, do you think?
2. What is the PURPOSE of Kadi's detailed calculations of cost and volume (paras. 3–4, 7–12)?
3. What does Kadi's last paragraph add to your understanding of her ARGUMENT? What is her purpose in using and manipulating the quotation from *Scientific American*?
4. **MIXED METHODS.** Kadi offers a detailed PROCESS ANALYSIS as an EXAMPLE of how the Internet works to limit a user's experience of diversity. Is this example effective as support for Kadi's argument, or should she have provided more or different kinds of EVIDENCE? Explain your answer.
5. **MIXED METHODS.** SUMMARIZE the pattern of CAUSES AND EFFECTS that Kadi sees in Internet use.

QUESTIONS ON LANGUAGE

1. Kadi accuses heavy Internet users of "religious fanaticism" (para. 2). Why does she use this phrase? What does it imply more generally about those who advocate the Internet?

2. What are the "intellectually negative implications" of writing and receiving only two paragraphs of text at once (para. 12)? Is Kadi being SARCASTIC?

3. Although Kadi defines *folders* and *posts*, she leaves a number of computer terms undefined. Refer to a book such as *The Internet for Dummies* or *Student's Guide to the Internet* for the meanings of any of these terms: bulletin board, e-mail, newsgroups, log on (para. 1); hardware (2); on-line services, modem, software, forum (3); shareware, downloads, scrolling (4).

4. Make sure you know the meanings of the following words from earthbound language: provocation, implicit, delirious (para. 1); regurgitated, rhetoric (2); repository, stringent, neophyte (3); scenario (6); genealogy (9); tiers, hierarchy (11); disgruntled, neanderthals (15); venture (17).

SUGGESTIONS FOR WRITING

1. **JOURNAL WRITING.** What do you think of this essay? Consider its examples, tone, overall argument—whatever strikes you.
   FROM JOURNAL TO ESSAY. Expand and refine your gut reaction to Kadi's essay. Do you like it? Is your liking or not liking based more on Kadi's argument or on her tone? Write an ANALYSIS and EVALUATION of this essay that makes clear what the essay's main elements are and what you think of them.

2. Kadi mentions "the Other" in paragraph 17, using a term that, when capitalized, refers to those who are different from ourselves in socioeconomic class, race, religion, or other fundamental ways and are thus unknown to us. In a brief essay, explain how "the Other" figures in Kadi's essay, perhaps more significantly than its appearance in parentheses would otherwise imply.

3. **CRITICAL WRITING.** What's wrong with the suburbs? Kadi clearly considers them unpleasant, or worse, but do you? Are people really all the same in a suburb, as Kadi implies? And what's wrong with sameness, anyway? Why shouldn't people seek out and associate with others like themselves? What's so valuable about diversity? Consider these questions in evaluating Kadi's METAPHOR of "cyberbia."

4. **CONNECTIONS (PART ONE).** Like Kadi, Robert B. Reich, in "Why the Rich Are Getting Richer and the Poor Poorer" (p. 346), also believes that the global community will disappoint and even reject many people. Drawing on the evidence in both essays plus your own experiences and observations, write an argument of your own about whether a cooperative, inclusive global community is possible or not.

5. **CONNECTIONS (PART TWO).** Esther Dyson, in "Cyberspace for All" (p. 640), and Kadi have similar but also widely dissimilar visions of cyberspace. Write an essay that COMPARES their visions. Consider who they think participates, what the responsibilities of the participants are, what the consequences are of being free to roam the Internet, what the limitations of the Internet are, and who does or should control the Internet.

APPENDIX

USING AND DOCUMENTING SOURCES

When you write about them, the essays in this book serve as your sources: Either you ANALYZE them or you use them to support your own ideas. Writing with sources will occupy you for much of your academic career, as you rely on books, periodical articles, interviews, electronic databases, and other materials to establish and extend your own ideas.

This appendix introduces the essentials of using sources: summarizing and paraphrasing (below), avoiding plagiarism (p. 656), integrating quotations into your own prose (p. 657), and documenting sources using the style of the Modern Language Association, or MLA (p. 658).

SUMMARIZING AND PARAPHRASING

To summarize or paraphrase is to express the ideas from a source in your own words. A SUMMARY condenses an entire passage, article, or even book into a few lines that convey the source's essential meaning. We discuss summary as a reading technique on pages 14–15, and the advice and examples there apply here as well. For another example, here is a summary of Barbara Lazear Ascher's "On Compassion," which appears on pages 145–47.

> Ascher shows how contact with the homeless can be unsettling and depressing. Yet she also suggests that these encounters are useful because they can teach others to be more compassionate (145–47).

Notice how the summary identifies the source author and page numbers and uses words that are *not* the author's. (Any of Ascher's distinctive phrasing would have to be placed in quotation marks.)

In contrast to a summary, a PARAPHRASE usually restates a single idea, again in words different from those of the original author. Here is a quotation from Ascher's essay and a paraphrase of it:

> QUOTATION: "Could it be that the homeless, like [ancient Greek dramatists], are reminding us of our common humanity? Of course there is a difference. The play doesn't end—and the players can't go home."

> PARAPHRASE: Ascher points out an important distinction between the New York City homeless and the characters in ancient Greek tragedy: The homeless are living real lives, not performing on a stage (147).

As with the summary, note that the paraphrase cites the original author and page number. Here is another example of paraphrase, this from an essay about immigration by David Cole.

> QUOTATION: "If we are collectively judged by how we treat immigrants—those who appear to be 'other' but will in a generation be 'us'—we are not in very good shape."

> PARAPHRASE: Cole argues that the way native-born Americans deal with immigrants reflects badly on the native-born citizens themselves. He also points out that today's immigrants will be part of tomorrow's mainstream society (110).

AVOIDING PLAGIARISM

Take a look at another attempt to paraphrase the sentence above by David Cole.

> Cole argues that if we are judged as a group by how we treat immigrants—those who seem to be different but eventually will be the same—we are in bad shape (110).

This is PLAGIARISM—the theft of someone's ideas or written work. Even though the writer identifies Cole as the source of the information, the language essentially remains the same. It is not enough to change a few words—"collectively" to "as a group," "in a generation" to "eventually," "not in very good shape" to "in bad shape." A paraphrase must express the original idea in an entirely new way, both in word choice and in sentence structure. (Even more blatant plagiarism, of course, would have repeated Cole's statement exactly as he wrote it, without quotation marks *or* a source citation.) Plagiarism also occurs when a writer neglects to cite a source at all—if, for example, a writer paraphrased Ascher's comparison of the homeless with actors in a Greek drama, as on the previous page, but did not mention Ascher's name.

Not all information from sources must be cited. Some falls under the category of common knowledge—facts so widely known or agreed upon that they are not attributable to a specific source. The statement "World War II ended after the United States dropped atomic bombs on Hiroshima and Nagasaki, Japan" is an obvious example: Most people recognize this statement as true. But some lesser-known information is also common knowledge. You may not know that President Dwight Eisenhower coined the term *military-industrial complex* during his 1961 farewell address; still, you could easily discover the information in encyclopedias, in books and articles about Eisenhower, and in contemporary newspaper accounts. The prevalence of the information and the fact that it is used elsewhere without source citation tell you that it's common knowledge.

In contrast, a scholar's argument that Eisenhower waited too long to criticize the defense industry, or the President's own comments on the subject in his diary, or an opinion from a Defense Department report in 1959—any of these needs to be credited. Unlike common knowledge, each of them remains the property of its author.

USING AND INTEGRATING QUOTATIONS

Quotations from your sources can serve as EVIDENCE for your own ideas (see p. 444) and can enliven your subject—*if* they are well chosen. Too many quotations can clutter an essay and detract from your own voice. Choose quotations that are relevant to the point you are making, that are concise and pithy, and that use lively, bold, or original language. Sentences that lack distinction—for example, a statement providing statistics on economic growth between 1985 and 1995—should almost always be paraphrased.

When you do quote from a source, you want to integrate the quotation into your own sentences and also set it up so that readers know what you expect them to make of it. In the passage below, the writer drops the quotation awkwardly into her sentence and doesn't clarify how the quotation relates to her idea.

NOT INTEGRATED: The problem of homelessness is not decreasing, and "It is impossible to insulate ourselves against what is at our very doorstep" (Ascher 147).

In the following revision, however, the writer indicates with "As Ascher says" that she is using the quotation to reinforce her point. These words also link the quotation to the writer's sentence.

> INTEGRATED: The problem of homelessness is not decreasing, nor is our awareness of it, however much we wish otherwise. As Ascher says, "It is impossible to insulate ourselves against what is at our very doorstep" (147).

You can integrate a quotation into your sentence by interpreting the quotation and by mentioning the author in your text—both techniques illustrated above. The introductory phrase "As Ascher says" has many variations:

> According to one authority...
>
> John Eng maintains that...
>
> The author of an important study, Hilda Brown, observes that...
>
> Ascher, the author of "On Compassion," has a different view, claiming...

For variety, such a phrase can also fall elsewhere in the quotation.

> "It is impossible," Ascher says, "to insulate ourselves against what is at our very doorstep" (147).

When you omit something from a quotation, use the three spaced periods of an ellipsis mark to signal the omission:

> "It is impossible to insulate ourselves...," says Ascher (147).
>
> In Ascher's view, "Compassion ... must be learned" (147).

CITING SOURCES USING MLA STYLE

On the following pages we explain the documentation style of the Modern Language Association, as described in the *MLA Handbook for Writers of Research Papers*, 4th edition (1995). This style—used in English, foreign languages, and some other humanities—involves a brief parenthetical citation in the text that refers to an entry in a list of works cited at the end of the text.

PARENTHETICAL TEXT CITATION

The homeless may be to us what tragic heroes were to the ancient
Greeks (Ascher 147).

Ascher, Barbara Lazear. "On Compassion." The Bedford Reader. 6th ed.

    Ed. X. J. Kennedy, Dorothy M. Kennedy, and Jane E. Aaron.

    Boston: Bedford, 1997. 145-47.

By providing the author's name and page number in your text citation, you're giving the reader just enough information to find the source in the list of works cited and then find the place in the source where the borrowed material appears.

MLA Parenthetical Citations

When citing sources in your text, you have two options: You can identify both the author and the page number within parentheses, as in the example at the bottom of the facing page, or you can introduce the author in your sentence and use the parentheses only for the page number, as here:

Wilson points out that sharks, which have existed for 350 million

years, are now more diverse than ever (301).

A work with two or three authors

More than 90 percent of the hazaradous waste produced in the United

States comes from seven major industries, all energy-intensive (Romm

and Curtis 70).

A work with more than three authors

With more than three authors, name all the authors, or name only the first author followed by "et al." ("and others"). Use the same form in your list of works cited.

Gilman herself created the misconception that doctors tried to ban her

story "The Yellow Wallpaper" when it appeared in 1892 (Dock, Allen,

Palais, and Tracy 61).

Gilman herself created the misconception that doctors tried to ban her

story "The Yellow Wallpaper" when it appeared in 1892 (Dock et al. 61).

An entire work

Reference to an entire work does not require a page number.

Postman argues that television is destructive because of the nature of

the medium itself.

A work in more than one volume

If you cite separate volumes of the same work, identify the volume number before the page number. Separate volume number and page number with a colon.

> According to Gibbon, during the reign of Gallienus "every province of the Roman world was afflicted by barbarous invaders and military tyrants" (1: 133).

Two or more works by the same author(s)

If you cite more than one work by the same author or authors, include the work's title. If the title is long, shorten it to the first one or two main words. (The full title for the first citation below is <u>Death at an Early Age</u>.)

> In the 1960s Kozol was reprimanded by his principal for teaching the poetry of Langston Hughes (<u>Death</u> 83).

> Kozol believes that most people do not understand the effect that tax and revenue policies have on the quality of urban public schools (<u>Savage Inequalities</u> 207).

An unsigned work

Cite an unsigned work by using a full or shortened version of the title.

> In 1995 concern about Taiwan's relationship with China caused investors to transfer large amounts of capital to the United States ("How the Missiles Help" 45).

An indirect source

Use "qtd. in" ("quoted in") to indicate that you found the source you quote within another source.

> Despite his tendency to view human existence as an unfulfilling struggle, Schopenhauer disparaged suicide as "a vain and foolish act" (qtd. in Durant 248).

A literary work

Because novels, poems, and plays may be published in various editions, the page number may not be enough to lead readers to the quoted line or passage. For a novel, specify the chapter number after the page number and a semicolon.

Among South Pacific islanders, the hero of Conrad's <u>Lord Jim</u> found "a totally new set of conditions for his imaginative faculty to work upon" (160; ch. 21).

For a verse play or a poem, omit the page number in favor of line numbers.

In "Dulce Et Decorum Est," Wilfred Owen undercuts the heroic image of warfare by comparing suffering soldiers to "beggars" and "hags" (lines 1-2) and describing a man dying in a poison-gas attack as "guttering, choking, drowning" (17).

If the work has parts, acts, or scenes, cite those as well (below: act 1, scene 5, lines 16–17).

Lady Macbeth worries about her husband's ambition: "Yet I do fear thy nature; / It is too full o' the milk of human kindness" (1.5.16-17).

More than one work

In the post-Watergate era, journalists have often employed aggressive reporting techniques not for the good of the public but simply to advance their careers (Gopnick 92; Fallows 64).

MLA List of Works Cited

Your list of works cited is a complete record of your sources. Follow these guidelines for the list:

- Title the list "Works Cited."
- Double-space the entire list.
- Arrange the sources alphabetically by the last name of the first author.
- Indent the second and subsequent lines of each entry one-half inch or five spaces.

Following are the essentials of a works-cited entry:

- Reverse the names of the author, last name first, with a comma between. If there is more than one author, give the others' names in normal order.
- Give the full title of the work, capitalizing all important words. Underline the titles of books and periodicals; use quotation marks for the titles of parts of books and articles in periodicals.

- Give publication information. For books, this means city of publication, publisher, date of publication. For periodicals, this often means volume number, date of publication, and page numbers for the article you cite.
- Use periods between parts of each entry.

You may need to combine the models below for a given source — for instance, combine "A book with two or three authors" and "A book with an editor" for a book with two or three editors.

Books

A book with one author

Tuchman, Barbara W. The March of Folly: From Troy to Vietnam. New
    York: Knopf, 1984.

A book with two or three authors

Silverstein, Olga, and Beth Rashbaum. The Courage to Raise Good Men.
    New York: Viking, 1994.

A book with more than three authors

You may list all authors or only the first author followed by "et al." ("and others"). Use the same form in your parenthetical text citation.

Kippax, Susan, R. W. Connel, G. W. Dowsett, and June Crawford. Gay
    Communities Respond to Change. London: Falmer, 1993.
Kippax, Susan, et al. Gay Communities Respond to Change. London:
    Falmer, 1993.

More than one work by the same author(s)

Kozol, Jonathan. Death at an Early Age: The Destruction of the Hearts
    and Minds of Negro Children in the Boston Public Schools. Boston:
    Houghton, 1967.
    Savage Inequalities: Children in America's Schools. New York:
    Crown, 1991.

A book with an editor

Gwaltney, John Langston, ed. Drylongso: A Self-Portrait of Black Amer-
    ica. New York: Random, 1980.

A book with an author and an editor

Orwell, George. The Collected Essays, Journalism and Letters of George
    Orwell. Ed. Sonia Orwell and Ian Angus. New York: Harcourt,
    1968.

A later edition

Mumford, Lewis. Herman Melville: A Study of His Life and Vision. 2nd
    ed. New York: Harcourt, 1956.

A work in a series

Hall, Donald. Poetry and Ambition. Poets on Poetry. Ann Arbor: U of
    Michigan P, 1988.

An anthology

Glantz, Michael H., ed. Societal Responses to Regional Climatic Change.
    London: Westview, 1988.

A selection from an anthology

The numbers at the end of this entry are the page numbers on
which the cited selection appears.

Kellog, William D. "Human Impact on Climate: The Evolution of an
    Awareness." Societal Responses to Regional Climatic Change. Ed.
    Michael H. Glantz. London: Westview, 1988. 283-96.

If you cite more than one selection from the same anthology, give
the anthology as a separate entry and cross-reference it by the editor's
or editors' last names in the selection entries.

Ascher, Barbara Lazear. "On Compassion." Kennedy, Kennedy, and
    Aaron 145-47.
Kennedy, X. J., Dorothy M. Kennedy, and Jane E. Aaron, eds. The
    Bedford Reader. 6th ed. Boston: Bedford, 1997.
Quindlen, Anna. "Homeless." Kennedy, Kennedy, and Aaron 149-51.

A reference work

Cheney, Ralph Holt. "Coffee." Collier's Encyclopedia. 1993 ed.
"Versailles, Treaty of." The New Encyclopaedia Britannica: Macropae-
    dia. 15th ed. 1990.

Periodicals:
Journals, Magazines, and Newspapers

An article in a journal with continuous pagination throughout the annual volume

In many journals the pages are numbered consecutively for an entire annual volume of issues, so that the year's fourth issue might run from pages 240 to 320. For this type of journal, give the volume number after the journal title, followed by the year of publication in parentheses, a colon, and the page numbers of the article.

Clayton, Richard R., and Carl G. Leukefeld. "The Prevention of Drug
    Use Among Youth: Implications of Legalization." Journal of Pri-
    mary Prevention 12 (1992): 289-301.

An article in a journal that paginates issues separately

Some journals begin page numbering at 1 for each issue. For this kind of journal, give the issue number after the volume number and a period.

Vitz, Paul C. "Back to Human Dignity: From Modern to Postmodern
    Psychology." Intercollegiate Review 31.2 (1996): 15-23.

An article in a monthly or bimonthly magazine

Fallows, James. "Why Americans Hate the Media." Atlantic Monthly
    Feb. 1996: 45-64.

An article in a weekly magazine

Gopnick, Adam. "Read All About It." New Yorker 12 Dec. 1994:
    84-102.

An article in a newspaper

Gorman, Peter. "It's Time to Legalize." Boston Sunday Globe 28 Aug.
    1994, late ed.: 69+.

The page number "69+" means that the article begins on page 69 and continues on a later page. If the newspaper is divided into lettered sections, give both section letter and page number, as in "A7."

An unsigned article

"How the Missiles Help California." Time 1 Apr. 1996: 45.

A review

Bergham, V. R. "The Road to Extermination." Rev. of Hitler's Willing
Executioners, by Daniel Jonah Goldhagen. New York Times Book
Review 14 Apr. 1996: 6.

Other Sources

A film or video recording

Achbar, Mark, and Peter Wintonick, dirs. Manufacturing Consent:
Noam Chomsky and the Media. Zeitgeist, 1992.

A television or radio program

"Cable TV Squeezes High Numbers and Aces Competition." All Things
Considered. PBS. WGBH, Boston. 9 Feb. 1994.

A recording

Mendelssohn, Felix. A Midsummer Night's Dream. Cond. Erich Leins-
dorf. Boston Symphony Orch. RCA, 1982.

A letter or e-mail

List a published letter under the author's name, and provide full
publication information.

Hemingway, Ernest. Letter to Grace Hemingway. 15 Jan. 1920. In
Ernest Hemingway: Selected Letters. Ed. Carlos Baker. New York:
Scribner's, 1981. 44.

For a letter or e-mail that you receive, list the source under the writer's
name, add "to the author," and provide the date of the correspondence.

Dove, Chris. Letter to the author. 7 May 1996.

Dove, Chris. E-mail to the author. 7 May 1996.

An interview

Kesey, Ken. Interview. "The Art of Fiction." <u>Paris Review</u> 130 (1994):
    59-94.

Macedo, Donaldo. Personal interview. 13 May 1995.

An electronic source

Electronic sources vary greatly, and the material available electronically is constantly increasing. Your aim in citing such a source should be to tell readers how they can find it for themselves. The models below go beyond MLA style, which does not include many kinds of sources and information, to incorporate the styles developed by Janice R. Walker of the University of South Florida and Michael N. Salda of the University of Mississippi.

For portable databases (CD-ROMs, diskettes, magnetic tapes), the content of the citation depends on whether the database is a periodical and whether it is also published in print. For a periodical also published in print, provide full print information (following the models given earlier), the title of the electronic source, the medium (for instance, "CD-ROM"), the name of the distributor, and the date of electronic publication:

Rausch, Janet. "So Late in the Day." <u>Daily Sun</u> 10 Dec. 1994, late ed.:
    C1. <u>Daily Disk</u>. CD-ROM. Cybernews. Jan. 1995.

For a periodical not also published in print, replace the print information after the title with a date for the source.

Mallan, Chris. "The Allegory of <u>Mommy Dearest</u>." 23 Mar. 1993.
    <u>Movie/Lit Abstracts</u>. CD-ROM. InfoCo. Dec. 1993.

Treat a portable database that is not a periodical as if it were a book, but provide the version or release number and the medium after the title.

Hardy, Joel P. <u>Rose Quartz: A Study in Geology</u>. Ver. 2. Magnetic tape.
    New York: Hestas, 1996.

For online sources — those reached over wires — the references can be more complicated. The reference for any source that is also published in print should include the print information, as indicated above for portable databases.

Sturgeon, Gregory D. "Study Right: A Guide to Better College Success."
    <u>Hipster Magazine</u>. May 1996: 18–21. <u>Magazine Index</u>. Online.
    Earshot. 21 Apr. 1996.

Monner, David M. "The Quiet Life." <u>Long Island Data</u>. Online. Nexis.
June 1996.

For a source reached over a computer network, provide the author, title, date, and medium as above, but also give the electronic address (after "Available" and the access mode, such as "http" or "gopher") and the date of your access to the source (in parentheses at the end of the entry). In the address, do not use any extra periods, spaces, or hyphens that the reader might mistake for part of the address. The following models show how to cite the most common Internet sources.

A site on the World Wide Web (WWW):

McClure, Mark. "Speakers." <u>On-line Calendar of Events</u>. 18 Apr. 1996.
Online. Internet. Available http://www.mwc. edu/-mmcclure/
sa_spkrs.html (23 May 1996).

A Telnet or Gopher site:

Johnson, Earl. "My House: Come On In." <u>Houses of Cyberspace</u>. 16
June 1995. Online. Internet. Available telnet edwin.ohms.bookso.
com 7777, @go #50827, press 10 (11 Aug. 1996).

Meacham, Jeffrey S. "The Beauty of Ohio." <u>Ohio Tourist Sites</u>. 2 July
1996. Online. Internet. Available gopher UofOhio/ohiodisk/Ohio
Tourist Sites (1 Sept. 1996).

A posting on a Listserv or newsgroup:

Forrester, Thomas. "Embracing Mathematics." 21 Sept. 1996. Online.
Internet. Available listserv@gargantuan.smartguy.newyork.uny.
edu (22 Sept. 1996).

An FTP (File Transfer Protocol) site:

Valezquez, Joel. "Wearing Out the Internet." <u>Internet Concerns</u>. 15 Apr.
1996. Online. Internet. Available ftp downtown.centaur.edu/new/
conc/internet/essay/valez.text (23 May 1996).

USEFUL TERMS

Abstract and concrete Two kinds of language. *Abstract* words refer to ideas, conditions, and qualities we cannot directly perceive: *truth, love, courage, evil, wealth, poverty, progressive, reactionary. Concrete* words indicate things we can know with our senses: *tree, chair, bird, pen, motorcycle, perfume, thunderclap, cheeseburger.* The use of concrete words lends vigor and clarity to writing, for such words help a reader to picture things. See IMAGE.

Writers of expository and argumentative essays tend to shift back and forth from one kind of language to the other. They often begin a paragraph with a general statement full of abstract words ("There is *hope* for the *future* of *motoring*"). Then they usually go on to give examples and present evidence in sentences full of concrete words ("Inventor *Jones* claims his *car* will go from *Fresno* to *Los Angeles* on a *gallon* of *peanut oil*"). Inexperienced writers often use too many abstract words and not enough concrete ones.

Allude, allusion To refer to a person, place, or thing believed to be common knowledge (*allude*), or the act or result of doing so (*allusion*). An allusion may point to a famous event, a familiar saying, a noted personality, a well-known story or song. Usually brief, an allusion is a space-saving way to convey much meaning. For example, the statement "The game was Coach Johnson's Waterloo" informs the reader that, like Napoleon meeting defeat in a celebrated battle, the coach led a confrontation resulting in his downfall and that of his team. If the writer is also showing Johnson's character, the allusion might further tell us that the coach is a man of Napoleonic ambition and pride. To make an effective allusion, you have

669

to be aware of your audience. If your readers do not recognize the allusion, it will only confuse. Not everyone, for example, would understand you if you alluded to a neighbor, to a seventeenth-century Russian harpsichordist, or to a little-known stock car driver.

Analogy   An extended comparison based on the like features of two unlike things: one familiar or easily understood, the other unfamiliar, abstract, or complicated. For instance, most people know at least vaguely how the human eye works: The pupil adjusts to admit light, which registers as an image on the retina at the back of the eye. You might use this familiar information to explain something less familiar to many people, such as how a camera works: The aperture (like the pupil) adjusts to admit light, which registers as an image on the film (like the retina) at the back of the camera. Analogies are especially helpful for explaining technical information in a way that is nontechnical, more easily grasped. In August 1981, for example, the spacecraft *Voyager 2* transmitted spectacular pictures of Saturn to Earth. To explain the difficulty of their achievement, NASA scientists compared their feat to a golfer sinking a putt from five hundred miles away. Because it can make abstract ideas vivid and memorable, analogy is also a favorite device of philosophers, politicians, and preachers. In his his celebrated speech "I Have a Dream" (p. 502), Martin Luther King, Jr., draws a remarkable analogy to express the anger and disappointment of African Americans that, one hundred years after Lincoln's Emancipation Proclamation, their full freedom has yet to be achieved. "It is obvious today," declares King, "that America has defaulted on this promissory note"; and he compares the founding fathers' written guarantee — of the rights of life, liberty, and the pursuit of happiness — to a bad check returned for insufficient funds.

Analogy is similar to the method of COMPARISON AND CONTRAST. Both use DIVISION or ANALYSIS to identify the distinctive features of two things and then set the features side by side. But a comparison explains two obviously similar things — two Civil War generals, two styles of basketball play — and considers both their differences and their similarities. An analogy yokes two apparently unlike things (eye and camera, spaceflight and golf, guaranteed human rights and bad checks) and focuses only on their major similarities. Analogy is thus an extended METAPHOR, the FIGURE OF SPEECH that declares one thing to be another — even though it isn't, in a strictly literal sense — for the purpose of making us aware of similarity: "Hope," says the poet Emily Dickinson, "is the thing with feathers / That perches in the soul."

In an ARGUMENT, analogy can make readers more receptive to a point or inspire them, but it can't prove anything because in the end the subjects are dissimilar. A false analogy is a LOGICAL FALLACY that claims a fundamental likeness when none exists. See page 451.

Analyze, analysis   To separate a subject into its parts (*analyze*), or the act or result of doing so (*analysis*, also called *division*). Analysis is a key skill in CRITICAL THINKING, READING, AND WRITING; see pages 15–16. It is also considered a method of development; see Chapter 6.

Anecdote   A brief narrative, or retelling of a story or event. Anecdotes have many uses: as essay openers or closers, as examples, as sheer entertainment. See Chapter 1.

Appeals   Resources writers draw on to connect with and persuade readers.

A **rational appeal** asks readers to use their intellects and their powers of reasoning. It relies on established conventions of logic and evidence.

An **emotional appeal** asks readers to respond out of their beliefs, values, or feelings. It inspires, affirms, frightens, angers.

An **ethical appeal** asks readers to look favorably on the writer. It stresses the writer's intelligence, competence, fairness, morality, and other qualities desirable in a trustworthy debater or teacher.

See also pages 444–45.

Argument   A mode of writing intended to win readers' agreement with an assertion by engaging their powers of reasoning. Argument often overlaps PERSUASION. See Chapter 10.

Assume, assumption   To take something for granted (*assume*), or a belief or opinion taken for granted (*assumption*). Whether stated or unstated, assumptions influence a writer's choices of subject, viewpoint, evidence, and even language. See also pages 16 and 445–48.

Audience   A writer's readers. Having in mind a particular audience helps the writer in choosing strategies. Imagine, for instance, that you are writing two reviews of the movie *Independence Day*: one for the students who read the campus newspaper, the other for amateur and professional filmmakers who read *Millimeter*. For the first audience, you might write about the actors, the plot, and especially dramatic scenes. You might judge the picture and urge your readers to see it — or to avoid it. Writing for *Millimeter*, you might discuss special effects, shooting techniques, problems in editing and in mixing picture and sound. In this review, you might use more specialized and technical terms. Obviously, an awareness of the interests and knowledge of your readers, in each case, would help you decide how to write. If you told readers of the campus paper too much about filming techniques, you would lose most of them. If you told *Millimeter*'s readers the plot of the film in detail and how you liked its opening scene, probably you would put them to sleep.

You can increase your awareness of your audience by asking yourself a few questions before you begin to write. Who are to be your readers? What is their age level? background? education? Where do they live? What are their beliefs and attitudes? What interests them? What, if anything, sets them apart from most people? How familiar are they with your subject? Knowing your audience can help you write so that your readers will not only understand you better but more deeply care about what you say.

Cause and effect   A method of development in which a writer ANALYZES reasons for an action, event, or decision, or analyzes its consequences. See Chapter 8. See also EFFECT.

Chronological order   The arrangement of events as they occurred or occur in time, first to last. Most NARRATIVES and PROCESS ANALYSES use chronological order.

Claim   The proposition that an ARGUMENT demonstrates. Stephen Toulmin favors this term in his system of reasoning. See pages 445–46. In some discussions of argument, the term THESIS is used instead.

Classification   A method of development in which a writer sorts out plural things (contact sports, college students, kinds of music) into categories. See Chapter 7.

Cliché   A worn-out, trite expression that a writer employs thoughtlessly.

Although at one time the expression may have been colorful, from heavy use it has lost its luster. It is now "old as the hills." In conversation, most of us sometimes use clichés, but in writing they "stick out like sore thumbs." Alert writers, when they revise, replace a cliché with a fresh, concrete expression. Writers who have trouble recognizing clichés should be suspicious of any phrase they've heard before and should try to read more widely. Their problem is that, so many expressions being new to them, they do not know which ones are full of moths.

Coherence   The clear connection of the parts in a piece of effective writing. This quality exists when the reader can easily follow the flow of ideas between sentences, paragraphs, and larger divisions, and can see how they relate successively to one another.

In making your essay coherent, you may find certain devices useful. TRANSITIONS, for instance, can bridge ideas. Reminders of points you have stated earlier are helpful to a reader who may have forgotten them—as readers tend to do sometimes, particularly if your essay is long. However, a coherent essay is not one merely pasted together with transitions and reminders. It derives its coherence from the clear relationship between its THESIS (or central idea) and all its parts.

Colloquial expressions   Words and phrases occurring primarily in speech and informal writing that seeks a relaxed, conversational tone. "My favorite chow is a burger and a shake" or "This math exam has me wired" may be acceptable in talking to a roommate, in corresponding with a friend, or in writing a humorous essay for general readers. Such choices of words, however, would be out of place in formal writing—in, say, a laboratory report or a letter to your senator. Contractions (*let's, don't, we'll*) and abbreviated words (*photo, sales rep, TV*) are the shorthand of spoken language. Good writers use such expressions with an awareness that they produce an effect of casualness.

Comparison and contrast   Two methods of development usually found together. Using them, a writer examines the similarities and differences between two things to reveal their natures. See Chapter 4.

Conclusion   The sentences or paragraphs that bring an essay to a satisfying and logical end. A conclusion is purposefully crafted to give a sense of unity and completeness to the whole essay. The best conclusions evolve naturally out of what has gone before and convince the reader that the essay is indeed at an end, not that the writer has run out of steam.

Conclusions vary in type and length depending on the nature and scope of the essay. A long research paper may require several paragraphs of summary to review and emphasize the main points. A short essay, however, may benefit from a few brief closing sentences.

In concluding an essay, beware of diminishing the impact of your writing by finishing on a weak note. Don't apologize for what you have or have not written, or cram in a final detail that would have been better placed elsewhere.

Although there are no set formulas for closing, the following list presents several options:

1. Restate the thesis of your essay, and perhaps your main points.
2. Mention the broader implications or significance of your topic.

3. Give a final example that pulls all the parts of your discussion together.
4. Offer a prediction.
5. End with the most important point as the culmination of your essay's development.
6. Suggest how the reader can apply the information you have just imparted.
7. End with a bit of drama or flourish. Tell an ANECDOTE, offer an appropriate quotation, ask a question, make a final insightful remark. Keep in mind, however, that an ending shouldn't sound false and gimmicky. It truly has to conclude.

Concrete   See ABSTRACT AND CONCRETE.

Connotation and denotation   Two types of meanings most words have. *Denotation* is the explicit, literal, dictionary definition of a word. *Connotation* refers to the implied meaning, resonant with associations, of a word. The denotation of *blood* is "the fluid that circulates in the vascular system." The word's connotations range from *life force* to *gore* to *family bond*. A doctor might use the word *blood* for its denotation, and a mystery writer might rely on the rich connotations of the word to heighten a scene.

Because people have different experiences, they bring to the same word different associations. A conservative's emotional response to the word *welfare* is not likely to be the same as a liberal's. And referring to your senator as a *diplomat* evokes a different response, from the senator and from others, than would *baby-kisser, political hack,* or even *politician*. The effective use of words involves knowing both what they mean literally and what they are likely to suggest.

Critical thinking, reading, and writing   A group of interlocking skills that are essential for college work and beyond. Each seeks the meaning beneath the surface of a statement, poem, editorial, picture, advertisement, or other "text." Using ANALYSIS, INFERENCE, SYNTHESIS, and often EVALUATION, the critical thinker, reader, and writer separates this text into its elements in order to see and judge meanings, relations, and ASSUMPTIONS that might otherwise remain buried. See also pages 15–17 and 269.

Data   The name for EVIDENCE favored by logician Stephen Toulmin in his system of reasoning. See pages 445–46.

Deductive reasoning, deduction   The method of reasoning from the general to the particular: From information about what we already know, we deduce what we need or want to know. See Chapter 10, pages 448–49.

Definition   A statement of the literal and specific meaning or meanings of a word, or a method of developing an essay. In the latter, the writer usually explains the nature of a word, a thing, a concept, or a phenomenon; in doing so the writer may employ NARRATION, DESCRIPTION, or any other method. See Chapter 9.

Denotation   See CONNOTATION AND DENOTATION.

Description   A mode of writing that conveys the evidence of the senses: sight, hearing, touch, taste, smell. See Chapter 2.

Diction   The choice of words. Every written or spoken statement contains diction of some kind. To describe certain aspects of diction, the following terms may be useful:

Standard English: the common American language, words and grammatical forms that are used and expected in school, business, and other sites.

Nonstandard English: words and grammatical forms such as *theirselves* and *ain't* that are used mainly by people who speak a dialect other than standard English.

Dialect: a variety of English based on differences in geography, education, or social background. Dialect is usually spoken, but may be written. Maya Angelou's essay in Chapter 1 transcribes the words of dialect speakers: people waiting for the fight broadcast ("He gone whip him till that white boy call him Momma").

Slang: certain words in highly informal speech or writing, or in the speech of a particular group. For example, *blow off, dis, dweeb.*

Colloquial expressions: words and phrases from conversation. See COLLOQUIAL EXPRESSIONS for examples.

Regional terms: words heard in a certain locality, such as *spritzing* for "raining" in Pennsylvania Dutch country.

Technical terms: words and phrases that form the vocabulary of a particular discipline (*monocotyledon* from botany), occupation (*drawplate* from die-making), or avocation (*interval training* from running). See also JARGON.

Archaisms: old-fashioned expressions, once common but now used to suggest an earlier style, such as *ere, yon,* and *forsooth.* (Actually, *yon* is still current in the expression *hither and yon;* but if you say "Behold yon glass of beer!" it is an archaism.)

Obsolete diction: words that have passed out of use (such as the verb *werien,* "to protect or defend," and the noun *isetnesses,* "agreements"). *Obsolete* may also refer to certain meanings of words no longer current (*fond* for foolish, *clipping* for hugging or embracing).

Pretentious diction: use of words more numerous and elaborate than necessary, such as *institution of higher learning* for college, and *partake of solid nourishment* for eat.

Archaic, obsolete, and pretentious diction usually has no place in good writing unless for ironic or humorous effect: H. L. Mencken delighted in the hifalutin use of *tonsorial studio* instead of barber shop. Still, any diction may be the right diction for a certain occasion: The choice of words depends on a writer's purpose and audience.

Discovery   The stage of the writing process before the first draft. It may include deciding on a topic, narrowing the topic, creating or finding ideas, doing reading and other research, defining PURPOSE and AUDIENCE, planning and arranging material. Discovery may follow from daydreaming or meditation, reading, or perhaps carefully ransacking memory. In practice, though, it usually involves considerable writing and is aided by the act of writing. The operations of discovery—reading, research, further idea-creation, and refinement of subject, purpose, and audience—may all continue well into drafting as well. See also pages 24–26, 29–30.

Division   See ANALYSIS.

Dominant impression   The main idea a writer conveys about a subject through DESCRIPTION—that an elephant is gigantic, for example, or an experience scary. See also Chapter 2.

Drafting   The stage of the writing process during which a writer expresses ideas in complete sentences, links them, and arranges them in a sequence. See also pages 26–27, 30–32.

Effect   The result of an event or action, usually considered together with CAUSE as a method of development. See the discussion of cause and effect in Chapter 8. In discussing writing, the term *effect* also refers to the impression a word, sentence, paragraph, or entire work makes on the reader: how convincing it is, whether it elicits an emotional response, what associations it conjures up, and so on.

Emotional appeal   See APPEALS.

Emphasis   The stress or special importance given to a certain point or element to make it stand out. A skillful writer draws attention to what is most important in a sentence, paragraph, or essay by controlling emphasis in any of the following ways:

> **Proportion:** Important ideas are given greater coverage than minor points.

> **Position:** The beginnings and ends of sentences, paragraphs, and larger divisions are the strongest positions. Placing key ideas in these spots helps draw attention to their importance. The end is the stronger position, for what stands last stands out. A sentence in which less important details precede the main point is called a **periodic sentence:** "Having disguised himself as a guard and walked through the courtyard to the side gate, the prisoner made his escape." A sentence in which the main point precedes less important details is a **loose sentence:** "Autumn is orange: gourds in baskets at roadside stands, the harvest moon hanging like a pumpkin, and oak and beech leaves flashing like goldfish."

> **Repetition:** Careful repetition of key words or phrases can give them greater importance. (Careless repetition, however, can cause boredom.)

> **Mechanical devices:** Italics (underlining), capital letters, and exclamation points can make words or sentences stand out. Writers sometimes fall back on these devices, however, after failing to show significance by other means. Italics and exclamation points can be useful in reporting speech, but excessive use sounds exaggerated or bombastic.

Essay   A short nonfiction composition on one central theme or subject in which the writer may offer personal views. Essays are sometimes classified as either formal or informal. In general, a **formal essay** is one whose diction is that of the written language (not colloquial speech), serious in tone, and usually focused on a subject the writer believes is important. (For example, see Bruce Catton's "Grant and Lee.") An **informal essay,** in contrast, is more likely to admit colloquial expressions; the writer's tone tends to be lighter, perhaps humorous, and the subject is likely to be personal, sometimes even trivial. (See James Thurber's "University Days.") These distinctions, however, are rough ones: An essay such as Judy Brady's "I Want a Wife" may use colloquial language and speak of personal experience, though it is serious in tone and has an undeniably important subject.

Ethical appeal   See APPEALS.

Euphemism   The use of inoffensive language in place of language that readers or listeners may find hurtful, distasteful, frightening, or otherwise objectionable—for instance, a police officer's announcing that someone *passed on* rather than *died,* or a politician's calling for *revenue enhancement* rather than *taxation.* Writers sometimes use euphemism out of consideration for readers' feelings, but just as often they use it to deceive readers or shirk responsibility.

Evaluate, evaluation   To judge the merits of something (*evaluate*), or the act or result of doing so (*evaluation*). Evaluation is often part of CRITICAL THINKING, READING, AND WRITING. In evaluating a work of writing, you base your judgment on your ANALYSIS of it and your sense of its quality or value. See also page 17.

Evidence   The factual basis for an argument or an explanation. In a courtroom, an attorney's case is only as good as the evidence marshaled to support it. In an essay, a writer's opinions and GENERALIZATIONS also must rest upon evidence. The common forms of evidence are **facts,** verifiable statements; **statistics,** facts stated numerically; **examples,** specific instances of a generalization; **reported experience,** usually eyewitness accounts; **expert testimony,** the opinions of people considered very skilled or knowledgeable in the field; and, in CRITICAL WRITING about other writing, **quotations** or **paraphrases** from the work being discussed. (See PARAPHRASE.)

Example   Also called **exemplification** or **illustration,** a method of development in which the writer provides instances of a general idea. See Chapter 3. *An example* is a verbal illustration.

Exposition   The mode of prose writing that explains (or exposes) its subject. Its function is to inform, to instruct, or to set forth ideas: the major trade routes in the Middle East, how to make a dulcimer, why the United States consumes more energy than it needs. Exposition may call various methods to its service: EXAMPLE, COMPARISON AND CONTRAST, PROCESS ANALYSIS, and so on. Most college writing is at least partly exposition, and so are most of the essays in this book.

Fallacies   Errors in reasoning. See pages 449–51 for a list and examples.

Figures of speech   Expressions that depart from the literal meanings of words for the sake of emphasis or vividness. To say "She's a jewel" doesn't mean that the subject of praise is literally a kind of shining stone; the statement makes sense because its CONNOTATIONS come to mind: rare, priceless, worth cherishing. Some figures of speech involve comparisons of two objects apparently unlike. A **simile** (from the Latin, "likeness") states the comparison directly, usually connecting the two things using *like, as,* or *than:* "The moon is like a snowball," "He's as lazy as a cat full of cream," "My feet are flatter than flyswatters." A **metaphor** (from the Greek, "transfer") declares one thing to be another: "A mighty fortress is our God," "The sheep were bolls of cotton on the hill." (A **dead metaphor** is a word or phrase that, originally a figure of speech, has come to be literal through common usage: "the *hands* of a clock.") **Personification** is a simile or metaphor that assigns human traits to inanimate objects or abstractions: "A stoop-shouldered refrigerator hummed quietly to itself," "All of a sudden the solution to the math problem sat there winking at me."

Other figures of speech consist of deliberate misrepresentations. **Hyperbole** (from the Greek, "throwing beyond") is a conscious exaggeration: "I'm so hungry I could eat a horse and saddle," "I'd wait for you a thousand years." Its opposite, **understatement,** creates an ironic or humorous effect:

"I accepted the ride. At the moment, I didn't feel like walking across the Mojave Desert." A **paradox** is a seemingly self-contradictory statement that, on reflection, makes sense: "Children are the poor person's wealth" (wealth can be monetary, or it can be spiritual). *Paradox* may also refer to a situation that is inexplicable or contradictory, such as the restriction of one group's rights in order to secure the rights of another group.

Flashback   A technique of NARRATIVE in which the sequence of events is interrupted to recall an earlier period.

Focus   The narrowing of a subject to make it manageable. Beginning with a general subject, you concentrate on a certain aspect of it. For instance, you may select crafts as a general subject, then decide your main interest lies in weaving. You could focus your essay still further by narrowing it to operating a hand loom. You can also focus your writing according to who will read it (AUDIENCE) or what you want it to achieve (PURPOSE).

General and specific   Terms that describe the relative number of instances or objects included in the group signified by a word. *General* words name a group or class (*flowers*); *specific* words limit the class by naming its individual members (*rose, violet, dahlia, marigold*). Words may be arranged in a series from more general to more specific: *clothes, pants, jeans, Levis*. The word *cat* is more specific than *animal*, but less specific than *tiger cat*, or *Garfield*. See also ABSTRACT AND CONCRETE.

Generalization   A statement about a class based on an examination of some of its members: "Lions are fierce." The more members examined and the more representative they are of the class, the sturdier the generalization. The statement "Solar heat saves homeowners money" would be challenged by homeowners who have yet to recover their installation costs. "Solar heat can save homeowners money in the long run" would be a sounder generalization. Insufficient or nonrepresentative EVIDENCE often leads to a hasty generalization, such as "All freshmen hate their roommates" or "Men never express their feelings." Words such as *all, every, only, never*, and *always* have to be used with care. "Some men don't express their feelings" is more credible than the statement above. Making a trustworthy generalization involves the use of INDUCTIVE REASONING (discussed on pp. 448–49).

Hyperbole   See FIGURES OF SPEECH.

Illustration   Another name for EXAMPLE. See Chapter 3.

Image   A word or word sequence that evokes a sensory experience. Whether literal ("We picked two red apples") or figurative ("His cheeks looked like two red apples, buffed and shining"), an image appeals to the reader's memory of seeing, hearing, smelling, touching, or tasting. Images add concreteness to fiction — "The farm looked as tiny and still as a seashell, with the little knob of a house surrounded by its curved furrows of tomato plants" (Eudora Welty in a short story, "The Whistle") — and are an important element in poetry. But writers of essays, too, find images valuable to bring ideas down to earth. See also FIGURES OF SPEECH.

Inductive reasoning, induction   The process of reasoning to a conclusion about an entire class by examining some of its members. See pages 448–49.

Infer, inference   To draw a conclusion (*infer*), or the act or result of doing so (*inference*). In CRITICAL THINKING, READING, AND WRITING, inference is the means to understanding a writer's meaning, ASSUMPTIONS, PURPOSE, fairness, and other attributes. See also page 16.

Introduction   The opening of a written work. Often it states the writer's subject, narrows it, and communicates the writer's main idea (THESIS). Introductions vary in length, depending on their purposes. A research paper may need several paragraphs to set forth its central idea and its plan of organization; a brief, informal essay may need only a sentence or two for an introduction. Whether long or short, good introductions tell readers no more than they need to know when they begin reading. Here are a few possible ways to open an essay effectively:

1. State your central idea, or thesis, perhaps showing why you care about it.
2. Present startling facts about your subject.
3. Tell an illustrative ANECDOTE.
4. Give background information that will help your reader understand your subject, or see why it is important.
5. Begin with an arresting quotation.
6. Ask a challenging question. (In your essay, you'll go on to answer it.)

Irony   A manner of speaking or writing that does not directly state a discrepancy, but implies one. **Verbal irony** is the intentional use of words to suggest a meaning other than literal: "What a mansion!" (said of a shack); "There's nothing like sunshine" (said on a foggy morning). (For more examples, see the essays by Jessica Mitford, Linnea Saukko, and Judy Brady.) If irony is delivered contemptuously with an intent to hurt, we call it **sarcasm:** "Oh, you're a real friend!" (said to someone who refuses to lend the speaker a quarter to make a phone call). With **situational irony,** the circumstances themselves are incongruous, run contrary to expectations, or twist fate: Juliet regains consciousness only to find that Romeo, believing her dead, has stabbed himself. See also SATIRE.

Jargon   Strictly speaking, the special vocabulary of a trade or profession. The term has also come to mean inflated, vague, meaningless language of any kind. It is characterized by wordiness, ABSTRACTIONS galore, pretentious DICTION, and needlessly complicated word order. Whenever you meet a sentence that obviously could express its idea in fewer words and shorter ones, chances are that it is jargon. For instance: "The motivating force compelling her to opt continually for the most labor-intensive mode of operation in performing her functions was consistently observed to be the single constant and regular factor in her behavior patterns." Translation: "She did everything the hard way."

Journal   A record of one's thoughts, kept daily or at least regularly. Keeping a journal faithfully can help a writer gain confidence and develop ideas. See also pages 24–25.

Metaphor   See FIGURES OF SPEECH.

Narration   The mode of writing that tells a story. See Chapter 1.

Narrator   The teller of a story, usually either in the first PERSON (*I*) or in the third (*he, she, it, they*). See pages 41–42.

Nonstandard English   See DICTION.

Objective and subjective   Kinds of writing that differ in emphasis. In *objec-*

tive writing, the emphasis falls on the topic; in *subjective* writing, it falls on the writer's view of the topic. Objective writing occurs in factual journalism, science reports, certain PROCESS ANALYSES (such as recipes, directions, and instructions), and logical arguments in which the writer attempts to downplay personal feelings and opinions. Subjective writing sets forth the writer's feelings, opinions, and interpretations. It occurs in friendly letters, journals, editorials, bylined feature stories and columns in newspapers, personal essays, and arguments that appeal to emotion. Few essays, however, contain one kind of writing exclusive of the other.

Paradox   See FIGURES OF SPEECH.

Paragraph   A group of closely related sentences that develop a central idea. In an essay, a paragraph is the most important unit of thought because it is both self-contained and part of the larger whole. Paragraphs separate long and involved ideas into smaller parts that are more manageable for the writer and easier for the reader to take in. Good paragraphs, like good essays, possess UNITY and COHERENCE. The central idea is usually stated in the TOPIC SENTENCE, often found at the beginning of the paragraph. All other sentences in the paragraph relate to this topic sentence, defining it, explaining it, illustrating it, providing it with evidence and support. Sometimes you will meet a unified and coherent paragraph that has no topic sentence. It usually contains a central idea that no sentence in it explicitly states, but that every sentence in it clearly implies.

Parallelism, parallel structure   A habit of good writers: keeping ideas of equal importance in similar grammatical form. A writer may place nouns side by side ("*Trees* and *streams* are my weekend tonic") or in a series ("Give me *wind, sea,* and *stars*"). Phrases, too, may be arranged in parallel structure ("*Out of my bed, into my shoes, up to my classroom*—that's my life"); or clauses ("Ask not what your country can do for you; ask what you can do for your country").

   Parallelism may be found not only in single sentences, but in larger units as well. A paragraph might read: "Rhythm is everywhere. It throbs in the rain forests of Brazil. It vibrates ballroom floors in Vienna. It snaps its fingers on street corners in Chicago." In a whole essay, parallelism may be the principle used to arrange ideas in a balanced or harmonious structure. See the famous speech given by Martin Luther King, Jr. (p. 502), in which each paragraph in a series (paras. 11–18) begins with the words "I have a dream" and goes on to describe an imagined future. Not only does such a parallel structure organize ideas, but it also lends them force.

Paraphrase   Putting another writer's thoughts into your own words. In writing a research paper or an essay containing EVIDENCE gathered from your reading, you will find it necessary to paraphrase—unless you are using another writer's very words with quotation marks around them—and to acknowledge your source. Contrast SUMMARY. And see page 656.

Person   A grammatical distinction made between the speaker, the one spoken to, and the one spoken about. In the first person (*I, we*), the subject is speaking. In the second person (*you*), the subject is being spoken to. In the third person (*he, she, it*), the subject is being spoken about. The point of view of an essay or work of fiction is often specified according to person: "This short story is told from a first-person point of view." See POINT OF VIEW.

Personification   See FIGURES OF SPEECH.

Persuasion   A mode of writing intended to influence people's actions by engaging their beliefs and feelings. Persuasion often overlaps ARGUMENT. See Chapter 10.

Plagiarism   The use of someone else's ideas or words as if they were your own, without acknowledging the original author. See pages 656–57.

Point of view   In an essay, the physical position or the mental angle from which a writer beholds a subject. Assuming the subject is starlings, the following three writers have different points of view. An ornithologist might write OBJECTIVELY about the introduction of these birds into North America. A farmer might advise other farmers how to prevent the birds from eating seed. A bird-watcher might SUBJECTIVELY describe a first glad sighting of an unusual species. Furthermore, the PERSON of each essay would probably differ: The scientist might present a scholarly paper in the third person; the farmer might offer advice in the second; the bird-watcher might recount the experience in the first.

Premise   A proposition or ASSUMPTION that supports a conclusion. See page 449 for examples.

Process analysis   A method of development that most often explains step by step how something is done or how to do something. See Chapter 5.

Purpose   A writer's reason for trying to convey a particular idea (THESIS) about a particular subject to a particular AUDIENCE of readers. Though it may emerge gradually during the writing process, in the end purpose should govern every element of a piece of writing.

　　In trying to define the purpose of an essay you read, ask yourself "Why did the writer write this?" or "What was this writer trying to achieve?" Even though you cannot know the writer's intentions with absolute certainty, an effective essay generally makes some purpose clear.

Rational appeal   See APPEALS.

Revision   The stage of the writing process during which a writer "re-sees" a draft from the viewpoint of a reader. Revision usually involves two steps, first considering fundamental matters such as purpose and organization, and then editing for surface matters such as smooth transitions and error-free sentences. See pages 27–28, 32–34.

Rhetoric   The study (and the art) of using language effectively. *Rhetoric* also has a negative connotation of empty or pretentious language meant to waffle, stall, or even deceive. This is the meaning in "The president had nothing substantial to say about taxes. Just the usual rhetoric."

Rhetorical question   A question posed for effect, one that requires no answer. Instead, it often provokes thought, lends emphasis to a point, asserts or denies something without making a direct statement, launches further discussion, introduces an opinion, or leads the reader where the writer intends. Sometimes a writer throws one in to introduce variety in a paragraph full of declarative sentences. The following questions are rhetorical: "When will the United States learn that sending people to the moon does not feed them on the earth?" "Shall I compare thee to a summer's day?" "What is the point of making money if you've no one but yourself to spend it on?" Both reader and writer know what the answers are supposed to be. (1) Someday, if the United States ever wises up. (2) Yes. (3) None.

Sarcasm   See IRONY.

Satire   A form of writing that employs wit to attack folly. Unlike most comedy, the purpose of satire is not merely to entertain, but to bring about enlightenment — even reform. Usually, satire employs irony — as in Linnea Saukko's "How to Poison the Earth" and Jonathan Swift's "A Modest Proposal." See also IRONY.

Scene   In a NARRATIVE, an event retold in detail to re-create an experience. See Chapter 1.

Sentimentality   A quality sometimes found in writing that fails to communicate. Such writing calls for an extreme emotional response on the part of an AUDIENCE, although its writer fails to supply adequate reason for any such reaction. A sentimental writer delights in waxing teary over certain objects: great-grandmother's portrait, the first stick of chewing gum baby chewed (now a shapeless wad), an empty popcorn box saved from the World Series of 1952. Sentimental writing usually results when writers shut their eyes to the actual world, preferring to snuffle the sweet scents of remembrance.

Simile   See FIGURES OF SPEECH.

Slang   See DICTION.

Specific   See GENERAL AND SPECIFIC.

Standard English   See DICTION.

Strategy   Whatever means a writer employs to write effectively. The methods set forth in this book are strategies; but so are narrowing a subject, organizing ideas clearly, using TRANSITIONS, writing with an awareness of your reader, and other effective writing practices.

Style   The distinctive manner in which a writer writes. Style may be seen especially in the writer's choice of words and sentence structures. Two writers may write on the same subject, even express similar ideas, but it is style that gives each writer's work a personality.

Subjective   See OBJECTIVE AND SUBJECTIVE.

Summarize, summary   To condense a work (essay, movie, news story) to its essence (*summarize*), or the act or result of doing so (*summary*). Summarizing a piece of writing in one's own words is an effective way to understand it. See pages 14–15. Summarizing (and acknowledging) others' writing in your own text is a good way to support your ideas. Contrast PARAPHRASE. See pages 655–56.

Suspense   Often an element in narration: the pleasurable expectation or anxiety we feel that keeps us reading a story. In an exciting mystery story, suspense is constant: How will it all turn out? Will the detective get to the scene in time to prevent another murder? But there can be suspense in less melodramatic accounts as well.

Syllogism   A three-step form of reasoning that employs DEDUCTION. See page 449 for an illustration.

Symbol   A visible object or action that suggests some further meaning. The flag suggests country, the crown suggests royalty — these are conventional symbols familiar to us. Life abounds in such relatively clear-cut symbols. Football teams use dolphins and rams for easy identification; married couples symbolize their union with a ring.

   In writing, symbols usually do not have such a one-to-one correspondence, but evoke a whole constellation of associations. In Herman

Melville's *Moby-Dick*, the whale suggests more than the large mammal it is. It hints at evil, obsession, and the untamable forces of nature. Such a symbol carries meanings too complex or elusive to be neatly defined.

Although more common in fiction and poetry, symbols can be used to good purpose in nonfiction because they often communicate an idea in a compact and concrete way.

Synthesize, synthesis   To link elements into a whole (*synthesize*), or the act or result of doing so (*synthesis*). In CRITICAL THINKING, READING, AND WRITING, synthesis is the key step during which you reassemble a work you have ANALYZED or connect the work with others. See page 16.

Thesis   The central idea in a work of writing, to which everything else in the work refers. In some way, each sentence and PARAGRAPH in an effective essay serves to support the thesis and to make it clear and explicit to readers. Good writers, while writing, often set down a **thesis sentence** or **thesis statement** to help them define their purpose. They may also include this statement in their essay as a promise and a guide to readers. See also pages 26–27.

Tone   The way a writer expresses his or her regard for subject, audience, or self. Through word choice, sentence structures, and what is actually said, the writer conveys an attitude and sets a prevailing spirit. Tone in writing varies as greatly as tone of voice varies in conversation. It can be serious, distant, flippant, angry, enthusiastic, sincere, sympathetic. Whatever tone a writer chooses, usually it informs an entire essay and helps a reader decide how to respond. For works of strong tone, see the essays by Annie Dillard, Joan Didion, Jessica Mitford, Judy Brady, A. M. Rosenthal, and Martin Luther King, Jr.

Topic sentence   The statement of the central idea in a PARAGRAPH. Often it will appear at (or near) the beginning of the paragraph, announcing the idea and beginning its development. Because all other sentences in the paragraph explain and support this central idea, the topic sentence is a way to create UNITY.

Transitions   Words, phrases, sentences, or even paragraphs that relate ideas. In moving from one topic to the next, a writer has to bring the reader along by showing how the ideas are developing, what bearing a new thought or detail has on an earlier discussion, or why a new topic is being introduced. A clear purpose, strong ideas, and logical development certainly aid COHERENCE, but to ensure that the reader is following along, good writers provide signals, or transitions.

To bridge sentences or paragraphs and to point out relationships within them, you can use some of the following devices of transition:

1. Repeat words or phrases to produce an echo in the reader's mind.
2. Use PARALLEL STRUCTURES to produce a rhythm that moves the reader forward.
3. Use pronouns to refer back to nouns in earlier passages.
4. Use transitional words and phrases. These may indicate a relationship of time (*right away, later, soon, meanwhile, in a few minutes, that night*), proximity (*beside, close to, distant from, nearby, facing*), effect (*therefore, for this reason, as a result, consequently*), comparison (*similarly, in the same way, likewise*), or contrast (*yet, but, nevertheless,*

however, despite). Some words and phrases of transition simply add on: *besides, too, also, moreover, in addition to, second, last, in the end.*

Understatement   See FIGURES OF SPEECH.

Unity   The quality of good writing in which all parts relate to the THESIS. In a unified essay, all words, sentences, and PARAGRAPHS support the single central idea. Your first step in achieving unity is to state your thesis; your next step is to organize your thoughts so that they make your thesis clear.

Voice   In writing, the sense of the author's character, personality, and attitude that comes through the words. See TONE.

Warrant   The name in Stephen Toulmin's system of reasoning for the thinking, or ASSUMPTION, that links DATA and CLAIM. See pages 445–48.

Richard N. Current et al., paragraph from *American History: A Survey* 6th. ed. (1983). Reproduced with permission of The McGraw-Hill Companies.

Meghan Daum. "Safe-Sex Lies." From *The New York Times Magazine* 1/21/96. Copyright © 1996 by Meghan Daum. Reprinted by permission of International Creative Management, Inc.

Joan Didion. "Marrying Absurd." From *Slouching Towards Bethlehem* by Joan Didion. Copyright © 1967, 1968 by Joan Didion. In "Joan Didion on Writing," excerpts from "Why I Write," first published in *The New York Times Book Review*.

Annie Dillard. "The Chase" pp. 45–49 from *An American Childhood* by Annie Dillard. Copyright © 1987 by Annie Dillard. Reprinted by permission of HarperCollins Publishers, Inc. "Annie Dillard on Writing" copyright © 1985 by St. Martin's Press, Inc.

Esther Dyson. "Cyberspace for All." First appeared as "If You Don't Love It, Leave It" in *The New York Times Magazine* on July 6, 1995. Reprinted by permission of the author. "Esther Dyson on Writing" copyright © 1996 by Bedford Books.

Barbara Ehrenreich. "In Defense of Talk Shows." Appeared in *The New York Times Magazine* December 4, 1995. Reprinted by permission of Time Inc. "Barbara Ehrenreich on Writing" copyright © 1987, Foundation for National Progress.

Peter Elbow. "Desperation Writing." From *Writing Without Teachers* by Peter Elbow. Copyright © 1975 by Peter Elbow. Used by permission of Oxford University Press, Inc. In "Peter Elbow on Writing," excerpts from "Closing My Eyes as I Speak: An Argument for Ignoring Audience" from *College English*, vol. 49, no. 1, January 1987, copyright © 1987 by the National Council of Teachers of English. Reprinted by permission of the publisher and the author.

Ralph Ellison. "On Being the Target of Discrimination." From *A World of Difference*, a special magazine supplement to the *New York Times*, April 16, 1989. Copyright © 1989 by Ralph Ellison. In "Ralph Ellison on Writing," excerpts from *Shadow and Act* by Ralph Ellison. Copyright © 1953 and 1964 by Ralph Ellison. Reprinted by permission of Random House Inc.

Louise Erdrich. "Beneath My House" as it appeared in *Harper's* Magazine March 1993. Reprinted as "Wild Kitten" in *The Blue Jay's Dance* by Louise Erdrich. Copyright © 1995 by Louise Erdrich. Reprinted by permission of HarperCollins Publishers, Inc. In "Louise Erdrich on Writing," excerpt from "Louise Erdrich" by Miriam Berkley. Reprinted from the August 15, 1986 issue of *Publishers Weekly*, published by Cahners Publishing Company, a division of Reed Elsevier Inc. Copyright © 1986 by Reed Elsevier Inc. Excerpt from interview with Michael Schumacher for *Writer's Digest*.

Stephanie Ericsson. "The Ways We Lie." © 1992 by Stephanie Ericsson. Notes for *Companion into the Dawn* to be published in 1997 by HarperCollins. Originally published in the *Utne Reader*. Permission granted by Rhoda Weyr Agency, NY.

M. F. K. Fisher. "The Broken Chain." From *To Begin Again* by M. F. K. Fisher. Copyright © 1992 by the M. F. K. Fisher Literary Trust. Reprinted by permission of Pantheon Books, a Division of Random House Inc.

Robert Francis. Excerpt from "Teacher." From *Pot Shots at Poetry* (1980). Reprinted by permission of the University of Michigan Press.

Stephen Jay Gould. "Sex, Drugs, Disasters, and the Extinction of Dinosaurs." Reprinted from *The Flamingo's Smile: Reflections in Natural History* by Stephen Jay Gould, by permission of W. W. Norton & Company, Inc. Copyright © 1985 by Stephen Jay Gould. In "Stephen Jay Gould on Writing," Prologue excerpts are

Spiro Kostof. Excerpt from *A History of Architecture: Settings and Rituals* by Spiro Kostof. Copyright © 1985 by Oxford University Press, Inc. Reprinted by permission.

Michael Kroll. "The Unquiet Death of Robert Harris." From the July 6, 1992 issue of *The Nation*. Reprinted with permission from *The Nation* magazine. © The Nation Company, L. P.

Christine Leong. "On Being a Chink." Reprinted by permission of the author. "Christine Leong on Writing," copyright 1996 by Bedford Books.

Brad Manning. "Arm Wrestling with My Father." Reprinted by permission of the author. "Brad Manning on Writing," copyright 1996 by Bedford Books.

Merrill Markoe. "The Day I Turned Sarcastic." Reprinted from *What the Dogs Have Taught Me* by Merrill Markoe. Copyright © 1992 by Merrill Markoe. Used by permission of Viking Penguin, a division of Penguin Books USA Inc.

H. L. Mencken. "The Penalty of Death." Reprinted from *A Mencken Chrestomathy* by H. L. Mencken. Copyright 1926 by Alfred A. Knopf Inc. and renewed 1954 by H. L. Mencken. Reprinted by permission of the publisher. In "H. L. Mencken on Writing," excerpts from "Addendum on Aims" by H. L. Mencken in *American Scene* and from "The Fringes of Lovely Letters" by H. L. Mencken in *Prejudices: Fifth Series*, all copyright © by Alfred A. Knopf, Inc. and reprinted by permission of Alfred A. Knopf, Inc.

Horace Miner. "Body Ritual Among the Nacirema." Reproduced by permission of the American Anthropological Association from *American Anthropologist* 58:3, June 1956. Not for further reproduction.

Jessica Mitford. "Behind the Formaldehyde Curtain." Reprinted from *The American Way of Death*. Simon & Schuster © 1963, 1968 by Jessica Mitford, all rights reserved. Reprinted by permission of Jessica Mitford. In "Jessica Mitford on Writing," excerpts from *Poison Penmanship: The Gentle Art of Muckraking* by Jessica Mitford, copyright © 1979 and from *A Fine Old Conflict* by Jessica Mitford, copyright © 1977, both reprinted by permission of Random House Inc.

Gloria Naylor. "The Meanings of a Word." First appeared in the *New York Times* Feb. 20, 1986 (Hers Column). Reprinted by permission of Sterling Lord Literistic, Inc. Copyright © 1986 by Gloria Naylor. In "Gloria Naylor on Writing," excerpt from W. Goldstein, " A Talk with Gloria Naylor" *Publisher's Weekly* 9/9/83.

George Orwell. "Politics and the English Language." Copyright 1946 by Sonia Brownell Orwell and renewed 1974 by Sonia Orwell. Reprinted from his volume *Shooting an Elephant and Other Essays* by permission of Harcourt Brace & Company and A. M. Heath, copyright © The Estate of the late Sonia Brownell Orwell and Martin Secker and Warburg Ltd. "George Orwell on Writing" excerpts from "Why I Write" from *Such, Such Were the Joys* by George Orwell, copyright 1953 by Sonia Brownell Orwell; renewed 1981 by Mrs. George K. Perutz, Mrs. Miriam Gross, Dr. Michael Dickson, Executors of the Estate of Sonia Brownell Orwell.

Diane E. Papalia and Sally Wendkos Olds. Paragraph from *Psychology* (1985). Reproduced with permission of The McGraw-Hill Companies.

Katha Pollitt. "Why Boys Don't Play with Dolls." First appeared in *The New York Times Magazine* October 8, 1995. Copyright © 1995 by The New York Times Co. Reprinted by permission. In "Katha Pollitt on Writing," excerpt from "Katha Pollitt," by Ruth Coniff, first appeared in *The Progressive*, Dec. 1994, pp. 38–39. Reprinted by permission from The Progressive, 409 East Main Street, Madison, WI 53703.

Michael Sorkin. Excerpt from "Faking It" from *Watching Television* (1986) edited by Todd Gitlin. Reprinted by permission of Random House, Inc.

Thomas Sowell. "Student Loans" from *Is Reality Optional? and Other Essays*. Hoover Institution Press Publication No. 418. © 1993 Stanford University. Reprinted by permission of the author.

Brent Staples. "Black Men and Public Space." From *Harper's* Magazine, December 1986. Reprinted by permission of the author. "Brent Staples on Writing," copyright © 1991 by St. Martin's Press, Inc.

Amy Tan. "Fish Cheeks." Copyright © 1987 by Amy Tan. As first appeared in *Seventeen Magazine*. Reprinted by permission of the author and the Sandra Dijkstra Literary Agency. In "Amy Tan on Writing," excerpts from "Mother Tongue," copyright © 1989 by Amy Tan. As first appeared in *Threepenny Review*. Reprinted by permission of the author and the Sandra Dijkstra Literary Agency.

Deborah Tannen. "But What Do You Mean?" Reprinted from *Talking from Nine to Five* by Deborah Tannen. Copyright © 1994 by Deborah Tannen. Reprinted by permission of William Morrow & Company, Inc.

Edward J. Tarbuck and Frederick K. Lutgens, excerpt from *The Earth: An Introduction to Physical Geology*.

Edward Tenner. "Voice Mail and Fire Ants." From *Why Things Bite Back* by Edward Tenner. Copyright © 1996 by Edward Tenner. Reprinted by permission of Curtis Brown, Ltd. "Edward Tenner on Writing" copyright © 1996 by Edward Tenner. Printed by permission of the author.

James Thurber. "University Days." Copyright © 1933, 1961 James Thurber. From *My Life and Hard Times*, published by HarperCollins. In "James Thurber on Writing," excerpts from "James Thurber" by Malcolm Cowley, editor, from *Writers at Work*, *First Series* by Malcolm Cowley, © 1986 by The Paris Review. Used by permission of Viking Penguin, a division of Penguin Books USA Inc.

John Updike "The Disposable Rocket." First appeared in the *Michigan Quarterly Review*, Fall 1993. © John Updike. Reprinted by permission of the author. In "John Updike on Writing," excerpt from *The Paris Review Interviews*, Fourth Series, Viking 1976.

Robert M. Veatch. Excerpt from "Models for Medicine in a Revolutionary Age." *Hastings Center Report*, June 1972. Reprinted by permission.

Gore Vidal. "Drugs." From *Homage to Daniel Shays: Collected Essays 1952–1972* by Gore Vidal. Copyright © 1968, 1970, 1971, 1972 by Gore Vidal. Reprinted by permission of Random House, Inc. In "Gore Vidal on Writing," excerpt from "Gore Vidal" by George Plimpton, Ed. Intro. Francine du Plessix Gray from *Writers at Work*, *Fifth Series* by George Plimpton, editor, introduced by F. du Plessix Gray. Copyright © 1981 by The Paris Review. Used by permission of Viking Penguin, a division of Penguin Books USA Inc.

Carole Wade and Carol Tavris. Paragraph from *Psychology* 3/e © HarperCollins 1993. Reprinted by permission of HarperCollins.

E. B. White. "Once More to the Lake." Reprinted from *One Man's Meat* by E. B. White. Copyright 1941 by E. B. White. Reprinted by permission of HarperCollins Publishers, Inc. In "E. B. White on Writing," excerpt reprinted from *Letters of E. B. White*, collected and edited by Dorothy Lobrano Guth. Copyright © 1976 by E. B. White. Reprinted by permission of HarperCollins Publishers, Inc.

Dennis L. Wilcox, Phillip H. Ault, and Warren K. Agee. Paragraph from *Public Relations: Strategies and Tactics* 4/e, © HarperCollins 1995. Reprinted by permission of HarperCollins.

Marco Wilkinson. "Exposing Truth for the Lie That It Is." Reprinted by permission of the author. "Marco Wilkinson on Writing" copyright 1996 by Bedford Books.

Marie Winn. "TV Addiction." Reprinted from *The Plug-In Drug*, Revised Edition by Marie Winn. Copyright © 1977, 1985 by Marie Winn Miller. Used by permission of Viking Penguin, a division of Penguin Books USA Inc. "Marie Winn on Writing" copyright 1986 by St. Martin's Press.

Linda Wolfe. Excerpt from *The Literary Gourmet: Menus from Masterpieces*. Copyright © 1962, 1985 by Linda Wolfe. Reprinted by permission of Simon and Schuster, Inc.

Tom Wolfe. "Pornoviolence." From *Mauve Gloves and Madmen, Clutter and Vine* by Tom Wolfe. Copyright © 1976 by Tom Wolfe. In "Tom Wolfe on Writing," excerpts from David Bellamy, *The New Fiction: Interviews with Innovative American Authors*. Copyright 1974 by the Board of Trustees of the University of Illinois. Used with permission of the University of Illinois Press.

INDEX

Page numbers in bold type refer to
definitions in the glossary.